A Casual Affair

A History Of The Casuals Football Club

Rob Cavallini

British Library Cataloguing in Publication Data
A catalogue record for this book is available from the British Library

ISBN 978-0-9550496-2-0

Copyright © 2009 Dog N Duck Publications

This edition published in 2017

All rights are reserved. No part of this publication may be reproduced, stored in a retrieval system or transmitted, in any form or by any means, electronic, mechanical, photocopying, recording, or otherwise, without the prior written permission of Dog N Duck Publications.

Printed in the UK by 4edge Ltd.

Contents

1	A Casual Beginning 1883-1890	5
2	Tragedy And Progress 1890-1895	25
3	All Change At The Top 1895-1900	47
4	The Re-emergence of the Casuals 1900-1907	61
5	The Southern Amateur League Years 1907-1914	79
6	Post War Depression 1919-1922	93
7	Good Times At The Palace 1922-1925	103
8	Richmond Road – The Early Years 1925-1929	118
9	Greenland's Revolution 1929-1933	135
10	Amateur Cup Chasing 1933-1936	152
11	A Casual End 1936-1939	178
	Casuals Results & Statistics	187
	Casuals All Time Appearances	292
	League Tables	307
	Casuals Reserve Team Record	312
	Bibliography & Thanks	313
	References	314
	Subscribers	316
	Also by this author	317

Chapter One
A Casual Beginning
1883-1890

The Casuals Football Club was founded in 1883 by a group of old boys from the leading public schools. Their intention was to establish one club for former pupils of the schools. The club's origins became shrouded in mystery, however, following the loss of the contemporary records prior to World War One. As a result, many legends about the Casuals have developed over time and it is now impossible to be completely certain of the facts surrounding their formative years.

The version put forward by the club in their 50th anniversary brochure states:

'Back in the early 'eighties some Public School old boys whiled away the journeys to their football games much as they do to-day - nap was the popular gamble. Anyhow, some of them left too much money behind one Saturday, and decided to have their own club, and so keep their money in the family. This new club was The Casuals, and membership was confined in the first place to old boys of Charterhouse, Eton and Westminster. Later, membership was thrown open to all old Public School and University players.'[1]

The Casuals is an interesting choice of name for a club whose membership was made up of the elite of British society and was perhaps intended to be ironical. The term 'casuals' in the 1880's was primarily associated with low class workers, who worked on a casual basis, as and when it was available; it was then practically a derogatory term. The name might have been influenced by an earlier team which operated under the same name between 1877 and 1881 and featured one of the new Casuals original committee, C.H. Last, in several of its games. There is however very little evidence to link these two clubs; the only other player to play for both Casuals being E.C. Bambridge. It is true that both Casuals teams drew their players from similar sources, but this is where the connections end. The most significant clue is that one of the founders T.W. Blenkiron, was present at the Casuals 50th anniversary dinner in 1933 and this would suggest that the two clubs were indeed unconnected.

Blenkiron and F. Bickley (the first captain) are the names that are most commonly associated with the foundation of the Casuals, but they were joined by an impressive array of sportsmen in the new venture. The first President was The Right Honourable Earl of Lathom, and the other committee members were E. Collins (Vice-President), A.C. Redshaw-Williams (Treasurer), H.G. Taunton (Secretary), Lord Skelmersdale, A.M. Walters, C.H. Last, T.W. Blenkiron, E.W.

Marshall, E.G. Church, and E.H. Taunton (Vice-Captain), six of whom played for the club in 1883/84.

It is interesting at this point to look at the credentials of these founding fathers. F. Bickley, who went on to become secretary and who was the driving force behind the club, was an Old Etonian, a vice-president of the Middlesex Football Association and is also known to have owned two racehorses: Alfred the Great and Chloris II. Thomas William Blenkiron, the other key founding member, again had a horse racing background. An Old Carthusian who was a Cambridge University football blue three times between 1885 and 1887, he also gained a blue for cricket. Blenkiron's family was heavily involved in horse racing and his father owned the Middle Park Stud. He was best remembered for being chairman of the directors of the Kempton Park Racecourse Company and a Steward under National Hunt Rules at the Gatwick Race Meetings.

The club's first President was The Right Honourable Earl of Lathom, Edward Bootle-Wilbraham who was educated at Eton and Christ Church, Oxford and owned 11,000 acres of land in Lancashire. He enjoyed a successful political career and was a Lord in Waiting (1866-1868), Captain of the Yeoman of the Guards (1874-1880) and eventually the Lord Chamberlain. He was also Deputy Grandmaster of freemasons in England, becoming the Grand Master in 1891.

The President's son was Lord Skelmersdale, Edward George Bootle-Wilbraham and he also served on the committee. He was the eldest of four sons, being educated at Eton and becoming a Major in the Royal Horse Guards. Skelmersdale was a Justice of the Peace for Lancaster, a Major and Honorary Lieutenant-Colonel of the Lancashire Hussars before succeeding his father in 1898 as the 2nd Earl of Lathom and 3rd Baron Skelmersdale. The family was extremely well connected and his sister married the second son of the Prime Minister, Lord Salisbury. His own son, William Bootle-Wilbraham, wrote plays under such titles as Ostriches, Wet Paint, The Way You Look At It, and Two Pence Coloured, under the nom de plume Edward Wilbraham.

The other interesting original committee members included C.H. Last and A.M. Walters. Last played for the Pilgrims (an entrant in the F.A. Cup between 1879 and 1884) and was described as *'a clever and indefatigable half-back; is a little wanting in weight. One of the leading players in the south.'*[2] Walters was one of the greatest players of his generation, playing regularly for Corinthian and England. He was educated at Charterhouse and Trinity College, Cambridge and became both a Senior Partner of Walters & Company Solicitors of New Square, Lincolns Inn and Chairman of the London Guarantee & Accident Co. Ltd. He also was a director of Phoenix Assurance Co. Ltd and, between 1911 and 1938, registrar of Charterhouse.

The Casuals clearly had one of the most well connected and influential committees of any football club in England, the majority having attended either Eton College or Charterhouse School. This is no doubt the source of the oft-recalled story that membership of the club was initially restricted to former pupils of Charterhouse, Eton and Westminster. One report from an early Casuals match emphasises this point as follows: *'This afternoon the Derby County Club were visited by the Casuals, a fine combination comprising, players from Old Westminsters, Old Carthusians, & c.'*[3] There is, however, no evidence to suggest that the club drew on players from Westminster School in the early days. The majority of the players were friends of the co-founders and of the 78 players known to have played in the first season 22 attended Charterhouse. Eton College supplied ten players, whilst Brighton College provided a further five. The remaining players came from a variety of schools or colleges: Forest, Lancing, Harrow, Brentwood and from Westminster (only one).

The first member to be elected was W.G. Morrison, the captain of Reigate Priory (an initial entrant to the F.A. Cup and winners of the first Surrey Senior Cup in 1882/83) for many years and an Old Carthusian who had been a childhood friend of Blenkiron. Although this is consistent with the legend that Casuals was a club for old boys of Charterhouse, Eton and possibly Westminster, it is doubtful whether a rule to this effect ever existed. It is just possible that the rule concerned membership, with the club being at liberty to play non-members as and when it was necessary to make up a full eleven. Regardless of whether the rule existed or not membership certainly opened up before long to include many more old boys of other schools and it was later said that the qualifying rule became *'Public Schoolboy to mean any boy whose school was represented at the Headmasters' Conference.'*[4] There was certainly an elitist policy but it is important to note that some of the greatest Casuals players did not attend the big public schools.

The Casuals quickly adopted their famous and wonderfully exotic chocolate and pink colours and therein lies another mystery. There are two versions of the origins of this eye catching combination: firstly, that they were the racing colours of F. Bickley. This has proved to be a red herring as Wetherbys (who act as the central administration of British Horseracing) have confirmed that F. Bickley never registered his racing colours with them and from newspaper sources it appears his racing interest was stronger towards the end of the 1890's rather than in 1883. Wetherbys were, however, able to confirm that T.W. Blenkiron did have his racing colours registered with them and it may be significant that his jockeys wore brown silks.

The second story associated with the choice of colours is they united those of Westminster and Charterhouse Schools. This is possible, but Westminster appears to have had very little connection with the early Casuals and surely there was a much stronger case for including Eton College's colours in the design. The two versions of events are inconclusive, and cannot be proved either way. It is perhaps noteworthy that Chocolate and Pink (or Salmon) were selected by a number of clubs around this time, so it may be the case that this was an easy strip for Casuals to acquire with no further significance behind the choice.

The Casuals F.C. was unique in that it had no rules, (except, conjecturally, one relating to player qualification) and the club was controlled by resolutions framed at the A.G.M. The Honorary Secretary effectively ran the entire club, although he did consult the committee and captain when necessary. The secretary was a busy man and every Friday spent £2 on telegrams alerting players to their selection and organising the various fixtures.

The final problem for the founders of the Casuals to resolve was the question of a home ground. The club soon adopted a pitch on Wandsworth Common (which is also commonly referred to as Upper Tooting), and the Surrey Hotel was chosen as its headquarters. The Surrey Hotel survived in name until recently, when it was converted to the 'Amici Bar and Italian Kitchen,'

Above: The Surrey Hotel in 2003

but the building itself remains and is situated on the junction of Bellevue Road and Trinity Road on Wandsworth Common. The author visited this establishment prior to its conversion to a restaurant and it was possible to imagine the players changing in one of several enclaves in the walls, behind a curtain. At its peak the Surrey Hotel must have been an impressive sight, it was a typical traditional Victorian style public house with its high ceiling and ornate decoration. One could almost feel the ghosts of those early footballing pioneers who must have made it their second home. The ground used by the Casuals was situated across the road on the land now managed by the Trinity Fields Trust. Contemporary reports mention Trinity Road, Burntwood Lane and Beechcroft Road which surround this sports ground on three sides. This is confirmed by F.J. Wall who recalled in his memoirs that *'The Rangers became quite a good club, and it was advisable to hire another field. This was near to Wandsworth Common, adjoining the ground of The Casuals, and adjacent to the county gaol. ... The Casuals used to dress at a tavern, and had to run 300 yards across the Common to their field.'*[5] The pitch may have moved at various times potentially (as it is possible to squeeze in four or five pitches on the area in question), but the aforementioned roads appear regularly under both the names Wandsworth Common and Upper Tooting, so it is safe to assume that this is the correct location.

Above: Casuals ground at Wandsworth Common in 2003

1883/84

The Casuals first season was a disappointing affair on the whole with the club struggling to achieve success. An unambitious fixture list saw the new club face mainly schools teams and old boy clubs, and it appears that the club struggled to find attractive opposition throughout. Casuals did not enter any cup competitions in this first season, which might have stimulated interest in the club, and in fact only 28 games have been traced, of which just six were won.

The first match took place on 29th September 1883 against Upton Park (a club which had entered every F.A. Cup campaign and had won the inaugural London Senior Cup final the previous season) and the following small report marked the occasion in *The Sportsman*:

UPTON PARK 3 CASUALS 3
'This, the first match of the newly-formed Casuals, was played at Upton on Saturday last, and resulted in a draw, each side obtaining three goals. For Upton Park the goals were obtained by R.D. Green, H. Brealey, and Norman Leete. D. Patrick scored twice, and H.N. Alston once, for Casuals. Besides those mentioned E.C. Lewis, E.D. Ellis, and S.R. Bastard played well for Upton Park, and amongst those most conspicuous for the Casuals were A.M. Walters and C.W. Foley.'[6]

Left: Casuals 1883/84 fixture card

This brief summary was not untypical of coverage in *The Sportsman*, which was practically the only newspaper to report on The Casuals. This has made telling the story of the first season's progress particularly difficult.

It took Casuals only another four days to register their first victory when Bruce Castle School were demolished 9-2, thanks to a four goal performance by L.A. Vintcent and a brace by founder F. Bickley. Casuals recorded further victories over Brighton College and Surbiton Wanderers, but also lost another three and drew one before playing their first home game at Wandsworth Common against St. Thomas's Hospital on 8th November 1883, which was reported briefly as follows:

CASUALS 2 ST. THOMAS' HOSPITAL 3
*'This match was played on Thursday on the Casuals ground at Wandsworth, and, after a very good game, resulted in a victory for the visitors by three goals to two (Alston and Nicholls). For the Casuals, Last, Nicholls, Bennett, and Williams played well, the latter being very useful in goal, saving several goals, though he did not use his hands freely enough.'*7

This match was the second in a five match losing streak with the club finding it tough going. Casuals recovered to beat Old Foresters and draw with Pilgrims and Guy's Hospital before Christmas, but a seven game losing run lasted until the end of February when E.C. Bambridge (the holder of 18 England International caps) was on hand to fire a hat-trick against Charterhouse School in a 3-2 victory. This was merely a brief recovery and of the last five games four ended in defeat and the club only had a 4-3 victory over Bradfield College to celebrate.

Regardless of whether the club had been successful it had completed its first season and built a foundation for the future. H.N. Alston recorded seven of the goals which have been traced to establish him (potentially) as the top scorer. He was also one of the mainstays of the team, making 13 appearances, with captain F. Bickley being just one ahead on 14.

1884/85

The Casuals made their competitive debut this season by entering the F.A. Cup and London Senior Cup for the first time and they also embarked on their first northern tour. The club showed improvement on the previous season winning 14 of their 42 games, although they suffered some heavy defeats along the way.

Casuals opened the season in promising fashion by defeating Upton Park 1-0, and following a defeat at Brentwood, recorded another 1-0 victory over Charterhouse School. One of the liveliest matches of the early season soon followed at Brighton College when Casuals found themselves three goals behind early in the game. The Casuals recovered to equalise by half-time, but Brighton added three more goals in the second half. This was probably the moment a young G.H. Cotterill first came to the notice of the amateur football world, as he fired in four of the College's goals that day; he would go on to play for England, Corinthian and the Casuals in future years.

Casuals went into their first ever competitive game on the back of five successive defeats, but still defeated Argus 2-0 in a London Senior Cup first round tie. Unfortunately only selective reports appear in The Sportsman for the early rounds of cup competitions and normally it was the more famous and established clubs which gained preference; Casuals were not quite there yet.

This reporting pattern continued for Casuals next game, their debut in the F.A. Cup, but fortunately the *Berkshire Chronicle* covered the match. Casuals were in fact the hot favourites and fielded a strong line up:

E. Cawston, Ingram, ? Morrison, C.H. Last, C.B. Crews, J.H. Farmer, H.M. Holman, H.R. Smith, W.G. Morrison, E.H. Atkinson, and F. Bickley.

CASUALS 1 SOUTH READING 4
'Four goals to one in favour of the latter was the result of the match played at Wandsworth on Saturday afternoon between South Reading and the Casuals, for the above mentioned cup. The play probably was one of the greatest surprises in the first round of this competition, and reflects great credit on our local team, who, nothing daunted by the knowledge that they had a very formidable eleven to meet, journeyed to London and expressed themselves confident of making the 'chance lot' work very hard indeed to effect victory. The success, however, with

which South Reading came out of the play was expected by none, and therefore all the more reason for congratulation...

Johnson having lost the toss drew up his men with the wind, sun and hill against them, and having sent the leather on its way at once attacked the enemy's fortress, the result being that Fry very neatly placed the ball between the posts. The goalkeeper was certainly caught napping, and no one was more surprised than himself when he was informed that the sphere had gone under the bar. This early downfall of the Casuals' colours much elated the Southerners and they were not long before another visit was paid by them to the Londoners' goal. This time, however, they found Cawston one too many for them, for by a good punch the 'case of air' was sent well out of danger. It was now the Casuals' turn to act the part of pressing, and, by the aid of Bickley, Last, Ingram and Farmer they pretty well managed to do so, but Steward and the other members of the back division were a very good match for them, and comfortably managed to keep their goal clear. Haydon, Embery, and Gregory now broke away, and taking the ball into the Casuals' quarters, the former sent in a hot shot, which was returned with apparent ease by the 'man in charge.' Bickley again led the way to the other goal, and passing to Atkinson, that player sent in a stinger, which was cleverly saved by Lusty. H.R. Smith then sent in another, which hit the post and bounded into play, thus giving Morrison time to rush up and send the globe flying beneath the bar. Of course the game now became more exciting, each team trying its utmost to gain an advantage, but without avail, as a half-time the state of the play was still one goal each, both goalkeepers having done remarkably good service.

For quite twenty-five minutes in the second half the game was of the most even description, both goals being in frequent danger, but nothing was scored, despite the fact that Johnson, Fry, Gregory, Haydon, Embery, Bickley, Smith, and Farmer were upon several occasions with in an ace of doing so for their respective sides. From here (twenty minutes to the expiration of play) South Reading had much of the best of it and although the Casuals broke away once or twice the Southerners completely outplayed them, and in rapid succession put on three goals, therefore at the call of time the Readingites – after a very pleasant game – were found to be the victors as before mentioned.'[8]

Casuals then met Cambridge University for the first time and crashed to a heavy 0-8 defeat at Parker's Piece, before their competitive hopes for the season were ended when the London Senior Cup holders Upton Park defeated them 0-2 in the second round. Casuals up and down season continued, but they were able to defeat Westminster School, Old Foresters (London Senior Cup winners 1885), Guy's Hospital and East Sheen (Surrey Senior Cup winners 1885) prior to their Christmas and New Year tour.

The tour began in stunning fashion when Derby County were defeated 2-1. Casuals took the lead after ten minutes when F. Bickley hit the cross bar and the ball bounced down behind the line. The score stayed unchanged until 25 minutes from time when Casuals hit Derby on the break: Bell evaded Morley, before passing to Hardman, who struck a hard shot which gave the home custodian little chance. Derby reduced the arrears with 15 minutes left, but to no avail. It was a good day for the club as another Casuals XI in London defeated Wimbledon 7-1.

Above: A Casuals team from the 1880's – Unfortunately the names have been lost

These impressive results were followed by another good performance at Long Eaton Rangers, another strong club. Casuals returned to London before recommencing the tour in the New Year with a visit to Blackburn Olympic (F.A. Cup winners in 1883) losing 0-2 on a heavy pitch after a close game. In their next match they crashed dramatically 1-12 at Bolton Wanderers. The Bolton game had seen Casuals take the lead after just four minutes before collapsing and conceding six goals in each half. The game was marked by an injury to F.W. Jansen who ruptured a kidney, and it was fortunate that one of his team mates was a doctor. The final game of the tour ended in a 0-3 defeat at Nottingham Forest.

Casuals returned to London and their poor form continued against Reigate Priory in the next match. Four Casuals players failed to turn up for the game so a resourceful captain managed to persuade four of the Clapham Rovers rugby team who had turned up (only to find no opposition) to play; his actions failed to prevent a 0-5 defeat.

The club began to scale down its activity after their return from the tour, and recorded just four victories before the end of the season against Guy's Hospital, Westminster School, Old Foresters and St. Thomas's Hospital. The latter match was the first of Casuals games to be reported in *The Times* and evidence that the club was slowly gaining some recognition:

ST THOMAS' HOSPITAL 0 CASUALS 1
'An interesting game resulted from the meeting of these Association elevens in the Lambeth Palace grounds yesterday. The afternoon was bright and the ground in excellent condition. Successful in the toss, St. Thomas's Hospital selected the goal nearest the Palace, and at 3

o'clock Miller set the ball rolling on behalf of the Casuals. The medicals soon drove it into their rivals' quarters, but Miller relieved his side by a good run. After some even play a determined attack was made by the Casuals, and Mills-Roberts (the home goal-keeper) had to use his hands several times. A free-kick for 'hands' next fell to the visitors, which was undertaken by A.J. Heath. Nothing resulted from it. Half-time was soon afterwards called, and positions were reversed. On resuming play both elevens showed excellent form, but for some time neither could score. At length after several loose scrimmages in front of the Hospital goal, Ibbs headed the ball under the cross-bar. This proved the deciding point of the game, and the Casuals thus won by one goal to none.' [9]

Casuals lethargic late season form reached its nadir in a 0-11 defeat at Forest School and a 0-8 defeat to Old Brightonians, but overall it could be regarded as a moderately successful campaign. Captain F. Bickley made the most appearances and was top scorer from the games which have been traced.

1885/86

Casuals third season marked a change in attitude towards the club as it began to gain the respect of its peers. The club recorded an impressive start to the season with a 5-0 victory over Old Brightonians, and this was followed by a 1-0 victory over Charterhouse School. A defeat against the Royal Engineers was followed by a 5-0 win against St. Thomas's Hospital and a 7-0 victory over St. Bride's in the London Senior Cup first round.

Casuals then faced the mighty Old Etonians (F.A. Cup winners in 1882) who featured famous international A.T.B. Dunn and nine time F.A. Cup finalist A.F. Kinnaird in their team. The club's problems were compounded as *'Casuals were greatly weakened owing to their being unable to draw from the first teams of the Old Carthusians and Old Westminsters, not to mention their opponents, who brought down a very hot eleven, seven of their cup team being in ranks.'* [10] This was to be a common theme for the club throughout its history as the calls of the Corinthian F.C., various representative teams and old boys clubs had a nasty habit of weakening the club at the most important moments. Old Etonians were triumphant by four goals to nil on this occasion.

The F.A. Cup tie with the Swifts was perhaps the most disappointing result of the season as Casuals conceded an own goal after just ten minutes. It was downhill from this point on as Swifts recorded a 7-1 victory to start a run to the semi-final where they lost by the odd goal in three to eventual winners Blackburn Rovers.

The Casuals bounced back with 6-3 win over Bruce Castle School before writing themselves into the Tottenham Hotspur history books by inflicting on the Spurs their first ever cup defeat. Tottenham's history explains the 8-0 London Senior Cup drubbing as follows:

'The result was to be expected. The Casuals were a powerful side who had at their command the cream of past and present Public Schools and University players. They fielded a side that in later years- after the advent of professionalism – would have done duty for an England amateur

international side. Better equipped in skill, and overwhelming in physique, they overshadowed the young, by no means tall, and still rather raw, Spurs side.'[11]

The improvement in the Casuals was emphasised in the next couple of games as Cambridge University were held 0-0 (after an 0-8 defeat at the hands of the same opponents the previous year), and Old Westminsters were beaten 3-2. The club bowed out of the London Senior Cup in the third round to Old St. Marks, but this defeat can be explained by the fact that Casuals started with nine men, prior to the arrival of one further player. The eleventh player, Arthur, never arrived.

Christmas was fast approaching (traditionally Casuals most active period prior to World War One) and the club was about to embark on another northern tour. The first match ended in a 1-2 defeat at Derby County and was followed by a 2-2 draw at Burnley, Casuals having held a 2-0 lead at half-time. The scheduled match against Blackburn Olympic was cancelled the next day, so allowing the Casuals some extra recovery time and this may have contributed to the club's most impressive victory in its short history. Aston Villa were the opponents and led 0-2 and 1-3 before Casuals roared back to steal a 4-3 victory from their illustrious opposition. Although the tour concluded with defeats against Nottingham Forest, Sheffield Club and Long Eaton Rangers, the club could be proud of an impressive showing against some of the leading clubs in England.

The season was significantly curtailed by the weather, as heavy rain between January and March meant Casuals only played another seven games after mid-January, of which only two, against Westminster School and West Kent, were victories.

Casuals could take great heart from a much improved season and as one reporter put it *'The Casuals always a good but rather nondescript team.'*[12] A curiosity from this season is that Casuals were members of the Middlesex Football Association, although this was probably due to F. Bickley's association with that county.

1886/87

The Casuals Football Club first broke through into the elite of London's amateur teams during the 1886/87 season when it reached the final of London Charity Cup and became the joint holder of the prestigious London Senior Cup. The club's progress was recognised in the press as it made its first appearance in *The Sportsmans* Chief Association Club's listings, an unofficial ranking system which was used prior to the commencement of organised league structures. Casuals were ranked as high as 11th in the country at the end of October, and climbed to ninth at the end of December, higher than Corinthian F.C., Bolton Wanderers, Derby County, Blackburn Rovers and Glasgow Rangers. Casuals finished in ninth position, and although clearly not a definitive guide, it was still evidence of the growing strength of the club.

During the campaign Casuals were assisted by Sir Charles Aubrey Smith the famous Old Carthusian who became a Hollywood movie star and whose credits included The Prisoner of Zenda and The Four Feathers. Smith had a interesting life and moved to South Africa in 1888/89 to prospect for gold; whilst there he developed pneumonia and was wrongly pronounced dead by the doctors. It was during his stay in South Africa that he captained the England cricket team (in his only test match) to victory in Port Elizabeth, and his love of this game led to him founding the Hollywood Cricket Club. Smith has a star on the Hollywood Walk of Fame.

Casuals' improvement in cup form can be attributed to the new policy of recruitment aimed specifically at achieving success in these competitions. This is another regular theme throughout the club's history and cup squads could contain seven or eight players who were not regular team members.

Casuals interest in the F.A. Cup was short lived as the club succumbed to Dulwich 2-4. Casuals were three goals behind at half-time, but fought back to score two goals before Dulwich sealed victory. Fortunately, though, the club saved its best performances for the two London cups.

In the London Senior Cup, Casuals overwhelmed Pilgrims 8-0 with Ingram hitting four and Charles Aubrey Smith scoring a hat-trick. The second round provided an even easier test and Waverley found themselves on the end of 12-0 drubbing as Currey hit seven goals. The third round was a tough game, on paper, against Clapham Rovers (F.A. Cup winners in 1880), and so it proved with the first game ending in a 1-1 draw. The second game was never played as Clapham Rovers withdrew, the reason for which was never established, but it is curious that on 18th December, only three days after the scheduled date for the replay Rovers played a friendly against Casuals which ended in a 9-1 win for the old boys.

Casuals were now in the fourth round and faced Hendon (not the present day club). The original game was postponed, although no one from Hendon had told the Casuals, so they arrived at the ground and in the absence of any opposition claimed the game. The London F.A. overruled this claim as the ground was unfit for play so the two sides met at the Oval two weeks later after another postponement. In any event Casuals had very little trouble in beating Hendon as the 6-0 score line testifies.

The semi-final beckoned and Casuals were drawn against their old rivals from Upton Park. A fast and exciting game ensued which was only decided when Evelyn scored with five minutes remaining. The final was to be Casuals' last game of the season:

OLD WESTMINSTERS 1 CASUALS 1
'For the second time with in a few days the Casuals have appeared in the final tie for a trophy under the management of the London Football Association, having as recently as Saturday tried conclusions with the Swifts in the final for the Charity Cup presented by the Lord Mayor. On this occasion they suffered defeat by three goals to none, but yesterday after looking like sustaining a further reverse, they managed to make a draw. The fixture should have been brought off on the 19th. Inst., but had to be postponed owing to snow and frost. Both teams were fairly representative, though the Casuals were decidedly weak forward on the left wing, but the interest in the fixture was apparently limited, and the attendance could not have numbered more than 400, and many of these were content to retire before the cessation of hostilities. It had been arranged, to suit the convenience of several City men, to postpone the start until half-past four, but it was nearly five before the game was started by F.M. Ingram, who kicked off from the

Vauxhall goal. For the first few minutes the past students of Westminster held the upper hand, but they were then gradually driven back, and the Casuals made several smart attacks, in which Amos and Smith were most conspicuous. The defence of Fevez, Janson and Squire proved excellent, and after a while the old boys assumed the offensive, Sandilands being especially active. A couple of corner-kicks fell to them, but without result, after which a very tough melee took place in the mouth of the Casual goal, but Mills-Roberts staved off disaster. Nothing was scored until just before half-time, when, after Jenner had put in a shot which was cleared by Mills-Roberts, Veitch got one between the post, and scored for Westminster amid slight applause.

Having crossed over, the game was carried on in a very even manner, though the Old Westminsters if anything held the advantage. Amos and Nickisson both had corner-kicks to no purpose, while Heath, Bain, Smith, and Veitch made good but ineffective dribbles for their respective sides, A.M. Walters also figuring to great advantage behind. About twenty minutes from the close F.M. Ingram put in a good kick with his left that equalised, and this put their rivals on their mettle. A corner-kick well placed by Nickisson was cleared by Wetton, but though directly afterwards Bain had a good opening for scoring, he lost time, and allowed Davies to get back and take the ball from him. At the expiration of the usual hour and a half the scores stood level – one goal each – and after some hesitation it was decided, amid cries of 'Play on,' to continue the game for another ten minutes each way, though it was now half-past six. During this extra period both played up well, but at its expiration the rival elevens left the field without having arrived at a definite conclusion, though a moment after the whistle blew, and in semi-darkness, Sandilands sent the ball through a second time. '[13]

The replay ended in controversial fashion without a ball being kicked:

A DISGRACEFUL FIASCO
'Some explanation ought to be given of the reason why no ball was provided at Sydenham yesterday. In consequence of this the game had to be postponed after the players had waited nearly two hours. The rival teams – Casuals and Old Westminsters – at first amused themselves by kicking about a couple of Rugby balls. The fun was evidently enjoyed by the spectators, despite the gale that was raging. When rain came on heavily, however, players and company were driven to the pavilion – if the shed in which shelter was sought could be called such. Meanwhile the district stores had been searched for a ball, and a telegram had also been despatched to London for one. Many of the players had dressed and gone when the article turned up – time 5.15. To begin then was out of the question, and nothing else remained but to postpone the game. It may be mentioned that when the rain came on the company slowly left the ground, but we subsequently met several people who had not had their money returned. Whether the storm was too much for the gatekeeper did not transpire.' [14]

There was no time during the season to replay the game and the London F.A. decided that the trophy would be shared between the finalists. As previously mentioned Casuals also reached the final of the London Charity Cup, just prior to the Senior Cup tie against Old Westminsters, by defeating Crusaders 3-1 after going behind in the first half. The final against the Swifts was delayed so both teams could watch the boat race:

SWIFTS 3 CASUALS 0

'In spite of the fact that the start was delayed until after half-past four in order to give intending spectators an opportunity of previously witnessing the Boat Race, there was but a very moderate attendance at the Oval on Saturday for the purpose of witnessing the final tie for the Cup presented by the Lord Mayor (Sir R. Hanson). The Casuals asserted their right to participation by defeating the Crusaders in the first tie on the 5th inst., but the Swifts only defeated their antagononists, the Old Westminsters, at the second time of asking, as recently as Wednesday last. Both sides were very powerfully represented the 'birds' playing their Cup team, while the Casual eleven included 'the prince of dribblers,' W.N. Cobbold, the Oxford three three-miler, F.M. Ingram, Dunn, Amos, and others. The latter won the toss, and played for the first half with a slight wind at their backs, Lindley starting the game from the gasometer end at twenty minutes to five, at which time there were about 1,500 spectators present. The Lord Mayor had signified his intention of honouring the game with his presence, but was prevented from so doing through a family bereavement.

For the first few minutes the Casuals looked like securing a definite advantage, and a couple of corner-kicks fell to them, without, however, definite result. The Swifts, aided by Challen, who was particularly active, then penned in their opponents, and with but short intervals continued to do so throughout the remainder of the game. A good shot by Challen struck the bar, but no score was obtained till about a quarter of an hour from the start, when after a free kick in front of goal Cotterill obtained the first point for the Swifts out of a melee, the ball rolling through out of reach of Mills-Roberts. On resuming Spilsbury and Brann made a plucky effort to score, and then Cobbold broke away, but finding Holden-White 'one too many' transferred to Dunn, but the effort died away. A little later Cobbold put in a rare shot, which was well cleared by Bambridge, but a dodgy run by Cotterill, who after beating Ingram, turned over to Spilsbury, resulted in a second goal from the foot of the latter. Give-and-take play followed, but in spite of the fact that the Casuals right wing were very active, while Cobbold – though not at his best – was equally vigilant, the Swifts had all the best of the play, and when ends were changed a pass by Challen to Spilsbury added a third goal by means of a very warm shot, which first struck the cross-bar and then went between the posts. In the second portion of the match the 'birds' continued to have the upper hand, though the play was scarcely of an interesting description. Cobbold lost one good chance of scoring, while but for a splendid save by Mills-Roberts a sharp shot by Lindley must have added still further disaster. A little sensation was thrown into the game by an unnecessary charge by Davies, which sent Dunn headlong against the seats near the touch-line, though the retirement of the Old Etonian shortly after was, we are glad to learn, in no way due to this circumstance. In the last few minutes Casuals rallied slightly, and a corner was obtained, followed by a free kick, after which Smith sent the ball through, but was ruled off-side. No alteration was effected in the score during the latter half of the game, and at the close the Swifts were left victorious by three goals to none – a result mainly due to their superiority of their defence.' [15]

The Christmas tour was less successful and was marred by appalling weather which saw Casuals lose 0-3 to Derby, the pitch being covered in two inches of snow. Casuals took the lead against Aston Villa on a waterlogged pitch before succumbing 1-2 and this was followed by a 3-6 defeat at Long Eaton Rangers, as the Casuals battled back to make a game of it after being 0-4 down at half-time, getting to within one goal at one stage. The bright spot was an impressive 0-0 draw at Stoke, soon to be founder members of the Football League.

1887/88

Casuals again reached the final of both the London Football Association competitions but once more failed to win in the all important match. The low point of the season came in the F.A. Cup when the club embarrassingly *'scratched to the Millwall Rovers as by accident their players were not registered until too late to permit their playing in the cup.'*[16] Apart from this the club was clearly thriving and a Smoking Concert was held in January at the Duval Restaurant on The Strand, which was well supported by the players who performed various cabaret acts.

The club was also present in December 1887 at the meeting which founded the Middlesex County F.A. Senior Challenge Cup (alongside Corinthian, Old Harrovians, Finchley, Oaks, Harrow Rovers, Olympic, Christchurch Rangers, Condors, St. Mary's Hospital, Tottenham Hotspur, Clapton and Amersham), but was destined never to play in this competition.

Casuals did, however, enjoy a reasonable Christmas tour although at times they found themselves overstretched and had to borrow players. The first game at Derby for example, saw Casuals arrive with only ten men and a guest player was required to complete the eleven. Despite this Casuals were leading 1-0 at half-time before conceding five second half goals. This was followed by a narrow 0-1 defeat at Aston Villa, before a disastrous 1-6 defeat at Gainsborough Trinity. Honour was restored with a 3-1 victory at Long Eaton Rangers.

The London Senior Cup campaign began with a comfortable 5-0 win over Hotspur at Merton, with Casuals receiving a bye in the next round. Round Three saw Casuals face Iona and another comfortable 4-1 win ensued, before Hendon proved sterner opposition, the old boys triumphing by the odd goal in five. In the semi-final against Old Harrovians, Casuals were losing until the 36th minute when a three goal burst in nine minutes, turned matters round and contributed to a 5-1 victory. The final ended in disappointing fashion and ironically the winning goal was scored by a player who represented the Casuals during the course of the season:

OLD WESTMINSTERS 1 CASUALS 0
'In seasonable weather the final tie in this competition between the representatives of Old Westminster and a strong contingent of the Casuals was decided at Kennington Oval on Saturday last, the turf, though rather slippery, being in tolerably good condition. Blenkiron, winning the toss, formed up his line of battle in front of the Crown baths side of the inclosure (sic) to take advantage of the wind that blew from that quarter, and at twenty minutes past three C.F. Ingram made a start from the gasometer end. C.R.W. Heath, at once following up, dribbled the ball well over till stopped by Walters. A corner by Janson failed to be productive, and a claim of hands, giving Fox a free kick, shared the same fate. The short runs by A.J. Heath and Higgins threatened much mischief, but they were all incontinently stopped before they could become dangerous. An attack by the Casuals, under the leadership of Dunn, looked like a probably success, but R.A. Ingram being in the way, the danger was cleverly placed aside, and a splendid side-kick by Dunn right across goal looked fatally directed, but, the ball going behind, the chance was lost. A good run by Jenner was put a stop to by Walters. Some fine

Left: T.W. Blenkiron – Casuals founder

dribbling and passing were now shown by Ingram and Higgins, and a corner by Squire, though well placed, proved ineffective. Westminster still continued to press their opponents, and the game was carried on as vigorously as at the commencement. At half-time the teams went over, nothing having been scored by either. At length, about ten minutes after the change of ends, out of a loose scrimmage in front of the Casuals' goal, Jenner was the means of gaining the only point made during the match, which thus came to an end in favour of the Old Boys by one goal to none.' 17

In the London Charity Cup, Casuals faced Old Foresters in the semi-final and strangely started with A.M. Walters in goal. He was later to swap positions and score Casuals fourth goal in a 4-1 victory. This set up a rematch with the Swifts in the final, but Casuals struggled and could only manage a repeat of the previous season's score line.

SWIFTS 1 CASUALS 0
'The former team on Saturday managed to retain possession of the handsome bowl presented by Sir Reginals Hanson by the narrow margin of one goal to none. Their opponents were the Casuals, who in the first round had beaten the Old Foresters, but though a somewhat better game than was witnessed a fortnight since, the contest was by no means of an inspiring character. The weather was dull and cheerless, and the ground at the Oval very greasy, but the attendance – a leading factor in a charity match was decidedly good, i.e., judging from the usual experiences of such fixtures in the metropolis. Both sides played as advertised, and Blenkiron having beaten Bambridge in the toss and chosen the gasometer goal, Lindley kicked off at 3.40. Regarded as a whole the play in the first half was in favour of the Casuals, though now and again their backs were called upon to repel smart attacks, in which Lindley was conspicuous. Ainger and Paul were busy for the Casuals, but at half-time neither side had scored. Nearly midway through the second portion, however, the Swifts ran the ball down to the Casuals' quarters, a fine centre from Lindley, almost on the goal-line, resulting in Bambridge

heading the ball through amid loud applause. The Swifts continued pressing, and for the rest of the game held decidedly the upper hand, though once Swepstone varied the monotony by running up field and leaving his goal unprotected for a moment. Alston nearly allowed a low shot to get past him, but no further points were registered, and when the whistle sounded for hostilities to cease the Swifts were left victorious as already mentioned.'[18]

1888/89

Casuals enjoyed another fine season in which they played 63 games, their record to date and in the course of it reached the London Senior Cup final and the semi-final of the Charity Cup. In another busy season the club who undertook its most extensive tour to the north and achieved some notable victories. During the season Casuals were assisted by W.P. Carpmael the founder of the famous Barbarians Rugby Union team.

The F.A. Cup was again a disappointment and after a walk-over against Hitchin who withdrew from the competition, Casuals went out immediately in the second qualifying round, 1-3 at the hands of Clapton.

The Christmas tour to the north started in positive fashion when West Manchester were defeated 3-2, but this was followed by a 3-6 defeat at Aston Villa on a quagmire of a pitch. Sheffield and Nottingham Forest were defeated 4-2 and 4-1 respectively to restore the impressive momentum, before the team tired badly due to the punishing schedule and lost successive games to Long Eaton Rangers (2-5), Burnley (0-4), Newton Heath (0-1), Notts County (0-1) and Derby County (0-6). Villa, Burnley, Notts County, and Derby were, of course, founder members of the Football League that season and it is worth noting that in their match against the latter club, Casuals were trailing only 0-1 at half-time.

The London Senior Cup provided Casuals with a much stiffer test than in the previous year, and after receiving a bye in the first round, Old Harrovians were defeated by the only goal of the game in round two. The third round resulted in a 2-0 victory over Brixton Rangers and then Casuals thrashed the holders Old Westminsters 3-0 to avenge their defeat in the previous year's final.

In the semi-final Casuals faced Hotspur and were severely weakened by the fact that the Walters brothers were representing the South in the international trial match. A close game which Casuals were never chasing ended in a 4-3 victory to set up a cup final tie with Clapton, a team destined to be one of the club's main rivals for many years to come.

CLAPTON 4 CASUALS 2
'The weather on Saturday was not very tempting, yet close upon 3,000 witnessed the encounter, among the spectators being Sir Charles Russell. Q.C., M.P., a patron of the victorious club. The turf, considering the recent variation in the temperature, was in fairly good condition, but the snowstorm that occurred before the interval rendered it terribly slippery during the later portion of the game. Cowan kicked off for the Claptonians from the Vauxhall goal at twenty minutes past three, and for a time the Casuals had much the best of the play, the ball remaining

for the most part in the Clapton territory, while the brothers Walters defended admirably, and were evidently dreaded by more than one of the opposing forwards. The shooting of the Casuals was, however, very erratic, Probyn missing one grand opening, whilst Glossop sent just over the cross-bar. Then for the first time Ford had to use his hands, and after a shot by Cowan conceded a corner. Nothing resulted, however, from the attack, and for a time the game was very evenly contested. A few minutes before the interval, Bryson ran down the left wing, and P.M. Walters, being hardly pressed gave away a corner. This Clark placed admirably, and from a melee in front of the Casuals' goal Connell headed through. This was the only score up to half-time, or, indeed, until nearly midway through the second portion. During this period Casselton put in some splendid work at back for the East-enders, who gained two fruitless corners, Glossop for the Casuals failing to make use of a golden opportunity by shooting wide. Then in the course of a few minutes the state of the game changed entirely, Sellar adding a second goal, Prior a third, after a pretty run down, and Sellar yet a fourth, the Claptonians having gained their usual confidence, and playing admirably together. This virtually settled the question, though the latter, somewhat slackening in their efforts, allowed Leman to obtain a soft goal for the Casuals, whilst Ainger, after a run down by the former player, added a second, and in the end Clapton retired the winners by four goals to two, a very popular victory. There can be no doubt that the poor combination of the Casuals forwards and their weakness at half-back lost them the game, though it must be admitted that Roe worked hard.' [19]

The London Charity Cup did not yield the same success as the previous two years, with Casuals failing to make the final. After beating Old St. Marks 4-1 in the first round, a ten man Old Westminster side triumphed 1-2 over the Casuals in the semi-final.

The club held another fundraising 'smoker,' but unfortunately this was not as well attended as in previous years. The players present were clearly enthusiastic, but bearing in mind the club used a minimum of 177 players during the season it certainly was disappointing:

'As mentioned in our issue yesterday, the attendance at the Falstaff, Eastcheap, on Thursday was extremely disappointing. Mr W.J. Seton presiding over a company of but fifty or sixty strong. This was all the more to be regretted as a really excellent programme had been arranged. Among the audience were, however, many crack players, who atoned for the smallness of numbers by the vehemence of their applause.' [20]

1889/90

The 1889/90 season was to be Casuals last season at Wandsworth Common and it was marked by their most ambitious programme of fixtures to date. So far as can be traced the club played an extraordinary 81 games and celebrated this by making an early season announcement:

'A really enormous card, is put forth by this leading club, quite one hundred contests being arranged, on one date no fewer than four engagements having to be fulfilled. Among the clubs to be met are Old Etonians, Old Westminsters, Old Harrovians, Old Foresters, Old Brightonians, Old Reptonians, Old Wykehamists, Old Lancing Boys, Oxford University, Cambridge University, United Hospitals, Clapton, Chatham, Royal Engineers, Royal Arsenal,

Charterhouse, Westminster School, Felsted School, Forest School, Repton School, Chiswick Park, West Kent, Old St. Mark's, Sunderland, Derby County, R.M.C., R.M.A, Lancing College, Brighton College, Bradfield College, Beckenham, Crusaders, Reigate Priory, Northamptonshire, Luton Town, &c. The Northern tour opens on December 26. and will include contests with Lincoln City, Derby County, Grimsby Town, Everton, East End (Newcastle), Sunderland and Sheffield United. Mr T.W. Blenkiron is captain, and Mr F. Bickley, 8, Georgeyard, Lombard-street, E.C., hon.sec.'[21]

Casuals, despite the increase in number of fixtures, failed to emulate the previous season's success and for the first time in several years failed to reach a cup final. Their F.A. Cup dreams ended in the second qualifying round with a 3-8 defeat to the Swifts, whilst the London Charity Cup witnessed Casuals' departure in the first round to Clapton. The club did however make progress in the London Senior Cup defeating Chiswick Park and Vulcan before bowing out, (following a bout of influenza) in a fourth round second replay to Old Westminsters, the eventual winners, who overcame Royal Arsenal in the final.

Casuals, though, could take heart from their games against the professional clubs. In October they helped Sunderland make history by playing their first game in London, the Wearsiders winning 1-3. The Christmas tour again saw Casuals visit the north and record some impressive results. A slow start saw the Old Boys lose at Lincoln City, but defeat Loughborough 2-1 with another Casual XI on the same day. The following day Casuals lost 3-4 to Derby County after taking a 3-0 lead. Sheffield United were held to a 3-3 draw, and the amateurs then lost 2-5 to Grimsby Town, and 2-3 to Everton; there was however, a strong end to the tour. Liverpool Ramblers (who were amateur) were defeated 3-0, before Newcastle East End (now United) were beaten 2-0. The final game saw a rematch with Sunderland and a close game ended in a 2-3 defeat. In subsequent matches against professional clubs, Casuals held Derby County to a 1-1 draw in London before losing 1-3 in the rematch whilst suffering defeats at Burslem Port Vale and Everton (2-7) and Aston Villa (0-4)

The club suffered a blow when founder F. Bickley resigned as Secretary with effect from 1st January 1890. He was succeeded by W.J. Seton and this change may well account for the discrepancy in the number of games quoted in the following summary of the season:

'The club has brought to a conclusion its seventh season. The programme was the largest it had ever attempted and resulted in 73 first team matches being played, a number never before equalled by any football club in one season.

In cup ties the club was not successful, but nevertheless played two drawn games with the ultimate winners of the London Cup (the Old Westminsters) before succumbing to them at the Oval, in a match in which both teams were disorganised by influenza. The 'fashionable complaint' treated the club very hardly, and deprived them of the services of such sterling and regular players as E.J.D. Mitchell and C.H. Jackson for the last three months of the season, as well as of others for a less period.

The most regular players for the club were R.R. Barker 36 matches (including a month's 'suspension' due to influenza), F. Bickley and W.J. Seton, the two secretaries 31 matches each;

S. Furber and F.E. Adams, 28; A.C. Nixon and H.H. Crawley, 26; A.G.B. Glossop (who was not available after January 11) 20 matches. At the head of the goal-getters H.M. Walters, who scored 35 goals in 18 matches; next to him comes the Rev. F.W. Pawson 18 goals in 16 matches, while W.H. Ainger and S. Furber scored 16 goals in 9 and 28 matches respectively. The interests of the club was materially affected at the beginning of the year by the resignation of the secretary, F. Bickley, who had held office since the foundation. An ample programme, including the usual northern tour at Christmas, is being arranged for next season when it is hoped all members will support the club with increased energy.'[22]

Chapter Two
Tragedy and Progress
1890-1895

The decade began in the saddest circumstances with the tragic death of Hugh Melmoth Walters (the youngest of the three Walters brothers) as a result of an accident on the field of play. This event overshadowed much of the 1890/91 season, but Casuals then rallied and went on to reach five cup finals in the following five seasons, winning two. The club continued to tour and arranged strong fixture lists which included frequent matches against professional clubs, producing some notable results. The club maintained a social side as resolutions passed regularly in the minutes of the 1890's show post match dinners being provided for their opponents.

1890/91

At the start of the 1890/91 season Casuals moved to a ground at Wormwood Scrubs and made Kensington Park Cricket Club their home for the next three seasons, (although on an infrequent basis). There are three possibilities for the location of the ground and the evidence for each is inconclusive. The first site was in Du Cane Road and could be the sports ground now occupied by Upper Latymer School. The second was close to Wormholt Farm (which was later used by Shepherd's Bush F.C.), and this is now covered by housing. The final site close to Little Wormwood Scrubs was St. Quinton Park. The Ordnance Survey map 1891-1893 shows three cricket grounds and five pavilions in this area, but there is no longer any evidence of these facilities (the site is now occupied by the St. Quinton Park estate). There was without doubt a large sporting interest in the area, but unfortunately no records survive from the Kensington Park Cricket Club which, it has been suggested, could also have been known as the West Kensington Park Cricket Club.

The season opened with a rip-roaring battle with Royal Arsenal which saw the Casuals go down by the odd goal in nine, after leading at the interval. Casuals then defeated Old Wykehamists and Chatham, before winning just one of their next six matches - a notable 10-0 victory over Somerset Rovers.

Victories were, however, proving hard to come by and only Bruce Castle (9-2) and Old Etonians (5-3) (who featured Casuals founder F. Bickley in their line-up) were defeated prior to November. At this point Casuals seemed to have got their house in order as St. Thomas's

Above: Little Wormwood Scrubs – A possible site of Casuals ground

Above: St. Quinton Park Estate which now occupies another possible site

Above: Upper Latymer School Playing Fields

Hospital, Old Westminsters and Forest School were all defeated whilst the powerful Oxford University were held to a 2-2 draw.

This recovery was to end in dramatic fashion, and was to plunge the club into crisis. On 12th November 1890 an unremarkable match against St. Bartholomew's Hospital was scheduled at Wormwood Scrubs.

CASUALS V ST BARTHOLOMEW'S HOSPITAL
For a mid-week match a fair few were present at the Kensington Ground, Wormwood Scrubs, on Wednesday. The turf was somewhat on the soft side, but not so much to prevent a very fast game being played. Unfortunately a nasty accident occurred in the second half, H.M. Walters, the Casuals centre forward, being injured in the abdomen. Falling to the ground he writhed in agony for some minutes, but ultimately was helped from the ground to the dressing room at the Pavillion Hotel adjacent to the field.[1]

The game was abandoned with the score being 2-7 to the medical men, Walters had scored both Casuals goals. Two weeks later H.M. Walters' death was announced in *The Sportsman*.

It is with very deep regret that we have to announce the death of Mr H.M. Walters, a member of the well known football family which has given us two of the greatest backs that Association football has ever known. The sad event occurred at the house of a medical friend in London at seven o'clock yesterday morning, and resulted from a kick in the abdomen accidentally received by him in the course of an Association match at Wormwood Scrubs, on the 12th inst., in which he was representing the Casuals against St. Bartholomew's Hospital. After writhing on the ground he was conveyed off the field, and it was soon seen that the injury was a serious one. Twelve days ago he was reported to be dying, and his brothers, 'A.M.' and 'P.M.,' were absent from the Cup tie played by the Old Carthusians against London Caledonians. A marked change for the better then occurred, though he was not pronounced out of danger, and only as recently as last Wednesday morning it was confidently announced that his two brothers would appear at the Oval to-morrow for London against a combined team of the Universities. The great change in the weather, however, doubtless had its effect upon the patient, and symptoms of acute peritonitis presented themselves, and to this he rapidly succumbed.

Deceased was educated at Haileybury, a public school more closely identified with the Rugby game, and on leaving there he went to Oriel College, Oxford. By this time he gave considerable promise at the Association game, and in the Spring of 1889 he was selected to represent the dark blues at the Queen's Club, West Kensington, partnering P.R. Farrant on the right wing. He afterwards became permanently identified with the Casuals, and should have represented that powerful organisation of amateurs, the Corinthians, at the Oval, in their opening engagement on the 15th inst. against the light blues. Deceased was a sterling forward, playing centre or right wing, and has taken part as a reserve man in of the London Association team.[2]

H.M. Walters was just 22 when he was laid to rest on 2nd December 1890 in the graveyard next to St. Mary the Virgin, Ewell. The Casuals placed a handsome wreath with the club's initials in pink flowers in the centre on the grave.

Casuals went into free fall and did not win for the next fifteen games, a run which overlapped the Christmas and New Year's tour to the north and Scotland. The tour began on Boxing Day and witnessed two games; a 3-3 draw at Lincoln City and a 2-4 defeat at Loughborough Town. Another two games were played on the following day and an over-stretched Casuals lost 2-7 to Aston Villa and 0-1 at Leicester Fosse. Casuals, however, finally got that elusive win two days later in a remarkable match with Football League strugglers, Derby County, which saw the amateurs demolish their opponents by ten goals to two after being 6-0 ahead at the interval. This was only a brief respite as Casuals again failed to win any of their next six games.

Sheffield United comfortably beat Casuals 0-7, before the tourists travelled to Scotland. There they held Kirkcaldy (3-3), before losing heavily to Abercorn (2-6), King's Park (5-9) and Third Lanark (1-4). An interesting insight into the Casuals' form from the latter part of the tour is provided by this extract of the report of the game at Paisley against Abercorn (who were founder members of the Scottish League):

The Casuals fairly took the breath away from the Underwood supporters as they bore down on the home goal and scored shortly after the start. The Casuals' centre played a grand individual game in the open, but failed perceptibly at goal.[3]

On their return from Scotland, Casuals next opponents were Aston Villa in an F.A. Cup First Round tie (last 32). Given Casuals' abysmal record in the F.A. Cup, having never won a game, it is somewhat surprising that they were awarded a bye to the first round proper. The Football Association announced the following exemptions the previous July:

The 18 clubs to take part in the second series of the national competition were selected thus:- Preston North End, Sunderland, Burnley, Accrington, Everton, West Bromwich Albion, Aston Villan, Derby County, Notts County, Casuals, Birmingham St. Georges, Old Westminsters, Darwen, Stoke, Royal Arsenal, Notts Forest, Clapton, and Crewe Alexandra. Blackburn Rovers, Sheffield Wednesday, Bolton Wanderers, and Wolverhampton Wanderers compete in that stage by right of being in last year's penultimate round.[4]

There is no logical reason for this exemption other than that of geography as few southern teams were chosen for a few years, but considering that the club had not reached the final of the two London F.A. competitions the previous season it is strange at the very least. It was even more surprising considering that the powerful Small Heath and Newton Heath (later known as Birmingham City and Manchester United) teams had to play through the qualifying rounds.

On the back of one win in twenty it is hardly surprising that Casuals were to suffer a humiliation at the hands of Aston Villa.

ASTON VILLA 13 CASUALS 1
The Perry Barr district seemed to have had a heavier sprinkling of snow than elsewhere, and the field was quite white and exceedingly hard....

The visitors who protested on account of the ground started uphill, and Dewhurst was stopped by Jones. The Villa left responded, and a couple of centres were put in by Campbell. Disbrowe spoilt the first and Seton dealt safely with a soft shot from the second. A corner fell to the home side, and the Casuals broke away. Back the Villa came, and Brown shot under difficult circumstances, and Seton stopped the progress of the ball. Another corner was obtained by the Villa, who penned their opponents in for a while. Graham shot splendidly into goal, and Seton stepped in between. The players on both sides had the greatest of difficulty in keeping their feet, and consequently the tactics of both sides were at a very low ebb. Topham got right right (sic) to the top of the field, and for the first time the Casuals really menaced the Villa position. Topham shot hard, and a loud cheer greeted Warner's success in repelling it. Almost directly the Villa forwards were seen racing down hill with the ball at the feet of Hodgetts. He passed quickly to Brown, who screwed in admirably. Campbell was just in time to meet it, and the Casuals goal came to grief for the first time. Two more shots had to be got rid of by Seton. Although the home team was by far the stronger, the Casuals got away now and again, but were never very powerful in goal. The Casuals backs had a lively time of it. Repeatedly their goal was assaulted. From the left the ball was dropped right in front. McKnight and Seton went for it, but the Villa man was there first, and cleverly scored....

Casuals kept the score respectable until half-time (0-2) before the floodgates opened.

The home team, in the second half, not only gave the game a more one-sided aspect than before, but put on goal after goal, as an indication of their superiority. The Casuals were hopelessly beaten. 5

Casuals protested to the Football Association following the game about the state of the ground, but this was not upheld and their only consolation was that it was not the biggest score of the round as Clapton had lost 0-14 against Nottingham Forest.

The Old Boys also made a relatively early exit from the London Senior Cup, losing to Royal Arsenal in the second round 2-3, after leading twice. This left the London Charity Cup as their only hope of collecting some silverware. Casuals started promisingly in this cup by defeating Clapton 8-1, and then a single goal by Perks was enough to beat Great Marlow in the semi-final. The final was to be the start of a great rivalry with the Old Carthusians:

CASUALS 1 OLD CARTHUSIANS 1
....Play was advertised to commence at 3.30, and three minutes later Currey set the ball in motion, kicking towards the pavilion goal. On settling down in earnest the Carthusians forced the work, and following some pretty combined play on the part of Parry, Wreford-Brown, Nixon, and Stanbrough, a judicious pass by the last named enabled Nixon to score the first point ten minutes from the start. The Old Boys continued to have the best of the game for the next twenty minutes, but could not get through, and at length a kick by Pelly let in Veitch, who got away and passed in turn to Sandilands, with the result that the latter, after a dashing run, shot a beauty and equalised. After this the Carthusians virtually played ten men, Currey's leg giving way, a loss that was severely felt by the Old Boys, as it necessitated a re-arrangement of the forwards. Sandilands sent in a couple of clinking shots, but Wilkinson saved grandly, and half-time arrived with the score one goal each. The second portion proved equally interesting. At the outset the Casuals, who had the wind and sun at their backs, pressed for some little time, but the defence of the Old Boys was good, and Guggisberg was in turn called upon to clear.

*Several times it appeared as though a deciding point would be obtained, Parry, Gilliatt, and Nixon working hard towards that end among the Carthusians, while Sandilands, Veitch, and Pryce-Jones made efforts to lower their rivals' goal. Wilkinson, however, was in grand form, and at the expiration of time neither side had been able to add anything, so that a draw of one goal each had to be recorded. There were shouts of 'Play on,' but the teams left the field, and at a subsequent meeting it was decided they should meet again next Saturday on the same ground. The game was contested throughout, and was noticeable for the absence of the slightest sign of rough play.*6

The replay followed one week later.

CASUALS 5 OLD CARTHUSIANS 2
*Three thousand spectators witnessed this match at Leyton on Saturday. The Carthusians failed to play with so much dash as hitherto, and although they had considerably the best of the contest the Casuals won by five goals to two. Both sides were almost identical with those that did duty the previous Saturday, the exception being that W.F. Stanbrough took the place of E.S. Currey, and W.J. Seton kept the Casuals' goal in lieu of F.G. Guggisberg, who is seriously ill. Owing to the teams being photographed it was twenty minutes to four when a start was made. The Casuals then kicked off from the pavilion goal, and faced a light wind. On settling down to work the Carthusian forwards were seen to the best advantage, and for close upon twenty minutes Seton was kept very busy indeed. At length a free kick for hands gave the Casuals an opening, and the ball being well placed by Cross, Knox got possession and sent in a beauty, which no custodian could save. The Old Boys returned to the attack on resuming, and Seton again had to put all he knew to keep his charge intact, despite the ponderous kicks of Pelly and partner. At length Veitch and Sandilands (both of whom had been very quiet) put in a combined run and got in very close quarters, the outcome being a second goal from the foot of Knox. Notwithstanding this reverse the Carthusian forwards played with renewed energy, and several times appeared certain to score. Luck, however, was on the side of their opponents, who just before half-time added a third, a run by Sandilands enabling Clarke and Knox between them to beat Wilkinson. This state of affairs did not suit the Carthusians, and at half-time they re-arranged their attack. Parry went centre, Gilliatt partnered M.H. Stanbrough, the latter's brother and Nixon playing on the right wing. This worked much better, as in less than three minutes they scored a goal. A corner-kick was taken by Streatfield, and M.H. Stanbrough heading right into the mouth of goal the ball was rushed through. This was quickly answered by one for Casuals, Clarke scoring after some good play by Pryce-Jones and Knox. The Old Boys stuck to their work, and following some pretty play Nixon obtained a goal from a splendid pass by M.H. Stanbrough. This proved to be their last point, notwithstanding the fact that they continued to press almost up to the end. The Casuals, on the other hand, secured a further item, a mis-kick by Shaw letting in Sandilands, who shot across and enabled Pryce-Jones to head the ball through. The Casuals thus secured a somewhat lucky victory by five goals to two.*7

The season thus ended on a high note, but the overall record was disappointing as Casuals only won 19 of the 74 games which have been traced, whilst losing 43. F.R. Pelly (24), T.L. Nelson (22), R.R. Barker (21) and F. Bickley (19) made the most appearances, whilst A.C. Nixon and R. Topham finished as top scorers with eleven. To highlight what a blow H.M. Walters' death was to the club, he still finished third top scorer with eight goals despite playing only four games prior to his untimely death.

1891/92

Casuals were the most active team in the country during the 1891/92 season having played one game more than Sheffield United who only managed to play 83 games! The club, still based at Wormwood Scrubs, was not to gather any silverware from cup success, but did finally break their F.A. Cup hoodoo and battle through the qualifying rounds to reach the last 32 or First Round Proper again. This season also witnessed the return of F. Bickley to the role of Club Secretary.

Not unexpectedly, Casuals began their F.A. Cup campaign this time in the first qualifying round and defeated Clapton 3-2 at the Oval when L.L. Cox scored a winner with ten minutes remaining of extra time. In the next round Casuals recovered from being one goal down against Old St. Marks, and hit five in reply. This set up an interesting third qualifying round tie with the Highland Light Infantry at Dover, the Old Boys running out comfortable 4-1 winners in the end. In the divisional final, Casuals met Chatham, to whom they succumbed 1-2 at Leyton after Cross was lamed early on in the game. Casuals, however, were reinstated after a successful appeal was upheld about the eligibility of two of Chatham's players. This set up a tie with Football League side Stoke in the First Round Proper which Casuals lost 0-3, but again the Old Boys protested, this time about the hard state of the ground. The protest was upheld, but it was to no avail this time as the game was replayed and ended exactly the same way as the first encounter. Casuals thus missed out on a chance to pit their skills against Burnley in the last sixteen. The club, however, did hold the distinction of being the last southern club to be knocked out of the cup that season.

In the London F.A. competitions they suffered a double first round exit at the hands of Millwall Athletic who within two seasons would be dominating the professional Southern League. The Casuals also entered the Middlesex Senior Cup for the only time, being drawn against Chiswick Park, before scratching.

The Casuals would probably have fared much better over the course of the season had they not overstretched their resources. On numerous occasions the side fielded several teams simultaneously against strong opposition, leading to some heavy defeats. In September the club lost 0-6 to Grimsby Town, 1-9 to Swindon Town and 1-2 to Marlow on the same day. This was followed in October when Football League leaders Derby County beat Casuals 0-4, and defeats against West Herts (0-6) and Westminster School (1-2) completed a miserable day. The only occasion this practice bore fruit was at the end of October when Sheffield United were beaten 3-0, although Reading comfortably won the other game 2-7.

The club again toured the north and Scotland at Christmas and New Year recording some impressive results. The tour opened with a 4-4 draw at Lincoln City after leading 3-0 at half-time. This was followed by a 3-3 draw at Gainsborough Trinity, prior to defeats at the hands of Derby County (2-5), Sheffield United (2-7), Heart of Midlothian (3-6, after drawing 3-3 with the Scottish Cup holders at half-time), Falkirk (3-7) and Third Lanark (0-1). The tour finished on a happier note, though, as Kirkcaldy were beaten 3-1 in the last game.

Casuals second half of the season was not overly successful and defeats followed against Royal Arsenal, Tottenham Hotspur, and Swindon Town. The best result was a 3-3 draw with Third Lanark when Furber saved Casuals with a last-second equaliser. The season closed with a tour to the north at Easter, and saw Casuals defeat Stockton and Sheffield United, whilst going down to Newcastle East End and Sunderland.

The problems facing a club secretary in the 1890's are highlighted by the following dialogue in regard to Casuals game against Hertfordshire which was cancelled.

CASUALS v. HERTFORDSHIRE
'Disappointed' writes – This match was arranged to take place on Saturday, at Hoddesdon, but through some unaccountable reason only one Casual put in an appearance, whereas Hertfordshire had their team and spectators waiting. (I should say the Herts XI was made up of players from Hitchin, Watford, St. Albans, Hertford, Hoddesdon, many travelling to London, and thence to Broxbourne. Thus a gentleman from Hitchin travelled eighty-six miles to take part in what turned out to be a 'pick up' match).

No one seemed to have the slightest idea that the Casuals would not turn up, and under these circumstances I trust the Herts secretary will report the matter to the Football Association. The gate-money, of course, was returned, and as this is the third consecutive disappointment Hoddesdon has received from the Casuals, I think you will see I am justified in calling attention to the matter through your valuable paper. For the information of your readers, the Casuals team was published in THE SPORTSMAN, and also time of train's departure.
(We are sure that Mr Bickley will satisfactorily explain matters. – ED., SPORTSMAN)[8]

Mr Bickley replied almost immediately:

CASUALS v. HERTFORDSHIRE
SIR – I saw in your paper a letter from 'Disappointed Player' re the Casuals failing to turn up last Saturday. The facts of the case are as follow: At the end of last season a match was arranged between the Casuals and Hertfordshire to take place on February 13, at Hoddesdon. The match was duly notified on the Casuals' card of fixtures. Upon February 8 I received a letter from the secretary of Hertfordshire informing me that the best train to go to Hoddesdon by was the 2.15, Liverpool-street to Broxbourne, and I accordingly wrote to my team, giving them that train. On Friday last (February 12), upon arriving at home too late too wire. I found two telegrams awaiting me. The first was 'wire at once if your team is coming to-morrow,' and the second, 'are you coming or not to-morrow.' I at once wrote to the secretary of the Herts team, saying that in consequence of his telegrams, if his team was not advertised in Saturday's SPORTSMAN, I should conclude the match was off, and that I could not understand why he should send wires as the Casuals had never disappointed the county team. On Saturday morning, as the Herts team was not advertised I wired to all my team putting them off, and also the Herts secretary to the same effect. – Yours, &c.
Feb. 18.   F.BICKLEY

P.S. – I may further add that it seriously inconvenienced some of my players being put off. (The Hertfordshire team was not received by us. ED. SPORTSMAN.)[9]

The Secretary of Hertfordshire responded again following this:

TO THE EDITOR OF THE SPORTSMAN
SIR, - I notice in your issue of this morning a letter from Mr Bickley re the Casuals v Herts fiasco on Saturday last. Mr Bickley's remarks are to a great extent correct, but not entirely so, and I must ask you to allow me, as hon. sec. of Herts, a few lines. As Mr Bickley states the match was arranged at the end of the last season and duly notified on both cards. He then goes on to state that I wrote to him on February 8, but does not say that I also wrote to him several days before that stating the arrangements I had made and asking him to let me know if they would suit. Receiving no answer I wrote again repeating my previous letter but this was also unanswered. Having heard nothing from him since the match was arranged I naturally felt anxious to know if they were coming as I had got my team team together and had made all arrangements for playing. On Friday morning, February 12. I received a wire from St. Albans F.C. asking if the match was coming off as they very much wanted two of their men who were playing for Herts. Of course, situated as I was, I was unable to reply so I immediately wired to Mr Bickley asking him to reply at once if they were coming. Receiving no answer I wired again and this was also unanswered, though this is perfectly explained by Mr Bickley's absence from home. I then determined to wait for the morning's SPORTSMAN to see if the Casuals' team was in, and in the meantime made final arrangements for playing, though I did not advertise my own team owing to the uncertainty I was in about the match. In the morning I saw the Casuals' team advertised, and this was the first imitation I had that they were coming. I immediately wired St. Albans saying that I could not spare the men, and directly afterwards received a telegram from Mr.Bickley, stating that he had concluded from my wires that the match was off and wired his men to that effect. I wired back instantly saying that all arrangements were made and we must play. He again did not answer my wire (though he had given me an address to wire to), so I naturally concluded that the match was on especially as on Mr.Bickley's own showing it is only necessary to reply when you are not coming. He also says that he received my wires on Friday too late for reply, so that he wrote at once. He may have written at once, but he certainly did not post it at once, as I did not receive his letter until 3.15 on Saturday afternoon. As to the inconvenience experienced by some of his players who were put off, how about the Herts' team and the one Casual who were not put off and made the fruitless journey to Hoddesdon? I appeal to any football secretary if they would not expect an answer from a visiting club saying if arrangements made would suit or not. I myself have had ten years of it and have always found it invariably the case. But apart from this, would it not have been an act of the merest courtesy to reply to my letters? Even now my wire of Saturday stating that the match must come off has not had the slightest notice taken of it. I should not have thought it would have been very difficult for Mr Bickley to understand why I wired to know if they were coming, and as to the Casuals having never disappointed the county before we only had one fixture with them. Apologising for taking up so much of your valuable space. I remain yours, etc.,
HERBERT W. PERKS, Hon. Sec. Herts C.F.A., Hitchen (sic), Feb. 19.[10]

Left: W.J. Oakley

There was no further correspondence, but following this the Casuals never played Hertfordshire again.

Three players made over thirty appearances for the Casuals during this season S. Furber and H. Knox both made 35, whilst F.R. Pelly played 31 games. Furber and Knox also lead the scoring charts with 27 and 25 goals respectively.

1892/93

Casuals built on the firm foundations of the previous campaign and produced a fine season. The club was in good hands as the list of officers shows. F. Bickley was Secretary, assisted by F.H. Walter, with T.W. Blenkiron being Treasurer. F.R. Pelly was captain and the committee consisted of A.C. Nixon, S. Furber, R.R. Barker, W.H. Bagshawe, F.J.K. Cross, H. Knox, H.C. Lowther, T.L. Nelson, W.J. Seton, H.P. Plumptre (Oxford University), and T.N. Perkins (Cambridge University).

Casuals record of playing 79 matches was even more impressive given that they were nomadic during the course of the season. The club played three times at Wormwood Scrubs, before wandering around grounds such as Leyton, the Oval, and Queen's Club.

The season opened with impressive victories over Swindon Town (4-2), Royal Arsenal (4-2) and Clapton (5-1) and although defeats were suffered in some of the minor matches, Casuals maintained their good form. In October Casuals beat Charterhouse School 4-2, significant in being the legendary G.O. Smith's first game for the club, and he duly scored on his debut.

Casuals continued to gain impressive victories, winning against Cambridge University, Old St. Marks, and Crusaders, whilst only going down narrowly against Oxford University and Sheffield United in the principal fixtures. Following the match against Guy's Hospital in November, the following report appeared:

It would hardly be accurate to describe the meeting of these clubs at Leyton, yesterday, as a football match – it partook more of the character of a scramble in the mud. Rain fell in torrents the whole time the game was in progress, and consequently it is not surprising that the spectators did number a dozen.[11]

In the F.A Cup, Casuals enjoyed a comfortable win over Wolverton in the first qualifying round, before cruising past Crusaders. In the third qualifying round only the heroics of W.R. Moon who was in goal for Old Westminsters kept the score line respectable as Casuals romped to a 5-2 victory. This was followed by a 5-0 demolition of Polytechnic. Casuals had made the last 32 for the third season running and were drawn against Division One side Nottingham Forest.

NOTTINGHAM FOREST 4 CASUALS 0
A great deal of interest was taken in this tie at Nottingham, and the result was that the 'gate' was the largest that has been seen at the Town Ground this season – fully 8,000 being present. The visitors had the disadvantage of playing against the wind in the first half, and added by this the home team commenced to press – a bit of nervousness on the part of Gostling (who was bothered by Shaw and kicked the ball right into his own goal instead of away), resulting in the 'reds' scoring soon after the start. Some pretty individual play on the part of some of the visitors was next seen, Sharples and Hope being very prominent, but bad shooting spoiled their final efforts, and the ball being returned McInnes headed to Higgins, who easily beat the Casual's custodian, the two goals having been scored in less than twenty minutes. Gostling, who was kept busy, was very soon afterwards again called upon, and in endeavouring to get away a high shot by McInnes, he inadvertently placed the ball almost at the feet of Pike, who dashed up and easily put it into the net. No further scoring took place till half-time. With the wind the visitors were expected to show up better, but the great pace at which the preceding portion of the game was taken was having its effect on some of the team, and as a consequence their play, to a certain extent, deteriorated. However, they went at it manfully, but it was a long while before they troubled Brown, the Forest backs playing a very good defensive game. About the middle of the half a pretty run on the Forest left wing carried the ball well into the visitors' quarters, and Higgins, taking steady aim, placed his side another point ahead. Both teams were now tiring now, and from this point to the finish Forest had the advantage, but no other material point could be added, and a good game ended in a victory for Forest by four goals to none. Brown, who has fully recovered from his illness, kept goal well, and as Allsop is ineligible through having played in the qualifying competition with Derby Junction, Brown will be the Forest Cup-tie goal-keeper throughout. Gostling, in goal, Sharples, Hope, and the backs were about the pick of the Casuals, who suffered from lack of condition as compared to their opponents.[12]

Prior to the Christmas Tour, Casuals crashed out of the London Charity Cup in the first round, and again at the hands of Millwall. The tour produced a few excellent results although it began with a 1-4 defeat at Leicester Fosse. The following day saw Casuals hold Lincoln City to a 1-1 draw whilst Luton Town were defeated 4-2. A defeat at Crewe Alexandra, preceded a 2-2 draw at Sheffield United and a 3-0 victory at Liverpool Ramblers. The next game at Southport Central was lost 2-3 as Casuals began to show signs of fatigue. Casuals then crashed 0-4 to King's Park, before defeating Third Lanark (3-2) and Kirkcaldy (1-0).

The second half of the season was dominated by Casuals' impressive form in the London Senior Cup. In the first round a late winner by Hope was enough to beat Tottenham Hotspur, before Old Harrovians were comfortably despatched 3-0. The Casuals were obviously feeling confident as they had sent a stronger team to face Third Lanark at the Oval on the same day! In the semi-final Casuals destroyed Clapton, as Robinson ran riot, creating three goals and scoring two in a 5-1 victory which set up a final against Old Westminsters.

OLD WESTMINSTERS 3 CASUALS 0
In weather more fitted for cricket than for football, a regular July sun prevailing, the final game for the London Senior Cup was played off on Saturday afternoon, on the Surrey County Ground, Kennington Oval. The clubs left to contend for the possession of the trophy were Casuals and the Old Westminsters, and there was enough interest in the result to attract fully 6,000 spectators to the ground spectators to the ground of play. Both sides had their full strength, and at 3.35 the Old Boys kicked off with the sun full in their eyes. After some even play the ball was taken down to the Westminsters' goal, but Robinson, with a fine opening, was too eager and kicked behind. Capital play by Simpkin and Robinson again gave Moon trouble, and the war was carried on in the Casuals half. Veitch made a fine run, and Sandilands sent the ball against the upright, and through the posts. The goal, however, was disallowed as 'off-side,' but five minutes later, or 25 minutes from the start, Street registered the first point for the Old Westminsters. Veitch, Sandilands, and Street now put in some grand work, with the result that Sandilands, amid considerable cheering, added a second goal, the score at half-time being: Old Westminsters, two points; Casuals, none. Changing ends the Casuals played up with marked spirit and energy. Bickley, Simpkin, and Robinson made desperate efforts to get away, and though Moon was now and again sorely pressed he kept his charge intact. In turn the Old Boys got the upper hand. Grand shots by Sandilands and Street were only saved by fine play of Seton, who once fell with the ball, but averted the danger when the score seemed certain. In the last 20 minutes the Casuals fell off somewhat, and Peck scored the third point, the game finally ending in a victory for the Old Westminsters by three goals to none. The back play of the winners was altogether superior to that of the Casuals. They were quicker on the ball, showed better combination, and proved much more accurate in passing. Street, Veitch, Sandilands, and Wetton were always prominent. For the losers, Robinson, Simpkin, Bickley, and Pelly did excellent work, but the first names, who often over-ran the ball, was too carefully watched to allow of him repeating his play in the semi-final against Clapton. Seton was a tower of strength in goal, but the best side certainly won a very enjoyable game.[13]

One of the more amusing games of the season occurred against Brighton College in February and it is worth quoting the following:

The referee, who was picked up on the ground, caused some amusement, and every now and then the two captains agreed to disregard his decisions.[14]

The season would not have been complete without the Easter Tour and again Casuals headed north. Casuals took the train to York on Good Friday, staying at the Station Hotel, before moving on to the Zetland Hotel in Saltburn-on-Sea prior to facing Newcastle United. Despite a goal-less first half Casuals were powerless to stop the Tynesiders scoring five second half goals.

Above: Casuals ground at Nightingale Lane, Hornsey

This was followed by a 0-4 reverse at Middlesbrough, before a victory was eventually achieved at Stockton.

The leading appearances chart was dominated by the committee as T.L. Nelson (30), F. Bickley (29), H. Knox (29), R.R. Barker (28), and F.R. Pelly (28) led the way. H. Knox was top scorer with 12.

1893/94

Casuals wrote themselves into the history books by reaching the first F.A. Amateur Cup final and also lifting the London Charity Cup to complete a successful season. After a nomadic existence season the previous year, Casuals began using two grounds for the next three years. The first and most regular venue during the 1893/94 season was at the bottom of Nightingale Lane in Hornsey, on the playing fields in the shadow of Alexandra Palace. This is still in use as a sporting venue with a cricket square and football pitch in evidence and it is quite feasible that there was an enclosure. A drainage ditch now surrounds the most likely location, around the boundary of the cricket pitch. This area is also the only flat land in the area as the terrain begins to climb sharply up to the eminence on which the Alexandra Palace is situated. It must have been an amazing venue with games being played with the majestic structure of the palace towering over the assembled crowds. The other popular venue at this point was the Lyttelton Ground, Leyton, the home of Essex County Cricket Club.

Casuals struggled against the professional clubs encountered in the early part of the season. The first game resulted in an impressive 1-0 victory over Tottenham Hotspur with F. Bickley scoring the winner. Casuals, though, soon came down to earth with 1-5 defeats at the hands of Woolwich Arsenal and the Football League champions, Sunderland. The latter was played in front of what was said to have been the biggest football crowd ever at Leyton.

There was further disappointment in the F.A. Cup when Casuals crashed out in the 2nd Qualifying Round at Wolverton after Blaker was injured and the Old Boys had to play the last half hour with ten men. Despite this set back, Casuals still produced some good results and only lost to the mighty Preston North End by the odd goal in seven in December.

The Christmas and New Year tour commenced with a 0-6 drubbing at Leicester Fosse, and on the same day a 1-1 draw at Northamptonshire. The following day saw narrow defeats at Luton and Derby. Casuals were struggling and went down 0-5 to Sheffield United and then 1-3 to Liverpool Ramblers. In Scotland, Casuals lost 0-4 in Edinburgh to St. Bernards before the New Year brought improved fortunes for the tourists as first Abercorn were defeated 4-2 at Paisley, thanks to four goals by R. Topham, and then Queen of the South Wanderers were held 2-2. The tour closed with defeats against King's Park (3-5) and Kirkcaldy (0-1).

The explanation for these poor results was given many years later:

During the Christmas tour in 1893-94, the Casuals played Derby County, Luton Town, Sheffield United, Liverpool Ramblers, St. Bernard's, Abercorn, Paisley, and King's Park, Dumfries. While on tour they joined the Corinthians, who were also up North, at a pantomime at Edinburgh. The outstanding players were W.R. Moon, R.R. Barker, J.E. Grieveson, and H.A. Rhodes. That the tour was not more successful from a playing point of view was due to the fact that – in the words of one of the players – 'most of our men were new to northern football, and could not understand why whenever they knocked a man over in fair charge, shoulder to shoulder, a free-kick was given, whereas when they were tripped, no award was given.' The northern tour was evidently a Spartan undertaking in those days; this particular trip was called 'The Casualty tour.'[15]

Casuals warmed up for their London Senior Cup campaign by playing St. Bartholomew's Hospital. After going 0-3 down after only ten minutes, the Old Boys recovered to win 4-3. In the Cup, Casuals had been drawn at home to City Ramblers who were beaten with a weak team. In the second round Casuals were held by Crouch End to a goal-less draw at home. In the replay Casuals contrived to lose 3-4 after being 3-1 up with ten minutes remaining.

The F.A. Amateur Cup First Round was to be played on 3rd February 1894 and Casuals had been drawn at home to Sheffield.

CASUALS 3 SHEFFIELD 1
Considering the many counter attractions in other parts of the metropolis it was surprising to find the ground at Nightingale-lane so well attended on Saturday, when these two clubs brought off their tie in the first round. The weather was all that could be desired, and the ground in capital condition. The Casuals were none too strongly represented, and many thought that they might go down. As it was, they only just scrambled home, and although they had a pretty good margin in their favour at the finish the score by no means represents the true state of the game.

*There was nothing much in it in the first half, and the only point scored was notched by Perkins for the home team about ten minutes after the start. On crossing over, Sheffield had decidedly the best of the game for the best part of twenty minutes, and then Barber placed them on level terms. On restarting, Sheffield went off with a rush, and tried hard to get ahead, but within ten minutes of the finish the Casual forwards again carried the ball in their opponents' quarters, and twice within five minutes Perkins beat Bolsover, who defended very finely all through. Nothing further transpired, and the Casuals thus won by three goals to one.*16

The victory set up a mouth-watering tie with Chatham, the team Casuals had protested against and had removed from the F.A. Cup only two years previously. As can be seen from the events which followed, it is clear many of the people of Chatham had not forgiven them for this.

CHATHAM 0 CASUALS 2
THE REFEREE DISGRACEFULLY MOBBED

The tie between these clubs, at Chatham, was regarded as likely to produce a close contest, the odds, slightly in favour of the Casuals. Expectations were verified, as the visitors won, after a remarkably even game, by two goals to none. Unfortunately the match did not end without a very unpleasant scene being witnessed. From the outset a large portion of the twelve hundred spectators displayed a large amount of feeling against the visiting players, and also against Mr C. Squires, the referee, who, while making a few mistakes, was, on the whole, up to his work. It may be well to state that in 1891 Chatham defeated the Casuals at Leyton by two to one, in the final of the division for the Association Cup, but were thrown out on protest. Since that period the Casuals have made several fixtures with Chatham, but subsequently scratched. At the close of the play a number of the onlookers blocked the entrances to the enclosure and pavilion, and the cry was raised, 'Remember the protest,' and 'Go for them!' A rush from all parts of the field was then made for the referee and players. Amidst loud hooting Mr Squires was surrounded and hustled. He was struck lightly on the shoulder with an umbrella, and L.V. Lodge, one of the visitors' backs, received a couple of knocks on the head with a similar weapon, and either from the effects of these or from a shove he fell to the ground. In the melee which followed a Casual struck a bystander, who had taken no part in the affray, a blow on the side of the face with his fist, but finding he had made a mistake at once apologized. As soon as the committee of the club saw what was passing several of their number went to the assistance of Mr Squires, and succeeded in getting him into the committee stand, though not before his macintosh had been badly torn. For some time the excited crowd remained hooting in front of the building, but eventually Mr Squires, escorted by the officials and police, was got a cab and driven away. The referee intimated that he should report the facts of the case to the Association. In fairness to the committee of the club, it should be said that they did what they could to keep order, and during the afternoon two or three men were ejected from the ground by the police. Dealing with the play, it may be said that the match was largely spoilt by the slippery state of the ground, rain falling during the whole time play was in progress. Chatham had the wind behind them during the first half, but although they had several chances of scoring the forwards did not avail themselves of them. The only point scored came from the foot of Rhodes a quarter of an hour from the start. The Casuals also had a penalty given because Pellatt fisted the ball within the twelve yard line, but Jones saved from Perkins. For a large portion of the second half the home side did most of the attacking, and Harrison had several warm shots to save. Jones also was not idle, and accounted for everything that came his way until ten minutes from the finish, when he was beaten by Rhodes.[17]

In the third round Casuals were drawn at home to Chirk. The Welsh club subsequently withdrew from the cup, however, which gave Casuals a bye to the semi-final. During the extended interval between rounds, Casuals beat Old Brightonians and Highgate School, but lost to R.M.C. Sandhurst. The day of the semi-final against Sherwood Foresters arrived on 17th March and a hard battle was anticipated.

CASUALS 1 SHERWOOD FORESTERS 0
This tie was decided on Saturday on the Essex County Ground at Leyton, before a company numbering about 3,000. The match was played under the most favourable conditions, the weather being fine and turf in first-rate order, while there was no wind to interfere with play. The Casuals were strongly represented and were a much heavier team than their opponents. The Sherwood Foresters were the first to attack, a long shot bringing Harrison out to save. The Casuals then pressed, and for some time the play was chiefly confined to the Sherwoods' ground. Perkins missed one good chance of shooting, but afterwards gave Cragg a particularly hot one to stop. Then, twenty minutes after the start, Landon headed through from a pass by Compton, a claim for off-side being disallowed. The Casuals had somewhat the best of the exchanges to the interval, but no further point was scored. In the second stage the play continued very fast, and was of a fairly even character, the Foresters making determined efforts towards the close to get on terms. They failed in the attempt, and the Casuals came out the victors of a hard fight by one goal to none. On both sides the defence was good, Lodge being particularly safe.[18]

Casuals were now the favourites for the cup, having beaten Old Carthusians heavily just weeks before the final.

OLD CARTHUSIANS 2 CASUALS 1
In the earlier stages of the competition for the Amateur Cup, presented this season by the Football Association, there was not very much enthusiasm shown by the general public; but on Saturday afternoon at Richmond some 4,000 spectators took a keen interest in the final tie to which Old Carthusians and the London Casuals had fought their way. The company at the athletic ground included the Duke and Duchess of Teck and the Duchess of York, who viewed the whole of the football from the pavilion. It was in every respect a fine game to watch; the fast pace of the forwards, the brilliant work of Stanbrough on the left wing of the Carthusians, the skill of Wreford-Brown at half-back, and the unerring kicking of A.M. Walters, also for the Carthusians, were points in the play that must have been patent to everybody. A weakness in the Carthusian front rank was the centre; G.O. Smith had been called away to help England at Glasgow, and his position was filled by Buzzard, who usually plays half. The last-mentioned did his best, but for a long while in the first half he did not get the ball out to the wings as he should have done, and this enabled the Casuals to have the better of the early play. R. Topham made some fine runs for the Casuals, who pressed severely to begin with and scored the first goal in five minutes from the kick-off, T.N. Perkins passing to R. Topham, who put the ball through. In the last 20 minutes of the first half the Carthusians fared well. Stanbrough executed some brilliant work on the left wing, and it was almost wholly through him that two goals were

recorded. Thus the Carthusians led at the interval. In the second three-quarters of an hour the play was full of excellence, but no further scoring occurred, and the victory was with the Old Carthusians by two goals to one. The winners were warmly cheered. Before the match began the captains of the teams – Wreford-Brown and R. Topham – were presented to the Royal visitors. 19

Casuals salvaged their season with victory in the London Charity Cup. London Caledonians were thrashed 5-1 in the first round, before Old Carthusians were swept aside 3-0 in the semi-final.

CASUALS 2 OLD WESTMINSTERS 1
In the eighth year of its existence the London Charity Cup, besides being very beneficial to the London Charity Fund, has awakened much more interest among the clubs than was hitherto noticeable.... The spectators on Saturday at the Lyttelton Ground, Leyton, mustered something like 5,000 strong, and they witnessed a very keen game between the Casuals and Old Westminsters for the possession of the cup. The Casuals, by reason of their defeat of the Old Carthusians in the penultimate tie, were, in most quarters, expected to win. And they did not disappoint their followers, although their success was not secured until the last five minutes of the match. From beginning to end the play proved interesting; and the many fine runs, the skilful passing, and the ability with which the defence was conducted were points pretty evenly distributed between the two sides. The fact that three of the Casuals and five of the Old Westminsters were internationals gave an idea of the calibre of the elevens. The play proceeded without any definite advantage to either side for a very long time in spite of many brisk attacks. The Casuals' football was, if anything, the more precise, and close upon the interval Guy kicked a goal for them. But the moments of the first period remaining proved sufficient for the Old Westminsters to get level, the honour of scoring, as the result of excellent passing, being with Sandilands. Thus were ends changed with the figures equal. The second three-quarters of an hour yielded play of a very similar character to that which had preceded it. Fine dribbling was shown by the forwards on each side, and at times the combination was excellent. It was left to the last few minutes to furnish the winning point, and the goal by Blaker enabled the Casuals to win the cup be two goals to one. 20

F. Bickley (28) and R.R. Barker (24) led the appearance totals, whilst T.N. Perkins was top scorer with 15 goals. R. Topham was the second top scorer with ten goals; Topham had collected an F.A. Cup winners medal with Wolverhampton Wanderers at the end of the previous season.

1894/95

Casuals had another memorable season, although they did not enjoy the success of the previous campaign. It was the last season that Casuals were to play in the F.A. Cup (except for two seasons in the early 1930's) and it also saw the club reach the final of the London Senior Cup.

Left: C.F. Drake

Casuals began with a 5-3 victory over Clapton, before losing 1-3 to Tottenham Hotspur and then 2-5 to Luton Town. Worse was to follow when Woolwich Arsenal demolished Casuals 0-8 in questionable circumstances:

We certainly must enter our protest against such a club as the Arsenal, considering its status in the football world, playing what is known as 'gallery.' On Saturday, as soon as they had seen the Casuals were 'no class,' the forwards began this detestable clowning. The spectators soon showed their disapproval in a most marked manner, and this caused the players to desist. 21

The club then lost only 3-4 to Nottingham Forest to mark an upturn in fortunes. Following this, Casuals won their last F.A. Cup tie for many years when Chesham were defeated 4-1 in the first qualifying round. In the next round Casuals drew 0-0 with Ilford (incidentally the old boys also played Preston North End on the same day losing 2-5), before bowing out in the replay.

CASUALS 1 ILFORD 3
Only about 500 spectators turned up at the Essex County Ground, Leyton, yesterday, when these clubs, who played a drawn game at Ilford on Saturday, met to decide which of the twain should enter the third round. Thoroughly representative elevens came to the fray, but whereas the Ilford men played with rare dash and vigour all through, their heavier opponents were slow to get to the ball, and suffered defeat by three goals to one. In addition to the fault already referred to several of the Casuals – notably Barker and Drake – were selfish, and neglected to pass, whilst the shooting at goal of Hannaford was bad. The game cannot be referred to as a scientific one, whilst towards the close an element of roughness was introduced, and the referee found it necessary to caution Linard (Ilford). At half-time the Casuals ranks were rearranged. Foy going full back, Bickley half, and Pelly forward, but this led to no improvement in the play.

The Casuals kicked off against the wind, but Ilford at once pressed, and a quarter of an hour from the start A. Porter opened the scoring for them. Bickley equalized from a fine centre by Hannaford, but A. Porter headed through for Ilford, who led at half-time by two to one. After change of ends Ilford continued to have more of the game than their rivals, and after a series of hot attacks by the Porters had been well saved by 'Wood,' the ball was centred to Gallon, and that player scoring. 22

In between the two rounds of the F.A. Cup Casuals produced one of the finest performances in their entire history when they defeated a Sunderland side who would go on to be the Football League champions at the end of the season:

CASUALS 4 SUNDERLAND 3
The Sunderland Club strengthened their team for the match with the Casuals, at Lyttelton-ground, Leyton, yesterday; but, in spite of this fact and also that the football was quite worthy of the reputation of the famous League side, they were beaten in a brilliant game by the Casuals. It was a triumph for amateurs against professionals in an encounter in which the styles of football were in marked contrast; Sunderland of course adopted the short passing game of great finish, whereas the Casuals went in for long passing, which, with their rushes, was very brilliant to watch. The Casuals thoroughly deserved their victory, although their game was not of the uniform of excellence which ran through the League side. Perhaps the player who was chiefly responsible for the Casuals' win was G.B. Raikes, of Oxford, in goal, and the way in which he stopped shot after shot from the Sunderland attack elicited repeated applause. C.B. Fry, G.O. Smith, and A.N. Guy all did excellently in the front rank of the amateurs, while Lodge, the Cambridge full back, worked with wonderful energy and vigour. Sunderland played beautifully together, but had the misfortune to meet a very determined defence. It was a splendid game, and was a case of goal and goal right through. The first point fell to Miller, of Sunderland, within five minutes of the start, and in a quarter of an hour G.O. Smith brought the score level, while a good piece of work between Fry and Guy enabled the latter to place the lead with the Casuals before half-time. After change the score was twice even, but 12 minutes from 'time' G.O. Smith kicked the deciding goal for the Casuals, who won by four to three. There were about 6,000 spectators. 23

Casuals' Christmas and New Year tour was certainly not as tough as in previous years, but the club still found victories elusive. It opened on with a defeat on 22nd December by 2-3 against Burslem Port Vale followed on Christmas Eve with 2-3 defeat at Leicester, before Kettering were defeated 2-1 on Boxing Day. A draw at Luton Town preceded a 1-4 defeat at Loughborough Town and another loss at division two side Burton Wanderers (0-3) which was played in a hurricane. Sunderland then gained their revenge on the Casuals (2-5), despite the Old Boys taking a 2-0 lead at half-time. Casuals travelled north of the border for their next game against Newton Stewart Athletic and recorded a 4-4 draw, before the defeats started again against Greenock Morton (2-3), Dumfries (2-4), and Third Lanark (1-4). Kirkcaldy were defeated 3-2 before the tour closed with a 0-4 defeat against Ayr Parkhouse.

The club's interest in the London Charity Cup ended at the first round stage, after losing a replay to London Caledonians who went on to win the competition this season. Casuals, however, missed a penalty in the first tie with the scores level, so were left to rue what might have been. The F.A. Amateur Cup provided even less joy: Casuals lost 1-3 to Reading after Manly had missed the train and thus the Old Boys had to play the whole game with ten men.

The only competition left open to the Casuals was the London Senior Cup and this certainly had its moments of controversy. In the first round Casuals defeated Ealing 5-3, and they were then drawn against Woodford. This tie was to drag on for the best part of a month after the referee deemed the pitch for the scheduled first meeting unfit for cup football. As often happened in those days, a friendly was played instead, which Casuals won 3-1.

The second attempt to play the tie saw the ground still in a poor condition, and Woodford were further aggrieved when only seven of the Casuals players turned up. This provoked the following complaint in the *Woodford Times*:

On Saturday the Woodford team were led by the Casuals on another wild-goose expedition to that Slough of Despond, the Crouch End ground, Nightingale Lane, Hornsey, with the ostensible object of deciding the London Senior Cup tie which was postponed on the previous Saturday, owing to the wretched condition of the ground. A recital of what had transpired in the interval between the two journeys to the Hornsey quagmire will enable people to judge whether the conduct of the Casuals towards Woodford has been either gentlemanly or sportsmanlike. On Thursday, the 28th ult., Mr. Bickley, the secretary of the Casuals, wired to Woodford: 'We play at Kennington Oval Saturday; kick-off 2.45.' After the Woodford team and the public had been notified of this fact Mr. Bickley wired again on Friday afternoon to the effect that the Oval Sub-Committee would not allow football on the Oval, and so the match would have to take place at Hornsey. Upon receiving this notice the Woodford secretary telegraphed back: 'As Hornsey is not fit, will you play at Woodford.' At 7.30 p.m., Mr. Bickley replied 'Train 2.15 Moorgate to Hornsey. Referee must decide.' The change of venue at the last moment entailed considerable outlay on telegrams to the members of the Woodford team, and as it proved, the money and trouble expended proved bootless. Despite the fact that they had a suspicion that the match would not come off, the Woodfordians, accompanied by a considerable number of their supporters, journeyed to Hornsey, where only seven Casuals put in an appearance. After looking at the ground they expressed the opinion that it was unfit for play, an opinion which the referee, Mr. Bisiker, acquiesced in. As the Casuals left they were loudly hooted by the crowd and one gentleman remarked 'I expect they will want to play football in a drawing room soon.' The opinion was freely expressed that the Casuals never meant to play on Saturday, because they were unable to put a good team into the field owing to several of their best men being engaged in the Oxford v Cambridge match, and they selected Hornsey because they knew the ground was unfit. The Casuals denied this, but they did not give any other explanation, and therefore, we think popular view is the correct one. If the Casuals had been acting in a bona-fide manner in the matter, they would not have turned up with only seven men and they would not have selected Hornsey as the rendezvous, knowing, as they must have known, that the referee had declared on the previous Saturday that the Crouch End ground would not be fit for a Cup tie within a month. Any team that had been anxious to have the fixture decided would have shown the same pluck at Woodville did, and would have tried conclusions on the Woodford ground, which was in admirable condition. Had the Casuals ordered the state of the Hornsey ground to be reported on before the match, with a view to saving Woodford the expense and trouble of going down, we should have been inclined to modify our view of the situation, but instead of doing that they caused their opponents all the inconvenience and loss they possibly could. After the extremely shabby conduct of the Casuals we consider that the London Association would only be doing its duty if it determined to stop such unjustifiable devices by ruling that the right to the choice of ground was now vested in Woodford, as they did in the Old St. Stephens v Old Westminsters match in 1893.

ACTION OF THE LONDON ASSOCIATION
A meeting of the Emergency Committee of the London Football Association was held on Wednesday evening to consider a request from the Woodford Club re their London Senior Cup tie with Casuals that the match might be postponed owing to illness among their players, and subsequently played on the Woodford ground. It was decided that certificates should be furnished by the Woodford Club with regard to their players laid up with influenza, and if the match will be postponed, otherwise the match must be played on a neutral ground provided by the Casuals; but failing that provision, to be played on the Woodford ground.[24]

The fact remained that Casuals had acted within the rules of the competition and had done nothing wrong. Woodford on the other hand were playing dirty, probably as they suspected it was their only chance of progressing. Their attempt to get the game postponed again due to a bout of influenza never materialised as they failed to provide the documentation and the following statements then ensued:

After a consultation the Woodford executive determined to play reserve men and so get the tie decided one way or the other, and telegraphed to that effect. On Friday evening, however, they received a wire stating that the match had been postponed; hence the meeting on Monday evening, when Mr. J. Grayston attended on behalf of Woodford and Mr. Bickley represented the Casuals. Eventually the committee decided that the tie be played on or before the 23rd inst., the Casuals to have choice of ground, and it was understood that it would probably by played at Leyton. In consequence of Woodford objecting to Mr Biseker acting as referee, Mr. Roston Bourke kindly offered to officiate in that capacity.[25]

At the fourth attempt the match was finally played and Casuals made short work of Woodford, recording another 3-1 victory, as Compton struck a hat-trick. Casuals were drawn against Ilford in the semi-final and avenged their F.A. Cup defeat with an emphatic 3-0 victory at Leyton. There was three weeks before the final and Casuals warmed up for this with victories over Tottenham Hotspur (2-1), Woodville (4-2), and Crouch End Thursday (3-2), whilst losing 1-3 to West Herts. The final was to be a disappointing affair.

OLD CARTHUSIANS 6 CASUALS 0
History has very nearly repeated itself this season in connection with the Charterhouse players. Last year, after reaching the final stage in the Amateur, London Senior, and Charity Cup contests they had to rest content with winning the first named trophy. This season they once more arrived in the closing scenes for all three, but in the Charity Competition lost to London Caledonians, whilst the Middlesborough team wrested the Amateur Cup from them. Last night, however, the Old Boys made some amending carrying off the London Senior, but although they won easily their display was far from being a high class tie. The weather was fine, but the turf at the Queen's Club was very long and caused the ball to travel somewhat slowly, whilst there

were not more than about 800 or 900 people present. Neither side was up to full strength, but in this respect the Casuals suffered most, and the lot they had to rely upon distinguished themselves by an utter lack of combination.

Toone kicked off from the top end of the ground at 4.35. The Casuals ran down, but Hewitt and Kirby at once returned, and were becoming exceedingly dangerous when Fry cleared. Kirby returned to the charge, and Smith headed into Lawrence's hands. The Corinthians (sic) kept up their pressure, and Buzzard came within an ace of scoring, whilst after a corner Tringham nearly got through, but nevertheless the play was not fast or particularly good. A quarter of an hour from the start a run by Tringham and 'Honeyball' ended in the former scoring, and this was the only point scored in the first half. After change of ends the game degenerated into a farce, almost, C.P. Wilson and Compton were continually making mistakes, whilst Hilleary was seldom dangerous. The Carthusians penned in their rivals, and after Smith had hit the bar with a swift shot, and the O.C.'s centre forward placed his side another point ahead. Then, from a pass by Smith, 'Honeyball' headed through, and directly after Kirby put on two goals in quick succession. Tringham then scored with a shot that hit Lawrence in the face and knocked him clean over. The goalkeeper was considerably shaken but he stopped a rare hot from 'Honeyball' directly after. [26]

C.F. Drake led the appearances with 31 matches, whilst J.F. Fernie was top scorer with 14 goals in as many games.

Chapter Three
All Change At The Top
1895-1900

At the start of the 1895/96 season F. Bickley stepped down for the last time as Secretary and was replaced by Roland Hilleary. This event heralded a change in policy as the club decided not to enter the F.A. Cup henceforth, a move which anticipated the club's withdrawal from the F.A. Amateur Cup at the end of the 1898/99 season. It also produced a reduction in the number of matches that were played on Christmas and New Year's tours. Unfortunately there is no written record to explain the motive for these actions, but the club continued to do well in the London F.A. competitions and were clearly one of the capital's leading clubs.

1895/96

The new era at the Casuals Football Club opened in dramatic fashion when the team contrived to throw away a 3-0 second half lead against Clapton and lose by the odd goal in seven. The next two games were losses at the hands of Tottenham Hotspur and Tunbridge Wells, before the 1st Grenadier Guards were beaten 2-0 at Nightingale Lane. The club progressed steadily, generally gaining the upper hand against the amateur clubs, but failing miserably against the professional clubs such as Southampton St. Mary's (0-5), Everton (1-2), Swindon Town (0-3), Preston (0-4), and Woolwich Arsenal (0-3).

Casuals' best form was saved for the F.A. Amateur Cup. After receiving a bye in the first qualifying round, they next overcame the 2nd Coldstream Guards in a match hindered by confusion as to which club was responsible for supplying the ball. The game eventually kicked off late and this led to a protest by the Guards who thought that the proceedings would end in darkness. In any event Casuals took control and were leading 3-0 by half-time, which proved to be the final result.

The next round saw Casuals record an easy 5-1 win over Queen's Park Rangers, the most notable event being a goal by R.R. Barker who scored from the half way line. The last qualifying round game pitted the club against their rivals Old Westminsters and despite having to start the game with ten men (as L.V. Lodge was twenty minutes late) and going a goal behind, Casuals recovered to win 2-1 with an 88th minute winner from H.J. Collier. The run came to an end in the first round when Shrewsbury Town won 2-4, Casuals having led twice.

December marked one of the performances of the season as Casuals held the mighty Sunderland to a 3-3 draw after trailing 1-3 at one stage. On the Saturday before Christmas, Casuals faced Tottenham Hotspur in their first game as a professional club. The professionals celebrated this occasion by recording a 1-3 victory over the Old Boys. On the same day Casuals suffered in the London Charity Cup at the hands of the Old Carthusians (2-3). This season's Christmas tour was a short-lived affair which began with a 2-2 draw at Clapton, followed by a mauling at Luton Town (1-7) and a narrow defeat at Leicester Fosse (5-6).

The New Year opened with defeats against New Brompton (0-2) and Luton Town (0-3), before Casuals began their London Senior Cup campaign. In the first round Casuals won an exciting game with Queen's Park Rangers 4-3, and followed this up with a 2-0 victory over St. Bartholomew's Hospital. In the semi-final Casuals faced the Vampires who hailed from Norbury and won a thrilling game 5-3 largely thanks to a hat-trick by J.F. Fernie.

Six weeks were to pass before the final was played, as their opponents, Old Carthusians, were still involved in the London Charity Cup. During this interval Casuals lost heavily at Woolwich Arsenal (1-4), but held Everton (who had just finished third in Division One of the Football League) to a 3-3 draw. This result failed to inspire Casuals in the London Senior Cup final as their bad luck at this stage of the competition continued.

OLD CARTHUSIANS 3 CASUALS 1
In the presence of about 2,000 spectators, the Old Carthusians, who were very strongly represented, defeated the Casuals yesterday by three goals to one. The match, which was of a rather tame character, was decided on the Essex County Ground at Leyton, which was in excellent order, but a rather high wind prevailed. The final score was by no means represented the actual superiority of the winners, who rarely allowed their rivals to cross the half-way line in the second half. It is only fair to mention, however, that after the first twenty-five minutes Hatton was injured, and for the rest of the time the Casuals had only four forwards. The whole of the scoring occurred after Hatton left the field. As already hinted, the match was a rather spiritless one until the last ten minutes when the exchanges were very exciting. Although having a lot the best of the game, the Carthusian forwards passed in very wild fashion, and neglected numerous opportunities of shooting. For the first half G.O. Smith was almost a passenger, but Kirby played very well all through. The gentleman who played as 'R.E. Ford' was a long way the best half-back on the field. Barker worked hard on the other side, but the backs were rather slow, and not too safe in their kicking, and Lawrence had a lot of hard work to do. He acquitted himself very well indeed. The Carthusians attacked directly after the kick-off, but after Kirby had passed to Tringham the latter shot wide. Then the Charterhouse representatives forced a corner, which Adams cleared, and 'R.E. Ford,' returning to the charge, had his shot fisted out by Lawrence. Keeping up the pressure, Tringham was next prominent and forced a corner, which, however, Hewitt sent behind. After Murdoch had hit the side of the net, the Casuals got a look in, and Drake wound up a fine run by shooting at Pritchett, who saved very nicely. Kirby returned, and caused Lawrence to handle, following which Smith missed a splendid opening. An attack by Hilleary and Taylor was broken up by Buzzard, who transferred to Kirby, and the latter opened the scoring for the Carthusians half an hour from the start. Following the centre kick, Hewett ran and passed to Smith, who shot. From the Press Box the ball certainly appeared

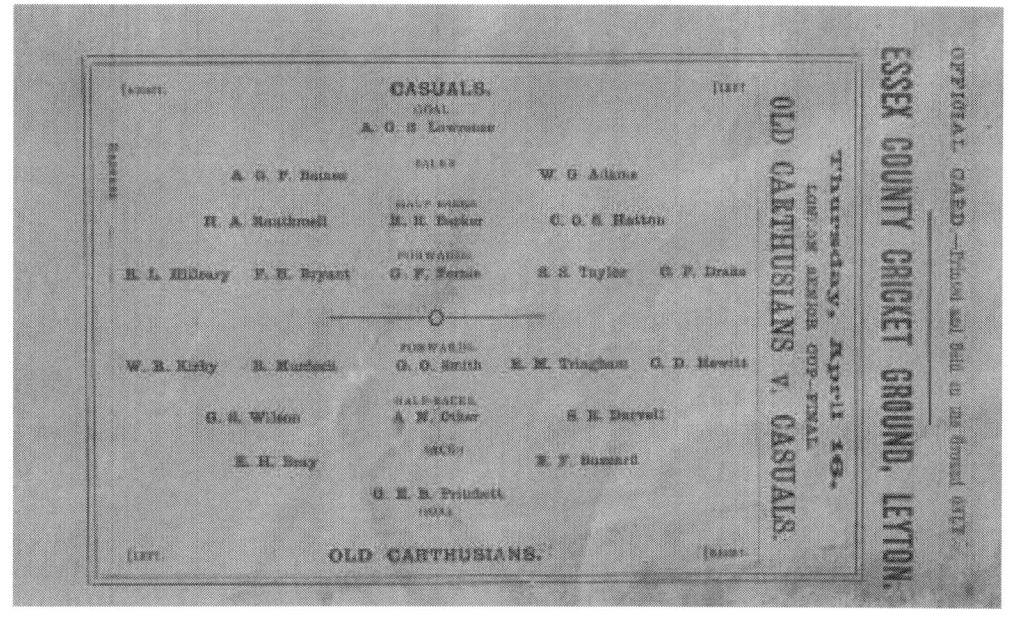

Above: London Senior Cup final programme 1895/96 - Casuals v Old Carthusians

to go under the bar before Lawrence fisted it out, but no appeal was made. From a corner, nicely placed by Hewitt, 'R.E. Ford' headed into the hands of the Casual goalkeeper, and three other corners, in as many minutes, fell to the Carthusians, but a half-time the score was still one goal to love in their favour. After crossing over the Carthusians continued to press, the rival halves and forwards being weak. Kirby (two) and Tringham made dangerous shots, and then, at the end of five minutes, Smith scored with a beauty. The Oxonian played very much better than in the opening half, but twice had the ill luck to hit the side of the net. Tringham sent wide and then Kirby rushed through, but he was offside. Hewitt and Smith were also pulled up for similar tactics. Ten minutes from time a mistake by Buzzard let in Bryant, who tricked the Carthusian backs and passed to Taylor, the latter kicking a goal for the Casuals. For a brief spell the 'Whites' played up superbly and looked like equalizing, Barker, Taylor, and Drake being very prominent, but Tringham then broke away and passing to Kirby, the latter beat Lawrence once more.[1]

The new secretary R.M. Hilleary led the appearances with a total of 37, and was followed by the top scorer J.F. Fernie who scored 30 goals in just 27 appcarances. Other prominent players included R.R. Barker (24), S.L. King (22), and A.G.S. Lawrence (20). The most impressive goal scoring feat was achieved by G.O. Smith who scored eight in a single game as Casuals romped to a 9-2 victory over Shrewsbury School.

1896/97

Casuals improved on the previous season by lifting the London Charity Cup and the team had a fine run to the quarter-final of the F.A. Amateur Cup. The club's A.G.M. at The Sports Club, St. James's Square on 24th September 1896, saw the members pay tribute to F. Bickley for all his years of service as club secretary and it was recorded:

The only other item of business of public interest was the presentation by Mr A.E. Harrison, on behalf of the club, of a handsome travelling bag to Mr. F. Bickley, who was chiefly instrumental in the formation of the club some fourteen years ago, and who in addition had rendered valuable assistance as honorary secretary. Mr Bickley in a few well chosen words expressed his thanks to the members for their gift.[2]

As a result of this meeting the following officials were elected; R.M. Hilleary (Secretary), S.L. King (Treasurer), R.R. Barker (Captain), J.F. Fernie (Vice-Captain) and the committee consisted of F. Bickley, A.E. Harrison, L.V. Lodge, G.O. Smith, E.H. Bray, F.R. Pelly, W.G. Adams, E.L. Hilleary, C.F. Drake, C.O.S. Hatton, W.J. Oakley, G.B. Raikes, H.A. Rauthmell, C.L. Alexander, S.S. Taylor, and W. McCowan.

Casuals relocated again during the Summer of 1896 to the Tufnell Park Athletic Ground, close to the Tufnell Park Hotel, whose address is listed in the Islington Suburban Directory of 1902 as 162 Tufnell Park Road and is now known as Tufnell's. The hotel is mentioned in contemporary reports and was clearly visible behind one of the goals. The sports ground survives in the form of the Tufnell Park playing fields and has the feel of an old football arena, even though little tangible remains. A line of trees which look like a new addition form a natural boundary at one end, and a wall stretches the length of the ground dividing the sports ground from the houses which overlooked the stadium. This looks likely to be the only surviving feature. It is known that in 1901 new timber terracing was installed behind the western goal and a year later wooden duck-boards were laid for the supporters around the ropes that kept the crowd from straying onto the pitch. A grandstand was present on the site at this time, so is it possible that the foundations are hidden beneath the concrete Tennis courts which now lie on the side closest to Campdale Road?

Casuals had to wait a couple of weeks before making their debut appearance at Tufnell Park, and things went badly during this period. The club crashed 2-7 at Clapton, when it was said that the team looked out of condition, and defeats followed 0-4 at Tottenham Hotspur and 1-4 at Gravesend.

The opening game at Tufnell Park saw Casuals continue this poor run losing 1-4 to Tottenham. The following game ended in another defeat, this time to Enfield (2-3) to complete a miserable September.

October did, however, bring about a change of fortunes as Ealing were defeated 3-1, prior to a

Left: The Tufnell Park Hotel in 2008

narrow defeat (0-1) against Southampton St. Mary's who were champions of the Southern League that season. Casuals faced their second professional side in three days when they defeated Millwall Athletic (2-0). On the 24th October Casuals contrived to play four games, which would have stretched any club's resources. In the process they suffered some heavy defeats, losing by a club record 0-13 (against Luton Town), 0-4 at Ipswich Town, 1-6 at Marlow (when Oxford University represented the Casuals) and by a marginally more respectable 2-3 score line at home to Old Etonians.

Following another defeat by Southampton St. Mary's, Casuals began their London Charity Cup fixtures with the visit of the 3rd Grenadier Guards. Casuals won comfortably by four goals to one, although the following amusing incident occurred:

The half-time whistle sounded before the proper interval had arrived, both the referee and linesman's watches having stopped, and play was then carried on for another five minutes.[3]

Ealing were defeated in the semi-final 4-0, which set up a final with the club's nemesis of recent years, Old Carthusians in January.

CASUALS 5 OLD CARTHUSIANS 0
Naturally enough the great Cup tie at Millwall detracted from the attendance at the encounter at the Essex County Ground, Leyton, which would otherwise have been the leading fixture in the metropolitan district on Saturday. Still, given favourable conditions, there was an attendance of fully four thousand to witness the contest, in which the pick of the amateur talent was engaged, and they had the satisfaction of seeing a splendid display of football for three-fourths of the time. At this point the Casuals speedily put on a couple of items, and it became evident that the Carthusians had 'shot their bolt.' Had it not been for two or three wild shots for goal on the part of Topham 'the previous highest score' in previous finals would have been eclipsed; as it was the Casuals won by five goals to none, securing for the third time possession of the handsome trophy presented for the competition by Sir Reginald Hanson, M.P. for the City of

London. It would be altogether wide of the mark to say that this was a true index of the play, as until the time of their sudden collapse – about twenty minutes from the finish – the Old Boys had had quite as much, if not more of the game than their adversaries. Both were at full strength, and played exactly as advertised, the Casuals having an eleven in the field which might with credit

HAVE REPRESENTED THE CORINTHIANS,

of which organization they are almost members. Drier weather had greatly improved the playing arena, but in parts it was yielding and greasy on the surface, though not sufficiently so to prevent a fast exposition of the game. Owing to the process of being photographed it was some dozen minutes after the advertised hour (2.30 p.m.) when Mr P.A. Timbs (who, owing to the indisposition of Mr E.E. Stewart, was called upon to officiate as referee) gave the signal for G.O. Smith to kick-off for the holders from the pavilion end. Little time was lost in getting to work, and the Stanbrough's were at once prominent. 'Hands' against the Casuals was followed by a corner in favour of the Old Boys, who, in spite of a 'dash' up field by Collier and Guy, had the best of the exchanges. G.O. Smith called forth loud applause for a dodgy run, and a little later, from a pass by Vassell, put in a low shot which Campbell cleverly saved with his foot. After a faultless corner the Casuals retaliated, and Alexander in turn made dangerous shots at the Old Boys' goal. At this point the holders were hard pressed, three corners and a free kick close in goal being in succession awarded the Casuals, but to no rank came to naught, while Bray put in a long dropping shot which, had it been a foot or two nearer the centre, would have caused Campbell anxiety. That custodian defended in brilliant style, in a yard of the post, dashed up and saved with the greatest coolness. Each side in turn attacked, and at last after the lapse of some thirty-five minutes, Alexander, at the close of a good run,

PUT INTO THE NET A SHOT,

with which Williamson had no chance. Nothing daunted by this disaster Hewitt and Vassall harassed the Casual defence, but found it too good, while at the opposite end Wilkinson made a magnificent save, footing out one of Topham's lightening shots. The Carthusians returned 'the ball to the Casuals' goal-line, and then half-time arrived with the score 1-0 in favour of the 'mixed' team. Upon resuming there appeared to be very little to choose between the two sides, the Carthusians if anything being more frequently dangerous, but rather lacking the combination of their opponents, though in extenuation it may be stated that their left wing was weak through M.H. Stanbrough falling very lame – his old trouble. They found, too, Oakley and Lodge virtually impassable, though twice openings were lost by M.H. Stanbrough and G.O. Smith, the former by hesitation, the latter by shooting over. After a 'free' against Oakley, Campbell was twice called upon, the first being an awkward low shot by Vassall, but he was equal to the occasion. With nearly half the second portion gone a change in a few minutes came over the scene. Topham ran brilliantly down the right wing and centred close on the touch-line to Collier, who dashed in and beat Wilkinson for the second time. This was bad enough, but in less than a couple of minutes he had added a third by a magnificent shot from a good distance, having previously made a pretty run on the ball being passed to him by Alexander. The rest of the game needs little description as it was evident

Above: Site of the Tufnell Park enclosure 2008

THE HOLDERS WERE A BEATEN SIDE.
Their backs with the exception of Ward offered but a feeble resistance and the rival front phalanx had matters their own way, the ball rarely traveling into the vicinity of the Casuals' goal. Collier, slightly assisted by Burnup, was responsible for the run which led up to the fourth – a low cross shot by the Godalming player into the corner of the net farthest from him, while Topham ran and shot the fifth, and afterwards missed two fine chances of increasing the lead, while Guy also nearly scored, Wilkinson saving.[4]

Between the semi-final and the final, the Casuals began their tradition of visiting some of the Midlands schools in December. The tradition was to continue for many years and on the inaugural journey Casuals beat Malvern College (7-0) and Shrewsbury School (3-2). Repton was later added to make it a three day tour for future years. December also witnessed a 0-3 defeat at home to Preston North End and the start of the Christmas and New Year tour.

The tour began on Boxing Day with a 3-1 victory over Clapton, before the party headed north and lost to Long Eaton Rangers (1-4). Casuals recovered from this and defeated Loughborough Town (4-3) and Mansfield (by the only goal). On reaching the north-east Casuals found things a bit harder, losing 1-3 to Stockton, and 0-8 at Middlesbrough; the only victory coming from their visit to Darlington (3-1).

On their return, Casuals began their F.A. Amateur Cup campaign with a 5-3 victory over Wycombe Wanderers. Casuals went two goals ahead, before Wycombe equalised by the end of normal time. Casuals, though, began playing again in extra time and at the end of the first period had rattled in three further goals. Although Wycombe subsequently pulled a goal back, there was no time for another fight back.

Casuals crashed out of the London Senior Cup the following week at the hands of Clapton, prior to the Amateur Cup second round clash with the Royal Artillery, Portsmouth. The soldiers were a strong side and later that season went on to win the Army Cup. Despite their strenuous efforts to out-muscle and foul the Casuals, however, they could not stop the Old Boys winning 3-2. In the quarter-final Casuals did not manage to get their strongest eleven on the field and in front of 3,000 partizan Stockton fans went down to a crushing 0-4 defeat.

It was the end of February and Casuals had nothing left to play for. Although the Old Boys did secure a notable 5-3 victory over Woolwich Arsenal a week later, their form suffered as further defeats followed against Stoke (0-3), Millwall (1-2), Notts County (1-2), and London Caledonians (0-1).

R.R. Barker made the most appearances (26), and he was followed closely by R.M. Hilleary (23), S.L. King (23) and H. Roper-Barrett (20). The top scorers were W.P. Toone who scored 14 goals in 19 appearances and S.S. Taylor who scored eleven in as many games.

1897/98

At the start of the season, Corinthians were touring South Africa and with them were a number of Casuals players, which is perhaps why the Old Boys only played one game in September (a 2-3 defeat at Clapton). Casuals, though, were to enjoy a successful season, reaching the latter stages of all competitions in which the club competed.

An impressive October saw Casuals achieve seven straight wins as Ealing were beaten 3-0 and West Herts (now Watford), who had just turned professional, were accounted for by three goals to one. These were followed by victories over 2nd Coldstream Guards (2-1), London Caledonians (6-0), Old Westminsters (4-2), Sheppey United (4-3), and Marlow (3-2).

From late October, Casuals adopted the policy of fielding two sides every Saturday and generally found opposition to suit the strength of the teams fielded. This ensured some close games with the Casuals players usually the happier at full time.

November opened with an impressive 2-2 draw with Oxford University, and was followed by a narrow defeat by Division Two leaders Manchester City. City had taken a two goal lead, but Casuals had levelled by half-time, only to concede a late goal and go down 2-3. This was followed by an extraordinary 8-2 victory over Cambridge University as G.O. Smith inspired the team with four goals.

Casuals now began their London Charity Cup ties and their good form continued with a narrow one goal victory over Old Westminsters and then a goal-less draw with Queen's Park Rangers at the Queen's Club. Casuals took no chances with the fast improving Q.P.R. and drafted in the sporting legend C.B. Fry (who was 20 minutes late) and other Corinthians W.J. Oakley and C.J. Burnup for the match. The replay took place in January without their reinforcements, but Casuals still won 1-0; the goal coming from R.G. Wright who would go on to be the club's all time leading scorer.

The final was not played until April when Casuals faced Old Carthusians yet again:

OLD CARTHUSIANS 3 CASUALS 0
Twelve months ago the Casuals wrested from the Old Carthusians the handsome charity bowl....., but on Saturday, at the Essex County Ground at Leyton, the Old Boys regained possession by a margin of three goals to love. Strong armies had been got together, though the holders, sadly lacked the services of C.J. Burnup – absent on the Continent – while at the last moment a substitute had to be found for W.N. Cobbold – at one time the prince of dribblers. The non appearance of the Old Cantab was a bitter disappointment, but it transpired that he had met with a slight strain. A substitute had to be secured on the ground and eventually D.M. Smith, a younger brother of 'G.O.,' was pressed into service. Happily the mid-day storm had passed away, but it left behind it a boisterous wind, which seemed to vary its direction greatly, and dropped considerably towards the close of the game. It kept off, however, further dampness, and so quickly dried the ground that it proved suitable for a very fast and interesting struggle. Spectators mustered in force, and altogether there could not have been far short of 6,000 present when Wilson started the ball at 6.40, the Old Carthusians defending the pavilion goal, deriving assistance from the wind. In the first few minutes each goal was attacked with vigour, Alexander missing a good opening. Wreford-Brown and Stanbrough were conspicuous for the Carthusians, but the Casuals were certainly having the better of the play. Darvell saved cleverly from a corner secured by a rebound off Bray from a kick by G.P. Wilson, and Gardiner cleared finely several times, notably from Wright. On the other side Hewitt put in a brilliant run, although harassed by Fry, this pair playing strongly against one another throughout. Harrison a little later had to clear by rather riskily bouncing the ball out after a run down by Stanbrough, who a few minutes later subsequently put just over the bar from a capital centre by Haig-Brown. Between the pair was sandwiched a further splendid save by Gardiner from a shot by Wright. G.O. Smith, who had taken a little time to settle down, next, made a marvelous kick, a long, low shot, which hit the post and rebounded, the International having only just brought himself within reach of the ball to make it. Shortly after he made another fine shot, Harrison having to bring himself to the ground at the corner of the goal to clear, which he just managed to do. Then the Casuals had another spell of attacking work, but found the Carthusian half-back line very strong, Wreford-Brown time after time evoking rounds of applause from the crowd in this, probably his final Cup-tie. Thirty-seven minutes elapsed without any score, and then, after 'G.O.' had received from his brother and made an effective dribble and pass, Stanbrough was afforded a good opening and sent the ball sideways in front of Harrison into the net, and opened account, for the Carthusians. 'G.O.' and Hewitt were both very prominent in the remaining minutes, during which Harrison twice had to cleverly save, though D.M. Smith lost a fine chance, and the interval arrived with the O.C.'s a goal in hand.

Having now the advantage of the wind it was thought that the Casuals who had perhaps done most of the pressing against it would speedily get on terms. Stanbrough now partnered Hewitt on the left, D.M. Smith going inside right, while at half Darvell and Ward changed over. At first the old boys were prominent, most of the work developing on the left wing, who 'worried' Fry considerably. The old Oxonian for his part infused vigour into his play, and was once penalized by Capt. Simpson (who refereed most ably) – the only foul awarded in the match. Wright had hard lines in not scoring from a pass by Drake, and Pickering got a nasty one from long range, but Gardiner saved very well. Harrison just managed to punch away a beauty from 'G.O.,' but at the end of seventeen minutes failed to stop a further one from the International centre, shot with irresistible force and accuracy some fifteen yards or so from goal. Again the Casuals attacked, and Barrett tested Gardiner, but unsuccessfully. From a low shot by Wright the Old Carthusian custodian had to concede a corner, and for a time the Casuals were very busy. The Carthusian goal had several narrow escapes, but the holders' front rank did not combine too well. Just before the close G.O. Smith repeated his previous success, the item being obtained in almost identical fashion, and a good game closed. 5

Before the final was played, Casuals still had plenty of other matters to attend to. In December, they overcame Liverpool Ramblers (2-0), before losing to Football League Division Two side Burton Swifts by 2-3. The club then went on their customary Christmas and New Year tour, beginning with a 6-0 victory at Clapton. Defeats followed at Lincoln City (2-3) and Long Eaton Rangers (3-5), but the visitors finally experienced some good cheer with wins against Bishop Auckland (3-2) and Darlington (6-1). The tour closed with a 2-4 defeat at Middlesbrough which was at least an improvement on the previous meeting.

The cup season now began in earnest and in addition to success in the London Charity Cup, Casuals were to enjoy good runs in both the London Senior Cup and the F.A. Amateur Cup. The London Senior Cup saw Casuals vanquish Old Foresters 7-0 after a weak Old Boys side scored six second half goals. The second round was just as comfortable as Barking Woodville, who plied their trade in the London League, were overwhelmed by nine goals to two with S.S. Taylor scoring five times. The game was marred by a broken collarbone suffered by the Barking goalkeeper: Casuals sportingly allowed a replacement, but he could do little about the result. In the semi-final Casuals faced the emerging Brentford F.C. team. Brentford were in fact lucky to still be in the competition after initially losing to Clapton, but were reinstated following an appeal about an ineligible player and won the subsequent replay. The match saw Casuals lose 3-4 and, *The Sportsman* diplomatically attributed the defeat to the shortcomings of one player: *Blaker, who kept goal for the Casuals, being about as much 'off colour' as it is possible for a custodian of ability to be.* 6

In the F.A. Amateur Cup, Casuals were drawn against Kirkley from Lowestoft, who had lost their place in the previous season's semi-final when they were disqualified for fielding an ex-professional. Casuals went a goal down but H. Roper-Barrett equalised for the visitors to rescue the tie. Casuals had in fact fielded a weak side: on the same day the club put out sides which defeated Oxford University 4-3 and Clapton 4-1! The replay resulted in a resounding 6-0 victory as Casuals took the game more seriously; C.L. Alexander scored four that day.

In the second round Casuals were drawn against Old Etonians and with nothing to choose between the teams the match finished goal-less, although Hilleary did hit the crossbar in extra time. The replay was more comfortable as Casuals established a 3-0 lead before conceding a late consolation goal. The quarter-final draw paired Casuals with Middlesbrough, but the Old Boys again failed to field their strongest line up and lost narrowly to a solitary second half strike by the eventual competition winners.

Amidst all the excitement of the cup ties Casuals lost 1-6 to Aston Villa, having been on level terms at half-time against a side that had completed a Football League and F.A. Cup double the previous year. The most impressive result came in March against Sheffield Wednesday who finished fifth in Division One that season:

CASUALS 4 SHEFFIELD WEDNESDAY 2

It was a thousand pities that with such an attractive fixture on as the above at Tufnell Park, the weather should have turned out of the most miserable description possible. Rain fell early in the metropolitan district and continued with annoying persistency throughout the greater portion of this match, while with a perfect gale raging matters for spectators and players alike were of the most uncomfortable nature. It was therefore not surprising that under the circumstances the attendance was a very small one; indeed, it could not possibly have exceeded a thousand, a fact much to be regretted. Still those who braved the elements were well rewarded, as they saw a thoroughly interesting game, in which the amateur combination decisively beat the professionals by four points to two.

It is true that the Sheffielders were without two of their best men in Spikesley and Earp, while C.B. Fry was absent from the Casuals' eleven, but on the day's play the visitors were deservedly beaten. The London front division, despite the slippery nature of the turf, gave a wonderfully pretty display, all their goals being gained through admirable tact and judgment. Burnup, on the extreme left, was a host in himself, and three out of the four points were due to his clever play. On the other side Wright, too, did some admirable work, and was ably backed up by all his confreres. Of the backs Barker and Bray were very prominent, while Harrison, in goal, saved very finely on more than one occasion. On the visiting side there was not quite so much cohesion, and at times some of the men did not over-exert themselves.

Starting at twenty minutes past four with the wind blowing straight across the ground, the Casuals soon attacked, and from a capital dribble on the right wing Hewitt sent in an oblique shot. The ball struck the left post and bounced into the net. This was within seven minutes of the start. Subsequently Wednesday forced two corners, but these proved unproductive though on more than one occasion Harrison had all his work cut out to clear. Eventually a grand combined passing run between Burnup, Alexander, and Wilson ended in the last named beating Massey with a beauty, but a few minutes afterwards Dryburgh sent in a long cross shot and Beech, dashing up, banged it into the net. At half-time Casuals were leading by two goals to one. On resuming, Wednesday played with renewed vigour and attacked hotly, but the defence was too good, and in turn another beautiful piece of concerted work between Burnup, Alexander, and Wilson ended in the third point with in fifteen minutes of the resumption, but once more the Sheffielders through a goal by Davis. Before the close, however, the Casuals' left were again busy and a fine centre by Burnup once more resulted in Wilson beating Massey.[7]

During the season Casuals fielded almost a regular side for their important games and H.J. Pickering, R.M. Hilleary, C.F. Drake, H. Roper-Barrett, R.R. Barker, H.R. Blaker, A.E. Harrison, C.O.S. Hatton, S.L. King, and top scorer R.G. Wright (with 14 goals) all made twenty or more appearances. G.O. Smith was second top scorer with eleven goals in just five games.

Left: H. Roper-Barrett – future Casuals president

1898/99

At this point S.L. King took over as secretary, a position he would hold until the eve of World War One. It was, however, certainly not the most successful season in the club's history and they struggled to make an impact in any of the competitions that were entered. The club made an unusually late start to the season, perhaps because of the secretarial change, and did not play their first match until October.

The delayed opening game was against the Casuals' co-tenants at the Tufnell Park enclosure, London Caledonians. Casuals found the Scotsmen in inspired form and crashed to a 0-3 defeat. Following this disappointment Casuals failed to turn up at their second scheduled game at Watford, despite confirming the fixture. No reason is given for this, but it might be another case of teething problems for the new secretary.

Casuals finally got going with an 8-0 victory over Great Marlow and followed this with an impressive 3-3 draw at home against Division Two club Grimsby Town. The team drew against Cambridge University in their next match then recorded their biggest victory of the season when Old Malvernians, minus some of their key players, were crushed 11-0 in the first round of the London Charity Cup. The cup run came to an abrupt end in early December when Old Carthusians again put paid to Casuals hopes of a trophy, by defeating them 0-3 at the Queen's Club ground.

The postponed match against Watford was played in late November and resulted in an impressive 4-2 win for the Old Boys. They were to meet with more success on the Christmas tour that season. Casuals lost 1-2 to London Caledonians, but then defeated Grimsby Town 7-5 after trailing 1-4 at half-time, thanks to a second half bombardment of the Mariners' goal. Casuals continued this good form in thrashing Long Eaton Rangers 8-1, and went on to share six goals with Bishop Auckland before losing the final match to Darlington 3-4 after leading 2-1 at half-time.

In January Casuals faced Old Westminsters in the London Senior Cup first round and were held to a 1-1 draw. The replay was won 2-1, setting up a tie with the Old Carthusians, who were by now the very last team the Casuals would have wanted to encounter. As was normally the case the ex-Charterhouse schoolboys gained the upper hand and ran out 2-4 winners, despite Casuals taking the lead after just ten minutes.

The F.A. Amateur Cup did not improve the club's plight: although Richmond Association were defeated 2-1 at Old Deer Park, Casuals were knocked out in the second round. The first match against Cheshunt was won 4-0, but it then discovered that R.G. Wright was ineligible and the Football Association ordered the tie to be replayed, a game which was lost 0-2. This was to be Casuals' last appearance in the competition until after the Great War. The competition had attracted considerable criticism in certain quarters and had not quite caught the public's imagination in the way it would in later years.

*There is far less interest in this competition than it was expected would be created. The Old Carthusians, the holders, did not even trouble to enter for the prize, and the old school clubs generally are content in the main to revert to the genuine sporting spirit, which needs no such competition for the enjoyment of a good game of football.*8

Casuals again had nothing to play for, although they did hold Southampton to a 2-2 draw, before losing 1-3 to Woolwich Arsenal and beating a Clapton side who had held the Corinthians the week before.

The new Secretary led the appearances with 29 and was followed by C.F. Drake on 22. E. Lowes was top scorer with eleven and R.G. Wright was two behind with nine goals.

1899/1900

This was without doubt Casuals worst season since the club began playing competitive football during the 1884/85 season. There seemed to be a change of policy with fewer games being scheduled, and although this may have been due to poor reporting, the records of the public schools certainly suggest Casuals had scaled down their commitments. Only 41 games have been traced for the entire season, although *The Sportsman* stated in May that 65 matches were played in total.

Casuals began with a 4-1 win over Barnes Incogniti, a victory only secured when Casuals scored three goals in the last 15 minutes of the match. The Old Boys then held London Caledonians to a 1-1 draw, before beating Walsall 3-2 and Gravesend United 4-3 after recovering from being three goals in arrears. Casuals came back from two goals behind against Cambridge University a couple of weeks later to record a 3-2 victory.

This did not help them in their London Charity Cup ties. In the first round Casuals achieved their only competitive win of the season, 7-0 over Ealing. The semi-final, though, saw the cup holders Clapton achieve a major upset by knocking out the Old Boys 2-3.

Casuals' form in December gave no indication as to what was to happen in the London Senior Cup: Lincoln City were beaten 3-2 despite Casuals having ten men and Bradfield Waifs were destroyed 9-0. Before Christmas, the Old Boys lost narrowly by the only goal to Southampton (F.A. Cup finalists in 1900) and 1-2 to London Caledonians. The northern part of the tour commenced with another victory over Lincoln City (1-0), prior to a 2-2 draw with Suffolk, and victories followed over three Northern League sides Bishop Auckland (3-1), Darlington (5-2), and Thornaby Uptonians (6-2). Football League division two side Middlesbrough were then defeated 4-2. This was Casuals most successful tour to date.

Ten days after the club's return from the north, they crashed out of the London Senior Cup 1-3 at Leytonstone, in the first meeting of two clubs who would become regular opponents. Casuals' only other hope of silverware was the minor West Ham Hospital Cup, but even this was too much as Clapton recorded a 1-3 victory over the Old Boys.

The only bright spot in the New Year was a 2-1 victory over Grimsby Town as Casuals largely failed to impress. S.L. King led the appearances featuring in 30 games, and was closely followed by C.E. Wilson on 26. The top scorer was E. Lowes with nine goals.

Chapter Four
The Re-emergence of the Casuals
1900-1907

The new century saw the Casuals re-emerge as one of the leading amateur clubs in the South after several lean years. Until 'The Split' in 1907, Casuals were to lift the London Charity Cup four times, and finished as runners-up on two further occasions. These years also saw the historic founding of the Isthmian League which was to be the club's primary competition for the majority of the next one hundred years. This period also witnessed the first overseas Casuals tours, to Prague, Budapest, and Germany in 1905 and Sweden two years later.

1900/01

Casuals were destined to win their first trophy since 1897, in the form of the London Charity Cup, during the course of this season. The campaign started slowly for the Old Boys as they suffered early reverses at the hands of London Caledonians, Clapton (twice) and Cheshunt. The only noteworthy positive result was a 2-1 victory over Richmond Association. It was not until the visit to Oxford University which resulted in a 3-2 victory that Casuals looked capable of improving on the previous season.

The season also was the first in many years when most of the professional opponents were dropped from the fixture list. Consequently a long procession of schools fixtures took place before Christmas and the only significant event was the start of the London Charity Cup.

In the first round Casuals easily defeated East Sheen (who were to win the Surrey Senior Cup that season) 5-1, before drawing Old Carthusians yet again in the semi-final. The first game resulted in a 1-1 draw as R.G. Wright scored the Old Boys goal. The replay was scheduled for 26th January 1901, but was postponed because of the death of Queen Victoria. Football was off the agenda on the following Saturday as it coincided with the late Queen's funeral, so it was not until the 9th February that the two teams renewed hostilities. The crowd numbered just 800, all paying one shilling admission, to see Casuals line up against a powerful Carthusian side containing G.O. Smith, C.F. Ryder and M.H. Stanbrough. C.O.S. Hatton and W.J. Oakley both had superb games in keeping the O.C.'s at bay and Casuals recorded a rare victory against their rivals by three goals to one. The final against Clapton was played at home at the end of March:

CASUALS 3 CLAPTON 1
On Saturday the Casuals secured for the fourth time possession of the handsome Charity bowl.... They were called upon to face the latter in the final, which place on Saturday in fine, bracing weather at the Tufnell Park Grounds, Holloway, and gained a well-deserved victory by three goals to one. They, had, it is true, the advantage of playing at home, but, on the other hand, the date was an inconvenient one, and but for clashing with the Corinthian fixture at the Queen's Club, they could have strengthened their side. Still, they placed a pretty powerful eleven in the field – a side which displayed in the first half more combination than might have been expected. Clapton had Evans back as centre, Mitchell standing out of their front rank, whilst Parson's leg was much better. Their game was an improvement on that played on the preceding Saturday, but yet disappointing, and it must be said that the Casuals fully justified the result. At the same time, Clapton, after the interval, had more of the game, and once only lost an almost certain goal by a bad failure on the part of Smith. Their half-back line was better than the previous week, and Earle, in goal, saved some marvellous shots. But for his defence the Casuals must have scored much earlier than they did, as after Smith had lost a good opening in a series of attacks by Clapton in the opening few minutes, the home team had much the better of the game. Earle just tipped a hot one from Green over the bar at the expense of a fruitless corner, and a little later, there was a prolonged bombardment of the visitors' goal. Taylor sent just across the goal mouth, and after Earle had run out to clear he had to negotiate a couple of hot ones whilst returning the second by stooping and throwing away. On another occasion he took the ball literally from Taylor's feet. At the opposite end Clapton then made several attacks, Brown, though, hampered, getting in a long low shot, and Evans making a fine single-handed run. Their passes and kicks were, however, not, as a rule, well directed, and at the end of half an hour the Casuals put on a couple of goals within a minute of each other, The first was the result of a pass by Taylor, who was playing a fine game. Green badly missed the centre, but the ball went out to Snell, who, with a hot, oblique shot, sent into the net. The second was a comparatively 'soft' affair. Stanley Briggs mis-kicked, and let in Taylor, who just got his foot to the ball and popped it into the corner of the goal before the backs could get to him. The Casuals did most of the pressing till the interval, Wright shooting over, but Wilson had to clear in turn from Brown and Folks. Half-time saw the Casuals still couple of goals to the good, but they did not settle down to work too well on resuming, and Clapton had the better of the play. Evans put the ball through, but the item was disallowed for offside. Then came a terrible miss by Smith with an open goal to shoot at, but at the end of a dozen minutes the ball came to Evans from the left wing, and he reduced the Casuals' lead to a goal. This put the latter on their mettle, and following an unsuccessful attack Taylor, by a clever run on the right, 'drew' the Clapton defence, and enabled Green to notch a third item. Only a fine save by Earle prevented Snell from being credited with a fourth, but for the next ten minutes the visitors did most of the pressing. Nearing the close the game fell off, and the Casuals had rather more of the play. They did not score again, winning by the margin stated, viz, 3-1. There was an attendance of about 3,500, who heartily cheered both teams at the close.[1]

The Christmas and New Year tour was a reasonable success as London Caledonians (2-1) and Scarborough (6-2) were both defeated. The first loss came against Sheffield Wednesday in a benefit game for Langley. Casuals were four goals behind at the break, but rallied to lose only 2-4. This was followed by defeats by Bishop Auckland (champions of the Northern League in

1901), Thornaby Utopians, and West Hartlepool. The only victory in this run was a 2-0 win at Darlington.

In the New Year, Casuals enjoyed a good run in the London Senior Cup and started in amazing fashion when they triumphed over the holders London Caledonians by 6-0, at one point scoring three goals in as many minutes. In the second round, Dulwich Hamlet were defeated 3-0, although Casuals only secured victory late in the game when they scored twice in the last four minutes. Casuals finally succumbed in the semi-final in an end to end and physical cup tie with Ilford (0-1).

Casuals again filled in most spare Saturdays with matches against schools teams, but did record an impressive 8-2 victory over Richmond Association after scoring four times in the last six minutes. The other games of note were the visits of Thornaby Utopians (4-0) and Darlington (1-1) at Easter.

The Casuals' fortunes were undoubtedly improved by the fact that they had four players who each scored at least 10 goals. R.G. Roper led the way with 18 and was followed by S.S. Taylor (14), R.B. Durrant (13) and P.A. Green (12). S.L. King made the most appearances again when he appeared in 28 games, closely followed by C.E. Wilson (24) and H. Roper-Barrett (23).

1901/02

Casuals failed to capitalise on the success of the previous season, but they were still making progress and were generally more than merely competitive. The season opened with a 2-2 draw against London Caledonians when the new wooden terracing installed at the western end of the Tufnell Park enclosure was used for the first time.

This heralded a somewhat inconsistent series of results as Casuals with a strong team surprisingly lost to Richmond Association, before beating Clapton and then sweeping away London Caledonians 9-1 in the first round of the London Charity Cup. Unfortunately Casuals' hopes of retaining the cup were laid to rest when Shepherd's Bush triumphed 1-2 over the Old Boys in the semi-final. It is interesting to look at the attendance figures up to that point in the season, which show Casuals regularly drawing crowds of over 2,000 for their matches at Tufnell Park, with as many as 3,700 present for the visit of Cambridge University.

Casuals suffered a heavy defeat (3-10) to West Hampstead who were the holders of the Middlesex Senior Cup in mid October, and this started a rocky period which saw the team lose at Marlow and then crash 0-9 to Ludgrove, The latter club featured a certain G.O. Smith in their eleven and he promptly scored six goals! Casuals bounced back with a 3-2 win over Cambridge University, this time with the assistance of G.O. Smith, before conceding five goals without reply at Dulwich Hamlet.

By the time Christmas arrived, Casuals had recorded victories over Old Westminsters (3-2), Old Foresters (4-0), Upton Park (6-0), and Old Cranleighans (6-2), but had not distinguished themselves in their other fixtures. The Christmas and New Year tour did spark some life into the team, however, and Casuals inflicted defeats on London Caledonians (7-1), Middlesbrough (2-1), Thornaby (2-1), Darlington (5-3), and West Hartlepool (4-0). The only defeats suffered came at the hands of Scarborough and Bishop Auckland who again won the Northern League at the end of the season.

On their return normal service was resumed in the London Senior Cup. Casuals, having drawn Old Carthusians in the first round went out following a replay to a solitary G.O. Smith goal. The remainder of the season was an anti-climax, although wins were recorded against Oxford University (2-0), Darlington (5-1), and Marlow (3-1).

S.L. King, who was well on his way to becoming the Casuals record appearance holder, played 32 matches and C.E. Wilson followed up again with 23. C.F. Drake was top scorer with 17 goals in 16 games.

1902/03

Casuals' return to form was marked by T.W. Blenkiron becoming President and M. Morgan-Owen assuming the role of captain. The Tufnell Park arena was also witnessing further developments with the directors arranging for wooden duck-boards to be laid around the ropes as dry standing for spectators and for repairs to be made to the grandstand.

After a slow start Casuals announced their intentions in emphatic fashion as they demolished Ealing 7-3 in the first round of the London Charity Cup. This was all the more impressive given that the score approaching half-time was 2-2. The semi-final saw a repeat performance as Old Westminsters were defeated by the same score line with R.G. Wright and C.W. Alexander both scoring hat-tricks.

The final played in late January, however, did not produce the same form. The week prior to the final, Casuals were due to play cup holders Clapton in a non-competitive game and as the weather was bad four players failed to appear. This was hardly the best preparation and not unexpectedly the match ended in a 1-3 defeat. Clapton then returned to give a repeat performance.

CLAPTON 3 CASUALS 1
Had it not been for the wretched weather that prevailed, a larger company would unquestionably have witnessed on Saturday the final struggle of this season's competition for the Challenge Bowl, presented by Sir Reginald Hanson, sixteen years ago, and the handsome medals that accompany the trophy. As it was the attendance at the Spotted Dog, Upton, can scarcely be regarded as sparse, seeing that every seat in the stand was occupied, and the total strength of the company was about three thousand. The ground was very much in order than might be expected after the recent rains, and the match, fast, and exciting one. At the interval the Casuals, who had whipped together a very powerful side, were a goal ahead, but after passing through a period of anxiety, the holders equalised a quarter of an hour after the restart, and subsequently added a couple of points. They were thus enabled to win by three goals to one

and secure possession of the trophy for the fourth time in the last five seasons – a record which they may well feel proud.

Except for the absence of Clyde Purnell, the holders who had won the toss for choice of ground, placed their full strength in the field, for the brothers Smith, who were assisting Oxford City in the Amateur Cup, can scarcely be reckoned as regular members of the side, although they appeared in the semi-final against the Old Carthusians. The Casuals had the Irish International, Nolan Whelan, between the uprights, and M. Morgan-Owen and B.O. Corbett were also assisting, but the last named found his master in the young Cantab, H.A. Milton, whose sturdy play had not a little to do with the success of his side. For the first half, the Casuals had to face the breeze, but they may be said to have held slightly the advantage, and, as already mentioned, registered the only point gained. They should, however, have been early placed in a minority, as less than three minutes from the kick-off the Clapton captain missed a penalty kick. G.S Farnfield had taken the ball down the left wing, and centred finely, but 'Micky,' who was attempting to clear head through, was fouled by Craig. A penalty was allowed and the kick essayed by Earle, who shot over the right corner of the goal. Thus was a rare chance lost. For a time the Casuals attacked with vigour, Durrant and Alexander both testing Earle, while Foot and P. Farnfield a little later assisted in warding off dangerous attacks at close quarters on the Clapton goal. It must not be supposed, however, that the play was in any way one sided for the Claptonians more than once were within an ace of scoring, a rattling shot by P. Farnfield being only just saved in falling by the Oxonian, Nolan Whelan, who turned aside at full length. 'Micky,' who twice had free kicks awarded against him, had hard luck with a shot in the corner, which led to the first of a couple of fruitless corner kicks, and could G.S. Farnfield have gauged an ackward overhead centre by Evans, following a breakaway, Clapton must have scored. For the Casuals Craig and Morgan-Owen, who was playing a fine game, both got in shots from long range, that from the latter striking the cross-bar, but Corbett was too well watched to prove the source of danger one would otherwise have found him. Nearing half-time, Evans broke away, and only missed scoring through Nolan Whelan literally picking the ball from his feet. A rare melee in front of the visitors' goal followed a corner conceded by Hatton (whose mis-kick might well have been a goal against his own side), and then the Casuals retaliated, and the ball being sent across from the left, Durrant took it fairly close to goal, and then beat Earle with a hot cross-shot, the latter apparently expecting his opponent to aim straight. A couple of minutes later, after a fine but abortive attempt by 'Micky' to equalise, half-time was sounded.

At the outset of the second stage, the visitors were, as their rivals had been, awarded a penalty for a foul charge within the area. Morgan-Owen put in a very hot shot, but almost straight to Earle, who, by shifting a pace to the side, caught the ball, which almost caused him to stagger, and cleared. For a time after this, the balance rested with the Casuals, who did most of the pressing. Twice Earle had to save, first from Alexander and then, at the expense of a corner, from Durrant, and had either of these taken effect the whole course of the game would have been altered. As it was, the holders, after the lapse of a quarter of an hour, pulled themselves together, and, in quick succession Evans equalised, and then gave the lead to his side. The first was from a nice centre from G.S. Farnfield, which gave him a capital opening at close range, and the second three minutes later by a diagonal shot from a centre by Folks, though in this case Nolan Whelan touched the ball as he slipped in the mud, the leather hitting the side of the *far upright, and finding the net. These successes caused Clapton to play up in vastly improved form, stimulated by much shouting, and though the Casuals strained every nerve to equalise, their defence was kept busy through the dashing onslaughts of the holders. With twelve minutes to go Evans, who had just previously been hurt in a collision with Craig, made a brilliant breakaway, and wound up a single-handed run by, for a third time, steering the ball into the net. Corbett and Wright, who had been but moderate changed places, but Clapton strengthened their defence and maintained to the end their advantage of three goals to one, thus winning a thoroughly interesting game.*[2]

The Christmas and New Year tour saw Casuals visit the south-west of England for the first time. London Caledonians were defeated 2-0 on Boxing Day and then Casuals moved on to Hastings St. Leonards who were thrashed 11-2. The club next travelled west and drew 3-3 with Oxford City before beating Bournemouth 3-1. The only defeat followed at Dorset, before Casuals destroyed Cornwall 7-1 having led 5-0 at half-time. The scoring was only checked after Pollock-Hodsoll dislocated his knee cap and Casuals were reduced to ten men. The Casuals moved on to the Pultenay Hotel in Bath prior to a match against Somerset. The game itself was to suffer a last minute change of venue as the original ground was waterlogged and was reduced to 35 minutes each way. This did not prevent the Old Boys securing a 3-1 victory to complete a successful tour.

Casuals got off to a good start in the London Senior Cup with a 4-1 win against London Caledonians 4-1 in the first round, the game having been decided by two goals in the last five minutes. The club then enjoyed some luck in the next round against Ilford, as the tie was abandoned in extra time with the Essex side leading 1-3. The replay went in favour of the Casuals who recorded a narrow 2-1 victory. The semi-final draw led to the Casuals facing Old Malvernians, but they were suffering at the time from a serious lack of match practice, because of calls on the club for the Varsity game and had not played a good standard team for several weeks. Casuals were no match for the Malvernians who scored through S.H. Day after only ten seconds and although Casuals were only 2-3 behind at the interval, this quickly became 2-5 ten minutes later. Despite Casuals pluckily battling on until the end, they went down 3-7.

Casuals lifted themselves to defeat Richmond Association 10-3 in March, and the team followed this with a 6-0 win over Marlow and then a 4-3 victory at home to East Sheen, the Mid Surrey League champions. The worst defeat in this late stage of the season was 0-4 at the hands of Metropolitan Amateur League champions Shepherd's Bush.

R.B. Durrant made the most appearances with 22 matches under his belt, and also finished as top scorer with 20 goals. C.W. Alexander was second top scorer with 15 goals.

1903/04

The season opened with news about the future of the Tufnell Park enclosure. There had been a continuing debate over the ground's future and Casuals received a special dispensation to complete the previous season as the lease had expired in 1903. The Northern Polytechnic took over this lease and in order for Casuals to continue playing there they were forced, along with co-tenants London Caledonians, to pay fifty per cent of the gate receipts to the institution.

Casuals began the season in disappointing fashion when they went down to the only goal against London Caledonians. The Old Boys then recovered to win their second game against Richmond Association 6-2, after being 1-2 down early in the second half. The previously unbeaten West Norwood were next to experience a rude awakening as Casuals cruised to a 5-0 victory.

A defeat at Ealing followed, before Casuals played their first match in the London Charity Cup. In a hard fought game, Casuals defeated Old Westminsters 4-2 and progressed to a semi-final tie with Old Carthusians. Casuals attacked from the start and recorded a fine 3-1 victory although it was not as comfortable as the score line suggests. The gate receipts for both these matches were later released publicly as it was a charity competition and the game against Westminster raised £36 and 14 shillings; the semi-final produced £42 9s and 7d for charity, which exceeded the receipts for the final (£40 6s 7d).

The final against Clapton had to be postponed because of adverse weather conditions on the original date as *The Sportsman* explains:

Though the overnight frost had been a sharp one, and there was no sunshine to obliterate its effects, there was not sufficient 'bone' in the ground to interfere with play, but the fog proved an insurmountable difficulty. Between one and two o'clock the mist lifted somewhat, and the sun tried to get the upper hand, but by the time the players and officials arrived the fog was steadily increasing in density. After waiting a while, only to find matters proceeding from bad to worse, there was no alternative but to postpone the tie – news of which decision was communicated to a fairly large crowd gathered outside the gates.[3]

The game was finally played in February, but unfortunately *The Sportsman's* report is almost unreadable and *The Times* could only offer this brief outline of Casuals 3-1 victory, which was achieved with the help of a hat-trick by C.W. Alexander.

CASUALS 3 CLAPTON 1
The Casuals won the London Charity Cup on Saturday, beating Clapton in the final tie, at the Essex County Ground, Leyton, by three goals to one. After the match, which attracted about 3,000 spectators, Lord Kinnaird presented the cup and medals to the winning team.[4]

Prior to Christmas, Casuals produced some impressive results with wins against Shepherd's Bush (5-1), Old Westminsters (4-3), Ilford (3-0) and Crouch End Vampires (2-0) as well as a host of schools. The only black mark was a 1-7 defeat by Cambridge University, but the Casuals was severely weakened by requests for their best players from old schools sides who were competing in the Arthur Dunn Cup that day.

The Christmas and New Year tour again saw Casuals travel west following a Boxing Day victory over London Caledonians. Oxford City were defeated 1-0, in what was described as the best game ever seen on the White Horse Ground, before McIver scored the only goal of the match to give Casuals victory against Bristol East of the Western League. In the next game Devon County were defeated 3-0, then Cornwall succumbed 3-2 at Plymouth. The first defeat came at West Somerset when Casuals were possibly suffering from the excesses of New Year's Eve and the following day the tourists lost again, this time against Dorset.

Casuals returned from the south-west in time to face Enfield in the London Senior Cup first round. The game ended tied at two goals each and Casuals were indeed fortunate to get a replay although the Old Boys did lead twice. During the game the referee awarded a penalty and was jeered by the crowd; he then proceeded to lecture them as to their conduct! The replay took place at Tufnell Park and Enfield brought a large following, one of whom had to be removed from the ground when he began to annoy the linesman after Casuals scored their fifth goal. The Old Boys were rampant and crushed Enfield by eight goals to one. The second round defeat against Leyton (the Essex Senior Cup holders) could have been avoided as the referee wanted to call the game off because of the state of the ground. It went ahead, however, as both teams were present and wanted to play, Casuals eventually losing by the only goal.

Casuals continued to produce good form in friendly matches, defeating Oxford University (4-1), St. John's School (15-1), Forest School (10-4), Uxbridge (3-0), Hampstead (4-0), Eastbourne (4-1) and Shepherd's Bush 6-5, despite trailing 3-5 late in this game.

S.L. King was the only player to appear in more than twenty games during the season when he played in 26 matches. The top scorers were C.W. Alexander who scored 13 in the same number of games and R.G. Wright who managed eleven in 13 games.

1904/05

In Casuals' last season before joining the newly formed Isthmian League, the club performed creditably and retained the London Charity Cup. The team made a slow start, however, only avoiding defeat against London Caledonians because the Scotsmen had a goal disallowed. The Old Boys then proceeded to lose heavily at Clapton and against Dulwich (3-4), despite leading 3-1 late in the game.

The first victory came in the home game with Ealing, and this was followed by a 1-1 draw in the London Charity Cup first round against London Caledonians. Casuals won the replay 2-1 with goals from G.S. Harris and R.G. Wright. In the semi-final Casuals defeated Old Westminsters with two goals from E.S. Ward in a five minute spell during the second half. The final was not played until February and was a repeat of the previous season's match,

CASUALS 1 CLAPTON 0
To the great disappointment of the three thousand spectators, who assembled on the Ilford F.C.'s ground on Saturday the game between the Casuals and Clapton was of only a moderate character. The forward play on either side was distinctly poor, except at intervals, the Casuals supplying the best display in the early part of the second half. The weather was fine and the ground in excellent order, so that there was no excuse for the moderate exhibition. Moreover,

both clubs were well represented, the only notable absentee being M. Morgan-Owen from the Casuals side....

The Casuals had the benefit of a slight breeze at starting, but Clapton had the better of the game. Purnell was early prominent with some capital dribbling but King and the half-backs of the Casuals defended finely. P.R. May was a trifle erratic, but after he had made two or three errors he settled down to good play, and his dash was useful thenceforth to the end. Purnell skimmed the bar with a hot drive and a good attempt by G.S. Farnfield directed the ball on top of the net. Then Driffield saved capitally from H.V. Farnfield, and another flying shot by Purnell sent the ball outside. Corners fell to both sides, but Clapton continued to have the better of the play, and but for their inability to make use of their chances, they should have been well ahead at half-time. But their efforts were scrambling, and, though the forward line was changed before the interval, it was still ineffective before the sturdy defence of the Casuals' half-backs, and the teams changed ends with no score.

*Straight from the restart the Casuals ran down and the only goal of the match was scored in less than half a minute. Alexander made an opening for Ward, who promptly centred to Durrant, and the latter drove the ball past Wilding with a fine shot. Then Clapton pressed hard, King clearing from a scramble. The play improved hereabouts, the Casuals passing being excellent. Their play was decidedly superior to Clapton's, but the latter were unlucky not score a quarter of an hour from the end, when H.V. Farnfield missed, a fine chance from a centre by Purnell. G.S. Farnfield obtained the ball after his brother had failed and shot hard at Driffield, who was brought to his knees. There was a claim for a goal, but the referee ruled against it, and although Clapton had more chances they allowed to slip, and the cup was retained by the Casuals, who won by one goal to love.*5

Meanwhile Casuals had further success in their friendly matches. They recovered from a 1-4 deficit to draw with West Norwood, and then held Oxford University (1-1), before losing heavily (2-8) to Cambridge University. This game was much closer than the score would suggest, however, as the students scored six goals in the last 15 minutes. The bitter taste of this defeat did not last long as both Shepherd's Bush and Old Malvernians were defeated 2-1. The club went down 0-3 to Ilford but secured further 2-1 victories over Richmond Association and London Caledonians.

Casuals travelled north for a Christmas and New Year tour for the first time in three years and met with overwhelming success. Six of the non-reserve teams in the Northern League were played: Scarborough and South Bank were held 3-3 and 1-1 respectively, whilst victories were recorded over Darlington St. Augustine's, West Hartlepool and Shildon. The last game resulted in a 3-3 draw with Darlington. The 6-2 victory over West Hartlepool deserves special mention and highlights the strength of the club, as Casuals' hosts would lift the F.A. Amateur Cup at the end of the season by beating Clapton.

The London Senior Cup competition that season again commenced on the first Saturday of January, when Casuals held Old Malvernians to a goal-less draw at Tufnell Park. In the replay, Casuals found themselves behind, but two goals from C.D. McIver enabled the club to progress to the next round. The second round again required a replay after a goal-less draw with Ealing, but this time Casuals succumbed 0-3.

The second half of the season saw Casuals lose again to Cambridge University (2-5), and defeat Oxford University (2-0), and West Norwood (2-1). The heaviest defeats came against London Caledonians (1-6) after the sides had been level at half-time, and 0-5 at home to East Sheen. The domestic season finished on the second Saturday in April as Casuals were about to break new ground with their first overseas tour.

1905 - Tour to Prague, Budapest, Germany

Casuals departed in the pouring rain for their new adventure on 11th April 1905. Aboard the 8.35am train from Victoria. The party, all in good spirits, consisted of: L.T Driffield, S.L. King, P.R. May, B.H. Willett, G.B. Pollock-Hodsoll, R. Cleave, H.A. Lowe, F.C.L. Pirkis, G.B. Canny, C.B. Magnay, B.S. Foster, P.P. Budge, and R. Corbett. They would be joined by W.H.B. Evans who was meeting up with the party in Prague, and C.W. Alexander who would be added in Vienna.

The tourists enjoyed a smooth crossing across the channel, arriving in Flushing in the early hours of the morning, and travelling from there to Leipzig. The tourists were entertained by their hosts on the morning of their arrival, and were taken on a tour of the city by motorcar.

Casuals clearly managed to put their hosts' hospitality aside when the football match started in the afternoon and the team produced a performance to remember in their first continental game against a club which had been the inaugural German champions in 1903 and which would repeat the feat in 1906:

VFB LEIPZIG 1 CASUALS 9

The Casuals kicked off against the wind at 3.50, and though the Leipzig men started one man short, yet for the first ten minutes they pressed hard and looked very much like scoring on several occasions. Corbett broke away once, but shot into the goal-keeper's hands. Friedrich made one magnificent shot, which Driffield saved grandly at the expense of a corner. This was unproductive. At length we got going, and, from some neat passing Budge scored the first goal. A good run down the wing by Canny gave Corbett a chance which was not taken. The second goal was scored by Foster, and shortly after Corbett shot over. For a time we were pressing round their goal, and Budge nearly headed through. Our halves were working splendidly, and hardly ever allowing their forwards to break away. From a pass by Pollock-Hodsoll, Corbett sent in a magnificent effort which the goal-keeper had no chance with. They had the best of the exchanges for the next few minutes, but their shooting was weak and wild, and never looked dangerous. Foster ought to have scored, and Budge hit the bar from a good distance. Shortly after, Corbett scored again from a pass by Budge, tricking the goal-keeper, who ran out to far. Corbett and Budge each scored one more goal before half-time, making the score six goals to nil in our favour.

Above: Casuals team photo versus Leipzig

*After ten minutes', interval we resumed with the wind and a slight slope in our favour. Soon after resuming, Leipzig made a determined attack, and looked like getting the ball through. Driffield had one or two shots to save and showed good judgement once in running out and clearing well down the field. The play of our opponents was marked by two distinct features in this half – firstly, the excellent passing of H. Riso, their centre forward, to his wing men; and, secondly, the splendid way the outside men centred when being pressed by our backs. The centres, unfortunately for them, where rarely taken advantage of, but given those sound inside forwards the result might have looked very different. Our halves and backs, playing a great game, kept us mostly within our opponents half of the field, and more goals should have been collected than the extra three. Once their forwards got going, every one of them touching the ball, left the inside right with a perfectly open goal. He missed it badly, and sent it behind. At last they were rewarded. Riso, sending a grand pass to his outside left, sent the ball right up to our goal, and, from a melee in front of goal, Richter netted the ball to the intense delight of the spectators. Foster scored twice this half, and Corbett once with a beautiful shot across the goalmouth which just entered the net. The attendance numbered about two thousand and keen interest was shown in our first match.*6

On the 13th April, Casuals departed for Prague via Dresden, arriving in good time for their match with Slavia Prague two days later. Slavia Prague were already the dominant force in the Bohemian region and would become the first club to defeat Corinthians on the continent. Casuals, though, were a strong side and despite the ground being almost entirely composed of hard gravel with no grass, they performed admirably. S.L. King opened the scoring when his shot from the half way line bounced over the Slavia goalkeeper. This was his third and final goal for the club, despite playing over 500 games for the Casuals. Slavia equalised before half-time, but R. Corbett scored the decisive goal ten minutes after the resumption. Casuals proceeded to control the remainder of the game, with the home side limited to a couple of half chances.

Casuals' second game in Prague was against a team representing Bohemia, not to be confused with the Bohemians club side who currently play in the Czech League. The match was practically a return match against Slavia as their team was chosen en bloc to represent Bohemia. Bohemia dominated the first half and should have scored three goals, instead of just the one by which they led. At half-time C.W. Alexander swapped positions with R. Corbett and G.B Canny and P.P. Budge did the same. These changes swung the course of the match in favour of the Casuals, and the Bohemians were reduced to rough tactics, which the referee's unorthodox interpretation of the rules only encouraged. R. Corbett scored a beautiful goal to bring the scores level, then Alexander scored with a volley and Canny hit the third with a low drive.

A banquet was given in Casuals' honour in the evening, after which G.B. Pollock-Hodsoll responded on behalf of the club and Cleave treated the assembly to his singing and dancing. The tourists then proceeded to Vienna where the team was rotated to give all the players a chance of playing. On the ground of the Vienna Football and Cricket Club, Casuals survived an early scare when L.T. Driffield saved a penalty, and then took the lead through a cross-shot by W.H.B. Evans. Evans next converted a penalty, before Vienna F.C. reduced the deficit. R. Corbett sealed victory when he tricked four players before shooting past the Vienna goalkeeper.

From Vienna, Casuals travelled to Budapest to play three games. The first was against Magyar Athletikai Club and resulted in a comfortable 4-0 victory in front of 700 spectators. The low attendance was the consequence of a 4 o'clock kick off which was too early to allow the local people to attend. A hailstorm had flooded the ground prior to the start, but this had been remedied with the aid of brooms and sawdust. Casuals then faced M.T.K. who had been champions of Hungary in 1904. This was supposed to have been the final match of the tour but had been brought forward. The ground was covered in sand and only had grass in the corners, whilst the crossbars were six inches too low. It was a strange game because of these factors and because Casuals were constantly penalised for charging, a tactic which was not permitted in Budapest. Despite these complications Casuals won convincingly by six goals to nil.

The final game of the tour took place on 24th April against Budapesti Torna Club, which had won the first two Hungarian League competitions in 1901 and 1902. The attendance was low again (2,500), this time because of the rival attraction of a race meeting being held just outside the town. Driffield saved his second penalty of the tour, and Casuals would have led through Evans early in the game had the crossbar been the correct height. The match was, however, scoreless at the interval and it was only goals by P. Willett and R. Corbett which maintained the tourists' one hundred per cent record. Casuals arrived back in England three days after this match.

1905/06

In 1905 Mr. T.H. Kirkup the secretary of the London Football Association, along with Mr. George Clark (Ilford) and Frank Evans (Clapton) proposed the formation of a league specifically for the leading amateur clubs in the capital. A meeting was held at Winchester House, Old Broad Street with representatives from the following clubs: Casuals, Civil Service, Clapton, Ealing Association, Ilford and London Caledonians. There was a positive response to the proposal, all the clubs being in favour of such a competition, and the Isthmian League was formally established on 8th March 1905. The league adopted the motto 'honour sufficit', and consequently no trophy was awarded to the champions or the players of that club, honour being seen as the appropriate reward for amateur sportsman in keeping with the ideals of the recently revived Olympic Games.

Casuals thus became founder members of the Isthmian League. This, however, had little effect on their previous commitments as the other member clubs, with the exception of Civil Service, were already regular opponents. Casuals played their first ever Isthmian League match on 16th September 1905 at Tufnell Park against their co-tenants London Caledonians, this particular game being regarded as an away fixture.

LONDON CALEDONIANS 1 CASUALS 1
Despite the warm weather, the game was carried on with unflagging energy throughout the full ninety minutes. The Scotsmen had the better of the exchanges, and the Casuals are in a great measure indebted to A.P. Day for saving them from defeat, the match terminating in a draw of one goal each. From the outset the Scots were the aggressors and Day experienced a very anxious time. Try all they knew, the Casuals were unable to break through the defence, and the Caledonians at length opened the scoring, as, after Day had saved a shot by Gibbons, Dale-Wilson found the net. Change of ends saw the Casuals do better but it was not until fifteen minutes of time that Wright equalised. Neither side was able to get the advantage after this and pleasant encounter ended in a draw of one goal each.[7]

It was appropriate that R.G. Wright, who would be Casuals all-time leading marksman, should score their first ever Isthmian League goal. It is also interesting to note that Casuals appear to have abandoned their traditional chocolate and pink colours during the ten years prior to World War One, the players sporting white shirts in the majority of their fixtures during this period.

Casuals went from strength to strength in their competitive fixtures, not losing until December, and still undertook a large number of friendly matches against various schools, old boys, and army teams. In the Isthmian League Casuals drew their first three games, the second of which was a tame draw with Clapton, and then the Old Boys came back from two goals behind to hold Ealing Association to a 2-2 draw. Their preparations for the latter game were not helped by the late arrival of the Casuals team, an action which attracted considerable criticism.

Casuals recorded their first victory of the season in the London Charity Cup first round tie against Old Westminsters, when, after a goal-less first half, the team scored six times without reply. Casuals first win in the Isthmian League followed this moral boosting result, Civil Service being defeated 3-2, with E.S. Ward hitting a last gasp winner.

The third successive win came in the London Charity Cup semi-final against Dulwich Hamlet, which saw Casuals gain revenge for an earlier heavy friendly defeat at the hands of Hamlet (0-4), with a hard fought 2-1 victory.

On 2nd December Casuals suffered their first Isthmian League defeat, losing 1-3 to Ealing Association, but they then bounced back to beat Ilford 3-1, a win which left the Old Boys in fourth position, one point behind the leaders Ealing, with two games in hand. Having secured a healthy league position, Casuals could now go and enjoy their two scheduled tours.

The first was the schools tour which resulted in victories over Shrewsbury School (8-0), Repton School (1-0) and Malvern College (2-1). On the last day of the tour, Casuals returned to Shrewsbury and played a benefit game against Aston Villa for the widow and children of Mr J.H. Wallett, a well-known sports journalist. Casuals performed well in their first match against a professional side for several years and were losing only 1-2 at half-time. The second half, however, saw Villa add three goals to their total.

Casuals travelled north again for the Christmas and New Year's tour and recorded an impressive 3-1 victory over Division Two side, Grimsby Town. This was followed by a 9-1 drubbing of Scarborough, who had taken the lead after just two minutes. West Hartlepool held the Old Boys to a 2-2 draw, but this was a prelude to victories over Stockton (4-3) and Shildon (5-1). The final game of the tour was a 0-0 draw with Darlington.

The resumption of the Isthmian League fixtures saw Casuals visit Clapton at the Spotted Dog and victory might have given the team top place for the first time. Casuals, however, slumped to a 0-2 defeat and the chance was lost. The club now turned its attentions to cup football until the end of March.

Casuals defeated West Norwood in the first round of the London Senior Cup, the team recovering from being two goals behind with 15 minutes left to win 3-2. In the next round Casuals faced the 2nd Grenadier Guards and, several players short, went a goal behind after only five minutes. When the absentees finally arrived, Casuals went on to record a 4-2 victory with C.D. McIver scoring a hat-trick. The run came to an end against Dulwich Hamlet in the semi-final where Casuals' hopes were dented by the loss of E.S. Ward who broke his collar bone after 17 minutes. The only goal came 14 minutes later when S.L. King put the ball in his own net to continue Casuals' hoodoo in the competition.

Two weeks prior to this match Casuals also lost in the London Charity Cup final. It was a case of history repeating itself as, for the third time, a club which had won back to back cups failed to complete a hat-trick of victories.

LONDON CALEDONIANS 2 CASUALS 0
The teams were in position prompt to time, and the Calies having lost the toss had to defend the entrance goal, facing the bright sunshine. At the very outset G.S. Harris received a nasty kick, but after a brief delay was able to continue, though the mishap may have had its effect on his play, which was scarcely so brilliant as usual. He forced the first corner of the match and the first 'free' also fell to his side, but there was a dash about the Scots which more than once

threatened danger. Their right wing was at the outset particularly prominent, and it was from this direction that the effort came that enabled Porter to give his side the lead at the end of seven or eight minutes' play. Dale Wilson centred into goal from the run-down and the ball came across to the outside left. Either Pollock-Hodsoll thought the player off-side or he left it to Driffield to stop the ball, but at any rate a complete misunderstanding occurred, and Porter sent the ball into the net – the softest of goals. Naturally such a galling incident was not conducive to the holders settling down, and the Calies certainly may be said to have held the upper hand on the first forty-five though they did not increase their advantage. This was not by individual, but rather collective merit the value of knowing one another's tactics to a nicety. More than once King had to bring his weight to bear, a 'free' being once awarded against him when it would have been to the advantage of his opponents had the game proceeded. Ward made several good runs, though his centres were sometimes too long delayed, and nearing half-time the Scots had an anxious period. Mention should be made of a long shot at the other end from Reid which Driffield just turned over the bar, Gibbons heading over from a scrimmage succeeding the corner.

*Early in the second stage the Casuals made desperate efforts to draw level, directing most of their energy to the left wing, where' Sim did surprisingly well in checking Ward. The Casuals goal had a narrow escape, through Gibbons and McEachrane each failing to turn to account a fine centre by Porter but after the lapse of a quarter of an hour came the Calies' second item. Ralston, during a Scottish attack, had advanced towards the centre line, when meeting a long kick from goal by Driffield he put remarkable force behind the return. The direction was perfect, the altitude equally so. Driffield with the sun in his eyes, was altogether nonplussed by the dropping shot and a roar of applause went up when the ball passed just under he bar into the net. A third nearly followed from a sharp scrimmage, and Melhuish hit the cross-bar a little later, whilst Driffield had to tip over it a good one from Dale Wilson. Brebner, who had made the journey from Darlington, had not very much to do, though once he had to dash in and clear, he and Wright falling together. As the second stage slipped by the Calies seemed content to depend largely on safety play. The Casuals, however strove hard and more than one hot shot was sent in, notably one by G.S. Harris, which found Reiston's chest in the way, and knocked him momentarily 'silly.' Numerouse corners were forced, but this was extent of the advantage, and just before the close Gibbons from a free kick, shot wide at the other end, and Rutherford put in one from long range that momentarily looked like repeating Raiston's sensational achievement. The result, however, was a two to nil victory for the Scots, after a match on rather heavy ground in which both sides, constituted as under, played for all they were worth.*8

Casuals had three Isthmian League games left to play and at this point, and the club still had an outside chance of the title. A 2-0 victory over Civil Service meant Casuals had to win their last two games and rely on having a superior goal average. These calculations were soon redundant because the following week, in what was effectively a championship decider, London Caledonians defeated the Old Boys 1-2. The final match, against Ilford, was a 0-0 draw but it is not certain that the game was actually played. *The Sportsman* and the local papers for Ilford fail to mention the match, so it would have been played midweek, if at all, and might therefore have passed unreported. However, Ilford played every Saturday in April and the league table published prior to the London Caledonians game indicates that Casuals still had two matches outstanding. These facts lead the author to conclude that it was an unfulfilled fixture with the league awarding a point to both sides. Whatever the truth of the matter, the final table issued by the Isthmian League formally records the result as a 0-0 draw.

It was a good season overall with Casuals achieving final position of third, a placing that was only bettered once in the club's entire history. S.L. King made the most competitive appearances during the season in playing 13 matches. C.W. Alexander was top scorer with seven goals in just eight appearances.

1906/07

This season was to be dominated by the events leading up to 'The Split' and as a result of the politics enveloping the amateur game at this point, Casuals would boycott the London Senior Cup with such clubs as New Crusaders and Old Malvernians. On the field of play it was also a hugely disappointing season as Casuals would finish in bottom place in the Isthmian League.

Casuals began the season by losing at home to the previous season's champions London Caledonians 0-1, although the Old Boys bounced back with a 5-0 victory over Ealing Association in the next match. The game against Ealing saw Casuals decline to take advantage of a penalty awarded to them: *'In the course of loose play near goal Ealing had a penalty awarded against them, but Morgan-Owen seemed reluctant to take it, and when he did so sent wide.'*[9]

This success was short-lived as the next three Isthmian League games all ended in defeat. Ilford beat Casuals 2-4 to maintain their one hundred per cent record at the top of the table, before Casuals threw away a two goal lead against Civil Service to lose 2-3, although they had played the whole game with ten men after the non-appearance of H.J. Beardsley. The last defeat of this bad run was a 1-3 reverse at Ealing Association.

Casuals' last league win of the season came in early December against Civil Service when, despite having only ten men again, the Old Boys battled their way to a 2-1 victory. In the last league match before Christmas, Casuals crashed 1-4 to the seemingly unstoppable Ilford who still had not dropped a point.

The Christmas and New Year tour again proved productive, as Casuals defeated Scarborough (4-1), Stockton (4-1), Darlington (8-2), and Bishop Auckland (5-1). Two other games were played. In the first of these, Casuals recovered from 1-3 down to draw with a Northern Nomads team which included the legendary goal-keeper Leigh Richmond Roose who was famed for carrying the ball out to the half way line (in the days before there was an 18 yard box) then throwing it deep into enemy territory. The second game was a 2-3 defeat at South Bank who finished the season as runners-up in the Northern League.

At the start of the New Year Casuals finally resolved their London Charity Cup first round tie with Clapton, at the third attempt, with a commanding 6-3 win. A 1-5 league defeat against London Caledonians caused Casuals to slip further into trouble, then another break for the London Charity Cup semi-final saw them draw 0-0 with New Crusaders. The Old Boys followed this with two Isthmian League games against Clapton in the space of a week. Casuals drew 1-1 at the Spotted Dog, and concluded their league programme with a heavy 0-4 defeat at Tufnell Park.

Casuals' last two games were the replayed London Charity Cup semi-final which was won 5-4 after a thrilling match in which the New Crusaders recovered from being 4-1 down to draw level, only for R.G. Wright to score the deciding goal and put the Old Boys through. In the final Casuals faced the London Caledonians in front of 4,500 people at Tufnell Park.

CASUALS 0 LONDON CALEDONIANS 0
*Extra time was played, at Tufnell-park, in the final tie of London Charity Cup competition on Saturday, but neither the Casuals nor the London Caledonians could score, and the match had to be left drawn. It was arranged that each club should hold the cup for six months, Lord Alverstone, who was to have presented the cup to winners, making the announcement. Quite 5,000 people were attracted to the game, which produced some very good football until rain set in. Then, with the ground and ball becoming greasy, the players lost their form to some extent. The greatest keenness, however, was shown throughout, and a fast pace was maintained. The London Caledonians combined smartly at times, but their chief strength was in defence. A.T. Rolston and R.D. Robertson were excellent at full back, and the half-backs did so well that the forwards constantly had the ball. Near goal, however, they were weak, very few good shots being put in, but one by D. Macrae was very finely saved by L.T. Driffield. For the Casuals, S.L. King and A.L. Beardsley, the backs, and R.D. Craig, M. Morgan-Owen, and F.H.G. Tudor-Owen, the half-backs, all showed to much advantage. The forwards never really settled down, but occasionally caused great trouble. The London Caledonians had the better of the game, and were rather unfortunate not to score.*10

Prior to the final tie, the London F.A. had made the draw for the 1907/08 London Charity Cup competition, which saw Casuals drawn away to Shepherd's Bush in the first round. This tie would never be played and the draw would be started again from scratch when Ealing Association and Old Malvernians joined the breakaway Amateur Football Alliance.

1907 TOUR OF SWEDEN

On 27th March Casuals sailed from Grimsby and enjoyed a smooth passage to Gothenburg where they arrived two days later, basing themselves at the Grand Hotel. The tour party consisted of the following players: R. Rogers, S.L. King, R.N. Balfour, G.B. Pollock-Hodsoll, H.L. Beardsley, R.D. Craig, F.H.G. Tudor-Owen, C.C. Matthews, E.S. Ward, B. Tuff, R. Turner, C.E. Brisley, and J. Simonds.

All three of the scheduled games were to be played at Idrottsplatts which as *The Sportsman* explained: *had till recently been flooded and in use as a skating rink. At first the ground presented some difficulty to those accustomed to play on grass, but except for a few bad places and loose stones, it was quite conducive to a fair exposition of football.* 11

The first game was played against Stockholm and a one sided game ended up 7-0 in the tourists' favour. Following the match, the tour party took the train 40 miles to Hindos where the team

Above: Casuals (in stripes) bombarding the Copenhagen goal

enjoyed a very pleasant weekend. On their return to Gothenburg, Casuals would face another touring side in the form of Copenhagen (who had just beaten Stockholm 6-0) and as a result a close game was expected. In the event Casuals secured a 4-1 victory over the Danish side who, despite showing good technique, would have lost by more had Ward not insisted on shooting from difficult angles. An excellent tour was rounded off with a 6-1 demolition of Gothenburg, victors over the Casuals' previous two opponents and again expected to be tough opposition.

Chapter Five
The Southern Amateur League Years
1907-1914

After a bitter war of words between many of the leading amateur clubs and the Football Association about the inclusion of professional clubs in the county Football Associations, the Amateur Football Association (A.F.A.) was formed on the 8th July 1907. Shortly after this historic announcement on 27th July, the Southern Amateur League was founded with two divisions. The league had an impressive list of members, the upper division consisting of the following clubs: New Crusaders (who had won the Middlesex Senior Cup in 1907 and the London Senior Cup in 1906), Civil Service (London Senior Cup winners in 1902), Casuals, Ealing Association (Middlesex Senior Cup winners 1897 and 1905, and Middlesex Charity Cup winners 1904 and 1905), Eastbourne (Sussex Senior Cup winners on eight occasions), Ipswich Town (Suffolk Senior Cup winners on nine occasions), Croydon (Surrey Senior Shield winners in 1905), Richmond Association (Middlesex Senior Cup winners in 1902 and 1904), and Townley Park (Surrey Senior Cup winners in 1903 and 1904). The need for strong opposition was made all the more essential by the fact that the Football Association banned the A.F.A. clubs from playing any of its members.

1907/08

Casuals' debut season in the Southern Amateur League was satisfactory, but the club achieved its greatest success by winning the inaugural A.F.A. Senior Cup. Unfortunately the new league struggled to secure major press coverage and following 'The Split' there was a perceptible shift in interest towards the professional clubs. Casuals' first game in the new competition was away to Townley Park.

TOWNLEY PARK 1 CASUALS 1
For this game at North Dulwich the Casuals were not at full strength, but, nevertheless, Townley Park did well to run them to a draw – one goal all. The weather was a trifle too warm for such a robust game as football; nevertheless, plenty of life and go were imparted into the contest, although, as was only natural, towards the end several players were showing signs of wear and tear. To commence with, the Casuals looked likely to prove the better side, for their forwards had almost a monopoly of the attacking for the opening ten minutes. Then the others rallied somewhat, but G.S. Harris then initiated a movement which ended in R.W. Crummack opening the scoring from the extreme outside. This roused the Townley Park forwards, and after some really smart work in midfield R. Holloway equalised, the teams crossing over with the

record one goal all. Following the change of ends play fell off somewhat, especially on the part of the Casuals. For one thing, G.S. Harris was shifted to left half-back, and in that position he can scarcely be written of as highly successful. When the Casuals forwards did get away they appeared more dangerous in front of goal than their opponents, but on the whole there was not a great deal to choose between the teams. There was nothing that could properly be termed a foul all through, and the referee's whistle for once had a rest.[1]

After a 3-1 away win in a friendly fixture against Reigate Priory (who finished as champions of Division B), a solid start was made in the next two games as Casuals won away at Eastbourne (2-0) and then drew at Ipswich Town (1-1). A rot then set in as Ealing brushed the Old Boys aside in a 0-5 rout and New Crusaders (who were to become the dominant force in A.F.A. football) won 1-4 at their Sidcup home after scoring two early goals. The final game of this run took place against Civil Service at Tidal Basin, where a 1-0 victory enabled Casuals' hosts to move to the top of the league.

It was fortunate at this point that Casuals met the new league's whipping boys Croydon because they were able to record a comfortable 4-0 victory. This was followed by a 2-2 draw with Ipswich Town, which was played away, despite the match being scheduleed as a home fixture for Casuals; such practice was to be repeated several times in the coming years. On the Saturday before Christmas, Casuals led four times against Ealing, before conceding a goal with just eight minutes left to lose 4-5.

For the first time in many years Casuals did not go on tour at Christmas, probably due to the uncertainty created because of 'The Split', and so were due to face Townley Park in a league fixture. Casuals, though, could muster only eight players so it was agreed that this match would not count towards the league. The Old Boys promptly borrowed two players and the two teams enjoyed a ten-a-side friendly which Casuals won 3-2.

Although the New Year opened with a 0-2 defeat at Richmond Association, the next match (in the first round of the A.F.A. Senior Cup against Ramsgate St. Georges), saw Casuals turn the corner and they would go unbeaten in competitive games for the remainder of the season. With seven minutes remaining in the game and with the scores level at one apiece, Casuals scored three goals in quick succession to seal a 4-1 victory.

Casuals defeated Townley Park 4-2 in the rearranged league match, before knocking Ipswich Town out of the A.F.A. Senior Cup with a 2-0 victory at Portman Road. A ten man Casuals side then produced an heroic performance to draw 2-2 at Eastbourne in another game where the Old Boys surrendered home advantage and played away. Casuals were on fire and next destroyed Civil Service 5-1, scoring three goals in the last half hour in the third round of the A.F.A. Senior Cup. The following week two fixtures were played on the same day. The first game saw a Casuals team overwhelm Croydon 10-1 in the league, whilst the second, the A.F.A. Senior Cup semi-final against Eastbourne, resulted in another convincing win, this time by six goals to two.

The Southern Amateur League fixtures were completed in style: first the champions elect New Crusaders were held to a 1-1 draw, before Casuals defeated the Civil Service and Richmond

Above: Casuals and Old Carthusians before the A.F.A. Senior Cup final in 1908

Back Row: (left to right) C.E. Brisley, A.H. Birks, C.E. Deacon, L.T. Driffield, O.L. Trenchman, H.G. Howell-Jones, P.A. Sergeant

Second Row: (left to right) Capt. Simpson (referee), B. Tuff, G.S. Harris, I.E. Snell, D. Grahame, H.J.E. Piers, C. Simmonds, E.W. Timmis, L.A. Fevez, H. Hughes-Onslow

Seated: T.S. Rowlandson, H.L. Beardsley, W.U. Timmis, M.M. Morgan-Owen, O.T. Norris, S.L. King, W.J.H. Curwen

In front (left to right) F.H.L. Rushton, B.O. Corbett

Association, both games ending 2-1. The latter match saw Richmond arrive late for the match which commenced at 5pm, and Casuals scored both their goals before Richmond had a full complement of players.

Casuals finest hour was saved for the last match of the season:

CASUALS 3 OLD CARTHUSIANS 1
The Casuals beat the Old Carthusians, Queen's Club, on Saturday, and won the cup given by the Corinthians for competition among clubs belonging to the Amateur Football Association. Perhaps the score of three goals to one flattered the winners to some extent; certainly it rather exaggerated their superiority, which was only noticeable forward. Of recent years the Old Carthusians have not had any specially good young forwards, and, in the absence of G.C. Vassall, their front line lacked combination and shooting power. On the other hand, the Casuals played capitally together in attack, their short passing, which was carried out at great pace,

frequently causing W.U. Timmis, O.T. Norris, and T.S. Rowlandson a great deal of trouble. With able help from W.J.H. Curwen and the other half-backs, the Old Carthusian defence held out for long periods under strong pressure, and their forwards did enough to keep the play fairly even, but almost all the dangerous attacks came from the Casuals, a well-balanced, skilful side. M. Morgan-Owen, at centre half-back, set the Casuals a splendid example by his indefatigable work in tackling, dribbling, and passing. Whenever possible he kept the ball low, giving numerous chances to his forwards, who, on occasions, were quite brilliant. In all respects it was a good game, marked by wonderful pace and dash; every one doing well, and Morgan-Owen and the Casuals forwards excelling. C.E. Brisley and R. Turner, on the right wing, and A.H. Birks, at inside left, were most consistent, but G.S. Harris and J. Symonds had a useful share in the success of their side. Brisley scored all three goals – the first just before half-time, from a centre by Symonds; the second from a pass by G.S. Harris, who had fallen, but managed to turn the ball over to his colleague; and the third from a centre by Symonds, after Rowlandson had kept out one of a few terrific shots put in by Harris. Played under pleasant conditions, the game aroused considerable enthusiasm among a company numbering about 2,000.[2]

Casuals finished in a creditable fifth position in the Southern Amateur League and had the honour of supplying five players for the A.F.A. International against Northern France: T.S. Rowlandson, M. Morgan-Owen, C.E. Brisley, I.E. Snell, and S.S. Harris. S.L. King and P.A. Sergeant made the most competitive appearances playing in 15 games, whilst the top scorers were R.W. Crummack and R.B. Durrant who both scored six goals.

1908/09

The Casuals repeated their fifth place finish in the Southern Amateur League, albeit in a slightly less convincing manner than the previous year and the club again reached the final of the A.F.A. Senior Cup. The club faced problems with their ground sharing arrangements at Tufnell Park, where the fixture list had become overcrowded. With the formation of Tufnell Park F.C. in 1907 there were now three clubs using the ground, which led to Casuals' home games being played away or switched to Leyton.

The season began with matches against the two teams promoted from Section B of the Southern Amateur League at the end of the previous season. The first was against Crouch End Vampires and ended in a convincing 4-1 win but the second was a wake up call for the Old Boys: Reigate Priory proceeded to cruise into 1-5 half-time lead, which finished as a crushing 2-8 defeat for the Casuals. Fortunately Casuals returned to winning ways when, despite only fielding ten men, the Old Boys defeated Eastbourne 5-3 and they followed this up by thrashing the defending champions New Crusaders 4-1.

The victory over New Crusaders was the high point for Casuals in the Southern Amateur League that season. A 1-2 defeat at Ipswich Town was followed by a 4-1 win at Richmond Association which left Casuals in fourth position. It was at this point that defeats started to pile up as Ealing, New Crusaders, and Reigate Priory all registered victories and it was not until January that Casuals next won a league match, by 6-0 against Ealing Association.

The team escaped from the pressures of these fixtures by reviving the New Year tour although the opponents were now restricted to A.F.A. clubs, and they visited Nottingham for what was intended to be five games, (two of which had to be cancelled because of bad weather). Casuals produced three good performances to defeat Notts Amateurs (4-1), Notts Magdala (1-0), and Derby Thornhill & Derwent (7-1).

The second half of the season was dominated by the A.F.A. Senior Cup run which began with a 7-1 victory over Lee who were struggling at the bottom of Section B. Casuals followed this up with a 3-0 win over Townley Park, and then a 3-1 victory against Ipswich Town in the quarter-finals. The semi-final against Civil Service was played at the University Ground in Cambridge and Casuals were always in control after taking a fifth minute lead, the final score being 2-0. Unfortunately for the Casuals, their opponents in the final were New Crusaders (playing many of the famous Farnfield brothers) who were also destined to win the league championsip:

NEW CRUSADERS 5 CASUALS 1
'At Ipswich on Saturday the New Crusaders gained possession of the Amateur Association Cup be beating the Casuals, the holders, by five goals to one. Some 4,000 people watched a capital game, which was much more even than might be imagined from the score. Until some time had elapsed in the second half there was little to chose between the sides.

The Casuals scored first, G.A. Joseph putting the ball through his own goal form a centre by J.S. Simonds. He was scarcely to blame for this, however, as he was charged when in the act of kicking, and the ball screwed off his foot through the posts. After ends had been changed the Casuals found their defence unequal to the strain. M. Morgan-Owen, who was unable to play, was much missed, and although W.G. Edwards, of Oxford University, his substitute, and P.A. Sergeant worked very hard, the Casuals' defence lacked certainty and resource. With a long shot the Rev. H.V. Farnfield got an equalizing goal, and soon afterwards Joseph gave the New Crusaders the lead. After that no doubt could be felt as to the result. Playing with their customary dash and pace the New Crusaders constantly had the ball, and showed to great advantage in passing and shooting. They frequently ran through the opposing defence, and their own half-backs and backs controlled the game, the Casuals rarely becoming dangerous. H.S. Buck, B.S. Farnfield, and A.J. Farnfield added goals, the Casuals being well beaten after a fast and interesting struggle.'[3]

Casuals, though, had more serious concerns by this stage of the season. Having lost to Richmond Association and Civil Service in the league since the turn of the year the club was now in danger of being relegated. The game against Civil Service appears to have been played as a double header as there is no evidence of a return fixture and the succeeding league table debits Casuals with two further defeats. This put Casuals dangerously close to the relegation zone, being two points ahead of Richmond with just three games to play.

As it transpired, Casuals' rivals failed to pick up the necessary points and the Old Boys escaped relegation with draws against Ipswich Town and Crouch End Vampires. Two games were left unplayed, the first being the possible double-header with Civil Service (evidently treated as a loss), whilst the second was the home game with Eastbourne (apparently treated as a 0-0 draw).

The secretary, S.L. King, made 16 appearances but P.A. Sergeant topped the appearance charts with 17 games, whilst R.C. Cutter was leading scorer with 12 goals. During the course of the season E.E. Paget-Tomlinson, a famous hurdler of the day, appeared in Casuals colours.

1909/10

It was another season of struggle for the Casuals as they again flirted with relegation. The club saved its best performances for the A.F.A. Senior Cup, but for the first time did not make the final. The league season began positively enough with a 6-0 victory over Townley Park, and this was followed by a narrow 2-3 defeat to New Crusaders who would win their third straight title at the end of the season. A 2-2 draw with newly promoted Norsemen and a 4-0 victory over Ipswich Town put the Old Boys in a strong position of third in the league at the end of October behind Civil Service and New Crusaders. The Ipswich game was notable in that Casuals scored three wind-assisted goals in three minutes from long range and also because Town refused to take advantage of a penalty awarded to them, as they felt it had resulted from a mere technical infringement.

Casuals still held third place in mid December after drawing at Eastbourne, (thanks to a late equaliser by P.A. Sergeant), crashing 1-6 at Civil Service and securing a 4-2 victory over Ealing. From here on Casuals found it difficult to pick up points although they progressed well in the A.F.A Senior Cup by overwhelming Old Etonians 7-1 in the first round and Crouch End Vampires 5-1 in the following round. Between these two games Casuals managed a 2-2 draw with Ealing in the league.

The New Year's tour was another resounding success as the Old Boys won all five of their games in Nottingham starting with a 7-1 victory over Derby Thornhill. This was followed by a 9-2 win against Notts A.F.A. when V. Edwards scored three goals in as many minutes. The other games saw wins against Notts Magdala (3-0), Notts Amateurs (4-0), and Northern Amateurs (4-1).

Following the return to league fixtures, successive defeats followed against Townley Park and Reigate Priory which plunged Casuals further into trouble. They could, however, take some consolation from a 2-0 win against an Old Carthusian side (which contained six Corinthians) in the A.F.A. Senior Cup quarter-final. This seemed to spark Casuals' league form into life as first Eastbourne were held to a 1-1 draw, (which kept the Old Boys one point clear of relegation), then Reigate Priory were comfortably beaten by five goals to two.

In the semi-final of the A.F.A. Senior Cup, Casuals suffered a 0-4 reverse against Civil Service, although the score-line did not reflect the play. Indeed, Casuals had the better of the first half despite conceding a second minute goal. Casuals' relegation fears returned after a worrying 0-1 loss to bottom club Ipswich Town, and a 0-6 defeat by New Crusaders. Relegation was finally averted after the points from an unplayed fixture against Civil service were shared, and two further points were secured from a 4-0 romp at home to Norsemen in the final match of the season. S.L. King and H.A. Milton led the way with 15 appearances, and E.G. Bisseker was the leading scorer with 10 goals in 14 games.

1910/11

A dramatic improvement in Casuals' Southern Amateur League form saw the club avoid the anxiety of the two previous seasons. The team began by recording their best start to a league campaign so far by registering four successive victories. Townley Park were despatched 1-0, then Hampstead were beaten 4-2, Casuals having recovered from being two goals behind. A 3-2 victory over Tunbridge Wells was followed by a stunning 6-3 win against Ealing after the Old Boys scored five first half goals.

Casuals were now sitting proudly at the top of the league, but unfortunately this was not to last long as defeats at Ipswich Town and at home to Civil Service saw the club slip down the table. Casuals did enjoy a mini-revival before Christmas as London County & Westminster Bank were swept aside 6-1 in the A.F.A. Senior Cup first round and Tunbridge Wells were beaten 4-1 in the league.

The Christmas and New Year tour was a somewhat up and down affair as Casuals lost the first three games before recovering to win the last three. Starting at Mansfield Amateurs (0-1), then proceeding to Northern Amateurs (1-4), and finally to Lincoln Lindum (0-3), Casuals were struggling. Against Derby Thornhill, the Old Boys' fortunes improved with a 6-1 victory, and this was followed by wins at Notts Magdala Amateurs (2-1) and Nottinghamshire (3-1).

1911 did not start well for the Casuals in the Southern Amateur League and their title hopes appeared to have disappeared following defeats at Civil Service and at home to Townley Park. Consequently all efforts could be concentrated on the A.F.A. Senior Cup. In the second round Casuals had no trouble in defeating Ealing 8-1, before Tunbridge Wells were beaten 3-0 in a tie which ended in controversy. The Kent club's officials claimed that the match had finished seven minutes early, but the referee stood his ground and the Old Boys progressed.

Casuals recovered their form in the league from the end of February and Eastbourne were beaten 1-0 at Tufnell Park then at the Saffrons, this time by two goals to one. At this stage it was still possible for Casuals to challenge for the title. Although they were eight points behind Civil Service they had three games in hand whilst New Crusaders, who still had to be played twice, were only one point ahead. There was, however, no margin for error.

Casuals defeated Civil Service in the A.F.A. Senior Cup semi-final (1-0), before their league hopes evaporated in the space of a week when New Crusaders drew 1-1 at the Tufnell Park ground and Ealing defeated the Old Boys by the odd goal in three. The defeats began to mount after this as Hampstead triumphed 0-4 against the Casuals and then Ipswich easily defeated the Old Boys 1-3. The final game against New Crusaders was never played and the points were shared.

The last game of the season was the A.F.A. Senior Cup final and Casuals faced tough opposition in the Old Malvernians, a team containing many members of the Casuals and Corinthians. The match was played in front of 3,000 spectators at Portman Road:

OLD MALVERNIANS 3 CASUALS 2

The final of the Amateur Football Association Cup, between the Old Malvernians and the Casuals, was played at Ipswich on Saturday, and resulted in a win for the Old Malvernians by three goals to two.

The expectations that the match would produce a keen struggle were to a large extent, realized. On the Casuals side C.E. Brisley showed to great advantage in the early part of the game, and was mainly responsible for the advantage held by his side at half-time. He manoeuvred excellently for position, and sent his colleague through time after time, P.J. Montgomery, taking advantage of his partner's skill, adopted forcing tactics, and rarely obtained the ball without gaining considerable ground and sending accurate passes to his inside men. A.L. Hosie worked hard, but the goal which he obtained was a lucky one. C.D. McIver played to score on many occasions and demonstrated his ability to go through, but he rather neglected E.S. Ward – often in a match-winning forward – at the latter end of the game. E.S. Ward showed all his old skill, and the manner in which he outwitted C.C. Page and scored brilliantly in the first half proved that enough use of him was not made. The great drawback to the Casuals' forward play lay first in their faulty shooting, and, in the later stages of the game, in a proneness to individual work when combination would have been more effective. K.C. Raikes was certainly the finest half-back on the field. He was very prominent in tackling, passing to his forwards, and shooting, and nearly won the match for his side. P.A. Sergeant and I.P.F. Campbell had hard work in order to cope with the intricate forward movements of their opponents, but their sturdy efforts kept them out on many occasions.

The Old Malvernians did not give an even display. At times they were a little slower than the opposing defence, and there were periods when their play approached perfection. The initiative power and deft foot-work of S.H. Day was to be seen in almost every advance, and the forwards, in their successful attacks, combined well. F.N. Tuff was a great success; his goal was obtained by a beautiful drive after a forward movement. S.E. Day played above his form, feinting well, and anticipating his brother's movements with extraordinary accuracy. J.W. Stretton was far and away the best back of the day. He tackled well, fed his forwards, and covered C.C. Page, who was obviously not in the best condition, in a very able manner.

There was little to choose between the two defences, but the sterling work of J.W. Stretton perhaps gave his side more confidence. The cup and medals were afterwards presented by Sir Daniel Goddard, M.P.[4]

Casuals enjoyed the services of a number of celebrities during the course of the season and G.D. Roberts, (Oxford University and Harlequins) the Rugby international featured, as did J. Densham another famous hurdler. Three players were selected to represent the Southern Amateur League against Oxford University namely, I.P.F. Campbell, H.A. Milton, and C.E. Brisley. The leading appearances were by P.A. Sergeant and P.J. Montgomery who each missed only one of the 20 competitive games played. C.E. Brisley was leading scorer with only five goals.

1911/12

This was to be Casuals' most disappointing season during their seven year stay in the Southern Amateur League. A lowly seventh placed position out of nine clubs, and an embarrassing first round exit from the A.F.A. Senior Cup meant there was little to play for except pride. There were also signs that 'The Split' would be resolved and although talks failed in April, things were beginning to move in the right direction.

Casuals opened the league season with three straight defeats at the hands of Ealing, New Crusaders, and Civil Service. In fact the team were to manage only one victory in the league until Christmas, a comfortable 3-0 victory over Hampstead. After this Casuals lost to Ipswich Town and Oxford A.F.A., whilst drawing with Townley Park and with Oxford A.F.A in the return fixture. The lowest point came in the A.F.A. Senior Cup first round when the club in a major upset crashed out to Carshalton, who were to gain admission to the lower division at the end of the season.

The last ever Christmas tour saw Casuals finally find their form, defeating Notts Magdala, Lincoln Lindum, Northern Amateurs, and Mansfield Amateurs, before losing the last match narrowly to Nottinghamshire.

The Old Boys started the New Year with further poor league results and struggled to draw with Alleyn Old Boys, then lost to Civil Service. Casuals were now firmly rooted to the bottom of the table having played more games than their rivals. At this point Casuals began to find their feet and Alleyn Old Boys were thrashed 7-1 with hat-tricks by E.F. Stokes and V. Edwards. That result did not alter the club's league position, but a 1-0 win over Ealing did lift the Casuals out of the danger zone.

Casuals managed a lucky draw with Townley Park, before crashing to a 1-4 defeat at home to Hampstead. Safety was finally secured with a 3-0 victory over Ipswich Town combined with a 2-1 win by Ealing over Townley Park in their last match. In the end Alleyn Old Boys were relegated but it was all too close for comfort, and not helped by selection of nearly 50 players for just 16 matches. R.W. Dower topped the list with 14 appearances ahead of several with 10 games. V. Edwards and E.F. Stokes led scoring with five of the 25 scored.

The strength of the club at this time is highlighted by the fact that A.F.A. International caps were awarded to H.G. Bache and S.H. Day, whilst M. Morgan-Owen, K.C. Raikes and V. Edwards were selected for the Welsh A.F.A. team.

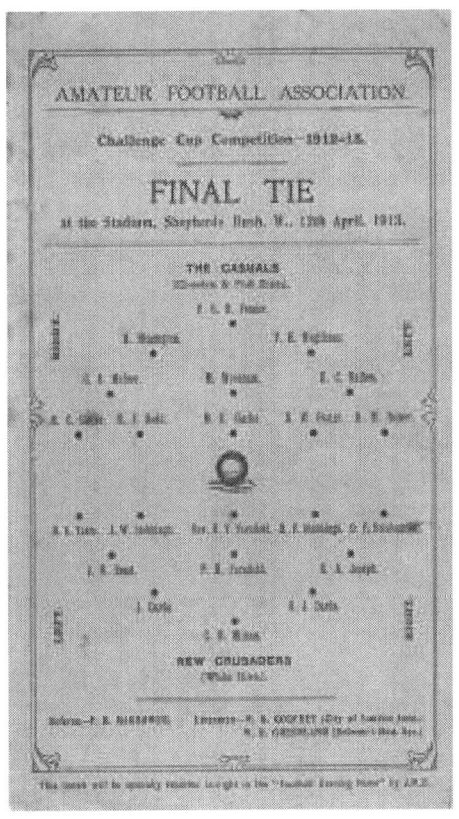

Left: Casuals v New Crusaders programme – A.F.A. Senior Cup final 1913

1912/13

Casuals recovered from the previous season's disappointment by gaining a creditable sixth place in the expanded ten team league, whilst recording an exceptional A.F.A. Senior Cup final victory over New Crusaders.

A slow start in the Southern Amateur League saw Casuals draw 1-1 with London County & Westminster Bank, before losing 0-3 at North Dulwich against Townley Park. The slide was halted with a 4-0 victory over Ipswich Town, as Casuals scored three goals in the last twenty minutes. Further victories against Eastbourne (6-1) and Oxford A.F.A. (2-0) saw the Old Boys climb the table, but this improvement could not be maintained and three successive defeats followed against Hampstead (0-2), New Crusaders (0-1), and Ealing (1-2). The only bright spot during this period was a 3-1 win at Notts Magdala Amateurs in the A.F.A. Senior Cup first round.

Casuals closed the year with a 4-3 win over Eastbourne, thanks to two goals scored in the last five minutes. A defeat against Civil Service was followed by further progress in the A.F.A. Senior Cup as London County & Westminster Bank were beaten 3-0 in a replay after Casuals

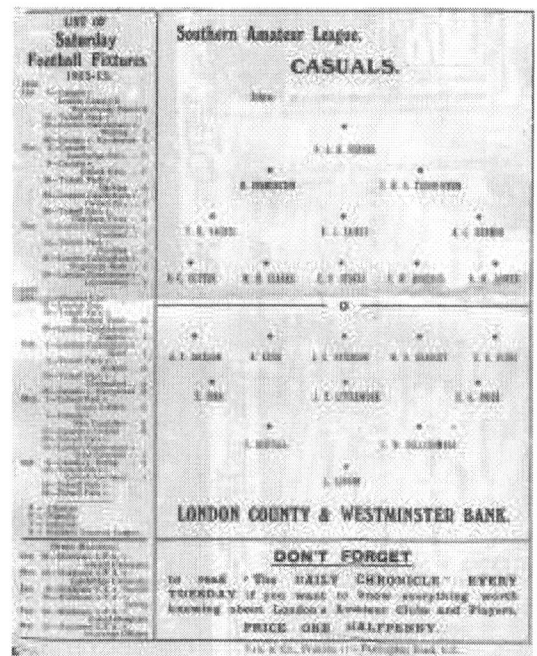

Left: Casuals v London County & Westminster Bank programme 1912/13

had scored a late equaliser in the first match. In the quarter-finals, the Old Boys defeated Hampstead 2-0, although the North London side soon got their revenge in the league game played only two weeks later when they ran out 1-2 victors.

London County & Westminster Bank were beaten again 3-0, before Casuals cruised into the final of the A.F.A. Senior Cup by beating the year's surprise package, Highgate. The Old Boys fielded a strong side, leaving nothing to chance and this policy paid dividends as they ran out 7-0 victors.

Casuals came down to earth with a bump in the next game as Oxford A.F.A. secured a narrow 0-1 victory, but the Old Boys then remained unbeaten until the end of the season. Ipswich Town were defeated 3-2, Townley Park held 1-1, and Ealing beaten 3-0 to finish Casuals' league programme in solid fashion. Two matches remained unplayed, these being home games against Civil Service and New Crusaders, who were league champions again (winning 13 of only fourteen games played). It was the highflying New Crusaders team that Casuals would play in the A.F.A. Senior Cup final:

CASUALS 3 NEW CRUSADERS 2
It is encouraging to find that there is real support for the best amateur Association football. The final for the Cup was played on Saturday in the Stadium, and, though in that immense space of seating the crowd did not look large, there must have been about 6,000 people there. The two

Above: Casuals team versus New Crusaders – A.F.A. Senior Cup final 1913

Back Row: (left to right) R.W. Dower, a linesman, M.H. Clarke, K.C. Raikes, P.G.H. Fender, A.W. Foster, H. Rimmington, P. Harrower (referee), a linesman

Seated: (left to right) M. Woosnam, R.C. Cutter, C.D. McIver (captain), F.H. Mugliston, T. Dodd

sides left in were the Casuals and the New Crusaders, who were unfortunately without the Rev. H.V. Farnfield at centre forward. He could not play owing to a weak knee, and no doubt his absence had an effect on the forward line. The result was a win for the Casuals by three goals to two, the deciding goal being scored in the last minute of the game.

The ground was in good order, but with a light ball and a certain amount of wind the conditions were not altogether easy. But if it was not great football it was a fast, very level, and exciting match, and there were some fine pieces of play. The centre half-backs were both excellent; P.H. Farnfield, for the New Crusaders, on the day being perhaps the better of the two, but M. Woosnam, who is only in his second year at Cambridge, with his pace, his strength, and the power he can put into his kicking – he made one splendid long and fast shot on Saturday which nearly scored – looks like becoming a really great player in this position. The defence on both sides was good, and the goalkeepers made no mistakes. In the forward line, both in skill and combination, the advantage was with the Casuals, though H.G. Yates, the New Crusaders' outside left, with his pace and his fine centring, often looked dangerous when he got away.

THE GAME
The New Crusaders had the wind to help them in the first half and as a whole they had rather more of the game. Their first goal came after several hard attacks, but was actually scored owing to K.C. Raikes, the Casuals' left half, attempting to kick the ball back to P.G.H. Fender,

*in goal and sending it just out of his reach. But before half-time the Casuals made the scores equal. There was some clever passing after a throw in, and A.W. Foster scored with a low cross shot. When ends were changed the Casuals, with the wind behind them, looked for a time as if they had the match in hand. R.W. Dower gave them the lead, and in the next quarter of an hour they were all always near their opponents' goal and were within an ace of scoring again more than once. At last the New Crusaders got away and a beautiful run down the wing by Yates ended with a fine centre and H.V. Stebbings scored. The rest of the match was most exciting, and play went quickly from end to end, but in the last minute R.C. Cutter, the Casuals' outside right, centred right into the goal, and M.H. Clarke got the ball through somehow with a twist of his body. There was an appeal for 'hands,' but the referee decided it was a goal, and so the Casuals won an exciting match.*5

Casuals' biggest defeat of the season came in the away friendly match against Cambridge University when the Old Boys were torn apart by the students and were 0-7 down after just twenty minutes. Fortunately Casuals only conceded two more goals during the remainder of the game.

Percy Fender made the most appearances playing all 22 matches in goal, and R.W. Dower played in 16 games. Fender also gained A.F.A. representative honours along with F.T. Vachell during the course of the season. Fender was regarded as the shrewdest county cricket captain of his generation, scoring over 19,000 runs and taking in excess of 1,900 wickets; he appeared in thirteen test matches during a first class career that stretched from 1910 to 1935.

1913/14

This was the year that Casuals finally made an impact on the Southern Amateur League by finishing as runners-up. It was also a season rocked by the tragic death of S.L. King, the club's secretary since 1897 and holder of the record number of team appearances. He had been a key figure for almost 20 years having been treasurer prior to his election as secretary. King's tragic death was the result of a mountaineering accident whilst he was attempting the ascent of Mount Cook in New Zealand, and as a mark of respect the match versus Reigate Priory on 28th February was called off. Prior to his voyage to the Southern hemisphere, King had stood down as secretary and had been succeeded by R.C. Cutter and P.G.H. Fender.

Casuals lost their only league game of the season on the opening day when they slipped to a 2-3 defeat against Civil Service. The next game, against Ealing, ended in 1-1 draw despite Casuals dominating the match. Casuals' first victory followed with a 3-1 defeat of Townley Park, before a 2-2 draw in the return fixture at the future champions Civil Service.

Seven successive victories quickly put Casuals season on track. The run started with a 3-1 victory over Old Carthusians in the A.F.A. Senior Cup first round, and was followed by league victories over Reigate Priory (3-1), Ipswich Town (8-1), and Crouch End Vampires (4-2). Further progress was made in the A.F.A. Senior Cup as Casuals completely overran Townley Park 6-0, and the team then secured a semi-final spot with a 3-2 victory at Ipswich Town. Sandwiched between these two cup ties was a 3-0 win over London County & Westminster

Bank, which was achieved notwithstanding that the Old Boys had only ten men for the entire game.

Casuals' league and cup hopes began to fade when London County & Westminster Bank held the Old Boys to a 1-1 draw, although they still had three Southern Amateur League games in hand. The league leaders Civil Service then knocked them out of the A.F.A. Senior Cup. A 1-1 draw with Crouch End Vampires left Casuals six points behind with the three games still in hand, and their hopes received a boost after a 7-2 mauling of Hampstead. Casuals played their last game on the 18th April against Ealing, when they were forced to play the first 15 minutes with seven men. It was therefore remarkable that they achieved a 1-1 draw, but it ended their hopes of the title. This was confirmed later when Civil Service beat London County & Westminster Bank 5-0. Casuals did not bother to schedule their four outstanding games against Ipswich Town, Reigate Priory, Hampstead and Townley Park.

Percy Fender made the most appearances during the season playing 16 matches, whilst E.J. Dodd was top scorer with eight goals in 12 games.

1914/15

Despite the resolution of 'The Split' at the end of the last season, Casuals were in no hurry to rejoin the Isthmian League. This competition was extended in time for the doomed 1914/15 season, and applications for membership were accepted from Ealing, West Norwood, and Woking. It is likely that Casuals took the place of Ealing on the resumption of peace time football in 1919, when the latter club decided to remain in the Southern Amateur League.

Casuals did, however, re-enter at least one of the London F.A. competitions in 1914 and were drawn away to London Caledonians in the first round of the London Charity Cup. It was around this time also that the club records were lost, which severely hampered the first post-war secretary A.M. Wilkinson in his efforts to contact all the players after the war.

Chapter Six
Post War Depression
1919-1922

The Great War was not kind to the Casuals Football Club. The huge death toll suffered by the country was reflected in a severely diminished club membership. Besides the Corinthian players who lost their lives in action having represented the club in the immediate pre-war years, (such as J.C.D. Tetley, L.A. Vidal, C.E. Brisley, R. Turner, H.G. Bache and G.B. Pollock-Hodsoll), the club inevitably experienced further loses with the passage of time. During the 1913/14 season, for example, the club called upon the services on no fewer than 141 different players, most of whom would not reappear when peacetime football was resumed.

Ten Casuals players are known to have died during the hostilities, although this is not a definitive list. Club stalwart L.T. Driffield was the only one of these not to die in the fighting as he passed away suddenly from heart disease at Leatherhead School, where he was an assistant master, in October 1917.

E.F. Gillett was killed on 29th September 1915 in France where he was a commissioned officer in the Royal Field Artillery. E.J. Dodd, the A.F.A. international, joined the Artists Rifles in September 1914, before being gazetted to the Royal Field Artillery the following year. Dodd survived being gassed in April 1916 and rejoined the front line in January 1917 where he was again injured and sent home in May. He returned to the front line at the start of July and was killed three weeks later, his death being reported in *The Times* on 27th July 1917.

C.L. Wilkinson was a commissioned officer in the Territorial Force from 1906 and was appointed to the command of a battery in October 1914. He was to see active service from April 1915 until his death on 7th April 1918. During the war he received the D.S.O. for gallantry in the field during the battle of Arras where he was wounded, having previously been mentioned in dispatches. Wilkinson held the rank of Major at the time of his death.

F.H. Bartley played for the Casuals in the last pre war season and was immediately gazetted to the West Yorkshire Regiment in August 1914, before leaving for the front in March 1915. After 16 months continuous service with his battalion he was severely wounded on 25th July 1916 and was granted three months leave. In January 1917 he rejoined his old battalion and on 31st July 1917, Bartley was slightly wounded whilst leading his company and was spotted being tended by stretcher bearers, none of whom was ever seen again. One of Bartley's contemporaries was moved to write:

'The adjutant writes: 'I cannot tell you what the loss of this gallant soldier has meant to the battalion. He had been with it longer than any other officer, and was twice recommend for bravery in the field, but unluckily had never received actual recognition of his services. He volunteered to come out to France a second time almost before he was fit. Those of us who are left will always remember him as straight, fair, and fearless under all circumstances. His memory will always be cherished in the battalion as an officer under whom his men were glad to serve, and as a gallant friend and gentleman by his fellow officers.' His colonel writes:- 'He was the very best type of officer, brave, efficient, and immensely popular and cheery. I had hoped soon to get him some further recognition of his fine services to his country.' [1]

C.B. Johnson, who was a Lieutenant Colonel in the Sherwood Foresters, was killed on 21st September 1917. G. Player, who played during the 1890's and was a second lieutenant in the Durham Light Infantry, was killed on 20th July 1916. F.A. Aston perished at Flanders on 31st July 1915 whilst serving as Captain in the 6th Duke of Cornwall's Light Infantry. P.S.C. Cadman died as a result of wounds sustained in the Great War on 31st March 1919 having served as a Major in the East Yorkshire regiment.

The last of this gallant band of men was H.H.A. Cooke, a career soldier who appeared for the club during the last ten pre-war seasons. Cooke was a captain in the Connaught Rangers, which was attached to the Nigerian Regiment. He was killed in German East Africa on 24th January 1917 after seeing active service in Nigeria and Cameroon.

1919/20

Casuals' post-war situation was unenviable. Not only were many experienced players no longer available, but there were fewer potential replacements and these were of a lower quality. The club's prospects were further damaged by the failure of the A.F.A. to re-establish itself promptly after the war. Many public schools were switching to the Rugby code partly as a result of 'the split' and Casuals had difficulties in arranging matches against suitable opponents.

It was only through the determination of M. Morgan-Owen that the club survived these troubles. His first action, in April 1919, was to call a meeting at the Sports Club, St. James' Square at which it was decided:

'...that the Casuals Football Club should be continued. Among those present were Lieutenant-Colonel M. Morgan-Owen, the Oxford Blue, Welsh international, and Corinthians' captain, who was also captain of the Casuals in 1914, and Captain R.C. Cutter, hon. Secretary of the club in 1914, the Old Rossallian, who got his Blue at Cambridge in 1908. M. Woosnam (Cambridge) and M. Howell (Oxford) wrote promising their support and assistance in every way to further the club's revival. The question of rejoining the Isthmian League will be considered at a meeting to be held on Tuesday week, at 5.30 p.m., at Captain Cutter's chambers, 2, Harcourt-buildings, Temple, E.C.' [2]

Above: The Lyttelton Ground – Casuals home for 1919/20

The resulting meeting agreed that the club should continue and rejoin the Isthmian League, whilst A.M. Wilkinson and R.C. Cutter became joint honorary secretaries.

'There were a few fine players, such as R. Sloley, H.G. Yates, P.A. Sergeant, R.W. Gandar Dower, M. Howell, and P.G.H. Fender 'left over,' but owing to the uncertain state of business they could only play occasionally. All the club records had been lost by a former secretary, there was no ground, and only about £40 in the bank.' [3]

A wide ranging and thorough search produced players such as A.E. Birch, W.G. Birch, C.R. Julian, A.J. Moore, H.F. Dubuis, H.G. Payne, A.H. Isaac and A.E. Batchelor whom it was hoped would provide a firm basis on which to rebuild the team. It should be noted, though, that the demands of Corinthian F.C. and the Arthur Dunn Cup teams were to be a constant drain on the club's resources from this point right up until World War Two.

Morgan-Owen arranged for Casuals to play their home games at the Essex County Cricket Club ground in Leyton and this was formally announced in August 1919. Despite all the hard work it was going to be a long hard season, with little cause for satisfaction at the conclusion.

The first game was played away and saw Casuals return to their previous home at Tufnell Park to face the London Caledonians in an Isthmian League fixture. Although the Old Boys scored immediately following the kick off, they were no match for the Scotsmen who responded with five goals as the Casuals collapsed. It was not all despondency in the early games: Nunhead were held to a 1-1 draw, largely due to the goal-keeping of A.J. Moore who was outstanding, before the first post war win was achieved in a 2-1 victory over Civil Service at Tidal Basin.

Casuals climbed to sixth in the Isthmian League table at the start of October following a 2-0 victory over West Norwood in their first game at Leyton. The rot quickly set in, however, and Casuals succumbed to a goal five minutes from time in their next game against Clapton (1-2). The Old Boys then crashed out of the London Charity Cup in the first round 2-4 at Dulwich Hamlet, although Gander-Dower hit the post with five minutes left with the score at 2-3.

The warning signs were plain enough and only more heroics by A.J. Moore helped Casuals record a goal-less draw with London Caledonians. Casuals proceeded to lose the next six games, starting with two close matches against West Norwood (2-3) and Tufnell Park (0-1). R.F. Popham and R.W. Gander-Dower were unavailable for the latter game because they had been selected to play for the England amateur international team against Ireland.

At this point that the results became wretched and Casuals suffered an 1-8 mauling at the hands of Dulwich Hamlet. This was followed by a 0-6 defeat at home to Ilford, when the club could only find nine players to start the game, although once more arrived later. The next game ended in a 1-5 defeat at Leytonstone, when all the scoring took place in the first half. Two further defeats 0-2 and 0-5 home and away at the hands of bottom placed Woking capped an appalling run.

The New Year began on a happier note, (albeit a brief break before the next run of defeats) when the Old Boys completed a league double over Civil Service. Three weeks later, though, normal service was resumed when a weak Oxford City side (who were resting the majority of the first choice players because of their involvement in the F.A. Amateur Cup) easily defeated Casuals 1-5. The state of affairs grew steadily worse when Casuals threw away a two goal lead against Clapton in losing 2-8, before a devastating double figure defeat at Ilford.

ILFORD 12 CASUALS 1

'Ilford beat The Casuals in a match in the Isthmian League, at Ilford, on Saturday, by 12 goals to 1.

The Casuals, who were advertised to play three Corinthian players – the Rev. K.R.G. Hunt, Captain H.A. Hambleton, and H.G. Yates, so that changes had to be made in their side, which contributed largely to their heavy defeat. The Casuals, who, before the war, fielded such fine sides, must feel a little disappointed at their efforts this season, and their lowly position in the Isthmian League is no doubt due to constant changes at the last moment.

The game, however, was not too one-sided, and the Casuals played a plucky game right to the end. In the first half of the game the Ilford forwards were fast, and kept the ball moving out to the wings, with the result that the wing men, W. Gatland and H.W. Still, repeatedly beat the defence, and the sure shooting of H.J. Eastwood, at inside right, enabled them to score five goals before the interval, to the one scored for the Casuals by F.V. Follett. The Casuals forward line adopted the inside passing game, which was quite ineffective, F.V. Follett, at centre, passing much too forward. H.G. Yates on the left wing was sadly neglected by his left half-back.

After the interval rain fell in torrents and the ground soon became waterlogged. The Casuals quite failed to keep their feet, and the Ilford players were able to add a further seven goals. The dribbling of E. Smith was very effective, and this player scored four goals.'[4]

The Casuals played on with no success and even contrived to lose 2-4 at home to Nunhead, despite the visitors playing the whole of the second half with only ten men. The team performed creditably in losing only 0-2 to the F.A. Amateur Cup finalists, Tufnell Park, but this was followed by defeats against Oxford City (0-4) and Dulwich Hamlet (0-3). The last match of the season was played away at Leytonstone, although it was technically a Casuals home game. Mustering only ten men Casuals held out for the first 35 minutes, before conceding nine goals in the remainder of the game. The club duly finished the season in last place, six points adrift of next from bottom West Norwood.

1920/21

After such a torrid season special efforts were made to improve the club's standing, but the attempt to restore the team to the pre-war level was unavailing. It was reported in *The Times*:

'Lieutenant-Colonel A.M. Wilkinson, owing to pressure of business, has given up the secretaryship, and Mr. H.F. Dubuis has undertaken the duties. His address is 26, High-street, Westminster, S.W.1. The ground of the East Molesey Cricket Club, five minutes' walk from Hampton Court Station, has been secured, and the first team will again compete in the Isthmian League.'[5]

The East Molesey Cricket Club Memorial Ground in Graburn Way is still in existence today close to Hampton Court. The club was destined to be based here only for one season as *'The owners decided that EMCC was unsuitable for any further football.'*[6]

During their stay at the East Molesey Cricket Club, Percy Sergeant (who was to go on and give sixty years service to the club), used to arrive early in the morning and proceed to mow, roll and mark the pitch. He would then go and collect the gate money, before changing quickly into his football kit in order to play in the game!

It was at this time that the club decided to take a firmer stance towards encroachments by the Corinthian F.C.:

'In 1920 there was such a continuous drain of their best players to the Corinthians that it was actually a toss up whether the club should pass out of existence altogether. Miles Howell and Sydney Hepburn took the view that if the club was preserve its' separate entity drastic steps must be taken. They adopted a certain policy towards the Corinthian F.C. (which decreed that any member who chose to play for Corinth in place of the Casuals was not again played by the Casuals), which succeeded in placing the Club on a sound practical basis. This resolute action paved the way to another amalgamation between the two famous clubs who, when they moved

to the Crystal Palace, had a joint selection committee, which included G.N. Foster of Corinthians and S.F. Hepburn of the Casuals.

*For a time this arrangement was highly satisfactory, but after G.N. Foster retired from the honorary secretaryship of Corinthians, difficulties began to crop up again.'*⁷

Casuals, though, suffered throughout the season and in March 1921 it was revealed that the club had had their resignation from the Isthmian League accepted and that they had made a formal application to join the Southern Amateur League. The club later withdrew this application and following eloquent appeals to the Isthmian League by H.F. Dubuis were allowed to retain their membership.

The season started promisingly with a 2-2 draw at Clapton, where Casuals led twice, and this was followed by the customary victory over the Civil Service in the first game at East Molesey. In front of what was described as an encouraging attendance, Casuals' secretary H.F. Dubuis scored the winner ten minutes from time to secure a 2-1 win.

From this point Casuals again began to struggle and went down 1-3 at Leytonstone, when an injury to Gander-Dower during the first half left him a virtual passenger for the rest of the game. This was followed by another defeat against the league leaders Nunhead. Casuals had led 1-0, before conceding five goals, although the play was of a high standard and was described as real Corinthian football.

Dubuis and his Casuals were struggling to stop the slide and a 1-8 defeat at Dulwich Hamlet, for the second season running, did little to suggest that this was going to change. It did, though, in the next game at home to West Norwood who were well beaten 4-1, with Casuals coming from a goal behind against nine men. As the visitors' complement of players increased so the Old Boys gradually improved their game. This was to be Casuals last competitive victory until April. Because the club had not entered any cup competitions this season, there were fewer distractions or easier friendly games to help turn the team's performances.

Casuals succumbed 0-5 at Tufnell Park and 2-3 at home to London Caledonians, where the Old Boys had held a 2-1 lead at half-time in front of *'quite a good crowd, the Casuals having become firmly established as a 'local' institution.'*⁸ The next game saw the visit of Nunhead and Casuals fielded three amateur internationals in the attack in an attempt to counter the obvious threat posed by the previous season's league runners-up. The plan failed and Casuals fell to a 1-4 defeat, although the Old Boys did hold Clapton to a 3-3 draw in the next game two weeks later (albeit after holding a two goal advantage).

London Caledonians displayed little Christmas spirit in disposing of Casuals 0-6, and in the New Year the Old Boys crashed 1-4 at West Norwood, despite leading and fielding the skilful future Corinthian star C.T. Ashton in their line-up. Casuals' form continued to dip and the club suffered its first defeat at the hands of Civil Service since the war when losing 1-4 at Hurlingham. It was also their opponent's first win of the season and pushed Casuals further towards the danger area.

Left: M.M. Morgan-Owen – Casuals saviour

Casuals lost again to Oxford City, before gaining their first point since November when Woking were held to a 1-1 draw thanks to A.J. Moore saving a penalty; a result which kept Casuals fourth from bottom of the Isthmian League.

A week later Casuals, despite producing a reasonable performance, lost 1-2 at Woking in the return; a crucial defeat in view of the forthcoming fixtures. The next match saw the visit of champions elect Ilford to East Molesey and the Essex club proceeded to crush Casuals, racing into a 1-7 half-time lead and eventually running out 3-9 winners. Tufnell Park, who were themselves still in with a chance of winning the Isthmian League, recorded a 0-3 victory when A.J. Moore again covered himself in glory by keeping the score respectable.

It was now the start of April and Casuals, who were by now desperate for points, had to face Ilford again. Despite a much improved performance, the Old Boys succumbed 1-2 in front of 4,000 supporters at Newbury Park. This form continued into the next match when a victory was achieved against Leytonstone by 3-2, largely due to a C.R. Julian hat-trick in the first 25 minutes of the game. Casuals still had a chance to preserve their honour and avoid a bottom two placing, but this dream was shattered in the first of these games at Oxford City when the Old Boys could only raise nine men and had to borrow two on arrival at the White House Ground. The 1-9 defeat which followed was hardly a surprise in such circumstances, Casuals conceding six goals before half-time. The last game of the season witnessed an Edgar Kail inspired Dulwich Hamlet side rattle in four goals in the first half hour, before finally triumphing 2-6. Casuals' only consolation at the end of a hard season was that they avoided the bottom place in the league table, which was at least some improvement on the previous season, but possible only because of the dire record of West Norwood who secured a mere six points from 22 games.

1921/22

The 1921/22 season was to be the worst season in the entire history of the club (including the separate records of Corinthian and Corinthian-Casuals) as the team did not win a single league game all season and, unsurprisingly, finished rock bottom. H.F. Dubuis continued as honorary secretary and Miles Howell, the Surrey cricketer, was club captain. The club though was strong, in the sense that it was running six teams on a regular basis, and if nothing else had a large pool of players from which to choose. 1921 was also the year that the club's saviour M. Morgan-Owen was elected to fill the position of President, a recognition which was richly deserved.

Casuals were still striving to improve their position and at a meeting in 1921 the following resolution was proposed by C. Wreford-Brown:

'that this meeting is of the opinion that efforts should be made to obtain a suitable ground in the London area which might be used by both the Corinthians and the Casuals Football Club, with a view to a mutually beneficial arrangement being arrived at for the future.' [9]

At the same meeting it was proposed also that Corinthian players would be invited to play for the Casuals whenever possible. In view of this it is difficult to see why the club performed so badly. Probably the root of the problem is to be found in the number of players used in Casuals' 26 league games. Certainly this cannot have been conducive to a settled or successful team.

The other factor which may have influenced the playing form was the choice of ground at St. Joseph's Road in Guildford. This ground was shared with Guildford who played in the Athenian League and Guildford United, soon to become Guildford City, who played as a professional club in the Southern League. This multiple tenancy meant that the reserve team had to play elsewhere and they spent the season based in Surbiton. Casuals failed to capture the local public's imagination and although their matches were played when the two Guildford clubs were away from home the attendances were poor. These improved with the visit of a successful club, but many numbered in the low hundreds.

The problems of ground sharing were highlighted early on as the first six games all had to be played away from home. The first was at Wimbledon and ended in 0-4 reverse in what was the Dons' first-ever match in the Isthmian League. This was followed by a heavy 2-7 reverse at Wycombe Wanderers, the other team in the expanded competition. A 0-2 defeat at Leytonstone, a 1-3 defeat at London Caledonians, a 0-5 thrashing at Dulwich and finally a 2-3 reverse at West Norwood completed the dismal run.

Casuals finally made their debut in Guildford on 10th October 1921 with a match against their landlords Guildford United and were outclassed in a 0-7 friendly defeat. Five days later, Casuals played their first Isthmian League match in the town and finally got off the mark when

Above: Casuals team versus Old Malvernians – December 1921

Back Row: (left to right) R.M. Gross, G.W. Shilcock, H.R. Munt, R.A. Evans, F.H. Plaistowe
Middle Row: (left to right) R.G. Pinfield, S.F. Hepburn, H.F. Dubuis, P.A. Sergeant, C.R. Julian
Front Row: (left to right) T.P. Symington, M. Howell

they recovered from two goals down to hold Clapton to a 2-2 draw. This was yet another short-lived glimmer of hope as Dulwich Hamlet recorded a 2-9 away victory the following week and Casuals' position was further compounded with defeats at Woking (1-2) and Wycombe (2-6) although the latter was formally a Casuals home game.

Despite all the doom and gloom surrounding Casuals' league form, the Old Boys had re-entered the A.F.A. Senior Cup and they saved their best form for this competition, going on to reach the semi-final. The first round was in early December and Casuals defeated Highgate 3-1 in front of only 100 spectators at Guildford. In the New Year they progressed through the competition, defeating the insurance company side Liverpool Victoria 4-3, and then London County Westminster and Parr's Bank 3-2 in a replay. Casuals' run ended in the semi-final against cup holders Ealing when, despite taking the lead, the Old Boys were hammered 1-5.

In the Isthmian League Casuals carried on their disastrous season with a 1-2 defeat at Woking, a 2-8 thrashing at Ilford, and a 0-3 reverse at Civil Service which meant the Old Boys started the New Year in the same way that they had finished the previous one. Another defeat followed at Tufnell Park (0-2) when Percy Fender gave a daring yet unorthodox performance in goal to keep the score respectable. Casuals lost 1-2 at Leytonstone in their next league game, although the Old Boys almost rescued a point late on.

The defeats continued to mount up and Clapton, Oxford City twice, Nunhead twice, and Wimbledon all recorded easy victories. In mid April the results at least began to get a bit closer when Casuals lost only 2-4 at Clapton and produced a battling performance. The Old Boys then led twice against Ilford before going down narrowly by the odd goal in five. A 0-3 reverse against Tufnell Park preceded a shock 2-2 draw at home to London Caledonians, a side who still had hopes of winning the Isthmian League. Casuals' last game of the season was also the last game they would play at Guildford and saw them lose 1-2 to West Norwood, thus completing the season without a single victory in the league.

In reviewing the season *The Times* reported:

'The Casuals have had a really bad season and have not won one League match. Individually their football has been quite good, but the side as a whole lacked cohesion and the defence have had a very hard time.'[10]

The Surrey Advertiser was almost in shock when it reported:

'It seems marvellous that a team of such resources should be in the undignified position of 'wooden spoonists.''[11]

There were, however, moves afoot which would shortly see Casuals' fortunes improve and the first part of the recovery plan was announced in April 1922:

'CORINTHIANS AND THE CRYSTAL PALACE
An agreement has been effected between the Crystal Palace Trustees and the Corinthians Football Club, by which the latter and the Casuals Football Club will make the old Cup-tie ground at the Palace their permanent headquarters.

The ground, stands, and pavilion are being thoroughly overhauled and repaired, affording comfortable seating accommodation for thousands of spectators, in addition to the vast area of terracing which has on many occasions been used by crowds numbering over 100,000.....

The programme of the Casuals Football Club will include league fixtures, the F.A. Amateur Cup, and probably some Surrey Cup competitions, all of which will be played, when necessary, at the club's new headquarters at the Crystal Palace. A great effort is being made to reinforce the playing strength of the club, and with the improved conditions it is confidently expected that a strong side will be available.'[12]

Chapter Seven
Good Times At The Palace
1922-1925

Casuals' move to the former cup final venue at the Crystal Palace promised to be the turning point in the club's history. Having won only six league matches since the end of the Great War, the Old Boys managed at last to get their house in order. So began a period which lasted until the amalgamation with Corinthians when they were always competitive and would rarely flirt with the lower reaches of the Isthmian League. The club would continue to be hampered by the calls of the Corinthian F.C. and the Arthur Dunn Cup sides, but overcame these problems and fielded reasonably settled teams in complete contrast to the pre-war seasons. During the Crystal Palace era Casuals again re-entered the F.A. Amateur Cup and various county F.A. cup competitions and this set the pattern for the coming years.

1922/23

The Summer of 1922 was a time of rebuilding for the Casuals in more than one way. S.F. Hepburn and G.N. Foster of the Corinthian F.C. had successfully negotiated a lease with the Crystal Palace Company which allowed the two clubs to play their home games at the gigantic arena in Sydenham. The two clubs set to work and duly renovated the pavilion, stands and dressing rooms; it was reported that:

'The scene of so many famous Cup finals looked very nice. The large stands, with a new coat of paint and new roofing, also the playing ground in fine condition, must make the Corinthian and Casual clubs feel proud of their new home.....

If only the great empty grassy slopes behind the playing ground had been filled with the pre-war crowds, both sides would have had a great reception at the end of the match.' [1]

The last sentence was prophetic of the clubs' problems with the tenancy in the long term,, but it must have been an exciting time for all concerned and no doubt helped the cause of secretary, S.F. Hepburn, who was also busy recruiting a new team. Hepburn was schooled on the oval ball game, having been educated at Rugby School, but during his service with the R.A.S.C. in the Great War, he turned his attention to football. Affectionately known as 'Sprouts' he obtained a Blue whilst at Oxford University and in 1921 toured America as part of the Oxford and Cambridge combined Tennis team. His enthusiasm no doubt helped him recruit an impressive list of players including J.H. Lockton, R.G. Pinfield, E. Martin and Miles Howell (who were all

Left: The Crystal Palace ground

county cricketers), and such fine players as future England internationals F.H. Ewer and A.G. Bower and ex-Chelsea captain Nils Middleboe, the Danish international.

It was an all star cast who formed the nucleus of the new Casuals team and this new generation who would help turn the club around deserve a proper introduction.

Reginald George Pinfield was known to the fans as the 'Glaxo Baby' and began his career at the age of 16 with Reading in the Southern League, gaining fame when he scored the goal which knocked Tottenham Hotspur out of the F.A. Cup in 1913. His career was halted by the war where he served as an observer in the Royal Flying Corps. On the cessation of hostilities he resumed his football career and joined Millwall, playing in their London Combination side and also captaining the R.A.F. team. Pinfield was a talented all-round sportsman who played cricket for Sussex and was an England amateur football international.

Miles Howell, who had already appeared occasionally for the club now began playing on a regular basis and also joined the committee. Howell was an opening batsman with the Surrey County Cricket Club having previously captained Oxford University Cricket Club in 1919.

Also joining from the Surrey County Cricket Club was the prolific goal scorer John Henry Lockton. Lockton had played both football and cricket for London University, and had appeared for Nottingham Forest prior to the Great War.

The last of the quartet of cricketers was Eric Martin who played for Middlesex and who was a pilot in the R.A.F.

The longest serving player of the new influx was Frederick Harold Ewer who, having served during the war in the Honorary Artillery Company, played for his regiment in the Southern Amateur League, before joining the Corinthian F.C. and Casuals F.C. Freddy Ewer was capped at both full and amateur level for England and also represented the Isthmian League and London

Above: Casuals team 1922/23

Back Row: (left to right) A. Tait (trainer), F.H. Ewer, H.H. Low, W.T. Coles, W.S. Watkinson, E.Martin

Middle Row: (left to right) A.G. Bower, R.G. Pinfield, Miles Howell (captain), H.F. Dubuis, S.F. Hepburn (Honorary Secretary)

Front Row: (left to right) H.G. Payne, R.L. Holdsworth

Above: Casuals Reserves 1922/23

Back Row: (left to right) T.P. Symington, F.V. Smith, A.W. Wallich, G.W. Shilcock, T.A. Ryder, A. Platts, E.H. Hallows

Front Row: (left to right) H.B. Kidd, A.W. Kay, P.A. Sergeant (captain), C.R. Julian, F.H. Plaistowe

F.A. In 1923 he represented the Amateurs against the Professionals in that year's F.A. Charity Shield.

H.F. Dubuis, the previous secretary, was also still playing regularly despite being wounded twice during the war. Dubuis had previously appeared for Oxford City, London Caledonians, Civil Service and had toured with the Middlesex Wanderers.

The Casuals, with all this talent available, seemed certain to improve on the previous season's debacle and the club appointed Sandy Tait (who had won an F.A. Cup winner's medal in 1901 with Tottenham Hotspur) as trainer. Everything was now in order and the Casuals began pre-season in enthusiastic fashion:

'The Casuals F.C. have been hard at it this week and two fast practice matches have been played at the Crystal Palace. The Casuals hold a prominent position in amateur football circles, but there are thousands of lovers of the great winter game within a ten mile radius of the Crystal Palace, who, having had no opportunity to witness their play, only know the club by name. The members of the club are all University men, and that fact alone constitutes a guarantee that they have a sound knowledge of the game and how it should be played. Last season they had one disappointment after another. When they played and lost their first match none of the players had kicked a ball by way of practice. They were right out of match winning condition and circumstances prevented them from developing a strong side. The practices of Monday and Wednesday served to bring their speed into operation, but several of the players still require to work hard at ball practice.

Many of those taking part came from long distances in order to participate in the games. For instance, one came from Bath and another from Brighton. That is a proof of their enthusiasm.'[2]

It was hoped that the club would build up a firm support base in their new location and season tickets details were announced in late August.

'Ground members' tickets, admitting the holder (and one lady, free) to the Crystal Palace and seats in stands A or B for all Corinthian and Casuals matches (F.A. Cup-ties excepted), can be had on application to the Assistant Secretary, the Corinthian F.C. and the Casuals F.C., Crystal Palace, S.E.19.'[3]

Casuals commenced the season by recording their first competitive victory since April 1921 when West Norwood were beaten 3-0, after the Old Boys raced into a 2-0 lead after 15 minutes. Tufnell Park then defeated Casuals (2-3) against the run of play, before a 2-2 drawn game with Dulwich Hamlet, when the Old Boys were denied victory only by a late equaliser.

At the end of September Casuals played their first F.A. Amateur Cup tie for 25 years with Redhill being defeated 4-2. A brief return to Isthmian League football then saw Casuals score twice in the last minute to steal a 2-1 victory over Oxford City. The second qualifying round of the F.A. Amateur Cup paired Casuals with Kingstonian and only an 87th minute equaliser by H.F. Dubuis prevented defeat. The replay was Casuals' first game at their new ground at the Crystal Palace and another late Old Boys equaliser deep into extra time saved the tie, which

 Left: Casuals v Nunhead programme 1923

ended 2-2. Casuals finally progressed at the third attempt when a hat-trick by H.M. Morris helped the Old Boys to a 4-1 victory in a match played at neutral Wimbledon.

Casuals' success in the F.A. Amateur Cup continued when Kingston team Leyland Motors were thrashed 5-1, despite the works side going ahead after just four minutes. A thrilling 4-4 league match with Dulwich Hamlet preceeded Casuals' next F.A. Amateur Cup tie with Wimbledon. The tie ended in another draw, one goal each, with both sets of forwards being largely ineffectual. The replay was also held at Wimbledon, (as the Corinthian F.C. had a match scheduled at the Crystal Palace that day) and this time Casuals were not so lucky, their hosts winning 2-6 and progressing to the first round proper.

Casuals were now free to concentrate on the Isthmian League for the rest of the season and their impressive form continued with a surprising 4-3 away victory over Wycombe Wanderers, a score-line which does not reflect the run of play as the Chairboys scored twice in the last few minutes. This was followed by an emphatic 8-0 victory over West Norwood (in their last season in the league) and a 3-0 win against the league leaders London Caledonians, both matches being played at the Crystal Palace.

A fortnight later Casuals again faced London Caledonians and came down to earth with a bump, when the Scots beat the Old Boys 5-1. At this point Casuals announced that they had made arrangements with London Welsh to play some league games at Herne Hill, although this never occurred at first team level at least.

The New Year began with a short tour to Spain (which is described separately) and on their return Casuals suffered a 1-2 defeat at home at the hands of Wimbledon. The Old Boys bounced back two weeks later with a 7-1 victory over Tufnell Park, when it was said that Casuals looked to be returning to their pre-war best. Casuals registered seven for the second successive week when they visited Civil Service, Johnny Lockton and H.F. Dubuis both recording hat-tricks. The victories continued to build up; Oxford City were defeated 2-0, then the current league leaders Nunhead were comfortably beaten 4-2 away. Ilford were despatched 3-2, with Lockton scoring the winner five minutes from time. This win put Casuals in second place, three points behind the leaders with two games in hand.

Unfortunately the team hit a poor run of form which coincided with the absence of H.M. Morris, while H.F. Dubuis (who had scored 18 goals) swapped places with J.H. Lockton in defence. The first match of this disappointing run was a 1-4 defeat at Ilford, which was followed by a goal-less draw with second from bottom Woking. Civil Service then visited the Crystal Palace and won 0-2 as the Old Boys were outplayed, before title rivals Clapton took both points in a victory by the odd goal in seven.

Casuals subsequently steadied the ship with two successive 2-2 draws against Leytonstone and Wycombe Wanderers, and got their title challenge back on track with a 1-0 win over Nunhead at the Crystal Palace; a match which was played immediately after a crowd of 14,000 saw London Caledonians win the F.A. Amateur Cup final at the same ground. Wimbledon were then swept aside 3-0, a result which could have set up an exciting end to the season.

Had Casuals won their last three matches of the season, they would have finished level at the top of the Isthmian League with Nunhead and might have won the title. As it happened Casuals returned to their losing ways and crashed 1-4 at both Woking and Clapton, before going down 1-2 at Leytonstone after taking the lead.

In the final table Casuals were destined to finish fifth, and although they could be disappointed by their late season slump, it should be remembered that their performance overall was a dramatic improvement on the previous three years. The move to the Crystal Palace had certainly sparked some interest locally and several crowds of 4,000 and 5,000 were recorded for league fixtures. The largest attendance was reserved for the visit of Luton Clarence (Athenian League champions in 1920) in a friendly fixture at Easter, when 10,000 were present to see Casuals romp to a 5-2 victory. The most impressive goal-scoring feat of the season was accomplished by Johnny Lockton who scored nine in a 16-1 victory over Gypsy Hill Police when he appeared for the midweek team (one of six elevens Casuals regularly fielded).

The first team had nine players who appeared in 20 or more (out of 33 competitive games), M. Howell and H.G. Payne missed two games. Dubuis led the goal scoring with 18 of the 87 goals and four others netted ten or more including A.G. Doggart (in only seven games).

Above: Casuals in Spain before playing Bilbao – January 1923

Left to Right: G. Davison-Brown (Team Manager), F.H. Pentland (Bilbao F.C.), A.M. Gamble, E. Martin, A.C. Kirby, F.V. Smith, W.S. Watkinson, R.W. de Koven, J.H. Lockton, F.H. Plaistowe, H.M. Morris, S.F. Hepburn, A. Platts, R.M. Gross, R.G. Pinfield (captain), H.F. Dubuis

Spain 1923

Casuals travelled to Spain between 4th and 12th January 1923 under the leadership of team manager G. Davison Brown. The playing contingent consisted of: W.S. Watkinson, H.G. Payne, F.H. Plaistowe, A.M. Gamble, F.V. Smith, A.C. Kirby, B.C.A. Patchitt, A. Platts, S.F. Hepburn, H.M. Morris, H.F.D. Dubuis, J.H. Lockton, E. Martin, and R.G. Pinfield.

The tourists played three matches, the first two being against Athletic Bilbao, who would win the northern regional championship, known as Campeonato de Vizcaya, which was played before the Spanish national league began in 1928. Athletic Bilbao were also destined to lift the Copa del Rey (the Spanish F.A. Cup) for the tenth time at the end of this season. In view of this Casuals did well only to slip to a 2-4 defeat in the first match and to hold Bilbao to a 4-4 draw the following day. The third game also ended in a draw, (2-2) with Real Union of Irun, founder members of the Spanish League with Athletic Bilbao in 1928 and cup finalists in 1922 and winners in 1918. Following the tour the following article appeared in *The Sportsman*:

'In the first game the tourists were 'travel tired,' J.H. Lockton, H.F. Dubuis, and R.G.C. Pinfield all being adversely affected, but they gave quite a good account of themselves in the other fixtures, though the grounds were ankle-deep in mud and water, and the matches played in continuous rain. Bilbao and Irun, my correspondent tells me, are quite up to the standard of Isthmian League clubs, and are well trained; he has especially a good word to say for Pentland, the old Middlesborough-Brentford International, who is coach of the former. The refereeing by

*Spanish officials was poor, the honest shoulder charge being very much disliked by them, but the hospitality, especially by Bilbao, great. After the second match there a dinner was given at which Count Villalonga (president Bilbao A.C.) made a charming speech for which I cannot find space to-day, in which he said that their greatest satisfaction would be to hear it said on their return home that the Bilbao A.C. understood and put into practise real sportsmanship.'*4

1923/24

Casuals were looking to build on the previous season's strong showing and retained the majority of the team whilst adding a number of new faces. The goal-keeper, A.M. Wilkinson, joined after Johnny Lockton had persuaded the committee to invite him to become a member. Wilkinson had represented the British Army and appeared for both Clapton Orient and Leyton. It was at Ilford, though, that he enjoyed his most successful period when he helped them win successive Isthmian League titles in 1921 and 1922. J.G. Knight joined the club from London University and would go on to play for the Corinthian F.C. and F.V. Smith stepped up from the reserves to win a regular spot in the team.

The season opened in sensational fashion as Wimbledon were blown away by eight goals to three. Johnny Lockton, who was not even due to play, recorded a double hat-trick, with four goals coming in the last ten minutes. Casuals, though, were brought down to earth when the reigning champions Clapton won 1-3 at the Crystal Palace, although the Old Boys had taken the lead after 13 minutes. Wimbledon then exacted their revenge by winning the return by the odd goal in five, Lockton scoring both goals for Casuals.

A 0-0 draw with Ilford in the London Charity Cup (Casuals lost the replay 0-3 two months later), was followed by five successive wins for the Old Boys. Casuals beat Nunhead 3-0 in front of 2,000 people at the Crystal Palace, before securing a 3-2 victory over Ilford. Clapton were then beaten 3-2 as Casuals came from behind and Leytonstone were beaten by the only goal of the game scored by Miles Howell in the seventh minute. The fifth match of the run saw Casuals recover from going two goals behind against London Caledonians to win 3-2.

The run was ended by league leaders Dulwich Hamlet who won by the only goal of the game at Champion Hill. Casuals recovered from defeat in the charity cup replay to record a flattering 4-1 victory over Oxford City, before slumping once again this time by 1-2 to the F.A. Amateur Cup holders London Caledonians. The year closed on a high note as Casuals defeated Ilford 6-2, despite a number of the regular side being on tour with the Corinthian F.C.

Casuals received a bye to the first round proper of the F.A. Amateur Cup for the first time since they re-entered the competition and were drawn away to Southall, a strong Athenian League club. A major shock occurred as Casuals literally slipped to a 1-3 defeat in tricky conditions. Bad weather then meant Casuals were forced to take a break until the end of January. Their next competitive game was a 5-2 victory over Civil Service, when the Corinthian, C.T. Ashton, scored four goals in a twenty minute spell. This was followed by a 4-1 victory over Tufnell Park, Eric Martin scoring all the Casuals' goals.

Above: Casuals 'B' XI 1923/24

Back Row: (left to right) R.W.V. Robins, G.A. Ashton, G.P. Mead, C. Otley, D.J.P. O'Meara, J.R. Escolme

Front Row: (left to right) J.S. Bunting, E.W. Dennes, H.L. Wallach (captain), J.G. Siewert, C.I. Record

Above: Practice Games – 1923

Back Row: (left to right) F.T. Boswell, L.J. Goddard, C.K. Part, W. Wright, C. Naef

Standing: (left to right) H.B. Kidd, E.M. Cruikshank, C.H. Kingsley, A.W. Crips, G. Coley, K.H. Lindsey, E.H. Hallows, R.J. Mander, E. Martin, J.H. Lockton, A. Platts, A.M. Wilkinson, K.M. Lindsay

Sitting: (left to right) F.H. Plaistowe, H.G. Payne, H.F. Dubuis, M. Howell, A.G. Bower, S.F. Hepburn, P.A. Sergeant, R.L. Holdsworth

In front: (left to right) G. Cruikshank, L. Stone, J.G. Knight, J. Bunting

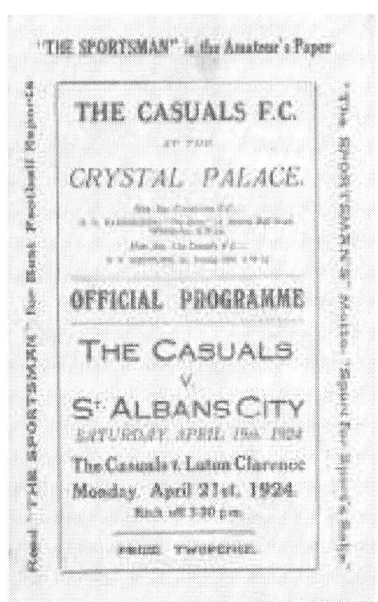

Left: Casuals v St. Albans City programme 1924

The Times suggested at this point that Casuals had a real chance of winning the Isthmian League title, but the Old Boys immediately confounded this prediction by going six games without a win. Oxford City inflicted a 1-3 defeat on the Casuals, who then drew 1-1 at Woking before losing 1-2 to Leytonstone. Any hopes Casuals had of retrieving the situation ended the following week when the Old Boys crashed 0-4 at Nunhead, and was further emphasised by a 1-3 defeat at St. Albans City.

Casuals did at least remember where the goal was when they visited Wycombe Wanderers, but still succumbed 4-5 to the Loakes Park side. The elusive win finally came when Woking visited the Crystal Palace in the second week of April, and were comprehensively defeated 5-1; a case of too little, too late. Tufnell Park were then despatched 1-0, before Casuals' woeful form returned and a 0-4 defeat by St. Albans City set the Hertfordshire club on their way to the Isthmian League title in their debut season. Further defeats against Civil Service (1-2) and Dulwich Hamlet (0-4) followed, before Casuals closed the season with a 6-2 victory at home to Wycombe Wanderers. Johnny Lockton and F.J. Boswell both scored hat-tricks against a Wanderers side who had been in contention for the title all season.

The season had finished with Casuals in a creditable seventh position in the Isthmian League, and the 'A' team collected the Surrey A.F.A. Junior Cup by beating Kew Association reserves 6-0 in the final. It was not all good news: the club was rocked in May when one of their star players, Eric Martin, was killed following a mid-air collision at Duxford, when his Bristol fighter struck an Avro during stunt flying. Martin, a prolific goalscorer, was only 29 years old.

This season A.M. Wilkinson, in goal appeared in all 29 competitive games with H.G. Payne missing just one. J.H. Lockton with 17 goals scored just two more than E. Martin.

The season was reviewed in the *Norwood News*:

'The Casuals have just completed a successful season. They hold the 7th position in the Isthmian League table, having won 13 matches out of 26 with an aggregate of 27 points. Generally speaking, they have played very good football, but a few displays have been disappointing. These have been due to fielding weak sides, but this is unavoidable in the Casuals Football Club, as so many players have interests elsewhere.

It speaks well for the spirit of the members when several have travelled long distances in order to play, and the fact that 152 different players have been called upon to fill the five weekly teams, is a great disadvantage if winning combinations are to be found.

However, the management of the club feel that they have fulfilled their object, which is to supply good, clean football to their patrons, and it is hoped that the Casuals will continue to give an exhibition of the highest class of amateur football at the Crystal Palace.'[5]

1924/25

Casuals last season at the Crystal Palace saw the club maintain the standard it had set in the previous two seasons and also reach its first post-war cup final. *The Times* previewed the forthcoming season as follows:

'Five teams will be run, four of which will turn out every Saturday throughout the season. In addition to the Isthmian League matches, the first eleven, which will be captained by H.G. Payne, will compete in the following competitions:- The F.A. Amateur Cup, the London Challenge Cup, the London Charity Cup, and the Surrey Senior Cup. The reserve team will compete in the London Intermediate Cup, the Surrey Intermediate Cup, and the South London Charity Cup competitions. Friendly games have been arranged with Oxford, Cambridge, and London Universities, Old Malvernians, Northampton Nomads, and Liverpool Ramblers. All their old players will be available, and among the new players who have offered their services are E.G. Norris and R. Jenkins (London University), G. Nicholson (Crystal Palace F.C.), and R.G. Seldon, F.H. Barnard, H.C. Boddington, and J.K. Reid, of last year's Oxford and Cambridge teams.

During the past three years the Casuals, like the Corinthians, have done much to encourage the game among the public schools, and their 'B' and 'mid-week' elevens will again meet all the leading schools in the country where the Association game is played.'[6]

In the course of the previous season, attendances had fallen from the levels initially achieved at the Crystal Palace. In an effort to arrest this decline Casuals cut admission prices from one shilling to sixpence, with transfers to the stand being priced at 8d. Although no attendance

Above: Casuals team photo 1924/25

Standing: (left to right) J.H. Lockton, T.C. Langley, C.E. Glenister, R. Sloley, A.S. Melville, A.C.J. German, F.H. Ewer, A.M. Wilkinson, J.P. Dickson, F.V. Smith

Sitting: (left to right) P.A. Sergeant, S.F. Hepburn, C.H. Sleightholme, M. Howell, N. Middleboe, A.G. Doggart, R.G. Pinfield, H.F. Dubuis, H.G. Payne

figures survive it is clear that this did not work and Casuals struggled to match the support enjoyed by their local rivals Dulwich Hamlet and Nunhead.

Casuals began the season with a 2-1 victory at home to Dulwich Hamlet, after going a goal down. The Old Boys then proceeded to throw away a two goal lead against Spartan League runners-up Great Eastern Railway, eventually going down 3-4 and departing from the London Senior Cup at the first qualifying round stage. A 3-1 victory over Wimbledon was some compensation for this disappointment and it gave the club maximum points from their first two league matches.

The Old Boys were to have an inconsistent season, however, and would never be serious challengers for the Isthmian League title at any stage. This was demonstrated by a 4-5 home defeat at the hands of London Caledonians in a topsy-turvy game and a 0-2 loss at Ilford. In true Casuals tradition they bounced back with a 5-3 win over Wycombe Wanderers on a day when A.G. Bower, C.T. Ashton and F.H. Ewer were all absent, having been selected for the England amateur international team.

This sparked a good run which saw Casuals progress in the London Charity Cup when Clapton were defeated 2-1 in a first round replay (the first game ending 1-1). This tie was followed by a 4-2 league win against Civil Service, and a 3-1 victory at Oxford City with Casuals coming from behind. This form was not maintained and Woking demolished the Old Boys 1-6, before London League side Tooting Town inflicted a Surrey Senior Cup reverse on Casuals, who were making their debut in the competition. The match ended in a 2-3 defeat, and was an exciting

Above: Casuals 'A' XI – A.F.A. Junior Cup finalists 1924/25
Standing: (left to right) S.F. Hepburn, C. Naef, B.M. Bulman, J.T. Barker, A. Jeacocke, C.I. Record, J.R. Speeding, H.J. Cory
Sitting: (left to right) C.A.E. Parker, J.G. Siewert, E.R. Mayer, E.H. Hallows, N.F. Zabell, R.A. Evans

affair which saw Casuals take a two goal lead, before surrendering this and being denied a blatant penalty with three minutes remaining.

The defeats continued to mount in December as Tufnell Park completed an Isthmian League double over Casuals in the space of two weekends, and the Old Boys began to struggle through injuries. The week before Christmas saw Casuals recover and beat Kingstonian 2-1 in the semi-final of the London Charity Cup, despite fielding a weakened side because of calls on their players from the Arthur Dunn Cup teams. This was all the more impressive as it was Kingstonian's first defeat by an amateur club in a competitive game that season.

The last game of 1924 ended in 0-0 draw with Ilford and was played in near farcical conditions as *The Times* reported:

'The ground was practically under water an hour before the match was begun, and rain fell, at times heavily, throughout the game, which was reduced to one hour's play. Naturally the players had great difficulty in obtaining a foothold, and during the first 15 minutes of the game they mostly walked about helplessly, only a few of them being able to break into a run.'[7]

The New Year began in exactly the same manner as the previous one, when Casuals bowed out of the F.A. Amateur Cup in the first round to Athenian League opposition; on this occasion the opponents were Hampstead Town (now better known as Hendon). Fortunately for the Old Boys, their form improved dramatically and Casuals reversed the result of the previous league meeting with Woking to gain revenge by six goals to one. Wycombe were then comfortably beaten 3-0, before local rivals Nunhead were outplayed 4-1. This was followed by a lucky victory over London Caledonians when Johnny Lockton scored the only goal of the match.

Casuals suffered their first defeat of the year when the team went down 1-2 at Leytonstone after conceding a last minute goal. Revenge was exacted two weeks later in the next game against the same opponents when Lockton scored twice to reverse the result. The win was all the more satisfying because Casuals had to play for 75 minutes with ten men after captain H.G. Payne was kicked in the face and was obliged to leave the field.

March was not to be a happy month for Casuals and further defeats followed against Civil Service (2-3), Clapton (2-3 and 0-3) and Nunhead (0-7). Casuals then found some form in April and defeated Dulwich Hamlet 2-0 and St. Albans City 3-0, before losing their last three league games to St. Albans City (3-5), Wimbledon (0-2) and Oxford City (3-4).

The last match of the season was the London Charity Cup final against London Caledonians and Casuals fielded a team which contained six internationals:

LONDON CALEDONIANS 1 CASUALS 0
'The meeting of the London Caledonians and the Casuals in the London Charity Cup final, on the ground of the Wimbledon club, last evening, produced a fast and thrilling game, the Caledonians winning by the only goal of the match.

The Casuals, who had six Internationals in their team, played clever football, Pinfield excelling on the extreme left. They were not so quick, however, as the Caledonians, whose forwards, splendidly led by Sloan, played a great game.

Wilkinson made a number of fine saves in the Casuals' goal, but the backs, Middelboe and Bower, were scarcely so reliable as the brothers Gates for the Caledonians. The winning goal was obtained a quarter of an hour before the interval by May, after Wilkinson had fisted away from Sloan.'[8]

Casuals again finished in seventh place in the Isthmian League and once more failed to finish the season with a trophy of some kind. The 'A' team (who played at the Malden Ground) once again performed well, this time reaching the final of the A.F.A. Junior Cup, but losing 1-2 to Civil Service reserves. Two of Casuals' friendly fixtures provided some interesting moments; in the game against Redhill, the Old Boys conceded seven goals in the last 25 minutes in losing 1-8, and against Old Malvernians the *Norwood News* was most surprised to see a penalty awarded in a game featuring the Casuals.

The Old Boys had more important issues to worry about as secretary S.F. Hepburn related:

'The fact is that there was not sufficient support in the Sydenham district for an Isthmian League club – even a winning one – so that the Old Boys had no option but to go elsewhere. During the last three seasons, although the standard of play in the club has steadily increased,

 Left: Miles Howell – club captain

as have its successes on the field, the lack of support (inspite of the introduction of a sixpenny gate this year) has steadily diminished, and the financial loss on the Casuals F.C. has been amazing. The officials of the club have felt that in the interests of the club it is impossible to continue bearing this burden indefinitely, and it is with very great regret that they have felt obliged to move to a district where the possibility is that the local supporters will be very much greater. The most important point, however, is that there is no reason to anticipate that the co-operation and close relations that have existed at the Crystal Palace between the Corinthians and the Casuals should in no way be affected; it is certainly to the great interests of both clubs that this relationship should remain as heretofore.'[9]

It was soon revealed that the club would relocate to Kingston-upon-Thames to groundshare with Kingstonian, then members of the Athenian League. A new era in the club's history was about to begin.

Denmark - 1925

Casuals' tour to Denmark consisted of three games in Copenhagen. The written records of the events of the tour are scarce, but it is known that Mr. G. Davison-Brown again acted as team manager. The touring players were: C.S. Trapp, H.G. Payne, H.F. Piper, F.H. Plaistowe, F.V. Smith, N.C.E. Ashton, C.E. Glenister, H.F. Dubuis, J.G. Knight, P.E. Mellor, H.C. Boddington, C.H. Sleightholme, S.F. Hepburn, M. Howell, J.G. Siewert, F.R. Mayer, J.H. Lockton, and R.G. Pinfield.

All three games ended in defeat, the first time Casuals had lost every game on tour, with the Old Boys losing 1-2 to Copenhagen BK (Danish Cup winners in 1925) twice and Boldklubben 1903 (Danish Cup winners in 1924) by the odd goal in five.

Chapter Eight
Richmond Road – The Early Years
1925-1929

Casuals hardly set the amateur football world alight during the early years at their new home at Richmond Road as tenants of Kingstonian F.C., but this period can be seen as the prelude to the successes of the 1930's. As time went by the Casuals F.C. became firm favourites with the local people and the club was destined to stay in Kingston until the amalgamation with the Corinthians in 1939.

1925/26

A spirit of co-operation was the order of the day, as Casuals began life in Kingston and the two clubs joined forces to issue joint season tickets with Kingstonian club members being charged 30 shillings and non members 35 shillings. Supporters favouring just one club could purchase a season ticket for 21 shillings (one guinea). The ground was in good order and the capacity makes interesting reading, as reported in *The Times*:

'The Kingstonians' ground, where the Casuals will play their home matches this season, has been considerably improved during the last two months, and it will now accommodate 20,000 spectators.'[1]

The *Surrey Comet* took the opportunity to explain the workings of the club, perhaps to avoid disappointment:

'Local spectators of the Casuals' matches will before long become familiar with a number of unusual features which are peculiar to such a club. In the first place it is not a football club in the usual sense of the term, but, like the Corinthians, it is really an association of players. There are no rules, but it is governed by the fact that the membership is elected and subject to special qualifications.

This means that the players, who have many other calls on their services, cannot be tied down to the Casuals. The result of this will be better understood as the season progresses; it will be found that owing to various fixtures clashing with important Corinthian (a term practically synonymous with Casuals), and other representative matches, the club is not able to field its strongest team every Saturday. The club finds itself in the curious position of being able to defeat a strong team one week and then suffer defeat at the hands of a much weaker team the

Above: Casuals team prior playing Wimbledon in September 1925

*following week. The reason for these fluctuations is because many of the leading players are also county cricketers, prominent golfers, or tennis players who find great difficulty in attending matches at the beginning and end of the season.'*2

Casuals again fielded five teams every week and were reinforced at first team level by Rex de Koven, and J. Fleming from Cambridge University, and J.R. Potts and A.R. Barker from Oxford University. J.G. Knight became the first team captain, a position he would hold for the next four years.

Casuals were wanting in the forward department, however, and the loss of players such as J.H. Lockton and Miles Howell led to the club struggling in front of goal all season. Despite playing attractive football, this became increasingly evident as the season progressed. The opening game was against Wimbledon in what was Casuals' debut at Richmond Road. Casuals started brightly and held a 3-2 lead, forcing the visiting goalkeeper into making two stunning saves, before Wimbledon stormed back with three goals to win 3-5. Casuals recovered from this setback to defeat Nunhead 2-1 and secure a 1-1 draw at Woking which together represented a solid start to the season.

The Woking match was in fact the first of six successive away games, which did little to help the club's cause. A 0-3 defeat at Nunhead was followed by further defeats at Wimbledon (2-3),

Above: A corner for Casuals in the 6-4 victory against Oxford City

and Clapton (3-6 in the London Charity Cup), before the trend was reversed with a 2-1 victory over Wycombe Wanderers, the Old Boys coming from behind to take the points.

Disappointingly, the team then slumped to a 1-4 defeat at London Caledonians, after numerous call ups by the Corinthian F.C. robbed Casuals of many of their starting eleven. The reserves who took their place finally succumbed to three goals scored at the start of the second half. The next match at Dulwich Hamlet saw another 1-4 defeat with many of the first team players again engaged elsewhere.

Casuals then returned to the Richmond Road ground and were held to a goal-less draw by Tufnell Park, despite the Old Boys making a blistering start to the game which should have put the result beyond all doubt. The next game in Kingston was not a happy experience, as London Caledonians outclassed Casuals to win the match comfortably 2-5.

A poor showing at home to Woking produced a 1-1 draw and was followed by Casuals' best performance of the season, a resounding 6-0 win against Civil Service, although the Old Boys only led by a solitary goal at half-time. The *Surrey Comet* report included a colourful description of the conditions in which this match was played:

'A piercing cold wind swept the carpet of snow that covered the Richmond-road ground on Saturday, when the Casuals met Civil Service in an Isthmian League match. The humorous cry

Above: Casuals team photo 1925/26

Back row: (left to right) F.R. Sanders, R.G. Pinfield, C.S. Trapp, R.G.H. Lowe, G.S. Watson, J. Fleming

Front row: (left to right) G.L. Worcester, C.H. Sleightholme, J.G. Knight, H.F. Piper, J. Harwood

of the box-office man, 'standing room only' unfortunately was belied in its full meaning by the large gaps which separated the little groups of enthusiasts who fringed the enclosure. The number of spectators increased, however, as the game wore on. Quite a Yuletide atmosphere was created by the group of bandsmen playing cheery music in front of the stand looking very much like a party of 'waits' making their Christmas rounds.'[3]

In December the team returned to their bad ways with three successive defeats. First, the visit to Ilford saw Casuals lose by the only goal of the game, only the goalkeeping of C.S. Trapp preventing a heavy defeat. St. Albans City then visited Kingston and recorded a 2-5 victory and this was followed by 2-3 loss at home to Dulwich Hamlet, when Casuals again suffered through a lack of forward power.

1926 opened with a home tie in the F.A. Amateur Cup against Oxford City. A thrilling match saw Casuals race into a two goal lead after just three minutes, and this increased to four goals after 20 minutes. Oxford City rallied briefly but Casuals finally ran out 6-4 winners, or so they thought. In the aftermath of the game, Oxford City lodged a protest about the Old Boys playing an ineligible player. As it happened this was only the tip of the iceberg with no fewer than six

Above: Kingstonians' team and the Casuals team, taking the field in April 1926

players eventually being ruled ineligible and inevitably the match was ordered to be replayed by the Football Association. The replayed match at Iffley Road, Oxford, resulted in a close contest, but Casuals lost to the only goal in extra time. The tie attracted a huge attendance which was reported to be the biggest crowd seen in Oxford since the visit of the All Blacks the previous year.

Casuals' cup tie disappointments continued as the club crashed out of the Surrey Senior Cup in waterlogged conditions at Woking. Casuals, at this time, were noted for struggling in muddy conditions and the 1-6 score line would seem to confirm this. A weak side was then humiliated 1-8 at Clapton, before the Old Boys' form improved. Two late goals were enough to beat Tufnell Park (2-0), before the Casuals gained revenge for their F.A. Amateur Cup exit with a 4-2 victory over Oxford City at Richmond Road.

The Old Boys then entertained Wycombe Wanderers and despite dominating the match could record only a 1-1 draw. Four successive defeats ensued as Leytonstone completed an Isthmian League double over Casuals in the space of three weeks, with Clapton winning the intervening game by the only goal to put the Old Boys deep into the re-election zone. The fourth match was a Surrey Charity Shield first round tie against their landlords Kingstonian and although the football was apparently a delight to watch, the result was another defeat, this time 2-4.

Casuals' form improved and three wins in the last four games helped the club climb to fourth from bottom. St. Albans City were defeated 4-1 at Clarence Park, before Ilford succumbed 3-2 in Casuals' last home match of the season. A 1-2 defeat at Oxford City preceded a 5-3 win over Civil Service, who had begun to struggle with the demands of Isthmian League football. The annual dinner at Gatti's Restaurant concluded the season and was presided over by Casuals stalwart and player from the turn of the century, H. Roper-Barrett.

J.G. Knight appeared in 30 out of 31 games scoring seven goals, but with eight goals C. Sleightholme was top scorer.

Portugal – 1926

Casuals travelled to Portugal during Easter 1926 for a short tour, where they would face future Portuguese giants Benfica and Sporting Lisbon. The touring party consisted of: C.S. Trapp, R.W. De Koven, H.F. Piper, J.G. Siewart, J.G. Knight, F.G. Frizzell, S.F. Hepburn, C.A.E. Parker, D.H. Couch, R.G.H. Lowe, T.D. Antill, H.G. Payne, J.H. Lockton, F.V. Smith, C.K. Part, G.S. Watson, and R.G. Pinfield.

It would be a few years before Benfica and Sporting Lisbon would start to dominate Portuguese football (although the latter had won the Portuguese Cup in 1923), and Casuals had mixed fortunes. Benfica were defeated 3-1, whilst the Sporting Lisbon match finished 2-2. The other match against Vitoria ended in a 0-2 reverse. It had originally been intended to extend the tour to Madeira, but owing to transport problems this idea was later abandoned. The tour was noteworthy in that it witnessed perhaps the first ever sending off of a Casuals player. In fact this is the only recorded instance at first team level of a player being dismissed, and ironically it seems to been the result of a misunderstanding:

'During a later trip in Portugal Rex de Koven, much to the amusement of the other members of the tour, was ordered off the field during a match in Lisbon. The referee had made some ridiculous decision and Rex had mildly remonstrated, 'How stupid!' But there is a word in the Portuguese language that sounds very like 'stupid,' which had a particularly offensive meaning, and the referee pointed to the touch line. However, as under Continental rules another player was allowed to take his place, the match proceeded with even forces.'[4]

1926/27

Casuals were optimistic about the new season, having retained most of the previous year's players and had added A.M. Russell, R.W. Robins, J. Hermon, R.W. Smith from Cambridge University and N.C. Ashton, H.C. Boddington, H.G. Lewis from Oxford University. An unsettled team, though, would militate against any improvement and Casuals slipped into the re-election zone by the end of the season. Rex de Koven was elected honorary secretary, succeeding S.F. Hepburn who remained involved by becoming Club Captain.

The Old Boys suffered what can only be described as a desperate start to the season. The first match was a 2-3 defeat at the hands of Kingstonian in the Surrey Charity Shield, and although the opening three league games produced five points, results soon began to deteriorate. Clapton were defeated 2-1 in the league opener, then Casuals shared six goals with Dulwich Hamlet after leading 3-1. Dulwich were defeated 1-0 in the return fixture, but Casuals next had a taste of what was going to be a hard season as Oxford City demolished the Old Boys 1-7. This was followed by a 1-3 loss at Wycombe Wanderers when Casuals fielded W.E. Barnie-Adshead, the England amateur international, who usually played for Aston Villa.

Casuals then let slip a two goal lead against the league leaders Leytonstone to draw 3-3, before the Old Boys lost 1-4 in the quagmire that was Tufnell Park. If this was not bad enough, Casuals completely collapsed in the away match with St. Albans City and found themselves eleven goals down by half-time. The Old Boys improved (or rather City eased off) in the second half and the final score was limited to 1-13, the joint second worst defeat suffered by the club in its entire history. The *Surrey Comet* reported:

'This solitary success for the Casuals might have been a winning goal for St. Albans in a cup final, so enthusiastically was it cheered by the crowd.'[5]

The *Herts Advertiser* was more generous:

'There was not 12 goals difference between the sides on the balance of exchanges.'[6]

Casuals almost achieved a dramatic turnaround of fortunes in the next game at Ilford when they led with 15 minutes to go, but contrived to lose 1-3. The result was the same in the next game as Wycombe Wanderers inflicted Casuals' first home defeat of the season. There was no respite for the Old Boys as they were outclassed 1-7 in their return fixture with Ilford which, although formally a home fixture, was actually played at Newbury Park. This miserable year finally came to an end on a high note as Tufnell Park were beaten 2-0 after wholesale changes were made to the team.

Casuals' improved form continued into the New Year as the team faced Hampstead Town for the second time in three years in the first round of the F.A. Amateur Cup. After a 3-3 draw the replay saw Casuals recover from two goals down to record a 3-2 victory; their first win in this competition since 1922. The second round was a week later when the Old Boys were to play at Portland United of the Western League Division Two. Casuals travelled to Weymouth on the Friday night before the game and stayed at the Gloucester Hotel. The match marked the last appearance of H.F. Piper, who was taking employment at a rubber firm based in Frankfurt. The game itself, which was played on the summit of Portland Bill, saw Casuals race into a two goal lead inside 15 minutes and ultimately hold on for a 3-2 victory.

The Old Boys were unable to maintain their momentum, and lost 1-3 to Sutton United in the Surrey Senior Cup with a team weakened by difficulties over the residential qualification rule. A week later, on the day of the England amateur international trial, Casuals went down by the odd goal in seven at home to Clapton.

The F.A. Amateur Cup dream then ended in the third round when Casuals succumbed 2-4 after extra time to Southall of the Athenian League who went onto lose in the semi-final. Casuals still had to plenty to do to avoid the ignominy of re-election and they improved their prospects with a 1-0 victory over Civil Service in a game devoid of thrills. Defeats followed against London Caledonians and Leytonstone, before Civil Service were defeated (2-1) again in a match that was described by the *Surrey Comet* as:

'A casual game by two of the most casual of teams in the Isthmian League resulted from the meeting of the Casuals and the Civil Service on Saturday.'[7]

Above: Casuals taking the field before the match against Tufnell Park in December 1926

This win spurred the Casuals on and the Old Boys defeated Wimbledon 2-1 on the day of the annual dinner which was held at Prince's Restaurant in Piccadilly. A week later the team recorded their third straight victory with a 1-0 win at home to Oxford City. Again Casuals failed to build on these foundations and with no Easter tour, endured a torrid end of season. Woking and St. Albans City both recorded victories over the Old Boys, before Casuals secured their last win of the campaign 3-2 over London Caledonians. The *Surrey Comet* commented on the useful advice given in the programme notes in the Casuals match day magazine:

"If the forwards would only shoot hard and well, the Casuals may be better off by two points at the end of the game.' The hint contained in this extract from the Casuals programme was acted upon to some purpose....

'During the second half the referee, Mr. G. Howlett, unintentionally stopped a hard drive with his head. It made him reel, and as he reeled into the arms of a player he blew the whistle.'

The last four matches yielded just one point, that coming from a hard fought game with Woking which ended 1-1. Nunhead then ran riot at home to Casuals who endured a 0-6 drubbing, but in the return fixture the Old Boys managed to go down only 1-2. The last game ended in a 1-4 defeat at Wimbledon when C.S. Trapp again played heroically in Casuals goal.

Casuals finally finished in 13th position in the Isthmian League, level with 12th placed Oxford City on points and three ahead of bottom placed Civil Service. Casuals, fortunately, were to succeed in the re-election vote and would survive to play Isthmian League football the following season. For the first time since 1924 the club had not gone on a foreign tour so there were no distractions or excuses for the teams poor performance during the course of the season. R.M. Robins finished as top scorer with eight goals which he achieved in just six matches. Leading appearances were J.G. Knight and F.G. Frizzell who both played in 27 games.

 Left: S.F. Hepburn –Club Secretary who donated the Casuals Cup

1927/28

The Casuals made early season promises in the press to be more competitive but although there was some improvement the team was never in a position to challenge for honours. Rex de Koven continued as secretary and was joined by S.F. Hepburn who shared the responsibilities pf the post. The players made encouraging noises about improving the club's league position and some even went so far as to indulge in pre-season training.

Casuals made a brilliant start to the season when a very strong Woking team was soundly beaten by four goals to one in a Surrey Charity Shield first round tie. This was followed by a 3-2 victory at Nunhead in the first Isthmian League match.

Casuals competed in a new cup competition from this season onwards, in the form of the so-called Casuals Cup, (which was also known at various times as the Hepburn Cup). The cup was presented by S.F. Hepburn and was to be played for annually by the Casuals and their landlords Kingstonian as an expression of good feeling between the two clubs. In the first of this series of contests Kingstonian were victorious (1-2), although Casuals were said to be the cleverer side.

The Old Boys returned to their Isthmian League campaign but showed only indifferent form in the early matches. Wimbledon defeated Casuals 2-3 at Plough Lane, although it was a creditable display given that F.R. Sanders dislocated his shoulder after only ten minutes play. A 1-0 victory at London Caledonians was followed by a 4-4 draw at Clapton, and a 0-0 draw in the return against the Scotsmen.

Casuals' cup hopes for the season took a hard knock when the club crashed out of the London Charity Cup in the first round, Nunhead winning 1-3 at Richmond Road. Casuals were obliged to field a weakened side that day as Ewer was at the amateur international trial and Whewell was unable to travel from Cambridge for the game.

Above: The Mayor of Kingston is presented to the Casuals before the Surrey Senior Cup tie with Kingston in January 1928

The club's return to Isthmian League duty saw little improvement and the Old Boys lost 2-4 at home to Civil Service in what was described as one of the worst performances since the move to Kingston. This was followed by a 2-2 draw at home to Dulwich Hamlet and a 1-2 defeat at Woking, which saw the Old Boys concede the decisive goal two minutes from time.

November opened with Casuals' first victory in over a month when Tufnell Park were defeated 3-0 at Richmond Road, all the goals coming in the first half. This success was short lived once more as Casuals lost 2-5 at home to league leaders St. Albans City and then conceded another five when the club visited Leytonstone in the following match.

A second half bombardment of the Wimbledon goal enabled Casuals to defeat the Dons by the odd goal in seven, before the Old Boys lost the next game through an act of sportsmanship at Wycombe. Two of the Old Boys' players were late and rather than delay the kick off, Casuals started with nine men; by the time the two missing players arrived the team was already 0-3 down, although the full side rallied to make the final score 2-4.

Casuals' involvement with the F.A. Amateur Cup that season began with a first round tie against Woking on New Year's Eve. The Old Boys had been drawn at home but were forced to play at their opponents ground as Kingstonian were also drawn at home. Alarmingly: *'When they arrived at Woking they found the playing pitch looking like a scene painter's canvass on which the colours had been permitted to wash together, like a piece of war camouflage.'*9 The

Above: Casuals, A. Cree encounters two Oxford City defenders – March 1928

match finished all square at two goals each, and was replayed the following week. Casuals should have been leading at the break in this game, but instead the half ended one all. In the second half Casuals conceded four goals to crash out of another cup competition at an early stage.

Casuals carried this poor form into the next league game and duly lost 2-5 at home to Ilford. Fortunately, though, the next match saw them visit fellow strugglers Civil Service. At half-time the match was goal-less, before a remarkable second half performance saw Casuals rattle in eight goals, with A.C. German leading the scoring with five goals. The *Surrey Comet* remarked

'*The Casuals surprised the Civil Service and, probably to some extent themselves, by their decisive Isthmian League victory...*'[10]

The Old Boys commenced their Surrey Senior Cup campaign after this emphatic win, the club being drawn away to landlords Kingstonian. Casuals were able to progress this time after a 4-2 victory when the Old Boys scored twice in the last ten minutes. After a 2-2 draw in the league against Woking, Casuals faced them again in the second round of the Surrey Senior Cup. Woking again proved to be the Old Boys' cup nemesis, on what was the sixth meeting of the two clubs that season, and Casuals bowed out after another defeat, this time 1-3.

Casuals finally pulled themselves together in the Isthmian League and went on a run of seven matches unbeaten. Champions elect St. Albans City were held to a 2-2 draw at Clarence Park, before Casuals completed a league double over Tufnell Park with A. Cree scoring the only goal of the game. Three successive draws followed at home to Clapton and Oxford City (both 1-1), and away at Oxford City in the return league game (2-2).

The only defeat during this period came against Tooting Town (1-3) in the semi-final of the Surrey Charity Shield, which ended Casuals hopes of a trophy for the year. Casuals responded by humiliating Nunhead 6-1, in what was the club's best performance of the season. Leytonstone were then defeated 2-1 after the Old Boys scored twice in a three minute spell early in the game. The season fizzled out with three defeats against Dulwich Hamlet (0-4), Ilford (0-2), and Wycombe Wanderers (1-3).

The club's tenth place finish was reviewed by the *Surrey Comet*:

'At first sight, a record of that kind for such a club as the Casuals, with a big reserve of first class amateur players, is not one to evoke enthusiastic praise. Yet, after consideration of the exceptional difficulties which the Casuals, as a club, have to face, they have cause to be thankful that they are not lower in the list.

The three seasons during which the Casuals have tenanted the Richmond-road ground, Kingston, have been sufficient to demonstrate to their loyal supporters that their very greatness is the cause of their weakness. And none more than the Casuals committee and officers realise the disappointments which are frequently caused by the club's inability to field regularly an eleven of representative merit.' [11]

The Casuals were also threatened, at this point, by the proposed creation of a new club, the Argonauts, by former player R. Sloley. It was hoped that the Argonauts would gain election to the Football League and play as an amateur club. This would no doubt have put more pressure on the Casuals to share its resources with yet another team, but the club supported the proposal as it was deemed to be 'in the best interests of amateur football.' However, the Argonauts' ambitious plans, which included the use of Wembley Stadium as a home ground, never came to fruition and after three failed attempts (with diminishing support) the project faded away. With the threat removed, Casuals went on to enjoy a successful next ten years.

The Guardian reported:

'In response to an invitation, Mr R. Sloley yesterday attended a meeting of the general committee of the Casuals Football Club in order to outline his general policy in creating the Argonauts F.C. It was resolved that 'In the opinion of the Casuals F.C. such an endeavour was in the best interests of amateur football. Accordingly, the Casuals F.C., representing as it does by it constitution the Public School Association footballer, welcomes this opportunity of giving their support whenever possible.' [12]

Both C.E. Glenister and M. Van der Borgh appeared in 26 games with A.C. German on 17 goals leading the scoring.

France – 1928

In April 1928, Casuals toured France with the following players making up the touring party; M. Van den Borgh, C.T. Bennett, S.F. Hepburn, J.H. Lockton, C.S. Trapp, P.S. Snow, D. Lomax, A.E. Fellowes, F.V. Smith, T.C. Johnson, J. Hermon, B.M. Bulman, G.S. Watson, A. Cree, J.A. Massey, W.E. Lingelbach, A.T. Barber, R.S. Jerome, W.C. Galbally, and C.H. Newland. Unfortunately no records survive, not even the results. It is known that Stade Harais and Le Havre were played at Havre, and that the team also played Rouen F.C.

1928/29

Casuals were again hopeful of enjoying a good season, but this optimism ultimately proved unjustified and the club continued to struggle. One memorable feature of the season, however, was that the Casuals played their only match at Wembley Stadium. The Old Boys retained most of the players from the previous campaign and, subject to availability, were able to add the following players to their squad: A.T. Barber, A. Bonham-Carter, M.B. Bower, G.S. Fletcher, P.G.T Kingsley, T.C. Johnson, N. Mace, W.F. Price, F.R. Sanders, E.C. Toye. The most famous name to appear for the club during the course of the season was D.G.A. Lowe, the Olympic sprinter who won gold in the 800 meters in both the 1924 and 1928 games.

The Isthmian League season commenced with a 2-0 win at Nunhead (who ended the season as champions), despite the Old Boys starting the game with ten men, R.G. Jenkins having been delayed. In true Casuals style the club then slumped to a 1-3 defeat at home to Tufnell Park and a 2-10 defeat against Kingstonian in the Casuals Cup.

Casuals' potential was shown when a Corinthian strength side defeated the reigning league champions St. Albans City 4-0, but again the club immediately slumped, losing 0-1 to London Caledonians. The decisive goal in this game was scored before the arrival of Jenkins, who was late once more. Five last minute changes did little to help the team in the next match at Dulwich Hamlet as they again went down by the only goal of the game. This was followed by a 1-4 defeat at London Caledonians.

Ilford were defeated 3-1 to help get the Casuals' season back on track, but the club was then immediately eliminated from the London Charity Cup after a 0-4 defeat at Nunhead - Jenkins was late yet again! The Old Boys' woes continued with a 2-4 defeat against Leytonstone, after they had led 2-1, and then Casuals were held 2-2 at Woking. Three goals in the last 15 minutes enabled the team to defeat Civil Service 6-3, prior to another 2-4 defeat in the return fixture at Leytonstone.

Casuals' next match was against Cambridge University at the magnificent Wembley Stadium:

CAMBRIDGE UNIVERSITY 5 CASUALS 2
'Cambridge University beat the Casuals in a fast game at the Wembley Stadium on Saturday by five goals to two. It was only in the last 20 minutes, in which time they scored four goals, that

Above: Casuals attack during the 4-2 home defeat against Leytonstone – October 1928

the Cambridge side were even as good as the Casuals, who, playing with the wind, had all the best of the play in the first half, and led by one goal to none.

The game was played at a great pace, and the Casuals fed their fast wing players, O.R. (sic) Fabian and G.S. Watson, with passes which were always well forward, so that the receiver of the pass was always reaching the ball when travelling at top speed instead of standing still to take the pass, or, worse still, being compelled to go back for the ball. The Casuals' forwards all went straight and hard, but the tackling of the Cambridge backs, M.B.S. Bower and J.A. Cook, and the sound anticipation of T.C. Johnson, their centre half-back, was of a high class, and a dozen dangerous attacks were broken up at the very last moment by the strong defence. Cambridge showed plenty of method in mid-field, but in the first half the chances in front of

goal were not taken. With the wind, Cambridge were quick on the ball, and in the last half-hour perhaps a little fitter than their opponents. It must be said, however, that the Casuals' side was unbalanced just as Cambridge were scoring their third goal to make the score 3 goals to 2 in their favour, by an accident to their right back, H.J. Enthoven. Enthoven was off the field for nearly ten minutes, and when he came back Cambridge had gained the attack and that peculiar sense of the power to win with which a side may become suddenly imbued.

After eight minutes' play G.S. Fletcher sent across a long forward pass to Fabian at outside right. Fabian took the ball some 20 yards and centred hard, and Watson, taking the ball in his stride, worked inwards and scored with a perfect low, hard shot into the left corner of the net. A hard shot from C.E. Glenister went just a matter of inches over the cross-bar, and another from R.G.H. Lowe was charged down when a goal looked almost a certainty. Watson put in another good shot from a centre from Fabian, but A.D. Bonham-Carter saved it at the expense of a corner. Cook, trying to clear, hit the cross-bar of his goal hard, but the ball was kicked away to safety. A good run and perfect centre by W.S. Parker left W. Lewis the Cambridge centre-forward, close in and with only the keeper to beat, but he hesitated for what seemed seconds and when at last he did shoot A. Fellowes had come across, and he charged the ball down and away to safety. H.M. Bulman nearly put through his own goal, but C.S. Trapp deflected the ball cleverly outside the post.

Two minutes after half-time a clever piece of heading by G.C. Grant gave B.H. Valentine a fine opening, but he shot straight into the goalkeeper. After a quarter of an hour Lewis equalized, putting a centre from Parker into the net from only a few yards out. Lewis looked to be standing off-side when Parker centred. Bonham-Carter tipped a hard shot from Fletcher just over the cross-bar for a corner, and the corner-kick was cleared. A long, quick dribble by Fabian followed by a centre right across the goal mouth was reached by Lowe, who came up at a great pace to score from only a couple of yards out. Shortly after clever combination by Grant and Parker, Lewis scored again from close in, finishing a good movement with a good shot. Trapp saved a hard shot from Valentine, and at the other end Bonham-Carter had to allow a corner to turn a shot from Watson outside the post. R.T. Vaughan, the Cambridge right half-back, came right up among the forwards with a long, clever dribble, and passed to Lewis, who shot at once to score his third goal. Ten minutes later Lewis, who was unmarked, met a good centre from Crowther and scored again with a well-placed shot. Just before the finish Crowther placed a corner almost into goal. It was headed out to him and he put the ball right across the goal mouth. O.R. (sic) Fabian, who was playing outside right for the Casuals, is at Cambridge University, and he was one of the best players on the field on Saturday.' [13]

After the thrill of appearing at Wembley the team experienced the greatest possible let-down with a 1-5 defeat by Clapton at the Spotted Dog. It has to be said, however, that Clapton scored most of their goals after J.G. Knight was injured within 15 minutes. This disappointing form continued in the next match when the Old Boys crashed 1-7 at Oxford City.

Casuals next held Wycombe Wanderers to a 1-1 draw prior to their F.A. Amateur Cup first round tie with Sussex County League champions Southwick. This was to prove a tricky game and Casuals had to recover from going two goals behind, only a brace by G.S. Fletcher securing a 2-2 draw. Casuals were naturally worried about the replay and called up several Corinthians in an effort to progress. Despite including leading lights such as C.S. Trapp, J.G. Knight, F.H. Ewer, and F.N.S. Creek, Casuals struggled after the late arrival of two players. The team found themselves three goals behind and although the players rallied and brought the score back to 2-3, they could not earn another replay.

A remarkable victory at Ilford could not dispel the disappointment, but it certainly provided a few talking points. Ilford had been unbeaten in two months at Newbury Park, so Casuals' 7-6 victory was most unexpected, especially as the Old Boys had led 7-4 with ten minutes to go. Casuals then slumped again and lost 0-1 to Kingstonian in the Surrey Charity Shield, before

Above: Casuals take the field before the home game with Wycombe Wanderers. Left to right: A. Cree, R.G.H. Lowe, A.H. Fellows, G.S. Watson, C.H. Sleightholme, and J.G. Knight

going down 0-2 at home to Woking, the side being weakened once more by call-ups for the Arthur Dunn Cup teams.

Casuals sprang back to life with a 7-0 demolition of Southern Amateur League side Kew Association in the Surrey Senior Cup first round, all the goals coming in the first half. This was followed by 4-2 victory over Clapton, and a 0-3 defeat at home to Wimbledon. The Old Boys then were surprisingly knocked out of the Surrey Senior Cup by Epsom Town (1-3) the reigning champions of the London League. The *Surrey Comet* remarked: '*The manner in which Epsom Town overwhelmed the Casuals in the second half can be well- illustrated by the fact that, for over 30 minutes, Watson the Casuals prominent forward, was keeping his hands warm in his pockets.*'[14]

Casuals had little left to play for except a safe position in the league, and this was achieved soon enough. Wimbledon were held 1-1 at Plough Lane, but the team then lost 1-2 to Nunhead. A 3-2 victory over Tufnell Park, when Casuals recovered from being two goals down with 27 minutes left, and a 0-0 draw at Wycombe Wanderers, edged Casuals closer to safety, before a 2-3 defeat at St. Albans City produced further anxiety. Casuals finally ensured their survival with a 4-0 victory over Oxford City, before a draw at home to Civil Service, and a defeat to Dulwich Hamlet completed the campaign.

At the end of season dinner S.F. Hepburn gave the following explanation for the problems faced by the club:

'There were two reasons, added Mr Hepburn, why the Casuals had not been successful during the past season. The first was that their committees did not view seriously enough the selection of teams, and secretaries of the various teams did not cooperate sufficiently. Five years ago it had been extremely difficult to get into the first eleven. Now the club was spending pounds on the telephone endeavouring to make certain of a definite team before each Saturday. He suggested that a better state of affairs would obtain if there were one selection committee for all the teams. The second reason for the non-success of the club was that they had not had the regular support of their best players, and there were not sufficient good players from Oxford, Cambridge and London Universities coming into the club. They had no machinery for recruiting from a junior team, and they were having to depend more and more on London University purples.' 15

Hepburn finished his speech and then resigned, citing personal commitments. He was followed by Roper-Barrett, the famous lawn tennis player, who commented:

'Hepburn was always a gloomy fellow regarding the club,' said Mr. Roper-Barrett in his reply. 'I became a member of the club in '92, and I know that it has such a spirit that it could never fail. Don't let us be down-hearted. Hepburn always makes me creep when he gets into a pessimistic mood.'

This was perhaps not the most diplomatic or generous reply to someone who had done so much work for the club and who had been obliged to wrestle with some of the club's most intractable problems. It is clear that some serious internal stresses existed and these were probably the reason for Hepburn's departure. Whatever the truth of the matter, this was an unsettling episode which the club could have done without.

B.M. Bulman and G.S. Watson both appeared in 26 games and J.A. Massey was top scorer with nine goals.

Madiera – 1929

Casuals travelled to Madiera at Easter in 1929 and the touring party included A.D. Bonham-Carter, M.B.S. Bower, D. Lomax, P.S. Snow, J.G. Stevenson, A.C.J. German, G.D. Kemp-Welch, A.H. Fabian, and G.S. Fletcher. The team left on the 9.10 a.m. train from Waterloo to Southampton. There they sailed for Madiera, where they were due to play three games. The details of the matches are again unknown, but it is known that two were drawn and one lost against, C.S. Maritimo. Nearly ten years later the *The Times* reported '*..supporters of Maritimo were not shy of speaking of the crushing defeat inflicted by their heroes on the Casuals a few years ago.*' 16 Casuals arrived back in Southampton on 8th April.

Chapter Nine
Greenland's Revolution
1929-1933

In October 1929 the secretary, Reginald Winthrop le Roy de Koven passed away a few days short of his 29th birthday:

'He will always be remembered at Cambridge, and elsewhere, for his genial disposition, and even when he had to have a leg amputated soon after going down from University his cheerfulness remained. Had this misfortune not overtaken him, it is certain that he would have made a still greater mark in amateur football, for he was a fine full-back and he was popular wherever he went.'[1]

This tragedy appears to have provoked debate within the Casuals' committee about team performances, which had been disappointing since the move to Kingston. Walter E. Greenland became the full time secretary of the club, having previously been involved in the A.F.A. Greenland had the job of providing football for the 150 playing members of the Casuals and he helped to improve the fortunes of the club by utilising his A.F.A. contacts. He was assisted by club captain Johnny Lockton, honorary secretary and treasurer G.P. Mead and honorary team secretary C.T. Bennett.

1929/30

Casuals' preparations for the season showed this determination to build a strong team. 17 players from the public schools were given trials, including F de L Evans of Bradfield College, and it was hoped that there would be greater harmony between the Casuals and Corinthian F.C.'s. A weekly paper called Casuals Weekly News was launched in an effort to keep all the members country-wide up to date with events at the club.

Although Casuals were to enjoy their most successful season since the end of the Great War, Rome was not built in a day, and the early season form was indifferent. The league fixtures opened with a 0-1 defeat at Nunhead, before Clapton were demolished 5-0 at Richmond Road. The Old Boys then lost the Casuals' Cup for the third successive year, when the team went down very unluckily 1-2 to Kingstonian.

Casuals' poor form continued, with defeats following against Wycombe Wanderers (2-3), and London Caledonians (0-1), but in the return match with the Scotsmen, Casuals overwhelmed

Above: Casuals versus Kingstonian in January 1930
Left to right: A.E. Knight, F. Macey, and A.M. Russell

their opponents 5-0, C.T. Ashton leading the goal scoring with a hat-trick. Casuals kept alive their interest in the Surrey Charity Shield with a 1-1 draw against Kingstonian, and also the London Charity Cup, after 2-2 draw at Dulwich Hamlet. Yet another draw followed, when St. Albans City were held 2-2 in a league game.

Casuals, though, were beginning to suffer from the claims of the Corinthian F.C. and with inadequate performances by the remaining players compounding their problems, the team failed to win any of the next nine games. A 1-2 defeat against Kingstonian was followed by a 1-3 loss at Oxford City. Dulwich Hamlet then beat Casuals 0-4 in the London Charity Cup replay, after the Old Boys were able to field only three regular players. A 1-1 draw at home to Tufnell Park, and a 2-2 draw at Dulwich Hamlet in the next two games were but a brief respite: Kingstonian then knocked Casuals out of the Surrey Charity Shield after a 0-2 win in the replay, the Old Boys again fielding a weak team.

After battling on with depleted forces for several weeks Casuals took a strong team to Leytonstone, and upset the local supporters with an impressive 5-2 victory. Casuals then held Wycombe Wanderers to a 2-2 draw before the commencement of the club's F.A. Amateur Cup campaign.

Above: Casuals clear a Kingstonian corner – January 1930.

The team's interest in the competition on this occasion was to be brief and the supposed cause of failure to progress brought about a new low in the relationship between the Casuals and Corinthian F.C. The facts are that Casuals were eliminated 0-4 by Dulwich Hamlet in the first round, after call-ups by the Corinthian F.C. caused havoc with the Old Boys' plans. The *Morning Post* explains:

'An open disagreement took place in December, 1929. The Casuals had an important Amateur Cup engagement with Dulwich Hamlet, and the Corinthians fixed up a club match with Luton; thus the Casuals had to take the field against Dulwich with a team that included only four members of the side originally chosen, and were beaten 4-0. This incident ended the entente that had existed between the Clubs for many years. The Corinthian point of view was that they could not afford to miss a single Saturday, prior to the third round of the F.A. Cup, which offered them an opportunity of opposing a professional side with their best available eleven.' [2]

Casuals were understandably furious, as the F.A. Amateur Cup was important for their own survival, and in a defiant act they entered the F.A. Cup the following season in direct competition with the Corinthian F.C.

Casuals' season was going downhill quickly and a 0-7 defeat at Ilford on Arthur Dunn Cup day was followed by a 2-3 defeat at home to Wimbledon, though Casuals at least made a game of it and were perhaps unlucky not to draw. The *Surrey Comet* reported:

'Wimbledon came to Kingston on Saturday expecting an easy victory over the Casuals in an Isthmian League game. Their supporters were so confident of gaining both points that they began to congratulate themselves audibly before the game started.'[3]

The New Year saw Casuals improve and in their first match held a Kingstonian side, then on an eight match winning streak, to a 1-1 draw. A 1-2 defeat at Clapton was followed by the commencement of the Surrey Senior Cup. The first round paired Casuals with London League champions Mitcham Wanderers and the Old Boys soon found themselves a goal down. Casuals missed so many chances that they scarcely deserved to win, but they eventually scraped through 2-1.

Casuals' good form continued and was emphasised by a 5-3 victory over Ilford (the previous meeting between the two clubs in December ended 0-7). Tufnell Park (1-0) and Oxford City (2-1) were then beaten prior to the team's second round tie with Tooting Town in the Surrey Senior Cup. Casuals, fielding six internationals, tantalised their opponents as a cat would play with a mouse, and the 6-1 victory was well merited.

At the start of March, Casuals defeated St. Albans City 1-0, before suffering only their second defeat of the year (1-3) at Woking. In the semi-final of the Surrey Senior Cup the Old Boys were drawn against landlords Kingstonian and fielded four internationals. Casuals' superior finishing allowed them to come from behind to record a 3-2 victory. Following the game the club held its annual dinner, the assembled company being entertained by a pianist and tenor.

Casuals continued to impress and only a late Woking equaliser deprived the Old Boys of both points from an Isthmian League fixture which ended as a 2-2 draw. Leytonstone were then easily defeated 5-3, before a the team took a well deserved point off the eventual champions Nunhead in a 1-1 draw at Richmond Road. Casuals enjoyed a brief break when the club won the Warminster Challenge Cup, beating the local side 5-1 and receiving gold medals in addition to the magnificent trophy.

The build up to the Surrey Senior Cup final was disappointing as Casuals lost to a late Edgar Kail goal in the match against Dulwich Hamlet (2-3), and then 0-3 at Wimbledon. Despite these defeats the first team still managed to secure eighth position in the Isthmian League, a significant improvement on the last few years. The reserves also impressed and finished as runners-up in the Isthmian League reserve section. Casuals' goalkeeper A.M. Russell also gained recognition when he was selected for the England amateur international team that played Scotland in March 1930. Casuals are alleged to have toured the Channel Islands at Easter in 1930, but there is no evidence of this and the only reference in the island newspapers is to Kingstonian's visit there.

Casuals were now ready for their finest moment in fifteen years:

CASUALS 2 NUNHEAD 1
'There was never any doubt about the result of Casuals' match with Nunhead at Guildford in the final tie for the Surrey Senior Cup last Saturday. The Casuals were superior always and

everywhere. They gave a great performance, fast, vigorous, alert and forceful; in fact, they played as if they, and not their opponents, were champions of the Isthmian League.

WHERE THE STRENGTH WAS.
With that clever international half-back, F.H. Ewer, in charge, the Old Boys were encouraged to fine work, and their leader compelled them to be as thorough in their attention to detail as he was himself. This combined with a calm, steady play, gave them a comparatively easy victory.

There was more than the usual sting in the front line, where E. Punnett and E.D. Shearer used speed and dexterous footwork to baffle the opposing defence. M.R. Soper's thrustful tactics at centre forward would have been better rewarded had he been quicker in his movements. F.K. Reeves and H.M. Barber did well on the wing on occasions, but they had not the keen insight which made the left wing so dangerous. The severest check to the Nunhead attack was the stalwart defence of those two giants, F. de L. Evans, at left-back, and the custodian A.M. Russell.

NUNHEAD NOT THEMSELVES
No one would have imagined that the team Nunhead fielded last Saturday had raised themselves to the championship of the Isthmian League. They played like a beaten team from the start.....

The Casuals were playing against the wind during the first half, a handicap which was overcome to some extent by close play, for long distance passing was quite out of the question. Within a couple of minutes Shearer and Punnett had forced a corner, but the kick went behind. In retaliation, Nunhead ran ahead and took the Casuals' defence by surprise. Stevenson nearly put the ball behind the line when Sidey captured it and attempted to kick a goal from about a yard from the post. In a frantic effort to clear Russell and Stevenson collided, and the goal was left unattended. Nunhead's forwards ran up and placed themselves for a pass, which Sidey never gave, for, as Russell and Stevenson staggered from the bump of their collision they obstructed the play and the ball and the ball was cleared. The incident seemed to shake up the Casuals's defence, and for some time afterwards they played with a show of anxiety and nervousness which did not look promising.

CASUALS OPEN THE SCORING
A powerful drive by Whitehouse roused Russell to an alertness, which he had lost only for a short time. At the end of fifteen minutes the Casuals were attacking hard and holding the Nunhead attack firmly. Several passes from Reeves were tried, but Soper always took too long before shooting, and he failed. Five minutes before half-time the Casuals got their first goal from a scramble in the mouth of Nunhead's goal. The ball was bobbing above the heads of a group of players when Soper shot up suddenly and headed the ball in just under the bar. The score had no apparent effect on Nunhead, but the Casuals finished this part of the game by maintaining a strenuous attack, during which Reeves missed the goal by about a foot.

Rain had begun to fall steadily, and in consequence, the Casuals had been forced to reduce their speed. This gave some relief to Nunhead, who woke up on the right wing, while there was an occasional show of promise from the steady, thrustful work of Ellis, on the left-wing. The opposing defence happened to be the weakest part of the Casuals' team, but Nunhead negatived *much of their work by complicated passing movements whenever they had raided and made more good ground. This was obviously wrong, and to rectify the blunder Ellis attempted some long distance shots whenever he got openings. From one of these, which sailed through three groups of defenders, he scored from about thirty yards out. Russell being taken unaware, or he probably had no view of the direction of the kick.*

THE ISSUE SETTLED
There was only ten minutes to go when this score happened, and the rain had made the ground so sodden that the Casuals hampered. But they obviously intended capturing the trophy, for they spurted with such effect that they ought to have scored three or four times during the last eight minutes. They were, however apparently content with a single winning goal, and this was scored with a little check by Reeves.'[4]

1930/31

Casuals, under Greenland's leadership, continued their improvement and ultimately finished fourth in the Isthmian League, their highest finish since 1906. F.H. Plaistowe became the Club Captain and E.H. Hallows took over as honorary secretary. The club's big signings of the Summer were Glyn Davies, the Welsh amateur international and A. Griffiths, the captain of Old Hamptonians. Following three practice games in August, the club was well set for a successful season.

Casuals could not have been given a harder start as they faced the reigning champions, Nunhead, in their opening game, but the team rose to the occasion and fought out a 2-2 draw. This was followed by a 5-3 victory over Clapton, when the Old Boys recovered from being 1-3 down at half-time.

Casuals' first defeat came in the Hepburn Cup which had previously being known as the Casuals Cup. The competition had now evolved into a charity cup in aid of the Kingston Victoria Hospital, Kingston Nursing Association, and Surbiton Hospital. Casuals lost the match 1-3 to Kingstonian, but a description of the Richmond Road ground written after this game is worth reproducing:

'I visited Kingstonian F.C. ground for the first time, and very fortunately saw it on Wednesday evening under the best possible conditions. Very heartily do I congratulate the club and the Royal borough on such an acquisition to the amenities of the district.

The ground resembled a huge tennis court, so perfect was the turf, and of the hundreds of similar enclosures, well known to me I can only say that Kingston easily takes the palm, not merely because of the ground's beautiful appearance, but also by reason of its convenience in relation to transport.'[5]

Casuals drew their next match at Wycombe Wanderers 3-3, (after playing half the game with ten men), then lost 1-3 at London Caledonians, following a lifeless performance by both teams. These games were a preparation for Casuals' first F.A. Cup tie for 35 years, against Redhill of the Athenian League. Playing high speed energetic football the team recorded a 3-1 and

Left: Casuals in action during the 1930's

progressed to the next round.

The Old Boys were held to a goal-less draw by London Caledonians in the next league match then went down 0-2 at Tufnell Park. A 2-1 victory over Nunhead lifted the team's spirits, but they were soon brought down to earth with 0-4 defeat at Woking in the F.A. Cup first qualifying round.

Casuals bounced back immediately with a thrilling 5-4 victory over St. Albans City after going two goals down after 20 minutes. Unfortunately this could not be maintained and despite a gallant display, the team slipped to a 3-5 reverse at Ilford followed by a 1-3 defeat at the hands of Kingstonian. Casuals, though, were resilient enough to hold Dulwich Hamlet to a 1-1 draw without a number of regulars and the team returned to winning ways with a 4-2 victory over Oxford City, when all the goals were scored in the opening 35 minutes. A 1-0 victory over Woking followed as the Old Boys gained revenge for their F.A. Cup defeat by the Cards.

Casuals lost by the odd goal in five to league leaders Wimbledon to remain in sixth place in the Isthmian League on 22nd November, and then lost again to Woking. An entertaining 3-3 draw at Dulwich Hamlet was the prelude to the season's F.A. Amateur Cup campaign. In the first round Casuals were drawn against the Royal Marines at Chatham. The Marines plied their trade in the Kent League and raced into a 1-3 half-time lead. Casuals, however, fought back strongly in the second period and managed to secure a 4-3 victory.

Casuals' promising season received a boost when Kingstonian were demolished 6-1 just after Christmas, E.D.R. Shearer hitting a hat-trick on a quagmire of a pitch. Tufnell Park were then defeated by five goals to three in the opening game of 1931, as Casuals scored four times in the opening 18 minutes.

The Second Round of the F.A. Amateur Cup paired Casuals with Ilford, who had won the competition in the two previous seasons. Casuals dominated for the majority of the match and led 2-1 with 15 minutes remaining, but in a frantic ending to the tie Ilford scored three times and progressed to the next round.

Casuals then surrendered the Surrey Senior Cup they had won the previous season when Mitcham Wanderers out-muscled the Old Boys to win 0-4 in the first round. Casuals were now left to concentrate on the Isthmian League and the team finished the season in impressive fashion. Leytonstone were easily despatched 5-1, but there was then a minor set-back in the form of a 0-2 defeat at Oxford City. Casuals next completed the double over Leytonstone (3-1), a result which took the Old Boys to third place, although they had played more games than their rivals. A 3-2 victory at home to Ilford witnessed a thrilling fight back after Casuals had found themselves two goals in arrears.

Casuals were now a most entertaining team, and they almost pulled off a remarkable victory over champions elect Wimbledon, who had been unbeaten in 15 games, when they led 3-1 at half-time. Wimbledon rallied, however, and ran out 4-5 winners. Casuals were then held by St. Albans City to a 2-2 draw, although Jenkins could have won it for the Old Boys had he not missed a penalty. In the penultimate game of the season Wycombe Wanderers, fresh from their F.A. Amateur Cup final victory over Hayes, were comfortably beaten 3-0 by an unfamiliar Casuals line up. The final match saw Casuals overwhelm Clapton 6-2 and secure fourth place with the club's record Isthmian League points total.

The reserves again performed well and recorded a runners-up position for the second year running in the Isthmian League reserve section. One match of interest during the season was against Downing College when two Casuals players, V.M. Rogers and G.A. Collins, scored double hat-tricks in the course of a crushing 15-4 victory. There was a mood of optimism within the club and those present at the annual dinner on 21st March 1931, could reflect on the fact that Casuals' standing was higher than it had been for many years.

1931/32

Casuals failed to build on the success of the previous campaign, although this was largely the result of a slump in the second half of the season. J. Whitehorn was appointed trainer and he obviously had a big impact on the early season form, whilst A.M. Russell took over as Club Captain and shared the first team captaincy with R.G.C. Jenkins. The hunt for talented amateurs continued and the following article appeared in *The Times*:

'The Casuals Football Club, which did extremely well in both divisions of the Isthmian League last season, would like to hear from old public school boys wishing to play in practice matches at Kingston at 6.15pm on August 24, 25, and 26, with a view to joining the club. The Casuals propose to field four Saturday elevens and a Wednesday side during the coming season, and, in

addition to the Isthmian League, will compete in the F.A. and F.A. Amateur Cups, the A.F.A. Senior Cup, and the Surrey Senior Cup. Visits will also be paid to the public schools, including Charterhouse, Repton, Shrewsbury, Westminster, Highgate, Aldenham, Bradfield, and Wellingborough. Communications should be addressed to Mr. W.E. Greenland, 26-27, Fenchurch-street, E.C.3.'[6]

It is interesting to note that J.C. Hayden, who was the assistant honorary secretary and was in charge of home games, was insured by the club as he had the responsibility of taking the gate money to the bank after every game!

The season opened disappointingly as Casuals lost 3-4 to Oxford City, the winning goal being scored three minutes from time. The Old Boys' cause was not helped by A.M. Russell missing the train and L.J. Kingston being forced to play in goal. A 1-2 defeat to Kingstonian followed with a late goal again proving costly.

Casuals then picked up and Woking were despatched 4-0, E.D.R. Shearer scoring all four goals. This sparked an encouraging club record run of six successive Isthmian League victories. Kingstonian were defeated 3-2 as Casuals played brilliantly in patches, and then Tufnell Park were beaten 5-4. A 5-0 victory over London Caledonians followed, as Casuals scored four second half goals. Unfortunately, on the way home Casuals' shirts were stolen when the trainer failed to look after them!

The new shirts obviously did not inspire the Casuals as a weak side promptly crashed out of the F.A. Cup. The Old Boys could not draw on most of the Corinthian players, and they were bound to struggle if forced to seek cover from their reserve teams. The match at Mitcham Wanderers was Casuals' last ever match in the F.A. Cup.

MITCHAM WANDERERS 6 CASUALS 2
'Mitcham Wanderers beat the Casuals on Saturday in the preliminary round of the F.A. Cup competition at Streatham Road Mitcham, by six goals to two.

This was Mitcham Wanderers' first home match and their first victory of the season. Their long passes, anticipation of each other's movements, and neat finishing near goal threw the Casuals defence out of gear. The Casuals were the heavier team and included three amateur international players. R.G.C. Jenkins and G. Davies made a great deal of ground on the wings, but A.M. Russell in goal was disappointing.

Play was fast throughout and the variations of fortune were kaleidoscopic. For 20 minutes the Casuals threatened goal the more often, and but for some misfortune and astonishing saves by Shoesmith would have gained a decisive lead. From the kick-off the Casuals' forwards carried out a neat movement up the field along the line, but Jenkins failed to centre. Mitcham Wanderers forced a corner immediately, but Davies took the ball back quickly along the wing towards goal, at which he shot high. Shoesmith saved well and a second later got somehow to a severe shot from F. Wheeler from a melee. The ball came out to Jenkins, who centred so that L.T. Couchman at inside-right was able to head past Shoesmith after five minutes' play. Mitcham Wanderers retaliated. A long pass from R.J. Wilson to S.A. Bleach on the left wing

Above: A.M. Russell arrives just in time to save as a Wycombe forward is poised. K.S. Ling looks on

passed G.H. Tidswell at right back and enabled T. Sealey to shoot. His shot was wide. Except during this movement the Casuals continued to attack. Jenkins centred to Couchman, who was unmarked, but lofted the ball over the bar, and then Davies raced ahead of the other forwards, tricked three of the opposition, and drove hard at Shoesmith, who just got a fist to the ball. After this the Casuals' chances were fewer. Mitcham Wanderers' combination began to tell. Sealey centred to H.E. Pullen, who headed past Russell, giving him no chance, to bring the scores level. Eight minutes later F. Burling centred through A.A. McCall, who shot obliquely at the extreme top right-hand angle of the goal. Russell was in position, but the force of the shot forced his hands back enough for the referee to allow a goal. Mitcham Wanderers scored twice more shortly before half-time and crossed over leading by four goals to one.

After 10 minutes in the second half Jenkins penetrated the defence on his own and, with Shoesmith at his mercy, easily put the ball past him to make the score 4-2. Jenkins and Davies, the Casuals' most dangerous and skilful players, had so far been somewhat wasted on the wings, so that an alteration of the forward formation was not surprising. Jenkins came to inside-right and Couchman went outside, Davies and Wheeler making a similar exchange on the left. With Pullen and Sealey both off the field with leg injuries, the Casuals had more scoring chances, but Mitcham Wanderers' defence survived a severe test, and, on the return of the injured, the Casuals were again put on the defensive. Wilson at left-half passed well forward to Pullen, who sent Sealey in so that Russell's only chance of guarding the goal was to come

Left: Action shot from Casuals versus Wycombe Wanderers – October 1931

*out. He dallied instead and was beaten. After several corner kicks at either end, and with three minutes' play to go, Sealey again got away down the right wing and passed hard across goal to McCall at inside-left. McCall tried a 'first-time' shot, but missed the ball, which came to Bleach. Bleach's shot, however, scored a sixth goal, which Russell might have saved by anticipation.'*⁷

Casuals responded to this set-back with a 4-0 victory at home to London Caledonians, and this was followed by a 2-1 win against Leytonstone. The latter game produced this incident as reported in the *Surrey Comet*:

'*Interest was soon reawakened, however, by a nasty collision between Benka and Adams, Leytonstone's centre-half, who dashed their heads together when going for the ball. Both were temporarily stunned, and had to be helped off the field. When they returned there was a ripple of amusement over the spectators at the sight of two men with clean white sticking plaster on their heads, a ripple that broke out when some wit called out 'Come on, you cripples.'*⁸

Casuals' good league form was halted by Nunhead who held the Old Boys to a 2-2 draw after scoring two late goals. The point enabled the team to retain the leadership, but they had at this stage played more games than their rivals. Casuals then returned to their bad ways and lost 1-2 at home to Wycombe Wanderers and 1-4 at Woking, when all the goals came in the last 20 minutes. A 3-2 victory over Nunhead allowed Casuals to regain the leadership of the Isthmian League thanks to a Jenkins hat-trick.

Two heavy defeats against Clapton (0-5) and Dulwich Hamlet (0-4) were separated by Casuals' 3-0 A.F.A. Senior Cup victory over Southern Amateur League team Lloyd's Bank. Casuals, however, could never regain their early season form and although Clapton were beaten 3-2, Walthamstow Avenue ended the Old Boys' F.A. Amateur Cup hopes in the first round. Casuals had been drawn at home, but so had landlords Kingstonian, and the match had to be switched to Walthamstow. Under the terms of the ground-share arrangement Kingstonian had first use of the Richmond Road stadium but Casuals were entitled to financial compensation should a clash of fixtures require them to play elsewhere. Avenue easily defeated Casuals 2-4 after the Old Boys got bogged down in the mud against the previous season's Athenian League runners up.

Casuals gave their followers little to smile about as defeats piled up. A 0-1 reverse at home to Wimbledon was followed by a 3-9 friendly defeat to Cambridge Town and then a 3-8 league loss to Ilford. A brief improvement in the A.F.A. Senior Cup second round saw Casuals beat another Southern Amateur League side Merton, 1-0. Included in their opponents' team that day was the future Old Boys goalkeeping legend Terry Huddle. This success was short-lived as Nunhead ended Casuals' Surrey Senior Cup hopes (3-4) in the first round. Casuals' last hope of a trophy was the A.F.A. Senior Cup and that dream ended in the third round after a 2-3 defeat away to Derbyshire Amateurs (who lost in the final to Hitchin Town).

It seemed that Casuals' luck would never change, particularly after a bad 0-4 home defeat to Ilford, but it did so briefly when the league leaders Oxford City were crushed 5-1 at Richmond Road. At this point Casuals had the honour of entertaining the touring Grasshoppers team from Switzerland; the visitors, it is worth noting, had become league champions of their country for a record eighth time in 1931.

CASUALS 0 GRASSHOPPERS 4
'The Grasshoppers, from Zurich, beat the Casuals yesterday on the ground of the Millwall Football Club at New Cross by four goals to none.

The Grasshoppers were lucky enough to have fine weather for the first match that they have ever played in England, and they created a most favourable impression. So few first-class Continental clubs visit this country that when two have come within a few weeks there is a natural tendency to compare them. The Grasshoppers, an amateur team, were not playing against the same class of opposition as that which the Spanish side met at Highbury before Christmas, but they lost nothing in comparison with the Spanish team in so far as their football was concerned, and they were much less theatrical.

....The Casuals, owing to the amateur international match against Wales to-morrow, were unable to call upon some of their players, and in the end they were run to a standstill and rather badly outplayed. T. Ross and J.R. Turnbull, however, put up a good defence, and no one worked harder than G.A.K. Collins.

Above: Dinner to the Grasshopper F.C. of Zurich, February 23rd, 1932, at the Criterion Restaurant.

The Casuals were the first to attack, but the Grasshoppers soon got into their stride, and Hitrec, taking a pass from A. Abegglen, crashed the ball against the crossbar. After Blasé had made a very good save from H.F. Benka, M. Abegglen finished off a good passing movement by scoring from close range. The Grasshoppers, keeping the ball well down, had most of the play, but M. Abegglen and Hitrec were both very slow in front of goal, and it was not until the first half was nearly over that they scored again. M. Abegglen began the movement with a pass into the centre, and Hitrec swung the ball out to Zivkovic. Zivkovic centred, and Hitrec had time to put the ball to his right foot and score. Just before half-time A. Abegglen shot hard against the under side of the crossbar.

A. Abegglen scored soon after the interval from a throw-in, and for some time after that the Grasshoppers had all the play. Adam tricked everyone who came near him, and Hitrec, when faced by a crowd of players near goal, gripped the ball between his ankles and hopped several yards before being stopped. A long pass from M. Abegglen to Adam, and an accurate centre from the outside-right, gave A. Abegglen another easy goal near the end.

It was a most enjoyable match, full of good football, and the Corinthians will have to struggle hard at the Crystal Palace on Saturday if they are to repeat the narrow victory that they gained over the Grasshoppers in Switzerland last year.'[9]

Finally free of re-election worries this season, Casuals plodded their way through their remaining Isthmian League fixtures. A 2-2 draw at Leytonstone preceded a 1-2 reverse at Tufnell Park, and further draws followed against St. Albans City, 3-3 and 4-4, the latter being City's first away point all season.

Casuals' tour to the West Country included wins against a pair of Western League teams; Frome Town (5-4) and Chippenham Town (6-0). This seemed to give Casuals confidence and Dulwich Hamlet's title aspirations were dented as the Old Boys recorded a rare victory by four goals to two. The season closed with 0-2 reverses against both Wimbledon and Wycombe Wanderers, the latter being significant in that it was Terry Huddle's first appearance for the Casuals.

Casuals ultimately finished in ninth position in the Isthmian League, with the reserves again finishing as runners-up in the reserve section. The fourth team deserves special mention as they reached the semi-final of the A.F.A. Minor Cup, which was quite an achievement in view of the calls on their numbers from Casuals' more senior sides. Casuals teams played 134 games in all during the course of the season with the following record; won 83, drawn 11, lost 40, goals for 517 and goal against 323. P.J. Rossage was the club's top scorer with 35 and L.J. Kingston was second with 23 goals in 48 games.

At the annual dinner held on 23rd April 1932, at the Northumberland Rooms, Charing Cross, the club's internationals were warmly congratulated. The players concerned were Glyn Davies (who was capped for Wales against England), Jenkins (who was capped for England against Wales) and Fabian (who was capped for England against Scotland).

1932/33

Casuals' Jubilee season saw the club improve on the previous campaign to finish fifth in the Isthmian League, but most of the teams were competitive this time and only two points separated fifth place from eleventh in the final table. W.E. Greenland continued his energetic reign as Casuals' full time secretary and he was assisted by Club Captain S.F. Hepburn and first team captain Tommy Ross.

Casuals' jubilee team was described in the *Morning Post*:

'The present first team are probably the youngest eleven that has ever turned out regularly for the Casuals. Roughly, I should estimate their average age at about twenty-three. L.T. Huddle is one of the cleverest and most dependable goalkeepers in the amateur game, and there is not a speedier nor a more accomplished outside-left in the Isthmian League than the Welsh amateur international, Glyn Davies. The other members of the side are tremendously keen fellows, whose play improves in every game. W.G. Lockey, the Surrey County inside forward, who played in the an Amateur Trial match last season, joined the club the other day.'[10]

The Times also gave their opinion:

'The Casuals are something of an unknown quantity. They have a fine selection of players from which to choose, but many of them cannot turn out regularly, with the result that the side may not settle down.'[11]

In contrast to previous years Casuals managed to field a settled team, which certainly contributed to the Old Boys' improved league form. Although they lost the services of the prolific E.D.R. Shearer who moved to Northern Ireland, A.H. Fabian committed himself to the club when he was not required by Derby County in the first division.

Above: Casuals team 1932/33

Back row: (left to right) W.E. Greenland (Secretary), J. Whitehorn (Trainer), P.K. O'Brien, F. de L. Evans, L.T. Huddle, F. Wheeler, M. Lampard, L.T. Couchman, E.H. Hallows (Hon. Sec. and Treasurer), J.C. Hayden (Assist. Hon. Treasurer)

Front row: (left to right) S.F. Hepburn (Club Captain), J.O.W. Webb, K.S. Ling, T. Ross (Captain), L.J. Kingston, Glyn Davies, and H.F. Dubuis (Chairman)

Casuals began the season with a 2-3 defeat at St. Albans City, but were unfortunate not to win. This false start was soon forgotten, however, as the team went on an impressive run with victories over London Caledonians 1-0, Kingstonian 1-0, Wycombe Wanderers 2-1 (after Soper scored a last minute goal) and the Calies again 1-0 which left the Old Boys top of the league. Another victory followed 3-0 against Oxford City, before a brief slump occurred with a 0-3 defeat against landlords Kingstonians and a 1-3 loss at Wimbledon.

Casuals then stormed back and recorded their first win over Wimbledon since 1927 when the Old Boys defeated them 4-2 at Richmond Road. This was followed by a 4-0 win at Tufnell Park which caused the *Surrey Comet* to get carried away, and suggest that Casuals were potential league champions.

The Old Boys had re-entered the London Senior Cup this season and began in the third qualifying round with a 2-0 victory over United Glass Blowers from the lower division of the London League. A 1-0 league victory over Leytonstone was followed by the fourth qualifying round tie against Wealdstone of the Athenian League. Casuals came through what was potentially a tricky tie, winning by four goals to two.

A 1-3 defeat at Dulwich Hamlet was Casuals' first loss in seven weeks, but fortunately it was followed by a 4-0 win at home to Oxford City. This win was Casuals' ninth in 13 Isthmian League games and put the club in third place. It was, however, the start of a poor run which nearly undid all the club's previous hard work.

December began with Casuals going out of the A.F.A. Senior Cup in the first round to Southern Amateur League Eastbourne 1-2 after leading at one stage. Casuals commenced a brief run in

Left: Casuals Jubilee Dinner Brochure

Left: Casuals v Dulwich Hamlet programme 1933

the F.A. Amateur Cup by beating Met Police of the Spartan League 3-2 in the first round. On that day the Met Police's new 300 seat grandstand at Imber Court was opened by Sir Noel Curtis-Bennett, but A.H. Fabian was the star of the show as he inspired Casuals to come back from a 1-2 deficit with 15 minutes remaining.

Casuals then lost to Ilford 1-2, although this was a much better result than expected as the Old Boys had lost seven players to Arthur Dunn Cup sides. New Year's Eve saw a dramatic 0-7 defeat at Walthamstow Avenue, when Casuals were again forced to surrender home advantage. One Casuals official was moved to say *'Funeral on Tuesday, no flowers by request.'* This was an unfortunate defeat only one week before the Casuals' Jubilee Dinner, which was held on 7th January 1933 at the Mayfair Hotel. The event was an outstanding success and a brochure was written by Ted Hallows and paid for by the ever generous S.F. Hepburn. The Sawyer Cup was presented to Tommy Ross, the first team captain, as was the tradition.

Casuals were eliminated from the F.A. Amateur Cup in the second round by Nunhead who scored the only goal with 25 minutes remaining, and the team then went down 0-1 again at home to Tufnell Park in a league game. The Old Boys finally returned to winning ways when St. Albans City were defeated 4-1 in a dull game at the start of February, and then a 2-2 draw at Wycombe Wanderers saw Casuals equalise twice.

Inexplicably, this was followed by a run of four successive defeats. First Nunhead scored a late goal to beat Casuals 0-1, the bright spot being the performance of C.H. Hiscock, a 17 year old centre half. The away match at Woking ended in 0-1 defeat, and this was followed by a 2-3 defeat at home to Ilford. The final game of this run was unfortunate in that Casuals were due to play Stade Rennais in France on Sunday 19th March. They therefore sought permission from the Isthmian League to postpone the game against Leytonstone which was scheduled for the 18th. This request was refused and so Casuals fielded a weak side which went down 1-2. The following day in France, the Old Boys lost to a goal scored two minutes from time.

On April Fool's Day, Casuals recorded their first victory in nearly two months when Woking were defeated 5-3 at Richmond Road. Nunhead were next held 0-0 in what was a tedious end of season game. The *Surrey Comet* remarked: *'There was one moment of real interest during the Isthmian League game between the Casuals and Nunhead, at Kingston on Saturday. That was when a little boy appeared, carrying a notice board with the Amateur Cup final half-time score chalked on it.'*[12]

Casuals lifted the Casuals Cup for the first time, by defeating Kingstonian 2-0, then secured fifth place in the league despite taking only two points from the final six points available. The team lost to Dulwich Hamlet (2-3) and Clapton (1-2), but demolished Clapton 5-0 in the return.

The Old Boys were building the foundations for future success and it was felt that had Casuals acquired a regular strong right wing and centre forward the team would have carried all before it. These weaknesses were all the more apparent because A.H. Fabian and K.H.L. Cooper were able to appear for the club only at the start and end of the season. The potential strength of the club was shown in November when Casuals held Tunbridge Wells Rangers to a 3-3 draw. Rangers were described as one of the strongest professional sides in the south outside the Football League at this time.

Chapter Ten
Amateur Cup Chasing
1933-1936

With the team's performances in the Isthmian League now improving, Casuals were determined also to make a better showing in the F.A. Amateur Cup. The Old Boys progressed to the quarter-finals, at the very least, in the next three years and in 1936 finally lifted the famous cup with what was said to be the finest team ever to win the trophy. There were several reasons for this success, including greater co-operation with the Corinthian Football Club, the appointment of F.G.I. Packington as secretary and the fact that the Arthur Dunn Cup committee showed a greater willingness to re-arrange fixtures which clashed with important Casuals matches.

1933/34

A fine season saw Casuals finish only six points behind the champions Kingstonian and reach the quarter-final of the F.A. Amateur Cup. During pre-season the club worked with Arsenal, Corinthians, and the Arthur Dunn Cup committee to provide football classes for boys, and this was the first step in achieving greater co-operation with their more famous sister club. *The Times* gave an optimistic preview of their chances:

'The Casuals are, as usual, full of life and enthusiasm, and if they can keep it up and get a regular side and persist with it they should do better than ever. They have many good players on whom to call.'[1]

It was to prove a sound prediction as A.H. Fabian and W.H. Webster had both agreed to play more matches for Casuals during the course of the season and their skills, added to what was already a talented side, would see a further dramatic improvement in the club's fortunes. The *News Chronicle* reported:

'The Casuals with the co-operation of the Corinthian club are anticipating a brilliant season, both from a playing point of view and a financial view point.'[2]

Casuals began the season on a sweltering day at the end of August with a 3-0 league victory over Tufnell Park. The team's good form continued and Casuals collected nine points from the first six games. Ilford were defeated 3-1 before the club experienced a surprising 1-3 reverse at the hands of a Wycombe side which contained six reserves. Ilford were defeated again, somewhat fortunately, when Casuals scored two goals in as many minutes midway through the second half to come from behind. A goal-less draw at Kingstonian preceded a 2-0 victory at home to St. Albans City.

Unfortunately this fine start could not be maintained and Casuals went down 1-2 at Woking in the next match, when a point would have been enough to send the Old Boys to the top of the table. The team's defeat was attributed to the fact that the forwards were inclined to try and walk the ball into the net. Casuals then lost at Leytonstone by the only goal of the match after the Old Boys had had a goal controversially ruled offside in the dying moments.

Casuals' next game was marginally better as a 0-0 draw was recorded at London Caledonians. It was obviously a poor game as the tone of the *Surrey Comet* report makes clear:

"What about a goal?' ' What about our money back?' These remarks shouted by a half-amused, half-board spectator, nearly expressed the feeling of his fellows at the Isthmian League match between the London Caledonians and the Casuals at Tufnell Park on Saturday, when, after a tedious game, neither side was able to score.'[3]

The next fixture produced a thrilling spectacle, however, as Casuals drew 2-2 with Kingstonian in what was said to be the most exciting derby match between the two clubs so far. This match was followed by a 4-0 victory against St. Albans City which left Casuals fourth in the Isthmian League.

The cup season opened in earnest on the second Saturday of November, and Casuals were not to return to Isthmian League action until mid-January. The team began in the third qualifying round of the London Senior Cup, with a comfortable 3-0 win over London League side Post Office Engineers. In the next round Casuals were held 2-2 by Cheshunt based club Hoxton Manor of the Spartan League, but came from behind in the replay to record a 4-2 victory. The fifth qualifying round tie turned into a three game epic against league rivals Clapton. The first match ended goal-less, with Casuals fielding a weak side. The *Surrey Comet* claimed that it would be a miracle if Casuals did not progress when they fielded their first choice team. As it was Casuals were unlucky not to win the replay which was stopped in extra time because of bad light at 1-1. Finally in the second replay, the Old Boys crashed 1-4 against a team which had not won a league game all season!

By the time of Casuals' defeat to Clapton, the F.A. Amateur Cup was underway and Casuals had disposed of Ilford. Casuals fielded a side containing the Corinthian element of the club including E.D.R. Shearer, who had flown over from Northern Ireland, A.H. Fabian, W.H. Webster, and Sussex cricketer G.A.K. Collins. Ilford rose to the challenge and held Casuals to a 1-1 draw, but in the replay they lost 3-0 to an Old Boys side then lacking its Arthur Dunn Cup contingent. During the game G.A.R. Green was injured, and but was placed at outside right with the hope that he might contribute something. This proved to be an inspired move, however, as he scored two goals to help send Casuals through.

The second round tie against Tufnell Park was played at neutral Ilford, as both teams ground shared at stadiums which were unavailable. Casuals won 2-1 thanks to a W.G. Lockey goal, remarkable in that this was his first game back after 18 months out of the game due to an injury.

During this period Casuals also went out of the A.F.A. Senior Cup to Old Westminsters. Casuals had cruised into a 2-0 lead before an injury to T. Ross required him to go off. In the end a goal scored in the final minute by Casuals' player K.H.L. Cooper, who was playing for his school on this occasion, saw Casuals go out 3-4.

Casuals finally returned to Isthmian League action with two games against Oxford City at the end of January. The first, at Kingston, saw the Old Boys recover from being 1-3 down with ten minutes left to win 4-3, the result being clinched by a brilliant goal from A.H. Fabian. The second ended all square at 2-2, with Casuals again leaving it late to equalise.

The third round of the F.A. Amateur Cup was next and Casuals were drawn to play away at Bournemouth Gasworks Athletic. Not a team to be underestimated, the works side had been F.A. Amateur Cup finalists as recently as 1930 and had reached the semi-final the year previously. Supporters were encouraged to attend the match and special train tickets were available at 11s 6d from Waterloo to Bournemouth; entrance to the stand being 1s 6d. In order to help the Casuals, three Arthur Dunn Cup ties were postponed and the Old Boys were able to get together a strong team. In the event, it was an even game for 80 minutes, before Casuals finally showed their class and scored four times to record a 5-1 victory.

Casuals were now on a roll it seemed and not even the withdrawal of eight players (six for Corinthian and two for Arthur Dunn Cup ties) from the team for the next league game at home to Wycombe Wanderers could stop the Old Boys winning 2-0. Casuals' bubble then burst with a disappointing 1-2 defeat at Clapton, prior to the F.A. Amateur Cup fourth round tie with Dulwich Hamlet, the reigning Isthmian League champions. Casuals were favoured to reach the semi-final because of the strength of their forward line:

CASUALS 1 DULWICH HAMLET 2
'After an exceptionally interesting match Dulwich Hamlet beat the Casuals in the fourth round of the F.A. Amateur Cup tournament at Kingston on Saturday by two goals to one.

The game was so full of incident and fluctuated so violently that impressions are difficult to sort out and conclusions hard to reach. Although the Casuals were a goal behind after five minutes' play, they looked by far the more dangerous side during the first quarter of an hour, but then they fell away surprisingly and Dulwich Hamlet took almost complete charge and were well worth their lead of two goals at the interval.

The two centre half-backs, B. Joy, for the Casuals and A.H. Hamer, for Dulwich, played the kind of football centre-forwards intensely dislike, and, taking the half-back lines as a whole, Dulwich had rather the more formidable one if only for the reason that C. Murray, at right half-back, was one of the outstanding players on the field. T. Ross, who seldom gets the recognition he deserves, and F. de L. Evans played heroically at full back for the Casuals, but Evans is rather slow and this once or twice led to a Dulwich forward being unmarked near goal. The Casuals failed where they were expected to be at their strongest – at forward. A.H. Fabian chopped and changed between the outside and inside-right positions, but completely failed to find his true form in either. E.D.R. Shearer scored a goal and must always have caused Hamer anxiety, but he could not produce that brilliance which might have inspired the whole line, and

G.A.K. Collins, who looked as though he would be dangerous, was seldom given the right kind of pass. W.G. Lockey and J.O.W. Webb dribbled cleverly at times, but their work was more effective in midfield than in the more important area round the goalmouth.

AN EXCITING START
The weather and the ground were everything that the crowd and the footballers could desire, and the match was exciting from the kick-off. The Casuals immediately forced two corners, and from the second Shearer should have scored. Joy from some yards out shot, Shearer touched the ball with his foot, and, instead of steering it between the posts, sent it a yard or so wide. Play was soon down the other end, and a scramble in the Casuals' goalmouth led to the ball going to Court, who gave L.T. Huddle no sort of chance with a cross-drive from the inside position.

For some time after this the Casuals were the cleverer and more impressive side, but they could not finish what they had so promisingly begun. They forced two more corners in quick succession, but the robust tackling of the Dulwich backs and half-backs began to upset the Casuals, who for a time looked a struggling and defeated side. Ten minutes before the interval a centre from Court was deflected to Goodliffe, who had moved over to the left, and he promptly hooked the ball into the corner of the net.

Court had a chance at the beginning of the second half of putting Dulwich farther ahead, but he sliced his shot badly, and the Casuals began to fight back in earnest. A centre from Collins led to trouble for Dulwich, and after seven minutes' play Shearer scored for the Casuals. Fabian got the ball on the right wing and swung it across the field to Collins, who ran on and centred. Shearer, who was going at full speed, got the ball on the volley with his left foot, and there was nothing for N. Cummings to do but pick it out of the back of the net. The game was now at its most exciting, and the Casuals were forcing the pace, but too often was their football a justification of the insistent advice, 'Shoot, Casuals, shoot!' offered them from the safe side of the touch-line.

Both goals had narrow escapes before the end, but the Casuals had rather the better of things, and an equalizing goal would have been the fair reward of work that was admirably clever and well co-ordinated until the penalty area was reached. Dulwich had few chances and took two of them; the Casuals had plenty and took one, and that is the way, regrettable though it be to those who like to see skill and finesse gain their proper reward, football matches are won and lost.'[4]

Dulwich Hamlet went on to win the F.A. Amateur Cup, but Casuals still had a good chance of winning the Isthmian League and bounced back from their disappointment with a hard fought 1-0 victory at Nunhead. During this match:

'There was an amusing incident before the whistle was finally blown. Hooton, Nunhead's veteran right back, finding himself well up field with the ball at his feet, decided to try for a goal. He sent in a beautiful low shot, dead in the centre of the goal, Huddle stooped down, saved and kicked the ball straight back to Hooton. Hooton tried again, and again Huddle saved and gave him another 'chance.' The third time was not lucky. The shot went badly astray.'[5]

Leytonstone were then beaten by a weak Casuals team 3-1, which left the Old Boys four points behind the leaders with two games in hand. A 3-3 draw at Wimbledon and a 0-2 loss at Tufnell Park were wasted opportunities, but then three successive wins restored Casuals' hopes. The first was a 6-1 victory over Clapton, which was secured with five second half goals. This was followed by a 2-1 victory at Wimbledon, thanks to a breakaway goal against the run of play, and a 2-0 win at home to Woking.

Casuals' form then deteriorated as players returned to cricketing duties in late April and three successive defeats, two against Dulwich Hamlet and one against London Caledonians, ended their title hopes. If Casuals had won these games they would have finished level on points with Kingstonian at the top of the Isthmian League table but the Old Boys would probably have been placed second on goal average. The final game of the season was a 1-0 victory over Nunhead, which meant Casuals finished sixth with a club record of 31 points for the season. On a bright note the 'A' team won the A.F.A. Minor Cup, beating Westminster Bank 1-0 in the final at New Malden.

1934/35

Casuals prepared for the new season in optimistic mood as nine of the previous season's successful side remained with the team. The club were to be hampered, however, by the age old difficulties in fielding a settled side and the club performed badly in the league, finishing rock bottom. In contrast the club fielded its strongest side in the F.A. Amateur Cup, and was rewarded with another appearance in the quarter-final.

One victory in the first ten Isthmian League games gave early warning of the hard times ahead. The campaign began with two 1-3 defeats at Wycombe Wanderers and at home to Dulwich Hamlet as the forwards laboured unavailingly. The first win followed shortly afterwards when, against the run of play, Casuals recorded a 1-0 victory over Tufnell Park but Dulwich Hamlet then completed the double over their struggling opponents (1-3). The late withdrawal of A.H. Fabian and L.J. Kingston disrupted Casuals' preparations for their next match at St. Albans City, which saw the Old Boys lose 1-2.

The poor form continued as Casuals were defeated 3-5 at home to Kingstonian. Their problems were compounded in the game when Terry Huddle, their inspirational goalkeeper, was injured and had to be carried off. This was followed by a 0-3 defeat against Nunhead in the battle of the basement clubs, a 2-2 draw at home to Woking and 1-2 defeat against bottom two side Clapton. Between these matches Casuals were the visitors to Alexandra Park for a friendly match to celebrate the opening of their hosts' pavilion, and although the Old Boys won 4-2, the team suffered another blow when T. Ross dislocated his shoulder.

Casuals next went down narrowly to Kingstonian 0-1, in what was their best performance of the season so far and halted their slide, temporarily, with a 1-0 win at Clapton. It was a brief respite only and Casuals soon returned to their bad habits, going down 2-3 at Oxford City after playing the first 15 minutes with nine men due to late arrivals. A 0-2 defeat at league leaders

Leytonstone was followed by 0-2 reverse against Kingstonian in the first round of the London Senior Cup.

The third win of the season came in the A.F.A. Senior Cup 4-1 against Old Cholmelians, the Old Boy side of Highgate School. It was a surprising victory as Cholmelians fielded a team which contained six Casuals players, including Webster and Fabian. In the second round Casuals lost 1-3 to Southern Amateur League leaders, Hastings St. Leonard's after losing C.A. Joliffe to an injury shortly after the Old Boys had equalised.

The year closed with a further two defeats and a draw. The first match was a 1-3 reverse at home to Oxford City, a result which sent the visitors to the top of the Isthmian League. There was a poor attendance for this match and the *Surrey Comet* was moved to comment:

'On the rain-swept terrace were no more than 40 spectators, and on one of them, which has accommodation for 500, stood six disconsolate figures under six dripping umbrellas.' [6]

Casuals then contrived to lose 1-5 at Tufnell Park in an awful game, the difference between the two sides being that the home side knew where the goal was. Casuals improved enough to secure a 4-4 draw at home to Wycombe Wanderers, and this was credited to the return of R.G. Jenkins to the side after an absence of two years.

The New Year brought with it the start of Casuals' F.A. Amateur Cup campaign and the Old Boys were drawn away to Oxford City in the first round. Casuals fielded their strongest side of the season so far and were rewarded with a 1-0 victory, despite T. Ross again dislocating his shoulder and playing the second half at outside right with his arm in a sling.

This cup upset spurred on the Casuals and they recorded an impressive 2-0 victory at home to Leytonstone the following week. The second round of the F.A. Amateur Cup followed as Casuals were rewarded for their efforts in the previous round with a trip to the Badgers Hill ground of Frome Town, who played in the Western League. Casuals' efforts were again hampered by a late withdrawal, but this time in unusual circumstances:

'Howard Fabian, unable to obtain release from school duties, could not travel by train with the rest of the team and was being flown to the ground by that enthusiastic pilot Graham Stevenson. There we were, with sheets spread out on a field near the pitch to facilitate the landing, but the plane never appeared. Gilbert, a reserve half back, took Fabian's place in the forward line and the game started.' [7]

Casuals raced into a three goal half-time lead before Frome rallied, and the game was only safe for the visitors when Webster scored scored a last minute goal to complete a 4-2 victory. Casuals form then fell away in the lead up to the third round as Wimbledon easily beat the Old Boys 0-2, both goals coming in the opening 17 minutes. This was followed by a 1-2 defeat against London Caledonians, notwithstanding that Casuals fielded three internationals (Jenkins, Fabian and Whewell) in their line up.

Casuals were drawn away to that season's Spartan League champions, Hitchin Town, in the third round of the F.A. Amateur Cup and Couchmen scored after only five minutes. A defence led by the legendary figure of Bernard Joy (later of Arsenal fame), then held out for 85 minutes against overwhelming pressure. The Old Boys subsequently recorded their fourth Isthmian League victory of the season when Nunhead visited Richmond Road, the win being attributed in large measure to the team's pluck and determination.

The Old Boys were then due to face mighty Bishop Auckland in the quarter-final of the F.A. Amateur Cup. Bishop Auckland had already achieved five of their record ten F.A. Amateur Cup wins at this point and unfortunately for Casuals (as it transpired) were only weeks away from securing their sixth success. Casuals had selection problems, with A.H. Fabian unable to play because of his Saturday morning work commitments. Unfortunately there was no offer of help from Graham Stevenson this time!

In the previous round Bishop Auckland had won 11-1 at home and this attracted a huge crowd of 7,640 which crammed into Bishops' Kingway ground, producing gate receipts of £231:

BISHOP AUCKLAND 1 CASUALS 0
'The contest in the fourth round between Bishop Auckland and the Casuals on the ground of the former, to reach the semi-final of the F.A. Amateur Cup competition did not produce anything in the nature of a noteworthy game. The vital issue associated with a match of so much importance probably had a good deal to do with the fact that although the tussle was by no means lacking in thrills very little really good football was seen.

NO FIREWORKS
Bishop Auckland did not produce any of those 'fireworks' in attack which have played so big a part in their cup progress this season. The resolute defence of the Londoners was a factor in this, and no individual player could claim greater responsibility for reducing the effectiveness of the home forwards than Bernard Joy who played a cool, dominating game in the middle of the field. Joy had the Auckland centre-forward (Wilson) well marked from the beginning, and the latter player was rarely seen in possession of the ball. If he did get it, it was not for long.

The home defence also played a strong game, and quick tackling, coupled with hefty kicking, while not tending to make the football any better to watch, certainly served to keep the Casuals' forwards at a fairly safe distance from the home goal. Generally, therefore the defenders carried off most of the honours and the forwards did not have a very good day.

WORTHY OF LEAD
On their first-half display Bishop Auckland were well worthy of their goal lead at the interval. Afterwards the visitors were very unlucky on two occasions when the ball struck the crossbar, with Hopps (the home goalkeeper) hopelessly beaten. Bryan (who was Auckland's cleverest forward) had a similar experience, so that a final reckoning serves to indicate that, if both sides had got their due, the scores should have been even, at any rate at the end of the first 90 minutes. What would have happened during any period of extra time is very difficult to judge. In the last half hour, Bishop Auckland were certainly showing signs of tiring but this could not be said of the Casuals, who made several strong efforts to save the game and would probably have

succeeded had it not been for the fine defence set up by Mitton and Scott (the full-backs), assisted by half-backs who gave no quarter and showed no hesitation in the tackle.

If Bishop Auckland had any distinct advantage which entitled them to the victory, it was that their team work was superior to that of their opponents. On the whole the Casuals played as individualists and this reduced the effectiveness of the attack to a great extent. Webster did a good deal of work for his colleagues, but the usual policy of the other members of the attack was to work for position and do the shooting themselves.

Rose did a good deal in this direction but shooting from anything between 20 and 30 yards does not usually produce goals. Many of his drives went very near the mark and they were always attended by danger. He had his best period in the first half, when the home supporters were always distinctly nervous upon his getting possession. Several flashing drives, taken unexpectedly and with astonishing power considering the scope in which he had to shoot, might have produced a couple of goals before the interval had Rose had the same good fortune as attended Straughan's only shot at goal.

The deciding point was scored after eight minutes' play. An Auckland attack had been repelled and the ball came out to Straughan, who was standing about twenty yards back watching the tussle which was going on in the Casuals' goalmouth. He did not hesitate, but shot and appeared to 'slice' the ball slightly. The Casuals' defence had hardly recovered from the attack in which they had engaged and it is doubtful whether Huddle realised what was happening until just a second too late for him to have an opportunity of judging the flight of a ball which appeared to swerve in a most disconcerting fashion.

He did the only thing possible in a situation which called for some quick thinking on his part. He went down full length in the hope of 'smothering' the ball, but he was not quite quick enough.

HOME TEAM STIMULATED

From that success until the interval Bishop Auckland did most of the attacking. The wing pairs combined well in several movements which were carried right to the Casuals' goal, but which could not be said to give Huddle much anxiety. Huddle handled the ball with confidence and his hefty throws almost to the centre of the field were good to see. For quite a time the Casuals' only efforts at goal were those essayed from long range, mainly by Rose, who sent one drive just inches wide of the upright. If this shot had been on the mark Hopps would have been well beaten. The other occasion upon which the visitors might have scored was when Collins centred well and Couchman headed in. It appeared to be a goal all the way, but Hopps made a wonderful save by throwing himself full length and turning the ball round the post.

The balance of play continued to run in favour of the home team, and this was mainly due to the foraging of Bryan, who created several good openings for Dodds (on the right wing) which were not turned to the best advantage. On two occasions the winger shot badly from good positions, and on another his centre passed right across the Casuals' goal without either Wilson or Stephenson being able to give it just the slight touch it needed for a goal.

CASUALS LIVELIER
In the second half by far the most of the danger came from the left wings of both sides. Huddle showed splendid anticipation in dealing with an awkward situation when Hogg headed in just after resuming. The ball was transferred from end to end very quickly, and the Casuals were much more dangerous, compared with their first-half display. Webster and Collins accomplished many clever things and between them gave Mitton a very warm time.

A strong kick down the field relieved an attack on the Casuals' goal and found Collins well placed for a run almost from the half-way line. He outpaced all opposition, and as Hopps advanced to meet him he sent a terrific drive which the home goalkeeper never saw. To the relief of Bishop Auckland players and supporters alike, the ball struck the cross bar with a resounding smack and rebounded into play almost the distance of an average goal-kick. Before this Couchman should have done better than fire wildly over the bar with a good opening from about ten yards out. Barely a minute after the home goal had escaped from the attentions of Collins, that player and Webster took the ball past all opposition, and this time it was Webster who found himself with only Hopps to beat. He also sent in the ball with tremendous force and again the crossbar saved the home team.

DEFENSIVE PLAN
At this period the Casuals were definitely all out to save the game and Bishop Auckland had to put in some strenuous periods of defence. Mitton and Scott were splendid defenders at this time and Hopps showed commendable agility in dealing with several shots. He was just in time to prevent a drive by Couchman entering the net when he made another of those spectacular full-strength saves.

In the last fifteen minutes, Bishop Auckland contented themselves mainly with defence, and this policy of playing five half-backs and three forwards undoubtedly did a good deal to crowd out many promising efforts by the visiting forwards. Both Bryan and Stephenson (the Auckland inside forwards) accomplished much strenuous work in resisting attack during this period, and the game petered out somewhat tamely with the home team hanging on grimly to their slender lead.'[8]

An improvement in Casuals' end of the season form at least gave the team's final points total some respectability, but it was not enough to spare the club the anxiety of another plea for re-election to the league. Woking were defeated 2-0 immediately after the F.A. Amateur Cup exit. This was followed by two games against Ilford, the first a 0-3 reverse, the second a 2-2 draw at Newbury Park, when Casuals conceded a last minute equaliser.

The last hope of cup success that season ended when Kingstonian easily defeated Casuals 0-4 in the semi-final of the Surrey Combination Cup. This opportunity only arose as Wimbledon had withdrawn from the competition because of other commitments. The Dons, that season's Isthmian League champions and F.A. Amateur Cup finalists, were held 1-1, in Casuals' next league match and would probably have been beaten had the Old Boys not missed a penalty. Casuals then completed the season by drawing with London Caledonians 3-3 after leading 2-0 after only ten minutes, and then overcoming St. Albans City 5-3, with all the Old Boys' goals coming in the opening 35 minutes.

1935/36

1935/36 was undoubtedly Casuals finest hour; not only did the club finally lift the F.A. Amateur Cup, it also achieved its highest ever Isthmian League position as runners-up. Casuals had most of the previous season's team still available, although Bernard Joy had signed amateur forms with Arsenal, (where he would collect a Football League championship medal in 1938). The most important acquisition was B.A. Clements, whose goal-scoring ability was the missing piece of the jigsaw, and the club emphasised that every effort would be made that season to field a settled team. Casuals also broke with recent tradition and withdrew from the A.F.A. Senior Cup because too many of their own players were appearing for other teams in the competition. The admission prices for the season were also revealed: adults 6d, boys 3d and a ticket for the stand 1s 3d, including tax.

The Observer previewed Casuals chances for the season:

'The entente between the Corinthians and the Casuals is to be continued, although it did not work out very satisfactorily for the Isthmian League club last season. The clubs have a joint selection committee, and except when the Casuals are engaged in the Amateur Cup, the Corintians usually have the first pick. Moreover, while the Corinthians can call upon the services of any Casual, the Casuals only play those Corinthians who are actually subscribing members of the Casuals club. Last season the Casuals at full strength were a formidable side; indeed, they were astonishingly unlucky to be defeated in the fourth round of the Amateur Cup by the ultimate winners at Bishop Auckland. On certain days, weakened not only by the claims of the Corinthians, but by the fact that several of their men were assisting Arthur Dunn Cup sides and Old Boy clubs competing in the A.F.A. Cup, they were only able to field weak sides, and consequently finished at the bottom of the Isthmian League table for the first time in history (sic).

The Casuals do an enormous amount of missionary work, fielding five of six teams every week and meeting over fifty public schools sides during the season, and it is obviously in the interests of the game that they should reach a dignified position in the League. Besides, it is obviously unfair to the other Isthmian clubs for the Casuals to field a powerful team one week and a mediocre one the next. For instance, if two clubs are fighting for the championship and one has to oppose a Casuals side that includes six or seven internationals and lose both points, they can justly feel aggrieved if their rivals move up as a result of a win over what is really a Casuals third eleven team.

THE REMEDY
My belief is – and I know my opinion is shared by several folk interested in Old Boy football – that the only way out of the difficulty is for the Casuals either to amalgamate or split. This season, more than ever, will the Corinthians be compelled to call upon the services of the Casuals players. Indeed, there is no disguising the fact that the Corinthians' committee are looking to the future with anxiety....

The Casuals who started the season yesterday with a League game against their old rivals, Kingstonian, should find the assistance of E. Tunnington, the amateur international half-back, who joined the club during the week, very useful indeed. He will not, however, be able to turn out for them regularly as he is still primarily a Lloyds Bank player and captains the side.'9

Casuals made their best start to a season since the 1910/11 season when they secured three successive victories. Kingstonian were defeated 3-1, as Casuals took their chances and Huddle, Evans and Ross kept the opposition forwards at bay. This was followed by a 2-1 victory at Woking when Lywood and Kingston scored two goals in nine second half minutes to help the Old Boys come from behind. The third victory was by the only goal of the match at Ilford, although Casuals had one or two narrow escapes.

Casuals were in fact destined to drop only four points from the opening ten games, two of which were in the next game when the Old Boys went down 1-3 at home to St. Albans City. A 1-1 draw with Woking followed, before the club returned to winning ways by coming from behind to beat Wimbledon 2-1 at Plough Lane. A last minute Tufnell Park equaliser in the next match robbed Casuals of another victory, but the Old Boys remained top of the Isthmian League.

It was Casuals' turn to score late in the next game when the club visited Leytonstone, and secured both points with a single goal scored by B.A. Clements with five minutes left. The Old Boys then lost in the Surrey Senior Cup second qualifying round to Surrey Senior League side Leyland Motors 0-1. It was a surprising defeat, but the qualification rule hindered a club like Casuals, as it required six players to live in Surrey. Regardless of this, the Old Boys used the wrong tactics during the match and duly lost.

Casuals completed a league double over Kingstonian, fighting back from two goals down to record a 4-3 victory. The Old Boys then recorded a stunning victory over Dulwich Hamlet, as A.H. Fabian inspired the team and assisted in all four goals scored by Casuals in a 4-1 victory. In the next match, Casuals went down 1-3 at London Caledonians and in the process surrendered top position. The team then bowed out of the London Senior Cup 0-1 at the hands of Kingstonian.

The Old Boys made a timely return to their best form with an easy 5-1 victory over Oxford City, Clements scoring four times. A 1-1 draw at Clapton kept the club on track, then Ilford were overwhelmed 6-2, Casuals having scored five goals in the first half. This victory left the Old Boys four points behind leaders Wimbledon with two games in hand, prior to the start of their F.A. Amateur Cup campaign against Horsham (who were in the process of winning four successive Sussex County League titles):

CASUALS 4 HORSHAM 1
'Two goals in the first hectic ten minutes scored by the Casuals as they spread-eagled and overwhelmed the opposing defence; Horsham gaining confidence as the Old Boys, rapidly tiring in the second half, were kept desperately on the defensive, and then alternate rallies by both teams. These were the features of the F.A. Amateur Cup tie in the first round proper between the Casuals and Horsham, at Kingston, last Saturday, when, before a crowd of 2,900, 700 of whom came from Horsham, the Old Boys won 4-1.

OLD BOYS IRRESTISTABLE AT OUTSET

In the first ten minutes the Casuals carried everything before them, scored from a penalty after three minutes, added a second goal five minutes later, and, had they been steadier in front of goal, could undoubtedly have been three and possibly four goals ahead at the end of this period.

Obviously somewhat awed by the occasion, Horsham, who are at the top of the Sussex County League, and have only lost twice this season, were badly shaken by the trend of the game in the opening stages, but they slowly settle down, and, for a period after the interval, before they suffered further reverses, put up a tremendous struggle to save the game.

DISSAPPOINTING LATER

Fortunately for the Old Boys Ross, Evans and Huddle were playing on top of their form, and, ably helped by Joy, managed to keep Horsham from scoring before the Old Boys added two further goals. If Horsham had drawn level during this concerted attack, the result might have been very different, for the Casuals were tiring rapidly – particularly those players who had appeared for the Corinthians in their mid-week game.

The Casuals fielded one of their strongest sides, but the team was often disappointing after showing dazzling form at the commencement. Sutcliffe and the forwards were inclined to be slow on the ball and lacking steadiness near goal. Fabian was the best of the Casuals' forwards, his second goal from 30 yards being a brilliant effort, and he and Kingston received useful assistance from Allen. In the Horsham goal Brooker rose to the occasion and saved his side from heavier defeat. Broadley and Hewitt kept the Old Boys' defence fully extended and Cope gave fine support. Horsham's weakness lay in their backs, who were markedly inferior to the opposing attack and luck often favoured them.

Although exciting and often tense the game was played in the best of spirits by both sides, and the refreshing sportsmanship of the Horsham supporters in the gauged remarks of many as they left the ground.

LEAD THROUGH PENALTY KICK

Three minutes after the kick-off the Casuals were awarded a penalty when Clements was brought down heavily, and Fabian made no mistake with the spot kick. Quickly settling down, the Old Boys continued to attack strongly and a neat run up the left wing by Riley spelt danger for the Horsham defence. The outside left sent across to Fabian, who shot over the bar from an awkward position.

Five minutes after scoring their first goal the Casuals went further ahead. Meyer effected a partial clearance in a concerted Casuals' raid and the ball went to Fabian, who sent a first-time shot from 30 yards into the top of the net. The Old Boys were now almost running the Horsham defenders off their legs and the visitors backs found it impossible to control the brilliant Old Boys forwards. Brooker made a remarkable dive across the goal to turn away a fine shot by Riley, who a few later, was unlucky not to see his centre into the goalmouth result in a third goal. Standing a few yards from goal, Joy completely missed the ball with only Brooker to beat. Kingston was narrowly off the mark with a long drive and Brooker did well to turn over the bar a shot from Webster.

HORSHAM MORE CONFIDENT
Becoming a little more confident, Horsham attacked through their right wing and Broadley's shot skimmed the crossbar. When the Horsham outside-right outpaced Joy the Casuals centre-half passed back to Huddle, who just managed to fall on the ball as Broadley dashed forward and shot. At the other end Brooker pulled down from underneath the crossbar a shot from Fabian and held a pass into the goalmouth from Kingston. From a pass from Hewitt, Ragless broke through, but with Joy and Evans in close attendance, shot into Huddle's hands when a yard from goal. As the game progressed Horsham gradually settled down and their forwards made made several promising attacks, where were usually foiled at the crucial stage by Joy. A corner on the right was accurately placed by Broadley and Huddle punched away. Falling full length, Brooker turned away a shot from Clements.

Horsham had a narrow escape at the beginning of the second half when Clements, close in, fired in a tremendous shot which hit Brooker and travelled along the goal line before going out of play. From Fabian, Kingston, with only Brooker to beat, shot across the goal. Getting more of the play then their opponents, Horsham strove desperately to break through on the right wing. After Ragless headed over the bar Broadley made a spectacular run up the right wing beating player after player before sending in one the best shots of the game, which Huddle, fully extended and with cool judgement, punched into the air. Ross scrambled the ball away as a number of Horsham forwards rushed in. At the other end a shot from Riley left Brooker standing, but passed across goal. As Hewitt dashed in Ross 'came out of the blue' and, in a desperate and successful effort to save his goal, kicked out. A melee in the goal mouth resulted from the corner-kick, but the Casuals managed to clear their lines.

STAND PACE BETTER
The Horsham players were going all out and as they were standing the pace much better than the Casuals excitement grew tense while they pressed with spirited persistency. The Casuals were tiring badly and it must have come as great relief to them when their forwards got moving. Brooker tipped over the bar a shot from Allen and the Horsham goalkeeper again came into prominence when he stopped a terrific drive from Clements, held a shot from close in from Allen and, although unsighted, pushed away at full length a drive along the ground from Fabian.

When Horsham next attacked Huddle dropped on to his knees to hold Ripley's hard shot and when Ragless went through the centre Ross foiled him by kicking away as the back fell. With only Brooker to beat Clements tamely shot into his hands. Running in, Ragless took the ball on the run and his first time drive had tremendous pace, but Huddle saved and cleared as the centre-forward somersaulted over his back.

EVENTFUL CLOSE
Nine minutes from the end the Casuals scored their third goal through Kingston, who, when unmarked, received a pass from Fabian. Two minutes later Riley, from near the half-way line dribbled forward, swerved past Norwood and scored the Old Boys' fourth goal. In the last minute Broadley scored Horsham's only goal from a corner taken by Hillman on the left.'[10]

Casuals continued their winning ways as Clements scored a hat-trick in a 4-0 victory at Tufnell Park, and the Old Boys followed this with a 5-2 victory at Wycombe Wanderers in what was a preview of the forthcoming F.A. Amateur Cup second round tie between the clubs. Casuals won this first encounter with an under strength team, eight of the club's players having been selected for the England amateur international trial match played the same day. The Casuals' first choice team was available for the cup game and the result was another win albeit by a narrower margin:

WYCOMBE WANDERERS 0 CASUALS 2

'The Casuals are thought this year to have a good chance of winning the Amateur Cup for the first time, and they beat Wycombe Wanderers at High Wycombe on Saturday in the second round by two goals to none. Loakes Park, with its pronounced slope, but so brilliantly did the Casuals start that they seemed set for an easy victory; yet in the end it was only their powerful defence which carried them to the next round.

...the Casuals soon went in front when Wycombe were penalized for no very obvious reason just outside the penalty area. Fabian took the free kick and Smith had no chance of saving a finely directed low drive. Wycombe fought back strongly, and twice Britnell threatened danger. Ross, however, is one of the ablest tacklers in amateur football and only allowed Britnell to put in high and hurried centres to be met each time by the well-placed defensive head of Joy. All the same, the Casuals were not without their anxious moments, for Young rounded Evans with his speed and Huddle made the first of many fine saves. Then, after half an hour, the Casuals should have gone further ahead, for Riley worked an opening for Clements, who this time took it splendidly. The centre-forward drew Smith to one side of his goal and then crossed the ball to Kingston, but the wing men tried to place his shot instead of hitting it first time, so that the goalkeeper was able to scramble it away.

In spite of the heavy ground the match continued at a great pace, but after the interval the long passing of Wycombe proved the better tactics. The solid phalanx of Casuals' defenders, with Joy ever prominent, stood firm but could not prevent Huddle being in constant action. Three times in quick succession he saved from Britnell, Brown and Andrews, yet perhaps in this period of pressure the Casuals most clearly emphasized their superior football skill. They declined to be put entirely out of their stride and gave their wing men chances of which they took full advantage. Indeed, halfway through the second period Riley more or less settled the issue when he robbed Gearing of the ball, tricked two further opponents, and finally side-stepped past the goalkeeper. Wycombe never gave up hope and once again Andrews tested all the skill of Huddle, but the brilliant individual goal of Riley, scored against the run of play, had proved a deciding influence.' [11]

Casuals were drawn at home in the next round to the holders, Bishop Auckland who had ended the Old Boys' hopes the previous season. Returning to their league programme, Casuals recovered from a two goal deficit to draw 2-2 with Dulwich Hamlet. The team then enjoyed the rare luxury of a week off to prepare for their F.A. Amateur Cup game. This tie caught the imagination of the Kingston public and 4,500 turned up for what promised to be an epic battle. The Casuals invited the residents of the Star and Garter home for disabled men to the game, whilst strengthening their team by bringing over E.D.R. Shearer from Londonderry by steamer and train. Bishop Auckland, in turn, ran a special train from the north east which brought 300 fans to London.

CASUALS 4 BISHOP AUCKLAND 0
'The Casuals beat the holders, Bishop Auckland, in the third round of the F.A. Amateur Cup by four goals to nothing at Kingston on Saturday, and they deserved their victory by playing football which, considering the conditions, reached a high standard.

Although four goals is a considerable margin in football, Bishop Auckland, if they looked to be playing against a team slightly but unmistakably better than themselves, put up a hard fight, and especially in the early stages of the game often looked like scoring. Their forwards, however, found themselves faced with a defence in which there was no discernible loophole. L.T. Huddle was remarkably cool and safe in goal; T. Ross and F. de L. Evans covered each other beautifully at full back, and B. Joy was the inspiration of a half-back line which took the game more and more into its own hands as time went on.

The one weakness in the Casuals' side was on the wings, and B.A. Clements, although he scored three goals, was not quite the ideal centre-forward. A.H. Fabian, too, made mistakes, but some of his work, especially his long and perfectly judged passes, was splendid, while W.H. Webster, at inside left, was perhaps the best player on the field. It was delightful to watch him retaining the ball, dribbling, and drawing the defence, instead of parting with it as though it had given him an electric shock, as so many modern players are apt to do. Webster had close rivals in J.G. Shield, Bishop Auckland's left half-back, a deliberate player who is much faster than he appears to be, and H. Mitton, their full back and captain.

LOST CHANCES
The first thing noticeable about the game was the disparity in the size between the teams – the Casuals must have averaged inches in height over their opponents. Twice in the first few minutes H.A. Taylor, the Bishop Auckland outside-left, had chances to give his side that lead which is of such importance in cup-ties. Once his shot was well saved by Huddle, and on the other occasion he drove the ball wide. The Casuals steadied themselves, and Joy, who was already making his presence felt, made a fine shot from long range.

The Casuals first goal came after 17 minutes' play, and an exceedingly good goal it was. Webster crossed the ball out to F. Riley, Clements met his centre on the volley and, with his foot, beat J.W. Hopps with a hook-shot that was both weird and wonderful. Just before the interval the Casuals went further ahead. Fabian had a shot blocked, but the ball went out to Riley and back again into the goal mouth for Fabian to put through.

Bishop Auckland started the second half by forcing a corner, but their opponents were carrying the heavier guns and any real hope of an exciting finish vanished when, after a quarter of an hour, the ball came off one of the Bishop Auckland players for Clements to run through a disorganized defence and shoot past Hopps. Bishop Auckland were handicapped by the fact that J. Birbeck seemed to be suffering from concussion and he was off the field when, five minutes before the end, Clements scored the Casuals' final goal. Shearer dropped over a centre from the right and Clements, standing close in, headed the ball through.'[12]

Casuals' league form began to fall off just as the feeling was growing that the team would finally win the F.A. Amateur Cup, and in their next match against St. Albans City when only five regulars were available, the Old Boys crashed to a 1-5 defeat. The following week Casuals played their F.A. Amateur Cup quarter-final against surprise package Manchester League side, I.C.I. Alkali, who were a Cheshire works team from Northwich.

CASUALS 3 ICI ALKALI 0
'The Casuals beat I.C.I. Alkali at Kingston on Saturday by three goals to none, thus entering the semi-final round of the F.A. Amateur Cup. The favourites won comfortably enough in the end, but I.C.I showed clearly that no mere chance had brought them so far in the competition at their first attempt.

Conditions were perfect, and a crowd of nearly 7,000, including a large contingent from Cheshire, gave the teams a warm reception. The Casuals started as if their opponents did not exist, with the valuable Fabian-Webster link firmly welded to their half-backs and the ball constantly moving towards the I.C.I. goal through both wings. Webster especially made two lovely openings for Riley, and also caused Lees to hold a long straight drive, but on the whole the Casuals' finishing was weak. For close on half an hour the Casuals pressed without result; the nearest approach to a goal, indeed, was at the other end when, in a sudden I.C.I. breakaway through Lowe, the redoubtable Joy nearly headed the ball through his own goal.

A DECEPTIVE PLAYER
Then at last came the expected score when Kingston cut in and from his pass Webster hit the post. The ball rebounded to Clements, who was able to turn it past Lees without difficulty. Clements, as in previous rounds, was to score further goals and must be a most deceptive opponent. For long periods slow and cumbersome, he will all at once make great haste and put in a shot of terrific power. Before he was to distinguish himself again, however, I.C.I. accomplished their best work of the match. Reeney was constructive at left, half and Hough, even if his energy was sometimes misplaced, caused Joy to put his best foot forward.

Most danger, however, came as expected through Marsh, whose long cross-passes opened up the game splendidly. Marsh, too, showed he could not shoot when Huddle did well to hold a low drive at the foot of the post. I.C.I. were again unlucky when Goulding was brought down close to goal just before the interval, and the game at this period seemed in a very open state, especially as the Casuals had Riley injured and hobbling on the left wing. A few minutes after half-time, however, the Casuals did much to settle the issue when Kingston forced a corner, and from it Allen headed down to Clements, who shot through. Some ragged play followed, but then came some fine football in which Couchman shone in both attack and defence. Both goals were in danger, but as time went on the Casuals strongly reasserted themselves, and Webster beat man after man in a wonderful dribble.

A chance was lost, but near the end a splendid piece of play concluded the scoring, the whole movement being carried out at top speed and the ball never once leaving the turf. A pass came to Fabian from Allen, and he quickly made ground before sending to Kingston, from whose centre Clements shot a grand goal on the run.'[13]

Casuals were in the semi-final for the first time since the competition's inaugural season. They were joined by Romford of the Athenian League, who defeated Sutton United 4-1, Maidenhead United of the Spartan League who beat Southall 1-0, and Ilford who overcame Cockfield in a replay. Following these results, Casuals were made favourites for the cup and were next drawn to play Romford.

Two league defeats followed, Wycombe Wanderers first recording a 2-3 victory at Kingston, after Casuals led 2-0. Several players were rested for the second match, at Oxford City, which ended in a 2-5 defeat. It was now time for the F.A. Amateur Cup semi-final and because Casuals were without key defender T. Ross, the Corinthian, W.T. Whewell was brought in as a replacement.

CASUALS 3 ROMFORD 2

'The Casuals beat Romford in the semi-final round of the F.A. Amateur Cup competition on the Dulwich Hamlet ground on Saturday by three goals to two.

It is seldom in football that a side which is faster on the ball loses, but Romford were faster on the ball on Saturday and they were beaten in a game which fell into some strangely contrasting periods. During the first 20 minutes or so Romford looked as though it was only a matter of time before they would score, but actually by the time the interval had arrived the Casuals were two goals ahead. Within 20 minutes of the start of the second half Romford had drawn level, and the Casuals were going through such a bad time that it seemed extremely probably that they would fall behind. As it turned out, however, it was the Casuals who got the decisive goal five minutes from the end, and they must have thought themselves fortunate to escape the ordeal of a replay. Physically they were a much bigger team then their opponents, and in B. Joy their centre half-back, they had the finest player on the field. It is difficult to refrain from using superlatives in writing of his play when is at the top of his form, and on Saturday he did not know what it was to put a foot wrong.

F. de L. Evans, apart from one or two miskicks, played splendidly at left back, and he, Joy, and W.T. Whewell showed throughout the game how well they understand each other. The Casuals' wing half-backs were not too strong, and although E.D.R. Shearer scored two of his side's three goals it was only in flashes that he was brilliant. The two inside forwards, however, by the subtlety of their passing and skill of their dribbling made the Casuals' forward line potentially more dangerous than that of their opponents, and one or two of the movements that carried out were beyond anything of which Romford were capable.

...To sum up, a draw would perhaps have been the fairest result, but if one side had to win then the Casuals just deserved to do so.

A LUCKY ESCAPE
The Casuals won the toss and Romford, who were handicapped by the fact that their regular right half-back, J.C. Anderson, was not able to play for them, had to face the sun. There was a large crowd, the ground was well covered with grass, and the ball was light. The Casuals made the first coherent attack, but it was nearly all Romford during the first half and Casuals' goal had a marvellous escape when Evans headed out from under the bar a shot which seemed

certain to score, since L.T. Huddle was yards away. The second real shot of the match led to the first goal. Riley broke through and E. Wingfield did well to save. He conceded a corner in doing so, A.H. Fabian placed it accurately and Clements had an easy chance of heading the ball through. Ten minutes later the Casuals went further ahead. G. Allen swung the ball out to Riley; Riley passed inwards to Clements; and Clements missed his shot. It deceived E. Wingfield, however, skidded across the goal-mouth, and Shearer, rushing up, had only to tap the ball across the line.

Romford dominated the beginning of the first half as much as they had done the first, but this time they had two goals to show for their pains. A burst down the middle by J. Osborne paved the way for the goal that G. Webb scored from point-blank range- for once the Casuals' marking seemed to be loose- and Romford's sustained pressure brought them another goal by G. Patterson a few minutes later. The Casuals pulled themselves together and kept hold of a game which threatened to get out of their control, and five minutes before the end Shearer beat Wingfield with a cross-shot which went into the corner of the net.'[14]

This narrow victory set up a final with Ilford (winners of the F.A. Amateur Cup in 1929 and 1930), who defeated Maidenhead United 4-1 in the other semi-final. The Romford result appears to have settled the team's nerves and the Old Boys went on to record victories over Leytonstone (2-1), and London Caledonians (4-0). The only blemish was a 0-2 reverse in the Surrey Charity Shield against Kingstonian. The London Caledonians match was memorable for the following incident:

'An amusing incident took place a few minutes before the end. A London Caledonian player had the ball when he heard a whistle blown by the referee of another game. The player picked up the ball and was walking off the field when he realised his mistake.'[15]

Casuals were red hot favourites to win the cup, not unexpectedly so, given the team's high quality. In goal was the exceptionally safe L.T. Huddle. B. Joy, widely regarded as the best amateur footballer of the day, played at centre half-back, with W.T. Whewell, who had appeared a record number of times for the Corinthian F.C., and was still capable of producing his best. Complementing this illustrious reargurd was a strong and experienced half-back line of F. de L. Evans, G. Allen and L.T. Couchman. The forwards, led by prolific goal scorer B.A. Clements, were a potent threat to any defence. W.H. Webster and F. Riley combined to make an impressive left wing, but the pairing of A.H. Fabian and E.D.R. Shearer on the right wing was without equal. The strength of this side is perhaps best shown by the fact that five of its members were selected to go to the 1936 Olympics, where Great Britain defeated China 2-0 before going out 4-5 to Poland in a game where all the Great Britain goal scorers (Joy 2, Clements and Shearer) were Casuals players.

CASUALS 1 ILFORD 1

'The Casuals and Ilford played extra time in the final round of the F.A. Amateur Cup on the Crystal Palace ground on Saturday, but even the added half-hour did not prevent the sides from

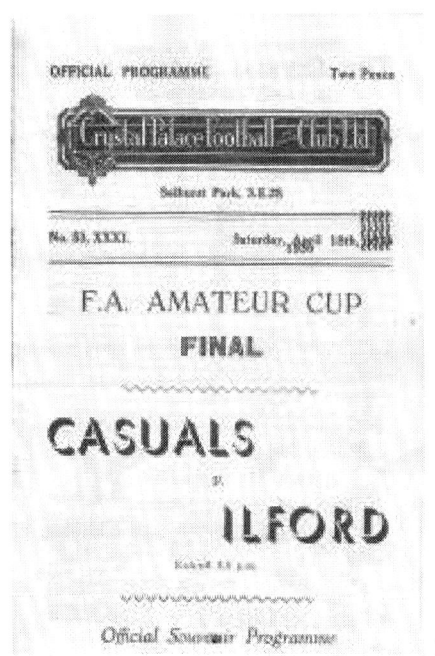

Left: Programme for the F.A. Amateur Cup final

having to meet again at Upton Park on May 2. The score was one all, and the wonder is – so much was the defence on top of the attack – that any goals were scored at all.

During the first quarter of an hour or so it seemed that the game would go according to expectations and that the polished and deliberate football played by The Casuals would would win them their reward. The goal they scored during this period was well contrived and well deserved, but after virtue seemed to desert them, and their forward line was never more than a shadow of its real self. F. Riley always looked capable of winning the match on his own, and E.D.R. Shearer must have alarmed A.C. Hayes by threats of brilliancy which once or twice became real. In the centre, however, The Casuals' attack was strangely weak. B.A. Clements was even more strongly held by A.E. Myers than J. Watts was by B. Joy, and W.H. Webster, although he brought off one or two characteristic dribbles, has seldom played a more inconspicuous game.

A.H. Fabian did a lot of work in taking corner-kicks- they were very well taken- and throwing-in, but he was not the influence in the forward line that he usually is. Joy seemed to be in three places at one and the same time, and L.T. Huddle kept goal remarkably well. The backs W.T. Whewell and F. de L. Evans covered each other with perfect understanding, and the longer the game lasted the better L.T. Couchman played at left half-back.

Left: L.T. Huddle in action during the final

SECOND HALF-BACKS
Ilford surpassed themselves. They had not the skill, man for man, of The Casuals, but they were exceptionally quick in their tackling and their kicking, and, although it was sometimes of the 'hit or miss' variety, more often succeeded in hitting than missing.

...The day was pleasant enough, although there was a breeze, which The Casuals had to face in the first half. They settled down immediately, however, and worked the ball so skilfully that there seemed little doubt as to what the result would be. After 10 minutes they scored. Webster and Clements burst down the centre and Clements passed the ball out to Riley, who converged on goal and beat N.F. Tietjen with a beautifully placed cross-shot.

Almost immediately the mood of the game changed, and Ilford, who had been desperately on the defence, took up the attack. The standard of the football was not high, but there was plenty of excitement in the air, excitement which became intensified when, within five minutes of the interval, Ilford equalized. A cross pass to E. Gilderson had the Casuals' defence spread-eagled, and E.J. Braund, standing close in, was able to get to Gilderson's centre and nod the ball into the net.

In the second half the play for a long period was dull, without initiative or ideas. The Casuals' forward line, except for an occasional thrust down the wings, ceased to exist and, although Ilford did the most of what attacking there was, there was never any real likelihood of a goal. The Casuals once forced three corners in succession, and the way Fabian took them must have given Tietjen considerable anxiety. Extra time, however, always seemed inevitable, and during it The Casuals seemed to last the better of two exceedingly tired sides.'[16]

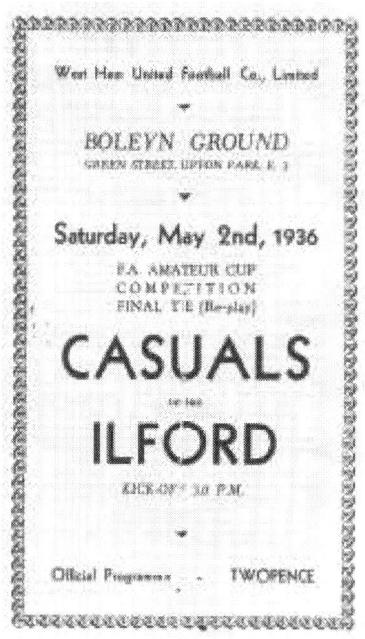

Left: Programme for the F.A. Amateur Cup replay

In the fortnight before the replay, the outstanding four league matches were to be played. Casuals' form slumped again and the team suffered a 1-3 defeat in the first game at home to Nunhead, despite opening the scoring. In the return at Nunhead, Casuals again led, but were forced to hold out against a rampant home side. The Old Boys then managed to beat Clapton 2-1, with two goals in the last 20 minutes, and this was enough to clinch the runners-up spot in the

Isthmian League. The remaining fixture, at home to the champion club Wimbledon, ended in another defeat for Casuals.

The replay of the F.A. Amateur Cup final was the last match of the season:

CASUALS 2 ILFORD 0
'The Casuals won the F.A. Amateur Cup for the first time in the long history of the club on Saturday, when, on West Ham United's ground at Upton Park, they beat Ilford in the replayed final round of the competition by two goals to none.

If only on account of the brilliance of their football in the second half, the Casuals deserved their victory, but before this a fast and efficient Ilford attack had established so complete a mastery over the defence that the most fervent and optimistic Casuals supporter could hardly then have expected a win for his side. Indeed, at this stage of the game, their defensive play generally showed unmistakable signs of panic, but there was one important exception, for

Above: Action from the cup final against Ilford

through it all B. Joy remained absolutely imperturbable. In their efforts to draw him away from the centre, Ilford tried every known trick, but Joy was the master of them all, and not only did he completely blot out the opposing centre-forward, but his certainty in anticipating the varied direction of the attack also enabled him to cover up the defensive mistakes made by the rest of the side. Joy's steadiness brought the Casuals safely through this critical period, but his success was, to a very large extent, made possible by L.T. Huddle's workmanlike display in the Casuals' goal.

TWO PERFECT ATTACKS
The first two attacks carried out by the Casuals' forwards were so brilliantly executed that even W.H. Webster's failure to get the ball through an open goal appeared to matter not at all, for it seemed certain that a side capable of constructing two such perfect movements would have little difficulty in overrunning Ilford's defence. This, however, was by no means the case, for A.E. Myers then began to gain a firm grip on B.A. Clements, and gradually the rest of the Ilford defence, influence by Myers's steadiness, settled down to disorganize the Casuals' attack, whose approach work not only lost its former brilliance, but also became decidedly wild.

A.R. Halcrow and T.G. Manley were accordingly relieved of any defensive responsibilities, and they immediately established a strong connecting link between their half-backs and forwards. Quick first-time passes to their outside forwards were followed by long and accurate centres, but, try as he might, J. Watts found it quite impossible to evade Joy. The rest of the Casuals'

Above: Huddle saves during the cup final

defence, however, were at sixes and sevens. The two Ilford inside forwards were left virtually unmarked. First Manley and then Halcrow sent in shots which might easily have given Ilford

the lead, but Huddle, whose anticipation in goal made really difficult shots seem to be comparatively simple, came to the rescue of his side.

The speed of Ilford's attack slackened after half-time, and, helped by the brilliant constructive play of Joy and L.T. Couchman, the Casuals' forwards rose in their might. G.G. Holmes cleared a dangerous movement on the Casuals' left wing by kicking the ball into touch, but, without waiting for the Ilford defence to get back into position, F. Riley threw the ball from touch to Webster, who quickly tapped it back to his outside left. Running very fast, Riley rounded Holmes, carried the ball to Ilford's goal-line and centred. His inside forwards were not up to take the pass, but E.D.R. Shearer ran in from the right, got his head to the ball, and that was a goal for the Casuals.

For a short time the earlier uncertainty crept back into the play of the Casuals' defence, but Joy steadied them, and once again the speed of their outside forwards had Ilford's defence in difficulties. Eventually Shearer broke away on the right and shot. N.F. Tietjen could do no more

Above: Casuals' captain F. de L. Evans being presented with the F.A. Amateur Cup

than knock the ball out to Webster, who, taking deliberate aim, made the game and the Cup safe for the Casuals.'[17]

Casuals returned to Kingston after the final and immense crowds gathered outside the Guildhall as the Old Boys received a civic reception:

'In the evening a great crowd thronged the Market-place and the space in front of the Guildhall to welcome the Casuals on their triumphant return to Kingston. When the motor coach conveying the Old Boys turned into Church Street it had to be slowed down to walking pace on account of the number of people in the road. By the time the Market-place was reached the police had to clear a way and the space in front of the Guildhall was a sea of people. Excitedly swaying to catch a glimpse of the approaching victors and of Evans and J. Whitehorn (the Casuals trainer), holding the cup aloft, and waiting to give them a tumultuous welcome.

At the entrance to the Guildhall the players were met by the Deputy-Mayor of Kingston (Sir Alfred Woodgate)....

Addressing the crowd, the Deputy-Mayor apologised for the absence of the Mayor, who was unable to be present. Sir Alfred said that he was honoured once again to receive the winners of the Amateur Cup and present the trophy to them....

Above: Casuals at the civic reception

Above: Huge crowds gather outside the Guildhall to welcome Casuals after the F.A. Amateur Cup final victory

At this point Sir Alfred's remarks were drowned by the cheers of the crowd. When these had died down Sir Alfred congratulated the Casuals on their victory and said that Kingston people were glad they had brought the cup back to them. Their victory was an example of dogged tenacity made all the greater because they had been trying to win the Amateur Cup for 40 years.

This was another signal for the crowd to roar its applause and once again the Deputy-Mayor could only wait for the noise of thousands of voices to subside....

At the conclusion of Sir Alfred's speech the crowd called for Evans, Joy and Huddle and persisted until those three players had shown themselves. Mr. Dubuis responded on behalf of the Casuals and said how genuinely honoured they were at being asked to come to Kingston that evening. At last the club had done something really great and he was glad that the people of Kingston wanted to share in their success.'[18]

Casuals' finances were greatly improved by the cup run: the club received £310 as its share of the gate from the semi-final, £320 (total gate receipts £1682 7s 2d) for the first final and £400-450 (total gate receipts £1898) from the replay.

The crowning moment of a memorable season was achieved when Bernard Joy was selected to play for the full England side against Belgium. In the process he became the last amateur to play for the full England international team.

'With England appearing to take things easily, the Belgians had plenty of opportunities for showing their worth, and their forwards made several raids, but without success. Joy, the amateur international, time after time broke up dangerous attacks, and he found time to open up forward movements. He once saved what seemed a certain goal by tackling Franckx, who had beaten Male and had the goal at his mercy.'[19]

Chapter Eleven
A Casual End
1936-1939

Casuals failed to build on the successes of the 1935/36 season and the record of the club in the three final seasons of its history was disappointing. The uncertainty over both their own future and that of the Corinthian Football Club no doubt played a part in this, and an amalgamation at this point might have been better than the continued sharing of resources, which did little to help either club.

1936/37

Speculation was rife about a possible merger and secretary F.G.I. Packington was obliged to issue a statement to the contrary. Casuals, though, now began making efforts to find a new home and a possible site was inspected in South East London. Nothing came of this initiative, however, and more than fifty years were to pass before the club, as Corinthian-Casuals, finally secured a ground of its own.

The season began with a 0-2 defeat by Kingstonian, but the Casuals team was honoured by its selection to face the touring Chinese Olympic team in a friendly at the Crystal Palace:

CASUALS 5 CHINA 2
'Although Wai-Tong Lee played another courageous game at centre-forward for China yesterday on the ground of the Crystal Palace club at Selhurst, his activities were curbed to a large extent by Joy, who put up a great defensive game. Yet in spite of that fact it was Wai-Tong Lee who scored after Collins had put the Casuals ahead late in the second half.

Soon after the interval, Kam-Shun Suen got China's second goal with a great drive and all through the closing period the Chinese were hardly flattered by their lead. They were speedier and controlled the ball better than the Old Boys.

FEELING THE STRAIN
Then the strain of playing against stronger and bigger opponents following a series of long journeys and torrid matches began to take effect, and the Casuals finished ever so much the fresher side. Riley equalised, the other goals being scored by Allen, Collins and Joy.

We had an exposition of Oriental courtesy while the last goal was scored. Riley was lying on the ground, and while our celestial defenders were solicitously inquiring what was the matter, Joy dashed up and banged the ball into the net.

The Chinese fielded nine members of their Olympic side and for long periods controlled the ball as well as any combination I have ever seen.'[1]

In Casuals' second Isthmian League game, the team slumped to a 0-4 defeat at home to Dulwich Hamlet, but immediately returned to form with a 4-0 win against St. Albans City, A.H. Fabian inspiring the Old Boys to their first win of the season. This success was the start of a good run, as the team took its revenge on Dulwich Hamlet by winning the return 2-1, and followed this up with a fine 4-0 victory over Wycombe Wanderers.

Casuals then shared the Casuals Cup with Kingstonian following a 2-2 draw at the neutral Alexandra Recreation Ground on the Surbiton/Tolworth border. The match was staged to celebrate Charter Day when Surbiton became the first borough to be created during King Edward VIII's reign.

The league victories continued, and Ilford were beaten 2-0 at Newbury Park in a rematch of the previous year's F.A. Amateur Cup final. Tufnell Park were then defeated 2-1, with the points taking Casuals to the top of the Isthmian League, and this was followed by a 3-1 success away to London Caledonians, equalling the club record of six consecutive Isthmian League wins. That was to be Casuals' last victory for two months as the team unexpectedly lost form, losing to Wycombe Wanderers (1-2), Wimbledon (2-3 and 0-3), Nunhead (0-4), and Clapton (1-2). The only points collected came in draws at home to Oxford City (2-2) and Woking (3-3), when Casuals recovered from being two goals behind with 15 minutes left.

In true Casuals style they bounced back and in a complete reversal of fortune, the team recorded seven successive victories. Kingstonian were defeated 4-1, despite the Old Boys conceding 23 corners in the process. Clapton were knocked out of the London Senior Cup 3-1, a lucky win, before Casuals overcame London Caledonians 2-1 in the Isthmian League.

Casuals took their good form into the F.A. Amateur Cup and defeated Oxford City 4-1. This game witnessed a terrible injury to L.T. Huddle, playing in goal for the Casuals, which would eventually end his football career. Wimbledon were then humiliated 6-1 in the second round of the London Senior Cup, and victories followed against Tooting & Mitcham (3-0) in the Surrey Senior Cup and Clapton 4-3 in the Isthmian League.

The run came to an end at the worst possible time, with Casuals being knocked out of the F.A. Amateur Cup in the second round by Dulwich Hamlet, who scored the only goal of the game and subsequently won in the final. Another Casuals goalkeeper, this time C.A. Joliffe, suffered an injury in this match, and the team's form was indifferent or poor for the remainder of the season. A 4-2 victory over Athenian League side Barnet in the London Senior Cup was, however, clinched with two late goals as the Old Boys used their sixth goalkeeper of the campaign.

Casuals then lost to Woking 3-4 after conceding three goals in the last five minutes, before gaining a 2-2 draw against holders Walthamstow Avenue in the semi-final of the London Senior Cup. This was followed by a 1-4 reverse at home to Ilford and a 3-1 victory over another Athenian League club, Sutton United, in the Surrey Senior Cup, when Casuals struggled to field a side due to the qualification rules.

Casuals then contrived to lose the next five games of which three, against Oxford City (2-3), Leytonstone (0-6), and St. Albans City (0-2) were in the Isthmian League. The first of the other two defeats came in the Surrey Senior Cup semi-final against Dulwich Hamlet (0-2) and the second came in the London Senior Cup semi-final replay by the staggering margin of 3-12 against Walthamstow Avenue. A promising season had collapsed in the space of a few games and Casuals had merely to play out the remaining fixtures; beating Tufnell Park 2-0, drawing with Nunhead 1-1 and losing to Leytonstone 1-5.

The club's last chance of success came in the Surrey Combination Cup final against Guildford City who had finished fifth in the professional Southern League. Casuals apparently received a bye to the final of this competition, which seems to have begun with only two teams.

GUILDFORD CITY 1 CASUALS 0

'Thrills and stylish footwork characterised the final of the Surrey Combination Cup final at Guildford on Monday, in which Guildford City defeated The Casuals by 1-0; scoring from a penalty kick, which had to be taken twice. The only disappointing feature was the poor attendance, the gate of 750 allowing only about £8 to be given to the Surrey County F.A. benevolent fund.

The winning of a final by a penalty goal is unsatisfactory in many respects, but it must be admitted that the City deserved to retain the trophy for their enterprise and persistency in the face of one of the keenest defences seen on their ground this season. Had the Casuals' forwards borrowed some of their rearguard's stoicism the cup might have changed hands, but they rarely approached within shooting distance. In the absence of any serious raids, the City defenders were never perturbed. Briggs dealt with a number of accurately-placed shots, but they were mostly long-distance hazards, and the heaviest burdens fell upon the shoulders of the half-backs. In this trio T. Jones, on the left displayed qualities as heroic as those of Caldwell, operating in a similar position for the visitors and by far their most outstanding man. Jones marked Allen so effectively that he spoilt the co-ordination of the forward line, while Caldwell negated much of McPheat's work. Ives, the City's centre-forward, made little headway against Partridge and Whewell, and after the interval he dropped back to right-half, Robinson taking over the leadership. Although this made little difference to the plan of attack, it overcame deadlock.

PENALTY GOAL AT SECOND ATTEMPT
Sessions, in the Casuals' goal, was called into action within fifteen seconds to save a shot by Bowater. An early goal seemed imminent, especially when Bytheway, following up from McPheat, beat Caldwell near the corner and swung the ball over to Bowater, Bowater centred, and Bytheway shot smartly goalwards, to see Partridge deflect. Bytheway tried again, receiving from Hunter, but the back repeated his performance. Edwards and Clements were prominent in

> THE CASUALS FOOTBALL CLUB.
>
> 181-9, Palmerston House,
> Old Broad Street, E.C.2.
>
> Dear Sir,
>
> A General Meeting of the Club will be held at the First Avenue Restaurant, Holborn, on Tuesday, 2nd March, commencing at 6.30 p.m.
>
> Yours faithfully,
>
> *[signature]*
>
> A G E N D A.
>
> To consider a recommendation by the General Committee for the amalgamation of the Club with the Corinthian Football Club.
>
> ———
>
> In view of the extreme importance of the decision to be made at this Meeting, the Committee earnestly hope that every Member will make the utmost endeavour to attend.

Above: Letter sent in March 1937 in regard to the proposed amalgamation with Corinthian F.C.

the visitors spontaneous sallies, but Wright and Oliver invariably checked them before the ball reached Briggs.

Twenty minutes after the interval Robinson was fouled in the penalty area, and took the kick. Sessions made a magnificent save, but one of the Casuals moved, and the referee ordered the kick to be retaken. This time Robinson drove at the side of the net, and the ball slipped in off the post. During the next ten minutes the visitors were given three free kicks and two corners, but nothing was forthcoming, and the match concluded with an example of perfect collaboration between Edwards, Clements and Lockey which brought warm applause from the crowd.'[2]

Consideration of the proposed merger with the Corinthians began in earnest during the second half of the season and Casuals' members gave the plan their full support:

'At the Casuals general meeting in London on Tuesday it was unanimously decided to support the general committee in their suggestion to amalgamate with the Corinthians. There were a few criticisms, but only of a minor nature.'[3]

No further steps were taken, however, as the two parties were not quite ready to join forces and a few days later it was reported that:

'At a meeting at the Sports Club last night between representatives of the Corinthians and the Casuals Football Clubs a project for amalgamation was discussed. In view of the diversity of opinions expressed no action was taken, and the meeting was adjourned.'[4]

As a compromise, the clubs agreed to establish a closer working relationship, but with the fortunes of both Casuals and Corinthians now in serious decline, this arrangement could be no more than the prelude to a full merger. In June 1937 it was reported:

'The Casuals at their annual general meeting, decided to agree with Corinthians that the two clubs should be run under a joint executive committee for at least the next three seasons. It is intended that the arrangement be permanent.'[5]

1937 – Corinthians and Casuals Tour to Jamaica

One of the new joint committee's first acts was to organise a tour to Jamaica in August 1937. The party consisted of G. Allen, J.T. Burrowes, K.P.S. Caldwell, P.T. Collins, H.A. Davies, V. Edwards, A.H. Fabian, E.O. Faulkner, R.W.E. Groves, C.R. Moreland, G.M. Partridge, H.S. Seaford, W.K. Sessions and P.H. Williams. This was not the strongest collection of players that the club could have selected, but the F.A. tour to New Zealand had robbed them of the services of L.T. Huddle, A.H. Woolcock, B. Joy, G.A. Strasser, L.C. Thornton and F. Riley. This was originally meant to be a Casuals tour, but following the events of the Summer it was opened up to both clubs. It was brought about to help the Kingston Club in Jamaica, celebrate their 100th anniversary.

The tourists set sail from Bristol on 19th July on the S.S. Bayano and on arrival stayed at the Manor House Hotel. The party quickly made themselves at home in their tropical surroundings and made the Glass Bucket Club their regular haunt. The Jamaican F.A. were busy preparing things for the visitors and even erected an extra stand in the south west corner of Sabina Park due to the amount of local interest.

The tourists opened their account on the island against St. Georges in front of one of the largest crowds (5,000) ever to see a sporting event in Jamaica. It was a social occasion and all the island's dignitaries gathered for this game. A fast game followed with the Corinthian and Casuals eleven securing a 3-1 win after goals by Allen, Edwards and Fabian.

The Corinthians and Casuals then faced the Jamaica First Colony and won 3-0 thanks to a hat-trick by Edwards. Following these two opening victories, the only defeat of the tour followed when Kingston Club won 1-2. The tourists, without Fabian or Caldwell, found them selves trailing 0-2 before a penalty by Williams reduced the deficit. The clubs returned to winning ways with a 1-0 victory over the Jamaica Second Colony. It was a slow game and the locals had given themselves odds of one hundred to one prior to the match. As it happened Jamaica had a goal disallowed towards the end and were unlucky not to draw level.

The final two fixtures were both against the Sherwood Foresters who were an army side currently based on the island. The first of these games saw the Foresters overrun the tourists early on and the army side took the lead. Following this the Corinthians and Casuals made a determined effort to equalise and one effort by Davis flew about twenty yards over the crossbar, before the ball got jammed in a tree, which led to a two minute delay while it was recovered. Fabian equalised from the penalty spot on 25 minutes and then Allen gave the tourists the lead. The army side equalised with 15 minutes remaining, but had the tourists converted their chances they would have been three or four ahead. It was said that this was the best game of football Jamaica had ever seen.

The party enjoyed the end of tour dinner, where there was a special floor show of native dancing at the Glass Bucket Club. Following this there were 300 people present at the dance held at the Lido Beach Club. After a day off to recover, the last game of the tour took place. It was a rematch against Sherwood Foresters and resulted in a 2-0 victory with goals by Edwards and Groves. The following day (17th August) the touring party sailed for England.

The tourists were popular visitors to the island and The Gleaner gave this glowing synopsis of the Corinthian and Casuals players:

'..a grand lot of fellows off the field, and a most interesting and attractive side to watch on it.

Off the field, while they're all first-class fellows, they display an intriguing amount of individuality in 'the General,' as effervescent as Eno's, and as irrepressible, who will surely become a legend in Jamaica football; Caldwell, dour and determined; the flying Collins, whose motto seems to be 'the farther, the faster'; Fabian, whose guileless good looks you would say no thought had ever marred, the greatest tactician of them all; Williams, who looks like a Welsh Bard, but is actually one of the few great captains of the game I have seen; to say nothing of Faulkner, whose robust displays at back are quite out of keeping with his 'gentlemanly' reputation.'[6]

1937/38

Casuals had high hopes for the new season and it was reported that the Old Boys were anticipating a comeback as spectacular as their fall from grace the previous season. It was thought that the agreement with the Corinthian F.C., would help, but the latter were not the power they once were. The Casuals' plans were further hindered by the F.A. tour to New Zealand which saw the Old Boys lose the services of L.T. Huddle, B. Joy, E. Tunnington, G.A. Strasser, and F. Riley for the early part of the season. The club managed to add one player of quality to their squad, J. Lee, an amateur with Blackburn Rovers who proved to be a most potent striker. It was also reported that Casuals were again looking at an unspecified ground in south east London as a possible future home.

Casuals were, in effect, having to field two first class elevens each week and it was clear that the club was having difficulty in maintaining its own standards let alone those of the Corinthian F.C. Corinthian was most active prior to Christmas and Casuals' results at that time were appalling. Casuals began with a 0-6 reverse at Leytonstone, and followed this up with a 2-4 defeat at home to Ilford. The defeats continued to pile up as Casuals lost 0-2 at home to Wimbledon, and then 2-5 at Dulwich Hamlet in the London Charity Cup.

Casuals' only victory prior to December came on the first Saturday of October when Wycombe Wanderers were defeated 3-2. This success was short-lived as the Old Boys went down 1-4 at Millwall in the London Challenge Cup (a competition Casuals had qualified for by virtue of reaching the previous season's London Senior Cup semi-final). Following this match F.G.I. Packington said:

'Apart from minor infringements by both sides, there was not a foul in the game. Our opponents took and gave some hard knocks in the very best spirits, and our fellows, although well beaten enjoyed it all immensely.'[7]

Casuals' fortunes did not improve, although the Old Boys managed to secure a 2-2 draw at Woking. This was followed by further defeats: against London Caledonians (1-2), Kingstonian (1-5), Nunhead (2-4), Ilford (0-6), Tufnell Park (0-2), and Leytonstone (2-4). Casuals then held on for a 2-2 draw with Kingstonian, having conceded an equaliser 13 minutes from time.

December provided some respite for the club as Clapton were overwhelmed 7-3 at Kingston. In the return a week later the Casuals recorded a narrow 2-1 victory at the Spotted Dog. Casuals then won their first cup tie of the season when Pinner (who won Division Two West of the Spartan League) were defeated 5-1 at Kingston in the London Senior Cup, the Old Boys scoring three late goals.

On New Year's Day, Casuals recorded their fourth successive win, as Oxford City were crushed 6-0 at Kingston. It was to be a poor January though, as the team was easily defeated 2-7 at Barnet in the London Senior Cup, despite taking a first minute lead. Casuals' remaining cup hopes were soon dashed. First the London League champions Finchley defeated Casuals 1-4 at Summers Lane in the F.A. Amateur Cup, the club being compelled to surrender home advantage. It was a disappointing performance because Casuals had fielded an impressive line up including seven internationals and nine Corinthians.

The following week Casuals suffered the ignominy of being knocked out of the Surrey Senior Cup by another London League side, Post Office Engineers. Yet again the Old Boys side was weakened by call ups from the Arthur Dunn Cup teams. Casuals continued to struggle in the league, losing 1-2 at home to Dulwich Hamlet and 1-4 to Tufnell Park after going two goals behind inside within eight minutes.

The selection committee rang the changes for the next match at home to Woking and it had the desired effect as the Casuals ran out 4-2 winners. This was followed by a surprise 4-0 victory at Isthmian League leaders Wycombe Wanderers, A.H. Fabian scoring three goals. The team could not maintain this form and lost by the odd goal in five at Oxford City. Casuals then lost 3-

4 at home to London Caledonians, after the Old Boys had gone 2-0 up after just five minutes. An 1-8 reverse debacle at Wimbledon followed although the Casuals were badly affected by an injury sustained by R.B. Guthrie who fractured his right leg after just five minutes. The losses continued with a disappointing 0-4 defeat at Nunhead and *The South London Press* sourly commented: '*Casuals hung together about as well as a Sunday School outing at the sea side.*'[8]

Casuals escaped the embarrassment of another application for re-election by defeating bottom club St. Albans City home and away, and holding Dulwich Hamlet to a 2-2 draw.

1938/39

Casuals' last season as a separate entity witnessed some improvement in form as the Old Boys achieved a creditable seventh place in the Isthmian League. This recovery may be attributed to the appointment of E. Magner as coach of both the Casuals and Corinthian F.C.. Magner had coached continental sides for 15 years and had played for Gainsborough Trinity and Everton. He later left to become manager of Huddersfield Town. Casuals' new players for the season included Maurice Edelston (later a war time England international), who was an amateur on Brentford's books and subsequently a regular for Reading. Another player worthy of mention was D.O. Finlay, an Olympic hurdler, who won a silver medal at the 1936 games in the 110 meter hurdles.

Casuals suffered from a lack of press coverage during the season as the *Surrey Comet*, not for the last time, either lost interest in or fell out with the club. As a result only Casuals' matches with Kingstonian and Wimbledon were covered during the entire season.

The Old Boys made a good start to the league campaign, starting with a 2-2 draw at Wycombe Wanderers. A defeat at home to Ilford (0-2), was then followed by three successive victories as J. Lee found his scoring boots. St. Albans City were beaten 3-2, prior to a 4-3 victory at Clapton, all seven goals for Casuals being scored by Lee. The run continued with another victory over St. Albans City (2-1) and a win against Oxford City (2-0), punctuated by a defeat at Leytonstone (0-2).

This form was not maintained as Woking visited Kingston and returned with a 0-3 victory. A 1-1 draw at London Caledonians followed, but the team then suffered defeats against Nunhead (2-3), Kingstonian (2-3 and 1-2), and Leytonstone (1-4). Casuals recovered again to defeat Wimbledon 4-3, and showed great spirit in reducing the deficit at Clapton to 2-3, after the Old Boys had trailed 0-3 only after 21 minutes.

Ilford were then held 1-1 at Newbury Park before Casuals crashed out of the London Senior Cup, losing 0-2 against Tufnell Park at Golders Green (now Hendon). This result was all the more frustrating as Tufnell Park were defeated comfortably by 3-1 in a league match only seven days later at Kingston. Casuals built on this result with a 4-2 victory at home to Wycombe, which preceded the start of Casuals' last F.A. Amateur Cup campaign.

It was no secret by this point that Casuals and Corinthians were to amalgamate at the end of the season. On 4th January 1939, at an E.G.M. in London, Casuals agreed in principle to join with the Corinthian F.C. and it was reported in the *Guardian* as follows:

"In the best interests of amateur football,' says C. Wreford Brown, a merger between the Corinthian and the Casuals Football Clubs, two of the best known amateur organisations in the country, has been agreed upon in principle and each club has appointed a committee to discuss and settle details. This was announced after an extra-ordinary meeting of the Casuals in London last night, and unless there is an unexpected hitch it is almost certain that the amalgamation will take place at the end of the present season. The committees will consist of eleven members each, and they will consider the numerous matters, including the name of the club and the rules.

The proposal to amalgamate with the Casuals was discussed by the Corinthians at a meeting on Tuesday night, and it is understood that a resolution they reached was put before last night's gathering. In June, 1937, the two clubs after several meetings decided to run under a joint executive committee for at least the next three seasons. It was then stated that this arrangement was intended to be permanent.

Corinthians particularly have found ever-increasing difficulty in getting together sides of the required strength, and in recent years they have been unable to produce the good displays which marked the earlier history of the club, especially in the F.A. Cup competition. The merging of the two clubs will permit fresh efforts for spreading the highest ideals of the amateur game with prospects of better results in various competitions.' [9]

With the amalgamation clearly on the players' minds, the team tore into Eastern Counties League side Harwich & Parkeston and recorded an emphatic 9-1 victory, with Lee scoring four goals. This was the last great Casuals performance in the F.A. Amateur Cup as the Old Boys lost by a single goal away to Leyton in the next round. Prior to this, Casuals were knocked out of the Surrey Senior Cup by Sutton United in a replay 0-1. The first match had seen Sutton build up a four goal lead, before Casuals staged a remarkable recovery to draw 4-4.

Casuals finished the season in excellent form, only losing one of their last eight matches. London Caledonians were defeated 4-0, prior to 1-1 draws at both Nunhead and Woking. Casuals recovered from going a goal behind after one minute to defeat Tufnell Park 4-1, before repeating that score-line a week later when Oxford City were entertained at Kingston.

The final season in Casuals' history drew to a close with a defeat at Dulwich Hamlet (1-5), and a 1-1 draw in the return fixture. The very last game was a 4-3 home victory over Wimbledon with goals coming from the whole forward line except, curiously, leading scorer Lee. The Casuals were no more and with war clouds gathering the new Corinthian-Casuals club faced an uncertain future – but that is another story.

CASUALS RESULTS
1883-1939

Every effort has been made to ensure the information in the following section is correct. If anyone has further information the author would be pleased to hear from you

All games prior to World War One are regarded as first team matches.

Venue Key

All home games between 1922 and 1925 were played at the Crystal Palace, and between 1925 and 1939 at Richmond Road, unless other wise stated.

H: Home   A: Away   N: Neutral

The above codes apply to the venues, many are followed by a letter:

@: Played Away
b: Barnes
c: Clapton
ca: Cambridge
cp: Crystal Palace
d: Dulwich
dh: Dulwich Hamlet
e: Ealing
em: East Molesey
g: Guildford
h: Hornsey
hh: Herne Hill
i: Ilford
ip: Ipswich

l: Leyton
o: The Oval
ox: Oxford
pl: Plumstead
qc: Queen's Club
s: Sidcup
sb: Shepherd's Bush
tp: Tufnell Park
u: Upton
w: Wimbledon
wc: Wandsworth Common
wh: West Ham
ws: Wormwood Scrubs

Competition Key

AC: F.A. Amateur Cup
AFASC: A.F.A. Senior Cup
CC: Casuals Cup
F: Friendly
FAC: F.A. Cup
HC: Hepburn Cup
IL: Isthmian League
LCC: London Charity Cup
LChC: London Challenge Cup

LSC: London Senior Cup
SAL: Southern Amateur League
SCC: Surrey Combination Cup
SCS: Surrey Charity Shield
SSC: Surrey Senior Cup
WCC: Warminster Charity Cup
WHC: West Ham Hospital Cup
WMC: Will Mather Cup
T: Tour

General Key

%: Goal scorers unknown
*: Goal described as a scrimmage or melee
og: Own goal
D-D: Match Drawn – result unknown
L-L: Match Lost – result unknown
W-W: Match Won – result unknown
v: Match void

1883/84

DATE	VEN	OPPONENTS	RES	COMP	ATT	1	2	3	4
29-Sep	A	UPTON PARK	3-3	F		MARSHALL EW	WALTERS AM	FOLEY CW	BOUSTEAD RN
03-Oct	A	BRUCE CASTLE SCHOOL	9-2	F		WILLIAMS ACR	WALTERS PM	WALTERS AM	KING AH
06-Oct	A	BRENTWOOD CLUB	2-4	F	%	WILLIAMS ACR	WALTERS PM	REEVES EA	BOUSTEAD RN
10-Oct	A	BRIGHTON COLLEGE	3-2	F		BEAUMONT H	BICKLEY F	LINGARD FC	KING AH
13-Oct	A	ROYAL ENGINEERS	1-2	F		WILLIAMS ACR	WALTERS PM	FORBES	BOUSTEAD RN
20-Oct	A	SURBITON W	3-1	F					
24-Oct	A	CHARTERHOUSE	1-1	F	%	CAWSTON E	PARAVICINI PJ	WALTERS AM	NICKISSON JL
03-Nov	A	FOREST SCHOOL	1-4	F		CAWSTON E	FORBES RAV	FORBES W	HANSELL AL
08-Nov	H wc	ST THOMAS' HOSPITAL	2-3	F		WILLIAMS ACR	HOTHAM FW	TAUNTON HG	KING AH
12-Nov	H wc	EAST SHEEN	1-4	F		STONE AE	TAUNTON HJ	KING AH	VIAN BA
01-Dec	A	RMC SANDHURST	0-6	F					
08-Dec	A	HIGHGATE SCHOOL	2-4	F	%	AN OTHER	NICHOLSON F	WEATHERHEAD TC	HAMILTON KA
15-Dec	A	OLD FORESTERS	2-1	F	%				
18-Dec	A	PILGRIMS	4-4	F		VAN LANGENBERG F	GUY H	BORROW SW	BLENKIRON TW
20-Dec	H wc	GUY'S HOSPITAL	2-2	F	%	BICKLEY F	HOTHAM FW	VIAN AR	HANSELL AL
22-Dec	A	BARNES	0-2	F		BICKLEY F	CORNWALLIS FSW	TAUNTON HG	LAST CH
05-Jan	H wc	UPTON PARK	2-3	F	%				
02-Feb	A	SURBITON W	0-4	F					
07-Feb	H wc	ST THOMAS' HOSPITAL	2-3	F					
13-Feb	A	WESTMINSTER SCHOOL	1-2	F		MILLS-ROBERTS RH	TOWNTON HC	FOLEY CW	LAST CH
13-Feb	A	BRADFIELD COLLEGE	1-2	F	%				
16-Feb	H wc	BURGESS HILL	1-4	F	%				
20-Feb	A	CHARTERHOUSE	3-2	F	#	FARMER JH	DIVER EJ	LINGARD FC	JANSON JW
01-Mar	H	OLD WESTMINSTERS	1-3	F					
04-Mar	A	FOREST SCHOOL	1-8	F	%				
08-Mar	A	OLD FORESTERS	1-3	F	%				
12-Mar	A	BRADFIELD COLLEGE	4-3	F	%				
05-Apr	H wc	JG FERN'S XI	0-2	F					

12 A SIDE GAME • NO. 12 = BICKLEY F

5	6	7	8	9	10	11
LAMING P	TAUNTON HG	CHURCH MB	BICKLEY F	FARMER JH	ALSTON HN 1	PATRICK D 2
BLENKIRON TW	VINTCENT LA 4	MARSON L	TAUNTON HG 1	FARDELL ES	BICKLEY F 2	ALSTON HN 2
BICKLEY F	MARSHALL EW	LAMING J	ALSTON HN	TAUNTON HG	CLEMENTS CT	FARMER H
CORNWALLIS AW	HOLDEN-WHITE C 1	TAUNTON HG	BREALEY H 1	ALSTON HN	BENNETT JH 1	FARMER JH
LAST CH	TAUNTON	TAUNTON HG	VINTCENT LA	PEARCE	BICKLEY F	ALSTON HN 1
		TAUNTON HG 1			CLEMENTS CT 1	ALSTON HN 1
BLENKIRON TW	BICKLEY F	VINTCENT LA	FARDELL ES	CROPPER C	ALSTON HN	CROPPER CE
					MARSHALL EW 1	
KING AH	BICKLEY F	VIAN BA	ATKINSON EH	ALSTON HN		CHURCH MB
LAST CH	TAUNTON EH	NICHOLLS H 1	ALSTON HN 1	FARMER H	BENNETT JH	BREALEY H
BICKLEY F	WALCH E	ALSTON HN 1	TAUNTON EH	CORNFORD JH		
BICKLEY F	KESTON HN	VIAN BA	MARSHALL EW	TWISS HW	CHURCH MB	TWIST A
VIAN AR	BREALEY H	FARDELL ES	PATRICK D 3	EDDIS KH 1	BICKLEY F	ALSTON HN
VIAN BA	HULL CPA	ALSTON HN	PATRICK D	FRERE WH	FARMER JH	
VIAN BA	FARMER H	BROWN FH	HULL CPA	THOMPSON C	ALSTON HN	
					BENNETT JH 2	
VINTCENT G	SMITH CM 1	PATRICK D	MACDONNELL J	MORTON PH	TWISS HW	BICKLEY F
CORNWALLIS AW	BARMBY FJ	CREWS AC	BAMBRIDGE EC 3	HARDMAN ET	PATRICK D	NICHOLLS H

1884/85

DATE	VEN	OPPONENTS	RES	COMP	ATT	1	2	3	4
27-Sep	A	UPTON PARK	1-0	F		CHARRINGTON E	WALTERS AM	SEWELL EB	BLENKIRON TW
04-Oct	A	BRENTWOOD	1-4	F	%	FARMER JH	WALTERS AM	WALTERS PM	BLENKIRON TW
08-Oct	A	CHARTERHOUSE	1-0	F		BARNETT WM	WALTERS AM	WALTERS PM	BLENKIRON TW
11-Oct	A	ROYAL ENGINEERS	1-3	F		CHARRINGTON E	SEWELL	SAVILLE AC	CREWS CB
15-Oct	A	BRIGHTON COLLEGE	3-6	F		RAYMOND L	BROWNLOW JR HON	COVENTRY CJ	LINGARD FC
18-Oct	H wc	OLD WESTMINSTERS	3-4	F	%				
18-Oct	A	FOREST SCHOOL	0-7	F		LAWRIE K	NICHOLSON F	TAUNTON HG	FARMER JH
23-Oct	A	ST THOMAS' HOSPITAL	0-2	F		ROBERTSON (SUB)	TAUNTON HG	HOTHAM FW	VIAN BA
25-Oct	A	ARGUS	2-0	LSC1	%				
08-Nov	H	SOUTH READING	1-4	FAC1		CAWSTON E	INGRAM	MORRISON ?	LAST CH
12-Nov	A	CAMBRIDGE UNIV	0-8	F		MILLS-ROBERTS RH	HASLOP RM	BLENKIRON TW	SANDERS FE
15-Nov	A	UPTON PARK	0-2	LSC2		CHARRINGTON E	WALTERS AM	SEWELL RB	VINTCENT J
19-Nov	A	WESTMINSTER SCHOOL	2-1	F		CHARRINGTON E	SEWELL FW	NICHOLLS H	LAST CH
22-Nov	A	BARNES	0-3	F		CHARRINGTON E	SEWELL EB	HARDMAN CJS	LAST CH
29-Nov	H wc	SOMERSET	2-2	F		GREENE HW	COLERIDGE GD	WARDE HP	ENGLAND GF
13-Dec	A	OLD FORESTERS	1-0	F		CHARRINGTON E	HOBBS WB	BRUNDETT JO	CREWS CB
18-Dec	H wc	GUY'S HOSPITAL	2-0	F		MILLS-ROBERTS RH	WALTERS AM	WALTERS PM	BLENKIRON TW
20-Dec	H wc	OLD BRIGHTONIANS	0-5	F		SOMERS-COCKS HL	JANSON JH	FARMER JH	JOBSON WS
22-Dec	H wc	EAST SHEEN	1-0	F		CHARRINGTON E	FEVEZ AL	RICHARDSON FJ	BLENKIRON TW
23-Dec	A	SWIFTS 'A'	2-3	F		SIRETT W	RICHARDSON FJ	SPRING-RICE G	JANSON JH
26-Dec	H wc	MR PEREZ'S XI	0-2	F	#	ROUGEMONT CH	HULL CPA	CREWS CB	CREWS AE
27-Dec	H	WIMBLEDON	7-1	F					
27-Dec	A	DERBY COUNTY	2-1	F		CHARRINGTON E	WALTERS PM	WALTERS AM	BLENKIRON TW
29-Dec	A	LONG EATON RANGERS	0-0	F		CHARRINGTON E	WALTERS PM	WALTERS AM	BLENKIRON TW
03-Jan	H	BARNES	2-2	F	%				
05-Jan	A	BLACKBURN OLYMPIC	0-2	F		CHARRINGTON E	WESTON WA	FEVEZ AL	WESTON W
07-Jan	A	BOLTON W	1-12	F		CHARRINGTON E	PEARSON CW	FEVEZ AL	RICHARDSON FJ
08-Jan	A	NOTTM FOREST	0-3	F		CHARRINGTON E	PEARSON CW	FEVEZ AL	SUGG FH
10-Jan	H wc	REIGATE PRIORY	0-5	F					
22-Jan	H wc	GUY'S HOSPITAL	5-3	F		CHARRINGTON E	JANSON JH	HOTHAM FW	HEATH CRW
31-Jan	H wc	BARNES	1-2	F					
04-Feb	A	WESTMINSTER SCHOOL	2-0	F		CHARRINGTON E	WARD FJ	SPRING-RICE G	BRIGGS H
07-Feb	A	SURBITON W	0-2	F					
12-Feb	A	ST THOMAS' HOSPITAL	1-0	F		CHARRINGTON E	IBBS RS 1	SCOTT HW	HEATH AJ
14-Feb	A	UPTON PARK	0-3	F		NICHOLSON F	TAUNTON HG	BENWELL JO	KING AH
21-Feb	A	ROYAL ENGINEERS	1-2	F	%				
21-Feb	A	FOREST SCHOOL	0-11	F		MARSHALL EW	SWISS J	BROWN J	TAUNTON HG
25-Feb	A	CHARTERHOUSE	1-2	F		MILLS-ROBERTS RH	RICHARDSON FJ	SPRING-RICE G	STEELE HS
28-Feb	A	OLD FORESTERS	5-1	F	%				
14-Mar	H	OLD BRIGHTONIANS	0-8	F		AN OTHER	THORNTON RG	FEVEZ AL	JANSON JH
25-Mar	A	CHARTERHOUSE	3-3	F	%	AN OTHER	WALTERS AM	WALTERS PM	BLENKIRON TW
?	H	OXFORD UNIVERSITY	2-1	F	%				

12 A SIDE GAME - NO. 12 - JH FARMER

5	6	7	8	9	10	11
JANSON FW 1	VINTCENT CH	BICKLEY F	PATRICK D	FARMER JH	CREWS AE	MARSHALL EW
CREWS CB	BOUSTEAD RN	HOLDEN-WHITE C	PATRICK D	BELL BW	BICKLEY F	CREWS AE
JANSON FW	COBBOLD WN	VINTCENT CH	PATRICK D	HARDMAN ET	BICKLEY F 1	FARDELL ES
FARMER JH	SAVILLE AC	BARNARD	PAUL JE 1	BICKLEY F	HOLMAN HM	DICKINSON
TAUNTON HG	MORICE HF 1	BENNETT JH	IBBS RS 1	FIENNES HEW	SMITH CA 1	
NICIN BA	SHEPPARD G	CHURCH MB	COTTON R	SMITH HR	ELLIS J	SAVILLE AC
CHARRINGTON E	BICKLEY F	HOLMAN HM	EVELYN EC	SMITH HR	PRICE WG	HUMPHREY EJ
CREWS CB	FARMER JH	HOLMAN HM	SMITH HR	MORRISON WG 1	ATKINSON EH	BICKLEY F
JANSON FW	WEATHERHEAD TC	PATRICK D	FARMER JH	IBBS RS	BICKLEY F	EASTON EG
LAST CH	BLENKIRON TW	EVELYN WA	ATKINSON EH	JANSON FW	HARDMAN CJS	PATRICK D
WETTON H	BICKLEY F 1	EVELYN EC	MORRISON WG 1	IBBS RS	JANSON FW	PAUL JE
JANSON FW	CURREY GE	HOLMAN HM	PAUL JE	MORRISON WG	REMNANT JF	BICKLEY F
FARMER JH	CREWS CB	TAUNTON HG 2	BETHEL V	BICKLEY F	NICHOLSON F	FRERE JWC
FARMER JH	WIGRAM EF	BICKLEY F	ROUGEMONT CH	MARSHALL EW 1	HULL CPA	HOLMAN HM
EVELYN WA	COLERIDGE GD	BICKLEY F 1	JANSON FW 1	HEATH AJ	WIGRAM EF	SETON WJ
HALL CPA	CREWS AE	HENLEY AK	ROUGEMONT CH			
HEATH AJ	EVELYN WA	HULL CPA	CREWS AE	BICKLEY F 1	WIGRAM EF	ROUGEMONT CH
ROUGEMONT CH	SETON WJ 1	JENNER ACW 1	CREWS AE	HUMPHREY EJ	BICKLEY F	
SOMER-COCKS HL	MUSPRATT PC	MUSPRATT FC	LEETE N	LEETE W	BUCKINGHAM HC	NICKISSON F
		HENLEY AK 2		FARMER JH 1	GREATOREX 2	BULLOCK 2
ENGLAND GF	RICHARDSON FJ	PAGE C	JANSON FW	HARDMAN ET 1	BELL BW	BICKLEY F 1
ENGLAND GF	RICHARDSON FJ	PAGE C	JANSON FW	HARDMAN ET	CREWS AE	BELL BW
BLENKIRON TW	ENGLAND GF	BELL BW	HARDMAN ET	PAGE C	JANSON FW	IBBS RS
BLENKIRON TW	ENGLAND GF	BELL BW 1	MUSPRATT FC	HURST J	JANSON FW	BICKLEY F
ENGLAND GF	RICHARDSON FJ	MUSPRATT C	BICKLEY F	BELL BW	HURST J	PAGE C
		HULL CPA	FARMER JH	CURREY GE		
MUSPRATT FC	BICKLEY F	PATRICK D 1	MILLER JS 4	PAUL JE	SAVILLE AC	
				FREEMAN 1		
ENGLAND GF	EVELYN EC	PATRICK D	IBBS RS 1	MILLER JS 1	PAUL JE	BICKLEY F
MUSPRATT FC	HEATH CRW	PAUL JE	MILLER JS	HUMPHREY EJ	BICKLEY F	HICKLEY CL
JOBSON WS	LOWE HP	ROUGEMONT CH	ATKINSON EH	MARSHALL PE	MARSHALL EW	THORNTON RG
WOOLLACOMBE W	NICHOL GN	BENWELL JO	TWISS HW	KING AH	VAN LANGENBERG F	
ENGLAND GF	PAUL JE	BICKLEY F	MILLER JS	IBBS RS 1	MOUNSEY OR	HOLDEN-WHITE C
BAKER B	MORRISON WG	HERBERT G	CROWDY C	HEATH CRW		
SCOTT HW	PEARSON CW	BICKLEY F	JENNER ACW 2	HARDMAN ET 1	PAUL JE	MOUNSEY OR

1885/86

DATE	VEN	OPPONENTS	RES	COMP	ATT	1	2	3	4
26-Sep	A	OLD BRIGHTONIANS	5-0	F		CHARRINGTON E	SEWELL EB	WALTERS AM	WETTON H
07-Oct	A	CHARTERHOUSE	1-0	F		PAUL JE	SQUIRES RT	WALTERS AM	AMOS A
10-Oct	A	ROYAL ENGINEERS	1-3	F		CHARRINGTON E	SEWELL EB	CREWS CB	WETTON H
15-Oct	H wc	ST THOMAS' HOSPITAL	5-0	F		HEATH AJ	SQUIRES RT	WARD HP	BICKLEY F
17-Oct	A	ST BRIDE'S (CLAPTON)	7-0	LSC1	og	CHARRINGTON E	SEWELL EB	BOUSTEAD RN	WETTON H
24-Oct	H wc	OLD ETONIANS	0-4	F		GRANT-WILSON CW	MOON WR	FRERE EC	CREWS CB
27-Oct	A	FOREST SCHOOL	6-1	F		EDDIS KH	SQUIRES RT	ROLLER CT 1	SCOTT HW
31-Oct	A	SWIFTS	1-7	FAC1		TRENT	BOUSTEAD RN	MOON WR	HOSKINS F
04-Nov	A	BRUCE CASTLE SCHOOL	6-3	F		MCLAREN J	JANSON JH	CHARRINGTON FH	STOKEN HS 1
07-Nov	H wc	TOTTENHAM H	8-0	LSC2		CHARRINGTON E	BOUSTEAD RN	SEWELL EB 1	WETTON H 1
11-Nov	A	CAMBRIDGE UNIV	0-0	F		MOON WR	SQUIRES RT	BEDFORD AER	HANGHAM HE
14-Nov	H wc	OLD WESTMINSTERS	3-2	F		WHEATEAR	FEVEZ AL	BOUSTEAD RN	ROPER WF
17-Nov	A	RMA WOOLWICH	2-2	F		WARD ER	CHARRINGTON FA	BICKLEY F	JANSON JH
18-Nov	A	WESTMINSTER SCHOOL	1-2	F		HEATH AS	ARTHUR SR	ROLLER CT	ENGLAND GF
21-Nov	A	BARNES	2-3	F		HEATH AS	BROWNLOW JR Hon.	CREWS CB	HOSKINS F
28-Nov	H b	OLD ST MARKS	1-2	LSC3	%	CHARRINGTON E	SEWELL EB	BOUSTEAD RN	WETTON H
02-Dec	A	BRIGHTON COLLEGE	1-1	F		COVENTRY CJ	HAY AT	LEETE W	LINGARD FC
09-Dec	H wc	LYNDHURST	1-1	F		GREENE HW	FOX CJM	SCOTT HW	FARMER JH
16-Dec	H wc	ST BARTHOLOMEWS H	1-3	F		BILBY EV	BICKLEY F	THORNE WC	KING AH
17-Dec	H wc	GUY'S HOSPITAL	1-3	F	#	PINGINS AR	ANDREWS FA	FOX CJM	SCOTT HW
19-Dec	H wc	CLAPHAM ROVERS	1-3	F	%				
21-Dec	H wc	CONDORS	7-0	F	%	GRANT-WILSON CW	FOX CJM	PEILE AB	BLENKIRON TW
22-Dec	H wc	EAST SHEEN	5-1	F		THORNTON RG	ROLLER CT 2	GRUNDTVIG HT	HARRISON HW
23-Dec	A	SWIFTS	2-5	F		MOON WR	GRUNDTVIG HT	HOLMES NT	HARRISON J
26-Dec	H wc	WIMBLEDON	5-2	F	%				
26-Dec	A	DERBY COUNTY	1-2	F	3,000	COOPER L	FOX CJM	FEVEZ AL	WETTON H
28-Dec	A	BURNLEY	2-2	F	% 200				
30-Dec	A	ASTON VILLA	4-3	F	3,000	JOHNSON	ANDREWS	INGRAM	NICKISSON JL
31-Dec	A	NOTTM FOREST	0-2	F	2,000	MOON WR	FOX CJM	BEDFORD AER	WETTON H
01-Jan	A	SHEFFIELD CLUB	0-2	F		MOON WR	ANDREWS WH	BEDFORD AER	WETTON H
02-Jan	A	LONG EATON RANGERS	0-4	F		MOON WR	ANDREWS A	BEDFORD AER	SAUNDERS FE
02-Jan	H	OLD BRIGHTONIANS	4-4	F	%	THORNTON RG	THORNE WC	BOUSTEAD RN	VIAN BA
04-Jan	H wc	CONDORS	10-4	F		THORNTON RG	HOLMES NT	GRUNDTVIG HT 1	BICKLEY F 1
16-Jan	A	OLD HARROVIANS	2-1	F		MOON WR	SEWELL EB	HOLMES NT	WETTON H
27-Jan	A	CAMBRIDGE UNIV	2-3	F		MOON WR	BEDFORD AER	SQUIRES RT	SCOTT HW
03-Feb	A	WESTMINSTER SCHOOL	4-1	F		CHARRINGTON E	HARDCASTLE ET	BEDFORD AER	SCOTT HW 1
20-Feb	H wc	CLAPHAM ROVERS	3-4	F	%	CHARRINGTON E	BOUSTEAD RN	HOSKINS F	LOCKER WA
24-Feb	A	CHARTERHOUSE	1-2	F	%				
06-Mar	A	WEST KENT	4-2	F		REPORTER A	THORNE WC	DENT WH	JANSON FW 1
13-Mar	H wc	OLD MALVERNIANS	0-1	F		AN OTHER	LOCKER WA	DRINKWATER AS	ADMIRAL JG
27-Mar	A	CHARTERHOUSE	0-1	F		CHARRINGTON E	WATKINS WF	LOWTHER HC	BICKLEY F

12 A-SIDE GAME - C PAGE NO. 12

5	6	7	8	9	10	11
BAILEY NC 1	BLENKIRON TW	BICKLEY F	HARDMAN CES 3	SAVILLE AC	FARMER JH	BAMBRIDGE EC 1
WETTON H	BLENKIRON TW	RICHARDSON FJ	COBBOLD WN	PAWSON FW	BICKLEY F 1	HOLDEN-WHITE C
ARTHUR SR	BICKLEY F	HOLDEN-WHITE C	PAWSON FW 1	FARMER JH	THORNE FG	
SCOTT HW 1	CAREY HL 2	SMITH HR 1	JENNER ACW 1	OLIVEY GS	PAUL JE	PECK HC
BLENKIRON TW 1	ENGLAND GF	CAREY HL	PAUL JE 2	MILLER JS	BICKLEY F 1	THORNE FG 2
ARTHUR SR	PINGUIS RG	BICKLEY F	KER-SEYMER E	THORNE FG	THORNE WC	FARMER JH
KING AH	HOSKINS F	CHURCH MB	STEVENS FH	MILLER JS 2	INGRAM CF 1	BICKLEY F 2
CREWS CB	ARTHUR SR	BICKLEY F	FARMER JH	HOLMAN HM 1	COOPER FJ	THORNTON RJ
PYKE AC	MOON WR	MACLEAN A	THOMAS FG	MILLER JS 3	TWISS AQ	CURRIE CE 2
HOSKINS F 1	ARTHUR SR	CURRIE CE 1	HOLMAN HM 1	PAUL JE 2	THORNE FG 1	BICKLEY F
SCOTT HW	ROLLER CT	HOLMAN HM	BICKLEY F	COLERIDGE GD	WELSH F	FARMER JH
MORGAN J	ROPER C	HOLMAN HM 1	BICKLEY F	LANGLEY C	SMITH Dr J 2	SMITH HR
MORGAN T	MACLEAN A	HICKLEY N	MILLER JS 2	MCCANCE HJ	ROLLER CT	SCOTT HW
HOSKINS F	ARLEY CH	THORNE FG	PAUL JE 1	HOLMAN HM	BICKLEY F	FARMER JH
RYDE FC	ROLLER CT	FARMER JH	PAUL JE 2	FIENNES HEW	THORNE FG	
ENGLAND GF	CURRIE CE	BICKLEY F	MORRISON WG	SMITH CA	PAUL JE	
STONE S	ELLIS H	LEETE N	SMITH CA	HAYMAN WHP	BENNETT JH 1	BONSELL AD
AN OTHER	BICKLEY F	CURRIE CE	MILLER JS 1	HICKLEY N	HEATH CRW	
HOWARD JE	PECK JH	PECK HC 1	THORNE FG	CREWS AE		
HOWARD TA	COLERIDGE HON. JC	FIENNES HEW	PECK HC	HURST AR 1	NORMAN L	BICKLEY F
GRUNDTVIG HT	BALFOUR AM	FARMER JH	HEATH CRW	SCOTT HW	BICKLEY F	CURREY ES
WYLDE HS	ARTHUR SR 1	SOMES FH	PECK HC 1	NIXON AC	SCOTT HW 1	BICKLEY F
CREWS AE	PECK HC	SCOONES O	BICKLEY F	BUCKLEY PF	LEETE N 2	CRONDY WM
			PAUL JE 1	FARMER JH 1	THORNE FG 1	
NICKISSON JL	BLENKIRON TW	SCOONES O	PAWSON FW	SMITH Dr J	PAGE C 1	PECK HC
BLEMKIRON TW	SCOONES O	PAWSON FW 1	SMITH Dr J 2	PAGE C	HURST AR 1	AN OTHER
BLEMKIRON TW	NICKISSON JL	SCOONES O	INGRAM FM	HURST AR	PECK HC	PAWSON FW
FOX CJM	HARRISON H	SCOONES O	HARDMAN ET	HURST AR	PAGE C	BICKLEY F
WETTON H	HARRISON H	PAGE C	BICKLEY F	HARDMAN ET	PECK HC	HURST AR
WRIGHT HE	MARSHALL EW	THORNE FG	BICKLEY F	FARMER JH 1	GRUNDTVIG HT	
BALFOUR AM	PECK HC 4	PECK JH 1	SCOTT HW 1	HARRISON H 2	CREWS AE	AN OTHER
KING AH	THORNE FG	BROOKS HT	CURRIE CE 2	CREWS AE	HARDMAN ET	FARMER JH
MITCHELL EJD	AUTOUEY R	BICKLEY F	MILLER JS 1	PAUL JE 1	HEATH CRW	FARMER JH
THOMPSON H	NICKISSON JL	BICKLEY F	HOLDEN-WHITE C 1	PAWSON FW	PAUL JE	MILLER JS 2
WYLDE HS	THORNE WC	CURRIE CE	HOLMAN HM	WATERFIELD N	PECK JH	HICKLEY N
CREWS CB	HEATH AJ	PECK HC	PAUL JE	THORNE FG	FARMER JH 2	INGRAM CF 1
ENGLAND GF	ASHBY G	SAVILLE AC	BICKLEY F	FARMER JH	VIAN BA	MOUNSEY OR
EVELYN EC	WYLDE HS	PROBYN PC	HURST AR	FARMER JH	HOLMAN HM	MOUNSEY OR

1886/87

DATE	VEN	OPPONENTS	RES	COMP	ATT	1	2	3	4
25-Sep	H ut	OLD BRIGHTONIANS	5-0	F		MOON WR	WALTERS PM	WALTERS AM	SQUIRE RT
02-Oct	A	LANCING OB'S	0-2	F					
06-Oct	A	CHARTERHOUSE	1-1	F		AN OTHER	HARRISON H	SHEPHERD WE	LOCKER WA
13-Oct	A	ST THOMAS' HOSPITAL	3-1	F		BICKLEY F	FORMER JN	ARTHUR SR	SQUIRE RT
16-Oct	H ut	PILGRIMS	8-0	LSC1		MILLS-ROBERTS RH	HARRISON H	LOCKER WA	AMOS A
21-Oct	A	OXFORD UNIVERSITY	1-3	F		LOCKHART-MUIR-IVES J	DAVIES AO	SQUIRE RT	SAUNDERS FE
27-Oct	A	BRUCE CASTLE SCHOOL	9-0	F		SUAL CA	FOX CJM 1	LOCKER WA 1	GORDON HH
30-Oct	H ut	DULWICH	2-4	FAC1		BICKLEY F	BOUSTEAD RN	FRERE EC	HARRISON H
03-Nov	A	BRUCE CASTLE SCHOOL	7-2	F		SUAL CA	HARRISON H	GORDON HH 1	STOCKEN HR
06-Nov	H ut	WAVERLEY	12-0	LSC2		MILLS-ROBERTS RH	BOUSTEAD RN	LOCKER WA 1	HARRISON H 1
10-Nov	A	CAMBRIDGE UNIV	2-2	F		FRANK FH	DAVIES AO	HARRISON H	SQUIRE RT
13-Nov	H ut	UPTON PARK	0-7	F		BICKLEY F	BOUSTEAD RN	LOCKER WA	HARRISON H
17-Nov	A	WESTMINSTER SCHOOL	1-2	F		WINCKWORTH WB	TURNER RJ	DICKINSON CF	ROE WN
20-Nov	A	ROYAL ENGINEERS	0-7	F					
27-Nov	H ut	OLD WESTMINSTERS	4-1	F		WELCHLAND P	BOUSTEAD RN	HASKETT-SMITH GB 1	NICHOLSON F
30-Nov	A	FOREST SCHOOL	3-2	F		VAN LANGENBERG F	FRASER FR 1	HASKETT-SMITH B 1	KING AH
04-Dec	H wc	CLAPHAM ROVERS	1-1 $	LSC3	%	MILLS-ROBERTS RH	INGRAM FM	BOUSTEAD RN	HARRISON H
04-Dec	H ut	GOUDHURST	D-D	F		SHEPHARD AS	CHAPMAN EL	KING AH	FARMER JH
18-Dec	H ut	CLAPHAM ROVERS	9-1	F		MOON EG	HARRISON H	BOUSTEAD RN	KING AH
23-Dec	H ut	ODD FELLOWS	6-0	F		MOON EG	FOX CJM	HARRISON H	SCOTT HW
24-Dec	H ut	ASHBURNHAM ROVERS	5-3	F					
27-Dec	A	DERBY COUNTY	0-3	F		MOON WR	FOX CJM	MOON EG	KING AH
28-Dec	A	ASTON VILLA	1-2	F		MOON WR	FOX CJM	INGRAM RA	NICKISSON JL
29-Dec	A	LONG EATON RANGERS	3-6	F	% *	MOON WR	MORLEY HA	WALTERS PM	FOX CJM
30-Dec	A	STOKE CITY	0-0	F		MOON WR	FOX CJM	WALTERS PM	INGRAM RA
30-Dec	H ut	EAST SURREY W	1-2	F		MOON EG	GRUNDTVIG HT	HARRISON H 1	LOCKER WA
07-Jan	H ut	EAST SURREY W	1-1	F	#	NOTES WJ	CHARLES MJ	WATT J	GRUNDTVIG HT
08-Jan	H ut	OLD WYKEHAMISTS	2-0	F		SETON WJ	BOUSTEAD RN	HASKETT-SMITH B	KING AH
22-Jan	N o	HENDON	6-0	LSC4	%	MILLS-ROBERTS RH	INGRAM FM 1	HARRISON H	LOCKER WA
26-Jan	A	WESTMINSTER SCHOOL	2-0	F		MILLS-ROBERTS RH	CHARLES CJ	WALTERS PM	BLENKIRON TW
05-Feb	N t	UPTON PARK	1-0	LSCsf	1,200	MILLS-ROBERTS RH	INGRAM FM	HARRISON H	EVELYN EC 1
16-Feb	A	CAMBRIDGE UNIV	2-3	F		TYLER CH	WALTERS PM	SALE RW	AMOS A
23-Feb	A	CHARTERHOUSE	2-3	F	%	THORNE FG	TOPHAM AG	LOCKER WA	WETTON H
28-Feb	H ut	GUY'S HOSPITAL	4-2	F	%				
01-Mar	A	FOREST SCHOOL	2-1	F		WINCKWORTH WB	LINGARD FC	NEILL B	LAURIE CC
05-Mar	N o	CRUSADERS	3-1	LCCsf	2,000	MILLS-ROBERTS RH	WALTERS AM	WALTERS PM	AMOS A
26-Mar	N o	SWIFTS	0-3	LCCf	1,500	MILLS-ROBERTS RH	HARRISON H	INGRAM FM	BLENKIRON TW
30-Mar	N o	OLD WESTMINSTERS	1-1	LSCf	400	MILLS-ROBERTS RH	DAVIES AO	WALTERS AM	NICKISSON JL

12 A SIDE GAME - NO. 12 F BURGE
$ CLAPHAM ROVERS WITHDREW FROM CUP

5	6	7	8	9	10	11
WETTON H	FEVEZ AL	BAIN FW	JANSON FW	BAMBRIDGE EC 4	HEATH CRW 1	SOMES FH
BLENKIRON TW	ARTHUR SR	BUCKLEY PF	BICKLEY F	CURREY ES	WATT J	MOUNSEY OR 1
HARRISON S	HOLDEN-WHITE C	POWELL EO	PAWSON FW 1	BAMBRIDGE EC 1	CURRIE CE 1	BUCKLEY PF
BLENKIRON TW 1	ARTHUR SR	SMITH CA 3	INGRAM FM 4	CURRIE CE	POWELL EO	BUCKLEY PF
NICKISSON JL	ARTHUR SR	BICKLEY F 1	CHARLES W	HARRISON H	BAIN FW	PAWSON FW
TILLEY A	THORNE FG	MARSHALL EW 2	PECK JH 2	FARMER JH 2	BUCKLEY PF 1	BICKLEY F
THORNE FG	HOWARD JE	COOPER FJ	HOLMAN HM	CURRIE CE 1	PETER J 1	EDDIS KH
MARSHALL EW 2	BAILEY NC 1	JACKSON NL	FARMER JH 1	PECK JH	BUCKLEY PF	BICKLEY F 2
THORNE FG	KING AH	PAGE C	NIXON AC 1	CURRIE CE 7	BUCKLEY PF	BICKLEY F 2
SAUNDERS FE	AMOS A	COTTERILL CH	COBBOLD WN 2	PAWSON FW	CURREY ES	WREFORD-BROWN C
HOWARD JE	KING AH	SCOONES FJ	ADAMS HN	CURRIE CE	POWELL EO	SMITH HR
FOX CJM	CREWS AE	HOLMAN HM 1	BICKLEY F	PAUL JE	THORNE FG	SOMES FH
LOCKER WA 1	KING AH	BUCKLEY PF	FRANKS F	HEATH CRW 1	ADAMS HN 1	HOWARD JE
LOCKER WA	MOUNSEY OR	GARRETT-CLARKE H	LEETE N 1	ADAMS HN	HASKETT-SMITH WP	
LOCKER WA	NICKISSON JL	SUAL ACA	CURRIE CE	MORRISON WG	NIXON AC	POWELL EO
BALFOUR AM	THORNE FG	SAVILLE AC	HEMMERDE AJ	BICKLEY F 3	BURGE F	
THORNE FG	MAINWARING CM	NIXON AC	VEITCH JG 3	BURGE F	BURGE F 3	
LOCKER WA	WETTON H 1	BURGE F	BICKLEY F	VEITCH JG 3	NIXON AC 1	MAINWARING CM 1
			JANSON FW 1	VEITCH JG 3	NIXON AC 1	
BLENKIRON TW	NICKISSON JL	VEITCH JG	BICKLEY F	CURTIS GF	SMITH Dr J	COOPER FJ
BLENKIRON TW	AN OTHER	SMITH Dr J	VEITCH JG	CURTIS GF 1	COOPER FJ	DAFT HB
NICKISSON JL	BLENKIRON TW	INGRAM RA	SCOONES O	SMITH Dr J 1	DAFT HB	CURTIS GF
REDFORD	BEDFORD AER	SCOONES O	CURTIS GF	LINDLEY T	SMITH Dr J	COOPER LJ
HAMILTON RE	WATT J	BURGE F	BICKLEY F	VEITCH JG	HEMMERDE AJ	SOMES FH
PAUL JP	LOCKER WA	HASKETT-SMITH WP	HASKETT-SMITH A 1	PECK HC	PECK C	BICKLEY F
PAUL JP	SOMES FH	PECK JH	PECK HC	PAUL JE		
BLENKIRON TW	NICKISSON JL	HOLDEN-WHITE C	SMITH CA 2	NIXON AC	BURGE F	BICKLEY F 2
WATT J	NICKISSON JL	HOLDEN-WHITE C	BICKLEY F	EVELYN EC	PECK JH 1	SOMES FH 1
LOCKER WA	NICKISSON JL	HOLDEN-WHITE C	NIXON AC	CURRIE CE	BICKLEY F	PRICE HC
MUNDAHL HS	NICKISSON JL	WALTERS AM 2	FARMER JH	NIXON AC	COBBOLD WN	WADDINGTON CW
KING AH	RYDE FC	PAGE C	SOMES FH	HARDMAN ET	BICKLEY F 1	HOLMAN HM
BURY L	BILBY EV	BICKLEY F 1	MARSHALL EW	NEWNHAM A	STEVENS H 1	PASCOE M
BLENKIRON TW	ROE WN	SMITH CA 2	NIXON AC 1	INGRAM FM	BICKLEY F	DUNN ATB
LINGARD FC	AMOS A	DUNN ATB	COBBOLD WN	SMITH CA	AINGER WH	VEITCH JG
BLENKIRON TW	AMOS A	SMITH CA	NIXON AC	INGRAM FM 1	BICKLEY F	HOLDEN-WHITE C

1887/88

DATE	VEN	OPPONENTS	RES	COMP	ATT	1	2	3	4
24-Sep	H ut	OLD BRIGHTONIANS	2-0	F	%	LEETE A	LOCKER WA	FOX CJM	MITCHELL EJD
01-Oct	H ut	OLD ETONIANS	2-3	F	%				
06-Oct	A	CHARTERHOUSE	0-1	F		KILLICH H	WALTERS PM	HEMMERDE CL	RUTTER EC
08-Oct	A	HOTSPUR (MERTON)	5-0	LSC1	%	ALSTON HN	WALTERS PM	WALTERS AM	SAUL CA
12-Oct	A	THE PHILBERDS	0-2	F		SAMSON EM	HEWETT HT	HEMMERDE CL	LOCKER WA
15-Oct	A	MILLWALL ROVERS	W/D	FAC1					
19-Oct	A	ST BARTHOLOMEWS H	1-3	F		ALSTON HN	FOX CJM	MOON EG	JANSON FW
22-Oct	H ut	CLAPHAM ROVERS	5-2	F		ALSTON HN	BOUSTEAD RN	RYDE FC	RUTTER NC
26-Oct	A	OXFORD UNIVERSITY	0-5	F		SAMSON EM	HARRISON H	HEMMERDE CL	WACE HC
02-Nov	A	CAMBRIDGE UNIV	0-3	F		SAMSON EM	WALTERS AM	FOX CJM	NICKKISON JL
05-Nov	A	CHARTERHOUSE	1-4	F		SMITH C	LOCKER WA	OTHER AN	RUTTER RC
07-Nov	A	SMALL HEATH ALLIANCE	2-4	F	%	MOON WR	HEMMERDE CL	LAWRENCE HC	HARRISON
15-Nov	A	FOREST SCHOOL	5-3	F	%	ALSTON HN	LOCKER WA	HASKETT-SMITH TB	BLENKIRON TW
19-Nov	H ut	IONA	4-1	LSC3		ALSTON HN	LOCKER WA	ROE WN	BLENKIRON TW
26-Nov	H ut	GUY'S HOSPITAL	3-1	F	%	CASUAL AC	LOCKER WA	RYDE FC	BLENKIRON TW
30-Nov	H ut	LYNDHURST	3-1	F		WINCKWORTH WB	LOCKER WA	RYDE FC	BLENKIRON TW
08-Dec	A	ROYAL ENGINEERS	1-3	F		ALSTON HN	COLERIDGE GD	FOX CJM	LEDWARD RH
12-Dec	A	RMA WOOLWICH	3-1	F		SETON WJ	LOCKER WA	LITTLE E	LEMAN GC
14-Dec	H ut	ST BARTHOLOMEWS H	6-2	F		OTHER AN	LOCKER WA	HARRISON H	BLENKIRON TW
15-Dec	H ut	GUY'S HOSPITAL	2-2	F		SETON WJ	HEMMERDE CL	FEVEZ AL	WACE HC
17-Dec	A	HENDON	3-2	LSC4	%	SETON WJ	BOUSTEAD RN	LOCKER WA	BLENKIRON TW
17-Dec	A	CLAPHAM ROVERS	1-2	F	# %	ALLBOY SM	HEMMERDE CL	RYDE FC	LEDWARD GH
19-Dec	A	CHISWICK PARK	2-2	F	%	WILKINSON LR	FOX CJM	HARRISON AH	HEMMERDE CL
21-Dec	H ut	OLD ETONIANS	2-4	F		AN OTHER	FOX CJM	ROE WN	MITCHELL RJD
21-Dec	A	LYNDHURST	1-1	F		SMITH W	LECKER WA	RYDE FC	HAYDEN AJF
22-Dec	H ut	EAST SURREY W	3-2	F		WATT J	FOX CJM	HARRISON AH	BICKLEY F
24-Dec	A	OLD LANCING BOYS	1-2	F	%				
26-Dec	A	DERBY COUNTY	1-5	F		SAMSON EM	WALTERS AM	FOX CJM	MITCHELL EJD
27-Dec	A	ASTON VILLA	0-1	F	5,000	SAMSON EM	WALTERS AM	MORLEY HA	NICKKISON JL
27-Dec	A	CLAPTON	0-5	F	500	ALSTON HN	LOCKER WA	DADLEY AB	PAUL JP
28-Dec	A	GAINSBOROUGH TRINITY	1-6	F		SAMSON EM	BEDFORD AER	MORLEY HA	MITCHELL EJD
29-Dec	A	LONG EATON RANGERS	3-1	F		SAMSON EM	MORLEY HA	BEDFORD AER	MITCHELL EJD
31-Dec	A	NEWTON HEATH	1-2	F		SAMSON EM	LAWRENCE HC	MORLEY HA	BLENKIRON TW
10-Jan	H ut	EAST SURREY W	1-4	F		ALSTON HN	LOCKER WA	HEMMERDE CL	PAUL JP
12-Jan	A	CHISWICK PARK	0-6	F		BEASLEY C	THORNTON RG	BICKLEY F	BLENKIRON TW
14-Jan	H ut	OLD HARROVIANS	3-2	F		BICKLEY F 1	BOUSTEAD RN	RYDE FC	POPHAM BG
21-Jan	N o	OLD HARROVIANS	5-1	LSCsf		ALSTON HN	BOUSTEAD RN	LOCKER WA	MITCHELL EJD
25-Jan	H ut	ST BARTHOLOMEWS H	4-3	F		NOTES WJ	LOCKER WA	PAUL JP	KING CH
28-Jan	A	OLD ETONIANS	4-2	F		SETON WJ	FORD HA	RYDE FC	BICKLEY F
04-Feb	H ut	BARNES	0-4	F		SETON WJ	FORD HA	FARRER FE	RYDE FC
11-Feb	A	ROYAL ENGINEERS	0-3	F		SOPPITT C	FORD HA	BOUSTEAD RN	PAUL
18-Feb	N o	OLD WESTMINSTERS	0-1	LSCf		ALSTON HN	BOUSTEAD RN	WALTERS AM	MITCHELL EJD
25-Feb	N o	OLD FORESTERS	4-1	LCCsf	500	WALTERS AM 1	BOUSTEAD RN	LAWRENCE HC	MITCHELL EJD
28-Feb	A	FOREST SCHOOL	2-2	F	%				
29-Feb	A	BECKENHAM	3-2	F		WALTERS PM	FORD HA	PAUL JP	BICKLEY F
21-Mar	A	EAST SURREY W	0-5	F		HETHERINGTON RE	RYDE FC	ANGER WH	PAUL JE
24-Mar	A	CHARTERHOUSE	2-2	F		HEMMERDE AJ	BOUSTEAD RN	ARTHUR SR	PAUL JP
24-Mar	A	GODALMING	3-3	F		MURPHY G	BOUSTEAD RN	COWIE RM	PAUL JP
31-Mar	N o	SWIFTS	0-1	LCCf		ALSTON HN	BOUSTEAD RN	LAWRENCE HC	MITCHELL RJD
14-Apr	A	CLAPTON	0-3	F		PAUL JP	LAWRENCE HC	FOX CJM	MITCHELL RJD

12 A SIDE GAME NO. 12 - BARRACLOUGH HC

5	6	7	8	9	10	11
JANSON FW	WACE HC	JOYCE R	HARRISON H	LEMAN DC	PATRICK D	NIXON AC
BLENKIRON TW	GRUNDTVIG A	HOLMAN HM	BICKLEY F	HARRISON AH	NIXON AC	WALTERS HM
BLENKIRON TW	LOCKER WA	PAGE C	NIXON AC	HARRISON H	THORNE FG	BICKLEY F
WACE HC	MITCHELL WG	AINGER WH	ESCOMBE RL	STEELE M	GRUNDTVIG HT	
GRUNDTVIG HT	BLENKIRON TW	FARMER JH	AINGER WH	PRICE WG 1	MARSHALL W	MOUNSEY OR
PAUL JP	BICKLEY F	MOUNSEY OR	PAUL JE 3	THORNE FG 1	PECK JH 1	MARSHALL EW
LOCKER WA	BICKLEY F	PAGE C	AINGER WH	PRICE HC	PATRICK D	CROSS FJK
SQUIRE RT	BLENKIRON TW	PARRY CW	HARRISON H	PATRICK D	SPILSBURY BW	WELCH FCB
PAUL JP	RYDE FC	BOUSTEAD R	LEDWARD RH	BICKLEY F	PAWSON FW 1	OTHER THE
JOHNSON	ARTHUR SR	PAGE C	GRUNDTVIG HT 1	HOGARTH RG	PRICE HC	PRINCEP
DASHWOOD L	LEDWARD RH	MARSHALL EW	HASKETT-SMITH WR	FARMER JH	HEMMERDE H	MARSH EC
RUTTER RC	NICKISSON JL	PAGE C	THORNE FG	PRICE HC 2	HARRISON H	HOGARTH RG 2
RUTTER RC	PAUL JP	LEDWARD RH	GRUNDTVIG HT	WALTERS AM 2	PAUL JE	MOUNSEY OR
LEDWARD GH	MARSHALL EW	GRUNDTVIG HT 1	SMITH Dr J 2	BURGE F	REDDY B	
PAUL JP	GRUNDTVIG HT	LEDWARD GH	PECK HC	BICKLEY F 1	SAUL CA	SLAUGHTER
LEDWARD GH	PAUL JP	NIXON AC 1	LEMAN DC	FOX CJM 2	BICKLEY F	BURGE F
WACE HC	GRUNDTVIG HT 3	JACKSON CH	PATRICK D	NIXON AC	BICKLEY F 2	THORNE FG 1
LEMAN GC	TAYLOR HS	PATRICK D 2	BICKLEY F	MAINWARING CM	LEMAN DC	GLOSSOP AGB
LEMAN GC	RUTTER EC	PAGE C	NIXON AC	PRICE HC	THORNE FG	BICKLEY F
POPHAM BG	PAUL JP	PECK JH	LEDWARD RH	PAUL JE	THORNTON RG	MAINWARING CM
LEDWARD GH	PAUL JP	PAGE C	PECK JH	PROBYN PC	WATT J	BICKLEY F
LEMAN GC	HEMMERDE CL	PRICE HC	PARTON FJ	HUMPHREY EJ 1	JACKSON CH 1	PARRY CW
POPHAM BG	PAUL JP	ADAMS FE	PAWSON FW	FAIRBAIRN T 1	PATRICK D	PROBYN PC
BLENKIRON TW	BALFOUR AM	FURBER S 1	PAGE C	PAUL JE	VEITCH JG 2	MARCH RC
BLENKIRON TW	NICKISSON JL	GLOSSOP AGB	PRICE HC	SMITH DR J 1	PARRY CW	AN OTHER
BEDFORD AER	MITCHELL WG	SMITH Dr J	PIKE	PRICE HC	FARRANT	NIXON AC
BAKER W	BILBY EV	ADAMS JR	PECK HC	FARMER JH	MARSHALL W	JACKSON CH
BLENKIRON TW	NICKISSON JL	GLOSSOP AGB	SMITH Dr J	NIXON AC	DAFT HB 1	PARRY CW
BLENKIRON TW	RADFORD T	GLOSSOP AGB	NIXON AC	THOMPSON W 1	PARRY CW	BURTON FE 2
MITCHELL EJD	NICKISSON JL	GLOSSOP AGB	NIXON AC	SMITH Dr J	JENNER ACW 1	PARRY CW
BICKLEY F	WEATHERHEAD TC	BUCKLEY PF	NASH RW	PECK HC	PAGE C	NORTH 1
BUCKLEY PF	SYMNS R	THORNE FG	SMITH Dr J	PECK JH		
PAUL JP	RUTTER EC	MARSHALL EW	BLENKIRON TW	PAUL JE 1	THORNE FG 1	SAVILLE AC
BLENKIRON TW	RUTTER EC	PAGE C	NIXON AC 1	PRICE HC 1	INGRAM FM 3	HARRISON H
BICKLEY F	BLENKIRON TW	GRUNDTVIG HT 1	BURGE F	FURBER S 3	PECK JH	MARSHALL EW
PAUL JP	LUSHINGTON G	MARSHALL EW 1	PECK JH 1	GRUNDTVIG HT 1	THORNE FG	BURGE F 1
LUSHINGTON G	LEDWARD RH	MARSHALL EW	MARSH EC	HILDYARD ED	SAVILLE AC	
RUTTER	LIDDELL	MARSHALL EW	LUSHINGTON G	BLENKIRON TW	BICKLEY F	BURGE F
BLENKIRON TW	RUTTER EC	PAGE C	NIXON AC	KNOX JJ	EVELYN EC	DUNN ATB
BLENKIRON TW	RUTTER EC	PAUL JE	AINGER WH 1	HOGARTH RG 1	EVELYN EC 1	BICKLEY F
BLENKIRON TW	MARSHALL EW	FOX CJM 1	FURBER S	AINGER WH 2	HOWELL EL	
BICKLEY F	FURBER S	BLENKIRON TW	PROBYN PC			
BLENKIRON TW 1	RUTTER EC	PAUL JE 1	PROBYN PC	MORRISON WG	FURBER S	BICKLEY F
BLENKIRON TW	ARTHUR SR	EARLE FA	HEMMERDE AJ 1	FURBER S 1	DICKINSON SC	BICKLEY F 1
BLENKIRON TW	RUTTER EC	PAUL JE	AINGER WH	HOGARTH RG	NIXON AC	BICKLEY F
BLENKIRON TW	ARTHUR SR	NIXON AC	AINGER WH	MORRISON WG	FURBER S	MITCHELL WG

1888/89

DATE	VEN	OPPONENTS	RES	COMP	ATT	1	2	3	4
29-Sep	H ut	OLD ETONIANS	2-2	F		BOOKER C	FEVEZ AL	PAUL JP	WATT J
03-Oct	A	CHARTERHOUSE	1-3	F	%	OTHER AN	CARSON HJ	ARTHUR SR	LEMAN GC
04-Oct	H ut	ROYAL ENGINEERS	3-3	F		AUSTIN HN	FOX CJM 1	ARTHUR SR	FEVEZ AL
06-Oct	H	HITCHIN	W/O	FAC1Q					
13-Oct	A	LONDON CALEDONIANS	1-5	F		CHARRINGTON E	FEVEZ AL	BELLHOUSE TW	POPHAM BG
13-Oct	A	LANCING OB'S	0-3	F					
17-Oct	A	ST BARTHOLOMEWS H	2-0	F		CARLYON S	ANDERSON EP	FEVEZ AL	POPHAM BG 1
20-Oct	H ut	RMC SANDHURST	3-1	F		GRANT-WILSON CW	BELLHOUSE JW	FORD HA	POPHAM BG
24-Oct	H ut	SWIFTS	3-4	F		CARLYON S	HASKETT-SMITH F	HASKETT-SMITH WP 1	POPHAM BG
25-Oct	H ut	GUY'S HOSPITAL	5-0	F		GRANT-WILSON CW	HALE G	LEETE N	WINCKWORTH WN
27-Oct	H ut	CLAPTON	1-3	FAC2Q		CHARRINGTON E	HARRISON H	FEVEZ AL	POPHAM BG
27-Oct	A	CHISWICK PARK	2-3	F		GRANT-WILSON CW	PAUL JP	PROTHERO AG	OLIVER FG
31-Oct	A	CAMBRIDGE UNIV	0-9	F		MURPHY JK	FEVEZ AL	SALE RW	POPHAM BG
03-Nov	A	OLD HARROVIANS	1-0	LSC2		STONE ACS	ROE WN	BELLHOUSE JW	MITCHELL EJD
03-Nov	A	RMA WOOLWICH	3-0	F	%				
10-Nov	N o	OLD ST MARKS	0-0	LCC1		SETON WJ	ROE WN	SALE RW	MITCHELL EJD
10-Nov	H ut	OLD CRANLEIGHANS	3-1	F		GRANT-WILSON CW	FEVEZ AL	FORD HA	BARKER RR
13-Nov	A	FOREST SCHOOL	5-0	F					
17-Nov	A	WESTMINSTER SCHOOL	0-1	F	%	GRANT-WILSON CW	OLIVER FG	FEVEZ AL	BALFOUR AM
19-Nov	H ut	CAPT JAMES XI	10-0	F	%				
21-Nov	H ut	INCOGNITI	4-1	F		GRANT-WILSON CW	FERNIE FE	LOCKER WA	BALFOUR AM
24-Nov	H ut	BRIXTON RANGERS	2-0	LSC3	*	STONE ACS	ROE WN	HARRISON H	POPHAM BG
24-Nov	A	BECKENHAM	0-1	F		SETON WJ	BOUSTEAD RN	MOON EG	RYDE FC
26-Nov	H ut	HOTSPUR	0-2	F		GRANT-WILSON CW	LOCKER WA	FORD HA	WINCKWORTH WN
28-Nov	H ut	LYNDHURST	4-1	F		SETON WJ	OLIVER FG	STONE AG	WINCKWORTH WN
01-Dec	A	OXFORD UNIVERSITY	2-4	F		SETON WJ	BARWELL CSW	ROE WN	LOCKER WA
05-Dec	A	BRIGHTON COLLEGE	3-1	F		PARSONS FW	FERNIE FE	PROTHERO AG	KING PV
08-Dec	H ut	OLD FORESTERS	3-2	F		GRANT-WILSON CW	BOUSTEAD RN	BARRACLOUGH HC	POPHAM BG
13-Dec	H ut	OXFORD UNIVERSITY	0-3	F		STONE ACS	ROE WN	ANDERSON EP	LOCKER WA
15-Dec	N 1	OLD WESTMINSTERS	3-0	LSC4		STONE ACS	WALTERS PM	WALTERS AM	POPHAM BG
17-Dec	H ut	EAST SURREY W	2-2	F		ROCK AC	ROE WN	BARRACLOUGH HC	BALFOUR AM
18-Dec	A	RIFLE BRIGADE	0-4	F		SHEPPARD	HASKETT-SMITH WP	ROE WN	PHILLIMORE JE
19-Dec	H ut	LYNDHURST	3-1	F		GRANT-WILSON CW	ROE WN	JACKSON CH	WACE HC
20-Dec	H ut	CHISWICK PARK	6-2	F		GRANT-WILSON CW	FOX CJM	HARRISON H	PHILLIMORE JE
21-Dec	H ut	FELSTED SCHOOL	5-0	F		GRANT-WILSON CW	FRY CB	JACKSON CH	WACE HC
22-Dec	H ut	LANCING OB'S	3-1	F	%	SETON WJ	FRY CB	BARKER RR	PAUL JP
24-Dec	H ut	EAST SURREY W	1-2	F	%	SETON WJ	FRY CB	HARRISON H	RUTTER EC
26-Dec	A	WEST MANCHESTER	3-2	F	* 3,000	SAMSON EM	WALTERS PM	JACKSON E	BLENKIRON TW
26-Dec	A	NORTHAMPTONSHIRE	2-4	F		GRANT-WILSON CW	JACKSON E	FRY CB	BICKLEY F
27-Dec	A	ASTON VILLA	3-6	F	500	SAMSON EM	ANDERSON EP	WALTERS PM	MITCHELL EJD
28-Dec	A	SHEFFIELD	4-2	F		SAMSON EM	ANDERSON EP	WALTERS PM	BLENKIRON TW
29-Dec	A	NOTTM FOREST	4-1	F	1,000	SAMSON EM	ANDERSON EP	JACKSON E	MITCHELL EJD
29-Dec	A	OLD HARROVIANS	3-5	F		GRANT-WILSON CW	JACKSON CH	FRY CB	BARKER RR
31-Dec	A	LONG EATON RANGERS	2-5	F		SETON WJ	SALE RW	LLOYD	MITCHELL EJD
01-Jan	A	BURNLEY	0-4	F		SETON WJ	MORLEY HA	LLOYD	MITCHELL EJD
02-Jan	A	NEWTON HEATH	0-1	F	1,000	SETON WJ	HARRISON H	MORLEY HA	BLENKIRON TW
03-Jan	A	NOTTS COUNTY	0-1	F		SETON WJ	MORLEY HA	HENDERSON J	MITCHELL EJD
05-Jan	A	DERBY COUNTY	0-6	F		SETON WJ	MORLEY HA	HENDERSON J	MITCHELL EJD
10-Jan	H ut	OLD REPTONIANS	3-3	F		OTHER AN	HARRISON H	BARRACLOUGH HC	BICKLEY F
12-Jan	A	OLD ST MARKS	4-1	LCC1		SETON WJ	ROE WN	FRY CB	MITCHELL EJD
12-Jan	H ut	OLD HARROVIANS	4-5	F					BICKLEY F
19-Jan	N o	HOTSPUR	4-3	LSCsf		STONE ACS	FRY CB	ROE WN	MITCHELL EJD
26-Jan	H ut	OLD ETONIANS	3-2	F		SHEPHERD W	ROE WN	BARKERS S	RAWLINSON JFP
30-Jan	A	WESTMINSTER SCHOOL	3-0	F	og	GRANT-WILSON CW	PROTHERO AG	LOCKER WA	MUNDAHL HS
02-Feb	H ut	BARNES	1-1	F		BAGSHAW WH	LOCKER WA	BARKER RR	RUTTER EC
06-Feb	H ut	ST MARYS HOSPITAL	2-0	F		ANDREWS F	PROTHERO AG	GRUNDTVIG HT	NASON FW
09-Feb	N o	OLD WESTMINSTERS	1-2	LCCsf		SETON WJ	WALTERS AM	WALTERS PM	BLENKIRON TW
09-Feb	A	REIGATE PRIORY	1-2	F		BAGSHAW F	PROTHERO AG	BOUSTEAD RN	RUTTER EC
19-Feb	A	FOREST SCHOOL	3-2	F		DEWDNEY EL	OLIVER FG	LOCKER WA	FARMER JH
20-Feb	A	CAMBRIDGE UNIV	0-4	F		SETON WJ	ANDERSON EP	ROE WN	GRUNDTVIG HT
02-Mar	N o	CLAPTON	2-4	LSCf	3,000	FORD FGL	WALTERS AM	WALTERS PM	LOCKER WA
09-Mar	A	RMC SANDHURST	0-2	F		DEWDNEY EL	LOCKER WA	SPRING-RICE G	GRUNDTVIG HT
13-Mar	A	ST MARYS HOSPITAL	8-1	F		DEWDNEY EL	BICKLEY F	FARMER JH	BLENKIRON TW
20-Apr	A	DERBY COUNTY	1-2	F	2,000	STONE ACS	MORLEY HA	MOON EG	DISBROWE EJ

5	6	7	8	9	10	11
BICKLEY F	WACE V	CRESSWELL CE	LEMAN DC	WOODHOUSE WM 2	PROBYN PC	GLOSSOP AGB
BLENKIRON TW	PROBYN PC	SAUL FJ	NIXON AC	LEMAN DC	NELSON JL	
CHRISTIAN FW	WALTERS JH 2	WACE HC	NELSON JL	WOODHOUSE WM		
LEETE N	PAUL JP	MUNRO CE	HEMMERDE AJ	PAUL JE 1	THORNE FG	HERVEY RM
WALTON GF	BLENKIRON TW	FOX CJM 1	PAWSON FW	CARPMAEL WP	THORNE FG	HASKETT-SMITH WP 1
BICKLEY F	RUTTER EC	CRESSWELL CE 1	HARVEY RM	WOODHOUSE WM 1	FOLEY AL	
FORD HA	BOND F	PECK HC	FARMER JH	FOX CJM 1	MARSHALL EW	HUMPHREY EJ 1
CARPMAEL WP	HUMPHREYS H 1	PAUL JE 1	PRINCEP PC	FOX CJM 1	COLEMAN S 2	FARMER JH
BICKLEY F	FORD HA	NELSON JL	THORNE FG	WOODHOUSE WM	PROBYN PC	GLOSSOP AGB 1
RYDE FC	WACE HC	MARSHALL HM 1	WACE A	HASKETT-SMITH WP	GRUNDTVIG HT 1	O'CONNOR J
WALTON GF	SHARPE HA	NIXON AC	LEMAN DC	WOODHOUSE WM	ANDREWS F	FARMER JH
HARRISON H	POPHAM BG	GLOSSOP AGB	PROBYN PC	PRICE HC	NIXON AC	LEMAN DC 1
BLENKIRON TW	HARRISON H	GLOSSOP AGB	AINGER WH	PRICE HC	HOGARTH RG	PROBYN PC
BALFOUR AM	WACE C	CRESSWELL CE	PIGGOTT MT 1	FOLEY AL 2	LISTER LH	BICKLEY F
RUTTER EC	WOODHOUSE WM	BICKLEY F	LISTER LH	PRICE HC	CURRIE CE	HOGARTH RG
POPHAM BG 1	OLIVER FG	CRESSWELL CE	PIGGOTT MT 1	SHEPHERD J	SMITH Dr J 2	ANDREWS F
BALFOUR AM	MITCHELL EJD	CRESSWELL CE	NIXON AC	LEMAN DC 1	LISTER LH	PROBYN PC
PAUL JP	HARVEY RM	PIGGOTT MT	MARSHALL EM	SAVILLE AC		
OLIVER FG	KNAPP T	SMITH Dr J	SHEPHERD W	FOX CJM	ANDREWS F	STOATS H
HUMPHREY EJ	JANSEN FW	MARSHALL EW	LUSHINGTON T	PAWSON FW 2	HASKETT-SMITH WP	FOX CJM 2
HARRISON H	FERNIE FE	HOGARTH RG	GLOSSOP AGB	NELSON JL 1	BAIN FW 1	PAUL JE
POPHAM BG	STREET EC	MARSHALL EW 1	BICKLEY F	SMITH Dr J 2	FORT HR	KING AL
BALFOUR AM	BARKER RR	LISTER LH	BICKLEY F	PAWSON FW 2	GRUNDTVIG HT 1	HOGARTH RG
HARRISON H	BLENKIRON TW	NIXON AC	LEMAN DC	PROBYN PC	AINGER WH	GLOSSOP AGB
HARRISON H	BLENKIRON TW	PROBYN PC 1	GLOSSOP AGB	AINGER WH 1	LEMAN DC 1	NIXON AC
WACE HC	HASKETT-SMITH GB	PECK JH	BICKLEY F	FOX CJM 1	HARRISON H	LEMAN DC 1
BALFOUR AM	TURNER H	HASKETT-SMITH GB	PECK JH	LEMAN RC	BROOKS	CONNOLLY
BALFOUR AM	WACE C	LEMAN DC	FOX CJM 1	PECK JH 2	BICKLEY F	
BALFOUR AM	WINSLOW G	BICKLEY F 1	PROBYN PC	NIXON AC 2	LEMAN DC 2	LEMAN RC 1
BARRACLOUGH HC 1	FOSTER A	ADAMS FE 1	GRUNDTVIG HT 1	MACDONALD CJ 1	LEMAN RC 1	PECK JH
RYDE FC	STEVENS GP	EARLE FA	GRUNDTVIG HT	PRICE HC	DICKINSON SC	ADAMS FE
BALFOUR AM	BICKLEY F	ADAMS FE	PECK JH	DICKINSON SC	GLOSSOP AGB	GRUNDTVIG HT
BELLHOUSE	HENDERSON	THOMPSON	AINGER WH 1	VEITCH JG 1	WALTERS HM	NELSON JL
BARKER RR	SUBSTITUTE	NIXON AC 1	LEMAN AC 1	LEMAN RC	LOUNDES M	GRUNDTVIG HT
WREFORD-BROWN C	BLENKIRON TW	AINGER WH	GRESSON CHR	VEITCH JG 1	WILSON GL 2	WALTERS HM
HARRISON H	MITCHELL EJD	BICKLEY F	GRESSON CHR	VEITCH JG 2	WALTERS HM 2	NELSON JL
HARRISON H	BLENKIRON TW	GRESSON CHR 1	AINGER WH 1	WALTERS HM	NELSON JL 1	VEITCH JG 1
FOSTER A	WINSLOW G	LEMAN RC	LEMAN DC 2	NIXON AC 1	ADAMS FE	GRUNDTVIG HT
BLENKIRON TW	HENDERSON	GRESSON CHR	AINGER WH 2	WALTERS HM	NELSON JL	VEITCH JG
BELLHOUSE TW	HENDERSON M	GRESSON CHR	AINGER WH	VEITCH JG	NIXON AC	NELSON GL
MITCHELL EJD	BELLHOUSE TW	NIXON AC	AINGER WH	VEITCH JG	PAUL JP	NELSON JL
BELLHOUSE EW	BLENKIRON TW	GRESSON CHR	AINGER WH	WALTERS HM	NIXON AC	VEITCH JG
BELLHOUSE EW	BLENKIRON TW	AINGER WH	BICKLEY F	VEITCH JG	NIXON AC	WALTERS HM
LEMAN GC	WATT J	LEMAN DC	AINGER WH	NIXON AC 3	LEMAN RC	
LEMAN GC	HARRISON H 1	ADAMS FE	WALTERS HM 3	NIXON AC	LEMAN DC	GLOSSOP AGB
		WOODHOUSE WM 1	BARRACLOUGH HC 1	LISTER LH 1	LEMAN DC 1	
BLENKIRON TW	HARRISON H	ADAMS FE	PROBYN PC 2	PAWSON FW	LEMAN DC 1	NIXON AC 1
PAUL	BLENKIRON TW	LOWNDES MJ	LEMAN RC 2	LISTER LH 1	GRUNDTVIG HT	CRESSWELL CE
BLENKIRON TW	FARMER JH	PECK HC 1	PECK JH	LEMAN RC 1	ANDREWS E	PIGGOTT MT
RYDE FC	STREET EC	CRESSWELL CE	LISTER LH	LEMAN RC	GRUNDTVIG HT	LOWNDES MJ 1
WACE C	WOODHOUSE WM	PECK JH	HOARE AR 1	LEMAN RC 1	LOWNDES MJ	EARLE FA
HARRISON H	BARKER RR	AINGER WH	STURGESS-JONES TO	HOGARTH RG 1	LEMAN DC	LEMAN RC
PAUL JP	RYDE FC	EARLE FA	GRUNDTVIG HT	PECK JH	HEMMERDE AJ	FURBER 1
LUSHINGTON G 1	ALEXANDER EB	MARSHALL HW	PECK JH 1	BICKLEY F	BURGE F	CASSWELL AE 1
HARRISON H	BICKLEY F	PARRY CW	LEMAN DC	DUNN ATB	STANBROUGH WF	PROBYN PC
BLENKIRON TW	ROE WN	LEMAN DC 1	NIXON AC	AINGER WH 1	PROBYN PC	GLOSSOP AGB
OLIVER FG	LUSHINGTON G	BURGE F	PECK JH	LOWNDES MJ	MARSHALL EW	GRAY
LUSHINGTON G	CARPMAEL WP	AINGER WH 7	LOWNDES MJ 1	MARSHALL EW	BURGE F	
BELLHOUSE EW	ANDERSON WC	AINGER WH	LOWNDES MJ	NIXON AC	WALTERS HM 1	COOPER FJ

1889/90

DATE	VEN	OPPONENTS	RES	COMP	ATT	1	2	3	4
14-Sep	A	ROYAL ARSENAL	0-6	F	2,500	STONE ACS	BARKER RR	WALTERS AM	BICKLEY F
21-Sep	A	CHATHAM	5-0	F	3,000	GRANT-WILSON CW	JACKSON CH	BARKER RR	FARMER JH 1
21-Sep	A	POLYTECHNIC WANDERERS	5-1	F		BAGSHAW WH	PAUL JP	BARRACLOUGH HC 1	MITCHELL EJD
25-Sep	A	ST MARKS COLLEGE	3-1	F		STONE ACS	BARKER RR	BARRACLOUGH HC	CARPMAEL WP
28-Sep	A	CLAPTON	0-1	F	1,000	STONE ACS	WALTERS AM	BARKER RR	PAUL JP
28-Sep	A	OLD ST MARKS	1-9	F	%	GRANT-WILSON CW	JACKSON CH	GRUNDTVIG HT	BLENKIRON TW
02-Oct	A	CHARTERHOUSE	3-3	F		MURPHY JK	SHEPPARD WF	BARKER RR	SHAW NF
03-Oct	A	ROYAL ENGINEERS	5-1	F	%				
09-Oct	A	ST MARYS HOSPITAL	7-5	F		GRANT-WILSON CW	LOCKER WA	BARKER RR	LEMAN RC
12-Oct	N o	SUNDERLAND	1-3	F	2,000	WILKINSON LR	WALTERS AM	WALTERS PM	HOLDEN-WHITE C
16-Oct	A	HERMOSA SCHOOL	6-4	F		BLACK R	FERNIE FE	FRERE E	CARPMAEL WP
19-Oct	H ut	RMC SANDHURST	13-2	F	%	BIGGS WH	BICKLEY F	POWELL JP	MITCHELL EJD
23-Oct	H ut	OLD ETONIANS	11-3	F		SOWLER T	BARKER RR	PELLY FR	PARES B
23-Oct	A	CAMBRIDGE UNIV	0-7	F		GRANT-WILSON CW	FERNIE FE	CARSON HJ	SHAW NF
26-Oct	N o	SWIFTS	3-8	FAC2Q		SAMSON EM	JACKSON CH	BARKER RR	ROE WN
30-Oct	H	HIGHGATE SCHOOL	4-0	F		SOWLER T	BARKER RR	PELLY FR	MUNDAHL HS
02-Nov	A	CHISWICK PARK	3-2	LSC2		SAMSON EM	PELLY FR	BARKER RR	HOLDEN-WHITE C
07-Nov	H ut	ST BARTHOLOMEWS H	5-5	F		DOBSON HL	MOON EG	BARKER RR	BICKLEY F 2
09-Nov	A	GREAT MARLOW	1-2	F		SETON WJ	OLIVER FG	JACKSON CH	WREFORD-BROWN C
12-Nov	A	FOREST SCHOOL	5-3	F	%	'SUB' A	OLIVER FG	BARKER RR	CROSS FJK
13-Nov	H ut	ST THOMAS' HOSPITAL	1-2	F		'DODGESON' EL	OLIVER FG	HASKETT-SMITH H	LUSHINGTON G
13-Nov	A	BRIGHTON COLLEGE	4-1	F		GREENWOOD WW	ANDERSON EP	PELLY FR	BARKER RR
18-Nov	A	BURSLEM PORT VALE	1-3	F		SOWLER T	BARKER RR	MORLEY HA	LORAINE WH
19-Nov	A	REPTON SCHOOL	2-6	F		SOWLER T	MORLEY HA	BARKER RR	FERNIE FE
20-Nov	A	RMA WOOLWICH	3-1	F		SETON WJ	PELLY FR	BARKER RR	CROSS FJK
23-Nov	H ut	VULCAN	6-0	LSC3	%	SOWLER T	BARKER RR	MUNDAHL HS	BALFOUR AM
23-Nov	A	BECKENHAM	0-0	F		ALSTON HN	COWLE J	PLATT GM	DRUMMOND EH
26-Nov	N1	EVERTON	2-7	F		MOON WR	WALTERS AM	MORLEY HA	CROSS FJK
27-Nov	H ut	INCOGNITI	4-2	F	%	WALKER A	PELLY FR	HASKETT-SMITH F 1	BICKLEY F
30-Nov	H	ST JOHN'S SCHOOL	5-2	F			COWIE RM	MUNDAHL HS	
10-Dec	H ut	GUY'S HOSPITAL	7-1	F	#	WALKER A	PELLY FR	BARKER RR	BICKLEY F
12-Dec	H o	OXFORD UNIVERSITY	1-2	F		SETON WJ	PELLY FR	BARKER RR	LORAINE WH
14-Dec	N1	OLD WESTMINSTERS	1-1	LSC4		SETON WJ	JACKSON CH	NELSON JL	BARKER RR
14-Dec	H o	DERBY COUNTY	1-1	F		VOGEL FL	WALTERS PM	WALTERS AM	HOLDEN-WHITE C
16-Dec	N qc	OLD ETONIANS	4-3	F		SETON WJ	MOON EG	WALTON GF	LORAINE WH
18-Dec	A	SUSSEX MARTLETS	4-3	F					
19-Dec	H ut	MR WH LORAINE'S XI	1-1	F		BLAKER HR	NESON F	BARKER RR	MUNDAHL HS
19-Dec	A	POLYTECHNIC WANDERERS	0-7	F		TROWEL JW (SUB)	PROTHERO AG	BROUGHTON L (sub)	KING CH
20-Dec	H ut	MR GRANT WILSON'S XI	4-2	F		WALKER A	SMITH WP	CRAWLEY HH	SMITH WD
21-Dec	A	OLD WESTMINSTERS	0-0	LSC4		SETON WJ	NELSON JL	JACKSON CH	MITCHELL EJD
21-Dec	A	LONDON CALEDONIANS	0-8	F		GRUNDTVIG HT	FRY CB	MUNDAHL HS	DRUMMOND EH
23-Dec	N o	SHEFFIELD UTD	1-0	F		MOON WR	FRY CB	NELSON JL	MITCHELL EJD
24-Dec	H ut	SOMERSET ROVERS	4-5	F		AN OTHER	JACKSON CH	FRY CB	BICKLEY F 1
26-Dec	N d	LONDON CALEDONIANS	0-6	F		SETON WJ	COWIE RM	HASKETT-SMITH WP	WATT J
26-Dec	A	OLD CRANLEIGHANS	5-2	F		GRUNDTVIG HT	PROTHERO AG	OLIVER FG	HAWES DM
26-Dec	A	NORTHAMPTONSHIRE	2-5	F	3,000	BLAKER HR	JACKSON CH	BARKER RR	CRAWLEY EC
26-Dec	A	LINCOLN CITY	1-6	F		MOON WR	WALTERS AM	NELSON JL	TOPHAM AG
26-Dec	A	LOUGHBOROUGH TOWN	2-1	F		GRANT-WILSON CW	MORLEY HA	FRY CB	PAUL JP
27-Dec	A	DERBY COUNTY	3-4	F		MOON WR	FRY CB	MORLEY HA	TOPHAM AG
27-Dec	A	SHEFFIELD UTD	3-3	F	2,000	GRANT-WILSON CW	HARRISON AH	NELSON TL	LORAINE WH
28-Dec	A	GRIMSBY TOWN	2-5	F	1,500	SETON WJ	NELSON JL	FRY CB	TOPHAM R
28-Dec	H ut	OLD HARROVIANS	4-3	F	og	SHEPHERD W	JACKSON CH	OLIVER FG	WACE HC
30-Dec	A	EVERTON	2-3	F	% 3,000	SETON WJ	FRY CB	NELSON JL	TOPHAM AG
31-Dec	A	LIVERPOOL RAMBLERS	3-0	F		GRANT-WILSON CW	MOON EG	NELSON JL	LORAINE WH
01-Jan	A	NEWCASTLE EAST END	2-0	F	*	SETON WJ	FRY CB	NELSON JL	TOPHAM AG
02-Jan	A	SUNDERLAND	2-3	F	4,000	SETON WJ	FRY CB	NELSON JL	MITCHELL EJD
08-Jan	N o	OLD WESTMINSTERS	0-4	LSC4		SETON WJ	JACKSON CH	FRY CB	NELSON JL
10-Jan	H ut	OLD BRIGHTONIANS	5-1	F		AN OTHER	FRY CB	NELSON JL	LORAINE WH 1
11-Jan	H ut	OLD WYKEHAMISTS	4-6	F	%				
18-Jan	H ut	CRUSADERS	3-2	F	% ##	BAGSHAW WH	FRY CB	PAUL JP	TEALE MA
18-Jan	A	WEST KENT	0-1	F					
22-Jan	H ut	ST BARTHOLOMEWS H	1-3	F		SETON WJ	FRY CB	NELSON TL	WINSLOW HP
25-Jan	H ut	CHATHAM	1-3	F		SETON WJ	NELSON TL	RYDE FC	BICKLEY F
01-Feb	A	CLAPTON	2-3	LCC1		SETON WJ	PELLY FR	NELSON TL	LORAINE WH
08-Feb	A	WESTMINSTER SCHOOL	4-4	F	%				
12-Feb	A	ST BARTHOLOMEWS H	1-1	F		SETON WJ	PELLY FR	SHEPPARD WF	HARRISON H
18-Feb	A	FOREST SCHOOL	7-0	F	%	MARSHALL EW	HASKETT-SMITH WP	HASKETT-SMITH H	COURT PH
24-Feb	A	ASTON VILLA	0-4	F		SETON WJ	MORLEY HA	NELSON JL	HARRISON H
26-Feb	A	PHILBERDS	1-4	F	%	MARSHALL EW	SHEPPARD WF	PELLY FR	MERK FH
01-Mar	A	ILFORD	1-4	F		BAGSHAW WH	CRAWLEY PAS	CHAPMAN WG	BLENKIRON TW
01-Mar	A	ROYAL ENGINEERS	4-1	F	%				
05-Mar	A	WESTMINSTER CRITERIONS	15-0	F	og	SETON WJ	HASKETT-SMITH WP 1	FARMER JH	HARRISON H

5	6	7	8	9	10	11
HARRISON H	FARMER JH	RATHBONE EP	LEMAN DC	FURBER S	ADAMS FE	LEMAN RC
GRUNDTVIG HT	CARPMAEL WP	FURBER S	COX LL 1	VEITCH JG 3	GLOSSOP AGB	ADAMS FE
BLENKIRON TW	RUTTER RC	CRESSWELL CE	LEMAN DC 1	PAWSON FW 1	LEMAN RC 2	BICKLEY F
FISHER LG	AN OTHER	COX LL	VEITCH JG	PAWSON FW 3	LEMAN RC	LEMAN DC
FISHER LG	SYMONDS RH	ADAMS FE	FURBER S	RATHBONE EP	HARVEY RM	
OLIVER TJ	WATT J	CRESSWELL CE	PAUL JP	PAWSON FW		MARSHALL EW
HARRISON H	RATHBONE EP	LEMAN DC 1	LEMAN RC	ADAMS FE	COTTERILL GH 1	VEITCH JG 1
BICKLEY F	CARPMAEL WP	GLOSSOP AGB	AINGER WH 4	PAWSON FW 2	COX LL	LEMAN DC 1
BLENKIRON TW	MITCHELL EJD	GLOSSOP AGB	HOGARTH RG 1	NIXON AC	COTTERILL GH	FURBER S
LORAINE WH	PARES B	WINSLOW HP 1	LEMAN RC	PAWSON FW 2	AINGER WH 2	BICKLEY F 1
FISHER LG	RATHBONE EP 1	WALTERS HM 5	AINGER WH 2	ADAMS FE 1	GLOSSOP AGB 3	
HOLDEN-WHITE C	CROSS FJK	FURBER S 3	ADAMS FE	AINGER WH 3	WALTERS HM 4	RATHBONE EP 1
FISHER LG	DANIEL AM	COX S	NIXON AC	PAWSON FW	PROBYN PC	STEWART HC
CROSS FJK	PARES B	GLOSSOP AGB	ADAMS FE	FURBER S 1	WALTERS HM 1	RATHBONE EP 1
STREET EC	EVORS CA	MARSHALL EW	FARDELL ES 1	BICKLEY F	WALTERS HM 2	COX LL 1
BLENKIRON TW	MUNDAHL HS	JACKSON CH 1	FURBER S	NIXON AC 1	DICKINSON SC	GLOSSOP AGB 1
GRANT-WILSON CW	PEARS AF	GLOSSOP AGB	ADAMS FE	PAWSON FW 1	WALTERS HM 2	WINSLOW HP
MERK C	CRAWLEY EC	PAGE C	MARSHALL EW	REEVE WG 1	WINSLOW HP	DAVIES GL
HASKETT-SMITH WP	'HARDWORKER' A	MARSHALL EW	LETTS SE	BICKLEY F	GLOSSOP AGB	ADAMS FE
MERK FH	THURWELL ES	MARSHALL EW	PERKS H	FOX CJM	PAWSON FW 1	BLAGDEN EJ
LETTE N	BOND CH	HUGHES-ONSLOW H	GREY CE	HOPKINS WH 1	BICKLEY F 1	LETTS SE 2
BLUNT E	FERNIE FE	ADAMS FE	DALGLEISH EF	NIXON AC	COX LL	CARTER WL 1
BLOUNT GB	DAVIES H	ADAMS FE	PALAIRET LCH 1	CHATTERTON W 1	DALGLEISH EF	BICKLEY F
HESELTINE C	CARPMAEL WP	GLOSSOP AGB 1	MARSHALL EW 2	BICKLEY F	LUSHINGTON G	SMITH WP
OTHER AN	HOLDEN-WHITE C	GLOSSOP AGB	DICKINSON SC	FURBER S	NELSON JL	RATHBONE EP
HUGHES-ONSLOW H	BURGE F	BEDFORD AER	MARSHALL EW			
DANIEL AM	LORAINE WH	GLOSSOP AGB	CLARK TP	FOX CJM 2	FURBER S	COX LL
BLENKIRON TW	PAWSON FW 1	ONSLOW HH	BURGE F	BEDFORD AER	MARSHALL EW	AN OTHER
BLENKIRON TW 2			DICKINSON SC 1		HEMMERDE J 1	RATHBONE EP 1
CRAWLEY HH	CARPMAEL WP	ADAMS FE 1	HUGHES-ONSLOW H 1	WINSLOW G 1	BARRACLOUGH HC 4	CRESSWELL CE
CROSS FJK	CRAWLEY EC	GLOSSOP AGB	BICKLEY F	FURBER S 1	LEMAN DC	COX LL
BICKLEY F	CRAWLEY HH	DICKINSON SC	GLOSSOP AGB 1	NIXON AC	LEMAN DC	FURBER S
CROSS FJK	TOPHAM AG	KNOX H	PAINE HN	LINDLEY T 1	COX LL	AMOS HGM
PROTHERO AG	TEALE MA 1	GLOSSOP AGB	STEWART HC 1	VEITCH JG 2	FURBER S	LEMAN DC
		PROBYN PC 2		VEITCH JG 2		
BALFOUR AM	CRAWLEY HH	WINSLOW G	DICKINSON SC	NIXON AC	PAGE C 1	LEMAN DC
HAWES DM	HASTINGS F (sub)	DAWSON GW	JONES FET	COWLEY HC	WALKER T	THINN F
WACE R	MITCHELL EJD	CRESSWELL CE	STEWART HC 3	MARSHALL F 1	THINN GA	KING CH
BICKLEY F	BARKER RR	GLOSSOP AGB	DICKINSON SC	NIXON AC	LEMAN DC	FURBER S
CRAWLEY HH	WALTER FH	ADAMS FE	SLINGER CW	CRESSWELL CE	BURGE F	
WREFORD-BROWN C	TOPHAM AG	GLOSSOP AGB	PECK HC	NIXON AC	KNOX H 1	STEWART HC
CRAWLEY HH	BALFOUR AM	GRANT-WILSON CW	ADAMS FE	ARMSTRONG PM 1	MARTYN AJK	MOON WR 2
COWAN T	PEILE AB	LUSHINGTON G	STIRLING W	ROGERSON W	MARSHALL EW	
DUDLEY-SMITH W	DRUMMOND EH	PARKS JH	HEMMERDE AF 2	PIGGOTT MT 2	LISTER LH 1	WALTER FH
BICKLEY F	BALFOUR AM	PROBYN PC	ADAMS FE 1	MARTYN AJK	BURGE F 1	SINGER
MUNDAHL HS	MITCHELL JP	TOPHAM R	WOODBRIDGE AR	NIXON AC	VEITCH JG 1	FURBER S
BELLHOUSE JW	LORAINE WH	MOON RG	PECK HC	AINGER WH 2	WALTERS HM	CARTER CC
MITCHELL EJD	CROSS FJK	WOODBRIDGE AR	NIXON AC	AINGER WH 1	WALTERS HM 1	SANDILANDS RR 1
BELLHOUSE EW	BARKER RR	STANBROUGH MH 1	FURBER S 1	ADAMS FE	PECK HC 1	TOPHAM HG
BELLHOUSE GW	MUNDAHL HS	SANDILANDS RR	WALTERS HM 1	NIXON AC	TOPHAM AG 1	AINGER WH
CRAWLEY HH	ARMSTRONG FC	BURGE F	MARSHALL EW	LISTER LH 3	DICKINSON SC	WALTER FH
MITCHELL EJD	CROSS FJK	WOODBRIDGE AR	NIXON AC	TOPHAM R	WALTERS HM 1	SANDILANDS RR
BELLHOUSE EW	BICKLEY F	WOODBRIDGE AR 1	BLENKIRON TW 1	TOPHAM R	SANDILANDS RR 1	CROSS FJK
MITCHELL EJD	CROSS FJK	WOODBRIDGE AR	NIXON AC 1	TOPHAM R	WALTERS HM	SANDILANDS RR
BELLHOUSE GW	TOPHAM AG	AINGER WH	NIXON AC	TOPHAM R 1	SANDILANDS RR	WALTERS HM 1
CARPMAEL WP	CRAWLEY HH	LEMAN DC	FURBER S	NIXON AC	DICKINSON SC	GLOSSOP AGB
MERK FH	WINSLOW G	BEASLEY C 1	SETON WJ	LISTER LH 1	BARRACLOUGH HC 2	HARVEY RM
WINSLOW HP	POLEHAMPTON FW	GLOSSOP AGB	AUSTIN W	FURBER S	HEMMERDE J	CRESSWELL CE
SAUNDERS FE	OLIVER FG	AINGER WH	WALTER FH	PAWSON FW 1	FOX CJM	ISWICK-PARKER CH
POLEHAMPTON EH	SHEPPARD H	WALTER FH	ADAMS FE 1	FORD FGJ	HEMMERDE J	MARSHALL EW
TEALE MA	POLEHAMPTON EH	PRYCE-JONES WE	NIXON AC	PAWSON FW	BARRACLOUGH HC 1	COX LL 1
CARPMAEL WP	BLENKIRON TW	WALTER FH	MARSHALL EW	PECK JH	HOPKINS JC 1	CRESSWELL CE
GRANT CW	CARTER WL	PECK JH	FORD FGJ	SINGER S		
TOPHAM AG	MUNDAHL HS	STREET F	PRYCE-JONES WE	TOPHAM R	HANSARD H	REAVE J
COURT PH	RAWLEY HC	MILLEN GMF	SEVIER-DAVIES G	LUSHINGTON G	BAIN FW	BEASLEY C
NOTCUTT SA	CRAWLEY HH	LUSHINGTON G	MARSHALL EW	FORD FGJ 1	CRESSWELL CE	
PROTHERO AG	FERNIE FE	FORD FGJ	SAUL CA	WALTERS HM 7	NIXON AC 2	FURBER S 4

08-Mar	A	CLAPTON	1-7	F	1,000	DEWDNEY EL	MUNRO CE	BARKER RA	MUNDAHL HS
08-Mar	A	RMC SANDHURST	2-3	F	%				
15-Mar	A	OLD ST MARKS	1-0	F	%				
19-Mar	A	OLD ETONIANS	4-1	F		SETON WJ	SHEPPARD WF	PROTHERO AG	HOLDEN-WHITE C
22-Mar	A	CHARTERHOUSE	2-2	F		SETON WJ	SHEPPARD WF	COWIE RM	BARKER RR
05-Apr	A	HUNTINGDON & DISTRICT	3-0	F		SETON WJ	BARKER RR	MUSPRATT FC	TOPHAM AG
07-Apr	A	KIDDERMINSTER OLYMPIC	2-2	F	3,500	SETON WJ	BARKER RR	MUNDAHL HS	BLENKIRON TW
08-Apr	A	DERBY COUNTY	1-3	F	1,500	SETON WJ	BARKER RR	MALDEN AW	TOPHAM AG
?	A	OXFORD UNIVERSITY	2-4	F	%				

12 A SIDE - NO12 - WINSLOW HP
12 A SIDE - NO12 - WALTER FH

CASUALS ALL TIME LEADING APPEARANCES

NAME	APPS
KING SL	518
BICKLEY F	259
BARKER RR	243
DRAKE CF	207
SERGEANT PA	195
COUCHMAN LT	192
POLLOCK-HODSOLL GB	189
DIXON GF	188
EVANS FL	169
KINGSTON LJ	158
BARRETT HR	149
ROSS T	139
HATTON COS	135
KNIGHT JG	135
DUBUIS HF	134
PAYNE HG	129
WRIGHT RG	128
FABIAN AH	124
HOWELL M	124
HUDDLE LT	124
DURRANT RB	116
PELLY FR	116
HILLEARY RM	113
NIXON AC	113
EWER FH	112
ALEXANDER CW	110
PINFIELD RG	110
BLENKIRON TW	109
WILSON CE	107
CUTTER RC	103
CLEAVE R	100

BARKER RR	NORMAN NC	FORD FGJ 1	BARRACLOUGH HC	WALTERS HM	HASKETT-SMITH WP	
HARRISON H	MERK FH	BARRACLOUGH HC	FURBER S	PAWSON FW 1	WALTERS HM 3	WALTER FH
COOPER NC	TOPHAM AG	WALTER JH	BLENKIRON TW 2	NIXON AC	SMITH HR	CRESSWELL CE
LORAINE WH	COOPER NC	WALTERS HM 1	BLENKIRON TW	NIXON AC 2	BARRACLOUGH HC	FURBER S
LORAINE WH	TOPHAM AG	BARRACLOUGH HC	FURBER S 1	RHODES HA	WALTERS HM 1	NIXON AC
COURT PH	LORAINE WH	BARRACLOUGH HC	NIXON AC	RHODES HA 1	WILSON	FURBER S

CASUALS ALL TIME LEADING GOAL SCORERS

NAME	GOALS
WRIGHT RG	84
DURRANT RB	82
ALEXANDER CW	77
DRAKE CF	55
EDWARDS V	55
CUTTER RC	52
FERNIE JF	52
DIXON GF	49
FURBER S	49
TAYLOR SS	49
KINGSTON LJ	48
CLEMENTS BA	48
MCIVER CD	46
KNOX H	46
TOONE WP	44
SHEARER EDR	44
NIXON AC	43
BICKLEY F	42
COUCHMAN LT	42
BRISLEY CE	42
TURNER R	42
SMITH GO	42
LEE J	41
FABIAN AH	40
LOCKTON JH	39
MONTGOMERY PJ	38
PERKINS TN	38
HOWELL M	37
JENKINS RG	37
WALTERS HM	36
DUBUIS HF	32

1890/91

DATE	VEN	OPPONENTS	RES	COMP	ATT	1	2	3	4
13-Sep	A	ROYAL ARSENAL	4-5	F		FABER	FRY CB	HARRISON AH	WINCKWORTH WN
20-Sep	H ws	OLD WYKEHAMISTS	5-3	F					
20-Sep	A	CHATHAM	3-2	F	og 3,000	KENNEDY AGO	WELLS WC	PELLY FR	TOPHAM AG
24-Sep	A	ST MARKS COLLEGE	2-3	F	%	BRANDON C	PELLY FR	MOON EG	BARKER RR
27-Sep	A	OLD ST MARKS	0-5	F		DEWDNEY EL	FEVEZ AL	WALKER EH	TEWSON S
27-Sep	A	SOMERSET ROVERS	10-0	F		GRANT-WILSON CW	STANCOMB FW	BARKER RR	COWIE RM
27-Sep	A	GREAT MARLOW	1-3	F		WALKER A	WISE W (SUB)	MOON EG	BLENKIRON TW
01-Oct	A	CHARTERHOUSE	1-2	F		BRANDON C	COWIE RM	PARES B	PELLY FR
04-Oct	?	CROUCH END	2-2	F	%				
08-Oct	A	BRUCE CASTLE SCHOOL	9-2	F		BLAKE GC	NELSON TL	BARKER RR	OLIVER FG 1
11-Oct	N o	OLD ETONIANS	5-3	F	500	WALKER A	NELSON TL	HARRISON AH	TEALE MA
15-Oct	A	SCOTS GUARDS	3-3	F	% 400	WALKER A	LORAINE WH	OLIVER FG	SMITH CA
18-Oct	A	SWIFTS	2-6	F		ELIOT MG	NELSON TL	MALDEN AW	BARKER MM
18-Oct	H ws	RMC SANDHURST	1-7	F	%	DEWDNEY EL	FLETCHER RH	WALKER WH	RUTTER EC
22-Oct	A	CAMBRIDGE UNIV	1-3	F		GUGGISBERG FG	WELLS WC	PELLY FR	BARKER RR
22-Oct	A	HIGHGATE SCHOOL	5-6	F		DEWDNEY EL	TEWSON S	WOODBRIDGE GH	BLOUNT GB
23-Oct	A	ROYAL ENGINEERS	1-6	F		WALKER RH	MILLS	PARES B	OLIVER FG
25-Oct	A	STOKE	2-4	F	%				
29-Oct	H ws	GUY'S HOSPITAL	1-4	F		CRESSWELL CE	JONES FET	MUSPRATT WE	OLIVER FG
01-Nov	A	READING	1-3	F		RICHARDS CJR	VEITCH HM	FORD HA	BICKLEY F
03-Nov	H ws	ST THOMAS' HOSPITAL	4-1	F	%	FRERE A	MUSPRATT WE	STEVENS GP	LORAINE WH
05-Nov	A	OXFORD UNIVERSITY	2-2	F		SETON WJ	PELLY FR	MOON EG	BICKLEY F
08-Nov	A	OLD WESTMINSTERS	3-0	F		SETON WJ	SHEPPARD WF	OLIVER FG	STEELE HS
11-Nov	A	FOREST SCHOOL	3-2	F		FOX RH	STEVENS GP	MUSPRATT WE	RUSSELL WH
12-Nov	H ws	ST BARTHOLOMEWS H	2-7	F		SUBSTITUTE	NELSON TL	OLIVER FG	TOPHAM AG
15-Nov	A	CHISWICK PARK	3-6	F		GRUNDTVIG HT	NELSON TL	BARKER RR	POLEHAMPTON EH
19-Nov	A	BRUCE CASTLE SCHOOL	3-6	F		KNOX H	MASON FW	SMITH WD 1	PATERSON JN
19-Nov	A	RMA WOOLWICH	1-3	F	%				
22-Nov	A	ROTHERHAM TOWN	0-6	F		SETON WJ	NELSON TL	PELLY FR	PARES B
22-Nov	A	ERITH	1-7	F		VOGEL FL			
24-Nov	A	BURSLEM PORT VALE	0-4	F	1,000	VOGEL FL	NELSON TL	MUSPRATT WE	BARKER RR
25-Nov	A	REPTON SCHOOL	1-1	F		VOGEL FL	NELSON TL	MUSPRATT WE	PARES GL
06-Dec	A	ROYAL ARSENAL	0-0	F		GUGGISBERG FG	PAULL JR	NELSON TL	BROOK AK
06-Dec	H ws	OLD FORESTERS	0-0	F		HAWKSWORTH M	WOODBRIDGE CM	WINSLOW G	RENSHAW JAK
09-Dec	H ws	OLD REPTONIANS	1-4	F		VOGEL FL	NELSON TL	PAULL JR	KITTERMASTER FJ
13-Dec	A	CLAPHAM ROVERS	2-4	F		BOUSTEAD WH	SHEPPARD WF	WOODBRIDGE GH	WACE HC
26-Dec	A	LINCOLN CITY	3-3	F		GUGGISBERG FG	NELSON TL	FRY CB	BROOK AK
26-Dec	A	LOUGHBOROUGH TOWN	2-4	F	% 1,000	SETON WJ	MALDEN AW	PELLY FR	MITCHELL EJD
27-Dec	A	ASTON VILLA	2-7	F	% 2,000	GUGGISBERG FG	NELSON TL	PELLY FR	DISBROWE EJ
27-Dec	A	LEICESTER FOSSE	0-1	F		SETON WJ	MALDEN AW	FRY CB	BARKER RR
29-Dec	A	DERBY COUNTY	10-2	F		SETON WJ	NELSON TL	FRY CB	BROOK AK
30-Dec	A	SHEFFIELD UTD	0-7	F	2,000	GUGGISBERG FG	NELSON TL	FRY CB	BARKER RR
31-Dec	A	KIRKCALDY	3-3	F		SETON WJ	MALDEN AW	PELLY FR	DISBROWE EJ
01-Jan	A	PAISLEY ABERCORN	2-6	F	% 4,000	GUGGISBERG FG	BARKER RR	NELSON TL	LECKY JG
02-Jan	A	KINGS PARK	5-9	F	%	SETON WJ	NELSON TL	PELLY FR	LECKY JG
03-Jan	A	THIRD LANARK	1-4	F	5,000	SETON WJ	NELSON TL	PELLY FR	MONTGOMERY RM
17-Jan	A	ASTON VILLA	1-13	FAC1		SETON WJ	NELSON JL	PELLY FR	DISBROWE EJ
24-Jan	A	CLAPTON	8-1	LCC1	%	GUGGISBERG FG	PAULL JR	MUNDAHL HS	WALL C
28-Jan	A	OXFORD UNIVERSITY	1-3	F		SAMSON EM	PELLY FR	MUNDAHL HS	LORAINE WH
31-Jan	N d	LONDON CALEDONIANS	4-3	LSC1		SETON WJ	PELLY FR	NELSON TL	TEALE MA
07-Feb	H ws	SWIFTS	2-1	F		BAGSHAW WH	BARKER RR	OLIVER FG	STEVENS GP 1
07-Feb	A	CAMBRIDGE UNIV	0-9	F		SETON WJ	MOON EG	MUNDAHL HS	RENSHAW JAK
11-Feb	A	BRIGHTON COLLEGE	0-1	F		GUGGISBERG FG	OLIVER FG	STEVENS GP	HUGHES JR
14-Feb	H ws	OLD CRANLEIGHANS	4-0	F		BAGSHAW WH	SHEPPARD WF	PAUL JP	HUGHES JR 1
14-Feb	A	WESTMINSTER SCHOOL	5-5	F	%	DEWDNEY EL	COWIE RM	OLIVER FG	BICKLEY F
17-Feb	A	FOREST SCHOOL	5-0	F		HAILEY H	PELLY FR	STEVENS GP	PARES B
21-Feb	A	ROYAL ARSENAL	2-3	LSC2	7,000	SETON WJ	COWIE RM	FORD HA	TOPHAM AG
21-Feb	H ws	CHISWICK PARK	1-3	F		VOGEL FL	SAVILL L	TEWSON S	COURT PH
21-Feb	A	SURBITON HILL	1-3	F		CARTER GC	VEITCH HM	BREMNER K	WACE R
25-Feb	H ws	KING'S COLLEGE HOSP	1-0	F		DEWDNEY EL	MUSPRATT WE	STEVENS GP	WACE R
02-Mar	H pl	THIRD LANARK	0-2	F	1,500	SETON WJ	PELLY FR	LAWRENCE HC	COURT PH
07-Mar	A	GREAT MARLOW	1-0	LCCsf		GUGGISBERG FG	PELLY FR	CUMMING G	BICKLEY F
14-Mar	A	READING	1-4	F		ELIOT MG	PELLY FR	MUNDAHL HS	CHURCH MR
25-Mar	A	CHARTERHOUSE	3-1	F	%				
28-Mar	A	PRESTON NE	2-5	F	* 3,000	GUGGISBERG FG	NELSON TL	PELLY FR	MONTGOMERY RM
30-Mar	A	STOCKTON	2-2	F	%				
30-Mar	A	KETTERING	0-5	F		BRERETON	SQUIRE RT	MUNDAHL HS	PAUL JP
31-Mar	A	MIDDLESBROUGH IRONOPOLIS	0-4	F	2,000	GUGGISBERG FG	NELSON TL	PELLY FR	BROOK AK
09-Apr	A	ROYAL ENGINEERS	2-2	F		THOMAS W	PELLY FR	CUMMING G	CROSS FJK
11-Apr	A	REIGATE PRIORY	4-1	F	%	BAGSHAW WH	BLOUNT GB	PELLY FR	HOLDSWORTH C
18-Apr	N 1	OLD CARTHUSIANS	1-1	LCCf	2,500	GUGGISBERG FG	PELLY FR	NELSON TL	CROSS FJK
18-Apr	A	SWINDON TOWN	0-3	F		BAGSHAW WH	LAWRENCE HC	LAWRENCE GH	BLOUNT GB
18-Apr	A	READING	3-4	F		DEWDNEY EL	MUNDAHL HS	BARKER RR	PAUL JP
25-Apr	N 1	OLD CARTHUSIANS	5-2	LCCf	3,000	SETON WJ	PELLY FR	NELSON TL	CROSS FJK

5	6	7	8	9	10	11
BARKER RR	PARES B	NIXON AC 1	BARRACLOUGH HC	VEITCH JG	SANDILANDS RR 3	COX LL
BICKLEY F	BARKER RR	SMITH CA	FURBER S	NIXON AC 2	SANDILANDS RR	COX LL
WOODBRIDGE MJ	LEMAN DC	BARRACLOUGH HC	HAY AS	TOPHAM R 1	PEAKE HE	ADAMS FE
BAGSHAW EC	RUTTER EC	CRESSWELL CE	PARES B	NIX JS	HEMMERDE AJ	MARSHALL RW
WREFORD-BROWN C	BICKLEY F	FURBER S 1	SMITH CA 2	NIXON AC 2	COX LL 4	WELCH FCB 1
WOODBRIDGE GH	TOPHAM AG	ADAMS FE	LEMAN DC	WALTERS AM 1	BARRACLOUGH HC	WINSLOW HP
ROFFEY GW	COWIE HN	SMITH CA	PAWSON FW	ARMSTRONG FP	LEMAN DC 1	ADAMS FE
BLOUNT GB	CRESSWELL CE 1	BOWRING W	PAWSON FW 5	BARRACLOUGH HC 2	ANDREWS F	
BARKER RR	RUTTER EC	SMITH CA	GLOSSOP AGB	NIXON AC 1	WALTERS HM 4	COX LL
CARPMAEL HP	LORAINE WH	WALTERS HM 1	VEITCH JG	HUGHES-ONSLOW H	GLOSSOP AGB	WALKER HW 1
TEALE MA	PEARS AF	COX LL	WELCH FCB	REEVE WG	FURBER S 1	WOOD GR 1
BLENKIRON TW	TEWSON S	CRESSWELL CE	GREGORY SH	NIXON AC	FURBER S	LEMAN DC
HOSSACK AH	MESELTINE C	KNOX H	DEWHURST GP	NIXON AC 1	REDDY F	LEWIS CE
STREET G	OLIVER FG	HASKETT-SMITH F	HAWES DM 1	CRAWLEY HH 2	MERK FH 1	CRESSWELL CE 1
CRAWLEY HH	WOODHOUSE WM	HASKETT-SMITH F 1	KNOX H	MARSHALL EW		
BICKLEY F	PARES B	BATTERSEY HF	PECK HC	PAWSON FW 1	PECK JH	MARSHALL F
STEELE HS	FLETCHER RH	FURBER S	WOODHOUSE WM	GOODWIN A	PAWSON FW 1	PARES B
TOPHAM AG	OLIVER FG	CRESSWELL CE	WOODHOUSE WM	TOPHAM R	PAWSON FW	HAY RS
TOPHAM AG	LORAINE WH	TRINGHAM E	COTTERILL LL 2	TOPHAM R	NIXON AC	KNOX H
MERK T	TEALE MA	PERKE FH	COTTERILL LL 1	NIXON AC 2	LEMAN DC	BLAINE T
BONSEY WH	OLIVER FG	CRESSWELL CE	COOPER EC 2	SMITH WP	FOY CA	WALTERS HM 1
CARPMAEL HP	SUBSTITUTE	HAY RS	ADAMS FE	WALTERS HM 2	COOPER EC	PECK JH
BICKLEY F	STEELE HS	ADAMS FE 1	LEMAN DC	CLARKE TBA 2	BLAIN CF	BALLANTINE T
BICKLEY F	HASKETT-SMITH WP	FURBER AL	SLOCOCK R 1	BEASLEY J 1	BEWRING W	
BELLHOUSE EW	BICKLEY F	ADAMS FE	FURBER AL	NIXON AC	ROBINSON GM	BARKER RR
BLENKIRON TW		WALTER FH	FURBER ? 1			
BELLHOUSE EW	PARES B	ADAMS FE	ROBINSON WE	CLUXON A	FURBER S	SINGER CW
BELLHOUSE EW	BARKER RR	BLAIN CF	ADAMS FE	DEWHURST GP	SINGER AM 1	ROBINSON GM
BICKLEY F	BARKER RR	ROBINSON GM	PRYCE-JONES AW	CLARKE TBA	FURBER S	PERKS JE
RYDE FC	SETON WJ	NIX JS	CADMAN PSC	LISTER RH	SINGER CW	WALTER FH
BICKLEY F	TEALE MA	PATERSON D	AN OTHER	NIXON AC	KNOX H	LISTER LR 1
WACE R	WHINNEY H	RYDE FC	HAY RS 2	WALTER FH	PRESTON WD	
DISBROWE EJ	MONTGOMERY RM	HALLAM	TOPHAM R 2	NIXON AC	NEWBERRY HC 1	SANDILANDS RR
BICKLEY F	BARKER RR	PRYCE-JONES WE	FURBER S 1	HOPE RB	PERKS JE	COX S
MONTGOMERY RM	FERNIE	PRYCE-JONES WE	RHODES HA	TOPHAM R 1	NEWBERRY HC	NIXON AC
RADFORD T	BICKLEY F	COX S	PERKS JE	COTTERILL LL	HOPE RB	FURBER S
DISBROWE EJ	LECKY JG	NEWBERRY HC 2	TOPHAM R 3	CLARKE TBA 5	RHODES HA	COTTERILL LL
BROOK AK	LECKY JG	FURBER S	HOPE RB	COX LL	RHODES HA	PRYCE-JONES WE
NELSON TL	MONTGOMERY RM	HOPE RB	COTTERILL LL	TOPHAM R	NEWBERRY HC 3	PERKS JE
DISBROWE EJ	MONTGOMERY RM	PRYCE-JONES WE	HOPE RB 1	TOPHAM R	NEWBERRY HC	PERKS JE
DISBROWE EJ	BICKLEY F	PRYCE-JONES WE 1	HOPE RB	TOPHAM R 1	NEWBERRY HC	COX LL
DISBROWE EJ	LECKY JG	PRYCE-JONES WE	HOPE RB	TOPHAM R 1	NEWBERRY HC	COX LL
TOPHAM AG	IZARD HC	PRYCE-JONES WE	DEWHURST GP	TOPHAM R 1	RHODES HA	STREET F
MONTGOMERY RM	TOPHAM AG	PRYCE-JONES WE	REEVE WG	CLARKE TBA	KNOX H	CADMAN PSC
PROBYN PC	CROSS FJK	ADAMS FE	BARRACLOUGH HC	KNOX H	CADMAN PSC 1	SANDILANDS RR
COWIE RM	BARKER RR	ROBINSON GM 2	ADAMS FE 1	NIXON AC 1	COTTERILL LL	PERKS JE
HUNNARD F	SHATTOCK GO	CRESSWELL CE 1	WALTERS JH	HOWELL DL	HEMMERDE AJ	NIX JS
PARES B	KITTERMASTER FJ	ADAMS FE	COTTERILL LL	ROBINSON GM	KNOX H	PIERCE A
JACKSON F	CARPMAEL WP	WALTER FH	PEARLESS SH	HANNARD F	CRESSWELL CE	BICKLEY F
HOWELL DL 1	WALTER FH	CRESSWELL CE	HAWES DM	HUNNARD F	WHINNEY E 1	HASKETT-SMITH WF 1
RYDE FC	SHATTOCK GO	HEMMERDE AJ	MOON EG	LEMAN DC	STEVENS GF	PERKS JE
MUSPRATT WE 1	COLLISON C	HASKETT-SMITH WE	ADAMS FE	PARES GL 2	CRESSWELL CE 1	HAWES DM 1
BARKER RR	FLETCHER RH	SMITH CA	FURBER S 1	NIXON AC 1	LEMAN DC	COX S
BICKLEY F	FLETCHER RH	ADAMS FE	HOWELL DL 1	HEMMERDE AJ	NIX JS	
RYDE FC 1	HASKETT-SMITH WP	BAGSHAW WH	CRESSWELL CE			
HUGHES JR	JONES A	HASKETT-SMITH WP	TRINGHAM J	CRESSWELL CE 1		
DISBROWE EJ	MONTGOMERY RM	PRYCE-JONES AW	REEVE WG	CLARKE TBA	NIXON AC	PROBYN PC
SHATTOCK GO	BARKER RR	ADAMS FE	WOODHOUSE WM	VEITCH JG	PERKS JE 1	CLARKE TBA
BICKLEY F	OLIVER FG	PAGE C	WOODHOUSE WM	KNOX H	NIX JS	REEVE WG
BROOK AK	CROSS FJK	PRYCE-JONES AW	NIXON AC	CLARKE TBA	KNOX H 1	CADMAN PSC
TEWSON S	SHATTOCK GO	TURNER (SUB)	SINGER	GLENURE	HEMMERDE AJ	WALTER FH
BLOUNT GB	CUMMING G	PRYCE-JONES AW	KNOX H	NIXON AC	CADMAN PSC	BLANE
FABER	OTHER AN	KNOX H 1	WALTER FH 1	CARPMAEL WP	HOBART H	IIILL
BROOK AK	BICKLEY F	WALTER FH	KNOX H	CLARKE TBA	COX S	COX LL
BROOK AK	CUMMING G	PRYCE-JONES AW	KNOX H	CLARKE TBA	VEITCH JG	SANDILANDS RR 1
BAGSHAW NC	FULTON R	WOOD GR	PAGE C	WILLIAMS C	COX LL	COX S
PROBYN PC	CHARMAN FH	BEASLEY J 1	HOPE RB 1	LORAINE GH	ELLICOTT AE	TOPHAM R 1
BROOK AK	CUMMING G	PRYCE-JONES AW	CLARKE TBA 1	KNOX H 3	VEITCH JG	SANDILANDS RR 1

1891/92

DATE	VEN	OPPONENTS	RES	COMP	ATT	1	2	3	4
05-Sep	A	NEWCASTLE EAST END	0-4	F		GOSTLING EV	FRY CB	PELLY FR	GRIEVESON JE
12-Sep	A	ROYAL ARSENAL	1-2	F	4,500	GOSTLING EV	BLOUNT R	PELLY FR	TOPHAM AG
16-Sep	H ws	1ST SCOTS GUARDS	6-2	F		RYDON HL	PELLY FR	FRY CB	TOPHAM AG
19-Sep	A	CHATHAM	2-3	F	3,000	GOSTLING EV	PELLY FR	FRY CB	TOPHAM AG 1
23-Sep	H ws	2ND SCOTS GUARDS	1-0	F		RYDON HL	PELLY FR	FRY CB	BROOK AK
26-Sep	A	GRIMSBY TOWN	0-6	F					
26-Sep	A	SWINDON TOWN	1-9	F		RYDON HL	OLIVER FG	ANDREWS A (SUB)	MARTEN AB
26-Sep	A	MARLOW	1-2	F		BAGSHAW WH	BARRACLOUGH HC	SAVILL L	BUCKMASTER WS
30-Sep	N 1	OLD ETONIANS	2-6	F		RYDON HL	PELLY FR	BLAKER HR	CHURCH MR
03-Oct	H o	CLAPTON	3-2 aet	FAC1Q		GUGGISBERG FG	PELLY FR	FRY CB	TOPHAM AG
07-Oct	A	ROYAL INDIAN ENGINEERING CO.	4-2	F	%				
10-Oct	H o	DERBY COUNTY	0-4	F	700	GUGGISBERG FG	PELLY FR	FRY CB	CUMMING G
10-Oct	A	WEST HERTS	0-6	F					
10-Oct	A	WESTMINSTER SCHOOL	1-2	F		DEWDNEY EL	SAVILL L	BLAKER HR	PROTHERO AG
14-Oct	A	CHARTERHOUSE	5-6	F		TOWNE WD	PELLY FR	BLAKER HR	LORAINE WH
17-Oct	H ws	RMC SANDHURST	1-1	F		BAGSHAW WH	SAVILL L	BLAKER HR	BROOK AK
17-Oct	A	BARNES	1-0	F	%	DEWDNEY EL	FARMER JH	JAMES NF	WACE R
21-Oct	A	CAMBRIDGE UNIV	2-4	F		GUGGISBERG FG	KNOX H 1	SAVILL L	BROOK AK
22-Oct	A	ROYAL ENGINEERS	1-0	F		DOBSON ED	PELLY FR	FOX CJM	HARRISON HA
24-Oct	A	OLD ST MARKS	5-1	FAC2Q		GUGGISBERG FG	FRY CB	WELLS WC	HOSSACK AH
27-Oct	A	FOREST SCHOOL	4-1	F		TIMBS PA	BLAKER HR	BARKER RR	SHARPE CC
31-Oct	H o	SHEFFIELD UTD	3-0	F	2,000	GAY LH	PELLY FR	BARKER RR	HOSSACK AH
31-Oct	A	READING	2-7	F		MANNERS J	BAGSHAW WH	COWIE RM	ALLEN B
04-Nov	A	OXFORD UNIVERSITY	1-2	F		BLAKER HR	PELLY FR	COWIE RM	MONTGOMERY RM
07-Nov	N o	OLD WESTMINSTERS	12-0	F		GUGGISBERG FG	DUNN ATB 1	BARKER RR	FARRER HM
10-Nov	A	REPTON SCHOOL	3-1	F		GUGGISBERG FG	NELSON TL 1	FREEBORN G	TEWSON S
11-Nov	A	BRIGHTON COLLEGE	2-0	F		TIMBS PA	NELSON TL 1	PHELPS GI	POLEHAMPTON EH
14-Nov	A	HIGHLAND 1ST INFANTRY	4-1	FAC3Q		GUGGISBERG FG	NELSON TL	PELLY FR	BROOK AK
14-Nov	A	CHISWICK PARK	5-1	F	%				
14-Nov	H ws	HAMPSTEAD	4-1	F	%				
18-Nov	A	RMA WOOLWICH	2-1	F		GUGGISBERG FG	FREELAND HE	WOODRUFFE W	BLOUNT GB
18-Nov	H ws	1ST SCOTS GUARDS	1-3	F		TIMBS PA	FARMER JH	FORD HA	COX AG
21-Nov	H ws	OLD CRANLEIGHANS	0-4	F		BAGSHAW WH	FARMER JH	CRAWLEY PAS	BAGSHAW EC
21-Nov	A	CLAPTON	2-6	F	#	MASON E	JOURDAIN RO	BARKER RR	RADFORD T
25-Nov	H ws	GUY'S HOSPITAL	4-1	F		BLAKER HR	FORD HA	HALSTEAD WF	PAWSON FW 1
28-Nov	A	WEST KENT	0-4	F		BLENKIRON TW	SHEPPARD WF	CRAWLEY PAS	PARES B
02-Dec	A	HIGHGATE SCHOOL	19-2	F		TIMBS PA	FARMER JH	HASKETT-SMITH WP	COX AG
05-Dec	H 1	CHATHAM	1-2 S	FAC4Q	2,500	BLAKER HR	PELLY FR	NELSON TL	TOPHAM AG
10-Dec	A	COLCHESTER	3-1	F		BLAKER HR	NELSON TL	BARKER RR	FARMER JH
12-Dec	A	MILLWALL ATHLETIC	1-2 v	LCC1	1,200	BLAKER HR	NELSON TL	BARKER RR	POLEHAMPTON EH
12-Dec	A	CLAPHAM ROVERS	0-4	F		DEWDNEY EL	FARMER JH	HASKETT-SMITH WP	INGE-GARDINER CH
17-Dec	A	SUSSEX MARTLETS	1-2	F	%				
19-Dec	A	OLD HARROVIANS	2-0	F		JOSSHOUSE A	MARSHALL AH	FARMER JH	FRERE GL
19-Dec	A	CROUCH END	1-5	F	%				
26-Dec	A	LINCOLN CITY	4-4	F	% 3,000	GUGGISBERG FG	PELLY FR	BARKER RR	POLEHAMPTON EH
28-Dec	A	GAINSBOROUGH TRINITY	3-3	F		GUGGISBERG FG	BARKER RR	OAKLEY WJ	POLEHAMPTON EH
29-Dec	A	DERBY COUNTY	2-5	F		GUGGISBERG FG	BARKER RR	PELLY FR	BROOK AK
30-Dec	A	SHEFFIELD UTD	2-7	F	% 2,000	GUGGISBERG FG	HARRISON AH	PELLY FR	MONTGOMERY RM
01-Jan	A	HEART OF MIDLOTHIAN	3-6	F	3,000	BLAKER HR	HARRISON AH	PELLY FR	BARKER RR
02-Jan	A	FALKIRK	3-7	F	1,500	BLAKER HR	PELLY FR	HARRISON AH	BARKER RR
04-Jan	A	THIRD LANARK	0-1	F	1,500	BLAKER HR	PELLY FR	BARKER RR	POLEHAMPTON EH
05-Jan	A	KIRKCALDY	3-1	F	og	GUGGISBERG FG	PELLY FR	BARKER RR	BROOK AK
09-Jan	N 1	MILLWALL ATHLETIC	1-3	LCC1	1,000	BLAKER HR	FRY CB	BARKER RR	BROOK AK
16-Jan	A	STOKE CITY	0-3 v	FAC1	2,000	GUGGISBERG FG	PELLY FR	WELLS WC	BROOK AK
23-Jan	H ws	SWIFTS	7-0	F		BLAKER HR	BARKER RR	SHEPPARD WF	CRAWLEY PAS
23-Jan	A	STOKE CITY	0-3	FAC1		GUGGISBERG FG	WELLS WC	PELLY FR	BROOK AK
27-Jan	H ws	KING'S COLLEGE HOSP	2-2	F		TIMBS PA	FRY CB	BUZZARD EF	POWELL WG
30-Jan	H o	MILLWALL ATHLETIC	0-1	LSC1	3,000	BLAKER HR	FRY CB	WELLS WC	BARKER RR
30-Jan	A	OLD WESTMINSTERS	0-5	F					
03-Feb	A	CAMBRIDGE UNIV	2-6	F		GUGGISBERG FG	FRY CB	JOURDAIN RO	LORAINE WH
06-Feb	H ws	OLD BRIGHTONIANS	1-1	F					
06-Feb	A	WESTMINSTER SCHOOL	3-2	F	%				
06-Feb	A	CHISWICK PARK	1-3	F	%				
13-Feb	N 1	OLD FORESTERS	0-2	F	1,000	GOSTLING EV	JOURDAIN RO	LODGE LV	BROOK AK
23-Feb	A	OXFORD UNIVERSITY	1-4	F		ROUTLEDGE MH	LODGE LV	JOURDAIN RO	BROOK AK
01-Mar	A	HIGHGATE SCHOOL	5-2	F		TIMBS PA	WALTER FH	FURBER S	HARRISON HA
05-Mar	A	SURBITON HILL	1-3	F		DEWDNEY EL	SALE EW	MUNDAHL HS	WACE R 1
09-Mar	H ws	2ND BATTN SCOTS GUARDS	3-4	F		SETON WJ	FARMER JH	HOARE G	CROSS FJK
10-Mar	A	ROYAL ARSENAL	1-3	F		SETON WJ	PELLY FR	LOWTHER HC	FOY RH
12-Mar	A	TOTTENHAM H	1-3	F		DEWDNEY EL	FARMER JH	SALE RW	MUNDAHL HS
12-Mar	H 1	THIRD LANARK	3-3	F	2,000	SETON WJ	PELLY FR	LAURENCE HC	MARTIN EB
19-Mar	H ut	OLD BRIGHTONIANS	6-0	F		DEWDNEY EL	SALE RW	MARSHALL AH	MUNDAHL HS
19-Mar	A	SHREWSBURY SCHOOL	1-2	F	%				
22-Mar	A	FOREST SCHOOL	14-2	F		TIMBS PA	FOY RH	BARKER RR	PARES B
26-Mar	A	SWINDON TOWN	0-5	F		BLAKER HR	LOWTHER HC	MARSHALL AH	MUNDAHL HS
30-Mar	N 1	OLD ETONIANS	2-0	F		ROUTLEDGE MH	PELLY FR	BARKER RR	MUNDAHL HS
02-Apr	A	MARLOW	0-3	F		ROUTLEDGE MH	MUNDAHL HS	SALE RW	BICKLEY F
06-Apr	A	CHESHAM	1-1	F	350	FRERE A	FOY RH	DEANS R	BICKLEY F
07-Apr	H 1	TRIDENTS	2-1	F		HALLEY HA	MUNDAHL HS	DEAN E	DRAN G
16-Apr	H 1	KINGSTON ROVERS (HULL)	3-0	F		ROUTLEDGE MH	OTHER AN	ALSTON GP	HARPER HA
16-Apr	A	STOCKTON	3-1	F		GOSTLING EV	LOWTHER HA	PELLY FR	BARKER RR

5	6	7	8	9	10	11
BLOUNT GB	BICKLE AG	HAY	PROBYN PC	FURBER S	COX S	BLOUNT R
WINCKWORTH WN	BROOK AK	NIXON AC	GLOSSOP AGB	SANDILANDS RR 1	COX S	COX LL
BLOUNT R	PARES B	BLAGDEN JJ	KNOX H 2	NIXON AC 3	BARRACLOUGH HC 1	REEVE WG
BICKLEY F	BROOK AK	FURBER S	KNOX H	NIXON AC	NEWBERRY HC 1	SANDILANDS RR
MARTEN AB	PARES B	PERKS JE 1	BARRACLOUGH HC	KNOX H	FURBER S	PARES GL
ARTHUR SR	CHURCH MR	WILLIAMS (SUB) 1	WALTER FH	ELLICOTT AE	WALTERS JH	PERKS JE
BROOK AK	BICKLEY F	COX LL 1	WELCH FCB	COX S	BRYANT FE	LEMAN DC
BROOK AK	ARTHUR SR	ADAMS FE	REEVE WG 2	NIXON AC	KNOX H	COX LL
CHURCH MR	BROOK AK	GLOSSOP AGB 1	REEVE WG	CLARKE TBA 1	KNOX H	COX LL 1
MALDEN AW	HOSSACK AH	FURBER S	KNOX H	NIXON AC	PECK HC	SANDILANDS RR
BUCKMASTER WS	BLOUNT GB	ADAMS FE	HEMMERDE AJ	LIDDELL FF	BUZZARD EF	PERKS JE 1
BAGSHAW EC	HALSTEAD WF	ADAMS FE	KNOX H 1	NIXON AC 1	FURBER S 3	GILLIATT WE
WARD HO	TEWSON S	PARES B	FURBER S	NIXON AC	PLUMPTREE HP 1	LEMAN DC
BLOUNT GB	BAGSHAW EC	FURBER AL	LIDDELL FF	ELLICOTT AE	ADAMS FE	BLUNT RA
BICKLEY F	HARRISON HA	NIXON AC	TURNER AE	PERKS JE	PLUMPTREE HP 1	
BLAKER AP	SHATTOCK GO	FURBER S 1	WINCKWORTH DP	KNOX H	CARPMAEL WP	PEYERS P
BROOK AK	CROSS FJK	GLOSSOP AGB 1	KNOX H 1	REEVE WG 1	PLUMPTREE HP 2	PERKS JE
LILL BA	BILSTOWE ES	PAGDON EH	ADAMS FE	FURBER S 3	CRUMP CW	FIE FM 1
POLEHAMPTON EH	BROOK AK	KNOX H	LEBAT W de	SIMKINS WA	PLUMPTREE HP 1	CROSS FJK 2
JOHNSON EA	WACE R	BLUNT RA 1	CARLTON FW 1	WALTER FH	SUTTON EW	NIX JS
BICKLEY F	IZARD HC	KNOX H	NIXON AC	GOSLING WS	PLUMPTREE HP	FURBER S 1
BICKLEY F 1	BROOK AK	ADAMS FE 1	KNOX H 4	SIMKINS WA 5	CROSS FJK	LABAT C de
BELLHOUSE EW	COX AG	PRYCE-JONES AW	KNOX H	FURBER S	BRYANT HJ	BLAKER H 2
TEWSON S	WOOD L	WOODHOUSE OW	BLUNT RA	FURBER S 1	CARPMAEL WP	COBBETT PG (SUB)
HOSSACK AH	POLEHAMPTON EH	ADAMS FE	KNOX H 1	FURBER S 1	LABAT C de	CROSS FJK 2
BICKLEY F	BAGSHAW EC	ADAMS FE	BRUNNER	FURBER S 1	WALTER FH	CROSS FJK 1
MONTGOMERY RM	WOODBRIDGE GH	BLUNT RA	KNOX H 1	NIXON AC	PARES GL	HASKETT-SMITH WP
COLVILLE PC	BLOUNT GB	BLUNT RA	WALTER FH	CRAWLEY HH	ELLICOTT AE	NIX JS
BICKLEY F	COX AG	COX S	HEWITT CD	SIMKINS WA 1	ADAMS FE	KNOX H
BICKLEY F	COX AG	NELSON TL 1	FURBER S 1	SUAL CA 1	HARRISON HA	WALTER FH
WOOD L	CRAWLEY HH	ADAMS FE	KNOX H	BLUNT RA	WALTER FH	FARMER JH
BICKLEY F	BAGSHAW EC	BLUNT RA 2	PARES GL 3	FURBER S 5	KNOX H 5	CROSS FJK 4
POLEHAMPTON EH	PARES B	GLOSSOP AGB	SIMKINS WA	FURBER S 1	KNOX H	CROSS FJK
BICKLEY F	BAGSHAWEC	BLUNT F	GLOSSOP AGB 1	FITZHUGH	KNOX H 2	HASKETT-SMITH WP
PARES B	BROOK AK	KNOX H	SIMKINS WA 1	COTTERILL GH	ADAMS FE	PERKS JE
CRAWLEY PAS	RYDE FC	BLUNT RA	ADAMS FE	MAORIE H	NIX JS	MATHER JW
CRAWLEY PAS	BUZZARD EF	HEWITT CD	CARLTON FW	FURBER S 1	PERKS JE	WALTER FH 1
				NIXON AC		
TOPHAM AG	BROOK AK	WOODBRIDGE AR	NIXON AC 1	FURBER S	KNOX H 2	LABAT C de
BROOK AK	COX AG	WOODBRIDGE AR 1	SIMKINS WA 1	NIXON AC	FURBER S 1	COX LL
MONTGOMERY RM	POLEHAMPTON EH	COX AG	PERKINS N 1	NIXON AC 1	SIMKINS WA	LABAT C de
TOPHAM AG	POLEHAMPTON EH	WOODBRIDGE AR	KNOX H 1	NIXON AC	FURBER S	COX LL
TOPHAM AG	POLEHAMPTON EH	KNOX H 1	SIMKINS WA 1	TOPHAM R 1	PLUMPTREE HP	COX LL
TOPHAM AG	COX AG	FURBER S 1	WOODBRIDGE AR 1	NIXON AC	LABAT C de	PERKINS N 1
TOPHAM R	MONTGOMERY RM	COX LL	PLUMPTREE E	SIMKINS WA	NIXON AC	WOODBRIDGE AR
TOPHAM AG	COX AG	WOODBRIDGE AR	PLUMPTREE E	NIXON AC 1	COX S	PERKINS N 1
TOPHAM AG	HOSSACK AH	KNOX H	COTTERILL GH	SIMKINS WA 1	PERKINS N	COX S
POLEHAMPTON EH	CROSS FJK	COX S	FURBER S	KNOX H	SIMKINS WA	BLUNT RA
POWELL WG	HARRISON HA	WALTER FA 1	PERKS JE	WILSON GL 6	CARLTON FH	CARLTON FW
POLEHAMPTON EH	FRY CB	HEWITT CD	FURBER S	KNOX H	SIMKINS WA	CROSS FJK
EBDEN FR	PELLY FR	KNOX H	NIXON AC 1	SETON WJ 1	CARLTON FW	
BICKLEY F	CRAWLEY PAS	GLOSSOP AGB	HARRISON HA	KNOX H	BLUNT RA	HEWITT CD
BICKLEY F	HARRISON HA	KNOX H 1	WILSON GL	NIXON AC	PLUMTREE HP	CROSS FJK 1
	STANBROUGH LK	HASKETT-SMITH WP	PARES GL 1			
BARKER RR	CRAWLEY PAS	GLOSSOP AGB	BLAIN GF	SALE RW	BLUNT RA	LABAT C de
POLEHAMPTON EH	NIGGER E	BLUNT RA	LABAT C de 1	GOSLING WS	KNOX H	FURBER S
BURROWS FR	NIXON AC 1	WILSON GL 2	BLUNT RA 1	KNOX H 1	BICKLEY F	
BAGSHAW EC	BLAKER HR	BLUNT RA	BARROW FR	HOPE RB	NIX JS	WALTER FH
COX AG	HARRISON HA	WINCKWORTH WN	STANBROUGH LK 1	BLACK W 2		
BROOK AK	HOARE G	ALINGTON CL	FURBER S 1	NIXON AC	PERKINS N	CROSS FJK
PARES CB	OTHER AN	BLUNT RA	STANBROUGH LK	HEWITT H	DICKINSON GN 1	WALTER FH
BROOK AK	BARKER RR	CROSS FJK	ASTON FM 1	NIXON AC	KNOX H 1	FURBER S 1
BICKLEY F	SHEPPARD NF	HASKETT-SMITH WP	BARKER RR 2	BRYANT FE 4	HEWITT HW	
'LEOPARD' WH	HARRISON HA	HASKETT-SMITH WP 3	DASHWOOD L 2	FURBER S 4	BRYANT FE	WILSON GL 5
BICKLEY F	SALE RW	HEWITT CD	BRYANT FE	NIXON AC	FURBER S	WALTER FH
HARRISON HA	FOY RH	WALTER FH	BRYANT FE 1	FURBER S	WILSON GL 1	LEWIS CE
MARTEN AB	BARKER RR	NIX JS	WINCKWORTH DP	FURBER S	MOON WR	WALTER FH
LANG LCV	DEANS G	HARRISON RHA	BRYANT FE	WILSON GL 1	WINCKWORTH DP	BARKER RR
LANG LCV	FOY RH	BRYANT FE	BARKER RR	FORD HA 2	BICKLEY F	WINCKWORTH WN
MILLS RO	MCNAIR JR	HEWITT CD	WALTER FE	GUY AN 1	TREVOR W 1	HEWITT HW 1
TOPHAM AG	BROOK AK	FURBER S	HOPE RB 2	NIXON AC 1	KNOX H	COX LL

207

18-Apr	A	NEWCASTLE EAST END	0-2	F		GOSTLING EV	PELLY FR	LOWTHER HC	TOPHAM AG			
19-Apr	A	SUNDERLAND	0-4	F		GOSTLING EV	LOWTHER HA	PELLY FR	BARKER RR			
21-Apr	A	SHEFFIELD UTD	3-1	F	500	GUGGISBERG FG	LOWTHER HA	PELLY FR	FOY RH			

S CHATHAM DISQUALIFIED
UNCLEAR WHETHER IT WAS AG OR S COX WHO SCORED

CASUALS TOP SCORERS SEASON BY SEASON

Season	Top Scorer	Goals	Season	Top Scorer	Goals
1883/84	ALSTON HN	7	1909/10	MONTGOMERY PJ	18
1884/85	BICKLEY F/ MILLER JS	5	1910/11	GREEN MA	17
1885/86	MILLER JS	11	1911/12	CUTTER RC/ EDWARDS V	10
1886/87	BICKLEY F	12	1912/13	DOWER RW	10
1887/88	GRUNDTVIG HT	7	1913/14	CUTTER RC	11
1888/89	AINGER WH	13	1919/20	GANDAR-DOWAR RD/ JULIAN CR	5
1889/90	WALTERS HM	30	1920/21	JULIAN CR	8
1890/91	NIXON AC/ TOPHAM R	11	1921/22	DUBUIS HF	7
1891/92	FURBER S	27	1922/23	DUBUIS HF	18
1892/93	KNOX H	12	1923/24	LOCKTON JH	17
1893/94	PERKINS TN	15	1924/25	HOWELL M	15
1894/95	FERNIE JF	14	1925/26	SLEIGHTHOLME CH	8
1895/96	FERNIE JF	30	1926/27	ROBINS RM	8
1896/97	TOONE WP	14	1927/28	GERMAN AC	17
1897/98	WRIGHT RG	14	1928/29	MASSEY JA	9
1898/99	LOWES E	13	1929/30	FLETCHER GS	10
1899/00	LOWES E	9	1930/31	SHEARER EDR	25
1900/01	ROPER RG	18	1931/32	JENKINS RG	11
1901/02	DRAKE CF	17	1932/33	COUCHMAN LT	13
1902/03	DURRANT RB	20	1933/34	COLLINS GAK	12
1903/04	ALEXANDER CW	13	1934/35	COUCHMAN LT	10
1904/05	WRIGHT RG	10	1935/36	CLEMENTS BA	27
1905/06	MCIVER CD	15	1936/37	CLEMENTS BA	20
1906/07	TURNER R	17	1937/38	LEE J	15
1907/08	DURRANT RB	10	1938/39	LEE J	26
1908/09	CUTTER RC	16			

BROOK AK	LANG LCV	CROSS FJK	COX S	NEWBURY	NIXON AC	FURBER S
TOPHAM AG	BROOK AK	FURBER S	HOPE RB 2	NIXON AC	NEWBERRY HC	FOX S
BARKER RR	BOX AR	CROSS FJK	SIMKINS WA 2	NIXON AC	COX S 1	FURBER S

CASUALS LEADING APPEARANCES SEASON BY SEASON

Season	Most Appearances	Apps	Season	Most Appearances	Apps
1883/84	BICKLEY F	14	1909/10	KING SL/ MONTGOMERY PJ	28
1884/85	BICKLEY F	22	1910/11	KING SL/ SERGEANT PA	35
1885/86	BICKLEY F	28	1911/12	DOWER RW	22
1886/87	BICKLEY F	22	1912/13	FENDER PGH	25
1887/88	BLENKIRON TW	28	1913/14	DOWER RW/ FENDER PGH	21
1888/89	BICKLEY F/ BLENKIRON TW	19	1919/20	BIRCH AE	18
1889/90	BARKER RR	29	1920/21	SERGEANT PA	21
1890/91	PELLY FR	24	1921/22	DUBUIS HF	26
1891/92	FURBER S/ KNOX H	35	1922/23	HOWELL M/ PAYNE HG	32
1892/93	NELSON TL	30	1923/24	WILKINSON AM	29
1893/94	BICKLEY F	28	1924/25	HOWELL M	28
1894/95	DRAKE CF	31	1925/26	KNIGHT JG	30
1895/96	HILLEARY RM	37	1926/27	FRIZZELL FG/ KNIGHT JG	27
1896/97	BARKER RR	26	1927/28	VAN DER BORGH M/ GLENISTER CE	26
1897/98	PICKERING HJ	34	1928/29	BULMAN BM/ WATSON GS	26
1898/99	KING SL	29	1929/30	MORRIS AE	27
1899/00	KING SL	30	1930/31	RUSSELL AM	27
1900/01	KING SL	28	1931/32	ROSS T	24
1901/02	KING SL	32	1932/33	COUCHMAN LT	31
1902/03	DURRANT RB	22	1933/34	COUCHMAN LT	34
1903/04	KING SL	26	1934/35	EVANS FL	29
1904/05	KING SL	38	1935/36	EVANS FL	31
1905/06	KING SL	40	1936/37	COLLINS PT/ PARTRIDGE GM	28
1906/07	KING SL	35	1937/38	WHEWELL WT	20
1907/08	KING SL	33	1938/39	LEE J	24
1908/09	KING SL/ WOODRUFF GG	24			

1892/93

DATE	VEN	OPPONENTS	RES	COMP	ATT	1	2	3	4
03-Sep	A	SWINDON TOWN	4-2	F		GOSTLING EV	BARKER RR	FOY RH	POWELL WG
10-Sep	A	ROYAL ARSENAL	4-2	F		GOSTLING EV	SHAW NF	BARKER RR	WINCKWORTH WN
17-Sep	A	CLAPTON	5-1	F	3,000	GOSTLING EV	PELLY FR	NELSON TL	BARKER RR
17-Sep	A	WEST HERTS	2-4	F	og	BLAKER HR	GRIEG RA	FEVEZ AL	FOY RH
21-Sep	A	CHESHAM	5-0	F		FREER AE	GRIEG RA	PELLY FR	FOY RH
24-Sep	A	MARLOW	0-2	F		NELSON MG	NELSON TL	FRY CB	POLEHAMPTON EH
24-Sep	A	ERITH	1-4	F	400	ROUTLEDGE MH	GRIEG RA	CRAWLEY FHP	BAGSHAW EC
28-Sep	A	NEWBURY	2-1	F		MOON WR	FRY CB	GREIG RA	MARTEN AB
01-Oct	A	REPTON SCHOOL	4-1	F	%	BLAKER HR	PELLY FR	GREIG RA	FOY RH
05-Oct	A	CHARTERHOUSE	4-2	F		BLENKIRON TW	SHAW NF	GREIG RA	MARTEN AB
08-Oct	A	LONDON CALEDONIANS	1-2	F	% 1,000	GOSTLING EV	CRAWLEY PAS	FRY CB	MARTEN AB
15-Oct	A	WOLVERTON (L AND N.W.R.)	3-1	FAC1Q		GOSTLING EV	FRY CB	LOWTHER L	POLEHAMPTON EH
19-Oct	A	CAMBRIDGE UNIV	3-2	F		BLAKER HR	PELLY FR	FOSTER HK	POLEHAMPTON EH
20-Oct	A	ROYAL ENGINEERS	2-2	F		BLAKER HR	PELLY FR 1	SALE RW	POWELL WG
22-Oct	A	OLD ST MARKS	3-2	F	%	RAIKES GB	OAKLEY WJ	LODGE LV	BROOK AK
22-Oct	H ws	OLD CRANLEIGHANS	0-4	F					
25-Oct	A	FOREST SCHOOL	2-0	F		TIMBS PA	STEVENS GP	BLAKER HR	HARRISON HA
26-Oct	A	ST JOHNS SCHOOL	1-5	F		RYDON HL	HARRISON AH	BAGSHAW EC	POLEHAMPTON EH
29-Oct	H1	CRUSADERS	3-0	FAC2Q	2,000	BLAKER HR	PELLY FR	NELSON TL	FOY RH
29-Oct	A	HILLINGDON	2-2	F	*	OTHER AN	HASKETT-SMITH WP	SALE RW	PHILLIPS J
02-Nov	A	OXFORD UNIVERSITY	2-3	F		BLAKER HR	PELLY FR	NELSON TL	CROSS FJK
05-Nov	N o	OLD WESTMINSTERS	1-1	F		BLENKIRON TW	NELSON TL	FORT CR	OTHER AN
09-Nov	A	WESTMINSTER SCHOOL	3-1	F		ROUTLEDGE MH	HARRISON AH	FLETCHER RH	BARKER RR
10-Nov	H1	SHEFFIELD UTD	1-2	F	og	GOSTLING EV	NELSON TL	PELLY FR	WHEELER A
12-Nov	A	BRIGHTON COLLEGE	1-2	F		RYDON HL	BLAKER HR	WALTER FH	NELSON MG
16-Nov	N1	GUY'S HOSPITAL	4-1	F	12	RYDON HL	BARKER RR	HASKETT-SMITH WP 1	WALSH AH
17-Nov	A	LANCING COLLEGE	2-4	FAC3Q	%	RYDON HL	GASKIN AL	POLEHAMPTON EH	HARRISON AE
19-Nov	N o	OLD WESTMINSTERS	5-2	F	* 4,500	GOSTLING EV	NELSON TL	SHAW NF	BARKER RR
19-Nov	A	BARNES	0-3	F		ROUTLEDGE MH	SALE RW	BAGSHAW EC	POWELL WG
23-Nov	A	RMA WOOLWICH	1-0	F		SETON WJ	PELLY FR	BLAKER HR	HAMMOND A
24-Nov	A	FRAMLINGHAM COLLEGE	4-0	F		FRERE WH	NELSON TL	GREARE H	NELSON MG
26-Nov	A	READING	1-4	F		'CROCK' A	NELSON TL	GRIEG EA	POWELL WG
01-Dec	A	1ST BATTN SHERWOOD FOR	1-3	F	%	SETON WJ	PELLY FR	NELSON TL	CROSS FJK
03-Dec	H o	ILFORD	4-2	F		SETON WJ	BARKER RR	BLAKER HR	BROOK AK
03-Dec	H ws	OLD BRIGHTONIANS	2-3	F	% #	VOGEL JF	FORD HA	SALE RW	PARES B
07-Dec	H ws	ST BARTHOLOMEWS H	1-5	F		ROUTLEDGE MH	HARRISON AH	BARKER RR	HARRISON HA
10-Dec	H o	POLYTECHNIC	5-0	FAC4Q	3,000	GOSTLING EV	NELSON TL	PELLY FR	BARKER RR
10-Dec	A	LONDON CALEDONIANS	0-3	F	3,000	SETON WJ	SHAW NF	LOWTHER HC	LECKY JG
13-Dec	H1	OLD ETONIANS	11-4	F		GOSTLING EV	BARKER RR	GREIG RA	TOPHAM AG
14-Dec	A	HIGHGATE SCHOOL	2-1	F		TIMBS PA	HASKETT-SMITH WP	GREIG RA	FOLEY B
15-Dec	A	SUSSEX MARTLETS	2-2	F		ROUTLEDGE MH	FRY CB	NELSON TL	BARKER RR
17-Dec	A	MILLWALL ATHLETIC	2-3	LCC1	2,000	SETON WJ	NELSON TL	FRY CB	BARKER RR
17-Dec	A	OLD HARROVIANS	2-10	F	%				
24-Dec	A	CLAPHAM ROVERS	0-0	F		JOHNSTON R	GREIG RA	ADAMS WG	EBDEN Fr
26-Dec	A	LEICESTER FOSSE	1-4	F	3,000	RAIKES GB	PELLY FR	NELSON TL	TOPHAM AG 1
27-Dec	A	LINCOLN CITY	1-1	F		RAIKES GB	PELLY FR	NELSON TL	BROOK AK
27-Dec	A	LUTON TOWN	4-2	F	3,000	BLENKIRON TW	BARKER RR	OAKLEY WJ	LECKY JG
28-Dec	A	CREWE ALEXANDRA	1-3	F	%	RAIKES GB	PELLY FR	OAKLEY WJ	LECKY JG
29-Dec	A	SHEFFIELD UTD	2-2	F	1,500	GOSTLING EV	OAKLEY WJ	PELLY FR	GRIEVESON JE
30-Dec	A	LIVERPOOL RAMBLERS	3-0	F					
31-Dec	A	SOUTHPORT CENTRAL	2-3	F		SETON WJ	NELSON TL	OAKLEY WJ	BARKER RR
02-Jan	A	KINGS PARK	0-4	F		GOSTLING EV	NELSON TL	FOSTER HK	LECKY JG
03-Jan	A	THIRD LANARK	3-2	F	% $	SETON WJ	NELSON TL	BARKER RR	LECKY JG
04-Jan	A	KIRKCALDY	1-0	F		SETON WJ	NELSON TL	BARKER RR	TOPHAM AG
14-Jan	A	GREAT MARLOW	2-4	F		NELSON MG	NELSON TL	BRAY EH	GRIEVESON JE
21-Jan	A	NOTTM FOREST	0-4	FAC1	8,000	GOSTLING EV	NELSON TL	PELLY FR	BARKER RR
28-Jan	A	TOTTENHAM H	1-0	LSC1	3,000	SETON WJ	NELSON TL	FRY CB	BARKER RR
01-Feb	H qc	CAMBRIDGE UNIV	1-0	F		SETON WJ	PELLY FR	NELSON TL	BARKER RR
04-Feb	H o	ROYAL ARSENAL	2-4	F	4,000	BLAKER HR	OWEN ML	BUZZARD EF	BARKER RR
04-Feb	A	REIGATE PRIORY	0-7	F		RYDON HL	FARMER JH	WACE R	POWELL WG
08-Feb	H qc	OXFORD UNIVERSITY	0-1	F		SETON WJ	PELLY FR	LOWTHER HC	MOON EG
11-Feb	H1	OLD HARROVIANS	3-0	LSC2		BLAKER HR	PELLY FR	BARKER RR	FOY RH
11-Feb	H o	THIRD LANARK	1-2	F		SETON WJ	FORT CR	SHAW NF	GRIEVESON JE
11-Feb	A	OLD BRIGHTONIANS	0-6	F					
15-Feb	A	CHARTERHOUSE	2-3	F		ROUTLEDGE MH	MUNDAHL HS	FOSTER HK	BLOUNT R
25-Feb	H o	CLAPTON	5-1	LSCsf	4,000	SETON WJ	NELSON TL	FORT CR	MONTGOMERY RM
08-Mar	A	RIEC	2-2	F		NELSON MG	MUNDAHL HS	PELLY FR	HOSSACK AH 1
11-Mar	A	HILLINGDON	2-2	F		NELSON MG	KING AH	FARMER JH	MONTGOMERY RM
15-Mar	A	SHREWSBURY SCHOOL	1-2	F		RAIKES GB	SALT RN	GREIG RA	STEVENSON
18-Mar	A	ST ALBANS	2-6	F		NELSON MG	FARMER JH	HOSSACK AH	KEYSELL FS
21-Mar	A	FOREST SCHOOL	4-3	F	og	TIMBS PA	GREIG RA	BICKLEY F	FOY RH
25-Mar	N o	OLD WESTMINSTERS	0-3	LSCf	6,000	MOON WR	MOON EG	SQUIRE RT	WINCKWORTH WN
29-Mar	H1	OLD ETONIANS	2-1	F	%	RUSSELL H	PELLY FR	GREIG RA	NICHOLSON RS
01-Apr	A	NEWCASTLE UNITED	0-5	F		SETON WJ	LODGE LV	NELSON TL	GRIEVESON JE
03-Apr	A	MIDDLESBROUGH	0-4	F					
04-Apr	A	STOCKTON	3-2	F	%	SETON WJ			
08-Apr	A	BURTON WANDERERS	1-3	F	%	SETON WJ	PELLY FR	NELSON TL	TOPHAM AG
08-Apr	A	REIGATE PRIORY	1-2	F		RYDON HL	FORT CR	GODWIN H (SUB)	BICKLEY F
15-Apr	A	ROYAL ARSENAL	0-3	F		MOON WR	PELLY FR	HARRISON AH	NELSON TL

12 A SIDE GAME - NO 12 - PERKS JE
$ ONE GOAL SCORED BY HA OR TB RHODES

5	6	7	8	9	10	11
TOPHAM AG	POLEHAMPTON EH	DE LABAT C 2	FURBER S 2	NIXON AC	COX S	LAMDIN
POLEHAMPTON EH	TOPHAM AG	VEITCH JG 2	HOPE RB	SANDILANDS RR 1	NIXON AC 1	COX S
WINCKWORTH WN 1	WALTERS PM	HOPE RB	NIXON AC 1	SANDILANDS RR 2	COX S 1	HILLEARY RM
BICKLEY F	MOON EG	KNOX H	DICKSON JE	MOON WR 1	HOPGOOD C	MARSHALL FJ
BICKLEY F	BARKER RR	GLOSSOP AGB	MOON WR 3	NELSON TL 1	PARES B 1	COX S
BICKLEY F	BARKER RR	FOLEY B	RECANO CM	NIXON AC	COX LL	HILLEARY RM
FLETCHER RH	PARES B	BLUNT RA	HANNARD F 1	CRAWFORD RO	HANNAFORD CH	FREER AE
POLEHAMPTON EH	FOY RH	FOLEY B	HUNNARD F	REEVE WG 1	KNOX H 1	PARES B
BICKLEY F	MONTGOMERY W	ADAMS FE 1	HOPE RB	FRY CB 1	KNOX H 1	BLUNT RA
BICKLEY F	FOY RH	SMITH GO 1	ADAMS FE	VEITCH JG 1	FRY CB	HEWITT CD 2
BROOK AK	POLEHAMPTON EH	BLUNT RG	HOPE RB	PERKINS N	KNOX H	HEWITT CD
PARES B 1	BROOK AK	ADAMS FE	FOLEY B 1	PERKINS N 1	KNOX H	HEWITT CD
PARES B	BROOK AK	ADAMS FE	POWELL JGT	DAVIES LI 3	PLUMPTREE HP	BICKLEY F
POLEHAMPTON EH	CARPMAEL W	HUNNARD F	STEVENS GF 1	PARES GL	KNOX H	PARES B
BICKLEY F	HAMMOND A	ADAMS FE	CARLTON FW	DAVIES LI 1	KNOX H 1	BLUNT RA
HARRISON AE	HAMMOND A	GLOSSOP AGB 1	SYMONDS JW	CRAWFORD RO 1	BICKLEY F	BURGE F
DEXTER AJ	PHILLIPS FW	HEATH FV	SMITH AF 1	HASKETT-SMITH F	BURGE F	HARRISON AE
MOORE AG	POLEHAMPTON EH	GLOSSOP AGB	CRAWFORD RO 1	PERKINS TN 1	KNOX H	HEWITT CD 1
LECKY JG	HUNNARD F	RECANO CM	PERKINS HW 1	HARRISON AE	PERKS JE	NELSON MG
RENDELL BA	POLEHAMPTON EH	BICKLEY F	REEVE WG	VEITCH JG	KNOX H 2	HEWITT CD
BICKLEY F	FORD HA	BLUNT RA	CRAWFORD RO	DAVIES LI	KNOX H	YOUNG R 1
POWELL WG	HARRISON HA	WOODBRIDGE AR	NELSON TL	MOON EG 3	BICKLEY F	BURGE F
GRIEVESON JE	BROOK AK	WOODBRIDGE AR	KNOX H	GOSLING WS	PERKINS TN	CROSS FJK
BROAD JD	POLEHAMPTON FW	HARRISON AE	KIRWAN BR	PARRY CF	DE LABAT C 1	BECKET SW
POLEHAMPTON FW	HARRISON HA	BICKLEY F	SIMKINS WA 1	DAVIES LI 1	KNOX H 1	
PARES B	POLEHAMPTON FW	DE LABAT C	KIRWAN RO	MOON EG	PARES ET	PARRY CF
TOPHAM AG	BROOK AK	GLOSSOP AGB	DAVIES LI 2	PERKINS TN 1	KNOX H	HEWITT CD 1
HAMMOND A	POLEHAMPTON FW	ADAMS FE	KIRWAN BR	BARRY CF	WALTER FH	
HUNTER	POLEHAMPTON FW	HARRISON AE	KIRWAN BR	BROAD JD 1	BICKLEY F	PARRY CF
BARKER RR	POLEHAMPTON FW	GLOSSOP AGB 1	HUBBARD LW	STEVENS GP 3	KNOX H	BICKLEY F
REYNOLDS LW	WALTER FH	BLAKER HR	FOLEY CP	WELSH FCB	'SPRINTEE' A	KIRWAN BR 1
GRIEVESON JE	HARRISON HA	GLOSSOP AGB	WOODBRIDGE AR	STEVENS GP	KNOX H	SMITH C
BICKLEY F	POLEHAMPTON EH	CROSS FJK	STANBROUGH LK	DAVIES LI 3	KNOX H 1	PRYCE-JONES AW
HAMMOND A	POLEHAMPTON FW	HASKETT-SMITH WP	ADAMS FE	BROAD JD	NELSON MG	PARRY CF
HAWE DK	OLIVER FG	WOODBRIDGE AR 1	KNOX H	STEPHEN GP	PARES GL	HASKETT-SMITH WP
TOPHAM AG	BROOK AK 1	GLOSSOP AGB	DAVIES LI	PERKINS TN 2	KNOX H 2	CROSS FJK
HALL GC	POLEHAMPTON EH	ADAMS FE	GUGGISBERG FG	BROAD JD	BLUNT RA	COX LL
KEYSELL FS	FOY RH	WOODBRIDGE AR 1	HOPE RB 2	PERKINS TN 4	FORD HA 3	HILLEARY RM 1
HARRISON CI	WALSH FA	EVORS CA 1	HOPE RB 1	CRAIK HD	HARRISON A	STEPHENSON FL
FARMER JH	HAMMOND A	DE LABAT C 1	BROOKER AGN	HOPE RB 1	WOODBRIDGE AR	BICKLEY F
TOPHAM AG	GRIEVESON JE	CROSS FJK	KNOX H 1	DAVIES LI	COX S 1	COX LL
BICKLEY F	WALTER FH	PERKS JE	SKILBECK W	KNOX H	LORD ENCOMBE	ADAMS FE
FOY RH	OAKLEY WJ	WOODBRIDGE AR	RHODES TB	RHODES HA	REEVE WG	FORD HA
TOPHAM AG	DISBROWE EJ	SIMPKINS H	NELSON TL	RHODES HA	COX S 1	RHODES TB
FOY RH	GRIEVESON JE 1	HOPE RB 2	KNOX H	REEVE WG	FORD HA	BICKLEY F 1
DISBROWE EJ	FOY RH	COX LL	DAVIES LI	TOPHAM AG	REEVE WG	KNOX H
TOPHAM AG	BARKER RR	RHODES C	RHODES TB	HOPE RB	RHODES HA 2	TOPHAM R
			DAVIES LI 1	REEVE WG 1		COX S 1
TOPHAM AG	LECKY JG	WOODBRIDGE AR	LLEWELLYN-DAVIES J	TOPHAM R	RHODES HA 1	COX S 1
TOPHAM AG	GRIEVESON JE	WOODBRIDGE AR	SIMKINS WA	RHODES HA	DAVIES LI	COX S
TOPHAM AG	GRIEVESON JE	WOODBRIDGE AR	RHODES TB	TOPHAM R	RHODES HA	COX S
LECKY JG	GRIEVESON JE	REEVE WG	RHODES TB	TOPHAM R 1	RHODES HA	DAVIES LI
REYNOLDS LW	FARMER MS	FORD HA 2	BICKLEY F	BORROW WS	CRAWFORD RO	FOLEY B
WARD ED	GRIEVESON JE	SHARPLES J	HOPE RB	PERKINS TN	RHODES TB	FORD HA
BLAKER HR	FOY RH	KNOX H	DAVIES LI	HOPE RB 1	BICKLEY F	BLUNT RA
LECKY JG	BROOK AK	GLOSSOP AGB	BICKLEY F	HOPE RB	KNOX H 1	CROSS FJK
LECKY JG	BROOK AK	BLUNT RA	KNOX H 1	HOPE RB	DE LABAT C 1	CROSS FJK
POLEHAMPTON FW	WALTER FH	HANNAFORD CH	CRAIK HD	FAWKS RAH	NELSON MG	HASKETT-SMITH WP
LECKY JG	FORD HA	WILSON GL	BICKLEY F	ROBINSON GM	KNOX H	STANBROUGH LK
BICKLEY F	PARES B	BLUNT RA	KNOX H	HOPE RB 2	SIMKINS WA 1	CRAWFORD RO
BROOK AK	MONTGOMERY RM	SHARPLES J	DEWHURST GP	PERKINS TN 1	ROBINSON GM	COX S
BICKLEY F	DAWSON GW	ADAMS FE	KNOX H	WILSON GL 1	GILLIATT WE	LEELE S 1
BICKLEY F	BARKER RR	ROBINSON GM 2	SIMKINS WA 2	HOPE RB 1	PARES B	BLUNT RA
MONTGOMERY RM	BICKLEY F	WINCKWORTH DP	NELSON TL	OTHER AN	YOUNG R	HANNAFORD CH 1
BARKER RR	WACE R	WALTER FH	CRAIK JD	PARES B 2	WOODBRIDGE AR	BLUNT RA
BUZZARD EF	TUDOR-OWEN E	WOOD GR	SALT RJ	THOMAS CM 1	WALKER J	BOWDLER JCH
COX AG	WALTER FH	HANNAFORD CH	EDGINTON AE 1	PERKINS TN 1	BICKLEY F	BLUNT RA
PARES B	KEYSELL FS	HILLEARY RM 1	HAYTER F	PERKINS TN 1	FARMER MS	KING AN 1
FERRERS GUY AW	WETTON H	WINCKWORTH DN	VEITCH JG	SANDILANDS RR 1	STREET F	PECK HC
KEYSELL FS	FRERE AE	HANNAFORD CH	NELSON MG	MOON EG 1	SCRIVEN J	HILLEARY RM
TOPHAM AG	PARES B	SHARPLES J	ROBINSON GM	KNOX H	HILLEARY RM	SIMKINS WA
STAPLES EP	PARES B	SHARPLES J	MANLY JH	SIMKINS WA	YOUNG R	LOWE C
WALTER FH	KNIGHT A (SUB)	MOON WR	COX LL	BLUNT RA	NELSON MG 1	HANNAFORD CH
GRIEVESON JE	BARKER RR	ROBINSON GM	BLUNT RA	WALTER FH	YOUNG E	COX S

1893/94

DATE	VEN	OPPONENTS	RES	COMP	ATT	1	2	3	4
16-Sep	A	CLAPTON	1-1	F	3,000	GOSTLING EV	NELSON TL	FORT CR	POLEHAMPTON EH
16-Sep	A	MAIDSTONE	1-2	F	½	LAWRENCE AGS	BLAKER HR	GREIG RA	BARKER RR
23-Sep	A	CROUCH END	6-2	F	1,500	GOSTLING EV	PELLY FR	NELSON TL	WINCKWORTH WN
27-Sep	A	NEWBURY	3-3	F		RYDON HL	GRIEG RA	FOY RH	MONTGOMERY RM
30-Sep	A	TOTTENHAM H	1-0	F		BLENKIRON TW	BLAKER HR	GREIG H	MONTGOMERY RM
30-Sep	A	IPSWICH TOWN	3-1	F		LAWRENCE AGS	NELSON TL	MARSH JW	DISBROWE EJ
04-Oct	A	CHARTERHOUSE	5-2	F		BLENKIRON TW	BLAKER HR	GREIG RA	SHAW NF
05-Oct	A	NORFOLK	4-2	F		GOSTLING EV	MARCH JW	GREIG CL	MONTGOMERY RM
07-Oct	A	WOOLWICH ARSENAL	1-5	F	6,000	GOSTLING EV	PELLY FR	NELSON TL	POLEHAMPTON EH
07-Oct	A	ILFORD	1-2	F		BAGSHAWE GC	FOY RH	FORD HA	FOY HC
07-Oct	A	WESTMINSTER SCHOOL	4-1	F		SIMPSON FA	BLAKER HR	GREIG RA	FOY CA
10-Oct	H1	SUNDERLAND	1-5	F	6,500	GOSTLING EV	PELLY FR	NELSON TL	SHAW NF
14-Oct	H1	RMC SANDHURST	3-1	F		BLENKIRON TW	CORNISH HH	KING SL	COLLIER JS
14-Oct	A	LONDON CALEDONIANS	1-1	F	3,500	LAWRENCE AGS	BARKER RR	MACDONALD TM	POLEHAMPTON EH
18-Oct	A	CAMBRIDGE UNIV	3-2	F		LAWRENCE AGS	PELLY FR	NELSON TL	BROOK AK
21-Oct	A	MARLOW	4-3	F	og	ROUTLEDGE MH	MACDONALD TM	NELSON TL	WILBERFORCE FR
21-Oct	A	ASHFORD	1-4	F	½	BLENKIRON TW			
24-Oct	A	FOREST SCHOOL	3-1	F		VOGEL JL	CORNISH HH	CORNISH HG	FOY HC
25-Oct	A	HILLINGDON	2-3	F		TIMBS PA	CORNISH HH	CORNISH HG	POWELL WG
26-Oct	A	ROYAL ENGINEERS	5-1	F		ROUTLEDGE MH	BLAKER HR	HILLEARY EL	FOY HC
28-Oct	A	2ND SCOTS GUARDS	0-2	F		BLENKIRON TW	KING SL	BLAKER HR	RAUTHWELL AW
01-Nov	A	OXFORD UNIVERSITY	0-2	F		BLAKER HR	PELLY FR	NELSON TL	RAUTHWELL AW
04-Nov	A	WOLVERTON (L AND N.W.R.)	0-2	FAC2Q		LAWRENCE AGS	NELSON TL	BLAKER HR	BARKER RR
11-Nov	A	LUTON TOWN	0-4	F	2,000	SIMPSON FA	BEASLEY EH	KING SL	HOSKINS CC
11-Nov	H h	OLD BRIGHTONIANS	1-0	F		BLENKIRON TW	NELSON TL	HATTON COS	BRAY EH
15-Nov	A	HIGHGATE SCHOOL	0-4	F		VOGEL JL	JACQUES (SUB)	BURT CCF	LOOKER WH
15-Nov	H ws	ST BARTHOLOMEWS H	2-1	F		SIMPSON FA	HOLLINGTON ET	MUNDAHL HS	FOY HC
18-Nov	H h	OLD ETONIANS	3-0	F	½	BLENKIRON TW	KING SL	HARRISON AE	WALTER FH
22-Nov	A	RMA WOOLWICH	0-7	F		SIMPSON FA	FOX CJM	FOY CA	BICKLEY F
23-Nov	A	LANCING COLLEGE	1-5	F		SIMPSON FA	COPPELSTON JH	TEMPLETON J	ADLER H
25 Nov	H h	OLD FORESTERS	1-2	F		BLENKIRON TW	KING SL	OTHER AN	FOSTER WL
29-Nov	H h	ST MARYS HOSPITAL	5-1	F		SETON WJ	WILSON GO 3	EBDEN FR	FOY HC
02-Dec	A	CRUSADERS	2-0	F	og	ROUTLEDGE MH	KING SL	FOY CA	BICKLEY F
05-Dec	A	REPTON SCHOOL	5-5	F		SMITH HF	BEASLEY EH	SALE RW	BROOK AK
06-Dec	H h	GUY'S HOSPITAL	1-1	F		ROUTLEDGE MH	PELLY FR	FARMER JH	LOOKER WH
09-Dec	A	LONDON CALEDONIANS	5-1	LCC1	½ 3,000	RAIKES GB	PELLY FR	NELSON TL	HOSSACK AH
09-Dec	A	BECKENHAM	0-2	F		SUB A	LOOKER WH	POWELL GL	SAUL AE
11-Dec	H1	WEST KENT REGIMENT	1-3	F		ROUTLEDGE MH	KING SL	NELSON TL	ALCOCK WG
12-Dec	H h	PRESTON NE	3-4	F	1,000	SETON WJ	PELLY FR	FRY CB	HOSSACK AH
14-Dec	A	SUSSEX MARTLETS	4-2	F		ROUTLEDGE MH	BRAY EH	FRY CB	FOY HC
18-Dec	A	EASTBOURNE	1-2	F	2,000	LAWRENCE AGS	NELSON TL	FRY CB	BUCKINGHAM HC
20-Dec	H1	OLD FORESTERS	3-1	F		LAWRENCE AGS	FRY CB	NELSON MG	GRIEVESON JE
23-Dec	A	CLAPHAM ROVERS	2-1	F		LAWRENCE AGS	FORT CR	KING SL	FARMER JH
26-Dec	A	LEICESTER FOSSE	0-6	F		LAWRENCE AGS	NELSON TL	FORT CR	GRIEVESON JE
26-Dec	A	NORTHAMPTONSHIRE	1-1	F		BLAKER HR	FOY CA	KING SL	FOY RB
27-Dec	A	LUTON TOWN	1-3	F	3,000	LAWRENCE AGS	KING SL	HATTON COS	FOY HC
27-Dec	A	DERBY COUNTY	1-2	F	2,000	MOON WR	NELSON TL	LODGE LV	GRIEVESON JE
28-Dec	A	SHEFFIELD UTD	0-5	F	2,000	MOON WR	LODGE LV	NELSON TL	FOY RH
29-Dec	A	LIVERPOOL RAMBLERS	1-3	F		BLAKER HR	LODGE LV	HATTON COS	PARES B
30-Dec	A	ST. BERNARDS	0-4	F	600	LAWRENCE AGS	BARBOUR RE	LODGE LV	BUZZARD EF
01-Jan	A	PAISLEY ABERCORN	4-2	F		LAWRENCE AGS	HATTON COS	LODGE LV	BUZZARD EF
02-Jan	A	QUEEN OF THE SOUTH WANDERERS	2-2	F		LAWRENCE AGS	HATTON COS	LODGE LV	BUZZARD EF
03-Jan	A	KINGS PARK	3-5	F					
04-Jan	A	KIRKCALDY	0-1	F		LAWRENCE AGS	HATTON COS	LODGE LV	BUZZARD EF
13-Jan	H h	ILFORD	4-0	F	300	LAWRENCE AGS	KING SL	ADAMS WG	BICKLEY F
17-Jan	H h	ST BARTHOLOMEWS H	4-3	F	*	ROUTLEDGE MH	MOON EG	ADAMS WG 1	BICKLEY F
20-Jan	H1	CITY RAMBLERS	2-0	LSC1	400	BLENKIRON TW	KING SL	FRY CB	BARKER RR
25-Jan	A	ROYAL ENGINEERS	4-2	F		ROUTLEDGE MH	DRAKE CD	MOIR JP	HARRISON HA
27-Jan	H h	OLD WESTMINSTERS	6-7	F		ROUTLEDGE MH	KING SL	BARKER RR	RAUTHMELL AW
27-Jan	A	CIVIL SERVICE	3-4	F	½				
31-Jan	A	CAMBRIDGE UNIV	1-3	F		HARRISON AE	PELLY FR	CRUIKSHANK WJ	RAUTHMELL AW
03-Feb	H h	SHEFFIELD	3-1	AC1		HARRISON AE	LODGE LV	HATTON COS	RAUTHMELL AW
03-Feb	A	CLAPTON	2-1	F		ROUTLEDGE MH	KING SL	CRUIKSHANK WJ	FARMER JH
07-Feb	A	OXFORD UNIVERSITY	0-2	F	300	HARRISON AE	KING SL	PELLY FR	LOW RA
10-Feb	H h	CROUCH END	0-0 aet	LSC2		BLAKER HR	GRIEG RA	ATHERLEY H	BARKER RR
14-Feb	A	CHARTERHOUSE	1-3	F		ROUTLEDGE MH	CATER GH	FORDYCE AD	FANE FL
17-Feb	A	CHATHAM	2-0	AC2	1,200	HARRISON AE	LODGE LV	BARKER RR	ANDERSON FJ
24-Feb	A	CROUCH END	3-4	LSC2r	2,500	BLAKER HR	FORD HA	GREIG A	BARKER RR
03-Mar	H	CHIRK	w/o	AC3					
03-Mar	A	OLD BRIGHTONIANS	1-0	F		ROUTLEDGE MH	KING SL	GREIG JL	LOOKER WH
07-Mar	A	HIGHGATE SCHOOL	5-0	F		BRIGHTON R	KORTRIGHT CJ	GREIG JL	MCCOWAN W
10-Mar	A	RMC SANDHURST	1-2	F		RYDON HL	GREIG JL	LOOKER WH	LEMAN RC
17-Mar	N1	SHERWOOD FORESTERS	1-0	Acsf	3,000	HARRISON AE	LODGE LV	HATTON COS	BARKER RR
31-Mar	H1	OLD CARTHUSIANS	3-0	LCCsf		RAIKES GB	PELLY FR	GREIG RA	FOY RH
05-Apr	H1	TRIDENTS	1-2	F	50	ROUTLEDGE MH	GREIG JL	GREIG RA	PLOWMAN J
07-Apr	N r	OLD CARTHUSIANS	1-2	AC.f	3,500	HARRISON AE	LODGE LV	HATTON COS	BARKER RR
12-Apr	A	SHEFFIELD UTD	0-3	F	800	BLAKER HR	GREIG JL	ADAMS WG	BARKER RR
21-Apr	H1	OLD WESTMINSTERS	2-1	LCCf	5,000	RAIKES GB	PELLY FR	HATTON COS	BARKER RR 1

5	6	7	8	9	10	11
WINCKWORTH WN	TOPHAM AG	BLUNT RA	MOORHOUSE HC 1	HOPE RB	KNOX H	BARKER RR
WREFORD-BROWN C	PARES B	FOLEY B	DE LABAT C	NELSON MG	BICKLEY F	DRAKE CF
POLEHAMPTON EH	PARES B	PERKINS TN 2	BLUNT RA	SANDILANDS RR 2	COX LL	COX S 2
PARES B	KEYSELL FS	FOLEY B	KNOX H 1	PERKINS TN 2	DYNE JB	HILLEARY RM
WREFORD-BROWN C	BARKER RR	NELSON MG	BICKLEY F 1	BROAD JD	KNOX H	STEVENS GP
POLEHAMPTON EH	GREIVESON JE	WHITTAKER LE 1	BLUNT RA	PERKINS TN 1	COX S 1	HILLEARY RM
BICKLEY F	FOY RH	TOPHAM R	KNOX H	SMITH GO 3	PERKINS TN 2	COX S
ALEXANDER ER	FOY HC	TOPHAM R 2	WHITTAKER LE 1	PERKINS TN 1	KNOX H	DRAKE CF
SHAW NF	BARKER RR	MOORHOUSE HC	TOPHAM R	SMITH GO 1	COX S	PERKINS TN
ALEXANDER ER	MONTGOMERY RM	WHITTAKER LE	BLUNT RA	SYMONS CBO 1	CARLTON FH	STANBROUGH LK
WALTER FH	WITHERINGTON C	BARWELL FR	KNOX H 1	STEVENS GP 1	BICKLEY F	NELSON MG 2
BARKER RR	WINCKWORTH WN	TOPHAM R	SMITH GO	GUY AN	PERKINS TN 1	WARD F
BICKLEY F	MONTGOMERY RM	NELSON MG	KNOX H	BROAD JD 2	CARLTON FH 1	WALTER FH
GREIVESON JE	WILBERFORCE FR	SHARPLES J	CARLTON WF	PERKINS TN 1	BLUNT RA	ORAMS E
POLEHAMPTON EH	MONTGOMERY RM	KNOX H	NELSON MG	GUY AN 2	BICKLEY F 1	WHITTAKER LE
POLEHAMPTON EH 1	BENSON EPS	MANLY JH	NEWBOLD JH	PERKINS TN 1	BLUNT RA 1	BARWELL FR
	MONTGOMERY RM		KNOX H	FARMER JH	BICKLEY F	NELSON MG
COLLIER JS	JONES GW	HARRISON HA	NELSON MG 1	WHITTAKER LE 1	PARES GL 1	POWELL WG
COLLIER JS	FOY HC	JAMES A 1	DRAKE CF 1	GUY AN	BICKLEY F	HANNAFORD CH
BICKLEY F	POWELL WG	FARMER JH 2	MOORHOUSE HC 2	GUY AN 1	DRAKE CF	HANNAFORD CH
HALL GC	ANDERSON FJ	NELSON MG	DRAKE CF	COMPTON ED	BICKLEY F	BLUNT RA
HALL E	HILLEARY EL	DRAKE CF	WHITTAKER LE	PARES B	BICKLEY F	BLUNT RA
POLEHAMPTON EH	GREIVESON JE	NELSON MG	DRAKE CF	MOORHOUSE HC	CARLTON FW	HANNAFORD CH
WALTER FH	LOOKER WH	STATTER RC	FARMER JH	FARRINGTON JM	FERRIS W	CARLTON FH
BICKLEY F	BARKER RR	COMPTON ED	NELSON MG	BROAD JD 1	HANNAFORD CH	ADAMS FE
EBDEN FR	KITCHING AL (SUB)	BRAY JE	ROUTLEDGE C	HEWITT HW	JENDWINE (SUB)	CLARKSON (SUB)
FARMER JH	BICKLEY F	HANNAFORD CH 1	HOPKINS W	DRAKE CF 1	PARES B	FERRIS W
BICKLEY F	MONTGOMERY RM	FARMER JH	CARLTON FR	COMPTON ED 1	NELSON MG 1	BLUNT RA
FOY CW	WALTER FH	FERRIS W	PARES B	JONES C	FARMER JH	INGRAM CF
BICKLEY F	FOY HC	MAYNE J	CLARKE HR (SUB)	DRAKE CF 1	HEWITT HW	FERRIS W
BICKLEY F	PARES B	BLUNT RA	STEVENS GP	SYMONS CBO 1	CARLTON FH	BROAD JD
WALTERS JH	BICKLEY F	BROAD JD 1	LISTER LH	GUY AN 1	STEPHENS GF	DRAKE CF
RAUTHMELL AW	MONTGOMERY RM	WALTER FH	BROAD JD	SYMONS CBO 1	COMPTON ED	HANNAFORD CH
'ELSE' SO	'OTHER' AN	ADAMS FE	BICKLEY F	SUAL ACA	WILSON GL 4	STANBROUGH MH 1
FOY HC	OTHER AN	HANNAFORD CH 1	HEWITT HW	STANBROUGH MH		
TOPHAM AG	BARKER RR	TOPHAM R	COMPTON ED 2	HATTON COS 1	CARLTON FW	PARES B 1
BUCKINGHAM HC	SUB A	RYDON HL	FARMER JH	HEWITT HW	BRAY EH	HULL
FOY HC	STOKES B	HANNAFORD CH	HATTON COS	GUY AN 1	PERKINS TN	HEWITT CD
TOPHAM AG	BARKER RR 1	TOPHAM R	PERKINS TN	SMITH GO	GUY AN 1	HEWITT CD
BICKLEY F	FARMER JH 1	TOPHAM R	COMPTON ED 2	DRAKE CF	SHARPLES J	CUMMING G 1
BRAY EH	BUZZARD EF	BOSWORTH-SMITH BN 1	BATEMAN W	DRAKE CF	POLEHAMPTON FW	BRAY JE
BICKLEY F	DE LABAT C	BOSWORTH-SMITH BN	ROBINSON CA	HOPE RB 2	SIMKINS WA 1	HANNAFORD CH
BARKER RR	EBDEN FR	NELSON MG	ROBINSON CA	NELSON TL 2	FARMER MS	HANNAFORD CH
BARKER RR	BUZZARD EF	SYMONS CBO	NEWBOLD JH	SIMKINS WA	ROBINSON CA	SHARPLES J
BICKLEY F	FOY HC	NELSON MG	CRAWFORD RO 1	HATTON COS	CARLTON FW	OTHER AN
BICKLEY F	FOY EH	NELSON MG	CRAWFORD RO 1	SYMONS CBO	COMPTON ED	PARES B
BUZZARD EF	BARKER RR	ROBINSON CA	CARLTON FW	RHODES TB 1	RHODES HA	SHARPLES J
GREIVESON JE	BUZZARD EF	SHARPLES J	RHODES HA	WILSON EG	CARLTON FW	TOPHAM R
BICKLEY F	FOY EH	SHARPLES J	SIMKINS WA	HOPE RB 1	CRAWFORD RO	NELSON MG
GREIVESON JE	FOY RH	TOPHAM R	CARLTON FW	HOPE RB	RHODES HA	COMPTON ED
CARLTON JE	FOY RH	BOSWORTH-SMITH BN	CARLTON FW	TOPHAM R 4	RHODES HA	COMPTON ED
GREIVESON JE	FOY RH	BOSWORTH-SMITH BN 1	CARLTON FW	NELSON MG 1	COMPTON ED	RHODES HA
		TOPHAM R	RHODES HA 1			
PARES B	FOY RH	CARLTON FW	RHODES HA	WILSON EG	RHODES TB	SHARPLES J
NELSON MG	FARMER JH	HANNAFORD CH	ROBINSON CA	DE LABAT C	HILLEARY RM 1	LANDON HE 3
HARRISON HA	SUB A	HANNAFORD CH	PATER A	CRAWFORD RO 2	ROBINSON CA	LANDON HE
ADAMS WG	NELSON MG	TOPHAM R	ROBINSON CA	HOPE RB 2	CRAWFORD RO	LANDON HE
BRAY JE	WHITE J	ADAMS FE	LEMAN DC	MOORHOUSE HC 3	PRIDHAM HR	HANNAFORD CH 1
FOSTER WL	MARTIN AR	HOGARTH RG 4	CRAWFORD RO 2	COMPTON ED	HILLEARY RM	
BROOK AK	HILLEARY EL	LEMAN RC 1	HOGARTH RG	RHODES HA	BICKLEY F	NELSON MG
BARKER RR	HENDERSON H	CARLTON FW	RHODES TB	PERKINS TN 3	RHODES HA	COMPTON ED
MONTGOMERY RM	HOSKINS CC	NELSON MG	ROBINSON CA	ATHERINGTON H	CARLTON FH	HANNAFORD CH 2
MONTGOMERY RM	NELSON MG	HANNAFORD CH	LEMAN RC	MOORHOUSE HC	ATHERLEY H	HOGARTH RG
MONTGOMERY RM	FARMER JH	HANNAFORD CH	SIMKINS WA	TOPHAM R	CARLTON FH	LANGDEN HE
WINCH AB	FARMER JH	HANNAFORD CH	DRAKE CF	HUNT R 1	LEMAN DC	LEMAN RC
MONTGOMERY RM	GREIVESON JE	HANNAFORD CH	ROBINSON CA	PERKINS TN	RHODES TB 2	MANLY JH
MONTGOMERY RM	FARMER JH	ROBINSON CA	SIMKINS WA	HATTON COS 1	CARLTON FH 1	HANNAFORD CH 1
MONTGOMERY RM	FARMER JH	HANNAFORD CH 1	HEWITT HW	ROUTLEDGE C		
CONOY FD	MAYNARD J	SCOTT A	HIBERT HR 3	BROAD JD	KNOX H 1	PERKINS HW 1
MONTGOMERY RM	FARMER JH	LEMAN DC	HEBERT HR 1	HEWITT HW	CARLTON FH	HANNAFORD CH
EDWARDS R	GREIVESON JE	BOSWORTH-SMITH BN	COMPTON ED	PERKINS TN	RHODES HA	LANDON HE 1
HATTON COS	BARKER RR	TOPHAM R	COTTERILL GH 1	PERKINS TN 1	GUY AN 1	RHODES HA
KORTRIGHT CJ	LOOKER WH	HANNAFORD CH	FORD HA	CARLTON FW	DRAKE CF 1	HEWITT HW
TOPHAM AG	GREIVESON JE	TOPHAM R 1	CARLTON FW	PERKINS TN	RHODES TB	RHODES HA
PLOWMAN A	FARMER JH	TOPHAM R	YOUNG R	SANDILANDS RR	MOORHOUSE CP	HANNAFORD CH
TOPHAM AG	FOY RH	MOORHOUSE HC	COTTERILL GH	PERKINS TN	GUY AN 1	RHODES HA

1894/95

DATE	VEN	OPPONENTS	RES	COMP	ATT	1	2	3	4
15-Sep	A	CLAPTON	5-3	F	2,500	LAWRENCE AGS	KING SL	FOY RH	BICKLEY F
22-Sep	A	TOTTENHAM H	1-3	F		BLAKER HR	PELLY FR	ADAMS WG	WETTON H
22-Sep	A	WOLVERTON (L AND N.W.R.)	1-6	F		LAWRENCE AGS	KING SL	MASTERMAN HA	RAUTHMELL LC
24-Sep	A	LUTON TOWN	2-5	F	2,000	LAWRENCE AGS	WETTON H	GREIG G	MONTGOMERY RM
26-Sep	A	UXBRIDGE	5-4	F	500	LAWRENCE AGS	GREIG RA	FOY RH	RAUTHMELL HA
29-Sep	H h	CROUCH END	5-2	F		BLAKER HR	KING SL	LANDALE N	MARTEN AB
29-Sep	A	IPSWICH TOWN	3-0	F		LAWRENCE AGS	TOWLE AF	TIMONEY F	HEIGHAM AF
03-Oct	A	CHARTERHOUSE	2-2	F		BLENKIRON TW	TIMMIS WU	BRAY EH	FOY RH
04-Oct	H1	WOOLWICH ARSENAL	0-8	F	2,500	IBBS RS	FOY RH	BRAY EH	BUZZARD EF
06-Oct	H1	IDLERS	0-2	F		WATSON WA	KING SL	FOY CA	BICKLEY F
11-Oct	H1	NOTTINGHAM FOREST	3-4	F		HARRISON AE	KING SL	FRY CB	WETTON H
13-Oct	A	CHESHAM	4-1	FAC1Q		RAIKES GB	OAKLEY WJ	KING SL	HILLEARY EL
13-Oct	A	HILLINGDON	0-2	F		TOWNE WD	KNOX H	HARPER EA	SMITH BF
16-Oct	A	SUNDERLAND	4-3	F	6,000	RAIKES GB	OAKLEY WJ	LODGE LV	GRIEVESON JE
17-Oct	A	CAMBRIDGE UNIV	1-4	F		HARRISON AE	THOMPSON J	FOY CA	KNOX H
27-Oct	A	WESTMINSTER SCHOOL	3-1	F	%	HALE JR	KING SL	SMITH ? 1	MARTEN AB
27-Oct	A	BRIGHTON COLLEGE	0-6	F		RYDON HL	BROWN GD	MASON G	STEVENS EH
31-Oct	H1	OXFORD UNIVERSITY	3-4	F	500	HARRISON AE	THOMPSON J	HILLEARY EL	FOY RH
03-Nov	H1	ILFORD	0-0	FAC2Q		LAWRENCE AGS	KING SL	FINNEY WW	HILLEARY EL
03-Nov	H1	PRESTON NE	2-5	F	10,000	HARRISON AE	BARKER RR	FORT CR	COOPER NC
03-Nov	H1	LIVERPOOL RAMBLERS	1-2	F					
07-Nov	H1	ILFORD	1-3	FAC2Q	500	'WOOD' GH	THOMPSON J	PELLY FR	HILLEARY EL
10-Nov	A	LONDON CALEDONIANS	1-1	LCC1	% 3,000	THOMPSON G	PELLY FR	FINNEY WW	HIGSON TA
17-Nov	A	OLD WESTMINSTERS	2-3	F	%	TOWNE WD	LANDALE N	BARLOW MY	MARTEN AB
17-Nov	A	WOOLWICH ARSENAL	1-4	F	3,000	BLAKER HR	GREIG RA	KING SL	BARKER RR
17-Nov	A	FELSTED SCHOOL	4-1	F	%	FARNIE MS	FORDYCE AS	GARNETT AW	MILLS HM
21-Nov	A	RMA WOOLWICH	4-3	F	%				
24-Nov		BEXLEY	0-1	F					
01-Dec	A	CRUSADERS	1-3	F	500	LAWRENCE AGS	KING SL	PELLY FR	BRAY EH
08-Dec	H1	OLD ETONIANS	7-4	F		MOSS HK	ADAMS WG	BRAY EH	HILLEARY EL
08-Dec	H1	OLD BRIGHTONIANS	2-3	F		MOSS HK	KING SL	MALDEN AW	MONTGOMERY RM
10-Dec	H1	ROYAL WEST KENT REGIMENT	2-1	F		SETON WJ	BRAY EH	BAINES AGP	DARVELL S
11-Dec	A	FOREST SCHOOL	7-2	F		TOWNE WD	FOY RH	GREIG RA	COOPER HES
12-Dec	A	SHREWSBURY SCHOOL	2-2	F		ALINGTON CL	OAKLEY WJ	FINNEY WW	ACKROYD E
13-Dec	H1	ST BARTHOLOMEWS H	1-2	F		FOY RH	BAINES AGP	THOMPSON J	DARVELL S
15-Dec	H1	OLD HARROVIANS	3-0	F		LAWRENCE AGS	KING SL	MALDEN AW	DARVELL S
17-Dec	A	EASTBOURNE	0-3	F		LAWRENCE AGS	BRAY EH	ADAMS WG	SALMON T
20-Dec	H1	OLD CHOMELIANS	6-1	F	og	COOKE CP	ADAMS WG	MALDEN AW	TOPHAM AG
22-Dec	A	BURSLEM PORT VALE	2-3	F		SETON WJ	SIMPSON GH	BAINES AGP	LE MESURIER G
24-Dec	A	LEICESTER FOSSE	2-3	F		SETON WJ	SIMPSON GH	BAINES AGP	LE MESURIER G
26-Dec	A	KETTERING	2-1	F		SETON WJ	HATTON COS	SIMPSON GH	SALMON T
27-Dec.	A	LUTON TOWN	2-2	F	og % 3,000	LAWRENCE AGS	KING SL	ADAMS WG	DARVELL S
27-Dec	A	LOUGHBOROUGH TOWN	1-4	F		SETON WJ	HATTON COS	SIMPSON GH	SALMON T
28-Dec	A	BURTON WANDERERS	0-3	F		SETON WJ	THOMPSON J	ADAMS WG	DARVELL TJ
29-Dec	A	SUNDERLAND	2-5	F		LAWRENCE AGS	SIMPSON GH	HATTON COS	FOY RH
31-Dec	A	NEWTON STEWART ATHLETIC	4-4	F	* %				
01-Jan	A	GREENOCK MORTON	2-3	F	%	HARRISON AE	HATTON COS	GREIG JL	HILLEARY EL
01-Jan	A	DUMFRIES	2-4	F		SETON WJ	GREIG	ADAMS WG	DARVELL S
02-Jan	A	THIRD LANARK	1-4	F		SETON WJ	HATTON COS	SIMPSON GH	HILLEARY EL
04-Jan	A	KIRKCALDY	3-2	F		HARRISON AE	SIMPSON GH	GREIG RA	HILLEARY EL
05-Jan	A	AYR PARKHOUSE	0-4	F		SETON WJ	HATTON COS	GREIG RA	HILLEARY EL
12-Jan	H1	LONDON CALEDONIANS	1-2	LCC1r	600	LAWRENCE AGS	SIMPSON GH	KING SL	GRIEVESON JE
16-Jan	A	SWANSCOMBE	2-3	F	%				
19-Jan	A	EALING	5-3	LSC1	%	BLENKIRON TW	FORT CR	ADAMS WG	HILLEARY EL
16-Feb	A	READING	1-3	AC1	2,000	RAIKES GB	SIMPSON GH	LODGE LV	BARKER RR
23-Feb	H h	WOODFORD	3-1	F	%	LAWRENCE AGS	KING SL	ADAMS WG	HIGSON TA
27-Feb	A	HIGHGATE SCHOOL	9-1	F	%	OTHER AN	KING SL	KING EL	PICKERING HJ
19-Mar	A	FOREST SCHOOL	4-4	F		BARKER RR 2	ADAMS WG	MCCOWAN W	ROOKE BE
20-Mar	A	CHESHAM	3-7	F	%	SHEEN F (SUB)	THOMPSON SJ	BAINES AGP	PAGE H
23-Mar	A	WOODFORD	3-1	LSC2		LAWRENCE AGS	KING SL	ADAMS WG	HILLEARY EL
04-Apr	H1	TRIDENTS	4-4	F		LAWRENCE AGS	PELLY FR	MCCOWAN W	PAGE H
06-Apr	H1	ILFORD	3-0	LSCsf	1,000	LAWRENCE AGS	FRY CB	ADAMS WG	ROOKE BE
06-Apr	A	TOTTENHAM H	2-1	F		BLAKER HR	SYMONS JA	MALDEN AW	RAUTHMELL HA
13-Apr	A	WOODVILLE	4-2	F	600	HARRISON AE	SYMONS JA	WHITTING AG	RAUTHMELL HA
18-Apr	H1	CROUCH END THURSDAY	3-2	F		HARRISON AE	KING SL	SYMONS JA	SYMONS CT
20-Apr	A	WEST HERTS	1-3	F		PENNEY J	KING SL	BARKER RR 1	TAYLOR J
30-Apr	N qc	OLD CARTHUSIANS	0-4	LSCf	850	LAWRENCE AGS	FRY CB	ADAMS WG	HILLEARY EL

5	6	7	8	9	10	11
MONTGOMERY RM	GRIEVESON JE	COLLIER HJ 2	DRAKE CF	FERNIE JF 2	LANDON HE	VEITCH JG 1
BICKLEY F	FOY RH	DRAKE CF 1	ROBINSON CA	PERKINS TN	BRYANT HJ	LEMAN DC
MONTGOMERY RM	MILLS HM	SMITH AS	HAYCOCK T (sub)	WHITTAKER LE 1	LANDON HE	OTHER AN
RAUTHWELL HA	MILLS HM	LANDON HE	PERKINS TN 1	FERNIE JF	ROBINSON CA	DRAKE CF 1
BROAD JD 1	DEAN E	DRAKE CF 3	PERKINS TN	ROBINSON CA	WELSH	HILLEARY RM 1
BARKER RR	RAUTHMELL HA	LEMAN DC	ROBINSON CA 1	FRY CB 3	BICKLEY F 1	HILLEARY RM
LYNCH F	GRIEVESON JE	MACKLIN W	PROCTER H 2	WARD JM	WITHERS A 1	MERRALL W
WETTON H	DRAKE CF	HILLEARY RM	BICKLEY F	SMITH GO 1	COLLIER HJ 1	VASSALL GC
BARKER RR	RAUTHMELL HA	VASSALL GC	DRAKE CF	FRY CB	HILLEARY RM	COLLIER HJ
BROAD JD	LINSELL MG	SMITH AE	CARLTON FW	GUY AN	BRYANT HJ	GIFFORD WJ
COOPER NC	FOY RH	DRAKE CF 2	CARLTON FW	FERNIE JF 1	BROWN CH	HILLEARY RM
RAUTHMELL HA	BICKLEY F	HANNAFORD CH	ROBINSON CA 1	CARLTON FW 2	SMITH RM 1	HILLEARY RM
BOROUGH RJ	SUB A	GIFFARD WJ	HARRISON AE	PARRY CF	ROUTLEDGE C	DURELL ED
COOPER NC	FOY RH	FRY CB 1	DRAKE CF	SMITH GO 2	GUY AN 1	RHODES HA
FOY RH	LOCKE EJ	HANNAFORD CH	ROBINSON CA	DRAKE CF	BICKLEY F	CRABTREE H 1
BARKER RR	BICKLEY F	HILLEARY EL	HANNAFORD CH	CATTLEY JF	BOLTON HE	ROOKE BE 1
HODSOLL B	MARSHALL EJ (SUB)	YOUNG CS (SUB)	SHARPLEY H	HARRISON AE	PARRY AF	RYDON AL
COOPER NC	MORTEN AB	HANNAFORD CH	BUZZARD EF 1	GOSLING WS 1	COLLIER HJ 1	DRAKE CF
RAUTHMELL HA	FOY RH	HANNAFORD CH	BICKLEY F	COMPTON ED	ROOKE BE	LANDON HE
WREFORD-BROWN C	BUZZARD EF	HEWETSON J	RHODES HA	HOPE RB 2 OLIVER 1	GUY AN	STANBROUGH MH
WETTON H	FOY RH	HANNAFORD CH	BICKLEY F 1	CATTLEY W	BARKER RR	DRAKE CF
BARKER RR	GRIEVESON JE	ROOKE BE	ROBINSON CA	HATTON COS	COLLIER HJ	RHODES HA
BICKLEY F	MACDONALD CN	HANNAFORD CH	SMITH AE	WILTSHIRE HP	NELSON MG	GUNNERY WR 1
MONTGOMERY RM	HILLEARY EL	HILLEARY RM	SANDERSON WB	BROADBENT HT 1	DRAKE CF	HEWETSON J
OPENSHAW J	LOWE HA	BARRETT-HAMILTON GE	MORTON L	RHODES HA 3	FORDYCE RD	ALEXANDER CL
COLLIER HJ	LOWE HA	BARWELL FR 1	WILTSHIRE HP	DRAKE CF	HILLEARY RM	
PICKERING HJ	BARKER RR 1	BARRETT-HAMILTON GE	ROBINSON CA 2	FERNIE JF 3	BARWELL FR 1	HILLEARY RM
COOPER HES	MACDONALD CN	WOODBRIDGE AR	ROOKE BE	CATTLEY JF 2	TOONE WP	HANNAFORD CH
ADAMS WG	PICKERING HJ	BOSWORTH-SMITH BN	CARLTON FW 1	PERKINS TN	ROOKE BE 1	TAYLOR SS
MCCOWAN W	HAMILTON GH	BARRETT-HAMILTON GE	BRAY EH 3	PERKINS TN 3	ROOKE BE 1	HILLEARY RM
RAUTHMELL HA	LOWE HA	HEWETSON J 1	RAIKES GB	CATTLEY TF	BOWDLER EH 1	HENDERSON TB
BARRETT-HAMILTON GE	LANDALE N	ROOKE BE	TOONE WP	PERKINS TN 1	BARWELL FR	HILLEARY RM
CARLTON FW	HILLEARY EL	BARWELL FR 1	PERKINS TN 1	COMPTON ED	HENDERSON TB 1	
LANDALE N	DARVELL S	D'ARCY-THOMPSON P	DRAKE CF	CARLTON FW	COMPTON ED	ROOKE BE
DARVELL S	LE MESURIER G	TOONE WP	CARLTON FW	PERKINS TN 3	HENDERSON TB 1	ROOKE BE 1
HATTON COS	HILLEARY EL	MANLY JH	ROBINSON CA 1	FERNIE JF 1	BARWELL FR	HILLEARY RM
HATTON COS	HILLEARY EL	BARWELL WT	GUY AN	FERNIE JF 2	ROBINSON CA	MANLY JH
HIGSON TA	DARVELL S	DRAKE CF 1	CARLTON FW	FERNIE JF	BARWELL FR 1	MANLY JH
RAUTHMELL HA	HILLEARY EL	HEWETSON J	ROBINSON CA	CARLTON FW	HENDERSON TB	BARWELL WT
HIGSON TA	FOY RH	DRAKE CF	TAYLOR SS	FERNIE JF	TOONE WP 1	MANLY JH
HIGSON TA	WETHERED WP	BARWELL FR	WILTSHIRE HP	FRANCIS PO	HENDERSON TB	HILLEARY RM
RAUTHMELL HA	SALMON T	MANLY JH	TOONE WP 1	FERNIE JF 1	TAYLOR SS	DRAKE CF
SALMON T	FOY RH	DRAKE CF	CARLTON FW	'MACHAGGIS' L 1	TAYLOR SS	HILLEARY EL
RAUTHMELL HA	FRANCIS PO	BARWELL WT	TOONE WP	BARWELL FR	WILTSHIRE HP 2	HENDERSON TB
SALMON T	FOY RH	DRAKE CF	TAYLOR SS 1	'HAGGIS' M 1	WILTSHIRE HP	BARWELL FR
RAUTHMELL HA	FOY RH	DRAKE CF 1	TAYLOR SS	FRANCIS PO	WILTSHIRE HP	BARWELL FR 1
RAUTHMELL HA	BARWELL	DRAKE CF	TAYLOR SS	WILTSHIRE HP	TOONE WP	BURNUP CJ
BARKER RR	SALMON T	DRAKE CF	TAYLOR SS	FERNIE JF 1	COLLIER HJ	MANLY JH
BARKER RR	MARTEN AB	TOONE WP 1	NELSON MG	CRAWFORD RO 1	HENDERSON TB 1	LANDON HE 1
HATTON COS	HILLEARY EL	DRAKE CF	FRY CB	FERNIE JF 1	PERKINS TN	
HATTON COS	HILLEARY EL	HENDERSON TB	HILLEARY RM	TOONE WP 1	NELSON MG	TAYLOR SS
MONTGOMERY RM	PAGE H	DRAKE CF	SMITH AE	FERNIE JF	'GOODUN' A 2	NELSON MG
HAMILTON GH	DRAKE CF	TOONE WP 1	FERNIE JF 1	HILLEARY EL	WALKER HJD	
ADAMS WG	MCCOWAN W	SMITH AE	WEST J (SUB) 1	TOONE WP 1	BARWELL WT	HILL T
BARKER RR	WILSON CP	DRAKE CF	COMPTON ED 3	TOONE WP	HENDERSON TB	LANDON HE
'SMITH' A	ROOKE BE	HILLEARY RM	TOONE WP 2	FERNIE JF 1	COMPTON ED 1	DRAKE CF
BARKER RR	WILSON CP	DRAKE CF	COMPTON ED	TOONE WP	HENDERSON TB	LANDON HE 1
BARRETT HR	SYMONS CT	FERNIE AE	COLLIER HJ 1	ROBINSON CA 1	SMITH AE	MCCOWAN W
SYMONS CT	MCCOWAN W	SMITH AE	ROBINSON CA	TOONE WP 1	COMPTON ED 2	LANDON HE 1
TURNBULL RM	ROOKE BE	LANDON HE 1	HENDERSON TB	TOONE WP	CARLTON FW 2	DRAKE CF
CARLTON FW	ROOKE BE	LANDON HE	HENDERSON TB	TOONE WP	GRIFFITHS C	DRAKE CF
BARKER RR	WILSON CP	LANDON HE	HENDERSON TB	TOONE WP	COMPTON ED	DRAKE CF

1895/96

DATE	VEN	OPPONENTS	RES	COMP	ATT	1	2	3	4
14-Sep	A	CLAPTON	3-4	F		LAWRENCE AGS	KING SL	SYMONS JA	PICKERING HJ
21-Sep	A	TOTTENHAM H	2-3	F	2,000	LAWRENCE AGS	BAINES AGP	SYMONS JA	PICKERING HJ
21-Sep	A	TUNBRIDGE WELLS	0-4	F		BLAKER HR	RYDON HL	CIOWAN WM	MONTGOMERY RM
25-Sep	H h	1ST GRENADIER GUARDS	2-0	F		LAWRENCE AGS	MALDEN AW	WHITTAKER LE	SYMONS JA
28-Sep	A	BARKING WOODVILLE	7-3	F	% 700	RYDON HL	BAINES AGP	SYMONS JA	WHITTING AG
02-Oct	A	UXBRIDGE	0-0	F		LAWRENCE AGS	SYMONS JA	MALDEN AW	BARRETT HR
05-Oct	A	CROUCH END	3-1	F		RYDON HL	BAINES AGP	SYMONS JA	KING SL
09-Oct	A	SOUTHAMPTON ST M	0-5	F		HARRISON AE	KING SL	MALDEN AW	SYMONS JA
12-Oct	H	LONDON CALEDONIANS	4-3	F	%	LAWRENCE AGS	ADAMS WG	KING SL	AUSTIN AE
15-Oct	H 1	EVERTON	1-2	F	5,000	HARRISON AE	BARKER RR	BRAY EH	WREFORD-BROWN C
16-Oct	A	CAMBRIDGE UNIV	2-2	F	og	HARRISON AE	MALDEN AW	FORDYCE AD	ECCLES A
19-Oct	A	WEST HERTS	2-1	F	%				
23-Oct	A	CHARTERHOUSE	7-3	F	%	HARRISON AE	FORDYCE AD	MALDEN AW	GARNETT EN
26-Oct	A	SWINDON TOWN	0-3	F	1,000	COODE CP	ADAMS WG	COOPER	PETTITT
26-Oct	A	IPSWICH TOWN	1-3	F		COOKSON RT	WILSON AB	BOUCHER C	MILLS HM
30-Oct	A	OXFORD UNIVERSITY	1-1	F		HARRISON AE	LODGE LV	MALDEN AW	HIGSON TA
02-Nov	H cp	2ND COLDSTREAM GDS	3-0	AC2Q	600	HARRISON AE	ADAMS WG	KING SL	GRIEVESON JE
06-Nov	H	ST BARTHOLOMEWS H	3-1	F		COODE CP	BAINES AGP	MALDEN AW	YOUNG W
07-Nov	A	ROYAL ENGINEERS	3-1	F		HALE JR	BAINES AGP	THOMPSON J	BRYANT HJ
09-Nov	A	ILFORD	1-2	F	400	HARRISON AE	KING SL	HILLEARY EL	MILLS HM
13-Nov	A	RMA WOOLWICH	4-6	F		RYDON HL	THOMPSON J	MCDONALD CR	JACKSON FM
16-Nov	H 1	PRESTON NORTH END	0-4	F	4,000	HARRISON AE	KING SL	PELLY FR	BUZZARD EF
16-Nov	H cp	OLD WESTMINSTERS	1-4	F	%				
20-Nov	A	SHREWSBURY SCHOOL	9-2	F		RAIKES GB	OAKLEY WJ	ADAMS WG	ECCLES A
20-Nov	A	FELSTED SCHOOL	4-2	F		COOKSON CF	WILSON AB	HARKNESS CL	SALE FA
21-Nov	H 1	WOOLWICH ARSENAL	0-3	F		LAWRENCE AGS	BRAY EH	PELLY FR	HOLLINGTON T
23-Nov	A	QUEEN'S PARK RANGERS	5-1	AC3Q	2,000	LAWRENCE AGS	KING SL	HILLEARY EL	WHITTING AG
23-Nov	H 1	OLD FORESTERS	1-4	F	%	COLLIER HJ	MACDONALD DR	FOULKES CH	WHITTING AG
30-Nov	H 1	LIVERPOOL RAMBLERS	6-0	F		COODE AP	KING SL 1	WHITTAKER LE	BARRETT FJ
30-Jan	A	BEXLEY	0-2	F		GODWIN WP	FOULKES CH	MACDONNELL CH	RYDON HL
04-Dec	H 1	ST MARYS HOSPITAL	6-3	F	og	GODWIN WP	BARRETT HR	BAINES AGP	FINCHAM E 1
07-Dec	H 1	OLD ETONIANS	3-0	F		HARRISON AE	BARKER RR	DROWN H	MONTGOMERY RM
07-Dec	A	OLD BRIGHTONIANS	1-0	F		GODWIN WP	KING SL	WILLIAMS SS	SMITH C 1
10-Dec	H c	SUNDERLAND	3-3	F	3,500	LAWRENCE AGS	BRAY EH	OAKLEY WJ	RAUTHMELL HA
10-Dec	A	FOREST SCHOOL	4-1	F		RYDON HL	COOPER HES	BOSTOCK AN	ROOKE BE
12-Dec	A	MALVERN COLLEGE	2-1	F		RAIKES GB	ECCLES A	OAKLEY WJ	RAUTHMELL HA 1
13-Dec	A	SHREWSBURY SCHOOL	5-1	F		RAIKES GB	OAKLEY WJ	ECCLES A	RAUTHMELL HA
14-Dec	H 1	OLD WESTMINSTERS	2-1	AC4Q	700	HARRISON AE	LODGE LV	PELLY FR	PICKERING HJ
14-Dec	A	HARROW ATHLETIC	4-2	F	og	GODWIN WP	KING SL	PHELPS J	MONTGOMERY RM
18-Dec	H 1	SOUTH EASTERN COLLEGE	5-2	F		RAUTHMELL HA	FINNEY CE	THOMPSON J	BARKER RR
21-Dec	H 1	OLD CARTHUSIANS	2-3	LCC1	1,500	HARRISON AE	LODGE LV	PELLY FR	HATTON COS 1
21-Dec	A	TOTTENHAM H	1-3	F	1,000	LAWRENCE AGS	BERWICK REH	ADAMS WG	NELSON JC
26-Dec	A	CLAPTON	2-2	F		TURNBULL H	ADAMS WG	KING SL	RAUTHMELL HA
27-Dec	A	LUTON TOWN	1-7	F		TURNBULL H	ADAMS WG	KING SL	RAUTHMELL HA
28-Dec	A	LEICESTER FOSSE	5-6	F		TURNBULL H	ADAMS WG	KING SL	RAUTHMELL HA
08-Jan	A	NEW BROMPTON	0-2	F		LAWRENCE AGS	BERWICK REH	KING SL	FOULKES CH
11-Jan	H cp	OLD HARROVIANS	0-2	F		LAWRENCE AGS	KING SL	WHITTING AG	HILLEARY EL
18-Jan	A	LUTON TOWN	0-3	F		BARTLEY TR	KING SL	BLAKER HR	LOWE HA
23-Jan	H 1	UNIVERSITY COLLEGE HOS.	1-1	F		COODE CP	MAYNARD-TAYLOR DC	MCDONNELL CH	BARRETT HR
25-Jan	A	QUEEN'S PARK RANGERS	4-3	LSC1	1,800	LAWRENCE AGS	BAINES AGP	ADAMS WG	BARKER RR
29-Jan	H 1	CAMBRIDGE UNIV	3-6	F		BARTLEY A	BAINES AGP	BARKER RR	HILLEARY EL
01-Feb	H	SHREWSBURY TOWN	2-4 aet	AC1		LAWRENCE AGS	ECCLES A	KING SL	HIGSON TA
01-Feb	A	WESTMINSTER SCHOOL	4-5	F		GODWIN WP	BLAKER HR	THOMPSON SL	REBOW MG
04-Feb	H 1	FOREST SCHOOL	1-1	F		GODWIN WP	ANDREWS HG	ROBERTSON GE	BOSTOCK FH
05-Feb	A	CHARTERHOUSE	3-4	F		BARTLEY PR	BLAKER HR	TRESTALL EA	ADAMS FE
08-Feb	H 1	ST BARTHOLOMEWS H	2-0	LSC2		LAWRENCE AGS	ADAMS WG	KING SL	WILSON CP
12-Feb	H 1	OXFORD UNIVERSITY	2-2	F	600	BARTLEY TR	PELLY FR	KING SL	PROBYN S
15-Feb	A	WESTMINSTER SCHOOL	2-2	F	%				
20-Feb	A	ROYAL ENGINEERS	3-3	F		GODWIN WP	ANDREWS HW	BARRETT HR	MARSHALL C
26-Feb	H 1	OLD ETONIANS	2-3	F		HOOPER E	MORTIMER RG	FORDYCE AD	BARRETT-HAMILTON GE
29-Feb	N tp	VAMPIRES	5-3	LSCsf	2,000	LAWRENCE AGS	BAINES AGP	ADAMS WG	HATTON COS
02-Mar	A	WOOLWICH ARSENAL	1-4	F		HARRISON AE	BRAY EH	KING SL	ECCLES A
05-Mar	H 1	NORTHAMPTONSHIRE	2-2	F		LAWRENCE AGS	ARCH MON	BAINES AGP	BRYANT HJ
14-Mar	A	BARKING WOODVILLE	3-0	F		LAWRENCE AGS	KING SL	BARRATT L	WILSON CP
21-Mar	H cp	CLAPHAM ROVERS	1-2	F	%				
02-Apr	A	WEYBRIDGE	7-0	F		LAWRENCE AGS	BAINES AGP	BRAY EH	BARRETT HR
14-Apr	H 1	EVERTON	3-3	F	2,000	LAWRENCE AGS	BRAY EH	PELLY FR	HATTON COS
16-Apr	H 1	OLD CARTHUSIANS	1-3	LSCf	2,000	LAWRENCE AGS	ADAMS WG	BAINES AGP	RAUTHMELL HA

5	6	7	8	9	10	11
BARRETT HR	COOKE AT	DRAKE CF	COLLIER HJ 2	FERNIE JF 1	HILLEARY RM	LANDON HE
BARRETT HR	PARES B	DRAKE CF	MOORHOUSE HC 1	FERNIE JF	TOONE WP 1	LANDON HE
SMITH C	BICKLEY F	MALDEN AW	HILLEARY RM	BARWELL WT	WINCKWORTH DP	SUB A
BARRETT HR	PARES B	HILLEARY RM	TOONE WP	FERNIE JF 1	TAYLOR SS	SMITH AE 1
LOW RA	ROOKE BE	ROOKE A	TOONE WP 1	FERNIE JF 2	TAYLOR SS 2	SMITH AE 1
BICKLEY F	PICKERING HJ	ROOKE BE	PARES B	FERNIE JF	TAYLOR SS	SMITH AE
WHITTING AG	SMITH C	SMITH AE	TAYLOR SS 2	FERNIE JF 1	HILLEARY RM	STANBROUGH MH
SMITH V	BARRETT HR	SMITH AE	BRYANT FH	BROWN TH	TOMBLESON JB	PARES B
HIGSON TA	RAUTHMELL HA	HILLEARY RM	MCKEAN H	FERNIE JF	TAYLOR SS	FRYER PA
HIGSON TA	BUZZARD EF	RHODES HA	TAYLOR SS	FERNIE JF 1	COMPTON ED	STANBROUGH MH
HIGSON TA	MASON L	RHODES HA	ROBINSON CA	FERNIE JF	MCKEAN H 1	HILLEARY RM
BARKER RR 1	BICKLEY F	HILLEARY RM	COLLIER HJ 3	FERNIE JF 1	BRYANT FH	FORDYCE RD 1
BRITTEN	WREFORD-BROWN G	MCKEAN H	BATHURST JA	CATTLEY JF	BOULTON	COCHRANE J
COOPER LP	WILBERFORCE S	SHINE EB	UNWIN LL 1	ALEXANDER CL	DAVIES HH	SEYMOUR
BARKER RR	TRESTALL EA	WILTSHIRE HP	BROAD JD	INGRAM FM 1	BELCHER AH	HILLEARY RM
BARKER RR	HIGSON TA	HILLEARY RM 1	BROWN TH 1	FERNIE JF 1	BRYANT FH	DRAKE CF
COX AG	WHITTING AG	DRAKE CF	BRYANT FH	RHODES HA	JACKSON FH	BRYANT HJ 3
BOSTOCK AH	JACKSON H	SMITH AE 1	BRYANT FH 2	GRANT DF	HEWITT HW	HILLEARY RM
BARRETT HR	LOW RA	RHODES HA	WINCH GB	GRANT DF	MACDONALD CN	HILLEARY RM 1
MACDONALD DR	SMITH AE	SUBSTITUTE A 2	BRYANT HJ 1	BRAY JE 1	MONTGOMERY RM	
HIGSON TA	HILLEARY EL	FRYER FA	PERKINS TN	FERNIE JF	BURNETT-STUART G	RHODES HA
RAUTHMELL HA	DONALDSON N	BARNETT-STUART E	COMPTON ED	SMITH GO 8	BARENS E 1	BRIGGS C
COOPER LP	LOWE HA	MARTIN WM	FARRAR PF 1	RHODES HA 2	WINCH GB	UNWIN SR 1
BARKER RR	WARD CB	'DUCK' A	'WARD' FOR	STREET F	BROWN TH	HILLEARY RM
BARKER RR 1	LOWE WW	DRAKE CF	ROBINSON CA 1	FERNIE JF 2	BROWN J 1	HILLEARY RM
PICKERING HJ	WILLIAMS SS	WALTON-EVANS J	MACDONALD CN	SMITH AE	NEWBOLD JC	SYMES-THOMPSON AH
MONTGOMERY RM	HILLEARY EL	SMITH AE	BARKER RR 1	FERNIE JF 3	WOODBRIDGE AR 1	HILLEARY RM
CANNON TH	WILLIAM F (SUB)	SMITH C	YOUNG W	NEWBOLD JC	MACDONALD CN	JACKSON FH
WHITTING AG	HAMILTON JB	HILLEARY RM 1	BARKER RR	'CROCK' A 1	HARRISON AE	SYMES-THOMPSON AH 2
WILSON P	HILLEARY EL	CATTLEY JF	BRYANT FH	FERNIE JF 3	NEIL MACDONALD C	HILLEARY RM
DARVELL S	SUAL ACA	SMITH AE	BRYANT HJ	BARRETT HR	TOMBLESON JB	
BARKER RR	WARD CB	STANBROUGH MH 1	COMPTON ED 1	FERNIE JF	OTHER AN	STREET F 1
BARRETT-HAMILTON GE	HARRIS PS	SYMES-THOMPSON AH	TOONE WP 1	BARTON GB 2	OTHER AN	SUBSTITUTE A 1
REYNOLDS LW	DONALDSON CH	VASSALL GC	MYTTON A	LAIRD RH 1	ROOKE BE	HILLEARY RM
REYNOLDS LW	DONALDSON JG	HILLEARY RM	ROOKE A 3	LAIRD RH 1	VASSALL GC 1	MYTTON A
HIGSON TA	BARKER RR	RHODES HA	COLLIER HJ 1	FERNIE JF 1	BROWN TH	FRYER PA
WILSON CP	WHITTING AG	HUNT	SMITH 1	HATTON COS	PHELPS N	STANBROUGH MH 2
FINCHAM W	BARRETT HR	SMITH AE	BATHURST JA 1	TAYLOR SS 2	SYMES-THOMPSON AH	OTHER AN
BARKER RR	GRIEVESON JE	PERKINS TN	TAYLOR SS	FERNIE JF	ALEXANDER CL	HILLEARY RM 1
PICKERING HJ	HARMSWORTH G	DRAKE CF	BRYANT FH	NEWBOLD JC 1	HENDERSON TB	ROOKE BE
HATTON COS 1	HILLEARY RM 1	SMITH RT	AGAIR CH	EKINS	HENDERSON TB	CLARKE B
HILLEARY RM	ECCLES A	SMITH RT	AGAIR CH 1	WILSON	HENDERSON TB	CORBETT BO
HATTON COS 3	DARVELL S	CORBETT BO	HENDERSON TB 1	SUAL ACA	WINGER E 1	HILLEARY RM
BARKER RR	OTHER AN	HILLEARY RM	THOMPSON AHS	SYMONS CBO	WINCH AB	CORBETT BO
TAYLOR SG	SMITH AE	BRAY JE	BRAY EH	HILLEARY RM		
GRIEVESON JE	PICKERING HJ	HILLEARY RM	MCKEAN H	FERNIE JF	WILLIAMS C	UNWIN SR
PICKERING HJ	FINCHAM E	BATHURST JA	MCKEAN H	BARWELL WT 1	SYMES-THOMPSON AH	
WILSON CP	ADAMS FE	TOONE WP	TAYLOR SS 1	FERNIE JF 2	BRYANT FH 1	HILLEARY RM
PICKERING HJ	'SOKER'	STANBROUGH MH	COLLIER HJ 1	FERNIE JF 2	WILTSHIRE HP	HILLEARY RM
BARKER RR	HILLEARY EL	FRYER PA	TAYLOR SS	LOWE WW 1	FERNIE JF 1	HILLEARY RM
WHITTING AG	WILSON CP	MANLY JH 2	BRYANT LH 2	SEWELL COH	NEWBOLD JC	TOONE WP
'SOFTUN' A	HOLLOCOMB JC	SMITH AE	CRAWFORD RO 1	BARTON GD	WETHERED P	ROGER RS
MONTGOMERY RM	BARRETT HR	TOONE WP 1	BRYANT HJ 1	LAIRD RH 1	TURNBULL ER	HILLEARY RM
BARKER RR	MONTGOMERY RM	DRAKE CF	HATTON COS 1	FERNIE JF	BRYANT FH	HILLEARY RM
BARKER RR	TRESTALL EA	STANBROUGH MH	RHODES HA 1	FERNIE JF 1	HILLEARY RM	'BROWN' A
GATES HW	POWELL C	HEWITT HW	THOMPSON RS	SEWELL COH	GEDDES EA	HAMILTON GH 3
TURNBULL H	COODE AP	SYMES-THOMPSON AH	LAIRD RH	COLLIER HJ 2	HEWITT HW	COCHRANE J
BARKER RR	MONTGOMERY RM	DRAKE CF	TAYLOR SS 1	FERNIE JF 3	BRYANT FH 1	HILLEARY RM
BARKER RR	TRESTALL EA	MANLY JH	STUART	FARNFIELD AS	WILTSHIRE HP	STANBROUGH MH 1
BARKER RR	MONTGOMERY RM	DRAKE CF	MOSELEY A	SUAL ACA 1	HILLEARY RM	SYMES-THOMPSON AH 1
GRIEVESON JE	WHITTING AG	HILLEARY RM	BRYANT	FERNIE JF 2	TOONE WP 1	LANDON HE
RAUTHMELL HA	STANBROUGH MH	DRAKE CF 3	HATTON COS 1	BRAY JE 1	HILLEARY RM 2	
BARKER RR	GRIEVESON JE	STANBROUGH MH	PERKINS TN 1	FERNIE JF 1	ALEXANDER CL 1	HILLEARY RM
BARKER RR	BARRETT HR	DRAKE CF	BRYANT FH	HATTON COS	TAYLOR SS 1	HILLEARY RM

1896/97

DATE	VEN	OPPONENTS	RES	COMP	ATT	1	2	3	4
12-Sep	A	CLAPTON	2-7	F	1,500	LAWRENCE AGS	KING SL	WREFORD-BROWN OE	PICKERING HJ
17-Sep	A	TOTTENHAM H	0-4	F	500	LAWRENCE AGS	BROWN RP	BAINES AGP	BROWN TH
19-Sep	A	GRAVESEND	1-4	F		HARRISON AE	KING SL	BARRETT HR	BROWN TH
26-Sep	H tp	TOTTENHAM H	1-4	F	2,000	HARRISON AE	TOVEY CH	KING SL	PICKERING HJ
30-Sep	A	ENFIELD	2-3	F		FOX	ANDREWS WH	CANE J	WOODARD EH
03-Oct	H tp	EALING	3-1	F	2,500	STOUT PW	KING SL	HATTON COS	WHITTING AG 1
05-Oct	A	SOUTHAMPTON ST M	0-1	F		COODE CP	BRAY EH	BROWN TH	COODE AT
07-Oct	H tp	MILLWALL ATHLETIC	2-0	F		HARRISON AE	KING SL	BRAY EH	WHITTING AG
10-Oct	H tp	LONDON CALEDONIANS	0-0	F	4,000	HARRISON AE	OAKLEY WJ	KING SL	PARES B
10-Oct	A	BRIGHTON ATHLETIC	0-4	F		STOUT PW	ARLINGTON GH	COOPER HES	WILSON CP
17-Oct	H tp	MIDDLESBROUGH	5-0	F	3,000	HARRISON AE	OAKLEY WJ	BRAY EH	MIDDLEDITCH B
24-Oct	A	LUTON TOWN	0-13	F		HARRISON AE	KING SL	LANDALE W	STOUT PW
24-Oct	A	IPSWICH TOWN	0-4	F		PRETTO DH	WILSON AB	AIREY TAA	SEDGWICK AV
24-Oct	A	OLD ETONIANS	2-3	F		MCGAW JT	HATTON COS	SMITH C	REBOW MG 1
24-Oct	A	MARLOW	1-6	F		TURNBULL HM	FINNEY WW	WILSON CH	ECCLES A
26-Oct	A	ST JOHNS SCHOOL	3-2	F	%				
31-Oct	H tp	LONDON WELSH	0-0	F	150	STOUT PW	KING SL	HATTON COS	'OPPER' ST
31-Oct	A	POLYTECHNIC	0-1	F					
02-Nov	A	SOUTHAMPTON ST M	0-3	F		HARRISON AE	SIMPSON GH	BRAY EH	PICKERING HJ
05-Nov	A	ROYAL ENGINEERS	3-5	F		GODWIN WP	PEARCE H	BAINES AGP	PARES B
07-Nov	A	CHARTERHOUSE	0-2	F		CAMPBELL W	KING SL	HATTON COS	WHITTING AG
11-Nov	A	RMA WOOLWICH	8-1	F		LANGTON JM	CANE J	LEA SE	MAYNARD-TAYLOR EG
14-Nov	A	3RD GRENADIER GUARDS	4-1	LCC1	1,000	HARRISON AE	HATTON COS	PELLY FR	HIGSON TA
14-Nov	H	CROUCH END	1-2	F		CANTAB' A	KING SL	LANDALE N	MAYNARD-TAYLOR DC
14-Nov	A	OLD BRIGHTONIANS	7-0	F		PRETTO DH	AIREY TAA	SMITH C	POPE WH
18-Nov	A	FELSTED SCHOOL	4-1	F					
21-Nov	A	CAMBRIDGE UNIV	1-2	F		CAMPBELL W	OAKLEY WJ	KING SL	LEA SE
21-Nov	H tp	LIVERPOOL RAMBLERS	5-1	F		'OXON'	TOVEY CH	MCCOWAN W	POPE WH
25-Nov	A	ST BARTHOLOMEWS H	2-0	F		CAMPBELL W	KING SL	FOX RHB	MAYNARD-TAYLOR
28-Nov	A	OXFORD UNIVERSITY	1-2	F	1,200	HARRISON AE	KING SL	FOULKES CH	BARRETT HR
28-Nov	A	WESTMINSTER SCHOOL	8-2	F		CAMPBELL W	BLAKER HR	AIREY TAA	BECKWITH EG
05-Dec	N cp	EALING	4-0	LCCsf		CAMPBELL W	HATTON COS	KING SL	BARKER RR
05-Dec	A	HIGHGATE SCHOOL	6-1	F	%				
05-Dec	A	BOROUGH-ROAD COLLEGE	2-2	F	%	PRETTO DH	AUSTEN HCM	HAVART HH	REBOW MG
08-Dec	A	FOREST SCHOOL	9-1	F		CANDY WF	LISS FJ	THOMPSON FL	GATES HW
10-Dec	A	MALVERN COLLEGE	7-0	F		PRETTO DH	MORTIMER H	SIMPSON GH	VICKERS H
11-Dec	A	SHREWSBURY SCHOOL	3-2	F		PRETTO DH	MORTIMER H	SIMPSON GH	VICKERS H
12-Dec	H tp	PRESTON NE	0-3	F	5,000	CAMPBELL W	PELLY FR	KING SL	BARRETT HR
18-Dec	A	SOUTH EASTERN COLLEGE	4-2	F		COODE CP	REBOW MG	TAYLOR CM	POLLOCK-HODSOLL GB
19-Dec	A	3RD GRENADIER GUARDS	4-4	F		GODWIN WP	PELLY FR	LOWTHER HC	BARRETT HR
26-Dec	A	CLAPTON	3-1	F		MCGAW JT	HATTON COS	SOPER NT	BARRETT HR
28-Dec	A	LONG EATON RANGERS	1-4	F		MCGAW JT	HATTON COS	TOPLIS NJ	WIILSON CH
29-Dec	A	LOUGHBOROUGH TOWN	4-3	F		MCGAW JT	HATTON COS	TOVEY	DARVELL S
30-Dec	A	MANSFIELD	1-0	F		MCGAW JT	KING SL	WILSON CH	BARRETT HR
31-Dec	A	STOCKTON	1-3	F		WILKINSON	TOVEY	HATTON COS	GRIEVESON JE
01-Jan	A	DARLINGTON	3-1	F	%				
02-Jan	A	MIDDLESBROUGH	0-8	F	2,000	WILSON CH	TOVEY		
09-Jan	H tp	OLD BRIGHTONIANS	7-1	F		HARRISON AE	LOWTHER HC	LANDALE N	SHILLITOE H
16-Jan	N 1	OLD CARTHUSIANS	5-0	LCCf		CAMPBELL W	LODGE LV	OAKLEY WJ	MIDDLEDITCH B
16-Jan	H tp	OLD WESTMINSTERS	1-11	F		'CANTAB' A	LANDALE N	BERWICK REH	POLLOCK-HODSOLL HE
30-Jan	A	WYCOMBE W	5-3 net	AC1		HARRISON AE	KING SL	LANDALE W	PICKERING HJ
06-Feb	A	CLAPTON	1-2	LSC1		HARRISON AE	OAKLEY WJ	BAINES AGP	BARKER RR
06-Feb	A	OXFORD UNIVERSITY	2-4	F		CAMPBELL W	LODGE LV	KING SL	LANDALE N
10-Feb	A	CHARTERHOUSE	1-1	F		WOODMAN A	KING SL	FORDYCE AD	VASSALL SH
13-Feb	H tp	ROYAL ARTILLERY	3-2	AC2	1,000	HARRISON AE	LANDALE N	HATTON COS	GRIEVESON JE
13-Feb	A	FELSTED SCHOOL	2-3	F		PRETTO DH	ORMSBY MH	KITCHING AL	HOWELL RGD
24-Feb	A	OLD MALVERNIANS	1-5	F		CAMPBELL W	BROWN RP	AUSTEN WAE	TAYLOR CM
24-Feb	A	HIGHGATE SCHOOL	4-1	AC3	80	AKESHIFT AM	THOMPSON JS	WHITTING AG 1	WILSON CP
27-Feb	A	STOCKTON	0-4	F	3,000	HARRISON AE	KING SL	LANDALE N	BARTON A
27-Feb	A	OLD ST MARK'S	1-1	F	%				
06-Mar	H tp	WOOLWICH ARSENAL	5-3	F	7,000	HARRISON AE	KING SL	LANDALE N	WILSON CP
06-Mar	A	ST JOHNS SCHOOL	3-1	F	%	TRESTALL EA	FRANCIS JA	ORMSBY MH	SHILLITOE FR
13-Mar	A	STOKE CITY	0-3	F	5,000	HARRISON AE	HATTON COS	KING SL	PICKERING HJ
15-Mar	A	MILLWALL ATHLETIC	1-2	F	700	HARRISON AE	THOMPSON JS	AIREY TAA	BARTON A
18-Mar	H tp	NOTTS COUNTY	1-2	F	1,500	HARRISON AE	KING SL	LANDALE N	WILSON CP
20-Mar	A	CLAPTON VETERANS	2-0	F	%	HILLEARY EL	BARRETT HR	BROWN RP	LEA SE
20-Mar	H tp	3RD GRENADIER GUARDS	3-2	F	%				
20-Mar	A	NEWBURY	3-2	F		HOOPER J	WREFORD-BROWN G	COOPER HES	TRESTALL EA
30-Mar	A	ETON COLLEGE	11-4	F	%	HILLEARY RM	WILSON CP	MAYNARD-TAYLOR C	DONALDSON JG
07-Apr	A	ATB DUNN'S XI	0-4	F		'OLD' J	TOONE P	MCALPIN J	PICKERING HJ
10-Apr	A	LONDON CALEDONIANS	0-1	F	3,000	FROST L	BROWN RP	SMITH GO	BARRETT HR

5	6	7	8	9	10	11
TEWSEY HJ	BARRETT HR	DRAKE CF	STOUT PW 1	FERNIE JF	BUZZARD EF 1	ROOKE BE
PRYCE-WHITE	DEANE F	DRAKE CF	HUGHES FW	THORBURN J	ALEXANDER CL	HAY A
FERNIE JF	PICKERING HJ	DRAKE CF	TAYLOR SS	SANDILANDS RR	STOUT PW	HAY A 1
LANDALE N	BROWN TH	CRUMP W	TAYLOR SS 1	DRAKE CF	BRYANT FH	CORBETT BO
WILSON CP	SIMPSON H	SMITH AE	TAYLOR SS	WRIGHT RG	TOONE WP 1	PARES B 1
WILSON CP	BARRETT HR	DRAKE CF	TAYLOR SS 1	WILSON GP 1	MCKEAN H	HILLEARY RM
FOULKES CH	MARSHALL	YOUNG W	HAYTER	AGAIR CH	CORBETT BO	DENNING
BARKER RR	PARES B	HILLEARY RM	TAYLOR SS	WRIGHT HW	ALEXANDER CL 2	CORBETT BO
BARKER RR	'OPPER' ST	HILLEARY RM	TAYLOR SS	WRIGHT RW	WILSON GP	BURNUP CJ
LANDALE N	LANG REV	YOUNG W	SPOONER WT	POTTER A	BOOKER AJN	TOONE WP
BARKER RR	'OPPER' ST	HILLEARY RL 1	TAYLOR SS 1	SMITH GO 1	ALEXANDER CL 2	BURNUP CJ
BARKER RR	'OPPER' ST	HAIG-BROWN A	MCKEAN H	WILSON GP	TOONE G	HILLEARY RM
CARTMAN PC	TRESTALL EA	LAIDMAN WE	SNELL HS	CHEALES F	POWELL NA	MITCHELL HA
WILSON CP	AUSTEN WAE	NEWITT JRH	CAUDWELL LS	FERNIE JF 1	YOUNG W	DAVIDSON W
RAUTHMELL HA	WREFORD-BROWN C	CATTLEY TF	BURNETT-STUART G	MORGAN-OWEN M 1	SEVERN AH	CAMPBELL RR
BARKER RR	PARES B	DRAKE CF	BROWN TH	TOONE WP	BRYANT FH	HILLEARY RM
BARKER RR	PARES B	HILLEARY RM	DRAKE CF	CARLTON FW	FERNIE AE	BURNUP CJ
BROWN TH	BARRETT HR	HILLEARY EL	ANDREWS WH	HEWITT HW 1	WILSON GP 2	MCKEAN H
BARRETT HR	WILSON CH	NEWITT JRH	WRIGHT RG	FERNIE JF	FERNIE AE	ANDREWS WH
POLLOCK-HODSOLL GB	DONALDSON JG	NEWCOME SL 1	SMITH AE 2	TOONE WP 4	THOMPSON AF 1	ANDREWS WH
BARKER RR	BARRETT HR	DRAKE CF	WRIGHT RG 1	COLLIER HJ 1	FERNIE JF 2	HILLEARY RM
WILSON CP	LEA SE	MITCHELL B	MCKEAN H	TOONE WP 1	BRYANT FH	WALL A
POLLOCK-HODSOLL GB 1	BECKWITH EC	SMITH AE	YOUNG W 1	NEWITT JRH 3	CAUDWELL E 1	DUVELL PD 1
				CAUSTON 1	FERNIE JF 3	
WILSON CP	BARRETT HR	DRAKE CF	FRYER PA 1	SYMONS LI	FERNIE JF	'DIS' A
LANDALE N	MCKEAN H	BOSWORTH-SMITH BN 2	COMPTON ED 2	TOONE WP 1	BRYANT FH	SYMES-THOMPSON AH
FERNIE JF	POLLOCK-HODSOLL GB	SYMES-THOMPSON AH	FERNIE AE 1	MASON S 1	WACE FH	
BARKER RR	PARES B	DRAKE CF	WRIGHT RG	FERNIE AE 1	WILSON GP	HILLEARY RM
WILSON CP	PECK HR	POLLOCK-HODSOLL HE	WATERHOUSE R 2	YOUNG 1	TOONE WP 3	DONALDSON JG 2
BARRETT HR	WILSON CP	BOSWORTH-SMITH BN 1	WRIGHT RG 1	WILSON GP 1	GUY AN 1	HILLEARY RM
POLLOCK-HODSOLL GB	TOVEY AG	SMITH AS 1	YOUNG E	NEWITT JRH	DUVELL PD	SAWYER T
BARRETT HR	BEASLEY HOC	WIGRAM R 3	WALTER A 1	DONALDSON WL 3	ANDREWS WH 1	HEWITT CD 1
FOSTER WL 1	RAUTHMELL HA	MYTTON H	PARES B 1	LOWE WW 2	TAYLOR SS 2	MACKEAN S 1
MCKEAN H	RAUTHMELL HA	MYTTON H	TAYLOR SS 1	PARES B	ANDERSON W 2	HILLEARY RM
BARKER RR	BEASLEY HOC	BOSWORTH-SMITH BN	WRIGHT RG	HATTON COS	HEWITT CD	STANBROUGH WF
WOODARD EH	PARES B	BATHURST JA 1	TAYLOR SS 2	WRIGHT RG 1	TOONE WP	ANDERSON W
BARKER RR	GRIEVESON JE	TOPHAM R 4	BRYANT FH	TOONE WP	ALEXANDER CL	BURNUP CJ
BARKER RR 1	WILSON CH	TOPHAM R	WRIGHT RG	GUY AN 1	TOONE WP 1	HILLEARY RM
BARKER RR	LOWE HA	TOPHAM R 1	COMPTON ED	WRIGHT RG	MOON LJ	RHODES HA
BARKER RR	BARRETT HR	JAMIESON W	WRIGHT RG 1	WILSON CP 2	MOON LJ 1	RHODES HA
BARKER RR	LOWE HA	JAMIESON W	TOONE WP	WILSON CP 1	PARES B	HILLEARY RM
BARKER RR	DARVELL S	JAMESON EM	WRIGHT RG 1	WILSON CP	MOON LJ	HILLEARY RM
			TOONE WP	WILSON GP		RHODES HA
BARKER RR 1	BARRETT HR	TAYLOR SS 3	WRIGHT RG 1	WILSON GP	CAUDWELL LS 1	BICKLEY F 1
BARKER RR	BARRETT HR	TOPHAM R 1	GUY AN	COLLIER HJ 3	ALEXANDER CL 1	BURNUP CJ
POPE WH	FERNIE JF	FROAT L	HENDERSON TB 1	HANNAFORD CH		
BARKER RR 1	BARRETT HR	DRAKE CF	'WINGER' R 1	COLLIER HJ 3	WILSON GP	HILLEARY RM
BARRETT HR	HATTON COS	TOPHAM R	WRIGHT RG	COLLIER HJ 1	WILSON GP	HILLEARY RM
WILSON CP	LEA SE	LAIRD RH 1	TOONE WP 1	INGRAM FM	FERNIE AE	WRIGHT OW
TURNBULL ER	FOX GH	UNWIN SR 1	RYDER GW	DRAKE CF	ROWE GH	SYMES-THOMPSON AH
BARKER RR	VICKERS H	BOSWORTH-SMITH BN	TOONE WP 2	WILSON GP	FERNIE AE 1	HILLEARY RM
FRANCIS CK	DURRELL HLV	UNWIN SR 1	ORWARD AF	CORFIELD EB 1	WEATHERHEAD HTC	MILMAN LCP
PICKERING HJ	CORFIELD A	HEWITT HW	FERNIE JF	WRIGHT RG 1	LAIDMAN WE	
POLLOCK-HODSOLL GB	DONALDSON JG 1	DRAKE CF	BRYANT HJ	TOONE WP	ANDREWS WH 1	SYMES-THOMPSON AH 1
BARKER RR	VICKERS H	FERNIE AE	DRAKE CF	WILSON GP	TOONE WP	HILLEARY RM
BARKER RR	VICKERS H	GUY AN 1	TOONE WP	WILSON GP	BURNUP CJ 2	ALEXANDER CL 2
WHITTING AG	YOUNG W	PATTERSON N	LARDMAN WE	FERNIE FE 1	DAVIDSON JL	EASYWOOD AE
BARKER RR	BARRETT HR	BOSWORTH-SMITH BN	TOONE WP	MORGAN-OWEN M	WILSON GP	HILLEARY RM
BEASLEY HOC	VICKERS H	UNWIN SR	WRIGHT RG 1	POWELL NA	LAWRENCE	WACE FH
BARKER RR	PICKERING HJ	TOONE WP	DRAKE CF	SYMONS CBO 1	MOON LJ	HILLEARY RM
WILSON CP	SHILLITOE FR	BATHURST JA	YOUNG W	HATTON COS	DAVIDSON JL	HILLEARY RM
RAUTHMELL RA	HARMSWORTH J	HOGARTH A	HOLLINS AM	CATTLEY TF	CORBETT BO 2	FRANCIS JA 1
RAUTHMELL RA	PICKERING HJ	BATHURST JA	MOON CT	WRIGHT RG	DRAKE CF	WATERHOUSE R
WILSON CP	DONALDSON JG	SYMES-THOMPSON AH	MOON LJ	HATTON COS	WRIGHT EG	HILLEARY RM
BARKER RR	PICKERING HJ	HEWITT CD	ORR E	WRIGHT RG	WATERHOUSE R	HILLEARY RM

1897/98

DATE	VEN	OPPONENTS	RES	COMP	ATT	1	2	3	4
18-Sep	A	CLAPTON	2-3	F		MCGAW JT	KING SL	LANDALE N	BARRETT HR 1
02-Oct	H tp	EALING	3-0	F		HARRISON AE	KING SL	OAKLEY WJ	PICKERING HJ
06-Oct	A	WEST HERTS	3-1	F		MUNRO H	OAKLEY WJ	LEA SE	WILSON CP
07-Oct	H tp	2ND COLDSTREAM GDS	2-1	F	250	FOX EH	GARNETT EN	HILLEARY EL	FOX WF
09-Oct	A	LONDON CALEDONIANS	6-0	F	4,000	BLAKER HR	HATTON COS	OAKLEY WJ	BARRETT HR
16-Oct	A	OLD WESTMINSTERS	4-2	F		HARRISON AE	ADAMS WG	KING SL	WILSON CP
16-Oct	H tp	SHEPPEY UNITED	4-3	F	%				
23-Oct	H tp	MARLOW	3-2	F	% 1500	HARRISON AE	OAKLEY WJ	HATTON COS	PICKERING HJ
23-Oct	A	CROUCH END VAMPIRES	0-1	F		BLAKER HR	KING SL	LANDALE N	LEA SE
26-Oct	A	FOREST SCHOOL	2-2	F		HAZELHURST FA	KING FR	HORTON L	PLAYER G
27-Oct	H tp	ATB DUNN'S LUDGROVE XI	4-8	F		ANDREWS WH 2 *	HATTON COS	LANDALE N	LEA SE
30-Oct	H tp	OLD ETONIANS	3-2	F	og	HARRISON AE	LANDALE W	PAULL JH	PICKERING HJ
30-Oct	A	HAMPSTEAD	3-0	F	%				
04-Nov	H tp	OXFORD UNIVERSITY	2-2	F	1,000	HARRISON AE	GARNETT EN	LANDALE N	PICKERING HJ
06-Nov	H tp	MANCHESTER CITY	2-3	F	5,000	BLAKER HR	BARRETT HR	HATTON COS	PICKERING HJ
13-Nov	H tp	OLD WESTMINSTERS	1-0	LCC1		HARRISON AE	OAKLEY WJ	HATTON COS	PICKERING HJ
13-Nov	A	OLD BRIGHTONIANS	2-2	F		BLAKER HR	BARFORD RF	SCOTT AL	TAYLOR CM
17-Nov	H tp	CAMBRIDGE UNIV	8-2	F	600	RICHARDSON AG	OAKLEY WJ	PAULL JR	PICKERING HJ
20-Nov	A	CHARTERHOUSE	2-1	F		GRANT AS	TOVEY CH	SCOTT AL	LEA SE
20-Nov	H tp	3RD GRENADIER GUARDS	4-0	F		THORNTON CF	OAKLEY WJ	HATTON COS	BARRETT HR
27-Nov	H tp	LONDON CALEDONIANS	2-0	F	4,000	HARRISON AE	LANDALE N	KING SL	TAYLOR CM
01-Dec	A	FELSTED SCHOOL	1-1	F		RICHARDSON AG	EVANS	LEA SE	LION
04-Dec	H qc	QUEEN'S PARK RANGERS	0-0	LCCsf	3,000	HARRISON AE	OAKLEY WJ	FRY CB	BARRETT HR
04-Dec	H tp	LIVERPOOL RAMBLERS	2-0	F	100	BLAKER HR	AUSTIN WSB	KING SL	TAYLOR CM
04-Dec	A	OLD FORESTERS	1-2	F	%				
08-Dec	A	WELLINGBOROUGH MASTERS	3-5	F		LAWRENCE AGS	MORTIMER RG	LANDALE N	COODE AT
08-Dec	A	HIGHGATE SCHOOL	3-1	F	%	SHARPE CA (SUB)	MCCOWAN W	KING SL	LEA SE
09-Dec	A	REPTON SCHOOL	3-3	F	%	LAWRENCE AGS	MORTIMER RG	LANDALE N	COODE AT
10-Dec	A	MALVERN COLLEGE	5-1	F		LAWRENCE AGS	MORTIMER RG	LANDALE N	COODE AT
11-Dec	H tp	BURTON SWIFTS	2-3	F	2,000	HARRISON AE	OAKLEY WJ	KING SL	PICKERING HJ
11-Dec	A	SHREWSBURY SCHOOL	1-1	F		LAWRENCE AGS	MORTIMER RG	LANDALE N	SULS W
11-Dec	A	OLD FELSTEDIANS	1-3	F	%				
18-Dec	H tp	MR NL JACKSON'S XI	2-4	F		HARRISON AE	HATTON COS	KING SL	BARKER RR
21-Dec	H tp	SOUTH EASTERN COLLEGE	6-1	F	%				
27-Dec	A	CLAPTON	6-0	F		BLAKER HR	BARRETT HR	KING SL	WILSON CH
28-Dec	A	LINCOLN CITY	2-3	F	1,000	BLAKER HR	MOSSER G	WRY ?	WILSON CH
29-Dec	A	LONG EATON RANGERS	3-5	F		BLAKER HR	TOVEY CH	MOSSER G	PICKERING HJ
31-Dec	A	BISHOP AUCKLAND	3-2	F	og	ROWLANDSON TS	ROBERTS AW	TOVEY CH	WILSON CH
01-Jan	A	DARLINGTON	6-1	F					
03-Jan	A	MIDDLESBROUGH	2-4	F		ROWLANDSON TS	TOVEY CH	MOSSER G	WILSON CH
08-Jan	A	CROUCH END VAMPIRES	2-3	F	2,000	BLAKER HR	SCOTT AL	KING SL	PLAYER G
15-Jan	H qc	QUEEN'S PARK RANGERS	1-0	LCCsf	3,000	HARRISON AE	KING SL	HATTON COS	PICKERING HJ
19-Jan	H tp	LONDON HOSPITAL	3-0	F	% 100	MALDEN AC	HATTON COS	ORMSBY MH	SCHOFIELD EH
22-Jan	H tp	OLD FORESTERS	7-0	LSC1	600	BLAKER HR	OAKLEY WJ	KING SL	PICKERING HJ
29-Jan	H tp	KIRKLEY	1-1 aet	AC1	4,000	HARRISON AE	TOVEY CH	MOSSER G	PICKERING HJ
29-Jan	A	OXFORD UNIVERSITY	4-3	F		THORNTON CF	PAULL JR	BLISS EC	FANE FL
29-Jan	A	CLAPTON	4-1	F		BLAKER HR	KING SL	OAKLEY WJ	LEA SE
02-Feb	H tp	ST BARTHOLOMEWS H	2-3	F		HARRISON AE	LEA SE	HARTLAND EL	OLD W
05-Feb	H tp	KIRKLEY	6-0	AC1r	3,000	HARRISON AE	OAKLEY WJ	TOVEY CH	PICKERING HJ
05-Feb	A	MARLOW	0-2	F		WEST H	ROBERTS AW	CORBETT LOWE	COOPER RG
10-Feb	H tp	ROYAL ENGINEERS	8-3	F		HEWITT CD	'TERISK' AS	BARTON A 1	SCHOFIELD EH
12-Feb	H tp	OLD ETONIANS	0-0 aet	AC2	2,000	HARRISON AE	HATTON COS	TOVEY CH	PICKERING HJ
12-Feb	A	CHARTERHOUSE	1-7	F		STURROCK WD	KING SL	SMITH GS	YOUNG
15-Feb	A	FOREST SCHOOL	2-3	F		DURRELL HLV	MOIR DE	ATKINSON AG	CROWTHER CNB
19-Feb	H tp	OLD ETONIANS	3-1	AC2r	1,000	HARRISON AE	OAKLEY WJ	TOVEY CH	PICKERING HJ
23-Feb	H tp	ASTON VILLA	1-6	F	4,000	HARRISON AE	OAKLEY WJ	'ORSEMAN' G N	HYMAN'H AS
23-Feb	A	HIGHGATE SCHOOL	7-2	F		SHARPE CA (SUB)	REBOW MG	MAIR WDK	PLAYER G
26-Feb	H tp	MIDDLESBROUGH	0-1	AC3	2,000	HARRISON AE	KING SL	MOSSER G	PICKERING HJ
05-Mar	H tp	BARKING WOULDVILLE	9-2	LSC2	1,500	BLAKER HR	HATTON COS	KING SL	PICKERING HJ
09-Mar	A	ST JOHNS SCHOOL	0-2	F					
12-Mar	N1	BRENTFORD	3-4	LSCsf	1,200	BLAKER HR	KING SL	ADAMS WG	PICKERING HJ
12-Mar	A	LONDON CALEDONIANS	1-0	F		GRANT AS	BOSANQUET J	TOVEY CH	WILSON CP
16-Mar	H tp	ROYAL VETERINARY COLL	4-4	F		SUB A	PLAYER G	GREENWOOD E	PICKERING HJ
23-Mar	H tp	SHEFFIELD WEDS	4-2	F	1,000	HARRISON AE	HATTON COS	BRAY EH	PICKERING HJ
30-Mar	A	READING AMATEURS	2-1	F					
09-Apr	A	OLD CARTHUSIANS	0-3	LCCF	6,000	HARRISON AE	FRY CB	OAKLEY WJ	PICKERING HJ
11-Apr	H tp	DARLINGTON	2-2	F	2,000	HARRISON AE	KING SL	BARRETT HR	HIGSON TA
12-Apr	H tp	MIDDLESBROUGH	0-2	F		ROWLANDSON TS	KING SL	OTHER AN	BLEWITT R

* PLAYED SECOND HALF IN GOAL, HILLEARY PLAYED THE FIRST HALF

5	6	7	8	9	10	11
DE PUTIE A	PICKERING HJ	DRAKE CF	TOONE WP 1	SANDILANDS RR	MOON LJ	HILLEARY RM
WILSON CP	BARRETT HR	DRAKE CF	TOONE WP	SMITH GO 2	WILSON GP 1	HILLEARY RM
FOX WF	POLLOCK-HODSOLL GB	HILLEARY RM	SMITH AR 1	SMITH GO 2	ANDREWS WH	CATTLEY TF
PICKERING HJ	WOODARD EH	CATTLEY TF	ANDREWS WH	HILLEARY R	MOON LJ 1	ROOKE BE 1
BARKER RR	PICKERING HJ	DRAKE CF	TOONE WP 2	WILSON GP 1	ALEXANDER CL 2	BURNUP CJ 1
LANDALE N	LEA SE	HANNAFORD CH	YOUNG W 2	TOONE WP	SNELL HS 2	WARE LH
BARKER RR	BARRETT HR	DRAKE CF	PERKINS TN 1	SMITH GO 1	HILLEARY RM	BURNUP CJ
WILSON CP	PLAYER G	BATHURST JA	FERNIE FE	YOUNG W	ARUNDEL AD	OTHER AN
CLARKSON F	YOUNG W	DRAKE CF 1	ARUNDEL AD	BICKLEY F	ANDREWS WH 1	DISS A
PICKERING HJ	POLLOCK-HODSOLL GB	WACE LH	SNELL HS 1	WILSON GP	HILLEARY RM 1	BURNUP CJ
WILSON CP	RAUTHMELL HA	DRAKE CF	SNELL HS 1	TOONE WP 1	HILLEARY RM	SMITH AE
'FORDIE' C	RAUTHMELL HA	DRAKE CF	WRIGHT RG 1	WILSON GP	HILLEARY RM	BURNUP CJ 1
BARKER RR	DARVELL S	DRAKE CF	TOONE WP 1	BLAKER RN 1	SNELL HS	WACE LH
BARKER RR	BARRETT HR	DRAKE CF	SNELL HS	TOONE WP	ALEXANDER CL 1	BURNUP CJ
WILSON CP	KING FR	CAMPBELL W	FERNIE FE	YOUNG W 1	PEARCE BG 1	HILLEARY RM
WILSON CP 1	TAYLOR CM	HILLEARY RM	TOONE WP 2	SMITH GO 4	WRIGHT RG 1	BURNUP CJ
PICKERING HJ	POLLOCK-HODSOLL GB	PARTON EG	GARNETT EN 1	GIBSON GH	ANDREWS WH 1	BUZZARD AD
BARKER RR 1	LANDALE N	ROBERTS AW	TOONE WP 1	WRIGHT RG 1	SNELL HS 1	HILLEARY RM
BARKER RR	BARRETT HR	DRAKE CF	TOONE WP	HATTON COS	WRIGHT RG 2	HILLEARY RM
SCOLLEAT	LANDALE N	BARRY	ESTRIDGE 1	OTHER AN	NICHOLS	BARNABY
BARKER RR	LANDALE N	DRAKE CF 1	TOONE WP	WRIGHT RG	SNELL HS	BURNUP CJ
WILSON CP	SYMES-THOMPSON AH	LEA SE 1	HILLEARY RL	SEWELL COH 1	ANDREWS WH	UNWIN G
BARKER RR	WREFORD-BROWN OE	WINCH GB	HILLEARY R	ANDREWS WH 3	ALEXANDER CL	BURNUP CJ
'WATSON' AG	POLLOCK-HODSOLL GB	'ORD' W 1	ARUNDEL AD	CLARKESON ES	FOESTON C	MARRIOTT HM
BARKER RR	WREFORD-BROWN OE	HILLEARY RM	POWELL HA	ANDREWS WH	ALEXANDER CL	BURNUP CJ 2
FOSTER WL	WREFORD-BROWN OE	ANDREWS WH	POWELL HA	LOWE WW 4	ALEXANDER CL	BURNUP CJ 1
BARRETT HR	POLLOCK-HODSOLL GB	DRAKE CF	TOONE WP 1	WILSON GP	WRIGHT RG	SEWELL COH 1
BARKER RR	COODE AT	MYTTON GH	POWELL HA 1	ANDREWS WH	ALEXANDER CL	HILLEARY RM
PICKERING HJ	SEWELL COH	TOONE WP	WILSON GP 1	WRIGHT RG 1	HILLEARY R	
BARKER RR	PICKERING HJ	ROBERTS AW 1	WRIGHT RG 2	BLAKER RN 2	MOON LJ 1	TOONE WP
WILSON CP	PICKERING HJ	ROBERTS AW	WRIGHT RG 1	BLAKER RN	MOON LJ 1	HILLEARY RM
WEY A	LEA SE	SNELL HS 1	JAMESON H	WRIGHT RG	MOON LJ 1	HILLEARY RM
WILSON CP	PICKERING HJ	SNELL HS	JAMESON H	BLAKER RN 1	MOON LJ 1	HILLEARY RM
		SNELL HS 1		BLAKER RN 2	MOON LJ 3	
WILSON CP	PICKERING HJ	SNELL HS	WRIGHT RG	BLAKER RN 1	MOON LJ 1	HILLEARY RM
BARKER RR	BARRETT HR	DRAKE CF 2	TOONE WP	WRIGHT RG	BRODIE TR	GRAHAM WM
BARKER RR	BARRETT HR	WRIGHT RG 1	DRAKE CF	WILSON GP	SNELL HS	HILLEARY RM
PICKERING HJ	ARUNDEL AD	BATHURST JA	FARRER CR 1	WRIGHT RG 1	LAIDMAN WE	UPWARD HA
BARKER RR	LEA SE	YOUNG W	BARRETT HR 3	HATTON COS 1	HENDERSON TB 3	ROOKE BE
BARKER RR	TAYLOR CM	DRAKE CF	WRIGHT OW	PERKINS TN	YOUNG W	BARRETT HR 1
HIGSON TA	DEANE F	CATTLEY TF	HENDERSON TB 1	HARMSWORTH SL 2	INGRAM FM	HOLLINS AF 1
BRAY EH	WREFORD-BROWN C	SNELL HS	FRYER PA	SMITH GO 2	BUZZARD EF 2	HEWITT CD
WILSON CP	PLAYER G	SIMPSON WH	NEWPORT GB	BRODIE HW 1	ARUNDEL AD 1	MARRETT HF
BARKER RR	BARRETT HR	DRAKE CF	WRIGHT RG 2	HATTON COS	ALEXANDER CL 4	HILLEARY RM
WILSON CP	LAIDMAN WE	SNELL HS	FERNIE AE	HARMSWORTH AH	HOLLINS FH	HOLLINS AM
FERNIE FE	YOUNG W	SNELL HS 3	FERNIE AE	MORGAN-OWEN M 2	JACKSON W 2	BARRETT-HAMILTON GE
LEA SE	BARRETT HR	DRAKE CF	WRIGHT RG	PERKINS TN	HENDERSON TB	HILLEARY RM
SCOTT AL	FRIEND RSI	JOHNSON GL	MURDOCH C	BUZZARD AD 1	NELSON AF	OTHER AN
OTHER AN	REBOW MG	WALTERS CR	GUY HM	NEWPORT GB 2	MUNN JS	HOWLETT
BARKER RR	BARRETT HR	DRAKE CF	PERKINS TN 1	HATTON COS	HENDERSON TB 2	HILLEARY RM
WILSON CP	POLLOCK-HODSOLL GB	HEWITT CD	'IGNOTUS' H	HATTON COS	HENDERSON TB 1	HOLLINS AM
LEA SE	DONALDSON JG	VICKERS H 1	COOPER SB 3	BRODIE HW	NEWPORT GB 2	CRAWFORD RC 1
BARKER RR	BARRETT HR	DRAKE CF	SNELL HS	HATTON COS	YOUNG W	HILLEARY RM
BARKER RR	WILSON CP	DRAKE CF 1	TAYLOR SS 5	WILSON GP 2	BARRETT HR 1	HILLEARY RM
				WARD	CRAWLEY (SUB)	EDWARDS (SUB)
BARRETT HR	LEA SE 1	DRAKE CF	TAYLOR SS	WILSON GP	HATTON COS 1	HILLEARY RM 1
FERNIE AE	DARVELL S	BUZZARD AD	PEARCE BG	BLACKBURN W 1	WRIGHT RG	SNELL HS
WILSON CP	VICKERS H	ARUNDEL AD 1	OLD W	WATERHOUSE R 1	NEWPORT GB 2	BURNUP CJ
BARKER RR	'ST HOPPER'	HEWITT CD 1	WRIGHT RG	WILSON GP 3	ALEXANDER CL	BURNUP CJ
				WATERHOUSE R 1	NEWPORT GB 1	
HATTON COS	BARRETT HR	DRAKE CF	WRIGHT RG	WILSON GP	ALEXANDER CL	HILLEARY RM
PICKERING HJ	'SLOWMAN' A	DRAKE CF	JAMESON H	BLAKER RN 2	MOON LJ	HILLEARY RM
PICKERING HJ	YOUNG W	DRAKE CF	WRIGHT RG	BLAKER RN	MOON LJ	HILLEARY RM

1898/99

DATE	VEN	OPPONENTS	RES	COMP	ATT	1	2	3	4
01-Oct	H tp	LONDON CALEDONIANS	0-3	F		BLAKER HR	OAKLEY WJ	KING SL	BARRETT HR
08-Oct	H tp	GREAT MARLOW	8-0	F	2,000	BLAKER HR	OAKLEY WJ	KING SL	BARRETT HR
08-Oct	A	BARNES INCOGNITI	2-3	F	%				
15-Oct	H tp	GRIMSBY TOWN	3-3	F	2,500	BLAKER HR	OAKLEY WJ	HATTON COS	BARRETT HR
15-Oct	A	WESTMINSTER SCHOOL	3-1	F	%				
05-Nov	H tp	CAMBRIDGE UNIV	2-2	F	4,500	BLAKER HR	OAKLEY WJ	PELLY FR	BARRETT HR
05-Nov	A	NEWBURY	0-1	F		DOCKER GAM	LANDALE N	FOULKES CH	MEERS RH
09-Nov	A	LUDGROVE MASTERS	0-6	F		JONES D	KING SL	HATTON COS	POLLOCK-HODSOLL GB
12-Nov	H tp	OLD MALVERNIANS	11-0	LCC1		BLAKER HR	OAKLEY WJ	HATTON COS	BARRETT HR
12-Nov	A	LANCING COLLEGE	4-3	F					
16-Nov	H tp	OXFORD UNIVERSITY	2-4	F	1,000	WILSON CE	OAKLEY WJ	KING SL	'CHOWEHOW' BF
19-Nov	H tp	WELLINGBOROUGH	1-1	F		RYDON HL	OAKLEY WJ	KING SL	BARRETT HR
19-Nov	A	CHARTERHOUSE	2-3	F	%	DOCKER GAM	SCOTT AL	WINGFIELD M	FOX GH
24-Nov	A	ROYAL ENGINEERS	4-0	F		KING SL	FOULKES CH	HEYSMAN A	POLLOCK-HODSOLL HE
29-Nov	A	FOREST SCHOOL	5-2	F		HENLEY FAH	KING SL	FOWLER TH	FARMER C
30-Nov	H tp	WATFORD	4-2	F		HARRISON AE	HATTON COS	TOVEY CH	BARTON GB
03-Dec	H qc	OLD CARTHUSIANS	0-3	LCCsf	3,000	HARRISON AE	OAKLEY WJ	HATTON COS	PICKERING HJ
03-Dec	A	OLD FORESTERS	3-2	F		SUB A	MYTTON HF	GREATOREX P	WESTBY HP
07-Dec	H tp	RNC GREENWICH	3-0	F		SUB A	POLLOCK-HODSOLL HE	ROBERTSON F	CHAUNCE KN
07-Dec	A	REPTON SCHOOL	1-4	F		DURRELL HLV	KING SL	TOVEY CH	LANDALE N
08-Dec	A	MALVERN COLLEGE	6-1	F	%	DURRELL HLV	KING SL	MOSER G	LANDALE N
09-Dec	A	SHREWSBURY SCHOOL	2-3	F		DURRELL HLV	KING SL	MOSER G	LANDALE N
10-Dec	H c	RUSHDEN	2-4	F		HOPPER AW	BARRETT HR	POLLOCK-HODSOLL HE	WESTBY A
14-Dec	A	HIGHGATE SCHOOL	6-0	F		DOCKER GAM	POLLOCK-NOTT HE	DIXON CE	BELCHER EA
17-Dec	H tp	MR WREFORD-BROWN'S XI	5-2	F	3,000	YOUNG W	OAKLEY WJ	LEA SE	PICKERING HJ
21-Dec	A	BRADFIELD WAIFS	1-1	F		WILSON CE	MOON LJ	SALWEY A	FOWLER TH
24-Dec	H tp	EALING	0-2	F		WILSON CE	KING SL	BARRETT HR	RAUTHMELL HA
26-Dec	H tp	LONDON CALEDONIANS	1-2	F	5,000	BLAKER HR	TOVEY CH	KING SL	BARRETT HR
27-Dec	A	GRIMSBY TOWN	7-5	F	%	LEE	KING SL	TOVEY CH	POLLOCK-HODSOLL GB
28-Dec	A	LONG EATON RANGERS	8-1	F	%				
30-Dec	A	BISHOP AUCKLAND	3-3	F		ROWLANDSON TS	KING SL	LEA SE	POLLOCK-HODSOLL GB
31-Dec	A	DARLINGTON	3-4	F		ROWLANDSON TS	KING SL	TOVEY CH	POLLOCK-HODSOLL GB
11-Jan	A	1ST GRENADIER GUARDS	1-0	F	%				
14-Jan	H tp	OLD WESTMINSTERS	1-1 aet	LSC1	2,500	WILSON CE	KING SL	BARRETT HR	PICKERING HJ
21-Jan	H tp	ILFORD	4-1	F		WILSON CE	KING SL	OAKLEY WJ	PICKERING HJ
23-Jan	A	OLD WESTMINSTERS	2-1	LSC1r	600	WILSON CE	KING SL	'COATS' P	'KIER' S
25-Jan	H tp	ROYAL VETERINARY COLL	2-1	F		DOCKER GAM	OAKLEY WJ	JOHNSON P	BOWRING FH
28-Jan	A	RICHMOND ASS	2-1	AC1	3,500	DOCKER GAM	OAKLEY WJ	TOVEY CH	PICKERING HJ
01-Feb	A	RNC GREENWICH	3-2	F		VAN WART RB	KING SL	FOULKES CH	'OLD' W
04-Feb	H tp	OLD CARTHUSIANS	2-4	LSC2		WILSON CE	HATTON COS	KING SL	PICKERING HJ
08-Feb	A	CAMBRIDGE UNIV	3-5	F		WILSON CE	SIMPSON-HAYWOOD GH	KING SL	BARTON EH
11-Feb	H	CHESHUNT	4-0 v	AC2	1,500	WILSON CE	KING SL	MOSER G	PICKERING HJ 1
11-Feb	A	CHARTERHOUSE	0-3	F		FULFORD CR	OLPHIN D	JOHNSON P	POLLOCK-HODSOLL HE
15-Feb	A	HIGHGATE SCHOOL	5-1	F		VAN WART RB	KING SL	FOULKES CH	REBOW MG
18-Feb	A	CHESHUNT	0-2	AC2	1,000	WILSON CE	KING SL	TOVEY CH	PICKERING HJ
25-Feb	H tp	OLD ETONIANS	2-1	F	800	DOCKER GAM	KING SL	JOHNSON P	PICKERING HJ
04-Mar	H tp	SOUTHAMPTON	2-2	F	4,000	WILSON CE	KING SL	HATTON COS	MORGAN-OWEN M
04-Mar	A	MARLOW	0-4	F		DOCKER GAM	JOHNSON P	FOULKES CH	BOWRING FH
08-Mar	A	ST JOHNS SCHOOL	6-2	F	%		KING SL		
09-Mar	H tp	ARSENAL	1-3	F	1,500	'REALING' W	KING SL	HATTON COS	'NETRAB' H
18-Mar	H tp	CLAPTON	2-1	F		WILSON CE	OAKLEY WJ	KING SL	PICKERING HJ
04-Apr	H tp	MIDDLESBROUGH	1-2	F	%				
08-Apr	A	ILFORD	1-2	F	%				

5	6	7	8	9	10	11
BARKER RR	PICKERING HJ	HILLEARY R	ALEXANDER CL	SMITH GO	WILSON CP	WRIGHT RG
BARKER RR	PICKERING HJ	WRIGHT RG 1	TAYLOR SS 3	SMITH GO 3	BLAKER RNR 1	ROOKE BE
BARKER RR	PICKERING HJ	DRAKE CF	WRIGHT RG 2	SMITH GO 1	ALEXANDER CL	ROOKE BE
BARKER RR	PICKERING HJ	DRAKE CF	TAYLOR SS	SMITH GO 2	ALEXANDER CL	HILLEARY R
POLLOCK-HODSOLL GB	WESTBY HP	MEERS DH	BARTON CT	LOWES E	LEBROCQ CN	SCOTT AL
DONALDSON JG	LEA SE	DRAKE CF	JAMESON H	ROUSE WS	PARTON EG	BRODIE WS
BARKER RR	PICKERING HJ 1	SNELL HS 3	TAYLOR SS 1	WRIGHT RG 4	ALEXANDER CL 1	LOWES E 1
			TOPHAM ? 4			
POLLOCK-HODSOLL GB	LEA SE	SNELL HS	WILSON GP	SMITH GO 2	WRIGHT RG	CATTLEY TF
BARKER RR	PICKERING HJ	HILLEARY R	TAYLOR SS	SMITH GO 1	LOWES E	HATTON COS
WESTBY HP	SHEPSTONE RA	YOUNG W	GORDON CW	GARNETT EN	JAMESON H	GIBSON LH
POLLOCK-HODSOLL GB	HIBBERT A	HILLEARY RM 1	'CANTAB' A	CHOWCHOW R	LOWES E 1	THOMAS R 2
'OLD' AW 2	WOODARD EH	FERNIE FE	KITCHENER HV	FERNIE JF	ARUNDEL AD 2	DRAKE CF 1
POLLOCK-HODSOLL GB	LEA SE	DRAKE CF	WOOLFENDER AR 3	PEARCE BG 1	LOWES G	LOWES E
BARKER RR	BARRETT HR	DRAKE CF	TAYLOR SS	WRIGHT RG	WILSON GP	LOWES E
LEA SE	LANDALE N	ROUSE WS 2	EVANS WA 1	YOUNG W	LEWIS EL	
POLLOCK-HODSOLL GB 2	ALSTON NH 1	'OLD' W	'CANTAB' A	OTHER AN		
RAUTHMELL HA	WOODARD EH	HILLEARY R	WOOLFENDER AR	MOSER G	ALEXANDER CW	LEWIS EL 1
RAUTHMELL HA	WILSON GP	HILLEARY R 1	ALEXANDER CW 1	BRODIE HW 1	BULLOCK GF 1	LEWIS EL
RAUTHMELL HA	WILSON CP	HILLEARY R	ALEXANDER CW 1	BRODIE HW	SUTTON AN	LEWIS EL 1
POLLOCK-HODSOLL GB	COLLIER GCB	WINCH GB	SNELL HS	TAYLOR SS	LOWES E 2	DOWSON TN
FORBES J	FERNIE H	MAKESHIFT A	FERNIE AE 1	PEARCE BG 4	ARUNDEL AD 1	DRAKE RE
BARKER RR	RAUTHMELL HA	DRAKE CF	BARRETT HR 1	WILSON GP 2	LOWES E 1	HILLEARY R 1
DARVELL S	'OLD' W	SMITH AE	BRODIE HW	PEARCE BG 1	DRAKE CF	DRAKE RE
BARKER RR	DARVELL S	HATTON COS	WOOLFENDER AR	WRIGHT RG	ALEXANDER CW	DRAKE CF
BARKER RR	HATTON COS	WOOLFENDER AR	WRIGHT RG	WILSON GP	SNELL HS	BARNBY LY 1
BARKER RR	MOSER G	DRAKE CF	HATTON COS	WRIGHT RG	WOLFENDEN E	SNELL HS
HARE BF	MOSER G	DRAKE CF	SNELL HS	LOWES E 1	ALEXANDER CW 2	BARNBY LY
BARKER RR	MOSER G	DRAKE CF	HATTON COS	WRIGHT RG	WOLFENDEN E 3	LOWES E
POLLOCK-HODSOLL GB	BARKER RR	DRAKE CF	TAYLOR SS	HATTON COS 1	LOWES E	HILLEARY R
MOSER G	HILLEARY R	SNELL HS 1	TAYLOR SS 1	WRIGHT RG	HENDERSON TB	LOWES E 2
BARKER RR	POLLOCK-HODSOLL HE	LOWES E 1	'GABY' A	DRAKE CF 1	POLLOCK-HODSOLL GB	'DIS' A
'OLD' W	MASTERMAN HW	WILSON HJ	PEARCE BG	BRODIE HW 1	FARRELL CL 1	ROOKE BE
BARKER RR	BARRETT HR	DRAKE CF	TAYLOR SS	WRIGHT RG	MOSER G 2	LOWES E
BELCHER RA 1	ARUNDEL AD 1	WILSON HJ	PEARCE BG	DURRANT RB 1	ALEXANDER CW	ROUSE WS
BARKER RR	BARRETT HR	LOWES E 2	TAYLOR SS	DRAKE CF	TOONE WP	HILLEARY R
POLLOCK-HODSOLL GB	MASTERMAN HW	DRAKE CF	DAY SH 1	WILLETT JA	ALEXANDER CW 1	SNELL HS 1
BARKER RR	BARRETT HR	DRAKE CF	TAYLOR SS 1	WRIGHT RG 1	MOON LJ 1	LOWES E
POLLOCK-HODSOLL GB	BOULTON A	SCOTT AL	FLOWER N	TOONE WP	GARNETT EN	LORD NORJOO
MASTERMAN HW	DONALDSON JG	JOHNSON B	ALEXANDER CW 1	BRODIE HW 3	DURRANT RB 1	WATSON HJ
POLLOCK-HODSOLL GB	BARRETT HR	DRAKE CF	TAYLOR SS	SNELL HS	MOSER G	LOWES E
BARRETT HR	FOULKES CH	SNELL HS	ALEXANDER CW	FERNIE FE 2	TOONE WP	LOWES E
POLLOCK-HODSOLL GB	PICKERING HJ	DRAKE CF	DAY SH 1	SEWELL COH	JAMESON H	LOWES E 1
WILSON CH	YOUNG W	MOSS W	BRODIE HW	TOONE WP	JAMESON H	PEARCE BG
				WILSON CP 1		
WREFORD-BROWN OE	BARKER RR	DRAKE CF	WRIGHT RG	MORGAN-OWEN M 1	JAMESON H	BURNUP CJ
OSBOURNE SE	BARRETT HR	DRAKE CF	TAYLOR SS	WRIGHT RG 1	WILSON GP	LOWES E 1

1899/1900

DATE	VEN	OPPONENTS	RES	COMP	ATT	1	2	3	4
23-Sep	A	BARNES INCOGNITI	4-1	F	%	WILSON CE	GREEN PA	KING SL	FOULKES CH
30-Sep	H tp	LONDON CALEDONIANS	1-1	F	2,000	WILSON CE	KING SL	OAKLEY WJ	JOHNSON H
07-Oct	H tp	WALSALL	3-2	F	1,000	DOCKER GAM	TOVEY CH	KING SL	PICKERING S
14-Oct	H tp	GRAVESEND UNITED	4-3	F	1,500	WILSON CE	KING SL	FOULKES CH	THWAITES H
14-Oct	A	MARLOW	1-3	F		DOCKER GAM	COLLIER CBG	WILD CH	GOLDBERG HW
18-Oct	A	RMA WOOLWICH	5-2	F		EDMUNDS HW	FOULKES CH	KING SL	PARSONS E 1
21-Oct	A	CLAPTON	0-1	F		WILSON CE	HATTON COS	KING SL	JOHNSON P
24-Oct	A	FOREST SCHOOL	1-0	F		EDMUNDS HW	KING SL	FOULKES CH	KING FJ
28-Oct	H tp	LONDON HOSPITAL	7-2	F		VAN WART RB	FOULKES CH	WESTRAIL AE	WESTBY HP
04-Nov	H tp	CAMBRIDGE UNIV	3-2	F		WILSON CE	BRAY EH	KING SL	JOHNSON P
11-Nov	A	EALING	7-0	LCC1		WILSON CE	HATTON COS	OAKLEY WJ	JOHNSON P
11-Nov	A	LANCING COLLEGE	4-5	F		CAMPBELL JA	KING SL	FERNIE AE	FERNIE FE
15-Nov	A	CHARTERHOUSE	2-3	F		PARSONS E	KING SL	MILBURN LE	TOMLINSON FW
18-Nov	H tp	ILFORD	3-3	F		WILSON CE	WILLIAMS RH	KING SL	AUSTEN WAE
18-Nov	A	EALING	2-4	F	%	DOCKER GAM	BRAMLEY HR	HATTON COS	WESTBY HP 1
25-Nov	A	OXFORD UNIVERSITY	0-4	F		WILSON CE	HATTON COS	KING SL	FOX WE
02-Dec	A	CLAPTON	2-3	LCCsf		WILSON CE	HATTON COS	OAKLEY WJ	JOHNSON P
09-Dec	H tp	LINCOLN CITY	3-2	F	800	WILSON CE	KING SL	HATTON COS	JOHNSON P
20-Dec	A	BRADFIELD WAIFS	9-0	F		DOCKER GAM	HARRISON EH	KING SL	DARVELL S
23-Dec	H tp	SOUTHAMPTON	0-1	F	2,000	WILSON CE	KING SL	BLISS EC	BARRETT HR
26-Dec	H tp	LONDON CALEDONIANS	1-2	F	1,500	WILSON CE	KING SL	GREEN PA	WILD CH
27-Dec	A	LINCOLN CITY	1-0	F		WILSON CE	TOVEY CH	HATTON COS	WILD CH
28-Dec	A	SUFFOLK COUNTY	2-2	F		WILSON CE	KING SL	TOVEY CH	BRAITHWAITE PP
30-Dec	A	BISHOP AUCKLAND	3-1	F					
01-Jan	A	DARLINGTON	5-2	F	%				
02-Jan	A	THORNABY UTOPIANS	6-2	F					
03-Jan	A	MIDDLESBROUGH	4-2	F	* og	WILSON CE	KING SL	TOVEY CH	ADDISON JS
13-Jan	A	LEYTONSTONE	1-3	LSC1		WILSON CE	HATTON COS	KING SL	BARRETT HR
20-Jan	H tp	OLD WESTMINSTERS	1-2	F		WILSON CE	BLISS EC	KING SL	BRAMLEY HR
24-Jan	H tp	MR HARRIS'S XI	4-2	F	200	JONES HA	KING SL	GREEN PA	'RUGER' K
27-Jan	H tp	CROUCH END VAMPIRES	3-0	F		WILSON CE	KING SL	TOVEY CH	RAUTHMELL HA
24-Feb	A	LONDON CALEDONIANS	0-1	F	1,500	WILSON CE	KING SL	BARRETT HR	RAUTHMELL HA
06-Mar	A	FOREST SCHOOL	4-3	F	%	KING AR	KING SL	ORTON L	GODSELL F
10-Mar	H tp	GRIMSBY TOWN	2-1	F	500	WILSON CE	HATTON COS	TOVEY CH	BRAITHWAITE PP
17-Mar	A	CHATHAM	1-3	F	1,000	WILSON CE	GREATOREX P	KING SL	ADDISON JS
31-Mar	H tp	OLD CITIZENS	8-1	F	%				
07-Apr	A	CLAPTON	1-3	WHC		WILSON CE	GREEN PA	KING SL	ADDISON JS
14-Apr	H tp	READING AMATEURS	3-0	F	500	WILSON CE	GREATOREX P	BARNBY AC	KING SL
16-Apr	H tp	THORNABY UTOPIANS	1-2	F	200	WILSON CE	TOVEY CH	KING SL	YOUNG W
17-Apr	H tp	DARLINGTON	2-1	F		WILSON CE	TOVEY CH	KING SL	ADDISON JS
21-Apr	H tp	LONDON CALEDONIANS	1-1	F		WILSON CE	KING SL	GREATOREX P	ADDISON JS

5	6	7	8	9	10	11
POLLOCK-HODSOLL GB	WHITE WN	DAVIDSON JL	TOONE WP	BRODIE HW	YOUNG W	DRAKE AB
THWAITES TW	WHITE WN	DRAKE CF	WRIGHT RG	SMITH GO	SEWELL COH 1	LOWES E
POLLOCK-HODSOLL GB	WHITE WN	DRAKE CF	WRIGHT RG	WOLFENDOE VJ	HATTON COS 1	LOWES E 2
BARKER RR	JOHNSON P	DRAKE CF	WRIGHT RG 2	WILSON GP	TOONE WP 2	LOWES E
FERNIE AE	BELCHER EA	HOGARTH AH	PEARCE BG	FERNIE PT 1	DAVIS CJ	EDMUNDS A
POLLOCK-HODSOLL HE	BELCHER BA	BRYANT FH 1	BRODIE HW 1	PEARCE BG 1	DRAKE EP 1	ROUSE WH
POLLOCK-HODSOLL GB	BRYANT FH	DRAKE CF	WRIGHT RG	FERNIE JF	TOONE WP	LOWES E
PARSONS E	COUPAR SE 1	DRAKE CF	BRODIE HW	ROPER RG	WELLS E	HOLLAND H
JOHNSON P	MOORE CA	DRAKE CF 1	TOONE WP	FERNIE JF 2	PEARCE BG 2	DAVIDSON JL 2
POLLOCK-HODSOLL GB	BARRETT HR	DRAKE CF	BRYANT FH 1	FERNIE FE	HENDERSON TB 2	LOWES E
POLLOCK-HODSOLL GB	BARRETT HR 1	DRAKE CF	TAYLOR SS 1	FERNIE FE 3	ALEXANDER CW 1	LOWES E 1
TRESTALL EA	MOORE CA	YOUNG W 1	HAMTIL N	BRODIE HW 3	PEARCE BG	CANDLER AL
WILSON CP	MOORE HL	GOOD GB	BRIGHT CH 2	BRODIE WS	WILSON CH	BRUCE WW
THWAITES H	MOORE CA	DRAKE CF	BRYANT FH	FERNIE JF	CANTAB A	LOWES E 3
TRESTALL EA	BARRETT HR	YOUNG W	WILLES	BRODIE WS	MACINTOSH C	DAVIDSON JL
POLLOCK-HODSOLL GB	TOMLINSON FW	MOORE CA	JAMESON H	FERNIE JF	PEARCE BG	LOWES E
BARKER RR	BARRETT HR	FERNIE JF	TAYLOR SS	FRYER PA 2	WRIGHT RG	LOWES E
POLLOCK-HODSOLL HE	BARRETT HR	TAYLOR SS	FERNIE JF	LOWES E 1	FRYER PA 2	
PARSONS E	DURRANT RB 5	DRAKE HB	TOONE WP	WARD VG 3	EVANS R 1	
WREFORD-BROWN C	DARVELL S	WRIGHT RG	SAREL WG	BLAKER RNR	WARD VE	HATTON COS
THWAITES H	BARRETT HR	HATTON COS	TOONE WP	GORDON (SUB)	RITCHIE (SUB)	WALKER PF (SUB) 1
BRAITHWAITE PP	BARRETT HR	CARRINGTON HW	UNWIN HR	FERNIE JF	CORBETT AL 1	TOONE WP
WILD CH	BARRETT HR 1	CARRINGTON HW	UNWIN HR 1	FRYER PA 1	ALEXANDER CW	FERNIE FE
		CARRINGTON HW 1	UNWIN HR 1		ALEXANDER CW 1	
		CARRINGTON HW 1	UNWIN HR			CORBETT AL 1
	FERNIE 1			RHODES TB 3	ALEXANDER CW 2	
WILD CH	FERNIE	CARRINGTON HW	UNWIN HR	RHODES TB 1	ALEXANDER CW	CORBETT AL 1
THWAITES H	ADDISON JS	TOONE WP	TAYLOR SS	FERNIE JF	DURRANT RB	LOWES E 1
THWAITES H	BRAITHWAITE PP	DAVIDSON JL 1	TOONE WP	FERNIE JF	TAYLOR SS	LOWES E
POLLOCK-HODSOLL GB	WHITE WN	DOWSON A	DRAKE CF 1	O'BRIEN C 1	WARD VG 2	WYLD HJ
POLLOCK-HODSOLL GB	WESTBY HP	FERNIE JF	TAYLOR SS	TOONE WP 2	MCINTOSH TW 1	LOWES E
POLLOCK-HODSOLL GB	'OXONIAN' AN	DIXON A	UNWIN HR	TOONE WP	LOWES E	LEPPELL H
POLLOCK-HODSOLL GB	WIMBLE HD	KILBY TA	POLLOCK-HODSOLL HE	O'BRIEN C	BEVAN CO	'OTHER' AN
POLLOCK-HODSOLL GB	RAUTHMELL HA	WRIGHT RG 1	FERNIE JF	ALEXANDER CW 1	CORBETT AL	LOWES E
POLLOCK-HODSOLL GB	BARRETT HR	DRAKE CF	O'BRIEN C 1	FERNIE JF	MACINTOSH C	TOONE WP
POLLOCK-HODSOLL GB	BRAITHWAITE PP	DRAKE CF	TAYLOR SS 1	LOWES E	MCINTOSH A	DAVIDSON JL
YOUNG W	DAVIDSON JL	WACE LH	DRAKE CF 1	WRIGHT RG	MACINTOSH C 1	KNIGHT C 1
WILD CH	WESTBY HP	DRAKE CF	MACINTOSH C 1	KNIGHT C		
GREENWOOD E	BARRETT HR	'O'ROSSA' 1	BARNLEY	WRIGHT RG	LOWES E 1	MACINTOSH C
POLLOCK-HODSOLL GB	BARRETT HR	DRAKE CF	YOUNG W	GREEN PA 1	TOONE WP	KNIGHT C

1900/01

DATE	VEN	OPPONENTS	RES	COMP	ATT	1	2	3	4
15-Sep	H tp	LONDON CALEDONIANS	2-3	F	3,000	WILSON CE	BARRETT HR	KING SL	BRAITHWAITE PP
29-Sep	H tp	RICHMOND ASS	2-1	F	2,000	WILSON CE	OAKLEY WJ	BARRETT HR	ADDISON JS
06-Oct	H tp	CLAPTON	2-4	F	2,000	WILSON CE	TOVEY CH	OAKLEY WJ	PICKERING HJ
13-Oct	H tp	EAST SHEEN	1-0	F		WILSON CE	TOVEY CH	WILLIAMS RH	PICKERING HJ
13-Oct	A	CHESHUNT	0-6	F					
16-Oct	A	FOREST SCHOOL	4-3	F		KING AR	KING SL	CRAWLEY E	PICKERING HJ
20-Oct	A	CLAPTON	1-6	F	2,000	WILSON CE	WILD CH	MERTONS R	CHURCHILL GS
20-Oct	A	WESTMINSTER SCHOOL	1-0	F		GRANT AS	WILLIAMS RH	RAUTHMELL HA	CARPENTER CE
24-Oct	A	OXFORD UNIVERSITY	3-2	F		WILSON CE	OAKLEY WJ	KING SL	POLLOCK-HODSOLL GB
27-Oct	H tp	MARLOW	1-2	F	600	GRANT AS	GREEN PA	KING SL	BARRETT HR
31-Oct	A	ATB DUNN'S XI	1-3	F		VAN WART RB	MOORE CA	KING SL	THWAITES H
03-Nov	H tp	CAMBRIDGE UNIV	0-3	F	3,000	WILSON CE	HATTON COS	KING SL	BEASLEY HOC
10-Nov	H tp	EAST SHEEN	5-1	LCC1	1,500	WILSON CE	OAKLEY WJ	HATTON COS	PICKERING HJ
17-Nov	H qc	OLD MALVERNIANS	4-2	F		WILSON CE	GREATOREX P	WILLIAMS RH	WESTBY HP
21-Nov	A	RMA WOOLWICH	9-0	F	%				
24-Nov	H tp	COLDSTREAM GUARDS	6-0	F		VAN WART RB	HATTON COS	TOVEY CH	BARRETT HR
24-Nov	A	WEST HAMPSTEAD	2-6	F	og 1,000	GRANT AS	KING SL	JESSOP GL	WESTBY HP
28-Nov	H tp	HIGHGATE SCHOOL	8-4	F	og	PAULL JD	JESSOP GL	KING SL	VAN WART RB
28-Nov	A	FELSTED SCHOOL	4-2	F	og	BRAITHWAITE PP	TIMMIS RB	THOMAS LS	RIVER-SMITH S
01-Dec	H tp	OLD CARTHUSIANS	1-1	LCCsf	2,000	WILSON CE	OAKLEY WJ	HATTON COS	BARRETT HR
08-Dec	A	MARLOW	2-2	F		'CUSTODIAN' A	KING SL	MARSH JW	BARRETT HR
08-Dec	A	BARNES INCOGNITI	2-0	F		GRANT AS	WRIGHT WR	SALWEY A	RAUTHMELL HA
12-Dec	A	MALVERN COLLEGE	1-1	F		WILKINSON GE	JOHNSON P	KING SL	BRAITHWAITE PP
13-Dec	A	REPTON SCHOOL	2-1	F		WILKINSON GE	JOHNSON P	KING SL	BRAITHWAITE PP
14-Dec	A	SHREWSBURY SCHOOL	2-1	F		WILKINSON GE	JOHNSON P	KING SL	BRAITHWAITE PP
15-Dec	A	ROSSALL SCHOOL	5-0	F	%				
15-Dec	H tp	ILFORD	4-4	F		VAN WART RB	MARSH JW	BRYDON P	THWAITES H
22-Dec	H tp	CHESHUNT	1-5	F	250	WILSON CE	HATTON COS	KING SL	BARRETT HR
26-Dec	H tp	LONDON CALEDONIANS	2-1	F	1,800	WILSON CE	KING SL	HATTON COS	LOWES E 1
27-Dec	A	SCARBOROUGH	6-2	F		WILSON CE	TOVEY CH	JOHNSON P	POLLOCK-HODSOLL GB
28-Dec	A	SHEFFIELD WEDS	2-4	F	2,000	WILSON CE	TOVEY CH	HATTON COS	POLLOCK-HODSOLL GB
29-Dec	A	BISHOP AUCKLAND	2-4	F		WILSON CE	KING SL		
31-Dec	A	THORNABY UTOPIANS	1-2	F		WILSON CE	KING SL		
01-Jan	A	DARLINGTON	2-0	F					
02-Jan	A	WEST HARTLEPOOL	0-2	F	2,000	WILD CH	KING SL	JOHNSON P	POLLOCK-HODSOLL GB
12-Jan	H tp	LONDON CALEDONIANS	6-0	LSC1		WILSON CE	HATTON COS	KING SL	TUBBS NH
19-Jan	A	LONDON WELSH	6-0	F		BARRETT HR 1	POLLOCK-HODSOLL GB	BRYDON P	RAUTHMELL HA
09-Feb	H qc	OLD CARTHUSIANS	3-1	LCCsf	800	WILSON CE	HATTON COS	OAKLEY WJ	BRAITHWAITE PP
13-Feb	A	CHARTERHOUSE	2-0	F		EDDIS BEG	WITHERINGTON GW	BROWN E	KING SL
20-Feb	A	ST JOHN'S SCHOOL	3-2	F	%			KING SL	WILSON AP
23-Feb	H tp	DULWICH HAMLET	3-0	LSC2	1,000	GRANT AS	HATTON COS	KING SL	TUBBS NH
27-Feb	A	HIGHGATE SCHOOL	9-0	F		EDMUNDS HW	KING SL	BRAMLEY HR	POLLOCK-HODSOLL GB
09-Mar	N c	ILFORD	1-2	LSCsf	3,000	WILSON CE	HATTON COS	MOORE CA	
13-Mar	A	RNC GREENWICH	3-1	F		SUB A	KING SL	WILSON CE	CARPENTER CE
16-Mar	A	RICHMOND ASS	8-2	F	1,000	WILSON CE	BLISS EC	GREATOREX P	BARRETT HR
22-Mar	A	OLD CITIZENS	2-4	F	%				
23-Mar	H tp	CLAPTON	3-1	LCCf	3,500	WILSON CE	KING SL	HATTON COS	BARRETT HR
30-Mar	H tp	READING AMATEURS	4-1	F		RICHARDS HW	GREEN PA	BRAMLEY HR	TUBBS NH
06-Apr	A	ILFORD	2-3	F	600	WILSON CE	GREATOREX P	KING SL	WESTBY HP
08-Apr	H tp	THORNABY UTOPIANS	4-0	F		WILSON CE	GREATOREX P 1	KING SL	TUBBS NH
09-Apr	H tp	DARLINGTON	1-1	F	800	PAULL JD	KING SL	HATTON COS	TUBBS NH

5	6	7	8	9	10	11
WESTBY HP	ADDISON JS	DRAKE CF	TAYLOR SS 1	SMITH J	LOWES E 1	KNIGHT C
THWAITES H	BRAITHWAITE PP	GREATOREX TA	TAYLOR SS 1	SMITH GO	STANBROUGH WF 1	LOWES E
THWAITES H	BARRETT HR	DRAKE CF	CORBETT AL 1	SMITH GO 1	STANBROUGH WF	STANBROUGH MH
THWAITES H	BARRETT HR	BRODIE HW	TAYLOR SS 1	HATTON COS	WARD VG	KINGHT C
LOCKER A	MOORE CA	KIRBY A	ROPER RG 3	WIMBLE HD 1	RUSSELL SH	
POLLOCK-HODSOLL GB	KING FL	STANBROUGH MH 1	COWAN DC	DURRANT RB	WOOD JL	LOWES E
WESTBY HP	BARNBY LY	MACKINTOSH C	BRODIE HW 1	BRYDON P	KNIGHT C	
WREFORD-BROWN C	MORGAN-OWEN M	VASSALL GC	FOSTER RE 1	SMITH GO 2	RHODES TB	LOWES E
CHURCHILL GS	THWAITES H	SNELL HS 1	PEARCE BG	HATTON COS	BRYDON P	LOWES E
CARPENTER CE	WIGRAM T	WOOD H 1	PEARCE BG	MORGAN-OWEN M	PICKERING HJ	LOWES E
CHURCHILL GS	BARRETT HR	WOOD JL	UNWIN HR	DRAKE CF	STANBROUGH WF	STANBROUGH MH
THWAITES H	BARRETT HR	DRAKE CF	TAYLOR SS 2	WRIGHT RG 2	UNWIN HR	LOWES E 1
SHEPHERD NP 1	ROBERTS AW	SNELL HS	TAYLOR SS 1	WARNER AC	STANBROUGH WF 1	STANBROUGH MH 1
RAUTHMELL HA	THWAITES H	ROBERTS AW	WARNER AC 4	TAYLOR SS 1	UNWIN HR	SNELL HS 1
FERNIE AE	SHEPHERD NP	BUTLER AF	PEARCE BG	MORRIS JF 1	BRYDON P	KNIGHT C
SHEPHERD NP 1	CARPENTER CE	DRAKE CF 1	BUTLER AF	MAIR WDK 3	VINTCENT CH 2	FERRIS W
DRIFFIELD LT	WILLIAMS GA	ELLISON HB	WARNER AC	WRIGHT RG 1	DAY SH 2	CANNY GB
THWAITES H	BRAITHWAITE PP	HATTON COS	TAYLOR SS	WRIGHT RG 1	ALEXANDER CW	LOWES E
POLLOCK-HODSOLL GB	MOORE CA	HATTON COS	BRODIE HW	ROPER RG 2	BRYDON P	GREEN PA
CARPENTER CE	FERNIE AE	HAMMELL N	MAIR WDK 1	PEARCE BG 1	MACKINTOSH C	BULLER AF
YOUNG F	WILD CH	GREATOREX TA	WRIGHT RG	MORGAN-OWEN M 1	ALEXANDER CW	HEPPLE TW
YOUNG F	WILD CH	GREATOREX TA	WRIGHT RG 1	MORGAN-OWEN M	ALEXANDER CW 1	STANBROUGH MH
YOUNG F	WILD CH	GREATOREX TA	WRIGHT RG	MORGAN-OWEN M 1	ALEXANDER CW 1	MOORE CA
POLLOCK-HODSOLL GB 2	FERRIS W	ROBERTS AW	BRODIE HW	ROPER RG 2	MACKINTOSH C	
RAUTHMELL HA	TUBBS NH	MACKINTOSH C	DURRANT RB	DEED SC	ROPER RG 1	FERRIS W
BARRETT HR	ROPER RG	DURRANT RB 1	WRIGHT RG	MACKINTOSH C		
POLLOCK-HODSOLL HE	BARRETT HR	CARRINGTON HW	DURRANT RB 1	GREEN PA 4	UNWIN HR	LOWES E 1
WILD CH	BARRETT HR	DOWSON FN	WRIGHT RG	DURRANT RB 2	LOWES E	TUFF B
			HEPPLE TW	GREEN PA 1	UNWIN HR 1	
			WRIGHT RG 1			
			DURRANT RB 1			
POLLOCK-HODSOLL HE	WRIGHT B	DOWSON FN	DURRANT RB	GREEN PA	UNWIN HR	DIXON CW
POLLOCK-HODSOLL GB	BARRETT HR	DRAKE CF 1	TOONE WP 1	GREEN PA 1	BRYDON P 3	LOWES E
THWAITES H	WILD CH	MCINTOSH W 1	DURRANT RB 2	GREEN PA 2	CHURCHILL GS	KNIGHT C
THWAITES H	BARRETT HR	DRAKE CF	TAYLOR SS 1	GREEN PA 1	WRIGHT RG	CORBETT BO 1
WILSON CP	MOORE CA	GIBSON RR	FRIEND RSI 1	ROPER RG 1	BRYANT FH	LOWES E
POLLOCK-HODSOLL GB	BARRETT HR	DRAKE CF 1	TAYLOR SS 1	GREEN PA	BRYDON P	LOWES E 1
CARPENTER CE	PEMMER A	DURRANT RB 4	ROPER RG 4	GIBSON RR	WARD VF 1	OTHER AN
POLLOCK-HODSOLL GB	BARRETT HR	DRAKE CF	TAYLOR SS	GREEN PA 1	BRYDON P	LOWES E
CAMERON J	WARD VF 1	ROPER RG 1	PEARCE BG	WRIGHT RG	WOODGATE GE	LITTLEJOHN E 1
POLLOCK-HODSOLL GB	BEASLEY HOC 1	SNELL HS 1	TAYLOR SS 4	WRIGHT RG 2	MOON LJ	STANBROUGH MH
		BARTLETT (SUB)				
THWAITES H	BRAITHWAITE PP	DRAKE CF	TAYLOR SS 1	WRIGHT RG	GREEN PA 1	SNELL HS 1
WESTBY HP	WHISH C	PEARCE BG	BRYDON P 1	ROPER RG 2	GOODMAN J	MAIR WDK 1
GREENWOOD E	BARRETT HR	ALLARD FM	DURRANT RB 1	HATTON COS 1	ROPER RG	WARD VG
GREENWOOD E	BARRETT HR	DRAKE CF	DURRANT RB 1	ROPER RG 1	SYMONDS J 1	WHISH C
POLLOCK-HODSOLL GB	GREENWOOD E	DRAKE CF	DURRANT RB	ROPER RG 1	LOWES E	SYMONDS J

1901/02

DATE	VEN	OPPONENTS	RES	COMP	ATT	1	2	3	4
21-Sep	H tp	LONDON CALEDONIANS	2-2	F	2,500	WILSON CE	KING SL	GREATOREX P	BRAMLEY HR
28-Sep	A	RICHMOND ASS	2-3	F		WILSON CE	KING SL	GREATOREX P	ADDISON JS
05-Oct	A	CLAPTON	3-2	F	2,000	WILSON CE	KING SL	GREATOREX P	ROBERTS AW
12-Oct	H tp	LONDON CALEDONIANS	9-1	LCC1	3,000	PAULL JD	KING SL	HATTON COS	BARRETT HR
15-Oct	A	FOREST SCHOOL	10-1	F	%	KING AR	KING SL	POLLOCK-HODSOLL GB	MOORE CA
19-Oct	A	WEST HAMPSTEAD	3-10	F	%	GRANT AS	MOORE CA	TOVEY CH	WILLIAMS CH
26-Oct	H tp	OXFORD UNIVERSITY	0-0	F	3,000	WILSON CE	HATTON COS	GREATOREX P	THWAITES H
26-Oct	A	MARLOW	1-3	F		KING AR	KING SL	STOCKS FL	GOODMAN J
30-Oct	A	LUDGROVE	0-9	F		SUB A	KING SL	WRIGHT WR	GREATOREX P
02-Nov	H tp	CAMBRIDGE UNIV	3-2	F	3,700	WILSON CE	KING SL	GREATOREX P	THWAITES H
02-Nov	A	DULWICH HAMLET	0-5	F	600				
06-Nov	A	ST BARTHOLOMEWS H	7-1	F		SUB A	ORTON L	WRIGHT WR	PLUMMER EN
09-Nov	H tp	OLD WESTMINSTERS	3-2	F	1,400	EDMUNDS HW	GREATOREX P	HATTON COS	CHATTERTON HF
09-Nov	A	ILFORD	1-3	F			KING SL		
13-Nov	A	BARNES	3-6	F		SUB A	BRAMLEY HR	WRIGHT WR	CARPENTER CE
16-Nov	A	OLD FORESTERS	4-0	F		ROWLANDSON TS	WRIGHT WR	SALWEY A	WILLIAMS CA
23-Nov	H tp	UPTON PARK	6-0	F	700	WILSON CE	KING SL	HATTON COS	POLLOCK-HODSOLL GB
26-Nov	A	CHARTERHOUSE	1-2	F		HORNER JF	WITHERINGTON JG	WRIGHT WR	HEYWOOD N
30-Nov	A	WEST HAMPSTEAD	0-4	F	800	WILSON CE	GREATOREX P	HATTON COS	LEACH-LEWIS AF
30-Nov	A	RMA WOOLWICH	0-2	F		HORNER JF	WRIGHT WR	BRAMLEY HR	CARPENTER CE
02-Dec	A	FELSTED SCHOOL	4-0	F	%	WRIGHT RG	WILLIAMS MB	GREEN GE	COOKE AT
07-Dec	A	OLD CRANLEIGHANS	6-2	F	%				
11-Dec	A	SHREWSBURY SCHOOL	5-0	F		NOLAN-WHELAN GN	KING SL	JOHNSON P	MOORE CA
14-Dec	A	EALING	1-2	F	% 300	WILSON CE	ORTON L	WRIGHT WR	FERNIE AE
21-Dec	H tp	SHEPHERD'S BUSH	1-2	LCCsf	1,000	WILSON CE	KING SL	HATTON COS	POLLOCK-HODSOLL GB
26-Dec	A	LONDON CALEDONIANS	7-1	F		WILSON CE	KING SL	GREATOREX P	CLEAVE R
27-Dec	A	SCARBOROUGH	1-2	F		WILSON CE	HOLLINS PL	GREATOREX P	CRAIG JD
28-Dec	A	BISHOP AUCKLAND	3-4	F		WILSON CE	STOCKS FW	GREATOREX P	BARRETT HR
30-Dec	A	MIDDLESBROUGH	2-1	F	1,000	WILSON CE	HATTON COS	JOHNSON P	CLEAVE R
31-Dec	A	THORNABY UTOPIANS	2-1	F		WILSON CE	KING SL	POLLOCK-HODSOLL GB	CLEAVE R
01-Jan	A	DARLINGTON	5-3	F		WILSON CE	KING SL	POLLOCK-HODSOLL GB	CLEAVE R
02-Jan	A	WEST HARTLEPOOL	4-0	F		WILSON CE	KING SL	JOHNSON P	CLEAVE JR
11-Jan	H tp	OLD CARTHUSIANS	1-1	LSC1		WILSON CE	GREATOREX P	KING SL	BARRETT HR
18-Jan	A	OLD CARTHUSIANS	0-1	LSC1r		WILSON CE	GREATOREX P	KING SL	CRAIG JD
18-Jan	A	BARNES	4-3	F		FONDER A de	SALWEY A	WRIGHT WR	PLUMMER EN
25-Jan	A	OXFORD UNIVERSITY	2-0	F		HOGARTH H	KING SL	GREATOREX P	CRAIG JD
29-Jan	A	GUY'S HOSPITAL	3-2	F		DAW JW	ORTON L	KING SL	MOORE CA
05-Jan	H tp	ST. MARY'S HOSPITAL	2-3	F		DAW JW	ORTON L	WRIGHT WR	TILLETT SJ
08-Feb	A	CAMBRIDGE UNIV	1-1	F		TOMPSON AH	KING SL	HATTON COS	LEACH-LEWIS AF
12-Feb	A	ST JOHN'S SCHOOL	4-1	F	%	DAW JW	ORTON L	ALLEN AR	MOORE CA
19-Feb	A	CHARTERHOUSE	0-1	F		ENGLAND RD	WITHERINGTON JG	KING SL	WRIGHT WR
22-Feb	A	WOODFORD	0-6	F		PALMER H (SUB)	KING SL	SALWEY A	HAMMILL V
01-Mar	H tp	ILFORD	3-3	F		WILSON CE	KING SL	WRIGHT WR	KINGHORNE (sub)
04-Mar	A	FOREST SCHOOL	6-2	F	og	DAW JW	KING SL	WRIGHT WR	PLUMMER EN
15-Mar	H tp	EAST SHEEN	5-3	F	%				
22-Mar	H tp	CLAPTON	0-0	F		WILSON CE	KING SL	GREATOREX P	YOUNG W
29-Mar	H tp	LONDON CALEDONIANS	1-1	F	1,000	WILSON CE	KING SL	GREATOREX P	KER J
01-Apr	H tp	DARLINGTON	5-1	F	500	WILSON CE	KING SL	KER J	ROPER RG
05-Apr	H tp	MARLOW	3-1	F	500	WILSON CE	KING SL	JOSEPH GA	CRAIG JD

5	6	7	8	9	10	11
POLLOCK-HODSOLL GB	BARRETT HR	DRAKE CF 1	WRIGHT RG 1	WARD VG	BRAMLEY FH	KNIGHT C
MORGAN-OWEN M	BRAITHWAITE PP	DRAKE CF	STANBROUGH WF	SMITH GO 1	WARD VG	SNELL HS 1
BRAITHWAITE PP	KING FL	HEWITT CD 1	ALEXANDER CW	HATTON COS 1	WARD VG 1	DRAKE CF
POLLOCK-HODSOLL GB	BRAITHWAITE PP	DRAKE CF	WARD VG 2	WRIGHT RG 5	ALEXANDER CW	SNELL HS 2
UPTON A	DRAKE HB 1	DRAKE CF 6	FEREDAY F	NASH CHC	ROPER RG 2	BRAMLEY FH
POLLOCK-HODSOLL GB	PUTY AD	SYMMS JM	WARD VG	ROPER RG	MACKINTOSH C	KNIGHT C
POLLOCK-HODSOLL GB	SIMMONDS A	STANBROUGH MH	TAYLOR SS	SMITH GO	ALEXANDER CW	SNELL HS
WILLIAMS CA	BAKER JM	SYMMS JM	WARD VG	ROBERTS AW 1	ROPER RG	KNIGHT C
MOORE CA	PLUMMER EN	FEREDAY F	ROPER RG	PEARCE BG	'CASUAL' A	BRYANT FH
POLLOCK-HODSOLL GB	BEASLEY HOC	WARD VG	TAYLOR SS 1	SMITH GO 1	ALEXANDER CW 1	SNELL HS
KING SL 1	MOORE CA	BIRD HJ	WARD VG 1	DRAKE CF 4	LIGHT F 1	YOUNG W
CHURCHILL GS	VENABLES FL	DRAKE CF 1	WILSON GP 1	MORGAN-OWEN M 1	HOWARD R	FERNIE AE
			WARD VG 1			
KING SL	SUB A	FERRIS W 1	WARD VF 2	PEARCE BG	HOWSE CA	SUB A
RAPAND C	FERNIE AE	ROBSON ST (sub)	WARD VG 1	DURRANT RB 1	SYMMS JM 2	KNIGHT C
THWAITES H	BRAITHWAITE PP	DRAKE CF	PEARCE BG 1	DURRANT RB 2	WILSON GP 2	SNELL HS 1
WILLIAMS CA	MOORE CA	SYMMS JM	MACDONALD CL 1	OXON A	PEARCE BG	MCCALL RF
POLLOCK-HODSOLL GB	KING FL	WARD VG	WILSON GP	TUFF B	ALEXANDER CW	KNIGHT C
COWPER SH	GOODMAN J	FERRIS W	GREENE R de V	OTHER AN	FERNIE AE	BRAMLEY FH
LEACH-LEWIS AF	HATHORNE AA	LIGHT P	HARRIS SS	BOMPAS HS	BRAITHWAITE PP	CANNY GB
CRAIG JD	BRAITHWAITE PP	GREATOREX TA	MORRIS JF 2	MCIVER CD	UNWIN HR 3	CANNY GB
POLLOCK-HODSOLL GB	MOORE CA	BRAMLEY FH	WILLIAMS CA	KER J	WARD VG	KNIGHT C
THWAITES H	BRAITHWAITE PP	DRAKE CF 1	FOSTER RE	WILSON GP	WARD VG	SNELL HS
CRAIG JD	COWAN DC	DEED A 2	ALEXANDER CW 4	MCIVER CD	KNIGHT C	CORBETT AL 1
POLLOCK-HODSOLL GB	BARRETT HR	UNWIN HR	DURRANT RB	DURRANT RB 1	MCIVER CD 1	DOWSON FN
CRAIG JD 1	DORRICK	CORBETT AL	ALEXANDER CW 1	DURRANT RB 1	UNWIN HR	DOWSON FN
POLLOCK-HODSOLL GB	CRAIG JD	DOWSON FN	UNWIN HR	DURRANT RB 2	ALEXANDER CW	CORBETT AL
SADDISON J	CRAIG JD	DOWSON FN	UNWIN HR	DURRANT RB 2	MCIVER CD	WOOD
SADDISON J	CRAIG JD	DOWSON FN	UNWIN HR 2	MCIVER CD 2	ALEXANDER CW 1	CORBETT AL
HOLLINS PL	CRAIG JD	DOWSON FN	UNWIN HR 1	MCIVER CD 1	ALEXANDER CW 1	CORBETT AL 1
CLEAVE JR	CRAIG JD	DRAKE CF	WILSON GP	DURRANT RB	WARD VG 1	MCIVER CD
MORGAN-OWEN M	BARRETT HR	DRAKE CF	WILSON GP	DURRANT RB	MCIVER CD	WARD VG
GOODMAN J 1	WILLIAMS CH	HAMMILL N	ROPER RG 1	MACKINTOSH C 2	FERRIS W	YOUNG W
POLLOCK-HODSOLL GB	BARRETT HR	DRAKE CF 1	WARD VG 1	RYDER CF	ALEXANDER CW	SNELL HS
WRIGHT WR	RUISER AB	BARNARD RL	PEARCE BG 1	FERRIS W	O'BRIEN CW 1	DRAKE CF 1
KING SL	MOORE CA	DRAKE CF	CROSDALE G 1	O'BRIEN CW 1	RUISER AB	FERRIS W
POLLOCK-HODSOLL GB	CHURCHILL GS	DRAKE CF	MCIVER CD 1	DURRANT RB	ALEXANDER CW	SNELL HS
FOWLER TH	WILLIAMS CA	BARNARD RL	WRIGHT WR	DRAKE CF	PEARCE BG	FERRIS W
WILSON CP	FERRIS W	MOORE CA	WARD VF	FOWLER TH	WYLD WH	BARROW J
YOUNG W	FERRIS W	'CANTAB' A	WARD VG	DURRANT RB	ROPER RG	MACKINTOSH C
			ROPER RG 1	DURRANT RB 1	ALEXANDER CW 1	
RUISER AB	MOORE CA 1	HARE A	CROSDALE G 4	O'BRIEN CW	WYLD WH	FERRIS W
POLLOCK-HODSOLL GB	COWPER SH	WRIGHT RG	WILSON GP	DURRANT RB	ALEXANDER CW	MCIVER CD
YOUNG W	FERNIE AE	BARNARD RL	WARD VF	O'BRIEN CW 1	ALEXANDER CW	WARD ES
YOUNG W	FERNIE AE 2	BARNARD RL	MCIVER CD 1	O'BRIEN CW 1	LOWES E 1	FERRIS W
DRAKE HB	YOUNG W	DOWSON FN	DRAKE CF 2	O'BRIEN CW	LOWES E 1	MACKINTOSH C

1902/03

DATE	VEN	OPPONENTS	RES	COMP	ATT	1	2	3	4
20-Sep	H tp	LONDON CALEDONIANS	2-0	F	2,000	WILSON CE	GREATOREX P	KING SL	CRAIG JD
27-Sep	H tp	CLAPTON	2-3	F		BARRETT HR	KING SL	CRAIG JD	SAMSON WL
04-Oct	A	MARLOW	1-7	F		BARRETT HR	JOSEPH GA	SUMMERS TH	COWPER SH
04-Oct	A	WESTMINSTER SCHOOL	8-0	F		TULL JE	FREEMAN H	GREATOREX P	MOORE CA
11-Oct	H tp	RICHMOND ASS	2-2	F	1,000	PAULL JD	KING SL	FREEMAN H	CRAIG JD
18-Oct	H tp	EALING	7-3	LCC1	1,000	WILSON CE	KING SL	GREATOREX P	CRAIG JD 1
18-Oct	A	BARNES	5-0	F	%				
25-Oct	H tp	OXFORD UNIVERSITY	2-1	F		CHEADE AR	KING SL	GREATOREX P	CRAIG JD
01-Nov	A	OLD ETONIANS	0-2	F		ESDAILE EGK	'LIATH' GO	HOUGHTON AJ	CRAIG JD
01-Nov	A	OLD CITIZENS	0-2	F					
05-Nov	A	RMC SANDHURST	4-2	F		STRATTON JC	POLLOCK-HODSOLL GB	SUMMERS TH	MOORE CA
08-Nov	N u	OLD WESTMINSTERS	7-3	LCC2sf	1,000	'KOGG' IN	HATTON COS	POLLOCK-HODSOLL GB	HOLLINS PL
12-Nov	H tp	UPTON PARK	1-1	F		CHEADE AR	MILLS WG	WRIGHT WR	DANIELL J
15-Nov	H tp	CAMBRIDGE UNIV	1-6	F	2,500	LOVEGROVE CD	GREATOREX P	MILLS WG	ROBERTS AW
15-Nov	A	OLD FORESTERS	5-2	F	%	BARRETT HR	PARNELL HS	WRIGHT WR	SALWEY A
19-Nov	A	CHARTERHOUSE	1-0	F		CHEALE AR	MILLS WG	WRIGHT WR	OTHER AN
22-Nov	A	EALING	1-3	F		CRISP	ROBERTS AW	WRIGHT WR	PRESTON AL
26-Nov	A	HIGHGATE SCHOOL	9-0	F		DANIELS GP (sub)	ESDAILE EGK	SUMMERS TH	ASHCROFT JM 1
29-Nov	A	OLD MALVERNIANS	2-1	F		BARRETT HR	MILLS WG	WRIGHT WR	WESTBY HP
02-Dec	A	FELSTED SCHOOL	4-2	F	%	OTHER AN	ROWLANDSON TS	CANNY GB	ASHCROFT JM
10-Dec	A	SHREWSBURY SCHOOL	2-0	F		ROWLANDSON TS	HAUGHTON AJ	BELL OB	POTTER GP
11-Dec	A	REPTON SCHOOL	1-4	F	%	ROWLANDSON TS	HAUGHTON AJ	BULL OB	BRAITHWAITE PP
12-Dec	A	MALVERN COLLEGE	6-1	F		ROWLANDSON TS	HAUGHTON AJ	HOLLINS PL 1	POTTER GP
20-Dec	H tp	SHEPHERD'S BUSH	2-6	F		DRIFFIELD LT			
26-Dec	H tp	LONDON CALEDONIANS	2-0	F	2,000	WILSON CE	KING SL	GREATOREX P	COWAN DC
27-Dec	A	HASTINGS ST L	11-2	F	3,000	DRIFFIELD LT	POLLOCK-HODSOLL HE 1	GREATOREX P	CLEAVE R
29-Dec	A	OXFORD CITY	3-3	F		DRIFFIELD LT	JOHNSON P	HAUGHTON AJ	CLEAVE R
30-Dec	A	BOURNEMOUTH	3-1	F					
31-Dec	A	DORSET	0-1	F	700	DRIFFIELD LT	JOHNSON P	POLLOCK-HODSOLL HE	CLEAVE R
01-Jan	A	CORNWALL	7-1	F	og			POLLOCK-HODSOLL HE	
03-Jan	A	SOMERSET	3-1	F		DRIFFIELD LT	JOHNSON P	POLLOCK-HODSOLL GB	CLEAVE R
10-Jan	H tp	LONDON CALEDONIANS	4-1	LSC1		DRIFFIELD LT	CRAIG JD	GREATOREX P	TUBBS NH
17-Jan	A	CLAPTON	1-3	F	og 1,000	ROWLANDSON TS	GREATOREX P	JOSEPH GA	CLEAVE R
24-Jan	A u	CLAPTON	1-3	LCCF	3,000	NOLAN-WHELAN JV	HATTON COS	POLLOCK-HODSOLL GB	CRAIG JD
24-Jan	A	OLD CRANLEIGHANS	1-4	F	%	GRANT AS	WRIGHT WR	PARNELL HS	YOUNG W
26-Jan	A	OXFORD UNIVERSITY	1-3	F		ROGERS R	KING SL	WITHERINGTON JG	WILLETT BH
28-Jan	A	GUY'S HOSPITAL	0-6	F		FORESTER A	DANKES SH	WRIGHT WR	PIRKIS FCL
31-Jan	A	ILFORD	1-3	LSC2	1,000	DRIFFIELD LT	CRAIG JD	GREATOREX P	TUBBS NH
07-Feb	H tp	ILFORD	2-1	LSC2r		DRIFFIELD LT	CRAIG JD	POLLOCK-HODSOLL GB	MORGAN-OWEN M
09-Feb	A	CAMBRIDGE UNIV	0-3	F		ANDERSON KB	WITHERINGTON JG	KING SL	TUBBS NH
11-Feb	A	HIGHGATE SCHOOL	5-3	F		DANIELS GP (sub)	WILLIAMS MR	KING SL	MOORE CA
21-Feb	N i	OLD MALVERNIANS	3-7	LSCsf	400	DRIFFIELD LT	POLLOCK-HODSOLL GB	GREATOREX P	TUBBS NH
24-Feb	A	FOREST SCHOOL	5-1	F		'SUB' A	KING SL	SUMMERS TH	MOORE CA
28-Feb	A	OLD FORESTERS	0-2	F					
04-Mar	A	CHARTERHOUSE	1-4	F	%				
07-Mar	H tp	RICHMOND ASS	10-3	F	%				
14-Mar	A	SHEPHERD'S BUSH	0-4	F		CROLY HP	DAVIES SJ	BENTON T	ASHCROFT JM
21-Mar	H tp	MARLOW	6-0	F		GRANT AS	SYMONS HJ	KING SL	TUBBS NH 1
04-Apr	H tp	EAST SHEEN	4-3	F	%				
11-Apr	H tp	LONDON CALEDONIANS	0-2	F	1,200	WILSON CE	KING SL	JOSEPH GA	CRAIG RD
13-Apr	H tp	DARLINGTON	2-2	F	500	WILSON CE	SHARP TS	JOSEPH GA	CURWEN WJH

230

5	6	7	8	9	10	11
CRAIG RD	BRAITHWAITE PP	BARNARD RL	DURRANT RB 1	MORGAN-OWEN M	MOON LJ 1	CANNY GB
MORGAN-OWEN M	CRAIG RD	DURRANT RB	MACKINTOSH C	O'BRIEN CW	MORGAN JS 2	DEED SC
SAMSON WL	ROBERTS AW	BARNARD RL	DEED SC	ROPER RG	WARD VG	YOUNG W 1
CHOON HU	DRAKE HB	DIXON GF	DONALDSON WL	DRAKE CF 3	WYLD 3	CORBETT BO 2
POLLOCK-HODSOLL GB	TUBBS NH	DRAKE CF	TUFF B 1	DURRANT RB 1	ALEXANDER CW	MORGAN JS
MORGAN-OWEN M	BRAITHWAITE PP 1	DRAKE CF 1	DURRANT RB	WRIGHT RG 2	ALEXANDER CW 2	MORGAN JS
ROBERTS AW	TUBBS NH	DRAKE CF	TUFF B	DURRANT RB	MCIVER CD 1	ALEXANDER CW 1
ROBERTS AW	WRIGHT WR	DONALDSON WL	TUFF B	DURRANT RB	ALEXANDER CW	O'BRIEN CW
PLUMMER EN	COWPER SH	GRANT AS	WARD VF 2	O'BRIEN CW 1	BRODIE HW 1	SYMONS HJ
MORGAN-OWEN M 1	BRAITHWAITE PP	DRAKE CF	DURRANT RB	WRIGHT RG 3	ALEXANDER CW 3	CRAIG JD
COUPER SB	STANBROUGH MH	WENTWORTH F	O'BRIEN CW	DIXON EF 1	MOORE CA	
POLLOCK-HODSOLL GB	TUBBS NH	DRAKE CF	DURRANT RB 1	O'BRIEN CW	ALEXANDER CW	SQUIRES AE
SHARP TS	POLLOCK-HODSOLL GB	DONALDSON OC	PEARCE BG	BRODIE HW	JOSEPH GA	MACKINTOSH C
WILSON CP	MOORE CA	LAMPTON WL	COWAN DC	O'BRIEN CW	WARD VG 1	FREEMAN EC
GUNN AH	POLLOCK-HODSOLL GB	DONALDSON WL	BRODIE HW	O'BRIEN CW	JOSEPH GA 1	MACKINTOSH C
WHITEINGTON B	WENTWORTH F 1	FREEMAN EC	BRYANT FH 1	GETHING HB 5	WALDRON LM 1	
YOUNG W	BARNARD RL	O'BRIEN CW 2	ALEXANDER CW	DIXON GF	PEARCE BG	
PESHALL F	DECHI SF	FARMER FR	BRAITHWAITE PP 1	DEACON PL	HOLLINS PL	HARRIS SS 2
HOLLINS PL	BRAITHWAITE PP	FARMER FR	ROBERTS FR 1	WALLER HK 1	CANNING GH	STEER G
HOLLINS PL	POTTER GP	FARMER FR	ROBERTS FR	MELLIN GL	WALLER HK	CANNY GB
CANNY GB	BULL DR	WALLER HK	ROBERTS FR 2	MELLIN GL 1	BRAITHWAITE PP 2	FARMER FR
		WRIGHT RG	DURRANT RB 2	TUFF B	BRAITHWAITE PP	SIMONDS J
CRAIG RD	CLEAVE R	MACKINTOSH C	DURRANT RB	LEACH R 2	MCIVER CD	SIMONDS J
CRAIG RD	WILLETT BH	COWAN DC	DURRANT RB 4	BLAKER RNR 3	ALEXANDER CW 3	SIMONDS J
CRAIG JD	WILLETT BH	SNELL HS 1	DRAKE CF	BLAKER RNR 1	DURRANT RB	PACKFORD CW (SUB) 1
			DRAKE CF 1	DOWSON FN 1	ALEXANDER CW 1	
CRAIG RD	WILLETT BH	DOWSON FN	COWAN DC	BLAKER RNR	ALEXANDER CW	SNELL HS
		DOWSON FN	ALEXANDER CW 1	DURRANT RB 3	BLAKER RNR 2	
COWAN DC	WILLETT BH	SIMONDS J	ALEXANDER CW 1	DOWSON FN 1	BLAKER RNR 1	DURRANT RB
POLLOCK-HODSOLL GB	CLEAVE R	DRAKE CF	DURRANT RB	GETHING HB 2	ALEXANDER CW 1	SIMONDS J
YOUNG W	MITCHELL A (SUB)	SMITH A (SUB)	HARRIS GH	DURRANT RB	DAVIS A (SUB)	PIPER SA (SUB)
MORGAN-OWEN M	TUBBS NH	DRAKE CF	DURRANT RB	WRIGHT RG	ALEXANDER CW	CORBETT BO
CASTLEY EG	'CANTAB' A	SYMONS HJ	MACKINTOSH C	O'BRIEN CW	JOSEPH GA	SUB A
CLEAVE JR	LOWE HA	PAWSON AC	MCIVER CD	BLACKBURN W 1	MASTER R	
PAINTON ER	FIELD WV	CLEAVE R	MOORE CA	WALDRON LM	DIXON EF	KING BW
WRIGHT WR	CLEAVE R	DURRANT RB	GETHING HB 1	MCIVER CD	ALEXANDER CW	SIMONDS J
CLEAVE R	TUBBS NH	FERRIS W	ALEXANDER CW 1	GETHING HB	DURRANT RB 1	DRAKE CF
LEACH-LEWIS AF	BEASLEY HOC	WARD VF	BLAKER RNR	GETHING HB	WILSON GP	WARD ES
PIRKIS FCL	CLEAVE R	FREEMAN W	PRIDEAUX 2	LEACH R 1	DICKSON JF 1	'SALOP' A 1
MORGAN-OWEN M 1	CLEAVE R	MORGAN JS	DURRANT RB 1	GETHING HB 1	ALEXANDER CW	SIMONDS J
PIRKIS FCL	LITCHFIELD PC 2	'SUB' A	FREEMAN W	'CANTAB' A 3	DIXON GF	
HALL J	FOYNE SM	DEACON FL	DURRANT RB	O'BRIEN CW	MACKIE S	BONSFORD AF
MORGAN-OWEN M	CRAIG RD	SIMONDS J	ALEXANDER CW 1	DURRANT RB 4	'CANTAB' A	GETHING HB
CURWEN WJH	MCIVER CD	BARNARD RL	O'BRIEN CW	TUFF B	WARD VF	WARD ES
CRAIG RD	MCIVER CD	BARNARD RL	SAMSON WL 1	O'BRIEN CW 1	WARD VF	DIXON GF

1903/04

DATE	VEN	OPPONENTS	RES	COMP	ATT	1	2	3	4
19-Sep	H tp	LONDON CALEDONIANS	0-1	F		WILSON CE	KING SL	JOHNSON P	TUBBS NH
26-Sep	H tp	RICHMOND ASS	6-2	F	1,500	YOUNG W	CRAIG JD	KING SL	CLEAVE R
03-Oct	H tp	WEST NORWOOD	5-0	F	%	GRANT AS	JOHNSON P	JOSEPH GA	MORGAN-OWEN M
10-Oct	A	EALING	2-4	F	%				
17-Oct	H tp	OLD WESTMINSTERS	4-2	LSC1	2,300	WILSON CE	KING SL	JOHNSON P	MORGAN-OWEN M
20-Oct	A	FOREST SCHOOL	8-2	F	*	SCORER AG	KING SL	BRENAN AR	PIRKISS FCL
24-Oct	A	CLAPTON	1-3	F	2,000	WILSON CE	KING SL	HATTON COS	THWAITES H
24-Oct	A	OLD FORESTHILLIANS	2-1	F	%				
31-Oct	H qc	OXFORD UNIVERSITY	3-1	F	400	DRIFFIELD LT	KING SL	STOCKS FC	THWAITES H
04-Nov	A	CHARTERHOUSE	3-1	F		NEWMAN GG	WITHERINGTON JG	SCOTT AL	GILLIATT W
07-Nov	H tp	OLD CARTHUSIANS	3-1	LCCsf	2,500	WILSON CE	KING SL	HATTON COS	MORGAN-OWEN M
07-Nov	A	OLD CITIZENS	2-5	F	%				
14-Nov	H qc	CAMBRIDGE UNIV	1-7	F	500	DRIFFIELD LT	KING SL	SYMONS HJ	TUBBS NH
18-Nov	A	HIGHGATE SCHOOL	6-3	F		GRANT AS	SYMONS HJ	BRUCE WW	TUBBS NH
21-Nov	A	CROUCH END VAMPIRES	2-0	F	%				
25-Nov	A	ST BARTHOLOMEWS H	4-0	F		ELLIOTT C	ORTEN L	BRUCE WW 1	PIRKIS FCL
28-Nov	H tp	SHEPHERD'S BUSH	5-1	F	og 500	WILSON CE	SYMONS HJ	JOSEPH GA	CLEAVE R
02-Dec	A	ST JOHNS SCHOOL	2-2	F		PHILLIPS S (SUB)	KING SL	LANGDEN JE	SALMON SW
12-Dec	H tp	OLD WESTMINSTERS	4-3	F	500	DAVIDSON JLM	KING SL	WRIGHT WR	CLEAVE R
14-Dec	A	SHREWSBURY SCHOOL	3-2	F		ROWLANDSON TS	KING SL	JOHNSON P	HACKING EM
16-Dec	A	MALVERN COLLEGE	2-2	F		ROWLANDSON TS	KING SL	JOHNSON P	HACKING EM
19-Dec	H tp	ILFORD	3-0	F	500	HOBART RC	BRENAN AR	JOSEPH GA	KING SL
26-Dec	H tp	LONDON CALEDONIANS	4-1	F	2,000	WILSON CE	JOSEPH GA	WILLETT BH	MCIVER CD
28-Dec	A	OXFORD CITY	1-0	F		WILSON CE	HATTON COS	JOHNSON P	MCIVER CD
29-Dec	A	BRISTOL EAST	1-0	F		WILSON CE	WITHERINGTON JG	KING SL	KING FL
30-Dec	A	DEVON COUNTY	3-0	F	500	WILSON CE	KING SL	KING FL	HATTON COS
31-Dec	A	CORNWALL	3-2	F		WILSON CE	WITHERINGTON JG	JOHNSON P	TOYNE SM
01-Jan	A	WEST SOMERSET	0-3	F		WILSON CE	KING SL	JOHNSON P	TOYNE SM
02-Jan	A	DORSET	2-3	F		WILSON CE	WITHERINGTON JG	JOHNSON P	KING FL
02-Jan	A	OLD XAVERIANS	0-2	F					
09-Jan	A	ENFIELD	2-2	LSC1	800	WILSON CE	KING SL	JOSEPH GA	MCIVER CD 1
16-Jan	H tp	ENFIELD	8-1	LSC1	1,500	WILSON CE	KING SL	JOSEPH GA	CRAIG RD
27-Jan	A	OXFORD UNIVERSITY	4-1	F		LOVEGROVE CD	KING FL	STOCKS FC	CLEAVE JR
30-Jan	H tp	LEYTON	0-1	LSC2		WILSON CE	KING SL	JOSEPH GA	CRAIG RD
06-Feb	A	CAMBRIDGE UNIV	3-6	F		ANDERSON KB	HATTON COS	KING SL	WILD CH
06-Feb	A	ST JOHNS SCHOOL	15-1	F	%				
20-Feb	N I	CLAPTON	3-1	LCCF	3,000	DRIFFIELD LT	HATTON COS	JOHNSON P	MORGAN-OWEN M
20-Feb	A	BARNES	3-4	F		BARRETT HR	JOSEPH GA	PARNELL HS	YOUNG W
23-Feb	A	FOREST SCHOOL	10-4	F		MILLER WW	KING SL	BRUCE TJ	GILLIATT W
27-Feb	A	UXBRIDGE	3-0	F		BARRETT HR	WRIGHT WR	JOSEPH GA	GILLIATT W
02-Mar	A	OXFORD CITY	1-1	F		HENLEY FAH	BRANSTON GC	STOCKS FC	WILLETT BH
02-Mar	A	CHARTERHOUSE	0-1	F		GRANT AS	KING SL	WITHERINGTON IG	STOCKS CL
05-Mar	A	WEST NORWOOD	3-4	F	og *	WILSON CE	WRIGHT WR	THOMAS TS	JOSEPH GA
12-Mar	A	CLAPTON	1-3	F	1,500	HENLEY FAH	KING SL	STOCKS FC	CRAIG JD
19-Mar	A	ILFORD	1-3	F		BARRETT HR	CULLING G	JOSEPH GA	WALLIS RWD
26-Mar	A	SHEPHERD'S BUSH	6-5	F	2,000	PEARCE HC	WARE RC	KING SL	JOSEPH GA
09-Apr	H tp	HAMPSTEAD	4-0	F		DRIFFIELD LT	KING SL	SUMMERS TH	NUGENT CN
16-Apr	A	EASTBOURNE	4-1	F		BARRETT HR	KING SL	CRAIG JD	CURWEN WJH

5	6	7	8	9	10	11
CRAIG RD	CLEAVE R	WARD VF	TUFF B	GETHING HB	HARRIS GS	SIMONDS J
POLLOCK-HODSOLL GB	SIMONDS J	MORGAN JS 1	GETHING HB 3	BLAKER RNR 2	HARRIS GS	WARD VF
POLLOCK-HODSOLL GB	CRAIG JD	TUFF B	GETHING HB	WRIGHT RG 2	ALEXANDER CW 2	CORBETT BO
POLLOCK-HODSOLL GB	CRAIG JD	WARD VF 1	DURRANT RB 1	WRIGHT RG	ALEXANDER CW 2	SIMONDS J
GARDINER JW	TUBBS NH	MILLER H 1	GUY JK 1	DRAKE CF 3	DIXON CE	CLEAVE R 2
POLLOCK-HODSOLL GB	CRAIG JD	WARD VF	DURRANT RB 1	MOON LJ	ALEXANDER CW	SIMONDS J
POLLOCK-HODSOLL GB	CLEAVE R	WARD VF	HARRIS GS 2	DURRANT RB 1	CORBETT AL	WARD ES
STOCKS CL	BRUCE TJ	DRAKE CF	BRYANT FH 1	BRUCE WW 2	DICKINSON HHR	DIXON GF
POLLOCK-HODSOLL GB	CRAIG JD	WARD VF	HARRIS GS	DURRANT RB 1	GETHING HB 1	CORBETT BO 1
POLLOCK-HODSOLL GB	THWAITES H	WARD VF	DURRANT RB	WRIGHT RG 1	DAY SH	STANBROUGH MH
PIRKIS FCL	STOCKS CL	WRIGHT WR	O'BRIEN CW 3	BRUCE TJ	MOON LJ 3	CLEAVE R
POLLOCK-HODSOLL GB	PLUMMER EN	MOORE CA	WRIGHT WR 1	O'BRIEN CW 1	BRUCE FJ	DIXON GF 1
HALL J	TOYNE SM	TUFF B	WARD VG 2	BUDGE PP	MECKLIN CB 2	FARMER FR
COOKE HHA	GARDINER JW	BARNARD RL	FREEMAN AC 1	CLEAVE R	DIXON GF	PEARCE BG 1
HALL J	BOLESIER AP	TUFF B 1	TOYNE SM 1	MCIVER CD 2	ALEXANDER CW	CRAIG JD
CRAIG RD	WATERS PB	BALFOUR-MELVILLE JE	WRIGHT RG 1	FARMER FR	BRYANT FH	HOLLINS PL 2
CRAIG RD	WATERS PB	BALFOUR-MELVILLE JE 1	WRIGHT RG	FARMER FR 1	BRYANT FH	HEPPELL
POLLOCK-HODSOLL GB 1	STOCKS CL	O'BRIEN CW	WARD VG	DURRANT RB	ALEXANDER CW 1	CORBETT AL 1
CRAIG RD	CRAIG JD	WARD ES	DURRANT RB 1	HARRIS GS 1	MOON LJ 2	SIMONDS J
CRAIG RD	KING FL	CORBETT AL 1	DOWSON FN	MORGAN JS	ALEXANDER CW	WARD ES
CRAIG RD	TOYNE SM	DOWSON FN	WARD VF	MCIVER CD 2	MORGAN GC	FARMER FR
SMITH A	TOYNE SM	WARD VF	DOWSON FN	MCIVER CD 2	ALEXANDER CW 1	CORBETT AL
CRAIG RD	KING FL	FARMER FR	DOWSON FN	ALEXANDER CW 1	MORGAN GC	CORBETT AL 2
CRAIG RD	KING FL	FARMER FR	MORGAN JS	MCIVER CD	DOWSON FN	WARD VF
CRAIG RD	TOYNE SM	DOWSON FN	MCIVER CD	BLAKER RNR 1	CORBETT AL	WARD VF 1
POLLOCK-HODSOLL GB	CRAIG JD	WARD VF	DURRANT RB	GETHING HB	ALEXANDER CW 1	MORGAN JS
POLLOCK-HODSOLL GB 1	CLEAVE R	WARD VF 2	WARD VG	HARRIS GS 2	WARD ES 2	MORGAN JS 1
POLLOCK-HODSOLL GB	LOWE HA	BRUCE WW	MCIVER CD	BLACKBURN REV W 3	DURRANT RB 1	VASSALL GC
MORGAN-OWEN M	CRAIG JD	WARD VF	WARD VG	DURRANT RB	ALEXANDER CW	MORGAN JS
MORGAN-OWEN M	CRAIG JD	WARD VF	WRIGHT RG 1	CANNY GB	ALEXANDER CW 2	WARD ES
			WARD VG 2			DONALDSON WL
POLLOCK-HODSOLL GB	CRAIG JD	WARD VF	DURRANT RB	WRIGHT RG	ALEXANDER CW 3	WARD ES
OTHER AN	GROOM AH	THOMAS TS 1	BUDGE PP 1	O'BRIEN CW 1	ROPER RG	DIXON GF
TUBBS NH	'SAUL ACA'	PERKISS FCL	SULMAN SW 4	BRUCE WW 1	SIMONDS SR 4	DIXON GF 1
HALL J	SUMMERS TH	YOUNG W	WARD VF	O'BRIEN CW	WARD ES 3	DIXON GF
CHEADE AR	TOYNE SM	SETH SMITH DF	BIRD WS	COLEBY AT 1	MCIVER CD	CHUTE JC
GILLIATT DE	CORBETT AL	LITCHFIELD ACA	VERREY BT	WRIGHT RG	CANTAB A	DIXON GF
POLLOCK-HODSOLL GB	GILLIATT W	WARD ES 1	FINLAY RV	O'BRIEN CW	HAMMOND CR	DOWSON FN
POLLOCK-HODSOLL GB	STOCKS CL	GETHING HB	ALEXANDER CW	WRIGHT RG 1	DURRANT RB	WARD VF
YOUNG W	GILLIATT W	THOMAS TS	DURRANT RB	WRIGHT RG	MATTHEWS CC 1	DONALDSON WL
POLLOCK-HODSOLL GB	PLUMMER EN	DONALDSON TH	BIRD FN 2	WRIGHT RG 2	FINLAY RV 2	MORGAN JS
POLLOCK-HODSOLL GB 1	STOCKS CL	MATTHEWS CC	GUY JK 1	WRIGHT RG 1	WARD ES	JOHNSON SM 1
POLLOCK-HODSOLL GB	COAST JP	MORGAN JS	BUDGE PP 1	WRIGHT RG 2	ALEXANDER CW	WARD ES 1

1904/05

DATE	VEN	OPPONENTS	RES	COMP	ATT	1	2	3	4
17-Sep	H tp	LONDON CALEDONIANS	0-0	F	1,500	BARRETT HR	KING SL	JOSEPH GA	CLEAVE R
24-Sep	A	CLAPTON	0-4	F	600	LOVEGROVE CD	KING SL	JOSEPH GA	CLEAVE R
01-Oct	A	DULWICH HAMLET	3-4	F		GRANT AS	TUFF B	THOMAS TS	JOSEPH GA
01-Oct	A	RMC SANDHURST	3-2	F		BARRETT HR	KING SL	WRIGHT WR	CLEAVE R
08-Oct	H tp	EALING	2-1	F	2,000	WILKINSON GE	KING SL	MAY PR	CLEAVE R
15-Oct	H tp	LONDON CALEDONIANS	1-1	LCC1	3,000	WILKINSON GE	KING SL	MAY PR	POLLOCK-HODSOLL GB
15-Oct	A	ST THOMAS' HOSPITAL	0-1	F		YOUNG W	WALLER HK	SAMSON WL	MEERS RH
19-Oct	A	RNC GREENWICH	5-0	F		GRANT AS	GRIMSDELL RE	KING SL	CLEAVE R
22-Oct	A	WEST NORWOOD	4-4	F	og 2,000	ESDAILE EGK	KING SL	WRIGHT WR	FROST RH
22-Oct	A	WESTMINSTER SCHOOL	2-0	F		BARRETT HR	SYMONS HJ 1	WALLER HK	YOUNG W
25-Oct	A	FOREST SCHOOL	13-1	F		MEERS RH	PIRKIS FCL	CLEAVE R	SULMAN SW
29-Oct	H tp	OXFORD UNIVERSITY	1-1	F	2,500	WILKINSON GE	KING SL	HATTON COS	POLLOCK-HODSOLL GB
29-Oct	A	CHARTERHOUSE	3-1	F		HOBART RC	WRIGHT WR	OTHER AN	WILLETT BH
02-Nov	A	GUY'S HOSPITAL	2-3	F	og	GRANT AS	BALFOUR RN	SYMONS HJ	CLEAVE R
05-Nov	H tp	LONDON CALEDONIANS	2-1	LCC1r	3,000	WILKINSON GE	KING SL	HATTON COS	CLEAVE R
09-Nov	A	HIGHGATE SCHOOL	5-1	F		CLEAVE R	SYMONS HJ	GRIMSDELL RE	PIRKIS FCL
12-Nov	H tp	CAMBRIDGE UNIV	2-8	F	1,800	FLOWER H	KING SL	HATTON COS	CLEAVE R
16-Nov	A	ROYAL ENGINEERS	4-4	F	%	BARRETT HR	KING SL	BALFOUR RN	PIRKIS FCL
19-Nov	A	SHEPHERD'S BUSH	2-1	F		ESDAILE EGK	BULL OB	'CANTAB' A	CLEAVE R
26-Nov	H tp	OLD MALVERNIANS	2-1	F	300	FINLAY JK	KING SL	WRIGHT WR	CLEAVE R
03-Dec	H tp	THE ARMY	5-1	F	1,200	ESDAILE EGK	KING SL	WRIGHT WR	POLLOCK-HODSOLL GB
12-Dec	A	SHREWSBURY SCHOOL	6-0	F		ROGERS R	KING SL	JOHNSON P	CRAIG JD
13-Dec	A	REPTON SCHOOL	4-0	F	%	ROGERS R	KING SL	JOHNSON P	CRAIG JD
14-Dec	A	MALVERN COLLEGE	0-0	F		ROGERS R	KING SL	JOHNSON P	CRAIG JD
17-Dec	A	ILFORD	0-3	F	1,500	DRIFFIELD LT	MAY PR	JOSEPH EH	CLEAVE R
24-Dec	H tp	RICHMOND ASS	2-1	F		GOODMAN GW	KING SL	MAY PR	CLEAVE R
26-Dec	H tp	LONDON CALEDONIANS	2-1	F		DRIFFIELD LT	KING SL	MAY PR	MCIVER CD
27-Dec	A	SCARBOROUGH	3-3	F					
28-Dec	A	DARLINGTON ST AUGUSTINE'S	3-1	F		DRIFFIELD LT	MAY PR	OWENS T	HOCKING
29-Dec	A	WEST HARTLEPOOL	6-2	F		DRIFFIELD LT	KING SL	MAY PR	CLEAVE R
30-Dec	A	SOUTH BANK	1-1	F					
31-Dec	A	SHILDON ATHLETIC	3-0	F		DRIFFIELD LT			
02-Jan	A	DARLINGTON	3-3	F	2,500	DRIFFIELD LT	TURNOUR	MAY PR 1	HACKING EM
07-Jan	H tp	OLD MALVERNIANS	0-0	LSC1	3,000	DRIFFIELD LT	KING SL	CRAIG JD	MCIVER CD
14-Jan	H tp	WAR OFFICE	5-4	F		DRIFFIELD LT	MAY PR	JOHNSON P	CLEAVE R
21-Jan	N l	OLD WESTMINSTERS	2-0	LCCsf	900	ESDAILE EGK	KING SL	JOHNSON P	POLLOCK-HODSOLL GB
21-Jan	A	OLD CITIZENS	1-0	F	%				
25-Jan	H tp	OLD MALVERNIANS	2-1	LSC1r	700	DRIFFIELD LT	KING SL	CRAIG JD	POLLOCK-HODSOLL GB
25-Jan	A	WESTMINSTER SCHOOL	5-2	F		FINLAY JK	BRUCE TJ	WRIGHT WR 1	PIRKIS FCL
01-Feb	A	HIGHGATE SCHOOL	9-1	F	%			WRIGHT WR 1	
04-Feb	A	CAMBRIDGE UNIV	2-5	F		ESDAILE EGK	KING SL	JOHNSON P	CLEAVE R
08-Feb	A	RMA WOOLWICH	3-2	F	%				
11-Feb	H tp	OLD ETONIANS	2-3	F	1,000	FINLAY JK	BRENAN AR	JOSEPH GA	CLEAVE R
15-Feb	A	OXFORD UNIVERSITY	2-0	F		HENLEY FAH	KING SL	JOHNSON P	CLEAVE R
15-Feb	A	ST JOHNS SCHOOL	8-2	F		FINLAY JK	BALFOUR RN	GRIMSDELL RE	COAST JP
18-Feb	H tp	EALING	0-0	LSC2	1,500	DAVIDSON JLM	KING SL	JOSEPH GA	POLLOCK-HODSOLL GB
18-Feb	A	FOREST SCHOOL	2-1	F	%				
22-Feb	A	ST THOMAS' HOSPITAL	1-3	F		FINLAY JK	BRUCE TJ	GRIMSDELL RE	JOHNSON AF
25-Feb	N i	CLAPTON	1-0	LCCf	3,000	DRIFFIELD LT	KING SL	MAY PR	POLLOCK-HODSOLL GB
01-Mar	A	BARNES	2-2	F		FINLAY JK	BALFOUR RN	KING SL	JOHNSON AF
04-Mar	A	EALING	0-3	LSC2		DAVIDSON JLM	KING SL	JOSEPH GA	CLEAVE R
08-Mar	A	CHARTERHOUSE	3-0	F		DAY AP	WALLER HK	LAPIN AB	CLEAVE R
11-Mar	N i	TOWNLEY PARK	1-3	F		BARRETT HR	KING SL	JOHNSON P	GILLIATT W
18-Mar	H tp	LONDON CALEDONIANS	1-6	F	1,500	ESDAILE EGK	KING SL	JOSEPH GA	CLEAVE R
22-Mar	A	MR BO CORBETT'S XI	0-2	F		DAY AP	JOHNSON P	WRIGHT WR	GRIMSDELL RE
25-Mar	H tp	WEST NORWOOD	2-1	F		DAVIDSON JLM	KING SL	MAY PR	CLEAVE R
29-Mar	A	2ND LINCS REGIMENT	2-3	F		DAY AP	KING SL	WRIGHT WR	PIRKIS FCL
01-Apr	A	ARTILLERY	0-1	F					
08-Apr	H tp	EAST SHEEN	0-5	F		FINLAY JK	KING SL	WRIGHT WR	CLEAVE R
12-Apr	A	VFB LEIPZIG	9-1	F	2,000	DRIFFIELD LT	KING SL	MAY PR	CLEAVE R
15-Apr	A	SLAVIA PRAGUE	2-1	F		DRIFFIELD LT	KING SL 1	MAY PR	WILLETT P
17-Apr	A	BOHEMIAN XI	3-1	F	5,500	DRIFFIELD LT	KING SL	MAY PR	CLEAVE R
19-Apr	A	VIENNA FC	3-1	F	1,000	DRIFFIELD LT	FOSTER BS	MAY PR	MAGNAY CBW
21-Apr	A	MAGYAR ATHLETIKAI CLUB	4-0	F	700	DRIFFIELD LT	KING SL	WILLETT P	CLEAVE R
22-Apr	A	MTK	6-0	F	3,300	DRIFFIELD LT	KING SL	MAY PR	CLEAVE R
24-Apr	A	BUDAPESTI TORNA CLUB	2-0	F	2,500	DRIFFIELD LT	WILLETT P 1	MAY PR	CLEAVE R

5	6	7	8	9	10	11
WRIGHT WR	STOCKS CL	BARNARD RL	DURRANT RB	HARRIS GS	GETHING HB	WARD ES
MORGAN-OWEN M	CRAIG JD	MCIVER CD	DURRANT RB	HARRIS GS	GETHING HB	MATTHEWS CC
MORGAN-OWEN M	MCIVER CD	WRIGHT RG 1	HARRIS GS 2	GETHING HB	SIMONDS J	
POLLOCK-HODSOLL GB	MEERS RH	CLEAVE A	DRUMMOND GH 3	WALKER HK	BLASSON CH	DIXON GF
MORGAN-OWEN M	MORGAN JS	WARD VF	GETHING HB	WRIGHT RG 1	ALEXANDER CW 1	WARD ES
MORGAN-OWEN M	CRAIG JD	DURRANT RB	WRIGHT RG 1	HARRIS GS	ALEXANDER CW	WARD ES
CLEAVE R	BLASSON EA	CLEAVE A	DRUMMOND GH	SYMONS SR	SIMONDS J	DICKSON SF
PIRKIS FCL 1	COAST JP	SYMONS SJ	SIMONDS J 4	SIMONDS SR	DIXON GF	BRUCE
MORGAN-OWEN M	CLEAVE R	DRAKE CF	ROBERTS FW 1	BUDGE PP 1	WARD ES 1	VERREY BT
MEERS RH	GRANT AS	WILKINSON GE	SIMONDS SR	DRUMMOND GH	ALEXANDER CW 1	DIXON GF
POLLOCK-HODSOLL GB	GILLIATT W	CLEAVE A	DRUMMOND GH 2	MCIVER CD 6	SIMONDS SR 4	DIXON GF 1
MORGAN-OWEN M	MCIVER CD	DRAKE CF	DURRANT RB 1	WRIGHT RG	ALEXANDER CW	WARD ES
MCKERROW	OTHER AN	VERREY BT 1	WALLER HK	DRUMMOND GH 1	SIMONDS SR 1	DIXON GF
COAST JP	GILLIATT W	CLEAVE A	SULMAN SW	DRUMMOND GH 1	SIMONDS SR	DIXON GF
MORGAN-OWEN M	CRAIG JD	CORBETT AL	WRIGHT RG 1	HARRIS GS 1	ALEXANDER CW	WARD ES
SULMAN SW	MEERS RH	CLEAVE A	MOODY WR 1	DRUMMOND GH 2	SIMONDS SR	DIXON GF 2
CANNY GB	SILVERTOP FS	DOWSON FN	TRECKMAN O	WRIGHT RG 1	ALEXANDER CW 1	MACKRILL OW
POLLOCK-HODSOLL GB	GILLIATT W	BARNARD RL	YOUNG W	MCNEIL H	SALMON SL	DIXON GF
WALLIS SR	TOYNE SM	HALL RS	MATTHEWS CC 1	WARD VG	ALEXANDER CW 1	SIMONDS J
POLLOCK-HODSOLL GB	WESTBY HP	BARNARD RL	VERREY BT 1	ALEXANDER CW	MATTHEWS CC 1	YOUNG RA
MORGAN-OWEN M 1	TOMLINSON FW	BARNARD RL	WRIGHT RG 2	HARRIS GS 1	MATTHEWS CC	WARD ES 1
CRAIG RD	CURWEN WJH	RYDER JS	ROBERTS FW	FOSTER GN 4	YOUNG RA	TOYNE SM 2
CRAIG RD	CURWEN WJH	RYDER JS	ROBERTS FW 1	TOYNE SM	FOSTER GN 2	YOUNG RA
CRAIG RD	CURWEN WJH	RYDER JS	ROBERTS FW	TOYNE SM	FOSTER GN	YOUNG RA
WRIGHT WR	WESTBY HP	BLASSON CA	CLARK J	FINLAY RV	ALEXANDER CW	SIMONDS J
DRIFFIELD LT	JOSEPH GA	DURRANT RB	FINLAY RV 1	WARD ES 1	SIMONDS J	
POLLOCK-HODSOLL GB	CRAIG JD	BARNARD RL	DURRANT RB	FINLAY RV 2	ALEXANDER CW	WARD ES
				TURNER R 2	CORBETT AL 1	
WILD CH	POTTER	DOWSON	DURRANT RB 2	TURNER R 1	CORBETT AL	MORGAN JS
POLLOCK-HODSOLL GB	HACKING EM	CARRINGTON HW 1	DOWSON	DURRANT RB 1	CORBETT AL 1	DOWSON FN 3
				TURNER R 1		
			DOWSON FN 1	TURNER R 2	CORBETT AL	
POLLOCK-HODSOLL GB	CLEAVE R	CARRINGTON HW	DURRANT RB 2	TURNER R	MORGAN JS	SIMONDS J
CRAIG RD	POLLOCK-HODSOLL GB	WARD VF	WARD VG	DURRANT RB	ALEXANDER CW	WARD ES
POLLOCK-HODSOLL GB	JOSEPH GA	DONALDSON LL	DECON PL	FINLAY RV 3	WARD VG 1	SIMONDS J 1
MORGAN-OWEN M	MCIVER CD	CORBETT AL	DURRANT RB	WRIGHT RG	ALEXANDER CW	WARD ES 2
MORGAN-OWEN M	CRAIG RD	WARD VF	DURRANT RB	MCIVER CD 2	ALEXANDER CW	WARD ES
GILLIATT W	COAST JP	SYMONS HJ	DONALDSON WL 1	MOODY WH 1	SIMONDS SR 1	DIXON GF 1
GILLIATT W 1			DURRANT RB 2	SYMONS SR 2	SIMONDS SR 1	DIXON GF 1
POLLOCK-HODSOLL GB	MCIVER CD	MACKRILL OW	FOSTER BS 1	WRIGHT RG 1	ALEXANDER CW	LOWNDES RG
WRIGHT WR	MEERS RH	BLASSON CA	HAMMOND CR	BUDGE PP 2	FINLAY RV	DIXON GF
WILD CH	GUY C	DOWSON FN	ALEXANDER CW 1	BLACKBURN W	WRIGHT CW 1	REES RM
WRIGHT WR	SHARP GF	SULMAN SW 1	SYMONS HJ 1	BUDGE PP 3	SIMONDS SR	DIXON GF 3
CRAIG RD	CRAIG JD	WARD VF	DURRANT RB	MCIVER CD	ALEXANDER CW	WARD ES
GILLIATT W	PIRKISS FCL	WARD VF 1	WRIGHT WR	SIMONDS SR	DIXON GF	
CRAIG RD	CRAIG JD	MACKRILL OW	DURRANT RB 1	TURNER R	ALEXANDER CW	WARD ES
WRIGHT WR	PIRKIS FCL 1	SYMONS HJ 1	SIMONDS SR	CLEAVE R	WILLIAMS WJ	
POLLOCK-HODSOLL GB	CRAIG JD	WARD VF	DURRANT RB	BARNARD RL	ALEXANDER CW	WARD ES
BRUCE TJ	WILLETT BH	BRUCE WW	WRIGHT RG 2	BUDGE PP	LEACH R 1	SYMONS HJ
CRAIG RD	MAGNAY CBW	HAMMOND CR	TURNER R 1	ALEXANDER CW	ROBERTS FW	THOMAS TS
MORGAN-OWEN M	MAGNAY CBW	DONALDSON TN	TOYNE SM	TRECKMAN CL	LOWNDES RG 1	WARD ES
CLEAVE R	PIRKIS FCL	GRANT AS	SYMONS HJ	WALLER HK	SULMAN SW	DIXON GF
HORLICK OP 1	WILLETT BH	DRAKE CF	HAMMOND CR	WALLER HK 1	FINLAY RV	MAGNAY CBW
CLEAVE R	GILLIATT W	SYMONS HJ	FOSTER A	WALLER HK	SIMONDS SR 1	DIXON GF 1
HORLICK OP	JOSEPH EH	BLASSON CA	DRAKE CF	CORRY HB	FINLAY RV	DIXON GF
POLLOCK-HODSOLL GB	LOWE HA	CANNY GB	BUDGE PP 2	FOSTER BS 3	CORBETT R 4	PIRKIS FCL
POLLOCK-HODSOLL GB	LOWE HA	CANNY GB	BUDGE PP	FOSTER BS	CORBETT R 1	MAGNAY CBW
POLLOCK-HODSOLL GB	PIRKIS FCL	CANNY GB 1	BUDGE PP	FOSTER BS	ALEXANDER CW 1	CORBETT R 1
CANNY GB	LOWE HA	BUDGE PP	ALEXANDER CW	EVANS 2	CORBETT R	PIRKIS FCL 1
CANNY GB	LOWE HA 1	PIRKIS FCL 1	CORBETT R	EVANS 1	ALEXANDER CW 1	MAGNAY CBW
POLLOCK-HODSOLL GB	MAGNAY CBW	BUDGE PP 1	EVANS 2	FOSTER BS 2	CANNY GB	ALEXANDER CW 1
POLLOCK-HODSOLL GB	LOWE HA	CORBETT R 1	ALEXANDER CW	EVANS	BUDGE PP	PIRKIS FCL

1905/06

DATE	VEN	OPPONENTS	RES	COMP	ATT	1	2	3	4
16-Sep	A	LONDON CALEDONIANS	1-1	IL		DAY AP	WHITTOW A	KING SL	POLLOCK-HODSOLL GB
23-Sep	H tp	CLAPTON	1-1	IL	1,500	DAY AP	CRAIG JD	KING SL	MORGAN-OWEN M
07-Oct	A	EALING	2-2	IL	500	DIXON CA	GROOM RG	MAY PR	POLLOCK-HODSOLL GB
14-Oct	H tp	OLD WESTMINSTERS	6-0	LCC1		DRIFFIELD LT	MAY PR	KING SL	POLLOCK-HODSOLL GB
21-Oct	A	CIVIL SERVICE	3-2	IL		ESDAILE EGK	MUGLISTON FH	KING SL	POLLOCK-HODSOLL GB
04-Nov	A	DULWICH HAMLET	2-1	LCC sf	3,000	DRIFFIELD LT	MAY PR	KING SL	POLLOCK-HODSOLL GB
02-Dec	H tp	EALING	1-3	IL		WILSON CE	KING SL	MUGLISTON FH	GREEN E
16-Dec	H tp	ILFORD	3-1	IL	1,000	ROWLANDSON TS	TIMMIS WU	MAY PR	POLLOCK-HODSOLL GB
06-Jan	A	CLAPTON	0-2	IL		WILKINSON GE	MAY PR	KING SL	POLLOCK-HODSOLL GB
13-Jan	H tp	WEST NORWOOD	3-2	LSC1		NESBITT P	LUKER SG	KING SL	POLLOCK-HODSOLL GB
10-Feb	H	2ND GRENADIER GDS	4-2	LSC2		ADAMS NP	LUKER SG	KING SL	POLLOCK-HODSOLL GB
03-Mar	A	LONDON CALEDONIANS	0-2	LCCF	6,000	DRIFFIELD LT	MAY PR	KING SL	POLLOCK-HODSOLL GB
17-Mar	N hh	DULWICH HAMLET	0-1	LSC sf		ADAMS NP	UDAL NR	KING SL	POLLOCK-HODSOLL GB
31-Mar	H tp	CIVIL SERVICE	2-0	IL		WILKINSON GE	GROOM RG	KING SL	TURNER PF
07-Apr	H tp	LONDON CALEDONIANS	1-2	IL		DRIFFIELD LT	MAY PR	KING SL	TUDOR-OWEN FHG
	A	ILFORD	0-0	IL					

Friendly Matches

DATE	VEN	OPPONENTS	RES	COMP	ATT	1	2	3	4
30-Sep	A	DULWICH HAMLET	0-4	F	2,000	ESDAILE EGK	CLEAVE R	KING SL	POLLOCK-HODSOLL GB
07-Oct	A	RMC SANDHURST	1-3	F	og	NESBITT P	SYMONS HJ	OWEN JD	LIDDELL NO
18-Oct	A	SUFFOLK REGIMENT	4-2	F	1,000	GRANT AS	BALFOUR RN	GRIMSDELL RE	POLLOCK-HODSOLL GB
24-Oct	A	FOREST SCHOOL	9-0	F		MOODY RH	WRIGHT WR	KING SL	COOKE HHA
28-Oct	H	OXFORD UNIVERSITY	4-4	F		ROGERS R	MUGLISTON FH	KING SL	POLLOCK-HODSOLL GB
28-Oct	A	CHARTERHOUSE	1-2	F		GRANT AS	WRIGHT WR	OWEN JW	CARTER EB
01-Nov	A	ST BARTHOLOMEWS H	6-1	F		GRANT AS	KING CE	GREATOREX P	WRIGHT WR
07-Nov	A	OLD FORESTERS	3-3	F		ADAMS NP	ROPER RG	SALWEY A	CARTER KB
08-Nov	A	ROYAL ENGINEERS	10-0	F		BARRETT HR	KING SL	BALFOUR RN	CLEAVE R
11-Nov	H tp	CAMBRIDGE UNIV	2-2	F	1,000	DIXON AS	LUKER SG	KING SL	POLLOCK-HODSOLL GB
15-Nov	A	GUY'S HOSPITAL	0-4	F		GRANT AS	KING SL	WRIGHT WR	GRIMSDELL RE
22-Nov	A	HIGHGATE SCHOOL	8-2	F		MOODY RH	BALFOUR RN	KING SL	GRIMSDELL RE
25-Nov	A	RMA WOOLWICH	8-1	F		WILSON W	WRIGHT WR	MILLS WG	TOMLINSON FW
28-Nov	A	ST JOHNS SCHOOL	6-2	F		SPOONER FD	MILLS WG	OWEN TD	EDWARDS FGB
06-Dec	A	RNC GREENWICH	3-1	F		GRANT AS	WRIGHT WR	GRIMSDELL RE	TUFF B
09-Dec	H tp	OLD MALVERNIANS	3-3	F		DIXON AS	GROOM RG	LUKER SG	CLEAVE R
11-Dec	A	SHREWSBURY SCHOOL	8-0	F		ROWLANDSON TS	UDAL NR	KING SL	PIRKIS FCL 1
12-Dec	A	REPTON SCHOOL	1-0	F		ROWLANDSON TS	UDAL NR	KING SL	PIRKIS FCL
13-Dec	A	MALVERN COLLEGE	2-1	F		MITCHELSON TR	UDAL NR	KING SL	TUDOR-OWEN FHG
14-Dec	A	ASTON VILLA	1-5	F	1,500	ROWLANDSON TS	CRAIG JD	KING SL	POLLOCK-HODSOLL GB
26-Dec	A	GRIMSBY TOWN	3-1	F		DRIFFIELD LT	MAY PR	KING SL	MCIVER CD
27-Dec	A	SCARBOROUGH	9-1	F		DRIFFIELD LT	MAY PR	KING SL	MCIVER CD
28-Dec	A	WEST HARTLEPOOL	2-2	F	600	DRIFFIELD LT	SNELL IE	KING SL	CORBETT AG
29-Dec	A	STOCKTON	4-3	F		DRIFFIELD LT	MAY PR	KING SL	HOWELL-JONES HG
30-Dec	A	SHILDON ATHLETIC	5-1	F					
01-Jan	A	DARLINGTON	0-0	F		DRIFFIELD LT	MAY PR	SNELL IE	HOWELL-JONES HG
17-Jan	A	GUY'S HOSPITAL	0-2	F		CLEAVE R	BALFOUR RN	KING SL	GILLIATT W
20-Jan	A	OLD CITIZENS	2-0	F	%	ADAMS NP	GREATOREX P	GOODMAN J	WESTBY HP
24-Jan	A	OXFORD UNIVERSITY	2-4	F		WILKINSON GE	SNELL IE	KING SL	CRAIG JD
27-Jan	A	CAMBRIDGE UNIV	0-3	F		ADAMS NP	LUKER SG	KING SL	POLLOCK-HODSOLL GB
27-Jan	A	WESTMINSTER SCHOOL	5-1	F	%				
31-Jan	A	ST THOMAS' HOSPITAL	7-1	F		GLENDALL AF	BALFOUR RN	KING SL	MILLS WG
03-Feb	H tp	OLD WESTMINSTERS	3-3	F		ADAMS NP	SIMONDS J	KING SL	CLEAVE R
13-Feb	A	WINCHESTER COLLEGE	8-1	F		ADAMS NP	KING SL	BALFOUR RN	GRIMSDELL RE
14-Feb	A	RMA WOOLWICH	8-1	F		GRANT AS	MILLS WG	BALFOUR RN	CLEAVE R
17-Feb	A	CHARTERHOUSE	2-3	F		NESBITT P	BRUTTON HL	BELCHER G	MEERS RH
21-Feb	A	HIGHGATE SCHOOL	15-4	F		GARNEY AH	GRIMSDELL RE	KING SL	POLLOCK-HODSOLL GB 1
24-Feb	A	THE ARMY	2-3	F	7,000	NESBITT P		BELCHER G	HOWELL-JONES HG
24-Feb	A	ALDENHAM SCHOOL	8-1	F	% 200				
28-Feb	A	ST JOHNS SCHOOL	4-1	F		SPOONER FD			TIMMIS WU
10-Mar	H tp	RICHMOND ASS	3-2	F	300	TAYLOR GMC	KING SL	MILLS WG	MAGNAY CBW
10-Mar	A	CRANLEIGH SCHOOL	4-0	F	% og	GRANT AS	ADAMS O	BOUTTON L	ROPER RE
14-Mar	A	MR SO CORBETTS XI	4-1	F	*	WILKINSON GE	KING SL	BALFOUR RN	SEEDORFF FJ
14-Apr	H tp	STOCKTON	1-3	F		DRIFFIELD LT	GRIMSDELL RE	KING SL	CRAIG JD

5	6	7	8	9	10	11
CRAIG RD	CLEAVE R	WARD VF	DURRANT RB	WRIGHT RG 1	GILLESPIE FW	BARNETT RO
CRAIG RD	CLEAVE R	FOSTER BS 1	DURRANT RB	WRIGHT RG	MCIVER CD	DAY SE
MORGAN-OWEN M	CRAIG JD	WARD VF	WRIGHT RG 1	HORLICK OP	ALEXANDER CW 1	WARD ES
MORGAN-OWEN M	CRAIG JD	WARD VF	WRIGHT RG 1	HARRIS GS 1	ALEXANDER CW 3	WARD ES 1
CLEAVE R	SIMONDS J	WARD VF	DRAKE CF	HARRIS GS 1	HAMMOND CR 1	WARD ES 1
MORGAN-OWEN M	CRAIG JD	WARD VF	DURRANT RB	HARRIS GS 1	ALEXANDER CW	WARD ES 1
MORGAN-OWEN M	CORBETT A	DRAKE CF	FINLAY RV	WRIGHT RG	GREY JN 1	HUMPHREYS CE
SIMONDS J	CLEAVE R	DRAKE CF	DURRANT RB 1	TUPPER GW	ALEXANDER CW 2	WARD ES
CRAIG RD	CLEAVE R	BROWN WL	FINLAY RV	BLAKER RNR	WARD ES	WARD VF
WESTBY HP	CLEAVE R	DRAKE CF	WARD VF 1	MCIVER CD 1	ALEXANDER CW	WARD ES 1
MORGAN-OWEN M	CRAIG JD	DRAKE CF	DURRANT RB 1	HARRIS GS	MCIVER CD 3	SIMONDS J
CRAIG RD	CRAIG JD	YOUNG RA	WRIGHT RG	HARRIS GS	ALEXANDER CW	WARD ES
MORGAN-OWEN M	SIMONDS J	DRAKE CF	BRYANT FH	HARRIS GS	ALEXANDER CW	WARD ES
RUSSELL EC	CLEAVE R	PAGET-TOMLINSON	DURRANT RB 1	FOSTER BS	ALEXANDER CW 1	TUPPER GW
SEEDORFF FJ	CLEAVE R	MOORHOUSE AC	DURRANT RB	SNELL IE 1	MCIVER CD	PAGET-TOMLINSON EE

5	6	7	8	9	10	11
MORGAN-OWEN M	LIDDELL NO	BLASSON CO	EASTERBROOK TE	HARRIS GS	HAMMOND CR	WIPPELL DP
SIMONDS J	MEERS RH	BLASSON CO	EASTERBROOK TE	TUPPER GW	GILLESPIE FW	DIXON GF
PIRKIS FCL	GILLIATT W	SYMONS HJ	SULMAN SW	SIMONDS SR 1	GILLESPIE FW 3	DIXON GF
CLEAVE R	SIMONDS J	DIXON GF	MCIVER CD 5	DRUMMOND GH 2	SIMONDS LR 2	'CASUAL' A
MCIVER CD	SIMONDS J	WARD VF 1	WRIGHT RG	HARRIS GS 2	DURRANT RB	WARD ES 1
MEERS RH	CLEAVE R	SYMONS HJ 1	SIMONDS SR	TUPPER GW	GILLESPIE FW	WIPPELL DP
GILLIATT W	GRIMSDELL RE	SYMONS HJ 1	SIMONDS SR	MORRIS JF 2	SIMONDS JF 1	DIXON GF 2
MEERS RH	CORBETT AG	SIMONDS SR 1	EASTERBROOK TE	TUPPER GW	GILLESPIE FW 2	DIXON GF
WRIGHT WR 1	POLLOCK-HODSOLL GB	PIRKIS FCL 1	SULMAN SW 3	SIMONDS SR 1	GILLESPIE FW 3	SIMONDS J 1
MORGAN-OWEN M	CRAIG JD	WARD VF	DURRANT RB 1	WRIGHT RG 1	ALEXANDER CW	WARD ES
BLACKSTONE AF	MEERS RH	MOODY RH	SULMAN SW	MCIVER CD	SIMONDS SR	DIXON GF
SIMONDS J	GILLIATT W	DESSEN CO	GILLESPIE FW 2	MCIVER CD 2	ALEXANDER CW 4	DIXON GF
SPRATT H	ROPER RG	SYMONS HJ	BLASSON CO 1	TUFF CT 2	GILLESPIE FW 3	DIXON GF 2
KING SL	TOMLINSON FW	POLLOCK-HODSOLL GB	SULMAN SW 1	CAMPBELL FC	WRIGHT WR 5	DIXON GF
POLLOCK-HODSOLL GB	SULMAN SW	SYMONS HJ	SIMONDS SR	TUFF CT 2	GILLESPIE FW 1	DIXON GF
GREEN E	CORBETT A	SYMONS HJ 1	DURRANT RB 1	FINLAY RV 1	GUY JK	TUPPER GL
CRAIG RD	CRAIG JD	HUMPHREYS CE	FOSTER GN 4	WAUGH AJ 2	ROBERTS FW 1	GREENWELL E
CRAIG RD	CRAIG JD	HUMPHREYS CE	FOSTER GN	WAUGH AJ 1	ROBERTS FW	GREENWELL E
CRAIG RD	CRAIG JD 1	HUMPHREYS CE	FOSTER GN	WAUGH AJ	ROBERTS FW	GREENWELL E 1
CRAIG RD	VICKERS H	CARRINGTON HW	GRESWELL R	FOSTER GN	ALEXANDER CW 1	WRIGHT EGD
CRAIG RD	CLEAVE R	CARRINGTON HW 1	FINLAY RV	SNELL IE 2	BIRKS AH	CORBETT AL
HOWELL-JONES HG 1	CORBETT AL	CARRINGTON HW 2	FINLAY RV 1	TURNER R 5	ROBERTS FW	YOUNG RA
CRAIG RD	CLEAVE R	YOUNG RA	BIRKS AH 1	TURNER R 1	ROBERTS FW	CORBETT AL
CRAIG RD	CLEAVE R 1	CORBETT AL	SNELL IE	TURNER R 2	MCIVER CD	CARRINGTON HW 1
					MCIVER CD 4	YOUNG RA 1
CRAIG RD	CLEAVE R	CARRINGTON HW	MCIVER CD	TURNER R	ROBERTS FW	YOUNG RA
GREEN G	GRIMSDELL RE	'OTHER' AN	SULMAN SW	WRIGHT RG	TUFF B	DIXON GF
RUSSELL EC	LIDDELL NO	BLASSON CO	EASTERBROOK TE	TUPPER GW	ROPER RG	DIXON GF
CLEAVE R	SIMONDS J	MCIVER CD	VASSALL GC 1	BLACKBURN W	ALEXANDER CW	CORBETT BO 1
MCIVER CD	CLEAVE R	PAGET-TOMLINSON EE	BRYANT FH	WRIGHT RG	DURRANT RB	SIMONDS J
CORBETT AG	CLEAVE R	SYMONS HJ 2	SIMMONS G 1	ROGERS R 1	EDWARDS V 2	DIXON GF
SPRATT H	GREEN G	TUPPER GW	DURRANT RB	WRIGHT RG	ROGERS R 1	WARD ES
CORBETT AG	CLEAVE R	SULMAN SW	BRYANT FH 3	WRIGHT RG 2	SIMONDS J 2	DIXON GF 1
CORBETT AG	TUFF B	SYMONS HJ	BRYANT FH	SIMONDS J 6	SULMAN SW 2	UNKNOWN
SPRATT H	BRUCE TJ	SYMONS HJ	EDWARDS V 1	EASTERBROOK TE 1	EDWARDS WG	WRIGHT EGD
CLEAVE R	CORBETT AG	WARD VF 1	BRYANT FH 5	FOSTER BS 7	SIMONDS ER 1	MILLER H
POLLOCK-HODSOLL GB 1	CLEAVE R	DRAKE CF	DURRANT RB	TURNER R 1	FOSTER BS	WARD ES
POLLOCK-HODSOLL GB	TUFF B 3				DIXON	SIMONDS J 1
GREEN E	CLEAVE R	DRAKE CF	COLEBY AT 1	SNELL IE	ALEXANDER CW 2	SIMONDS J
MOUNT SC	DIXON GF	CROSS AB	SYMONS HJ	'BRIGHTONIAN' A	EDWARDS O	CORBETT AL 1
TUFF B	GRIMSDELL RE	SYMONS HJ 1	SULMAN SW 1	SIMONDS J 1	HODGES HF	DIXON GF
SEEDORFF FJ	CORBETT AG	SEYMOUR HJ	BIRKS AH	SIMONDS J	MARWOOD G 1	DIXON GF

1906/07

DATE	VEN	OPPONENTS	RES	COMP	ATT	1	2	3	4
22-Sep	H tp	LONDON CALEDONIANS	0-1	IL	2,000	BEARDSLEY GL	KING SL	GRIMSDELL RE	SERGEANT PA
06-Oct	H tp	EALING	5-0	IL	700	HENLEY FAH	KING SL	MAY PR	GREEN G
13-Oct	A	CLAPTON	1-1	LCC1	1,500	BEARDSLEY GL	KING SL	MAY PR	POLLOCK-HODSOLL GB
03-Nov	H 1	ILFORD	2-4	IL		TAYLOR GMC	KING SL	THEW VG	SEEDORFF FJ
17-Nov	H tp	CIVIL SERVICE	2-3	IL	400	HENLEY FAH	KING SL	THEW VG	TUDOR-OWEN FHG
01-Dec	A	EALING	1-3	IL		DRIFFIELD LT	KING SL	SERGEANT PA	BEARDSLEY HL
08-Dec	A	CIVIL SERVICE	2-1	IL		DRIFFIELD LT	KING SL	BEARDSLEY HL	POWELL WA
15-Dec	A	ILFORD	1-4	IL		TAYLOR GMC	KING SL	LUKER SG	POWELL WA
22-Dec	H tp	CLAPTON	0-0	LCC1r	1,000	DRIFFIELD LT	KING SL	MUGLISTON FH	SIMONDS J
12-Jan	A	CLAPTON	6-3	LCC1r	1,000	DRIFFIELD LT	KING SL	LUKER SG	LEACH-LEWIS AF
09-Feb	H	LONDON CALEDONIANS	1-5	IL		HOLMES CB	KING SL	SEEDORFF FJ	GREEN G
02-Mar	N 1	NEW CRUSADERS	0-0	LCCsf	1,000	DRIFFIELD LT	KING SL	THEW VG	BEARDSLEY HL
16-Mar	A	CLAPTON	1-1	IL		TAYLOR GMC	KING SL	TIMMIS WU	EDWARDS WG
23-Mar	H	CLAPTON	0-4	IL		ROGERS R	KING SL	LUKER SG	POWELL WA
13-Apr	N 1	NEW CRUSADERS	5-4	LCCsf	1,200	DRIFFIELD LT	KING SL	LUKER SG	CRAIG RD
27-Apr	N tp	LONDON CALEDONIANS	0-0	LCCf	4,500	DRIFFIELD LT	KING SL	BEARDSLEY HL	CRAIG RD

Friendly Matches

DATE	VEN	OPPONENTS	RES	COMP	ATT	1	2	3	4
29-Sep	H tp	RICHMOND ASS	4-1	F	700	BEARDSLEY GL	KING SL	MAY PR	GREEN G
29-Sep	A	CHARTERHOUSE	1-0	F		DYKES WR	THEW VG	BRUTTON HL	EASTERBROOK TE
20-Oct	A	DULWICH HAMLET	0-4	F	2,500	ADAMS NP	KING SL	SERGEANT PA	CLEAVE R
24-Oct	A	CHARTERHOUSE	1-5	F		DYKES WR	KING SL	GRIMSDELL RE	CORBETT AG
27-Oct	H tp	OXFORD UNIVERSITY	1-2	F	1,800	HENLEY FAH	KING SL	TIMMIS WU	POLLOCK-HODSOLL GB
31-Oct	A	HIGHGATE SCHOOL	7-2	F		ADAMS NP	BALFOUR RN	GRIMSDELL RE	TUFF B
07-Nov	A	ST THOMAS' HOSPITAL	4-3	F		ADAMS NP	BALFOUR RN	COOKE HHA	CLEAVE R
10-Nov	H tp	CAMBRIDGE UNIV	0-6	F		DAY AP	SERGEANT PA	SEEDORFF FJ	POLLOCK-HODSOLL GB
10-Nov	A	BERKHAMSTED SCHOOL	3-0	F	½				
14-Nov	A	GUY'S HOSPITAL	6-3	F		CLEAVE R	KING SL	SULMAN SW	CORBETT AG
17-Nov	A	OLD CRANLEIGHANS	3-1	F	½			WINSLOE (SUB)	
20-Nov	A	FOREST SCHOOL	10-1	F	½	'PLAYER A'	BALFOUR RN	KING SL	CLEAVE R
24-Nov	A	OLD CITIZENS	2-1	F	½	BARRETT HR	GOODMAN J	SERGEANT PA	MOUNT SC
08-Dec	A	WESTMINSTER SCHOOL	6-0	F		BARRETT HR	NICHOLLS PS	CLEAVE R	MEERS RH
10-Dec	A	SHREWSBURY SCHOOL	1-1	F		ROWLANDSON TS	MUGLISTON HG	KING SL	FOSTER GN
11-Dec	A	REPTON SCHOOL	2-0	F		ROWLANDSON TS	KING SL	MUGLISTON FH	POLLOCK-HODSOLL GB
12-Dec	A	MALVERN COLLEGE	1-0	F		ROWLANDSON TS	MUGLISTON HG	KING SL	FOSTER GN 1
15-Dec	A	SURBITON HILL	2-1	F	og	BARRETT HR	NICHOLLS PS	GOODMAN J	MOUNT SC
27-Dec	A	SCARBOROUGH	4-1	F		DRIFFIELD LT	KING SL	LUKER SG	POWELL WA
28-Dec	A	NORTHERN NOMADS	3-3	F		DRIFFIELD LT			
29-Dec	A	SOUTH BANK	2-3	F					
31-Dec	A	STOCKTON	4-1	F					
01-Jan	A	DARLINGTON	8-2	F		DRIFFIELD LT		LUKER SG	
02-Jan	A	BISHOP AUCKLAND	5-1	F	og 500				
23-Jan	A	OXFORD UNIVERSITY	0-5	F	100	ROGERS R	KING SL	BALFOUR RN	GRIMSDELL RE
02-Feb	A	SHEPHERD'S BUSH	0-2	F		HOLMES CB	KING SL	BRITTEN AF	SERGEANT PA
06-Feb	A	HIGHGATE SCHOOL	12-1	F	og	DREW N	KING SL	CLEAVE R	WEAVER LT
16-Feb	A	CHARTERHOUSE	6-1	F		BARRETT HR	GOODMAN J	SERGEANT PA	MEERS RH
19-Feb	A	FOREST SCHOOL	9-0	F		DIXON AS	KING SL	BALFOUR RN	BONE J 1
23-Feb	A	ROYAL NAVY	3-1	F		DRIFFIELD LT	KING SL	SERGEANT PA	WOODRUFF GG
26-Feb	A	WINCHESTER COLLEGE	5-3	F		LANGLEY CK	KING SL	CLEAVE R	TUFF CT
02-Mar	A	BECKENHAM	1-1	F	½	HOLMES EB	SERGEANT PA	GOODMAN J	MEERS RH
09-Mar	H tp	THE ARMY	2-2	F		HENLEY FAH	BEARDSLEY HL	DAY GD	CORBETT AG
30-Mar	A	STOCKHOLM	7-0	F		ROGERS R	KING SL	BALFOUR RN	POLLOCK-HODSOLL GB
01-Apr	A	COPENHAGEN	4-1	F	½	ROGERS R	KING SL	BALFOUR RN	BEARDSLEY HL
03-Apr	A	GOTHENBURG	6-1	F		ROGERS R	KING SL	BALFOUR RN	BEARDSLEY HL

5	6	7	8	9	10	11
CANNY GB	SEEDORFF FJ	DRAKE CF	GUY JK	DURRANT RB	HAMMOND CR	DAY SE
CRAIG RD	SERGEANT PA	DRAKE CF	MORGAN-OWEN M 1	TURNER R 3	HARRIS SS 1	SYMONS HJ
HOWELL-JONES HG	HUNT KRG	DRAKE CF	MORGAN-OWEN M 1	HARRIS GS	TURNER R	MATTHEWS CC
MORGAN-OWEN M	SERGEANT PA	DRAKE CF	DURRANT RB	HARRIS GS 2	TURNER R	SIMONDS J
GREEN G	SERGEANT PA	DURRANT RB	EDWARDS V 1	BIRD WS 1	CORBETT AL	
MORGAN-OWEN M	CLEAVE R	DURRANT RB	BRYANT FH	SAYER GR 1	SHAW GL	CORBETT AL
SEEDORFF FJ	PAGET-TOMLINSON EE	BRYANT FH	DURRANT RB 1	BRISLEY CE 1	EDWARDS V	
SEEDORFF FJ	CLEAVE R	MOUNT SC	BEARDSLEY HL	CRUMMACK RW 1	EASTERBROOK TE	SIMONDS J
CRAIG RD	HUNT KRG	DIXON GF	BIRKS AH	HARRIS GS	DURRANT RB	CORBETT AL
MORGAN-OWEN M	MCIVER CD	DOWSON FN	BIRKS AH 2	HARRIS GS 3	DURRANT RB 1	SIMONDS J
LEACH-LEWIS AF	WOODRUFF GG	PAGET-TOMLINSON EE 1	EDWARDS V	CRUMMACK RW	TURNER R	SIMONDS J
MORGAN-OWEN M	MCIVER CD	WRIGHT RG	DURRANT RB	MORGAN-OWEN H	BIRKS AH	TUDOR-OWEN FHG
POLLOCK-HODSOLL GB	TUDOR-OWEN FHG	CLARKE A	COLEBY AT	TUFF B	BRISLEY CE 1	SIMONDS J
POLLOCK-HODSOLL GB	GREEN G	WRIGHT RG	DURRANT RB	DRAKE CF	SIMONDS J	ROUSE AH
MORGAN-OWEN M	TUDOR-OWEN FHG	WRIGHT RG 1	BIRKS AH 1	HARRIS GS 2	BRYANT FH 1	PAGET-TOMLINSON EE
MORGAN-OWEN M	TUDOR-OWEN FHG	WRIGHT RG	DURRANT RB	HARRIS GS	BRYANT FH	PAGET-TOMLINSON EE

5	6	7	8	9	10	11
CRAIG RD	SERGEANT PA	WARD VF	BIRKS AH 1	HARRIS GS 2	MATTHEWS CC 1	SYMONS HJ
WILLETT BH	GOODMAN J	JAMESON EM	EDWARDS V	ROPER RG 1	BLASSON CH	DIXON GF
BEARDSLEY HL	SEEDORFF FJ	POLLOCK-HODSOLL GB	BRISLEY CE	SHAW CL	DUNNETT HW	SYMONS HJ
CLEAVE R	GILLIATT W	SYMONS H	BRYANT FH 1	POYSER AV	DIXON EF	JAMESON EM
MORGAN-OWEN M	SERGEANT PA	CLARKE A	DURRANT RB	GORDON WG 1	DUNNETT HW	SIMONDS J
CORBETT AG	WEAVER LT	CLEAVE R	BRYANT FH 5	POYSER AV 2	GALE D (SUB)	'PLAYER' A
TUFF CT	CORBETT AG	CUTCHIE B (SUB)	EDWARDS V 2	WEAVER LT	SULMAN SW 2	DIXON GF
MORGAN-OWEN M	GREEN G	PAGET-TOMLINSON EE	DUNNETT HW	HARRIS GS	HARRIS SS	WARD ES
COOKE HHA	WEAVER LT	SYMONS HJ	BRYANT FH	TABERNACLE G 3	BRYDONE RM 3	DIXON GF
CORBETT AG	WEAVER LT	DIXON GF	BRYANT FH	BRYDONE RM	POYSER AV	DENISON-PENDER JC
SPRATT H	MEERS RH	LIPPELL DP	LUBBOCK HT	COOKE HHA	ROPER RG	DIXON GF
CORBETT AG	SYMONS CT	WIPPELL DP	EASTERBROOK TE	ROPER RG	CRUMMACK RW	DIXON GF
WREFORD-BROWN C	POLLOCK-HODSOLL GB	CRAIG RD	HUMPHREYS CG	CORNELIUS NS 1	GRESWELL EA	TUDOR-OWEN FHG
WREFORD-BROWN C	FOSTER GN	CRAIG RD	HUMPHREYS CG	CORNELIUS NS 2	GRESWELL EA	TUDOR-OWEN FHG
WREFORD-BROWN C	CRAIG RD	OWEN F	CRESSWELL	CORNELIUS NS	HUMPHREYS CG	POLLOCK-HODSOLL GB
CORBETT AG	COOKE HHA	SYMONS CT	LUBBOCK HT	EDWARDS V 1	ROPER RG	DIXON GF
LEACH-LEWIS AF 1	SEEDORFF FJ	EDWARDS V	BRISLEY CE 1	SAYER GR	TURNER R 2	CORBETT AL
HOWELL-JONES HG 1			BRISLEY CE 1	EDWARDS V	TURNER R 1	
					TURNER R 2	
				EDWARDS V 2	TURNER R 2	
			BRISLEY CE 1	SAYER GR 2	TURNER R 5	
			BRISLEY CE 1	EDWARDS V 3	TURNER R	CORBETT AL
POLLOCK-HODSOLL GB	MCIVER CD	VASSALL GC	BRYANT FH	BLACKBURN W	BRISLEY CE	SIMONDS J
GOODMAN J	POLLOCK-HODSOLL GB	EDWARDS V	DURRANT RB	SAYER GR	CRUMMACK RW	SIMONDS J
DIXON GF	TUFF CT 1	WARD OW 2	SYMONS HJ	ROPER RE 3	TUFF B 5	DENISON-PENDER JC
SYMONS HF	SYMONS CT	SIMONDS F	BRYANT FH 3	SIMONDS SR 2	EDWARDS V	DIXON EF
COCKELL FH 1	HARTLEY A	MILLER H 2	SIMONDS J	BRISLEY CE 1	DIXON GF 1	DENISON-PENDER JC 2
BEARDSLEY HL	SEEDORFF FJ	TUFF B 1	BRISLEY CE 1	DURRANT RB 1	BIRKS AH	TUDOR-OWEN FHG
GRIMSDELL RE 2	BONE J	MILLER H	BRYANT FH 3	BRYDONE RM	DIXON GF	PENDER JCD
RUSSELL EC	SYMONS CT	SYMONS HJ	EASTERBROOK TE	EDWARDS V	ROPER RG	DIXON GF
HOWELL-JONES HG	ROSS	DRAKE CF	TUFF B 1	BRISLEY CE 1	GRESWELL EA	TUDOR-OWEN FHG
BEARDSLEY HL 1	TUDOR-OWEN FHG	MATTHEWS CC	TUFF B 3	BRISLEY CE	SIMONDS J 1	WARD ES 2
CRAIG RD	POLLOCK-HODSOLL GB	MATTHEWS CC 1	TUDOR-OWEN FHG 1	BRISLEY CE 2	TUFF B	SIMONDS J
CRAIG RD	POLLOCK-HODSOLL GB	WARD ES	TURNER R 2	BRISLEY CE 1	TUFF B 3	TUDOR-OWEN FHG

1907/08

DATE	VEN	OPPONENTS	RES	COMP	ATT	1	2	3	4
28-Sep	A	TOWNLEY PARK	1-1	SAL		TAYLOR GMC	KING SL	ROBERTSON FG	SIMONDS J
12-Oct	A	EASTBOURNE	2-0	SAL		FLINN OS	KING SL	MAY PR	BEARDSLEY HL
02-Nov	A	IPSWICH TOWN	1-1	SAL		BARRETT HR	KING SL	LUKER SG	CARR AL
16-Nov	A	EALING	0-5	SAL		ACKLAND BM	KING SL	SERGEANT PA	BEARDSLEY HL
23-Nov	A	NEW CRUSADERS	1-4	SAL	1,000	FLINN OS	MAY PR	LUKER SG	POLLOCK-HODSOLL GB
30-Nov	A	CIVIL SERVICE	0-1	SAL		ROGERS R	KING SL	SERGEANT PA	WOODRUFF GG
07-Dec	A	CROYDON	4-0	SAL		TAYLOR GMC	SERGEANT PA	KING SL	DIXON GF
14-Dec	H @	IPSWICH TOWN	2-2	SAL	1,000	BARRETT HR	KING SL	BEARDSLEY HL	CRAIG RD
21-Dec	H tp	EALING	4-5	SAL		ADAMS NP	LUKER SG	MAY PR	SERGEANT PA
11-Jan	A	RICHMOND ASS	0-2	SAL		DRIFFIELD LT	MAY PR	SERGEANT PA	POLLOCK-HODSOLL GB
18-Jan	H tp	RAMSGATE ST GEORGES	4-1	AFASC1		DRIFFIELD LT	KING SL	MAY PR	POLLOCK-HODSOLL GB
25-Jan	H @	TOWNLEY PARK	4-2	SAL	%	ADAMS NP	KING SL	BEARDSLEY HL	SEEDORFF FJ
15-Feb	A	IPSWICH TOWN	2-0	AFASC2	2,000	DRIFFIELD LT	KING SL	BEARDSLEY HL	POLLOCK-HODSOLL GB
29-Feb	H @	EASTBOURNE	2-2	SAL		BARRETT HR	KING SL	LUKER SG	SERGEANT PA
07-Mar	H qc	CIVIL SERVICE	5-1	AFASC3	400	DRIFFIELD LT	KING SL	BEARDSLEY HL	HOWELL-JONES HG
14-Mar	A	CROYDON	10-1	SAL		HERMAN GL	MAY PR	JOHNSON WW	SEEDORFF FJ
14-Mar	H qc	EASTBOURNE	6-2	AFASCsf		DRIFFIELD LT	KING SL	BEARDSLEY HL	HOWELL-JONES HG
26-Mar	H tp	NEW CRUSADERS	1-1	SAL		DAY AP	TETLEY JCD	TUDOR-OWEN FHG	MCIVER CD
01-Apr	H tp	CIVIL SERVICE	2-1	SAL		ROGERS R	KING SL	MAY PR	BEARDSLEY HL
09-Apr	H tp	RICHMOND ASS	2-1	SAL		NICHOLLS EP	MAY PR	GRIMSDELL RE	WEAVER LT
11-Apr	N qc	OLD CARTHUSIANS	3-1	AFASCF	2,000	DRIFFIELD LT	KING SL	BEARDSLEY HL	HOWELL-JONES HG

Friendly Matches

DATE	VEN	OPPONENTS	RES	COMP	ATT	1	2	3	4
05-Oct	A	REIGATE PRIORY	3-1	F	%	FLINN OS	KING SL	MAY PR	SIMONDS J
05-Oct	A	CARSHALTON	5-2	F	%	ROPER RE	DIXON GF	GOODMAN J	NICHOLLS PS
09-Oct	A	CITY OF LONDON SCHOOL	5-2	F		AN OTHER	KING SL	BALFOUR RN	WEAVER LT
12-Oct	A	OLD FORESTERS	2-0	F		FLINN OS	KING SL	MAY PR	BEARDSLEY HL
19-Oct	H tp	OXFORD UNIVERSITY	4-2	F	2,000	ROGERS R	KING SL	MAY PR	BEARDSLEY HL
19-Oct	A	WESTMINSTER SCHOOL	6-0	F	%	FLINN OS	GOODMAN J	SEEDORFF FJ	GILLIATT W
23-Oct	A	WELLINGBOROUGH SCHOOL	7-1	F	%	NICHOLLS EP	KING SL	GRIMSDELL RE	GILLIATT W
26-Oct	A	BOWES PARK	6-2	F		DAVIDSON JLM	KING SL	BEARDSLEY HL	SEEDORFF FJ
26-Oct	A	CHARTERHOUSE	1-4	F		TAYLOR GMC	GOODMAN J	NICHOLLS PS	SYMONS CT
30-Oct	A	HIGHGATE SCHOOL	10-2	F	%	NICHOLLS EP	GRIMSDELL RE	WEAVER LT	GILLIATT W
06-Nov	A	ST THOMAS' HOSPITAL	2-2	F		NICHOLLS EP	BALFOUR RN	KING SL	WEAVER LT
09-Nov	H tp	CAMBRIDGE UNIV	2-1	F	1,500	HENLEY FAH	KING SL	LUKER SG	CRAIG RD
09-Nov	A	BERKHAMSTED SCHOOL	3-4	F		FLINN OS	SALWEY A	BONE J	MEERS RH
19-Nov	A	FOREST SCHOOL	7-0	F	og	NICHOLLS EP	BALFOUR RN	BRYDONE RM	ASHLEY FA
23-Nov	A	CARSHALTON	1-3	F	%	ADAMS NP	MEERS RH	SERGEANT PA	GREEN G
27-Nov	A	ST JOHNS SCHOOL	12-0	F		NICHOLLS EP	TETLEY JCD	GRIMSDELL RE	CLEAVE R
30-Nov	A	HAMPSTEAD	1-0	F	%	ADAMS NP	MORGAN-OWEN JG	CLEAVE R	GREEN G
09-Dec	A	SHREWSBURY SCHOOL	4-0	F		LANGLEY CK	KING SL	DARBYSHIRE CS	HOOPER FH
10-Dec	A	REPTON SCHOOL	3-4	F		LANGLEY CK	KING SL	STOCKS FC	HOOPER FH
11-Dec	A	MALVERN COLLEGE	6-1	F		LANGLEY CK	KING SL	DARBYSHIRE CS	DIXON S
26-Dec	A	TOWNLEY PARK	3-2	F	% 400	BARRETT HR	KING SL	SAYER GR	DIXON GF
04-Jan	A	GUILDHALL	3-2	F		TRELEAVEN CW	SERGEANT PA	LAMBERT CN	EASTERBROOK TE
22-Jan	A	ST THOMAS' HOSPITAL	0-2	F		NICHOLLS EP	KING SL	BALFOUR RN	CHATTERTON AF
25-Jan	A	WESTMINSTER SCHOOL	5-4	F	%	BARRETT HR	LAMBERT CN	BONE J	GILLIATT W
29-Jan	A	OXFORD UNIVERSITY	0-6	F		CRANSTOUN JC	KING SL	TETLEY JCD	POLLOCK-HODSOLL GB
01-Feb	A	ALDENHAM SCHOOL	0-2	F		ADAMS NP	MAY PR	SERGEANT PA	GILLIATT W
05-Feb	A	HIGHGATE SCHOOL	3-1	F	og	DOW MK	BALFOUR AJ	HUGHES HJ	GRIMSDELL E
08-Feb	A	CAMBRIDGE UNIV	2-5	F		ADAMS NP	KING SL	MAY PR	CRAIG RD
08-Feb	A	OLD ETONIANS	8-2	F	%	FLINN OS	GOODMAN J	SERGEANT PA	SEEDORFF JF
12-Feb	A	RMA WOOLWICH	6-1	F		NICHOLLS EP	CLARK HN	ASHBURNER WT	TUFF B
15-Feb	A	CHARTERHOUSE	1-0	F		NICHOLLS EP	SHEPPARD JHD	GOODMAN J	SEEDORFF FJ
18-Feb	A	FOREST SCHOOL	3-0	F	%	NICHOLLS EP	CLARK AM	BALFOUR RN	MOORS RH
29-Feb	A	BECKENHAM	1-2	F	%				
03-Mar	A	WINCHESTER COLLEGE	2-0	F	%	NICHOLLS EP	KING SL	TETLEY JCD	MILLS WG
07-Mar	A	CRANLEIGH SCHOOL	5-0	F	%	ADAMS NP	GOODMAN J	CARR AJ	MEERS RH
28-Mar	A	SURBITON HILL	7-2	F	%	BARRETT HR	KING SL	GOODMAN J	MCCALL RF

5	6	7	8	9	10	11
GOODMAN J	POYSER AV	CRUMMACK RW 1	TUFNELL NC	HARRIS GS	SAYER GR	KING RM
HOWELL-JONES HG	SERGEANT PA	TUPPER GW	MORGAN-OWEN M	HARRIS GS	CRUMMACK RW 1	BIRKS AH 1
LUDOLPH FJ	SERGEANT PA	DRAKE CF	TUPPER GW	PINK HS	REUNERT F	ACKLAND BM 1
POLLOCK-HODSOLL GB	WOODRUFF GG	DRAKE CF	BIRD WS	SAYER GR	PINK HS	CRUMMACK RW
MORGAN-OWEN M	MAGNAY CBW	TUDOR-OWEN FHG	PINK HS	HARRIS GS	CRUMMACK RW 1	SIMONDS J
CRAIG RD	KING FL	SAYER GR	BIRKS AH	CRUMMACK RW	ALEXANDER CW	DENISON-PENDER JC
POLLOCK-HODSOLL GB	CARR AL	LEAKE CL	BANN	POYSER AV 3	SAYER GR 1	TUFNELL NC
CRAIG JD	EDWARDS WG	TUDOR-OWEN FHG	DURRANT RB	CRUMMACK RW 1	SAYER GR 1	SIMONDS J
CRAIG RD	BEARDSLEY HL	POYSER AV	BIRKS AH 1	CRUMMACK RW 1	EDWARDS V 2	SIMONDS J
SEEDORFF FJ	GREEN E	TUPPER GW	CUTTER RC	SAYER GR	BIRKS AH	SIMONDS J
CRAIG RD	BEARDSLEY HL	LEAKE CL 1	DURRANT RB 2	SAYER GR	BIRKS AH 1	SIMONDS J
POLLOCK-HODSOLL GB	SERGEANT PA	LEAKE CL	DURRANT RB	VANN BW	BIRKS AH	DENISON-PENDER JC
MORGAN-OWEN M	SERGEANT PA	DRAKE CF 1	DURRANT RB 1	HARRIS GS	TURNER R	SIMONDS J
HOWELL-JONES HG	BEARDSLEY HL	CORBETT AL	TURNER R	HARRIS GS 2	SIMONDS J	
MORGAN-OWEN M	SERGEANT PA	TURNER R 1	DURRANT RB 1	HARRIS GS 1	BRISLEY CE 1	CORBETT AL 1
CRAIG RD 1	TUDOR-OWEN FHG	EDWARDS V 1	SAYER GR	VANN BW 5	ALEXANDER CW 3	ROBERTS FW
MORGAN-OWEN M	SERGEANT PA	CORBETT AL	DURRANT RB 2	HARRIS GS 2	TURNER R 2	SIMONDS J
SUAL CA	SERGEANT PA	PAGET-TOMLINSON EE 1	TUFF B	SNELL IE	BIRKS AH	SIMONDS J
POLLOCK-HODSOLL GB	SERGEANT PA	KING RM	EDWARDS V 1	CUTTER RC 1	BIRKS AH	DENISON-PENDER JC
WOODRUFF GG	MAGNAY CBW	KING RM	EDWARDS V 1	TUDOR-OWEN FHG 1	CUTTER RC	DENISON-PENDER JC
MORGAN-OWEN M	SERGEANT PA	TURNER R	BRISLEY CE 3	HARRIS GS	BIRKS AH	SIMONDS J

5	6	7	8	9	10	11
MORGAN-OWEN M	SERGEANT PA	DRAKE CF 1	SAYER GR	HARRIS GS	TUFNELL NC 1	ROBERTS FW
MINNS SC	SEEDORFF FJ	RUSSELL EC	EASTERBROOK TE	CRUMMACK RW	POYSER AV	BOURNE AC
HYME WM	SIMONDS J	DIXON GF	TUFF B 1	EDWARDS V 2	BRYDONE RM 1	DENISON-PENDER JC 1
HOWELL-JONES HG	SERGEANT PA	TUPPER GW	MORGAN-OWEN M	HARRIS GS	CRUMMACK RW 1	BIRKS AH 1
HOWELL-JONES HG	SERGEANT PA	DRAKE CF	MORGAN-OWEN M	HARRIS GS 2	CRUMMACK RW 2	SIMONDS J
MOUNT SC	MEERS RH	WIPPELL DP	TOYNE SM	TUPPER GW	ROPER RG	DIXON GF
MILLER H	DIXON GF	BRYDONE RM	ROPER RG	POYSER AV	BOURNE AC	DENISON-PENDER JC
MOUNT SC	SERGEANT PA	DRAKE CF	DURRANT RB 4	HARRIS GS 1	POYSER AV 1	SIMONDS J
GILLIATT W	TOYNE SM	EASTERBROOK TE	LEAK CS	MORRIS JF	CRUMMACK RW 1	DIXON GF
HYNE WM	TUFF B	ASHLEY FN	DIXON GF	DENISON-PENDER JC	MILLER H	KING SL
MILLER H	HYNE WM	LEAKE CL 1	EASTERBROOK TE	TUFF B 1	BRYDONE RM	DENISON-PENDER JC
LEACH-LEWIS AF	BEARDSLEY HL	TUDOR-OWEN FHG 1	DURRANT RB	MORGAN-OWEN M	BIRKS AH 1	SIMONDS J
GOODMAN J	NEWBERRY RE	OTHER AN	BOURNE AC	MORGAN JL	ROPER RG	DIXON GF
POLLOCK-HODSOLL GB	TUFF B	LEAKE CL	MORGAN-OWEN JG 2	SIMONDS SR 1	DIXON GF 2	DENISON-PENDER JC 1
GOODMAN J	EASTERBROOK TE	WIPPELL DP	MORGAN-OWEN JG	TUPPER GW	ROPER RG	DIXON GF
ASTLEY FW 1	HYNE WM	LEAKE CL	TUFF B 4	DENISON-PENDER JC 2	BRYDONE RM 5	DIXON GF
CARR AJ	OLIVER K	EASTERBROOK TE	DONALDSON TH	TUPPER GL	BRYDONE RM	DIXON GF
CRAIG	SPOOKE	ALEXANDER CW	GRESWELL EA	TUFF B	HICKSON	HUGHES JL
TUFF B	DARBYSHIRE CS	ALEXANDER CW	VASSALL GC 2	GRESWELL EA	TURNER R	DIXON GF
TUFF CT	HOOPER FH	PEERS HC	GRESWELL EA 1	TURNER R 3	ALEXANDER CW 1	HUGHES JL
CRAIG JD	PRICKETT H	LEAKE CL	CUTTER RC	POYSER AV	BROUGHTON H	
GILLIATT W	MEERS RH	LEAKE CL	SIMONDS SR	OTHER AN	ROPER RG	DIXON GF
POLLOCK-HODSOLL GB	AN OTHER	LEAKE CL	EASTERBROOK TE	DIXON GF	ALEXANDER CW	DENISON-PENDER JC
MOUNT SC	MOORS RH	WIPPELL DP	EASTERBROOK TE	TUPPER GW	EVANS RS	DIXON GF
CRAIG RD	MCIVER CD	VASSALL GC	DURRANT RB	PIDCOCK RG	SAYER GR	SIMONDS J
EASTERBROOK TE	NEWBERRY RE	LEAKE CL	CANTAB A	EVANS RS	BRYDONE RM	DIXON GF
WEAVER LT	CHATTERTON FV	NICHOLLS EP 1	DIXON GF 1	GRIMSDELL RG	EASTERBROOK TE	LEAKE CL
POLLOCK-HODSOLL GB 1	BEARDSLEY HL	PAGET-TOMLINSON EE	DURRANT RB	POYSER AV	BIRKS AH 1	KENYON MA
GILLIATT W	CARR AJ	LEAKE CL 1	EASTERBROOK TE	FOREMAN H 2	BRYDONE RM 2	DIXON GF 1
HYNE WN	MILLAR B	LEAKE CL	CLEAVES CF 3	INGRAM W 1	DIXON GF 2	RICKETT G
CARR AJ	LAMBERT CN	DIXON GF	BRYDONE RM	TUPPER GL 1	EASTERBROOK TE	FORDER FG
GLASGOW SG	CHATTERTON RB	HUGHES JS	SIMONDS SR	MILLER H	DIXON GF 1	WATKINS PMC 1
CRAIG RD	BALFOUR RN	LEAKE CL	SULMAN SW	MILLER H	ALEXANDER CW 1	DIXON GF
CORBETT AG	NEWBERRY RE	EASTERBROOK TE	BONE J	TUPPER GW	MCCALL RF	DIXON GF
CORBETT AG	MEERS RH	EASTERBROOK TE	DURRANT RB	HARRIS GS	TUPPER GW	DIXON GF

1908/09

DATE	VEN	OPPONENTS	RES	COMP	ATT	1	2	3	4
26-Sep	A	CROUCH END VAMPIRES	4-1	SAL	500	TAYLOR GMC	KING SL	SERGEANT PA	TUFF B
03-Oct	A	REIGATE PRIORY	2-8	SAL	%	FLINN OS	KING SL	SERGEANT PA	TUFF B
10-Oct	A	EASTBOURNE	5-3	SAL		TRELEAVEN CW	KING SL	WOODRUFF GG	HOWELL-JONES HG 1
17-Oct	H tp	NEW CRUSADERS	4-1	SAL	3,000	LACY-SCOTT G	THEW VG	KING SL	SEEDORFF FJ
24-Oct	A	IPSWICH TOWN	1-2	SAL		LACY-SCOTT G	MAY PR	KING SL	SERGEANT PA
31-Oct	A	RICHMOND ASS	4-1	SAL		LACY-SCOTT G	KING SL	LUKER SG	SEEDORFF FJ
21-Nov	A	EALING	2-4	SAL		ADAMS NP	KING SL	CARR AJ	WOODRUFF GG
28-Nov	A	NEW CRUSADERS	3-4	SAL	1,000	LACY-SCOTT G	THEW VG	KING SL	CRAIG RD
19-Dec	A	LEE	7-1	AFASC1		LACY-SCOTT G	KING SL	LUKER SG	WOODRUFF GG
26-Dec	H @	REIGATE PRIORY	0-1	SAL	1,000	HERMON GL	KING SL	CARR AJ	WOODRUFF GG
09-Jan	H 1	EALING	6-0	SAL		LACY-SCOTT G	KING SL	SERGEANT PA	WOODRUFF GG
16-Jan	A	TOWNLEY PARK	3-0	AFASC2	%	LACY-SCOTT G	KING SL	SERGEANT PA	EDWARDS WG
23-Jan	H 1	RICHMOND ASS	0-1	SAL		LACY-SCOTT G	KING SL	CARR AJ	WOODRUFF GG
13-Feb	H 1	IPSWICH TOWN	3-1	AFASC3	og	LACY-SCOTT G	KING SL	MAY PR	WOODRUFF GG
20-Mar	N ca	CIVIL SERVICE	2-0	AFASCsf		LACY-SCOTT G	KING SL	MAY PR	WOODRUFF GG
27-Mar	H tp	CIVIL SERVICE	0-2	SAL		LACY-SCOTT G	MAY PR	SERGEANT PA	WOODRUFF GG
03-Apr	N ip	NEW CRUSADERS	1-5	AFASCf	og 5000	LACY-SCOTT G	MAY PR	SERGEANT PA	WOODRUFF GG
10-Apr	H @	IPSWICH TOWN	0-0	SAL		LACY-SCOTT G	KING SL	BELCHER C	POLLOCK-HODSOLL GB
24-Apr	H @	CROUCH END VAMPIRES	3-3	SAL	%	LACY-SCOTT G	LUKER SG	GOODMAN J	WOODRUFF GG
NOT P	A	CIVIL SERVICE	#	SAL					
NOT P	H	EASTBOURNE		SAL					

There is no record of this match being played - the previous match against Civil Service was potentially a double header

Friendly Matches

DATE	VEN	OPPONENTS	RES	COMP	ATT	1	2	3	4
26-Sep	A	WEYBRIDGE	1-2	F	*	DAVIDSON JLM	WHITE FS	DIXON GF	GILLIATT W
08-Oct	A	COLCHESTER LEAGUE	2-2	F	+				
10-Oct	A	SURBITON HILL	1-1	F	%	LACY-SCOTT G	GOODMAN J	WADE CH	MOUNT SC
21-Oct	A	RMA WOOLWICH	0-1	F		STEPHENS A	CLARK HN	SAINSBURY PC	GRIMSDELL RE
24-Oct	A	CHARTERHOUSE	3-1	F		ADAMS WP	WADE CH	WILLETT BH	GILLIATT W
28-Oct	A	BERKHAMSTED SCHOOL	2-2	F	%	DIXON AS	WADE CH	SAINSBURY PC	WEAVER LT
04-Nov	A	HIGHGATE SCHOOL	11-1	F		STEPHENS A	MILLS WG	SAINSBURY PC	GRIMSDELL RE
07-Nov	H tp	CAMBRIDGE UNIV	0-2	F		HERMON GL	TIMMIS WU	MAY PR	WOODRUFF GG
14-Nov	H tp	OXFORD UNIVERSITY	0-1	F		LACY-SCOTT G	SERGEANT PA	MAY PR	WOODRUFF GG
17-Nov	A	FOREST SCHOOL	3-2	F		STEPHENS A	MEERS RH	HUGHES JS	DIXON AS
21-Nov	A	EAST LONDON COLLEGE	3-0	F	%	BARRETT HR	SAINSBURY PC	THWAITES H	GILLIATT W
05-Dec	A	CHESHUNT	4-1	F	%	LACY-SCOTT G	SERGEANT PA	THWAITES H	WOODRUFF GG
05-Dec	A	ALDENHAM SCHOOL	1-2	F	%	ADAMS NP	BENNET EO	GOODMAN J	OTHER AN
14-Dec	A	SHREWSBURY SCHOOL	10-0	F	%	NICHOLLS EP	THEW VG	KING SL	COOPER FH
15-Dec	A	REPTON SCHOOL	3-0	F		NICHOLLS EP	KING SL	THEW VG	COOPER FH
16-Dec	A	MALVERN COLLEGE	3-1	F		NICHOLLS EP	THEW VG	KING SL	COOPER FH
29-Dec	A	NOTTS AMATEURS	4-1	F		HERMON GL	KING SL	WADE CH	WOODRUFF GG
01-Jan	A	NOTTS MAGDALA	1-0	F		WADE CH	KING SL	LEACH-LEWIS AF	WOODRUFF GG
02-Jan	A	DERBY THORNHILL & DERWENT	7-1	F		WADE CH	KING SL	HACKING EM	WOODRUFF GG
23-Jan	A	OLD CRANLEIGHANS	1-2	F	%	OTHER AN	BRIGHT AS	GOODMAN J	CORBETT AG
06-Feb	A	CAMBRIDGE UNIV	2-1	F		TOWNSEND M	KING SL	MAY PR	WOODRUFF GG
10-Feb	A	CHARTERHOUSE	1-2	F		NICHOLLS EP	JOHNSON P	WILLETT BH	O'BRIEN T
23-Feb	A	FOREST SCHOOL	3-4	F		DIXON AS	KING SL	MALLINSON	GRIMSDELL RE
20-Mar	A	ETON COLLEGE	14-4	F	%	HERMAN GL	GOODMAN J	SHEPHARD JHD	MOUNT SC

5	6	7	8	9	10	11
MORGAN-OWEN M	EDWARDS WG	SAYER GR	VANN BW 1	CUTTER RC 2	BIRKS AH 1	EDWARDS V
MORGAN-OWEN M	SIMONDS J	KING RM	BIRKS AH	SAYER GR	HODGES HF 1	CUTTER RC
SERGEANT PA	WRIGHT RG 1	EDWARDS V	LESLIE KD 2	SIMONDS J	CORBETT AL 1	
CRAIG RD	SERGEANT PA	CUTTER RC 1	HOFFMEISTER CE 2	MORGAN-OWEN M	BIRKS AH 1	CORBETT AL
CRAIG RD	POLLOCK-HODSOLL GB	WRIGHT RG 1	VANN BW	CUTTER RC	SEEDORFF FJ	KING RM
WOODRUFF GG	SERGEANT PA	WRIGHT RG	DRAKE CF	CUTTER RC 3	CARDEW AE 1	SIMONDS J
GOODMAN J	SEEDORFF FJ	WRIGHT RG	PINK HS	CUTTER RC 1	CARDEW AE 1	KING RM
MORGAN-OWEN M	SERGEANT PA	CUTTER RC	HOFFMEISTER CE	BRISLEY CE 2	EDWARDS V 1	CORBETT AL
CRAIG RD	SERGEANT PA	WRIGHT RG 1	CUTTER RC 3	BRISLEY CE 2	EDWARDS V 1	TURNER R
PIRKIS FCL	HERMAN AE	TUPPER GL	CUTTER RC	VANN BW	MCIVER CD	DIXON GF
MORGAN-OWEN M	HERMAN AE	WARD ES	BRISLEY CE 1	LEACH-LEWIS AF 3	CUTTER RC 2	SIMONDS J
MORGAN-OWEN M	SEEDORFF FJ	CUTTER RC	BIRKS AH	BRISLEY CE	EDWARDS V	SIMONDS J
SEEDORFF FJ	SERGEANT PA	WRIGHT RG	BRISLEY CE	VANN BW	WARD ES	DENISON-PENDER JC
SEEDORFF FJ	SERGEANT PA	PAGET-TOMLINSON EE	CORBETT AL 2	VANN BW	PINK HS	SIMONDS J
SEEDORFF FJ	SERGEANT PA	CORBETT AL	EDWARDS V 1	BRISLEY CE	BIRKS AH 1	SIMONDS J
POLLOCK-HODSOLL GB	SEEDORFF FJ	BRISLEY CE	MCIVER CD	LEACH-LEWIS AF	BIRKS AH	CORBETT AL
EDWARDS WG	SEEDORFF FJ	SIMONDS J	BRISLEY CE	SAYER GR	BIRKS AH	CORBETT AL
SEEDORFF FJ	SERGEANT PA	WOODRUFF GG	GREEN G	LEACH-LEWIS AF	SAYER GR	DIXON GF
SEEDORFF FJ	SERGEANT PA	DIXON GF	BISSEKER EG	'OTHER' AN	BIRKS AH	SIMONDS J

5	6	7	8	9	10	11
CROFT T de C	STUART VD	LEAKE CL	VIDAL HSG	TUPPER GW	BISSEKER EG	TOMSON DV
				SIMONDS 1		
SEEDORFF FJ	GILLIATT W	MEERS RH	VIDAL HSG	TUPPER GW	BISSEKER EG	DIXON GF
COOKE HHA	BALFOUR RN	BIRKS AH	DIXON GF	CUTTER RC	NICHOLLS EP	DENISON-PENDER JC
GOODMAN J 1	WOODRUFF GG	WIPPELL DP 1	LESLIE KD	TUPPER GW 1	WILSON AP	DIXON GF
GRIMSDELL RE	WOODRUFF GG	MANN R	NICHOLLS EP	SKEWES V	DIXON GF	DENISON-PENDER JC
WOODRUFF GG	COOKE HHA	LEAKE CL 4	NICHOLLS EP 2	CUTTER RC 3	TUFF B 2	DIXON GF
HOWELL-JONES HG	SERGEANT PA	WRIGHT RG	HOFFMEISTER CE	CUTTER RC	SIMONDS J	CORBETT AL
HOWELL-JONES HG	SIMONDS J	WRIGHT RG	MORGAN-OWEN M	CUTTER RC	TURNER R	KING RM
POLLOCK-HODSOLL GB	COOKE HHA	DENISON-PENDER JC	CROLE-REES HB 1	NICHOLLS EP	WEAVER LT 2	DIXON GF
GOODMAN J	HYNE WM	TOMSON DV	MCCALL RF	TUPPER GW	'CANTAB' A	DIXON GF
SEEDORFF FJ	HYNE WM	KING RM	CUTTER RC	DIED CV	TUNKS GW	'CANTAB' A
HACKING EM	GILLIATT W	TOMSON DV	MCCALL RF	BAGNALL R ST V	HERRING J	DIXON GF
EDWARDS WG	PREST HEW	PEARS HT	SQUIRE CE 2	BRISLEY CE 5	EDWARDS V 2	CARDEW AE
EDWARDS WG	PREST HEW	PEARS HT	SQUIRE CE	BRISLEY CE 2	EDWARDS V 1	CARDEW AE
EDWARDS WG	PREST HEW	PEARS HT	SQUIRE CE 1	BRISLEY CE	EDWARDS V 2	CARDEW AE
LEACH-LEWIS AF	HERMAN AE	DOWSON FN	VANN BW 1	CUTTER RC 1	EDWARDS V 2	RAYNOR K
EDWARDS WG	HERMAN AE	DOWSON FN	RAYNOR K	CUTTER RC	EDWARDS V	ROBERTS FW 1
EDWARDS WG 1	HERMAN AE 1	CUTTER RC	VANN BW	LEACH-LEWIS AF 4	ROBERTS FW	RAYNOR K 1
MOUNT SC	HYNE WM	TOMSON DV	'CANTAB' A	MEERS RH	BRYDONE RM	DIXON GF
SEEDORFF FJ	SERGEANT PA	WRIGHT RG	MCIVER CD	VANN BW 1	PINK HS 1	SIMONDS J
WOODRUFF GG	OTHER AN	D'ETONIAN' OL	FORWARD MO	DIXON GF	DENISON-PENDER JC 1	
DIXON GF	STUBBINGS	NICHOLLS EP 2	MONTGOMERY PJ	DENISON-PENDER JC	'FORESTER' A	SIMONDS SR 1
CORBETT AG	MEERS RH	MCCALL RF	BISSEKER EG	ORWARD AF	BURROWS LR	DIXON GF

1909/10

DATE	VEN	OPPONENTS	RES	COMP	ATT	1	2	3	4
02-Oct	A	TOWNLEY PARK	6-0	SAL	og 300	TOWNSEND M	TETLEY JCD	KING SL	SERGEANT PA
09-Oct	H tp	NEW CRUSADERS	2-3	SAL	1,500	TOWNSEND M	MAY PR	KING SL	WOODRUFF GG
16-Oct	A	NORSEMEN	2-2	SAL		ADAMS NP	LUKER SG	KING SL	MILTON HA
23-Oct	A	IPSWICH TOWN	4-0	SAL	1,000	TOWNSEND M	KING SL	MAY PR	POLLOCK-HODSOLL GB
13-Nov	A	EASTBOURNE	1-1	SAL		TOWNSEND M	SHEPHERD JH	KING SL	MILTON HA
20-Nov	A	CIVIL SERVICE	1-6	SAL	%	NORRIS GH	SHEPHERD JH	SAINSBURY PC	GREEN G
27-Nov	H 1	EALING	4-2	SAL		TOWNSEND M	MILTON HA	OWEN RCD	HERMAN AE
18-Dec	A	OLD ETONIANS	7-1	AFASC1	%	TRELEAVEN CW	KING SL	MILTON HA	HERMAN AE
08-Jan	A	EALING	2-2	SAL		KING SL	LUKER SG	MALTBY FE	MILTON HA 1
15-Jan	H e	CROUCH END VAMPIRES	5-1	AFASC2		WADE CH	KING SL	CARR AJ	MILTON HA
22-Jan	H 1	TOWNLEY PARK	1-2	SAL		WADE CH	OWEN RCD	MILTON HA	SERGEANT PA
05-Feb	A	REIGATE PRIORY	0-1	SAL		QUICK CF	KING SL	WADE CH	RAIKES KC
26-Feb	H tp	OLD CARTHUSIANS	2-0	AFASC3		DRIFFIELD LT	KING SL	MILTON HA	HOWELL-JONES HG
05-Mar	H @	EASTBOURNE	1-1	SAL		ROGERS R	KING SL	MILTON HA	HOWELL-JONES HG
12-Mar	H 1	REIGATE PRIORY	5-2	SAL	og	DAVIDSON JLM	KING SL	MAY PR	WOODRUFF GG
19-Mar	N s	CIVIL SERVICE	0-4	AFASCsf		DRIFFIELD LT	KING SL	MILTON HA	HOWELL-JONES HG
26-Mar	H @	IPSWICH TOWN	0-1	SAL	1,500	LACY-SCOTT G	KING SL	WADE CH	MILTON HA
02-Apr	A	NEW CRUSADERS	0-6	SAL		TAYLOR GMC	SERGEANT PA	MILTON HA	RAIKES KC
13-Apr	H tp	NORSEMEN	4-0	SAL		DRIFFIELD LT	KING SL	MILTON HA	FITZGIBBON DF
NP	H	CIVIL SERVICE	NP	SAL					

Friendly Matches

DATE	VEN	OPPONENTS	RES	COMP	ATT	1	2	3	4
25-Sep	A	WEYBRIDGE	2-3	F	%	COWIE A	SHEPHERD JH	WADE CH	GILLIATT W
06-Oct	A	ST JOHNS SCHOOL	4-2	F	%	STEPHENS A	LAMBERT CN	KING SL	CLARK HN
09-Oct	A	SURBITON HILL	3-0	F	%	ADAMS NP	SAINSBURY PC	BECK PL	SALE HB
13-Oct	A	LANCING COLLEGE	8-1	F	%	STEPHENS A	KING SL	ESDAILE EGK	HUGHES JS
16-Oct	A	WESTMINSTER SCHOOL	2-0	F	%	DIXON AS	GOODMAN J	SAINSBURY PC	BIRRELL HA
20-Oct	A	RMA WOOLWICH	11-2	F		STEPHENS A	LAMBERT CN	KING SL	FRANCIS HW
23-Oct	A	CHARTERHOUSE	1-2	F		BURDON NE	SAINSBURY PC	SHEPPARD JH	SALE HB
27-Oct	A	BERKHAMSTED SCHOOL	14-1	F	%	'OTHER' AN	RIMMINGTON H	FRANCIS HW	TOMLINSON FW
30-Oct	H tp	OXFORD UNIVERSITY	0-2	F		LOVEGROVE CD	KING SL	MAY PR	MILTON HA
30-Oct	A	WELLINGBOROUGH SCHOOL	6-1	F	og	BARRETT HR	SHEPHERD JH	GOODMAN J	FRANCIS HW
03-Nov	A	HIGHGATE SCHOOL	5-3	F		STEPHENS A	HUGHES JS	WEAVER LT	FRANCIS HW
06-Nov	H tp	CAMBRIDGE UNIV	1-6	F	500	NEWMAN GG	KING SL	MILTON HA	SERGEANT PA
06-Nov	A	CRANLEIGH SCHOOL	5-0	F		NICHOLLS EP	GIMINGHAM CH	MENZIES T	WOODRUFF GG
10-Nov	A	CITY OF LONDON SCHOOL	5-2	F	%	STEPHENS A	RIMMINGTON H	CLARK HN	COOKE HHA
17-Nov	A	FELSTED SCHOOL	3-1	F		ALLEN HC	RIMMINGTON H	OWEN JH	LUCAS AL
24-Nov	A	ST THOMAS' HOSPITAL	3-4	F		STEPHENS A	HUGHES JS	GOLDSMITH BE	FRANCIS HW
27-Nov	A	BANK OF ENGLAND	4-1	F	%				
13-Dec	A	SHREWSBURY SCHOOL	5-0	F		APPLETON JA	KING SL	OWEN RCD	EDWARDS
14-Dec	A	REPTON SCHOOL	3-1	F		NEWMAN GG	KING SL	OWEN RCD	SALE HB
15-Dec	A	MALVERN COLLEGE	7-0	F	%	NEWMAN GG	TUFF FN	KING SL	SALE RB
28-Dec	A	DERBY THORNHILL	7-1	F	og	TOWNSEND M	KING SL	WADE CH	SALE RB
29-Dec	A	NOTTS AFA	9-2	F		TOWNSEND M	KING SL	WADE CH	CARR AL
30-Dec	A	NORTHERN AMATEURS	4-1	F		TOWNSEND M	MALTBY FE	WADE CH	POLLOCK-HODSOLL GB
31-Dec	A	NOTTS MAGDALA	3-0	F		WADE CH			MONTGOMERY PJ
01-Jan	A	NOTTS AMATEURS	4-0	F		WADE CH			
19-Jan	A	ST THOMAS' HOSPITAL	5-0	F		ALLEN HC	HUGHES HS	RIMMINGTON H	MANN R 1
29-Jan	A	CAMBRIDGE UNIV	2-4	F		TAYLOR GMC	MILTON HA	CARR AJ	MONTGOMERY PJ
02-Feb	A	GUY'S HOSPITAL	1-4	F		ALLEN HC	SERGEANT PA	LAMBERT CN	DYAS GE
05-Feb	A	HIGHGATE SCHOOL	7-6	F	%	MACKAY GR	SHEPPARD JH	SALE HB	FRANCIS HW
09-Feb	A	CHARTERHOUSE	4-0	F		ALLEN HC	TETLEY JCD	WILLETT BH	DYAS GE
12-Feb	A	WESTMINSTER SCHOOL	3-1	F	% og	GRANT AS	SHEPPARD JH	SAINSBURY PC	SALE HB
16-Feb	A	RMA WOOLWICH	4-4	F		STEPHENS A	KING SL	CLARK HN	SERGEANT PA
01-Mar	A	WINCHESTER COLLEGE	4-2	F	%	GRANT AS	KING SL	CLARK HN	DYAS GE

5	6	7	8	9	10	11
MILTON HA	LUKER SG	BIRKS AH 1	BISSEKER EG 2	BRISLEY CE 1	SAYER GR	TUFF B 1
CARR AJ	MILTON HA 1	CUTTER RC	BISSEKER EG 1	BRISLEY CE	MCIVER CD	SIMONDS J
RAIKES KC	SALE HB	CUTTER RC 1	BISSEKER EG 1	BRISLEY CE	BIRKS AH	JOHNSON AF
ASHTON HO	GREEN G	CUTTER RC 1	BISSEKER EG 1	TUFF FN 1	PINK HS 1	BIRKS AH
SERGEANT PA 1	GILLINGHAM CH	HALL KL	TURNER R	BISSEKER EG	MONTGOMERY PJ	CUTTER RC
POLLOCK-HODSOLL GB	SERGEANT PA	WATHAN AR	BISSEKER EG	CUTTER RC	ARKWRIGHT CH	MONTGOMERY PJ
SERGEANT PA	RAIKES KC	TURNER R 2	BISSEKER EG	BRISLEY CE 1	BIRKS AH 1	WARD ES
HOWELL-JONES HG	SERGEANT PA	POLLOCK-HODSOLL GB	BECK PL	TURNER R	MONTGOMERY PJ	WARD ES
LEACH-LEWIS AF	SERGEANT PA	TURNER R	BISSEKER EG 1	MCIVER CD	MONTGOMERY PJ	WATHAN AR
MORGAN-OWEN M	SERGEANT PA	TURNER R 1	BISSEKER EG 2	BRISLEY CE 2	CUTTER CE	RAYNOR K
RAIKES KC	MONTGOMERY PJ	PAGET-TOMLINSON EE	BISSEKER EG	BRISLEY CE	CUTTER RC 1	WARD ES
HERMAN AE	THOMPSON CB	HALL KL	HOSIE AL	CUTTER RC	MONTGOMERY PJ	WARD ES
POLLOCK-HODSOLL GB	SERGEANT PA	TURNER R	FITZGIBBON DF	CUTTER RC	BRISLEY CE 1	WARD ES 1
EDWARDS WG	SERGEANT PA	DIXON GF	MONTGOMERY PJ 1	TURNER R	BRISLEY CE	WARD ES
RAIKES KC	SERGEANT PA	TURNER R	BISSEKER EG	MONTGOMERY PJ 1	WARD ES 3	JOHNSON H
EDWARDS WG	SERGEANT PA	TURNER R	BRISLEY CE	MORGAN-OWEN M	BISSEKER EG	WARD ES
POLLOCK-HODSOLL GB	CARR AJ	DIXON GF	FITZGIBBON DF	ASHTON HO	BROOKS AH	WARD ES
MORGAN-OWEN M	FITZGIBBON DF	KING RM	BISSEKER EG	MONTGOMERY PJ	BRISLEY CE	WARD ES
HOWELL-JONES HG	SERGEANT PA	BRISLEY CE	BISSEKER EG 2	BACHE HG 2	BIRKS AH	WARD ES

5	6	7	8	9	10	11
LEACH-LEWIS AF	SAINSBURY PC	TOMSON DV	MEERS RH	CARTER AJ	KER AWW	DIXON GF
WOODRUFF GG	FRANCIS HW	MANN R	WEAVER LT	WILSON CP	SANDROVD A	DIXON GF
TOMLINSON FW	BIRRELL HA	TOMSON DV	MONTGOMERY PJ	LESLIE KD	KER AWW	DIXON GF
FRANCIS HW	MCCALL MM	MONTGOMERY PJ	WAUGH AJ	BRISLEY CE	MORICE CS	DIXON GF
TOMLINSON FW	GILLIATT W	TOMSON DV	MONTGOMERY PJ	LESLIE KD	KER AWW	DIXON GF
MONTGOMERY PJ	TOMLINSON FW	MANN R 1	CUTTER H 3	WAUGH AJ 3	KER AWW 2	DIXON GF 2
HOCKING EM	GILLIATT W	TOMSON DV	HUNTER JW	LESLIE KD 1	KER AWW	DIXON GF
BRUCE-HALL M		MANN R	WAUGH AJ	MONTGOMERY PJ	MORGAN JS	DIXON GF
POLLOCK-HODSOLL GB	SERGEANT PA	CUTTER RC	BISSEKER H	BRISLEY CE	SNELL IE	WARD ES
GILLIATT W	SALE RB	HALL AL	DIXON GF 3	MONTGOMERY PJ 1	MCCALL RF 1	MEERS RH
ALEXANDER EB 1	COOKE HHA	MANN R	MONTGOMERY PJ 2	DIXON EF 2	CROLE-REES HB	DENISON-PENDER JC
LEACH-LEWIS AF	FITZGIBBON DF	CUTTER RC	BISSEKER EG 1	BRISLEY CE	SIMONDS J	
GOODMAN J	SALE RB	THOMPSON CB	MCCALL RF 1	DIXON GF 1	KER AWW 3	HALL KL
TOMLINSON FW	BRUCE HALL R	FRANCIS HW	LEARMAN VS	MONTGOMERY PJ	CUTTER RC	DIXON GF 1
GREEN G	HILL JE	FRANCIS HW	FOX-WILMER B 1	PIKE SA 1	CLIFFORD EC 1	DIXON GF
BRUCE HALL R	GIMINGHAM CH	MANN R	MONTGOMERY PJ 3	DIXON EF	STEPHENS L	SHEARMAN V
RAIKES KC	SALE RB	THOMPSON	ARKWRIGHT CH 1	BACHE HG 2	VIDLER JS 2	HARRISON
EDWARDS WG	TUFF B	SHORT HS 1	VIDLER JS 1	BACHE HG	ARKWRIGHT CH 1	THOMPSON CB
RAIKES KC	THOMPSON CB	SHORT HS	VIDLER JS	BACHE HG	ARKWRIGHT CH	TUFF B
POLLOCK-HODSOLL GB	GREEN BG	CUTTER RC	FITZGIBBON DF 1	MONTGOMERY PJ 3	CORBETT AL 2	RAYNOR K
FITZGIBBON DF	GREEN BG	CUTTER RC 2	EDWARDS V 4	MONTGOMERY PJ 1	RAYNOR K	CORBETT AL 2
FITZGIBBON DF	CARR AL	RAYNOR K	MONTGOMERY PJ 1	DIXON GF	CUTTER RC 3	CORBETT AL
		RAYNOR K		DIXON GF	CUTTER RC	CORBETT AL 3
		RAYNOR K	EDWARDS V 2	MONTGOMERY PJ	CUTTER RC 1	CORBETT AL 1
WILKINSON CL	KING SL	FRANCIS HW	WILMER-FOX B	BRISLEY CE 2	MONTGOMERY PJ 1	DIXON EF 1
SERGEANT PA	HYNE WM	PAGET-TOMLINSON EE	BISSEKER EG 2	BRISLEY CE	CUTTER RC	WARD ES
BRUCE HALL R	WILKINSON CL	FRANCIS HW	FOX WILMER B 1	WAUGH AJ	MONTGOMERY PJ	DIXON GF
WILKINSON CL	CORBETT AG	MENZIES WK	TOMSON DV	TOWNSEND FW	DIXON GF 3	MCCALL MM
NAYLOR WA	WILKINSON CL	GRIMSDELL RE	FOX WILMER B	MONTGOMERY PJ 4	TOWNSEND FW	DIXON GF
CORBETT AG	SERGEANT PA	BECK PL	HUNTER JW	TOWNSEND FW	KER AWW	DIXON GF
'OTHER' AN	WILKINSON CL	FRANCIS HW	FOX WILMER B	MONTGOMERY PJ	TOWNSEND FW	DIXON GF
NAYLOR WA	WILLETT BH	SULMAN SW	FOX WILMER B	GRIMSDELL RE	TOWNSEND FW	DIXON GF

1910/11

DATE	VEN	OPPONENTS	RES	COMP	ATT	1	2	3	4
01-Oct	A	TOWNLEY PARK	1-0	SAL		TOWNSEND M	CAMPBELL IPF	DOLL MHC	MILTON HA
08-Oct	H tp	HAMPSTEAD	4-2	SAL	1,500	NEWMAN GG	SERGEANT PA	CAMPBELL IPF	RAIKES KC
22-Oct	H tp	TUNBRIDGE WELLS	3-2	SAL		NORRIS GH	DOLL MHC	CAMPBELL IPF	SERGEANT PA
29-Oct	A	EALING	6-3	SAL		TOWNSEND M	KING SL	MAY PR	HYNE WM
19-Nov	A	IPSWICH TOWN	0-1	SAL	1,000	NORRIS GH	KING SL	DOLL MHC	RAILTON NG
26-Nov	H tp	CIVIL SERVICE	2-5	SAL		NORRIS GH	KING SL	SERGEANT PA	WHARTON AW
17-Dec	A	LONDON CO & WB	6-1	AFASC1	%	NORRIS GH	KING SL	SERGEANT PA	RAILTON NG
24-Dec	A	TUNBRIDGE WELLS	4-1	SAL		DRIFFIELD LT	DOLL MHC	WADE CH	SERGEANT PA
07-Jan	A	CIVIL SERVICE	1-2	SAL		TOWNSEND M	CAMPBELL IPF	DOLL MHC	RAILTON NG
14-Jan	H 1	TOWNLEY PARK	0-1	SAL		TOWNSEND M	KING SL	MILTON HA	SERGEANT PA
21-Jan	A	EALING	8-1	AFASC2	og	TOWNSEND M	KING SL	SERGEANT PA	HOWELL-JONES HG
18-Feb	A	TUNBRIDGE WELLS	3-0	AFASC3		HERMAN GL	DOWEN RC	SERGEANT PA	HOWELL-JONES HG
25-Feb	H tp	EASTBOURNE	1-0	SAL		TOWNSEND M	KING SL	CAMPBELL IPF	SERGEANT PA
04-Mar	A	EASTBOURNE	2-1	SAL		ROGERS R	KING SL	CARR AJ	SERGEANT PA
11-Mar	N ox	CIVIL SERVICE	1-0	AFASCsf		TOWNSEND M	SERGEANT PA	CAMPBELL IPF	HOWELL-JONES HG
18-Mar	H tp	NEW CRUSADERS	1-1	SAL		TOWNSEND M	KING SL	SERGEANT PA	MILTON HA
25-Mar	H tp	EALING	1-2	SAL		TOWNSEND M	KING SL	CAMPBELL IPF	SNELL IE
29-Mar	A	HAMPSTEAD	0-4	SAL		TOWNSEND M	KING SL	CLARK HN	HILL JE
01-Apr	H @	IPSWICH TOWN	1-3	SAL		LANGLEY LE	KING SL	SERGEANT PA	MILTON HA
08-Apr	N ip	OLD MALVERNIANS	2-3	AFASCf	3,000	TOWNSEND M	SERGEANT PA	CAMPBELL IPF	MILTON HA
	A	NEW CRUSADERS	NP	SAL					

Friendly Matches

DATE	VEN	OPPONENTS	RES	COMP	ATT	1	2	3	4
24-Sep	A	CROUCH END VAMPIRES	7-0	F		TAYLOR GMC	KING SL	DOLL MHC	SERGEANT PA 1
24-Sep	A	WEYBRIDGE	1-2	F	%	ALLEN HC	WILKINS FC	DOWER JF	BIRRELL HA
01-Oct	A	RMC SANDHURST	3-0	F	%	MEERS RH	BECK PL	HANNAY WA	SALE HB
05-Oct	A	ST JOHN'S SCHOOL	9-3	F	%				
15-Oct	A	WESTMINSTER SCHOOL	1-1	F		GRANT AS	KING SL	SERGEANT PA	MEERS RH
22-Oct	A	CHARTERHOUSE	3-0	F	*	NICHOLLS EP	SHEPPARD JH	RATHBONE B	WYATT CP
26-Oct	A	BERKHAMSTED SCHOOL	2-0	F	%	GRANT AS	KING SL	SERGEANT PA	HAYES V
29-Oct	A	WELLINGBOROUGH SCHOOL	7-1	F	%	ESDAILE EGK	GILLIATT W	MCCALL RF	WYATT CP
02-Nov	A	HIGHGATE SCHOOL	11-1	F	%	'OTHER' AN	KING SL	LAMBERT CN	GILLIATT W
05-Nov	H tp	CAMBRIDGE UNIV	0-0	F		ROGERS R	MUGLISTON FH	MAY PR	SERGEANT PA
05-Nov	A	CRANLEIGH SCHOOL	9-1	F	%	GRANT AS	HANNAY WA	MCCALL RF	WYATT CP
09-Nov	A	CITY OF LONDON SCHOOL	7-1	F	%	NICHOLLS EP	KING SL	LAMBERT CN	HAYES V
12-Nov	H tp	OXFORD UNIVERSITY	0-5	F		TOWNSEND M	KING SL	MAY PR	SERGEANT PA
16-Nov	A	FELSTED SCHOOL	4-2	F	og	COLLIN ALLEN H	KING SL	GRIMSDELL RE	HAYES V
23-Nov	A	ST THOMAS' HOSPITAL	1-3	F		NICHOLLS EP	KING SL	LAMBERT CN	HILL JE
30-Nov	A	UNITED HOSPITALS	2-1	F		TOWNSEND M	WADE CH	KING SL	SERGEANT PA
07-Dec	A	BRIGHTON COLLEGE	4-4	F		NICHOLLS EP	KING SL	HOLFORD GT	HILL JE
12-Dec	A	SHREWSBURY SCHOOL	9-1	F	%	NORRIS GH	KING SL	OWEN RCD	RAILTON NG
13-Dec	A	REPTON SCHOOL	4-2	F	%				
14-Dec	A	MALVERN COLLEGE	1-1	F		NEWMAN GG	KING SL	CAMPBELL IPF	RAILTON NG
26-Dec	A	MANSFIELD AMATEURS	0-1	F		HERMAN GL	KING SL	DOLL MHC	HACKING EM
27-Dec	A	NORTHERN AMATEURS	1-4	F		HERMAN GL	DOLL MHC	CARR AT	HALL EF
28-Dec	A	LINCOLN LINDUM	0-3	F		HERMAN GL	DOLL MHC	CARR AT	HALL EF
29-Dec	A	DERBY THORNHILL	6-1	F		HERMAN GL	KING SL	DOLL MHC	HOWELL-JONES HG
30-Dec	A	NOTTS MAGDALA	2-1	F		HERMAN GL	CARR AT	SERGEANT PA	HACKING EM
31-Dec	A	NOTTINGHAMSHIRE	3-1	F		HERMAN GL	CARR AT	SERGEANT PA	LYMBERY
07-Jan	A	HAMPSTEAD DRUIDS	1-2	F					
18-Jan	A	ST THOMAS' HOSPITAL	2-1	F		NICHOLLS EP	KING SL	GRIMSDELL RE	HAYES V
21-Jan	A	OLD FELSTEDIANS	3-4	F	%	NICHOLLS EP	SHEPPARD JH	OLIVER CM	MCCALL RF
25-Jan	A	OXFORD UNIVERSITY	1-4	F		NEWMAN GG	KING SL	OWEN RCD	SERGEANT PA
01-Feb	A	GUY'S HOSPITAL	2-3	F		NICHOLLS EP	KING SL	CLARK HN	WALLACE A
04-Feb	A	CAMBRIDGE UNIV	1-5	F		TAYLOR GMC	KING SL	MUGLISTON FH	SERGEANT PA
08-Feb	A	CHARTERHOUSE	0-2	F		GRANT AS	KING SL	TIMMIS WU	SERGEANT PA
11-Feb	A	WESTMINSTER SCHOOL	5-1	F	%	HANNAY WA	SERGEANT PA	SHEPPARD JH	POLLOCK-HODSOLL GB
15-Feb	A	RMA WOOLWICH	12-2	F		STEDIAN F	KING SL	CLARK HN	POLLOCK-HODSOLL GB
22-Feb	A	ALDENHAM SCHOOL	3-2	F	%				
28-Feb	A	WINCHESTER COLLEGE	2-0	F		NICHOLLS EP	KING SL	CLARK HN	SERGEANT PA
08-Mar	A	CITY OF LONDON SCHOOL	5-1	F	%	NICHOLLS EP	KING SL	GRIMSDELL RE	HILL JE
11-Mar	A	RMC SANDHURST	0-2	F		GRANT AS	SHEPPARD JH	'OTHER' AN	POLLOCK-HODSOLL GB
18-Mar	A	SURBITON HILL	7-1	F		BARRETT HR	WADE CH	SHEPPARD JH	BIRRELL HA
01-Apr	A	WEYBRIDGE	0-6	F		ALLEN HC	HILL JE	BIRRELL HA	MCCALL RF

5	6	7	8	9	10	11
GREEN G	SERGEANT PA	BRISLEY CE	BISSEKER EG	GREEN MA	CLARKE MH 1	MONTGOMERY PJ
HOWELL-JONES HG	MILTON HA	BRISLEY CE 1	EDWARDS V 3	GREEN MA	CLARKE MH	MONTGOMERY PJ
HOWELL-JONES HG	MILTON HA	DRAKE CF	TUFF B	SNELL IE 2	BRISLEY CE	MONTGOMERY PJ 1
GREEN G	SERGEANT PA	DRAKE CF	CARTER AJ	HOFFMEISTER CE 4	CLARKE MH 1	MONTGOMERY PJ 1
SERGEANT PA	MILTON HA	JOHNSON CB	BRISLEY CE	CLARKE MH	MONTGOMERY PJ	
RAILTON NG	GREEN G	MONTGOMERY PJ	CLARKE MH 1	RUDD CT	PINK HS 1	WARD ES
'OTHER' AN	MILTON HA	MONTGOMERY PJ	EDWARDS V	BRISLEY CE	CLARKE MH	WARD ES
GREEN G	CARR AT	GREEN MA	CLARKE MH 1	BRISLEY CE 2	BIRKS AH 1	MONTGOMERY PJ
HERMAN AE	SERGEANT PA	DRAKE CF	CLARKE MH	MCIVER CD	VANN BW	MONTGOMERY PJ 1
MORGAN-OWEN M	HOWELL-JONES HG	MONTGOMERY PJ	MCIVER CD	HOSIE AL	WAUGH AJ	WARD ES
HERMAN AE	GREEN G	MONTGOMERY PJ	CUTTER RC 3	MCIVER CD 2	BRISLEY CE 2	WARD ES
HERMAN AE	MILTON HA 1	MONTGOMERY PJ 1	BRISLEY CE	MCIVER CD 1	CORBETT AL	WARD ES
RAIKES KC 1	GREEN G	MONTGOMERY PJ	CLARKE MH	CUTTER RC	BIRKS AH	YOUNG RA
HOWELL-JONES HG 1	MONTGOMERY PJ	GREEN G 1	CUTTER RC	HOSIE AL	CORBETT AL	WARD ES
RAIKES KC	MILTON HA	MONTGOMERY PJ	BRISLEY CE	MCIVER CD 1	BIRKS AH	WARD ES
CORNELIUS-BROWN JG	RAIKES KC	YOUNG RA	BRISLEY CE	BACHE HG 1	FLEMING AL	WARD ES
SERGEANT PA	WILKINSON CL	MONTGOMERY PJ	CLARKE MH	CUTTER RC	BIRKS AH 1	BRISLEY CE
BRUCE-HALL R	DOLL MHC	MONTGOMERY PJ	GREEN MA	MCIVER CD	HERYCE V	DIXON GF
GREEN G	WILKINSON CL 1	MONTGOMERY PJ	WAUGH AJ	MCIVER CD	CUTTER RC	WARD ES
RAIKES KC	HOWELL-JONES HG	MONTGOMERY PJ	BRISLEY CE	HOSIE AL 1	MCIVER CD	WARD ES 1

5	6	7	8	9	10	11
GREEN G	RATHBONE R	MONTGOMERY PJ	BISSEKER EG 2	GREEN MA 2	EDWARDS V 1	CARTER AJ 1
CORBETT AG	WYATT CP	TOMSON DV	MEERS RH	HUNTER JW	TOWNSEND FW	DIXON GF
WYATT CP	MCCALL RF	DENSHAM JB	PALMER HB	CARTER AJ	TOWNSEND FW	DIXON GF
			POTTS 1	SERGEANT PA 3	BIRD FA 1	DIXON GF 1
BIRRELL HA	RATHBONE B	DENSHAM JB	PALMER AB	PARKER O	DRAKE CF	DIXON GF
NAYLOR WA	MCCALL RF	DENSHAM JB	PARKER O 2	PIKE SA	MACDONALD WIF	DIXON GF
HOLFORD GT	GOOD RH	COULTHURST TT	FOX WILMER B	GRIMSDELL RE	NICHOLLS EP	DIXON GF
SALE HB	HANNAY WA	TOMSON DV	BECK PL	DENSHAM JB	PALMER AB	DIXON CB 1
GROSVENOR RL	BRUCE-HALL R	GRIMSDELL RE	LEE RT	GREEN MA	CROLE-REES HB	DIXON GF
NAYLOR WA	MILTON HA	MONTGOMERY PJ	EDWARDS V	HOFFMEISTER CE	CLARKE MH	PINK HS
DIXON EF	TOMSON DV	DRAKE CF	HALL RS	GREEN MA	CARTER AJ	BIRD FA
GRIMSDELL RE	GILLIATT W	SIMPSON L	COULTHURST TT	ROBERTS GD	GREEN MA	DIXON GF
HOWELL-JONES HG	MILTON HA	YOUNG RA	MONTGOMERY PJ	MCIVER CD	PINK HS	WARD ES
GREEN G	HALFORD FB	COULTHURST TT	FOX WILMER B	GREEN MA 3	NICHOLLS EP	HALFORD GT
LEE RT	HALFORD GT	BECK PL	DENSHAM JB	GREEN MA 1	FOX-WILMER B	DIXON GF
GRIMSDELL RE	HILL JE	SIMPSON L	MONTGOMERY PJ 1	GREEN MA 1	CLARKE MH	DIXON EF
HOWELL-JONES HG 3	CLOUSTON OR	CARR AJ	FOX WILMER B	HAYES V	CORBETT AL 1	ROGERS R
THOMPSON CB	COOKE EM	KERRY AHG	HOSIE SL	BACHE HG 1	TUFF B	OTHER AN
			HOSIE SL 2			JOHNSON CB 1
HALL EF	MURRAY G	KERRY AHG	TUFF B 1	HOSIE SL	THOMPSON RG	JOHNSON CB
HALL EF	DYAS GE	DOWSON FN	CLARKE MH	GREEN MA	EDWARDS V	MONTGOMERY PJ
GREEN G	DYAS GE	JOHNSON CB	CLARKE MH	MONTGOMERY PJ 1	PINK HS	DOWSON FN
GREEN G	HACKING EM	DOWSON FN	HOLFORD F	EDWARDS V	ROBERTS FW	MONTGOMERY PJ
GREEN G	SERGEANT PA	MONTGOMERY PJ	ROBERTS FW 2	EDWARDS V 1	PINK HS 2	JOHNSON CB 1
GREEN G	HILL JE	JOHNSON CB	MONTGOMERY PJ	PINK HS	ROBERTS FW 1	DOWSON FN 1
GREEN G	KING SL	DOLL MHC	MONTGOMERY PJ 1	EDWARDS V 1	ROBERTS FW 1	DOWSON FN
HILL JE	COOKE HHA	COOK JA	FOX-WILMER B	GREEN MA 1	CHEVELLY HC	MONTGOMERY PJ 1
BIRRELL HA	RATHBONE B	DENSHAM JB	PARKER O	GREEN MA	EASTERBROOK TE	TOMSON DV
ROBERTS FW	HILL JE	SERGEANT PA	BRISLEY CE	VIDAL LA 1	PAWSON AG	MONTGOMERY PJ
LEE RT	HILL JE	SIMPSON L	GREEN MA 1	DENSHAM JB	CHADWICK GE	COULTHURST TT
GREEN G	THOMPSON CB	MONTGOMERY PJ	CLARKE MH	CUTTER RC	FLEMING AL 1	HALL RS
NAYLOR WA	DOLL MHC	DENSHAM JB	CLARKE MH	GREEN MA	WILLETT BH	HOLFORD GT
WILKINSON CL	HALL RS	DENSHAM JB	CLARKE MH	GREEN MA	HUNTER JW	DIXON GF
LEE RT	HAYES V	HOLFORD GT	HILL JE 1	GREEN MA 6	ROBERTS GD 4	DIXON GF 1
HAYES V	HILL JE	HOLFORD GT	SULMAN SW	GREEN MA 2	FOX-WILMER B	DIXON GF
HAYES V	MILTON HA	COULTHURST TT	ROBERTS GD	GREEN MA	HOLFORD GT	DIXON GF
SALE HB	MCCALL RF	DENSHAM JB	CUTTER RC	GREEN MA	EASTERBROOK TE	DIXON GF
NAYLOR WA	WILKINSON CL	MONTGOMERY PJ 3	CLARKE MH 2	DALTON GT 1	MCCALL RF	DIXON GF 1
HAYES V	GRIMSDELL RE	ROBINSON F	DIXON GF	GREEN MA	EASTERBROOK TE	PARKER O

1911/12

DATE	VEN	OPPONENTS	RES	COMP	ATT	1	2	3	4
30-Sep	A	EALING	1-2	SAL		NORRIS GH	CAMPBELL IPF	KING SL	DOLL MHC
07-Oct	A	NEW CRUSADERS	0-4	SAL		NEWMAN GG	CAMPBELL IPF	VARDY AT	DOLL MHC
21-Oct	H tp	CIVIL SERVICE	1-3	SAL		NEWMAN GG	SNELL IE	DOLL MHC	MILTON HA
28-Oct	A	HAMPSTEAD	3-0	SAL		TOWNSEND M	KING SL	OWEN RCD	MCIVER CD
18-Nov	A	IPSWICH TOWN	0-1	SAL	500	TOWNSEND M	KING SL	DOLL MHC	SERGEANT PA
25-Nov	A	TOWNLEY PARK	1-1	SAL		TOWNSEND M	KING SL	VARDY AT	SERGEANT PA
02-Dec	H tp	OXFORD AFA	2-2	SAL		TOWNSEND M	KING SL	DOLL MHC	SERGEANT PA
16-Dec	H e	CARSHALTON	0-2	AFASC1		TOWNSEND M	SERGEANT PA	KING SL	WILKINSON CL
23-Dec	A	OXFORD AFA	1-3	SAL		TOWNSEND M	KING SL	CAMPBELL IPF	MILTON HA
06-Jan	A	ALLEYN OB	1-1	SAL		TOWNSEND M	CAMPBELL IPF	OWEN RCD	SERGEANT PA
13-Jan	A	CIVIL SERVICE	1-2	SAL		HENNAN GC	RIMMINGTON H	HOWELL-JONES HG	SERGEANT PA
27-Jan	H @	ALLEYN OB	7-1	SAL		EDGE AS	SERGEANT PA	RIMMINGTON H	CUTTER RC
24-Feb	H tp	EALING	1-0	SAL		HOPEWELL ER	SERGEANT PA	CAMPBELL IPF	CUTTER RC
02-Mar	H l	TOWNLEY PARK	2-2	SAL		EDGE AS	RIMMINGTON H	SERGEANT PA	MILTON HA
16-Mar	H tp	HAMPSTEAD	1-4	SAL		TOWNSEND M	SERGEANT PA	CAMPBELL IPF	MILTON HA
30-Mar	H @	IPSWICH TOWN	3-0	SAL	1,500	TOWNSEND M	RIMMINGTON H	JOHNSON WL	HERMAN AE
NP	H	NEW CRUSADERS		SAL					

Friendly Matches

DATE	VEN	OPPONENTS	RES	COMP	ATT	1	2	3	4
23-Sep	A	WEYBRIDGE	0-0	F		HODGKINSON GS	SERGEANT PA	SAINSBURY PC	WILKINSON CL
30-Sep	A	BRENTWOOD ROVERS	3-1	F	%				
11-Oct	A	BRIGHTON COLLEGE	3-1	F		WOODARD EN	KING SL	RIMMINGTON H	HAYES V
18-Oct	A	RMA WOOLWICH	4-1	F		WOODARD EN	KING SL	OSBORN JENKIN CO	SMIT NA
21-Oct	A	CHARTERHOUSE	1-2	F	%	GRANT AS	WILLETT BH	WITH PA	WILKINSON CL
25-Oct	A	BERKHAMSTED SCHOOL	10-0	F	%	WOODARD EN	KING SL	ALLEN HC	HAYES V
28-Oct	A	WELLINGBOROUGH SCHOOL	4-3	F		WOODARD EN	SHEPPARD JH	EDWARDS HC	WILKINSON CL
01-Nov	A	HIGHGATE SCHOOL	W-W	F	%	LANGLEY LE	KING SL	OSBORN JENKIN CO	LEE RT
04-Nov	H tp	CAMBRIDGE UNIV	0-1	F		NEWMAN GG	KING SL	DOLL MHC	MILTON HA
04-Nov	A	GUY'S HOSPITAL	1-2	F					
08-Nov	A	CRANLEIGH SCHOOL	8-1	F	%	GRANT AS	KING SL	CLARK HN	RIMMINGTON H
11-Nov	H tp	OXFORD UNIVERSITY	2-1	F		TOWNSEND M	KING SL	SNELL IE	MILTON HA
18-Nov	A	ST BARTHOLOMEWS H	1-0	F		GRANT AS	RIMMINGTON H	VARDY AT	EASTERBROOK TE
22-Nov	A	ST THOMAS' HOSPITAL	2-2	F		GRANT AS	KING SL	CLARK HN	RIMMINGTON H
25-Nov	A	BANK OF ENGLAND	4-2	F	%	GRANT AS	SHEPPARD JH	RIMMINGTON H	WILKINSON CL
02-Dec	A	ALDENHAM SCHOOL	1-5	F	*	DIXON GF	CHAMPNEYS J	BIRRELL HA	RATHBONE P
06-Dec	A	CITY OF LONDON SCHOOL	4-1	F	%	FELSTEDIAN' H	KING SL	CLARK HN	RIMMINGTON H
09-Dec	A	MERTON	2-1	F		DRIFFIELD LT	RIMMINGTON H	BUXTON SJ	SERGEANT PA
11-Dec	A	SHREWSBURY SCHOOL	13-0	F	%	HOPEWELL ER	KING SL	CAMPBELL IPF	KIRBY AC
12-Dec	A	REPTON SCHOOL	2-1	F		HOPEWELL ER	KING SL	CAMPBELL IPF	KIRBY AC
13-Dec	A	MALVERN COLLEGE	2-0	F		HOPEWELL ER	KING SL	CAMPBELL IPF	VACHELL FT
26-Dec	A	NOTTS MAGDALA	2-0	F	og	HERMAN GL	KING SL	DOLL MHC	GREEN G
27-Dec	A	LINCOLN LINDUM	3-1	F		HERMAN GL	KING SL	DOLL MHC	POPHAM RF
28-Dec	A	NORTHERN AMATEURS	4-2	F		HERMAN GL	GREEN G	VIDAL	BURROWS
29-Dec	A	MANSFIELD AMATEURS	6-1	F		HERMAN GL	GREEN G	POPHAM RF	CUTTER RC
30-Dec	A	NOTTINGHAMSHIRE	1-2	F		HERMAN GL	FROST R	GREEN G	BOROUGH J
17-Jan	A	ST THOMAS' HOSPITAL	0-1	F		COVINGTON CK	RIMMINGTON H	GREEN MA	HAYES V
20-Jan	A	OLD FELSTEDIANS	4-0	F		DENSHAM JB	LEANARD L	MILTON HA 1	MCCALL RF
24-Jan	A	OXFORD UNIVERSITY	1-2	F		LANGLEY LE	RIMMINGTON H	OWEN RCD	KIRBY AC
10-Feb	A	WESTMINSTER SCHOOL	4-0	F		GRANT AS	BUXTON SJ	SHEPPARD JH	DOLL MHC
21-Feb	A	ALDENHAM SCHOOL	5-0	F		LAWN CF	CLARK HN	GRIMSDELL RE	HAYES V
29-Feb	A	WINCHESTER COLLEGE	3-2	F		ALLEN HC	DOLL MHC	HICKS FM	FOX WILMER B
09-Mar	A	HARROW SCHOOL	5-1	F		TOWNSEND M	WITH PA	RIMMINGTON H	HACKING EM
16-Mar	A	ST BARTHOLOMEWS H	3-3	F		DAVIDSON JLM	VARDY AT	SHEPPARD JH	WILKINSON CL

5	6	7	8	9	10	11
GREEN E	MCIVER CD	KING RM	MONTGOMERY PJ	CUTTER RC	BIRKS AH 1	DOWER RW
THOMPSON CB	RAIKES KC	MONTGOMERY PJ	CARDEW AE	CLARKE MH	EDWARDS V	DOWER RW
GREEN G	MCIVER CD	MONTGOMERY PJ	BRISLEY CE	CUTTER RC 1	BIRKS AH	DOWER RW
THOMPSON CB	CARR AL	MONTGOMERY PJ	CLARKE MH	CUTTER RC 1	EDWARDS V 1	DOWER RW 1
WITH PA	MCIVER CD	MONTGOMERY PJ	BRISLEY CE	CUTTER RC	BIRKS AH	DOWER RW
GREEN G	DOLL MHC	MONTGOMERY PJ	CLARKE MH 1	STOKES EF	JAMES AC	DOWER RW
CARR AJ	WILKINSON CL	MONTGOMERY PJ	CARDEW AE 1	HOFFMEISTER CE	STOKES EF 1	DOWER RW
RAIKES KC	MCIVER CD	MONTGOMERY PJ	CLARKE MH	PINK HS	EDWARDS V	WARD ES
CROMMELIN-BROWN JL	GREEN G	YOUNG RA 1	CLARKE MH	BACHE HG	BRISLEY CE	DOWER RW
RAIKES KC	MILTON HA	DOWER RW	CLARKE MH 1	CUTTER RC	BIRKS AH	WARD ES
GREEN G	MILTON HA	MONTGOMERY PJ	CLARKE MH	CUTTER RC 1	STOKES EF	DOWER RW
RAIKES KC	GREEN E	CARDEW AE	EDWARDS V 3	STOKES EF 3	BIRKS AH 1	DOWER RW
GREEN G	MILTON HA	CARDEW AE	CLARKE MH 1	MONTGOMERY PJ	BIRKS AH	DOWER RW
GREEN G 1	CUTTER RC	BRISLEY CE	EDWARDS V	STOKES EF	WARD ES 1	DOWER RW
RAIKES KC	GREEN G	CARDEW AE	CUTTER RC	MCIVER CD	EDWARDS V 1	WARD ES
RAIKES KC	MILTON HA	HOWELL-JONES HG 1	STOKES EF 1	COX NJ 1	OSMOND JE	DOWER RW

5	6	7	8	9	10	11
GREEN G	BIRRELL HA	DIXON GF	TURNER TR	HUNTER JW	MONTGOMERY PJ	DOWER RW
FOX-WILMER B	WITH PA	GRIMSDELL RE	GREEN MA 1	HOWELL-JONES HG 1	DIXON GF 1	SIMPSON L
WITH PA	DELL HC	SUBSTITUTE A 1	GRIMSDELL RE 1	HAYES V	ROBERTS GD 2	GRANT AS
NAYLOR WA	BIRRELL HA	DENSHAM JB	THOMPSON DLN	PARKES O	MCCALL RF	TOMSON DV
FOX-WILMER B	GREEN MA	HARDY N	SIMPSON L	MORGAN J	OTHER AN	DIXON GF
MCCALL RF	CHAMPNEYS J	HARDY N	BARDEN YMH	GREEN MA	TOMSON DV	OTHER AN
THOMPSON CB	HAYES V	DRAKE CF	ROBERTS GD	GREEN MA	GRIMSDELL RE	DIXON GF
RAIKES KC	THOMPSON CB	SHORT HS MONTGOMERY PJ 1	CLARKE MH	CUTTER RC	BIRKS AH	DOWER RW
WITH PA	HAYES V	HARDY N	SIMPSON L	GRIMSDELL RE	BIRD FN	DIXON GF
RAIKES KC	SERGEANT PA	MONTGOMERY PJ	CLARKE MH	BRISLEY CE 1	EDWARDS V 1	DOWER RW
OTHER AN	BIRRELL HA	MCCALL MM	BARDEN VM	BUDD CT	PINK HS	DIXON GF
GRIMSDELL RE	FOX-WILMER B	HARDY N	ROBERTS GD	YOULE JS 1	SIMPSON L	DIXON GF 1
BIRRELL HA	RATHBONE B	DENSHAM JB	MCCALL RF	WITH PA	'CANTAB' A	DIXON GF
ADAMS HF	MCCALL RF	DENSHAM JB	EASTERBROOK TE	RUDD CI	PINK HS	BARDEN YMH
FOX-WILMER B	GRIMSDELL RE	SIMPSON L	ROBERTS GD	GREEN MA	YOULE JS	DIXON GF
RAIKES KC	WILKINSON CL	MONTGOMERY PJ	CLARKE MH	GREEN MA	DIXON EF	WARD ES
RAIKES KC	VACHELL FT	JOHNSON CB	HOSIE AL	WOOSNAM M	SULMAN H	PARRY JH
RAIKES KC	VACHELL FT	JOHNSON CB	HOSIE AL 1	WOOSNAM M 1	SULMAN H	PARRY JH
RAIKES KC	KIRBY AC	PARRY JH 1	SULMAN SW	WOOSNAM M 1	HOSIE AL	JOHNSON CB
CROMMELIN-BROWN JL	POPHAM RF	DOWER RW	STOKES EF	GREEN MA 1	BOROUGH J	JOHNSON CB
CROMMELIN-BROWN JL	GREEN G	DOWSON FN	FROST R	STOKES RF 3	EDWARDS V	DOWER RW
CROMMELIN-BROWN JL	POPHAM RF	DOWSON FN	EDWARDS V 1	CUTTER RC 2	FROST F 1	JOHNSON CB
CROMMELIN-BROWN JL	DOWSON FN	DOWER RW 1	EDWARDS V 3	STOKES RF 2	FROST F	JOHNSON CB
CROMMELIN-BROWN JL	POPHAM RF	DOWER RW	EDWARDS V	STOKES RF 1	CUTTER RC	DOWSON FN
SMITH DH	LEONARD RL	COOKE RC	MONTGOMERY PJ	YOULE YS	DIXON GF	
SMIT HN	WILKINSON CL	EASTERBROOK TE	SERGEANT PA	GREEN MA 2	DIXON GF 1	CARDEW AE
RAIKES KC	DOLL MHC	THEW VG	FOX WILMER B	JAMES AC	MCIVER CD 1	DOWER RW
BIRRELL HA	WILKINSON CL 1	MCCALL MM	CLARKE MH	MONTGOMERY PJ 2	RYAN JH 1	DIXON GF
HACKING EM	HILL JE	FOX-WILMER B 1	GREEN MA 2	CUTTER RC 1	DIXON GF 1	'OTHER' AN
HAYES V	JACKSON HA	HAWKER ML	DIXON GF 1	GREEN MA 1	MAPLES RC 1	LAMBERT WR
SHIPTON CH	STRACHAN A	'SUB' A	MONTGOMERY PJ	CLARKE MH	CUTTER RC 4	WARD ES 1
SHIPTON CH	WITH PA	DENSHAM JB	MONTGOMERY PJ 2	LETTS HM 1	MCCALL RF	DIXON GF

1912/13

DATE	VEN	OPPONENTS	RES	COMP	ATT	1	2	3	4
05-Oct	H tp	LONDON CO & WB	1-1	SAL		FENDER PGH	RIMMINGTON H	TUDOR-OWEN FHG	VACHELL FT
12-Oct	A	TOWNLEY PARK	0-3	SAL		FENDER PGH	RIMMINGTON H	VARDY AT	BIRRELL HA
19-Oct	A	IPSWICH TOWN	4-0	SAL	1,500	FENDER PGH	RIMMINGTON H	VARDY AT	VACHELL FT
26-Oct	H1	EASTBOURNE	6-1	SAL	og	FENDER PGH	RIMMINGTON H	VARDY AT	VACHELL FT
16-Nov	A	OXFORD AFA	2-0	SAL		FENDER PGH	DOYLE NHC	VACHELL FT	MCIVER CD
23-Nov	A	HAMPSTEAD	0-2	SAL		FENDER PGH	VACHELL FT	AN OTHER	GREEN G
30-Nov	A	NEW CRUSADERS	0-1	SAL		FENDER PGH	VARDY AT	DOLL MHC	VACHELL FT
14-Dec	A	NOTTS MAGDALA	3-1	AFASC1		FENDER PGH	RIMMINGTON H	VACHELL FT	CROMMELIN-BROWN
21-Dec	A	EALING	1-2	SAL		FENDER PGH	DOLL MHC	WHITE RSM	STOKES EF
28-Dec	A	EASTBOURNE	4-3	SAL		FENDER PGH	KING SL	BUXTON SJ	DOLL MHC
11-Jan	A	CIVIL SERVICE	0-1	SAL		FENDER PGH	HOWELL-JONES HG	WHITE RSM	MUGLISTON FH
18-Jan	A	LONDON CO & WB	1-1	AFASC2		FENDER PGH	MUGLISTON FH	VACHELL FT	RAIKES KC
25-Jan	H tp	LONDON CO & WB	3-0	AFASC2		FENDER PGH	MUGLISTON FH	VARDY AT	VACHELL FT
08-Feb	A	HAMPSTEAD	2-0	AFASC3		FENDER PGH	RIMMINGTON H	MUGLISTON FH	SEEDORFF FJ
22-Feb	H tp	HAMPSTEAD	1-2	SAL		FENDER PGH	SNELL IE	RIMMINGTON H	EDGAR SC
01-Mar	A	LONDON CO & WB	3-0	SAL		FENDER PGH	MUGLISTON FH	RIMMINGTON H	VACHELL FT
08-Mar	N e	HIGHGATE	7-0	AFASCsf		FENDER PGH	MUGLISTON FH	RIMMINGTON H	RAIKES KC
15-Mar	A	OXFORD AFA	0-1	SAL		FENDER PGH	MONTGOMERY H	VARDY AT	RAIKES KC
29-Mar	H @	IPSWICH TOWN	3-2	SAL		FENDER PGH	SNELL IE	RIMMINGTON H	MONTGOMERY PJ
02-Apr	H tp	TOWNLEY PARK	1-1	SAL		FENDER PGH	RIMMINGTON H	VARDY AT	CUTTER RC
05-Apr	H tp	EALING	3-0	SAL		FENDER PGH	MUGLISTON FH	RIMMINGTON H	BURY HV
12-Apr	N sb	NEW CRUSADERS	3-2	AFASCf	9,000	FENDER PGH	RIMMINGTON H	MUGLISTON FH	RAIKES KC

Friendly Matches

DATE	VEN	OPPONENTS	RES	COMP	ATT	1	2	3	4
21-Sep	A	WEYBRIDGE	3-3	F	%				
09-Oct	A	BRIGHTON COLLEGE	4-4	F		RUTHERFORD PW	CLARK HN	GRIMSDELL RE	DOWER LF
12-Oct	A	WESTMINSTER SCHOOL	0-3	F		GRANT AS	SLEIGH GB	KENT-LEMON AC	COOKE WH
16-Oct	A	BERKHAMSTED SCHOOL	2-2	F	%	LANGLEY LE	BECK PL	HAYES V	HACKING EM
19-Oct	A	CHARTERHOUSE	4-1	F	%	GRANT AS	MCCALL RF	WILLETT BH	NAYLOR WA
26-Oct	A	WELLINGBOROUGH SCHOOL	1-4	F		GRANT AS	BECK PL	LANGLEY CK	MCCALL RF
30-Oct	A	HIGHGATE SCHOOL	3-4	F	%	'OTHER' AN	VARDY AT	GRIMSDELL RE	BIRRELL HA
02-Nov	H tp	CAMBRIDGE UNIV	0-1	F		FENDER PGH	RIMMINGTON H	VARDY AT	EDGAR SC
02-Nov	A	WEYBRIDGE	1-3	F		NOTT-BOWER RE	MONTGOMERY PJ	SLEIGH GB	FLOWERS AD
06-Nov	A	CRANLEIGH SCHOOL	7-1	F	og %	TAYLOR GMC	RUSSELL D	CLARK HN	GRIMSDELL RE
09-Nov	H tp	OXFORD UNIVERSITY	1-0	F		FENDER PGH	SERGEANT PA	SNELL IE	EDGAR SC
27-Nov	A	ST JOHNS SCHOOL	4-1	F		DRIFFIELD LT	CLARK HN	CARTWRIGHT EH	OTHER AN
30-Nov	A	ALDENHAM SCHOOL	2-4	F		NOTT-BOWER RE	SLEIGH GB	KING A	BIRRELL HA
04-Dec	A	CITY OF LONDON SCHOOL	11-4	F	%	ESDAILE EGK	CLARK HN	'MAKESHIFT' A	TUDOR-OWEN FHG
09-Dec	A	SHREWSBURY SCHOOL	5-2	F	*	CARR JL	KING SL	CLARK HN	BOROUGH J
10-Dec	A	REPTON SCHOOL	1-0	F	ABAN	CARR	KING SL	WHITE RSM	BURY HV
11-Dec	A	MALVERN COLLEGE	2-1	F	%	CARR LC	KING SL	WHITE RSM	BURY HV
15-Jan	A	ST THOMAS' HOSPITAL	2-3	F		'SUB' A	KING SL	CLARK HN	SMIT NH
22-Jan	A	OXFORD UNIVERSITY	2-6	F		LANGLEY LE	ESDAILE EGK	SMITH NH	BOROUGH J
29-Jan	A	GUY'S HOSPITAL	3-7	F		TOWNSEND M	ESDAILE EGK	KING SL	SEEDORFF FJ
01-Feb	A	CAMBRIDGE UNIV	0-9	F		FENDER PGH	RIMMINGTON H	VACHELL FT	SEEDORFF FJ
05-Feb	A	CHARTERHOUSE	4-2	F	%	GRANT AS	WITHERINGTON IG	LANGLEY CK	GILLETT EF
08-Feb	A	WESTMINSTER SCHOOL	4-1	F		GRANT AS	PALLDITCH PH	LANGLEY CK	SHIPTON CH
05-Mar	A	CITY OF LONDON SCHOOL	1-1	F	%	TOWNSEND M	CLARK HN	KING SL	WITH PA

5	6	7	8	9	10	11
RAIKES KC	HERMAN AE	CUTTER RC	CLARKE MH	STOKES EF	ROBERTS FW 1	DOWER RW
GREEN G	SERGEANT PA	MONTGOMERY PJ	CUTTER RC	STOKES EF	AN OTHER	OWEN RCD
SERGEANT PA	DOLL MHC	SPACKMAN L	CLARKE MH	VERNON DF	BIRRELL HA 1	DOWER RW 3
RAIKES KC	DOLL MHC	CUTTER RC 1	CLARKE MH 1	MCIVER CD 2	DODD EJ 1	DOWER RW
RAIKES KC	BOROUGH J	CUTTER RC	TUDOR-OWEN FHG	BRISLEY CE	WILKINSON AM 2	DOWER RW
RAIKES KC	EDGAR SC	CUTTER RC	CLARKE MH	WILKINSON AM	WARD ES	DOWER RW
YOUNG SG	BOROUGH J	CUTTER RC	GILBERT EW	CLARKE MH	BISS JCV	DOWER RW
MORGAN-OWEN M	RAYNOR K	CUTTER RC	STOKES EF 1	PINK HS 1	FOSTER AW 1	WINCH HS
GREEN G	BURY HV	MORRIS CW	CLARKE MH	WHITE K	FOSTER AW	DOWER RW 1
DOWER LF	CASTLES A	WARD ES	DODD EJ	MCIVER CD	STOKES EF 1	DOWER RW 3
JOHNSON AF	BURY HV	STOKES EF	CLARKE MH	WHITE K	GREEN MA	DOWER RW
GREEN G	BIRRELL HA	DODD EJ	CUTTER RC 1	CLARKE MH	AN OTHER	MONTGOMERY PJ
FOSTER FJN	VACHELL FT	STOKES EF 1	DODD EJ 1	CLARKE MH	AN OTHER	DIXON GF 1
RAIKES KC	MCIVER CD	CUTTER RC	DODD EJ	CLARKE MH 2	HOFFMEISTER CE	DOWER RW
RAIKES KC	VACHELL FT	WARD ES	GILBERT EW 1	CLARKE MH	FOSTER AW	DOWER RW
RAIKES KC	BURY HV	JOHNSON CB	STOKES EF 2	CUTTER RC	FOSTER AW 1	WARD ES
WOOSNAM M 1	MCIVER CD	CUTTER RC	DODD EJ	CLARKE MH 1	FOSTER AW 5	DOWER RW
SHIPTON CH	STOKES EF	JOHNSON CB	DODD EJ	CLARKE MH	EDWARDS V	DOWER RW
RAIKES KC	STOKES EF	DIXON GF	DODD EJ	CLARKE MH 2	HOFFMEISTER CE 1	DOWER RW
GREEN G	MCIVER CD	JOHNSON CB	DODD EJ 1	STOKES EF	MONTGOMERY PJ	DOWER RW
RAIKES KC	MCIVER CD	CUTTER RC	STOKES EF	WHITE RSM 2	FOSTER AW 1	MONTGOMERY PJ
WOOSNAM M	MCIVER CD	CUTTER RC	DODD EJ	CLARKE MH 1	FOSTER AW 1	DOWER RW 1

5	6	7	8	9	10	11
GREEN G	HAYES V	CUTTER RC	GREEN MA 2	RYAN JH 1	DIXON GF 1	DOWER RW
WILLIAMS WL	DOWER LF	DENSHAM JB	RAILTON WJ	MCCALL RF	DIXON GF	
MORGAN JS	'OTHER' AN	DIXON GF	GREEN MA	RYAN JH	CUTTER RC	MOORE JG
GREEN E	HILL PG	RAYNOR K	RYAN JP 2	WINCH HS	BIRKS AH	DIXON GF
DOWER LF	HILL LO	RAYNOR K 1	MCKAY RG	DENSHAM JB	MALLORY TC	SMITH AG
GREEN E	FOX-WILMER B	TUDOR-OWEN FHG	GREEN MA	LEXHAM AH	COX JR	DIXON GF
GREEN G	VACHELL FH	CUTTER RC	CLARKE MH	STOKES EF	TUDOR-OWEN FHG	WARD ES
HILL JG	DIXON GF	DENSHAM JB	RAYNOR K	LEXHAM AH	WINCH HS	MALLORY TC
BIRRELL HA	WINSTON RC	LEXHAM AH	EVANS R	GREEN MA	RAYNOR K	DIXON GF
GREEN G	TUDOR-OWEN FHG	CUTTER RC	DODD EJ	MCIVER CD	EDWARDS V 1	WARD ES
BIRRELL HA	WITH PA	RAYNOR K	GREEN MA 3	KYLE J	EVANS LR 1	DIXON GF
HUGHES-DAVIES HE	POWELL HN	RAYNOR K	EASTERBROOK TE	WINCH HS 2	BECK PL	DIXON GF
BRUCE-HALL R	WITH PA	RAYNOR K	EVANS LR	GREEN MA	CUTTER RC	DIXON GF
RAIKES KC	BURY HV	NICHOLAS FW	WILKINSON AM	GILBERT H	VERNON HD 2	DOWER RW 2
RAIKES KC	CROMMELIN-BROWN JL	NICHOLAS FW	WILKINSON AM	GILBERT H 1	VERNON HD	DOWER RW
RAIKES KC	BOROUGH J	NICHOLAS FW	YOUNG D	GILBERT H 1	PENNING VH	DOWER RW
WHITE J	EDGAR SC	SIMPSON L	HOOPER FH	WHITE K	GREEN MA 1	DIXON GF 1
RAIKES KC	EDGAR SC	CARDEW AE 1	MCIVER CD	VIDAL LA 1	RICHARDSON JN	KERRY AHG
VACHELL FT	BRUCE-HALL R	STREET MG	FILOSE AA 3	DIXON GF	MOORE JD	'OTHER' AN
RAIKES KC	EDGAR SC	CUTTER RC	DODD EJ	MCIVER CD	RICHARDSON JN	ROLAND H
BRUCE-HALL R	MELLOR AA	WILLETT BH	WOOLLAN EB	FILOCE AA	MALLETT KL	DIXON GF
EDGAR SC	EASTERBROOK TE	RAYNOR K	MARTYN RV	WINCH HS 4	MONTGOMERY PJ	DIXON GF
VACHELL FT	BURT WJ	SIMPSON L	MALLETT ML	BRUCE-HALL R	JONES GV	DIXON GF

1913/14

DATE	VEN	OPPONENTS	RES	COMP	ATT	1	2	3	4
04-Oct	H tp	CIVIL SERVICE	2-3	SAL		FENDER PGH	VACHELL FT	DOLL MHC	KIRBY AC
18-Oct	H tp	EALING	1-1	SAL		FENDER PGH	ROBERTSON ARG	VARDY AT	KIRBY AC
25-Oct	A	TOWNLEY PARK	3-1	SAL	%	FENDER PGH	ROBERTSON ARG	'OTHER' AN	SHIPTON CH
22-Nov	A	CIVIL SERVICE	2-2	SAL		FENDER PGH	RIMMINGTON H	VARDY AT	DOLL MHC
13-Dec	A	OLD CARTHUSIANS	3-1	AFASC1	%	FENDER PGH	HOWELL-JONES HG	MUGLISTON FH	VACHELL FT
20-Dec	A	REIGATE PRIORY	3-1	SAL		FENDER PGH	DOLL MHC	BURTENSHAW G	RAIKES KC
03-Jan	A	IPSWICH TOWN	8-1	SAL	2,500	FENDER PGH	RIMMINGTON H	ROBERTSON ARG	NEWMAN D
10-Jan	A	CROUCH END VAMPIRES	4-2	SAL		FENDER PGH	RIMMINGTON H	DOLL MHC	CUTTER RC
17-Jan	A	TOWNLEY PARK	6-0	AFASC2		FENDER PGH	ROBERTSON ARG	CAMPBELL IPF	CUTTER RC
24-Jan	H tp	LONDON CO & WB	3-0	SAL		FENDER PGH	DOLL MHC	VARDY AT	WHITE J
14-Feb	A	IPSWICH TOWN	3-2	AFASC3	3,500	FENDER PGH	RIMMINGTON H	ROBERTSON ARG	RAIKES KC
07-Mar	A	LONDON CO & WB	1-1	SAL		FENDER PGH	HOWELL-JONES HG	SNELL IE	RAIKES KC
14-Mar	N tp	CIVIL SERVICE	1-3	AFASCsf	1,500	FENDER PGH	HOWELL-JONES HG	ROBERTSON ARG	RAIKES KC
28-Mar	H @	CROUCH END VAMPIRES	1-1	SAL	%	FENDER PGH	ROBERTSON ARG	RIMMINGTON H	DOLL MHC
04-Apr	A	HAMPSTEAD	7-2	SAL		FENDER PGH	ROBERTSON ARG	KYLE J	WALKER AR
18-Apr	A	EALING	1-1	SAL		FENDER PGH	ROBERTSON ARG	KYLE J	WALKER AR
NP	H	IPSWICH TOWN	NP	SAL					
NP	H	REIGATE PRIORY	NP	SAL					
NP	H	HAMPSTEAD	NP	SAL					
NP	H	TOWNLEY PARK	NP	SAL					

Friendly Matches

DATE	VEN	OPPONENTS	RES	COMP	ATT	1	2	3	4
27-Sep	A	WEYBRIDGE	0-1	F		FENDER PGH	SLEIGH GB	CUTTER RC	RAIKES KC
08-Oct	A	BRIGHTON COLLEGE	14-0	F		MEEK RG	ROBERSON AJE	RIMMINGTON H	HACKING EM 1
11-Oct	A	WESTMINSTER SCHOOL	8-0	F	%	DAVIDSON JLM	WITHERINGTON JG	BUXTON SJ	BIRRELL HA
18-Oct	A	CHARTERHOUSE	3-2	F	%	GRANT AS	WITHERINGTON JG	PILDITCH PH	BIRRELL HA
22-Oct	A	RMA WOOLWICH	3-2	F		MEEK RG	CLARK HN	VARDY AT	GILLETT EF
25-Oct	A	WELLINGBOROUGH SCHOOL	2-6	F		NOTT-BOWER RE	WHITE J	HASELTON WE	LANGLEY CK
29-Oct	A	HIGHGATE SCHOOL	5-1	F		YATES HG	VARDY AT	DAWBARN GM	GILLETT EF
01-Nov	H tp	CAMBRIDGE UNIV	3-5	F	800	FENDER PGH	RIMMINGTON H	SNELL IE	KIRBY AC
01-Nov	A	FOREST SCHOOL	4-1	F	%	NOTT-BOWER RE	SLEIGH GB	VARDY AT	LANGLEY CK
08-Nov	H tp	OXFORD UNIVERSITY	1-4	F	1,200	FENDER PGH	RIMMINGTON H	ROBERTSON ARG	MONTGOMERY PJ
08-Nov	A	LONDON HOSPITAL	1-3	F	%	NOTT-BOWER RE	SLEIGH GB	HASELTON WE	DAWBARN GM
12-Nov	A	FELSTED SCHOOL	2-2	F		ALLEN HC	CLARK HN	EAGEN R	GILLETT EF
15-Nov	A	CAMBRIDGE UNIV	2-2	F	og	SCOTT BJ	WHITE J	DUNKERLEY CL	MCIVER CD
29-Nov	A	ALDENHAM SCHOOL	4-1	F		NOTT-BOWER RE	PILDITCH PH	HASELTON WE	BIRRELL HA
06-Dec	A	LONDON CO & WB	2-5	F	%	NOTT-BOWER RE	VARDY AT	VACHELL FT	BARTLEY EH
08-Dec	A	SHREWSBURY SCHOOL	13-3	F		EDGE AS	CLARK HN	ROBERTSON ARG	DOLL MHC
09-Dec	A	REPTON SCHOOL	5-0	F		EDGE AS	CLARK HN	ROBERTSON ARG	PALMER B
10-Dec	A	MALVERN COLLEGE	3-0	F		EDGE AS	ROBERSON AJE	CLARK HN	PALMER B
13-Dec	A	ST JOHNS SCHOOL	2-0	F	%				
22-Dec	A	OLD WYKEHAMISTS	2-3	F		NOTT-BOWER RE	WHITE J	LANGLEY CK	MONTGOMERY PJ
14-Jan	A	ST THOMAS' HOSPITAL	3-2	F	%	ALLEN HC	DAWBARN GM	NEWMAN D	DOWER LF
17-Jan	A	OLD FELSTEDIANS	4-1	F		NOTT-BOWER RE	DAWBARN GM	BARTLEY EH	KERREY C
21-Jan	A	OXFORD UNIVERSITY	2-3	F		SCOTT BJ	RIMMINGTON H	CAMPBELL IPF	MCIVER CD
24-Jan	A	LONDON HOSPITAL	2-6	F		NOTT-BOWER RE	DAWBARN GM	SLEIGH GB	BIRRELL HA
28-Jan	A	GUY'S HOSPITAL	1-4	F		GRANT AS	VARDY AT	WEBDALE CF	DAWBARN GM
31-Jan	H tp	CAMBRIDGE UNIV	2-0	F		FENDER PGH	RIMMINGTON H	ROBERTSON ARG	DOLL MHC
04-Feb	A	CHARTERHOUSE	6-4	F	%				
14-Feb	A	BANK OF ENGLAND	5-1	F		NOTT-BOWER RE	VARDY AT	BUXTON SJ	EDGAR SC
18-Feb	A	ALDENHAM SCHOOL	1-1	F		SMITH ER	NEWMAN D	DAWBARN GM	SIMPSON FC
04-Mar	A	CITY OF LONDON SCHOOL	9-1	F	%	RANT JCG	DAWBARN GM	TRYWICK JA	KYLE J
21-Mar	A	SURBITON HILL	5-4	F		NOTT-BOWER RE	VARDY AT	MARTYN O	PILDITCH PH

5	6	7	8	9	10	11
RAIKES KC	WHITE J	CUTTER RC 1	HOWELL M	CLARKE MH 1	DOWER RW	DIXON GF
RAIKES KC	DOLL MHC	CUTTER RC	CLARKE MH 1	MCIVER CD	HOFFMEISTER CE	DOWER RW
KIRBY AC	GREEN G	CUTTER RC	'FORWARD' A	STOKES EF	YATES HG	DOWER RW
RAIKES KC	VACHELL FT	CUTTER RC 1	DODD EJ	CLARKE MH 1	YATES HG	DOWER RW
RAIKES KC	MCIVER CD	CUTTER RC	DODD EJ	WOOSNAM M	YATES HG	DOWER RW
HOWELL-JONES HG 1	DOWER GL	DODD EJ 1	HOWELL M	CLARKE MH 1	YATES HG	DOWER RW
DOLL MHC 2	WHITE J	DOWER RW 1	DODD EJ 2	GUNTER RC 1	YATES HG 1	KERRY AHG 1
RAIKES KC	VACHELL FT	DODD EJ	HOWELL M 1	MCIVER CD 1	YATES HG 1	KERRY AHG 1
HOWELL-JONES HG	VACHELL FT	DOWER RW	DODD EJ 2	CLARKE MH 2	YATES HG	KERRY AHG 2
RAIKES KC	SHIPTON CH	DODD EJ 1	BAIRD F 1	WOOD JL	DOWER RW 1	
HOWELL-JONES HG	MCIVER CD	CUTTER RC	DODD EJ 1	MILLER RW	WAUGH AJ 2	LAW H
		CUTTER RC	DODD EJ		YATES HG	DAVIES AT 1
WOOSNAM M	MCIVER CD	CUTTER RC	DODD EJ	FOSTER AW 1	YATES HG	DAVIES AT
HOWELL-JONES HG	DOWER LF	CUTTER RC	DODD EJ	CLARKE MH	GREEN MA	STOKES EF
HOWELL-JONES HG 1	DOLL MHC	MORRISON CL	DODD EJ 1	GREEN MA 1	CUTTER RC 2	STOKES EF 2
DAVIES NH	SWAINSON CG	GRICE OG	RAYNOR K	CUTTER RC 1	HOWELL-JONES HG	

5	6	7	8	9	10	11
SHIPTON CH	WHITE J	RAYNOR K	HOWELL M	DODD EJ	DOWER RW	DIXON GF
GREEN G	KIRBY AC	RAYNOR K	HOWELL M	SQUIRE CE 5	CUTTER RC 6	DIXON GF 2
SHIPTON CH	PILDITCH PH	RAYNOR K	HOWELL M	STOKES EF	CLARKE DH	DIXON GF
GREEN G	NEWMAN D	RAYNOR K	MONTGOMERY PJ	HARRIS G	CLARKE DH	DIXON GF
LEE RT 1	NEWMAN D	BECK PL	ASTE GA	DOWER RW 1	CLARKE DH 1	WATSON TW
DOWER LF	NEWMAN D	RAYNOR K	RAYNER J 1	MACKAY RJ	CARTER RD 1	GRANT AS
SMIT NH	SHIPTON CH	MACKAY RJ	JAMESON GD 1	LYONS JH 4	DIXON GF	COLLINS EH
RAIKES KC	VACHELL FT	CUTTER RC	CLARKE MH	BRISLEY CE 2	YATES HG 1	DOWER RW
SHIPTON CH	BIRRELL HA	RAYNOR K	HARRIS JB	MONTGOMERY PJ	CLARKE DH	DIXON GF
KIRBY AC	STOKES EF	RAYNOR K	HOWELL M	SLOLEY R	DOWER RW 1	
PILDITCH PH	EDGAR SC	'OTHER' AN	HOLLINS FH	MONTGOMERY PJ	LANGLEY CK	BIRRELL HA
EDGAR SC	NEWMAN D	BECK PL 1	HUNTER EI	ROBINSON F	FENDER PGH	DOWER RW 1
RAIKES KC	TONKIN RS	CUTTER RC 1	WOOD JL	CLARKE MH	HOFFMEISTER CE	DOWER RW
SHIPTON CH	LANGLEY CK	RAYNOR K	HARRIS JB 1	MONTGOMERY PJ 2	DIXON GF 1	RAYNOR J
RAIKES KC	LANGLEY CK	RAYNOR K	HARRIS JB	CUTTER RC	MONTGOMERY PJ	DIXON GF
WOOSNAM M	PALMER B	WETHERED WT	HINMERS W 3	RUDD GB 3	MILLER RW 6	DOWER RW 1
WOOSNAM M 1	DOLL MHC	LAW H	HINMERS W	RUDD GB 1	MILLER RW 3	DOWER RW
WOOSNAM M 1	DOLL MHC	LAW H	MILLER RW	RUDD GB 2	HINMERS EC	DOWER RW
COOKE HHA	ANDERSON ET	RAYNOR K	HARRIS JB	CLARKE DH	CUTHBERTSON H	DIXON GF
VACHELL FT	GRAST JC	DOWER RW	RAYNOR K	STOKES EF	ROBINSON F	DIXON GF
GOTTING H	CUTHBERTSON H	RAYNOR K 1	STOKES EF 1	MONTGOMERY PJ 2	DIXON GF	RAYNOR J
HOWELL-JONES HG	RAIKES KC	DOWER RW	DAVIES PH 1	JAMES HC	VERNON HD 1	KERRY AHG
SHIPTON CH	MONTGOMERY PJ	RAYNOR K	HARRIS JB	WALFORD PF 1	CLARKE DH 1	DIXON GF
SMIT HN	NEWMAN D	DIXON GF 1	THORNE WRP	DOWER GL	SMITH G	RAYNOR K
RAIKES KC	WHITE J	LAW H	DODD EJ 2	CUTTER RC	MCIVER CD	DOWER RW
GREEN G	PILDITCH PH	RAYNOR K	WALFORD PF	RYAN JH	MONTGOMERY PJ	DIXON GF
DOWER EL	KYLE J	ROBINSON F	THORNE WRP	CLARKE MH 1	DODD EJ	WOODS A
RABONE M	NEWMAN D	DIXON GF	YATES HG 2	CLARKE MH	COVERDALE H	OTHER AN
VANN BW	MACKENZIE J	RAYNOR K	HARRIS JB	WALFORD PF	MONTGOMERY PJ	DIXON GF

1919/20

DATE	VEN	OPPONENTS	RES	COMP	ATT	1	2	3	4
06-Sep	A	LONDON CALEDONIANS	1-5	IL	3,000	CROSSLAND GL	SERGEANT PA	WILKINSON AM	POPHAM RF
13-Sep	A	NUNHEAD	1-1	IL		MOORE AJ	SERGEANT PA	BADHAM JT	MORRIS E
20-Sep	A	CIVIL SERVICE	2-1	IL					
11-Oct	H1	WEST NORWOOD	2-0	IL		MOORE AJ	SERGEANT PA	WILKINSON AM	COCKBURN GE
18-Oct	H1	CLAPTON	1-2	IL		MOORE AJ	SERGEANT PA	WILKINSON AM	BIRCH AE
22-Oct	A	DULWICH HAMLET	2-4	LCC1	1,500	NEWHAM OE	SERGEANT PA	JOHNSON HL	BIRCH AE
25-Oct	H1	LONDON CALEDONIANS	0-0	IL		MOORE AJ	SERGEANT PA	SKEY HO	VAN THIEL HF
01-Nov	A	WEST NORWOOD	2-3	IL		MOORE AJ	SKEY HO	WHITE J	LEE RT
15-Nov	H1	TUFNELL PARK	0-1	IL		MOORE AJ	SKEY HO	HOWELL-JONES HG	WHITE J
29-Nov	A	DULWICH HAMLET	1-8	IL		MOORE AJ	DAVIS V	VAN THIEL HF	BIRCH AE
06-Dec	H1	ILFORD	0-6	IL		MOORE AJ	SKEY HO	WILKINSON AM	VAN THIEL HF
13-Dec	A	LEYTONSTONE	1-5	IL		SCOTT BJ	SERGEANT PA	DEWBARN GM	BIRCH AE
20-Dec	A	WOKING	0-5	IL	1,000	MOORE AJ	SKEY HO	SERGEANT PA	SHEPHERD GS
10-Jan	H1	WOKING	0-2	IL		MOORE AJ	SKEY HO	SERGEANT PA	BIRCH AE
31-Jan	H1	CIVIL SERVICE	3-2	IL		MOORE AJ	SERGEANT PA	PLAISTOWE FH	WOOD JL
21-Feb	A	OXFORD CITY	1-5	IL		CROSSLAND GL	COOK H	VAN THIEL HF	STERN A
28-Feb	A	CLAPTON	2-8	IL		MOORE AJ	SERGEANT PA	BOWER AG	POTTER R
06-Mar	A	ILFORD	1-12	IL	1,000	DEERING SB	WILKINSON AM	SERGEANT PA	BIRCH WG
13-Mar	H1	NUNHEAD	2-4	IL		MOORE AJ	JOSEPH GA	WILKINSON AM	WILLIAMS HR
27-Mar	A	TUFNELL PARK	0-2	IL	2,000	MOORE AJ	SERGEANT PA	COOK H	HUNTER CB
03-Apr	A	OXFORD CITY	0-4	IL		OATES M	COOK H	PLAISTOWE FH	MUNRO HH
08-Apr	H @	DULWICH HAMLET	0-3	IL		MAY RC	SERGEANT PA	COOK H	BIRCH WG
17-Apr	H @	LEYTONSTONE	0-9	IL		MAY RC	SERGEANT PA	COOK H	DAKINS HF

Friendly Matches

DATE	VEN	OPPONENTS	RES	COMP	ATT	1	2	3	4
23-Oct	H1	OXFORD UNIVERSITY	3-4	F	og	MOORE AJ	RUTHERFORD CC	BRADSHAW J	BOROUGH B
30-Oct	A	CAMBRIDGE UNIV	1-7	F		NEWHAM OE	WILJINSON AM	BADHAM JT	COOPER SH
26-Nov	H1	CAMBRIDGE UNIV	5-1	F		MOORE AJ	SERGEANT PA	COUTANCHE WJ	BIRCH OW
24-Jan	A	OXFORD UNIVERSITY	1-5	F					
07-Feb	A	LONDON CALEDONIANS	3-6	F	1,000	MOORE AJ	COOK F	GANDER-DOWER RW	POTTER R
14-Feb	A	BANK OF ENGLAND	8-1	F	%				

1920/21

DATE	VEN	OPPONENTS	RES	COMP	ATT	1	2	3	4
04-Sep	A	CLAPTON	2-2	IL		MOORE AJ	SERGEANT PA	BOWER AG	VAN THIEL HF
11-Sep	H em	CIVIL SERVICE	2-1	IL		MOORE AJ	SERGEANT PA	WRIGHT W	VAN THIEL HF
18-Sep	A	LEYTONSTONE	1-3	IL	3,000	MOORE AJ	SERGEANT PA	BOWER AG	LEE RT
25-Sep	A	NUNHEAD	1-5	IL		MOORE AJ	SERGEANT PA	NICHOLSON JCD	BIRCH WG
16-Oct	A	DULWICH HAMLET	1-8	IL		MOORE AJ	SERGEANT PA	NICHOLSON JCD	BERRY EA
23-Oct	H em	WEST NORWOOD	4-1	IL		KIDD HB	SERGEANT PA	DAVIES V	ISAAC HF
30-Oct	A	TUFNELL PARK	0-5	IL	2,000	LOMAX E	SERGEANT PA	POTTS AE	SULLIVAN SH
06-Nov	H em	LONDON CALEDONIANS	2-3	IL		MOORE AJ	SERGEANT PA	PAYNE HG	HUMPHREYS CM
13-Nov	H em	NUNHEAD	1-4	IL		BUNTROY HE	SERGEANT PA	DAVIES V	PAYNE HG
27-Nov	H em	CLAPTON	3-3	IL		MOORE AJ	SERGEANT PA	PAYNE HG	BODDINGTON N
18-Dec	A	LONDON CALEDONIANS	0-6	IL		MOORE AJ	SERGEANT PA	PAYNE HG	UNKNOWN
08-Jan	A	WEST NORWOOD	1-4	IL		MOORE AJ	SERGEANT PA	PAYNE HG	LEE RT
15-Jan	A	CIVIL SERVICE	1-4	IL		MOORE AJ	SERGEANT PA	PAYNE HG	SUTTON NP
22-Jan	H em	OXFORD CITY	0-4	IL		MOORE AJ	SERGEANT PA	PAYNE HG	DONKIN HAL
12-Feb	H em	WOKING	1-1	IL		MOORE AJ	PLAISTOWE FH	PAYNE HG	POTTER R
19-Feb	A	WOKING	1-2	IL	1,500	MOORE AJ	MORRISON JSF	PAYNE HG	SERGEANT PA
26-Feb	H em	ILFORD	3-9	IL		MOORE AJ	SERGEANT PA	DUBUIS HF	SUTTON NP
19-Mar	H em	TUFNELL PARK	0-3	IL		MOORE AJ	SERGEANT PA	STOKES A	SANDER MR
02-Apr	A	ILFORD	1-2	IL	4,000	HUMPHREYS CM	SERGEANT PA	SAWYER GS	LATTEN RC
16-Apr	H em	LEYTONSTONE	3-2	IL		HUMPHREYS CM	PLAISTOWE FH	SANGER GFD	MARRABLE SA
23-Apr	A	OXFORD CITY	1-9	IL	1,500	HUMPHREYS CM	PLAISTOWE FH	SERGEANT PA	HAYES EA
28-Apr	H@	DULWICH HAMLET	2-6	IL	1,700	HUMPHREYS CM	PLAISTOWE FH	PAYNE HG	SERGEANT PA

Friendly Matches

DATE	VEN	OPPONENTS	RES	COMP	ATT	1	2	3	4
03-Nov	A	OXFORD UNIVERSITY	0-3	F		DOBSON KWC	PLAISTOWE FH	WHINNEY JC	DAVIS FV
24-Nov	A	CAMBRIDGE UNIV	1-5	F		DOBSON KWC	MORRISON JSF	PLAISTOWE FH	PAYNE HG
01-Jan	H em	PUBLIC SCHOOLS XI	5-2	F					
05-Feb	A	SURBITON HILL	4-2	F					
23-Feb	H em	CAMBRIDGE UNIV	1-2	F		HUMPHREYS CM	PLAISTOWE FH	MORRISON JSF	LEVER FW
05-Mar	H em	OXFORD UNIVERSITY	2-1	F		MOORE AJ	PLAISTOWE FH	WHINNEY JC	PRINCE A

5	6	7	8	9	10	11
BIRCH AE	SHEPPARD SN	MITCHELL JF	BODDINGTON N	POPHAM CH	COLLINS CH 1	GANDAR-DOWAR RD
KIRBY AC	BIRCH AE	POPHAM CH	WILKINSON AM	BODDINGTON N	GIBBS F	GANDAR-DOWAR RD 1
				JULIAN CR 1	GRAY DHA 1	
KIRBY AC	POPHAM RF	NICHOLAS FWH	JULIAN CR 1	GRAY DHA	YATES HG 1	GANDAR-DOWAR RD
KIRBY AC	POPHAM RF	COCKBURN GE	WOOD JL 1	GRAY DHA	O'CONNOR D	GANDAR-DOWAR RD
MUNRO HH	DEWBARN GM	COCKBURN GE	VAN THIEL HF	GRAY DHA	SLOLEY R	GANDAR-DOWAR RD 2
POPHAM RF	BIRCH AE	SMITH E	JULIAN CR	GRAY DHA	HANCOCK	GANDAR-DOWAR RD
BIRCH AE	VAN THIEL HF	COCKBURN GE	STUART-LOVE C	JULIAN CR 1	WILLIAMS HR	GANDAR-DOWAR RD 1
BIRCH AE	VAN THIEL HF	WOOD JL	WILLIAMS HR	GRAY DHA	HAMBLETON HA	WHURR GT
KIRBY AC	PLAISTOWE FH	BAZELL R	MORRIS H	GRAY DHA 1	WADE PV	ALLAN HC
KIRBY AC	BIRCH AE	EDWARDS LS	DUBUIS HF	SLOLEY R	MORRIS H	
EDWARDS WT	VAN THIEL HF	MOORE AJ	WILKINSON AM 1	DUBUIS HF	APPLETON RM	POPHAM CH
BIRCH AE	GIEVE RW	WADE PV	EDWARDS CS	JULIAN CR	HAMBLETON HA	ELLIOTT-SMITH J
BODDINGTON N	BATTEN J	MORRIS H	JULIAN CR	HAMBLETON HA	DUBUIS HF	GANDAR-DOWAR RD
POLLOCK J	BIRCH JF	BAZELL H	BAZELL R 1	JULIAN CR 1	YATES HG	GANDAR-DOWAR RD 2
BIRCH AE	MASCALL WH	GANDAR-DOWER E	HAMBLETON HA	JULIAN CR 1	WOOD JL	GANDAR-DOWAR RW
BIRCH AE	VAN THIEL HF	ELLIOTT-SMITH J	HAMBLETON HA 1	GRAY DHA	HOWELL M	GANDAR-DOWAR E 1
DUBUIS HF	VAN THIEL HF	JULIAN CR	FOLLETT RV 1	GRAY DHA	YATES HG	
BIRCH AE	REISS RQ	HEPBURN SF	JULIAN CR	GRAY DHA	HAMBLETON HA 2	YATES HG
BIRCH AE	WOOD JL	WILLIAMS LG	JULIAN CR	REISS RQ	HAMBLETON HA	WILLIAMS HR
VAN THIEL HF	SHEPPARD SN	DAWSON P	DUBUIS HF	JULIAN CR	JONES R	AN OTHER
BIRCH AE	DUBUIS HF	WILLIAMS HR	HOWELL M	GRAY DHA	BAZELL R	BAZELL H
BIRCH AE	VAN THIEL HF	MITCHELL JF	HOWELL M	JULIAN CR	REISS RQ	WILLIAMS HR

5	6	7	8	9	10	11
WATT HM	BAILEY AJ	WILKINSON AM 1	JULIAN CR	CRUISE W 1	WADE H	GANDAR-DOWAR RD
MCLEAN WW	DOUGLAS JWHT	MOORE	WOOD JL	GRAY DHA	DUBUIS HF 1	GANDAR-DOWAR RD
KIRBY AC	VAN THIEL HF	POPHAM CH	LEWIS TH 1	BAZELL H 3	YATES HG 1	GANDAR-DOWAR RW
				JULIAN CR 1		
BIRCH AE	DUBUIS HF	MORRIS HM	GANDAR-DOWER E	JULIAN CR 3	YATES HG	SMITH T

5	6	7	8	9	10	11
BIRCH AE	DUBUIS HF	WILLIAMS JG	ISAAC AH	MORGAN WM 1	JULIAN CR	GANDAR-DOWAR RW 1
BIRCH AE	LEE RT	GRAY KR	MORGAN WM	DUBUIS HF 1	ISAAC AH	GANDAR-DOWAR RW 1
BIRCH AE	DUBUIS HF	BAZELL R	MORGAN WM	BAZELL H 1	ISAAC AH	GANDAR-DOWAR RW
BIRCH AE	THOMAS RM	LLOYD TGA 1	HOWELL M	BAZELL H	ISAAC AH	WILSON CT
BIRCH AE	DUBUIS HF	MORRIS HM	GRAY DHA	JULIAN CR 1	BODDINGTON N	MOORE JD
DUBUIS HF	BIRCH AE	MORRIS HM	GRAY DHA 2	JULIAN CR 1	BAZELL H 1	MOORE JD
DUBUIS HF	BIRCH AE	MORRIS HM	BUNTROY HE	GRAY DHA	CAMPBELL LN	ELLIOTT-SMITH J
DUBUIS HF	BIRCH AE	CAMPBELL LN	BUNTROY HE	GRAY DHA 1	SLOLEY R 1	MOORE JD
DUBUIS HF	BIRCH AE	MORRIS HJ	HOWELL M	JULIAN CR	SLOLEY R 1	VAN DER BORGH M
DUBUIS HF	WILLIAMS HR	WILLIAMS JG	MORRIS HM 2	GRAY DHA	LEWIS RP	ELLIOTT-SMITH J
DUBUIS HF	BIRCH AE	HEPBURN SF	MORRIS HM	GRAY DHA	BODDINGTON N	BOREHAM HR
DUBUIS HF 1	BIRCH AE	HEPBURN SF	SORENSON IM	GRAY DHA	ASHTON CT	VAN DER BORGH M
BIRCH AE	HEPBURN SF	VAN DER BORGH M	GRAY DHA	KAY AW	DUBUIS HF 1	
MILLER GT	BIRCH AE	HEPBURN SF	DUBUIS HF	GRAY DHA	OWEN RH	
DUBUIS HF	SERGEANT PA	DONKIN HAL	VAN DER BORGH M	JULIAN CR	GRAY DHA 1	ATWOOD WH
DUBUIS HF 1	MILLER GT	DONKIN HAL	MORRIS HM	JULIAN CR	GRAY DHA	OWEN RH
MILLER GT	HUMPHREYS CM	HEPBURN SF	JULIAN CR 2	DAWE LS 1	COLEY GH	GRAY DHA
DUBUIS HF	UNKNOWN	WILLIAMS JG	VAN DER BORGH M	DAWE LS	WILLIAMS HR	GRAY DHA
EWER FH	WILLIAMS HR	WILLIAMS JG	VAN DER BORGH M	DAWE LS	GRAY DHA 1	BATCHELOR AE
EWER FH	BEESON NW	WILLIAMS JG	JULIAN CR 3	DAWE LS	VAN DER BORGH M	BATCHELOR AE
USILL HV	BARTLETT V	PHILLIPS D	JULIAN CR	DAWE LS 1	BATCHELOR AE	RICE-OXLEY AE
DUBUIS HF	POTTER R	WILLIAMS JG	JULIAN CR 1	DAWE LS	GRAY DHA 1	BATCHELOR AE

5	6	7	8	9	10	11
DUBUIS HF	BIRCH AE	LINDSAY KM	HOWELL M	JULIAN CR	MORRIS HM	MOORE JD
DUBUIS HF	BIRCH AE	MORRIS HM 1	ROGERS RS	BAZELL H	HOWELL M	MOORE JD
DUBUIS HF 1		VAN DER BORGH M 1		GRAY DHA 1	BODDINGTON N 1	ELLIOTT-SMITH J 1
DUBUIS HF 1			SUTTON 1	GRAY DHA 2		
DUBUIS HF	SERGEANT PA	WILLIAMS JG	JULIAN CR	DAWE LS	BAZELL R 1	GRAY DHA
DUBUIS HF	SERGEANT PA	VAN DER BORGH M	WILSON EHE	DAWE LS 2	COLEY GH	GRAY DHA

1921/22

DATE	VEN	OPPONENTS	RES	COMP	ATT	1	2	3	4
27-Aug	A	WIMBLEDON	0-4	IL	5,000	MOORE AJ	PAYNE HG	SERGEANT PA	BERRY EA
10-Sep	A	WYCOMBE W	2-7	IL		BOUCHER N	PAYNE HG	MOULD WAH	BIRCH AE
17-Sep	A	LEYTONSTONE	0-2	IL		MOORE AJ	PAYNE HG	PLAISTOWE FH	EWER FH
24-Sep	A	LONDON CALEDONIANS	1-3	IL		MOORE AJ	PAYNE HG	SERGEANT PA	EWER FH
01-Oct	A	DULWICH HAMLET	0-5	IL		MOORE AJ	PAYNE HG	PLAISTOWE FH	EWER FH
08-Oct	A	WEST NORWOOD	2-3	IL		MOORE AJ	SERGEANT PA	PLAISTOWE FH	EWER FH
15-Oct	H g	CIVIL SERVICE	2-2	IL	200	MOORE AJ	PAYNE HG	PLAISTOWE FH	EWER FH 1
29-Oct	H g	DULWICH HAMLET	2-9	IL		MOORE AJ	PAYNE HG	SERGEANT PA	EWER FH
05-Nov	A	WOKING	1-2	IL	2,000	BALDWIN WW	SERGEANT PA	PLAISTOWE FH	BERRY EA
12-Nov	H g	WYCOMBE W	2-6	IL		JARDINE DR	SERGEANT PA	PLAISTOWE FH	EWER FH
03-Dec	H g	HIGHGATE	3-1	AFAS1	100	MOORE AJ	PAYNE HG	PLAISTOWE FH	PHILLIPS E
24-Dec	A	WOKING	1-2	IL		MOORE AJ	PLAISTOWE FH	CAVILL WV	SERGEANT PA
31-Dec	H @	ILFORD	2-8	IL	2,000	MOORE AJ	PAYNE HG	CAVILL WV	SERGEANT PA
07-Jan	A	CIVIL SERVICE	0-3	IL		MOORE AJ	PAYNE HG	CAVILL WV	WHARTON LE
14-Jan	A	TUFNELL PARK	0-2	IL	1,500	FENDER PGH	PAYNE HG	CAVILL WV	WHARTON LE
21-Jan	A	LIVERPOOL VICTORIA	4-3	AFAS2		FENDER PGH	PAYNE HG	CAVILL WV	WHARTON LE
11-Feb	H g	LEYTONSTONE	1-2	IL	3,000	FENDER PGH	PAYNE HG	PLAISTOWE FH	WHARTON LE
18-Feb	H g	LCW & PARRS BANK	1-1	AFAS3		FENDER PGH	PAYNE HG	PLAISTOWE FH	WHARTON LE
25-Feb	H g	CLAPTON	2-4	IL		WATKINSON WS	PAYNE HG	SMITH FV	SERGEANT PA
04-Mar	A	LCW & PARRS BANK	3-2	AFAS3		WATKINSON WS	PAYNE HG	CAVILL WV	WHARTON LE
11-Mar	A	OXFORD CITY	0-4	IL		WATKINSON WS	PAYNE HG	SMITH FV	EWER FH
18-Mar	N1	EALING	1-5	AFAS sf		WATKINSON WS	PAYNE HG	CAVILL WV	GROSS RM
23-Mar	A	NUNHEAD	0-5	IL		WATKINSON WS	PAYNE HG	PLAISTOWE FH	SERGEANT PA
25-Mar	H g	WIMBLEDON	0-8	IL		WATKINSON WS	PLAISTOWE FH	SMITH FV	HARRISON WFN
30-Mar	H g	OXFORD CITY	0-4	IL		WATKINSON WS	PLAISTOWE FH	SERGEANT PA	BRITTAN EM
08-Apr	A	NUNHEAD	0-8	IL		WATKINSON WS	PAYNE HG	PLAISTOWE Fh	BRITTAN EM
12-Apr	A	CLAPTON	2-4	IL		KIDD HB	PAYNE HG	PLAISTOWE FH	WALLACE AW
17-Apr	A	ILFORD	2-3	IL	4,000	WARD-CLARKE HM	PAYNE HG	PLAISTOWE FH	BULTEN
22-Apr	H g	TUFNELL PARK	0-3	IL	900	KIDD HB	PAYNE HG	PLAISTOWE FH	BRITTAN EM
26-Apr	H g	LONDON CALEDONIANS	2-2	IL		KIDD HB	PLAISTOWE FH	SERGEANT PA	WALLACE AW
29-Apr	H g	WEST NORWOOD	1-2	IL		KIDD HB	SERGEANT PA	PLAISTOWE FH	WRIGHT W

Friendly Matches

DATE	VEN	OPPONENTS	RES	COMP	ATT	1	2	3	4
12-Oct	H	GUILDFORD UNITED	0-7	F		MOORE AJ	PLAISTOWE FH	PAYNE HG	EWER FH
19-Nov	H	CAMBRIDGE UNIV	2-3	F		MOORE AJ	PAYNE HG	SERGEANT PA	EWER FH
21-Nov	H	OXFORD UNIVERSITY	3-5	F		MOORE AJ	PLAISTOWE FH	SERGEANT PA	EWER FH
17-Dec	A	AQUARIUS	5-4	F	%				
27-Dec	A	OLD MALVERNIANS	4-2	F	%				
28-Jan	A	IPSWICH TOWN	2-6	F	og 3,000	MOORE AJ	PAYNE HG	MOULD WAH	GROSS RM
04-Feb	A	CAMBRIDGE UNIV	1-3	F		FENDER PGH	PAYNE HG	PLAISTOWE FH	WHARTON LE
02-Mar	A	OXFORD UNIVERSITY	2-6	F					

5	6	7	8	9	10	11
EWER FH	DUBUIS HF	GLASSCOCK F	COLLINS EH	GILBERT A	EVANS AN	MOORE TD
DUBUIS HF	EWER FH	COCKBURN GE 1	WILLIAMS RW	GROSS RHW 1	MOORE JD	O'KELLY JW
DUBUIS HF	SERGEANT PA	O'KELLY D	WILLIAMS RW	DAWE LS	GROSS RM	PINFIELD RG
BUTCHER AH	SHILCOCK GW	KELLY JD	GROSS RM 1	DAWE LS	DUBUIS HF	PINFIELD RG
DUBUIS HF	SERGEANT PA	WILLIAMS RW	AN OTHER	DAWE LS	VAN DER BORGH M	PINFIELD RG
DUBUIS HF 1	PAYNE HG	WILLIAMS RW 1	MANDER RJ	DAWE LS	VAN DER BORGH M	PINFIELD RG
DUBUIS HF	SERGEANT PA	KELLY JD	JULIAN CR	VAN DER BORGH M	PHILLIPS E 1	AN OTHER
DUBUIS HF	SHILCOCK GW	PINFIELD RG 1	GRIFFIN LG	PHILLIPS E 1	DAWE LS	WILLIAMS RW
DUBUIS HF	MANDER RJ	WILLIAMS RW 1	EWER FH	PHILLIPS E	HOWELL M	LAWSON MB
SANGER GFD	AN OTHER	WILLIAMS RW	VAN DER BORGH M	DUBUIS HF	HOWELL M 2	PINFIELD RG
EWER FH	SERGEANT PA	LAWSON MB	DAWE LS	DUBUIS HF 2	HOWELL M 1	PINFIELD RG
DUBUIS HF	SHILCOCK GW 1	LAWSON MB	JULIAN CR	PHILLIPS E	VAN DER BORGH M	PINFIELD RG
DUBUIS HF	SHILCOCK GW	HEPBURN SF	JULIAN CR	SYMINGTON TP 1	HOWELL M 1	PINFIELD RG
GROSS RM	PLAISTOWE FH	HEPBURN SF	JULIAN CR	DUBUIS HF	HOWELL M	PINFIELD RG
DUBUIS HF	SHILCOCK GW	WILLIAMS RW	DYER R	SYMINGTON TP	VAN DER BORGH M	LAWSON MB
DUBUIS HF 1	SHILCOCK GW	WILLIAMS RW 1	GROSS RM	SYMINGTON TP 1	HOWELL M 1	PINFIELD RG
DUBUIS HF	LOW HH	WILLIAMS RW	JULIAN CR	DAWE LS 1	VAN DER BORGH M	SERGEANT PA
DUBUIS HF 1	LOW HH	SERGEANT PA	MORRIS	SYMINGTON TP	DAWE LS	PINFIELD RG
DUBUIS HF	LOW HH	HEPBURN SF	HOWELL M	JULIAN CR	PINFIELD RG 2	WILLIAMS RW
DUBUIS HF	LOW HH	WILLIAMS RW 1	HOWELL M	SYMINGTON TP	PINFIELD RG 1	SERGEANT PA
DUBUIS HF	SERGEANT PA	WILLIAMS RW	HOWELL M	SYMINGTON TP	PINFIELD RG	LAWSON MB
DUBUIS HF	LOW HH	WILLIAMS RW	HOWELL M	SYMINGTON TP 1	PINFIELD RG	LAWSON MB
BIRCH AE	LOW HH	HEPBURN SF	HOWELL M	DAY AT	JULIAN CR	VAN DER BORGH M
DUBUIS HF	WALLACE AW	VAN DER BORGH M	HOWELL M	JULIAN CR	CRUIKSHANK WR	SERGEANT PA
BEESON NW	WALLACE AW	HEPBURN SF	KAY AW	CRUIKSHANK WR	BROWN A	POPHAM CH
DUBUIS HF	SERGEANT PA	CRUIKSHANK G	HOWELL M	SYMINGTON TP	CRUIKSHANK WR	WASSELL H
BEESON NW	LOW HH	HOWELL M	WRIGHT W	DUBUIS HF 1	CRUIKSHANK WR 1	PINFIELD RG
DUBUIS HF 1	WALLACE AW	MARDEN	CRUIKSHANK WR	SYMINGTON TP	HOWELL M	PINFIELD RG 1
STONE RN	LOW HH	POPHAM CH	CRUIKSHANK WR	SYMINGTON TP	MANDER RJ	PINFIELD RG
LOW HH	BRITTAN EM	WILLIAMS RW	CRUIKSHANK WR	KAY AW 1	HOWELL M 1	PINFIELD RG
LOW HH	WALLACE AW	WILLIAMS RW	MANDER RJ	KAY AW 1	HOWELL M	PINFIELD RG

5	6	7	8	9	10	11
DUBUIS HF	SERGEANT PA	HEPBURN SF	JULIAN CR	GROSS RM	VAN DER BORGH M	KELLY JD
DUBUIS HF	SHILCOCK GW	WILLIAMS RW	JULIAN CR	DAWE LS 2	HOWELL M	PINFIELD RG
WOODING CS	SHILCOCK GW	MOUNSEY JW 1	PHILLIPS E	DUBUIS HF 1	JULIAN CR 1	LAWSON MB
DUBUIS HF	LOW HH	VAN DER BORGH M	JULIAN CR	SYMINGTON TP 1	HOWELL M	PINFIELD RG
DUBUIS HF 1	LOW HH	VAN DER BORGH M	JULIAN CR	SYMINGTON TP	COLES WT	POPHAM CH
		WILLIAMS RW 1	WILLIAMS J 1			

1922/23

DATE	VEN	OPPONENTS	RES	COMP	ATT	1	2	3	4
02-Sep	A	WEST NORWOOD	3-0	IL		KIDD HB	PAYNE HG	BOWER AG	WALLICH AD
09-Sep	A	TUFNELL PARK	2-3	IL	2,000	KIDD HB	PAYNE HG	BOWER AG	WALLICH AD
23-Sep	A	DULWICH HAMLET	2-2	IL	4,000	WATKINSON WS	PAYNE HG	BOWER AG	LOW HH
30-Sep	A	REDHILL	4-2	AC1Q		WATKINSON WS	PAYNE HG	BOWER AG	EWER FH
07-Oct	A	OXFORD CITY	2-1	IL	3,000	WATKINSON WS	PAYNE HG	BOWER AG	LOW HH
14-Oct	A	KINGSTONIAN	1-1	AC2Q	8,000	WATKINSON WS	PAYNE HG	BOWER AG	LOW HH
21-Oct	H	KINGSTONIAN	2-2	AC2Q	4,000	KIDD HB	PAYNE HG	BOWER AG	BUTCHER AH
25-Oct	N w	KINGSTONIAN	4-1	AC2Q		WATKINSON WS	PAYNE HG	BOWER AG	LOW HH
28-Oct	A	LEYLAND MOTORS	5-1	AC3Q		WATKINSON WS	PAYNE HG	BOWER AG	LOW HH
04-Nov	H	DULWICH HAMLET	4-4	IL	4,000	WATKINSON WS	PAYNE HG	BOWER AG	LOW HH
18-Nov	A	WIMBLEDON	1-1	AC4Q		WATKINSON WS	PAYNE HG	BOWER AG	LOW HH
25-Nov	H @	WIMBLEDON	2-6	AC4Q	8,000	KIDD HB	PAYNE HG	BOWER AG	SHILCOCK GW
02-Dec	A	WYCOMBE W	4-3	IL	4,000	WATKINSON WS	PAYNE HG	PLAISTOWE FH	SHILCOCK GW
09-Dec	H	WEST NORWOOD	8-0	IL		WATKINSON WS	PAYNE HG	BOWER AG	LOCKTON JH
16-Dec	H	LONDON CALEDONIANS	3-0	IL	1,000	KIDD HB	PAYNE HG	BOWER AG	LOCKTON JH
30-Dec	A	LONDON CALEDONIANS	1-5	IL	3,000	KIDD HB	PAYNE HG	BOWER AG	LOCKTON JH
20-Jan	H	WIMBLEDON	1-2	IL		WATKINSON WS	PAYNE HG	PLAISTOWE FH	LOCKTON JH
10-Feb	H	TUFNELL PARK	7-1	IL		KIDD HB	PAYNE HG	BOWER AG	SHILCOCK GW
17-Feb	A	CIVIL SERVICE	7-2	IL	2,000	KIDD HB	PAYNE HG	PLAISTOWE FH	EWER FH
03-Mar	H	OXFORD CITY	2-0	IL	og	WATKINSON WS	PAYNE HG	PLAISTOWE FH	LOCKTON JH
10-Mar	A	NUNHEAD	4-2	IL		KIDD HB	PAYNE HG	PLAISTOWE FH	LOCKTON JH 1
17-Mar	H	ILFORD	3-2	IL	og	KIDD HB	PAYNE HG	BOWER AG	LOCKTON JH 1
24-Mar	A	ILFORD	1-4	IL		KIDD HB	PLATT W	PLAISTOWE FH	LOCKTON JH
31-Mar	H	WOKING	0-0	IL		KIDD HB	PAYNE HG	PLAISTOWE FH	LOCKTON JH
07-Apr	H	CIVIL SERVICE	0-2	IL		KIDD HB	PAYNE HG	PLAISTOWE FH	SHILCOCK GW
11-Apr	A	CLAPTON	3-4	IL		KIDD HB	PAYNE HG	PLAISTOWE FH	MELLOR PE
14-Apr	H	LEYTONSTONE	2-2	IL		KIDD HB	PAYNE HG	PLAISTOWE FH	LOCKTON JH 1
18-Apr	H	WYCOMBE W	2-2	IL		KIDD HB	PAYNE HG	PLAISTOWE FH	DUBUIS HF
21-Apr	H	NUNHEAD	1-0	IL	5,000	KIDD HB	PAYNE HG	BOWER AG	DUBUIS HF
25-Apr	A	WIMBLEDON	3-0	IL		KIDD HB	PAYNE HG	BOWER AG	SERGEANT PA
28-Apr	A	WOKING	1-4	IL	2,000	WATKINSON WS	PAYNE HG	PLAISTOWE FH	DUBUIS HF
03-May	A	CLAPTON	1-4	IL		KIDD HB	PAYNE HG	PLAISTOWE FH	SHILCOCK GW
05-May	A	LEYTONSTONE	1-2	IL		KIDD HB	PAYNE HG	PLAISTOWE FH	DUBUIS HF

Friendly Matches

DATE	VEN	OPPONENTS	RES	COMP	ATT	1	2	3	4
11-Nov	A	OXFORD UNIVERSITY	1-4	F		KIDD HB	PAYNE HG	SMITH FV	LOW HH
28-Dec	A	OLD MALVERNIANS	3-3	F	%				
03-Feb	A	CAMBRIDGE UNIV	2-3	F		WATKINSON WS	PAYNE HG	PLAISTOWE FH	LOCKTON JH
24-Feb	A	OXFORD UNIVERSITY	3-4	F		KIDD HB	PAYNE HG	PLAISTOWE FH	SHILCOCK GW
07-Mar	A	CAMBRIDGE UNIV	3-1	F					
02-Apr	H	LUTON CLARENCE	5-2	F	10,000				

1923 - Tour to Spain

DATE	VEN	OPPONENTS	RES	COMP	ATT	1	2	3	4
06-Jan	A	ATHLETIC BILBAO	2-4	T	%	WATKINSON WS	GAMBLE AH	PLAISTOWE FH	DUBUIS HF
07-Jan	A	ATHLETIC BILBAO	4-4	T	%	WATKINSON WS	GAMBLE AM	PLAISTOWE FH	DUBUIS HF
10-Jan	A	REAL UNION	2-2	T	%	WATKINSON WS	GAMBLE AH	PLAISTOWE FH	DUBUIS HF

5	6	7	8	9	10	11
EWER FH	PLATTS A	HOWELL M 1	MARTIN E	DUBUIS HF 1	GLENISTER CE	PINFIELD RG 1
EWER FH	LOW HH	HOWELL M	MARTIN E 2	DUBUIS HF	GLENISTER CE	PINFIELD RG
EWER FH	PLATTS A	HOWELL M	LOCKTON JH	DUBUIS HF 2	MARTIN E	PINFIELD RG
MIDDLEBOE N	LOW HH	HOWELL M 2	LOCKTON JH 1	DUBUIS HF 1	MARTIN E	PINFIELD RG
EWER FH	PLATTS A	HOWELL M 2	LOCKTON JH	DUBUIS HF	MARTIN E	PINFIELD RG
EWER FH	COLES WT	HOWELL M	HOLDSWORTH RL	DUBUIS HF 1	MARTIN E	PINFIELD RG
EWER FH	LOW HH	HOWELL M	HOLDSWORTH RL 1	DUBUIS HF	MARTIN E 1	PINFIELD RG
BUTCHER AH	EWER FH	HOWELL M	MORRIS HM 3	DUBUIS HF 1	LOCKTON JH	PINFIELD RG
EWER FH	BUTCHER AH	HOWELL M	MORRIS HM 2	HOLDSWORTH RL 3	LOCKTON JH	PINFIELD RG
EWER FH	BUTCHER AH	HOWELL M	MORRIS HM 1	DUBUIS HF 1	LOCKTON JH	PINFIELD RG 2
BUTCHER AH	EWER FH	HOWELL M	MORRIS HM	DUBUIS HF 1	LOCKTON JH	PINFIELD RG
DUBUIS HF	EWER FH	HOWELL M	MORRIS HM	HOLDSWORTH RL	DOGGART AG 2	PINFIELD RG
MIDDLEBOE N	EWER FH	HOWELL M	MORRIS HM 2	DUBUIS HF	LOCKTON JH 2	MARTIN E
MIDDLEBOE N	EWER FH	HOWELL M	MORRIS HM 1	DUBUIS HF 2	DOGGART AG 4	PINFIELD RG 1
MIDDLEBOE N	EWER FH	HOWELL M	MORRIS HM 1	DUBUIS HF 1	DOGGART AG	PINFIELD RG 1
LOW HH	PLATTS A	HOWELL M	GLENISTER CE	DUBUIS HF 1	MARTIN E	PINFIELD RG
LOW HH	HUNT KRG	HOWELL M	MORRIS HM	DUBUIS HF	MARTIN E 1	PINFIELD RG
HUNT KRG	EWER FH	HOWELL M 1	MARTIN E 1	DUBUIS HF 1	DOGGART AG 4	PINFIELD RG
HUNT KRG	PLATTS A	HOWELL M	MARTIN E 1	DUBUIS HF 3	LOCKTON JH 3	PINFIELD RG
EWER FH	PLATTS A	MORRIS HM 1	MARTIN E	DUBUIS HF	HOWELL M	PINFIELD RG
HUNT KRG 1	EWER FH	MORRIS HM	MARTIN E	DUBUIS HF 1	HOWELL M 1	PINFIELD RG
EWER FH	PLATTS A	HOWELL M	MARTIN E 1	DUBUIS HF	DOGGART AG	PINFIELD RG
EWER FH	PLATTS A	MORRIS HM	DAWE LS	DUBUIS HF	HOWELL M	PINFIELD RG 1
EWER FH	SHILCOCK GW	HEPBURN SF	MARTIN E	DUBUIS HF	HOWELL M	PINFIELD RG
EWER FH	PLATTS A	HEPBURN SF	MARTIN E	DUBUIS HF	LOCKTON JH	PINFIELD RG
LOCKTON JH	EWER FH	HOWELL M	MARTIN E	DUBUIS HF 1	GLENISTER CE 2	PINFIELD RG
BOWER AG	PLATTS A	HOWELL M	MARTIN E	DUBUIS HF	GLENISTER CE 1	PINFIELD RG
SHILCOCK GW	PLATTS A	HOWELL M	LOCKTON JH	MARTIN E	GLENISTER CE 1	PINFIELD RG 1
KIRBY AC	EWER FH	HOWELL M	MARTIN E	LOCKTON JH 1	GLENISTER CE	PINFIELD RG
DUBUIS HF	EWER FH	HOWELL M	MARTIN E 2	LOCKTON JH	DOGGART AG	PINFIELD RG 1
KIRBY AC	EWER FH	HOWELL M 1	MARTIN E	LOCKTON JH	DOGGART AG	PINFIELD RG
KIRBY AC	EWER FH	GLENISTER CE	HOWELL M	LOCKTON JH 1	CRUIKSHANK WR	MARTIN E
HUNT KRG	SERGEANT PA	HEPBURN SF	HOWELL M	LOCKTON JH	MARTIN E 1	PINFIELD RG

5	6	7	8	9	10	11
BUTCHER AH	COLES WT	HEPBURN SF	MORRIS HM 1	LOCKTON JH	MARTIN E	PINFIELD RG
LOW HH	PLATTS A	HOWELL M	MORRIS HM	DUBUIS HF	MARTIN E 1	PINFIELD RG 1
HUNT KRG	PLATTS A	MORRIS HM 1	MARTIN E	LOCKTON JH 1	HOWELL M 1	RYDER TA
			MARTIN E 1	LOCKTON JH 1	HOWELL M 1	
		HEPBURN SF 1	MARTIN E 1	LOCKTON JH 1	SYMINGTON TP 2	

5	6	7	8	9	10	11
	PLATTS A	HEPBURN SF	MORRIS HM	LOCKTON JH	MARTIN E	
KIRBY AC	PLATTS A	HEPBURN SF	MORRIS HM	LOCKTON JH	MARTIN E	PINFIELD RG
	PLATTS A	HEPBURN SF	MORRIS HM	LOCKTON JH	MARTIN E	PINFIELD RG

1923/24

DATE	VEN	OPPONENTS	RES	COMP	ATT	1	2	3	4
15-Sep	H	WIMBLEDON	8-3	IL		WILKINSON AM	PAYNE HG	BOWER AG	HOWELL M
22-Sep	H	CLAPTON	1-3	IL	og	WILKINSON AM	PAYNE HG	SMITH FV	HOWELL M
29-Sep	A	WIMBLEDON	2-3	IL	8,000	WILKINSON AM	PAYNE HG	BOWER AG	HOWELL M
06-Oct	A	ILFORD	0-0	LCC1	3,000	WILKINSON AM	PAYNE HG	BOWER AG	HOWELL M
13-Oct	H	NUNHEAD	3-0	IL	2,000	WILKINSON AM	PAYNE HG	SMITH FV	EWER FH
20-Oct	A	ILFORD	3-2	IL		WILKINSON AM	PAYNE HG	SMITH FV	EWER FH
27-Oct	A	CLAPTON	3-2	IL		WILKINSON AM	PAYNE HG	SMITH FV	DUBUIS HF
10-Nov	A	LEYTONSTONE	1-0	IL		WILKINSON AM	PAYNE HG	SMITH FV	DUBUIS HF
17-Nov	H	LONDON CALEDONIANS	3-2	IL	1,000	WILKINSON AM	PAYNE HG	SMITH FV	DUBUIS HF
24-Nov	A	DULWICH HAMLET	0-1	IL		WILKINSON AM	PAYNE HG	BOWER AG	DUBUIS HF
01-Dec	A	ILFORD	0-3	LCC1		WILKINSON AM	PAYNE HG	SMITH FV	DUBUIS HF
15-Dec	H	OXFORD CITY	4-1	IL		WILKINSON AM	PAYNE HG	SMITH FV	DUBUIS HF
22-Dec	A	LONDON CALEDONIANS	1-2	IL	1,000	WILKINSON AM	PAYNE HG	SMITH FV	DUBUIS HF
29-Dec	H	ILFORD	6-2	IL		WILKINSON AM	PAYNE HG	SMITH FV	GLENISTER CE
05-Jan	A	SOUTHALL	1-3	AC1		WILKINSON AM	PAYNE HG	SMITH FV	DUBUIS HF
26-Jan	H	CIVIL SERVICE	5-2	IL		WILKINSON AM	PAYNE HG	SMITH FV	GLENISTER CE
09-Feb	H	TUFNELL PARK	4-1	IL		WILKINSON AM	PAYNE HG	SMITH FV	GLENISTER CE
16-Feb	A	OXFORD CITY	1-3	IL		WILKINSON AM	PAYNE HG	SMITH FV	EWER FH
23-Feb	A	WOKING	1-1	IL		WILKINSON AM	PAYNE HG	SMITH FV	GLENISTER CE
01-Mar	H	LEYTONSTONE	1-2	IL		WILKINSON AM	PAYNE HG	PLAISTOWE FH	EWER FH
08-Mar	A	NUNHEAD	0-4	IL		WILKINSON AM	PAYNE HG	SMITH FV	GLENISTER CE
15-Mar	A	ST.ALBANS CITY	1-3	IL		WILKINSON AM	PAYNE HG	SMITH FV	CAREY HR
05-Apr	A	WYCOMBE W	4-5	IL	5,000	PIPER HF	PAYNE HG	SMITH FV	GLENISTER CE
12-Apr	H	WOKING	5-1	IL		WILKINSON AM	PAYNE HG	SMITH FV	GLENISTER CE
14-Apr	A	TUFNELL PARK	1-0	IL		WILKINSON AM	PAYNE HG	SMITH FV	GLENISTER CE
19-Apr	H	ST.ALBANS CITY	0-4	IL		WILKINSON AM	PAYNE HG	PIPER HF	MELLOR PE
26-Apr	A	CIVIL SERVICE	1-2	IL		WILKINSON AM	PAYNE HG	PIPER HF	GLENISTER CE
28-Apr	H	DULWICH HAMLET	0-4	IL		WILKINSON AM	PLAISTOWE FH	PIPER HF	PAYNE HG
03-May	H	WYCOMBE W	6-2	IL		WILKINSON AM	PAYNE HG	BOWER AG	GLENISTER CE

Friendly Matches

DATE	VEN	OPPONENTS	RES	COMP	ATT	1	2	3	4
03-Nov	H	OXFORD UNIVERSITY	6-1	F		WILKINSON AM	PAYNE HG	SMITH FV	DUBUIS HF
08-Jan	A	PUBLIC SCHOOLS XI	8-1	F		KIDD HB	SERGEANT OA	SMITH FV	MANDER PJ
16-Jan	A	LONDON UNIVERSITY	2-4	F	%	KIDD HB	PLAISTOWE FH	SERGEANT PA	BODDINGTON HC
19-Jan	A	IPSWICH TOWN	L-L	F					
02-Feb	A	CAMBRIDGE UNIV	3-1	F					
06-Mar	A	OXFORD UNIVERSITY	2-2	F					
29-Mar	H	NORTHAMPTON NOMADS	3-0	F		WILKINSON AM	PAYNE HG	SMITH FV	GLENISTER CE
21-Apr	H	LUTON CLARENCE	0-2	F					

5	6	7	8	9	10	11
KNIGHT JG	HOLDSWORTH RL	GODDARD LJ	MARTIN E 1	DUBUIS HF 1	LOCKTON JH 6	PINFIELD RG
KNIGHT JG	EWER FH	GODDARD LJ	HOLDSWORTH RL	DUBUIS HF	LOCKTON JH	PINFIELD RG
KNIGHT JG	EWER FH	GODDARD LJ	GLENISTER CE	DUBUIS HF	LOCKTON JH 2	PINFIELD RG
KNIGHT JG	EWER FH	GODDARD LJ	MARTIN E	DOGGART AG	LOCKTON JH	PINFIELD RG
KNIGHT JG	HOLDSWORTH RL 2	GODDARD LJ	LOCKTON JH 1	HOWELL M	DOGGART AG	PINFIELD RG
KNIGHT JG	ASHTON CT	GODDARD LJ	HOWELL M	HOLDSWORTH RL 1	DOGGART AG 2	MARTIN E
KNIGHT JG	ASHTON CT	GODDARD LJ	HOWELL M	HOLDSWORTH RL	LOCKTON JH 1	MARTIN E 2
KNIGHT JG	PLATTS A	GODDARD LJ	HOWELL M 1	HOLDSWORTH RL	LOCKTON JH	MARTIN E
KNIGHT JG	EWER FH	GODDARD LJ	HOWELL M 1	HOLDSWORTH RL 2	LEWIS HG	RYDER TA
KNIGHT JG	EWER FH	GODDARD LJ	HOWELL M	HOLDSWORTH RL	DOGGART AG	MARTIN E
KNIGHT JG	EWER FH	GODDARD LJ	HOWELL M	HOLDSWORTH RL	LEWIS HG	RYDER TA
KNIGHT JG	EWER FH	GODDARD LJ	HOWELL M	LOCKTON JH 3	BARNARD FH	MARTIN E 1
KNIGHT JG	PLATTS A	GODDARD LJ	BARNARD FH	LINDSAY KM	LOCKTON JH	MARTIN E 1
DUBUIS HF	PLATTS A	MORRIS HM 1	HOWELL M	MARTIN E 4	LOCKTON JH 1	MILLAR-INGLISS KA
KNIGHT JG 1	EWER FH	MORRIS HM	HOWELL M	MARTIN E	LOCKTON JH	MILLAR-INGLISS KA
KNIGHT JG	PLATTS A	LINDSAY KM	HARWOOD CS 1	ASHTON CT 4	LOCKTON JH	MILLAR-INGLISS KA
KNIGHT JG	PLATTS A	GODDARD LJ	HOWELL M	MARTIN E 4	DUBUIS HF	MILLAR-INGLISS KA
KNIGHT JG	PLATTS A	LINDSAY KM	DUBUIS HF	MARTIN E 1	LOCKTON JH	GODDARD LJ
DUBUIS HF	PLATTS A	HEPBURN SF	MORRIS HM	MARTIN E 1	LEWIS HG	GODDARD LJ
DUBUIS HF 1	PLATTS A	GODDARD LJ	HOWELL M	MARTIN E	BARNARD FH	LOCKTON JH
DUBUIS HF	PLATTS A	GODDARD LJ	HOWELL M	LOCKTON JH	MILLER A	RYDER TA
MIDDLEBOE N	EWER FH	PLATTS A	DUBUIS HF	GLENISTER CE	MARTIN E	ASHTON CT 1
DUBUIS HF	EWER FH	CRUIKSHANK G 2	BARNARD FH	PARTRIDGE GB 2	HOWELL M	RYDER TA
DUBUIS HF	EWER FH	GODDARD LJ	ASHTON G 2	ASHTON CT 1	CRUIKSHANK G 2	RYDER TA
DUBUIS HF	MELLOR PE	GODDARD LJ	ASHTON G	LOCKTON JH	CRUIKSHANK G 1	RYDER TA
DUBUIS HF	PLATTS A	LINDSAY KM	MARTIN E	HOWELL M	HALLOWS EH	RYDER TA
DUBUIS HF	PLATTS A	LINDSAY KM	HOWELL M	CRUIKSHANK G 1	LOCKTON JH	RYDER TA
SERGEANT PA	DUBUIS HF	LINDSAY KM	HOWELL M	LOCKTON JH	RYDER TA	AN OTHER
DUBUIS HF	EWER FH	HEPBURN SF	BOSWELL FJ 3	LOCKTON JH 3	CRUIKSHANK G	RYDER TA

5	6	7	8	9	10	11
KNIGHT JG	EWER FH	HEPBURN SF	HOWELL M 3	HOLDSWORTH RL 3	LOCKTON JH	MARTIN E
GLENISTER CE	WOOLNER LR	HEPBURN SF	HARWOOD CS 1	MARTIN E 2	LOCKTON JH 4	MILLAR-INGLISS KA 1
GLENISTER CE	MANDER RJ	HEPBURN SF	CRUIKSHANK WR	BOSWELL FJ	LOCKTON JH	PINFIELD RG
				MARTIN E 2	HOWELL M 1	
GLENISTER CE 1	PLATTS A 1					
DUBUIS HF	PLATTS A	HEPBURN SF	BARNARD FH	LOCKTON JH 2	HOWELL M 1	RYDER TA

1924/25

DATE	VEN	OPPONENTS	RES	COMP	ATT	1	2	3	4
13-Sep	H	DULWICH HAMLET	2-1	IL		WILKINSON AM	PAYNE HG	BOWER AG	CAREY HR
15-Sep	H	GREAT EASTERN	3-4	LSC1Q		WILKINSON AM	PAYNE HG	COUCHMAN RH	HOWELL M
17-Sep	H	WIMBLEDON	3-1	IL		WILKINSON AM	PAYNE HG	BOWER AG	HOWELL M
20-Sep	H	LONDON CALEDONIANS	4-5	IL		WILKINSON AM	PAYNE HG	BOWER AG	MELLOR PE
27-Sep	A	ILFORD	0-2	IL	4,000	WILKINSON AM	SMITH FV	BOWER AG	GLENISTER CE
04-Oct	A	CLAPTON	1-1	LCC1	3,000	WILKINSON AM	PAYNE HG	BOWER AG	GLENISTER CE
11-Oct	H	WYCOMBE W	5-3	IL	og	WILKINSON AM	PAYNE HG	SMITH FV	PLAISTOWE FH
18-Oct	H	CLAPTON	2-1	LCC1		WILKINSON AM	PAYNE HG	SMITH FV	DUBUIS HF
25-Oct	H	CIVIL SERVICE	4-2	IL		WILKINSON AM	PAYNE HG	SMITH FV	EWER FH
15-Nov	A	OXFORD CITY	3-1	IL		KIDD HB	PAYNE HG	SMITH FV	DUBUIS HF
22-Nov	A	WOKING	1-6	IL	og	KIDD HB	PAYNE HG	SMITH FV	HOLDSWORTH RL
29-Nov	A	TOOTING TOWN	2-3	SSC1		MELVILLE AS	SMITH FV	PAYNE HG	EWER FH
06-Dec	A	TUFNELL PARK	1-3	IL	3,000	MELVILLE AS			
13-Dec	H	TUFNELL PARK	0-2	IL		MELVILLE AS	ADAMS FA	SMITH FV	GLENISTER CE
20-Dec	A	KINGSTONIAN	2-1	LCCsf	5,000	MELVILLE AS	DUBUIS HF	MIDDLEBOE N	GLENISTER CE
27-Dec	A	ILFORD	0-0	IL		TRAPP CS	MIDDLEBOE N	PIPER HF	GLENISTER CE
03-Jan	A	HAMPSTEAD TOWN	0-2	AC1	3,000	MELVILLE AS	MIDDLEBOE N	DUBUIS HF	GLENISTER CE
10-Jan	H	WOKING	6-1	IL		TRAPP CS	PIPER HF	SMITH FV	GLENISTER CE
17-Jan	A	WYCOMBE W	3-0	IL		TRAPP CS	BOWER AG 1	PIPER HF	GLENISTER CE
07-Feb	A	NUNHEAD	4-1	IL					
21-Feb	A	LONDON CALEDONIANS	1-0	IL		TRAPP CS	PAYNE HG	MIDDLEBOE N	GLENISTER CE
28-Feb	A	LEYTONSTONE	1-2	IL		TRAPP CS	PAYNE HG	MIDDLEBOE N	GLENISTER CE
14-Mar	H	LEYTONSTONE	2-1	IL		TRAPP CS	PAYNE HG	BOWER AG	GLENISTER CE
21-Mar	A	CIVIL SERVICE	2-3	IL		TRAPP CS	PIPER HF	COUCHMAN RH	STEVENSON JG
28-Mar	H	CLAPTON	2-3	IL		TRAPP CS	PAYNE HG	PIPER HF	GLENISTER CE
30-Mar	A	CLAPTON	0-3	IL		MELVILLE AS	PIPER HF	STEVENSON JG	PLAISTOWE FH
21-Apr	H	NUNHEAD	0-7	IL					
23-Apr	A	DULWICH HAMLET	2-0	IL	%				
25-Apr	H	ST.ALBANS CITY	3-0	IL		TRAPP CS	PAYNE HG	BOWER AG	GLENISTER CE
27-Apr	A	ST.ALBANS CITY	3-5	IL		WILKINSON AM	PAYNE HG	DUBUIS HF	GLENISTER CE
29-Apr	A	WIMBLEDON	0-2	IL		WILKINSON AM	PAYNE HG	STEVENSON JG	DUBUIS HF
02-May	H	OXFORD CITY	3-4	IL		TRAPP CS	PAYNE HG	STEVENSON JG	GLENISTER CE
07-May	N	LONDON CALEDONIANS	0-1	LCC F		WILKINSON AM	BOWER AG	MIDDLEBOE N	

Friendly Matches

DATE	VEN	OPPONENTS	RES	COMP	ATT	1	2	3	4
01-Nov	H	OXFORD UNIVERSITY	2-4	F		WILKINSON AM	PART CK	SMITH FV	SERGEANT PA
19-Nov	H	CAMBRIDGE UNIV	0-4	F		KIDD HB	PAYNE HG	PIPER HF	BEESON NW
17-Dec	H	LONDON UNIVERSITY	3-2	F		JEACOCKE A	ADAMS FA	PIPER HF	GLENISTER CE
24-Jan	H	OLD MALVERNIANS	2-1	F		HOMER H	BARKER JT	RECORD CI	BODDINGTON HC
31-Jan	A	REDHILL	1-8	F		WARD-CLARKE HM	DUBUIS HF	SMITH SF	CRAWFORD JL
07-Mar	A	OLD GRAMMARIANS	1-1	F	%				

1925 - Tour to Denmark

DATE	VEN	OPPONENTS	RES	COMP	ATT	1	2	3	4
10-Apr	A	COPENHAGEN BK	1-2	F					
12-Apr	A	BOLDKLUBBEN 1903	2-3	F					
13-Apr	A	COPENHAGEN BK	1-2	F					

5	6	7	8	9	10	11
ASHTON CT 1	EWER FH	HOWELL M	LOCKTON JH 1	DOGGART AG	CRUIKSHANK G	MILLAR-INGLISS KA
EWER FH	CAREY HR	HEPBURN SF	SLEIGHTHOLME CH 1	DOGGART AG 2	CRUIKSHANK G	MILLAR-INGLISS KA
ASHTON CT 1	EWER FH	HEPBURN SF	CRUIKSHANK G	MAYER ER	DOGGART AG 2	RYDER TA
ASHTON CT 2	EWER FH	SLEIGHTHOLME CH	HOWELL M 1	MAYER ER	DOGGART AG 1	RYDER TA
DUBUIS HF	EWER FH	SLEIGHTHOLME CH	HOWELL M	ASHTON CT	DOGGART AG	RYDER TA
DUBUIS HF	EWER FH	SLEIGHTHOLME CH	HOWELL M 1	ASHTON CT	DOGGART AG	PINFIELD RG
CHADDER AH	PLATTS A	SLEIGHTHOLME CH	HOWELL M 1	SLOLEY R 3	DOGGART AG	PINFIELD RG
ASHTON CT	PLATTS A	SLEIGHTHOLME CH	HOWELL M 1	HOLDSWORTH RL 1	DOGGART AG	PINFIELD RG
DUBUIS HF	PLATTS A	SLEIGHTHOLME CH	HOWELL M 2	HOLDSWORTH RL 2	SLOLEY R	PINFIELD RG
MIDDLEBOE N	KNIGHT JG	SLEIGHTHOLME CH 1	HOWELL M 1	HOLDSWORTH RL	BARNARD FH 1	PINFIELD RG
KNIGHT JG	EWER FH	SLEIGHTHOLME CH	HOWELL M	DUBUIS HF	BARNARD FH	PINFIELD RG
KNIGHT JG	DUBUIS HF	RYDER TA	LOCKTON JH 1	HOLDSWORTH RL	HOWELL M 1	HEPBURN SF
KNIGHT JG		SLEIGHTHOLME CH	HOWELL M 1	SLOLEY R	DOGGART AG	PINFIELD RG
ASHTON CT	EWER FH	SLEIGHTHOLME CH	HOWELL M	MAYER ER	DOGGART AG	PINFIELD RG
GERMAN AC	EWER FH	SLEIGHTHOLME CH	HOWELL M 1	SLOLEY R 1	DOGGART AG	PINFIELD RG
DUBUIS HF	LOCKTON JH	SMITH FV	HOWELL M	SLOLEY R	SLEIGHTHOLME CH	PINFIELD RG
GERMAN AC	EWER FH	SLEIGHTHOLME CH	HOWELL M	SLOLEY R	CHADDER AH	PINFIELD RG
KNIGHT JG	DUBUIS HF	HEPBURN SF 1	SLEIGHTHOLME CH 1	MAYER ER 2	LOCKTON JH 1	PINFIELD RG 1
MIDDLEBOE N	DUBUIS HF	HEPBURN SF	SLEIGHTHOLME CH 1	LOCKTON JH 1	HOWELL M	PINFIELD RG
GERMAN AC			HOWELL M 1	MAYER ER 3	CHADDER AH	
DUBUIS HF	PLAISTOWE FH	PARKER CA	HOWELL M	MAYER ER	LOCKTON JH 1	PINFIELD RG
DUBUIS HF	STEVENSON JG	LINDSAY KM	SLEIGHTHOLME CH 1	MAYER ER	LOCKTON JH	PINFIELD RG
DUBUIS HF	EWER FH	SLEIGHTHOLME CH	HOWELL M	KNIGHT JG	LOCKTON JH 2	PINFIELD RG
KNIGHT JG 1	DUBUIS HF	SLEIGHTHOLME CH 1	HOWELL M	MAYER ER	LOCKTON JH	PINFIELD RG
KNIGHT JG	STEVENSON JG	SLEIGHTHOLME CH	HOWELL M 1	SMITH FV	DUBUIS HF 1	PINFIELD RG
KNIGHT JG	MELLOR PE	HEPBURN SF	HOWELL M	DUBUIS HF	STUART JG	SMITH FV
KNIGHT JG	DUBUIS HF	SIEWART JG	SLEIGHTHOLME CH	LOCKTON JH 1	HOWELL M 2	PINFIELD RG
PARTRIDGE GB	KNIGHT JG	SLEIGHTHOLME CH 2	ASHTON CT	LOCKTON JH 1	HOWELL M	PINFIELD RG
KNIGHT JG	SERGEANT PA	SIEWART JG	SLEIGHTHOLME CH	LOCKTON JH	HOWELL M	SMITH FV
PARTRIDGE GB	DUBUIS HF	SLEIGHTHOLME CH	KNIGHT JG 1	HOWELL M 1	LOCKTON JH 1	PINFIELD RG
						PINFIELD RG

5	6	7	8	9	10	11
MIDDLEBOE N	PLATTS A	SLEIGHTHOLME CH	HOWELL M 1	LOCKTON JH	HOLDSWORTH RL 1	PINFIELD RG
PART CK	SERGEANT PA	HEPBURN SF	MORRIS HM	SLOLEY R	LOCKTON JH	PINFIELD RG
PLAISTOWE FH	MILLER GC	HEPBURN SF	LOCKTON JH 1	MAYER ER 2	MILLER HFR	CRUICKSHANK GS
NAEF CA	PLATTS A	LINDSAY RM	SLEIGHTHOLME CH	LOCKTON JH 2	HALLOWES AE	ZABELL NF
GLENISTER CE	MANN HC	KEHYANIAN JG	HOWELL M	PARTRIDGE GB 1	LOCKTON JH	PINFIELD RG

5	6	7	8	9	10	11

1925/26

DATE	VEN	OPPONENTS	RES	COMP	ATT	1	2	3	4
12-Sep	H	WIMBLEDON	3-5	IL	5,000	WILKINSON AM	PAYNE HG	KNIGHT JG	ASHTON CT
16-Sep	H	NUNHEAD	2-1	IL		WILKINSON AM	PAYNE HG	BOWER AG	SANDERS FR
19-Sep	A	WOKING	1-1	IL		WILKINSON AM	PAYNE HG	PARTRIDGE GB	POTTS R
24-Sep	A	NUNHEAD	0-3	IL		WILKINSON AM	PAYNE HG	BOWER AG	EWER FH
26-Sep	A	WIMBLEDON	2-3	IL		WILKINSON AM	PAYNE HG	PLAISTOWE FH	STEVENSON JG
03-Oct	A	CLAPTON	3-6	LCC1	3,000	WILKINSON AM	PAYNE HG	FLEMING J	KNIGHT JG
10-Oct	A	WYCOMBE W	2-1	IL		WILKINSON AM	PAYNE HG	FLEMING J	STEVENSON JG
17-Oct	A	LONDON CALEDONIANS	1-4	IL		WILKINSON AM	PAYNE HG	DUBUIS HF	POTTS R
24-Oct	A	DULWICH HAMLET	1-4	IL		WILKINSON AM	PAYNE HG	FLEMING J	SIEWART JG
07-Nov	H	TUFNELL PARK	0-0	IL		WILKINSON AM	DUBUIS HF	FLEMING J	SIEWART JG
14-Nov	H	LONDON CALEDONIANS	2-5	IL		WILKINSON AM	PAYNE HG	FLEMING J	SMITH FV
21-Nov	H	WOKING	1-1	IL		TRAPP CS	PAYNE HG	FLEMING J	HOWELL M
28-Nov	H	CIVIL SERVICE	6-0	IL		TRAPP CS	PAYNE HG	DUBUIS HF	HOWELL M
05-Dec	A	ILFORD	0-1	IL		TRAPP CS	PAYNE HG	FLEMING J	WORCESTER LO
12-Dec	H	ST.ALBANS CITY	2-5	IL		TRAPP CS	PAYNE HG	FLEMING J	GERMAN AC
19-Dec	H	DULWICH HAMLET	2-3	IL		TRAPP CS	PAYNE HG	SMITH FV	WORCESTER LO
02-Jan	A	OXFORD CITY	6-4	AC1		TRAPP CS	PAYNE HG	FLEMING J	KNIGHT JG
09-Jan	A	OXFORD CITY	0-1	AC1R		TRAPP CS	STEVENSON JG	FLEMING J	BODDINGTON HC
23-Jan	A	WOKING	1-6	SSC1		TRAPP CS	SMITH FV	FLEMING J	NAEF C
06-Feb	A	CLAPTON	1-8	IL	3,000	TRAPP CS	DE KOVEN R	FLEMING J	NAEF C
13-Feb	A	TUFNELL PARK	2-0	IL	2,000	TRAPP CS	FLEMING J	PIPER HF	BULMAN BM
20-Feb	H	OXFORD CITY	4-2	IL		TRAPP CS	SMITH FV	FLEMING J	WORCESTER LO
27-Feb	H	WYCOMBE W	1-1	IL		TRAPP CS	STEVENSON JG	FLEMING J	KNIGHT JG
06-Mar	A	LEYTONSTONE	1-2	IL		TRAPP CS	PIPER HF	FLEMING J	WORCESTER LO
13-Mar	H	CLAPTON	0-1	IL		TRAPP CS	FLEMING J	PIPER HF	KNIGHT JG
17-Mar	A	KINGSTONIAN	2-4	SCS1		JEACOCKE A	STEVENSON JG	BOWER AG	SANDERS FR
20-Mar	A	LEYTONSTONE	1-2	IL		TRAPP CS	FLEMING J	PIPER HF	WORCESTER LO
27-Mar	A	ST.ALBANS CITY	4-1	IL		RUSSELL AM	SMITH FV	PIPER HF	WORCESTER LO
17-Apr	H	ILFORD	3-2	IL		TRAPP CS	DE KOVEN R	PIPER HF	ANTILL DS
22-Apr	A	OXFORD CITY	1-2	IL		WILKINSON AM	FRIZZELL FG	PART CK	SIEWART JG
24-Apr	A	CIVIL SERVICE	5-3	IL		TRAPP CS	DE KOVEN R	PIPER HF	ANTILL DS

Friendly Matches

DATE	VEN	OPPONENTS	RES	COMP	ATT	1	2	3	4
31-Oct	H	OXFORD UNIVERSITY	1-3	F	5,000	WILKINSON MA	PAYNE HG	FLEMING J	SIEWART JG
18-Nov	H	CAMBRIDGE UNIV	0-3	F		JEACOCK A	SMITH FV	FLEMING J	LINDSAY KM
16-Dec	H	LONDON UNIVERSITY	1-4	F		MCBRIDE WN	MILLER GC	FRIZZELL FG	ANTILL DS
06-Jan	H	PUBLIC SCHOOLS XI	8-2	F		JEACOCKE A	COUCHMAN RH	SIEWART JG	BODDINGTON HC
30-Jan	A	CAMBRIDGE UNIV	2-1	F		JEACOCKE A	DE KOVEN R	FLEMING J	NAEF C
04-Mar	A	OXFORD UNIVERSITY	3-3	F		HAMMOND 1	HEPBURN SF 1	COUCH 1	

1926 - Tour to Portugal

DATE	VEN	OPPONENTS	RES	COMP	ATT	1	2	3	4
02-Apr	A	BENFICA	3-1	F					
03-Apr	A	VITORIA	0-2	F					
04-Apr	A	SPORTING LISBON	2-2	F					

5	6	7	8	9	10	11
PARTRIDGE GB 1	EWER FH	PARKER CA 1	HOWELL M	MAYER ER	DOGGART AG 1	PINFIELD RG
KNIGHT JG	EWER FH	PARKER CA	DUBUIS HF	HOWELL M 2	DOGGART AG	HAMMOND LG
KNIGHT JG	EWER FH	LOWE DGA	HOWELL M	ASHTON CT 1	DOGGART AG	SMITH FV
PARTRIDGE GB	SANDERS FR	LOWE DGA	KNIGHT JG	BAXTER	LOCKTON JH	SMITH FV
PARTRIDGE GB	EWER FH	LOWE DGA	SMITH JG	ASHTON CT 1	DOGGART AG 1	PINFIELD RG
PARTRIDGE GB	STEVENSON JG	PARKER CA	HOWELL M	ASHTON CT 2	DOGGART AG 1	PINFIELD RG
KNIGHT JG	EWER FH	BARKER AR 2	SLEIGHTHOLME CH	WEIGHTMAN H	DOGGART AG	PINFIELD RG
KNIGHT JG	PLAISTOWE FH	BARKER AR	SLEIGHTHOLME CH	WATSON GS	HOWELL M 1	PINFIELD RG
KNIGHT JG	BULMAN BM	LINDSAY KM	SLEIGHTHOLME CH	WATSON GS	HOWELL M 1	RYDER TA
KNIGHT JG	LOCKTON JH	LINDSAY KM	SLEIGHTHOLME CH	WATSON GS	HOWELL M	PINFIELD RG
KNIGHT JG	DUBUIS HF	HOWELL M	SLEIGHTHOLME CH	ROWLEY R	WATSON GS 2	PINFIELD RG
KNIGHT JG	LOCKTON JH	SLEIGHTHOLME CH	BARKER AR	ROWLEY R 1	WATSON GS	PINFIELD RG
KNIGHT JG	MILLER GC	LOWE DGA	BARKER AR 2	PART CK 2	WATSON GS 1	PINFIELD RG 1
KNIGHT JG	DUBUIS HF	SLEIGHTHOLME CH	BARKER AR	PART CK	WATSON GS	HOWELL M
KNIGHT JG	WORCESTER LO	SLEIGHTHOLME CH	BARKER AR 1	PART CK 1	HOWELL M	PINFIELD RG
TREISMAN WB	FRIZZELL FG	LINDSAY KM	KNIGHT JG 2	WILLIAMS LS	HAMMOND LG	PINFIELD RG
GERMAN AC	HARWOOD J	SLEIGHTHOLME CH 4	BARKER AR 1	PIPER HF 1	DOGGART AG	PINFIELD RG
PARTRIDGE GB	FRIZZELL FG	HOWELL M	BARKER AR	SLEIGHTHOLME CH	KNIGHT JG	PINFIELD RG
KNIGHT JG	FRIZZELL FG	HEPBURN SF	STEVENSON JG	WILLIAMS LS	HOWELL M 1	RYDER TA
KNIGHT JG	STEVENSON JG	SLEIGHTHOLME CH 1	BARKER AR	WILLIAMS LS	WATSON GS	PINFIELD RG
BOSWELL FT	HARWOOD J	SLEIGHTHOLME CH 2	KNIGHT JG	WATSON GS	LOWE DGA	PINFIELD RG
KNIGHT JG 1	HARWOOD J	LOWE DGA 1	SLEIGHTHOLME CH 1	WILLIAMS LS 1	HAMMOND LG	PINFIELD RG
GERMAN AC	EWER FH	LOWE DGA	SLEIGHTHOLME CH	PARTRIDGE GB	HAMMOND LG	PINFIELD RG 1
GERMAN AC 1	STEVENSON JG	LOCKTON JH	KNIGHT JG	HAMMOND LG	COUCH DH	PINFIELD RG
GERMAN AC	SANDERS FR	PARKER CA	SLEIGHTHOLME CH	WATSON GS	STEVENSON JG	PINFIELD RG
GERMAN AC 1	FRIZZELL FG	HEPBURN SF	PARKER CA	KNIGHT JG 1	LOWE DGA	PIPER HF
KNIGHT JG 1	FRIZZELL FG	PARKER CA	SLEIGHTHOLME CH	FISH AFB	HOLLAND LT	RYDER TA
GERMAN AC	SANDERS FR	PARKER CA	SLEIGHTHOLME CH	KNIGHT JG 2	COUCH DH 1	PINFIELD RG 1
GERMAN AC 2	SANDERS FR	PARKER CA 1	BARKER AR	KNIGHT JG	COUCH DH	PINFIELD RG
KNIGHT JG	EWER FH	PARKER CA	SLEIGHTHOLME CH	PARTRIDGE GB 1	COUCH DH	FISH AFB
KNIGHT JG	EWER FH	PARKER CA	BARKER AR	SLEIGHTHOLME CH	STEVENSON JG 4	PINFIELD RG 1

5	6	7	8	9	10	11
KNIGHT JG	BULMAN BM	LINDSAY K	SLEIGHTHOLME CH 1	WATSON GS	HOWELL M	PINFIELD RG
KNIGHT JG	CLARK R	HEPBURN SF	SLEIGHTHOLME CH	ROWLEY R	WATSON GS	PINFIELD RG
KNIGHT JG	BODDINGTON HC	MAYER ER	CRUIKSHANK WR	DOGGART AG 1	JEACOCKS J	LINDSAY KM
LOCKTON JH	FRIZZELL FG	HEPBURN SF	MAXWELL TA	WILLIAMS LS 6	HARWOOD CS	WATSON GS 2
KNIGHT JG	FRIZZELL FG	LOWE DGA	BARKER AR 2	WILLIAMS LS	WATSON GS	PINFIELD RG

5	6	7	8	9	10	11

1926/27

DATE	VEN	OPPONENTS	RES	COMP	ATT	1	2	3	4
04-Sep	H	KINGSTONIAN	2-3	SCS1	3,000	TRAPP CS	FRIZZELL FG	PIPER HF	SANDERS FR
11-Sep	A	CLAPTON	2-1	IL		TRAPP CS	FRIZZELL FG	PIPER HF	SANDERS FR
16-Sep	A	DULWICH HAMLET	3-3	IL	%	RUSSELL AM	FRIZZELL FG	SMITH FV	ANTILL DS
25-Sep	H	DULWICH HAMLET	1-0	IL		TRAPP CS	FRIZZELL FG	PIPER HF	ANTILL DS
09-Oct	A	OXFORD CITY	1-7	IL		TRAPP CS	FRIZZELL FG	ANTILL DS	BODDINGTON HC
16-Oct	A	WYCOMBE W	1-3	IL		WILLIAMS AW	ASHTON NC	PIPER HF	BODDINGTON HC
23-Oct	H	LEYTONSTONE	3-3	IL		TRAPP CS	ASHTON NC	PIPER HF	ANTILL DS
06-Nov	A	TUFNELL PARK	1-4	IL		WILLIAMS AW	DE KOVEN R	PIPER HF	WORCESTER BL
13-Nov	H	ST.ALBANS CITY	1-13	IL		WILLIAMS AW	ASHTON NC	PIPER HF	BARNIE-ADSHEAD WR
20-Nov	A	ILFORD	1-3	IL		TRAPP CS	FRIZZELL FG	PIPER HF	ANTILL DS
27-Nov	H	WYCOMBE W	1-3	IL		TRAPP CS	FRIZZELL FG	PIPER HF	ANTILL DS
04-Dec	H@	ILFORD	1-7	IL		WILLIAMS AW	FRIZZELL FG	PIPER HF	WORCESTER BL
18-Dec	H	TUFNELL PARK	2-0	IL		COLDHAM JM	FRIZZELL FG	SMITH FV	VAN DER BORGH M
01-Jan	H	HAMPSTEAD TOWN	3-3	AC1		TRAPP CS	FRIZZELL FG	SMITH FV	ROBINSON HF
08-Jan	A	HAMPSTEAD TOWN	3-2	AC1r		TRAPP CS	SMITH FV	PIPER HF	STEVENSON JG
15-Jan	A	PORTLAND UNITED	3-2	AC2	2,000	RUSSELL AM	STEVENSON JG	PIPER HF	WHEWELL WT
22-Jan	A	SUTTON UNITED	1-3	SSC		TRAPP CS	FRIZZELL FG	SMITH FV	VAN DER BORGH M
05-Feb	H	CLAPTON	3-4	IL		RUSSELL AM	FRIZZELL FG	PAXTON GN	VAN DER BORGH M
12-Feb	A	SOUTHALL	2-4	AC3		RUSSELL AM	STEVENSON JG	SMITH RW	WHEWELL WT
19-Feb	H	CIVIL SERVICE	1-0	IL		RUSSELL AM	SMITH FV	SMITH RW	VAN DER BORGH M
05-Mar	A	LONDON CALEDONIANS	1-2	IL		TRAPP CS	STEVENSON JG	SMITH FV	VAN DER BORGH M
12-Mar	A	LEYTONSTONE	1-3	IL		RUSSELL AM	FRIZZELL FG	SMITH FV	VAN DER BORGH M
26-Mar	A	CIVIL SERVICE	2-1	IL		TRAPP CS	FRIZZELL FG	FELLOWES AE	WORCESTER BL
02-Apr	H	WIMBLEDON	2-1	IL		MCBRIDE WN	FRIZZELL FG	VAN DER BORGH M	FELLOWES AE
09-Apr	H	OXFORD CITY	1-0	IL		MCBRIDE WN	FRIZZELL FG	HESLOP RH	VAN DER BORGH M
13-Apr	A	WOKING	1-2	IL		MCBRIDE WN	FRIZZELL FG	BOWER AG	BULMAN BM
21-Apr	A	ST.ALBANS CITY	1-3	IL		MCBRIDE WN	STEVENSON JG	FRIZZELL FG	VAN DER BORGH M
25-Apr	H	LONDON CALEDONIANS	3-2	IL		TRAPP CS	FRIZZELL FG	BOWER AG	BULMAN BM
27-Apr	H	WOKING	1-1	IL		BENNETT CT	FRIZZELL FG	SMITH FV	VAN DER BORGH M
28-Apr	A	NUNHEAD	0-6	IL		RUSSELL AM	SERGEANT PA	ANTILL DS	VAN DER BORGH M
02-May	H	NUNHEAD	1-2	IL		WAKEFORD RP	FRIZZELL FG	COLEBROOK D	VAN DER BORGH M
07-May	A	WIMBLEDON	1-4	IL		TRAPP CS	FELLOWES AE	COLEBROOK D	ANTILL DS

Friendly Matches

DATE	VEN	OPPONENTS	RES	COMP	ATT	1	2	3	4
30-Oct	H	OXFORD UNIVERSITY	2-2	F		TRAPP CS	DE KOVEN R	PIPER HF	BODDINGTON HC
17-Nov	H	CAMBRIDGE UNIV	4-5	F		BENNETT CT	DE KOVEN R	BIRD E	BODDINGTON HC
16-Dec	H	LONDON UNIVERSITY	3-6	F	%				
05-Jan	H	PUBLIC SCHOOLS XI	4-3	F	%	HILDER AL	SERGEANT PA	BIRD E	WATTS MA
19-Mar	A	FINCHLEY	0-3	F		BENNETT CT	FRIZZELL FG	IRWIN HC	VAN DER BORGH M

5	6	7	8	9	10	11
KNIGHT JG	EWER FH	PARKER CA	BARKER AR 1	VAN DER BORGH M	FISH AFB	COUCH DH 1
GERMAN AC	EWER FH	PARKER CA 1	CREEK FNS 1	KNIGHT JG	BARKER AR	COUCH DH
KNIGHT JG	EWER FH	PARKER CA	BARKER AR	CREEK FNS	VAN DEN BORGH M	COUCH DH
GERMAN AC	SANDERS FR	PARKER CA	BARKER AR	KNIGHT JG	JANSEN A	COUCH DH 1
KNIGHT JG	EWER FH	PARKER CA	BARKER AR	WATSON GS	STEVENSON JG	COUCH DH 1
BARNIE-ADSHEAD WR	FRIZZELL FG	PARKER CA	KNIGHT JG	JANSEN A	COUCH DH 1	PINFIELD RG
BARNIE-ADSHEAD WR	FRIZZELL FG	SLEIGHTHOLME CH	PARKER CA 1	KNIGHT JG	JANSEN A 2	PINFIELD RG
BARNIE-ADSHEAD WR	ANTILL DS	PARKER CA	BARKER AR	JANSEN A	COUCH DH	SMITH FV 1
KNIGHT JG	FRIZZELL FG	SLEIGHTHOLME CH	PARKER CA	BARKER AR	JANSEN A 1	COUCH DH
KNIGHT JG	BARNIE-ADSHEAD WR	BARKER AR 1	COUCH DH	WORCESTER BL	JANSEN A	PINFIELD RG
GERMAN AC	BARNIE-ADSHEAD WR	BARKER AR	COUCH DH	WORCESTER BL 1	JANSEN A	PINFIELD RG
KNIGHT JG	BARNIE-ADSHEAD WR	LOWE RGH	BARKER AR	BARKER JT 1	COUCH DH	PINFIELD RG
SANDERS FR	WORCESTER BL	ZABELL NF	PARKER CA	PIPER HF 1	COUCH DH	PINFIELD RG 1
SANDERS FR	STEVENSON JG	PARKER CA	KNIGHT JG	ROBINS RM 3	COUCH DH	PIPER HF
WHEWELL WT	SANDERS FR	FRIZZELL FG 1	KNIGHT JG	ROBINS RM 2	COUCH DH	PINFIELD RG
GERMAN AC	SANDERS FR	SLEIGHTHOLME CH	KNIGHT JG 2	ROBINS RM 1	COUCH DH	PINFIELD RG
GERMAN AC	KNIGHT JG	HEPBURN SF	MAXWELL TA	LOCKTON JH	JEACOCKE A 1	COUCH DH
PLAISTOWE FH	WORCESTER BL	SLEIGHTHOLME CH 1	WILLIAMS LC 1	KNIGHT JG	COUCH DH	PINFIELD RG
GERMAN AC	EWER FH	ROBINS RM	FLETCHER GS 2	KNIGHT JG	LOWE RGH	COUCH DH
SANDERS FR	FRIZZELL FG	SLEIGHTHOLME CH	JANSEN A	WATSON GS	FLETCHER GS 1	GREENSTOCK JW
KNIGHT JG	FRIZZELL FG	BARKER AR	PARKER CA 1	SLEIGHTHOLME CH	FLETCHER GS	JANSEN A
KNIGHT JG	BULMAN BM	BARKER AR	PARKER CA	SLEIGHTHOLME CH 1	MACE N	JANSEN A
SANDERS FR	BULMAN BM	PARKER CA	KNIGHT JG	SLEIGHTHOLME CH 1	JANSEN A	JANSEN A
KNIGHT JG	BULMAN BM	MAYER ER	ROBINS RM 1	SLEIGHTHOLME CH 1	FLETCHER GS	CRUMP RD
KNIGHT JG	BULMAN BM	SLEIGHTHOLME CH	WILLIAMS LC	MAYER ER 1	MACE N	BUSH JT
GERMAN AC	EWER FH	SLEIGHTHOLME CH	VAN DER BORGH M	KNIGHT JG 1	MACE N	BUSH JT
EWER FH	BULMAN BM	SLEIGHTHOLME CH	KNIGHT JG	MAYER ER 1	MACE N	JANSEN A
KNIGHT JG 1	EWER FH	PARKER CA	VAN DER BORGH M	STEVENSON JG 2	MACE N	JANSEN A
EWER FH	BULMAN BM	PARKER CA	KNIGHT JG 1	STEVENSON JG	MACE N	JANSEN A
KNIGHT JG	MAXWELL TA	HEPBURN SF	WILLIAMS LC	BARKER AR	JANSEN A	ZABELL NF
ANTILL DS	PLAISTOWE FH	MAXWELL TA	KNIGHT JG	SOOLE AS	WILLIAMS LC 1	CRUMP RD
KNIGHT JG	BULMAN BM	WORCESTER BL	WILLIAMS LC	BAKER J	WATSON GS	CRUMP RD 1

5	6	7	8	9	10	11
KNIGHT JG	FRIZZELL FG 1	PARKER CA	BARKER AR	JANSEN A 1	COUCH DH	PINFIELD RG
BARNIE-ADSHEAD WR	ANTILL DS	PARKER CA	MORRIS RJ	COUCH DH 1	JANSEN A 3	SMITH FV
ANTILL DS	LOCKTON JH	HEPBURN SF	DOGGRELL D	GENDER CH 2	STOW RM	CRUMP RD
ANTILL DS	BULMAN BM	PARKER CA	MAXWELL TA	LOCKTON JH	MACE N	JANSEN A

1927/28

DATE	VEN	OPPONENTS	RES	COMP	ATT	1	2	3	4
03-Sep	H	WOKING	4-1	SCS1		TRAPP CS	FRIZZELL FG	MIDDLEBOE N	BULMAN BM
08-Sep	A	NUNHEAD	3-2	IL		MCBRIDE WN	HESLOP RH	FRIZZELL FG	BULMAN BM
14-Sep	H	KINGSTONIAN	1-2	CC	og	MCBRIDE WN	FRIZZELL FG	STEVENSON JG	VAN DER BORGH M
17-Sep	A	WIMBLEDON	2-3	IL		MCBRIDE WN	FRIZZELL FG	STEVENSON JG	VAN DER BORGH M
22-Sep	A	LONDON CALEDONIANS	1-0	IL	og	MCBRIDE WN	FRIZZELL FG	MORRIS AE	VAN DER BORGH M
24-Sep	A	CLAPTON	4-4	IL		MCBRIDE WN	FRIZZELL FG	FELLOWES AE	VAN DER BORGH M
28-Sep	H	LONDON CALEDONIANS	0-0	IL		MCBRIDE WN	FRIZZELL FG	MORRIS AE	VAN DER BORGH M
01-Oct	H	NUNHEAD	1-3	LCC1		MCBRIDE WN	FRIZZELL FG	HESLOP RH	VAN DER BORGH M
08-Oct	A	CIVIL SERVICE	2-4	IL		MCBRIDE WN	FRIZZELL FG	HESLOP RH	VAN DER BORGH M
15-Oct	H	DULWICH HAMLET	2-2	IL		MCBRIDE WN	FRIZZELL FG	COLEBROOK D	GLENISTER CE
22-Oct	A	WOKING	1-2	IL		TRAPP CS	FRIZZELL FG	HESLOP RH	GLENISTER CE
05-Nov	A	TUFNELL PARK	3-0	IL		TRAPP CS	FRIZZELL FG	IRWIN HC	GLENISTER CE
19-Nov	H	ST.ALBANS CITY	2-5	IL		WAKEFORD RP	FRIZZELL FG	IRWIN HC	GLENISTER CE
03-Dec	A	LEYTONSTONE	0-5	IL		WAKEFORD RP	FRIZZELL FG	IRWIN HC	GLENISTER CE
10-Dec	H	WIMBLEDON	4-3	IL		TRAPP CS	FRIZZELL FG	SMITH FV	GLENISTER CE
17-Dec	A	WYCOMBE W	2-4	IL		WAKEFORD RP	LOMAX D	COLEBROOK D	FRIZZELL FG
31-Dec	A	WOKING	2-2	AC1		TRAPP CS	SNOW PS	LOMAX D	GLENISTER CE
07-Jan	H	WOKING	1-5	AC1r		MCBRIDE WN	SNOW PS	LOMAX D	GLENISTER CE
14-Jan	A	ILFORD	2-5	IL		WAKEFORD RP	FRIZZELL FG	LOMAX D	HERMON J
21-Jan	A	CIVIL SERVICE	8-0	IL		CLOKE HP	SNOW PS	FLEMING J	GLENISTER CE
28-Jan	A	KINGSTONIAN	4-2	SSC1		MCBRIDE WN	LOMAX D	FLEMING J	GLENISTER CE
11-Feb	H	WOKING	2-2	IL		DEUCHAR JD	SNOW PS	LOMAX D	GLENISTER CE
18-Feb	A	WOKING	1-3	SSC2		WILKINSON AM	LOMAX D	SMITH FV	WORCESTER GL
25-Feb	A	ST.ALBANS CITY	2-2	IL		ELLENGOWAN S	SNOW PS	LOMAX D	GLENISTER CE
03-Mar	A	TUFNELL PARK	1-0	IL		BONHAM-CARTER AD	PRITCHARD HK	LOMAX D	BULMAN BM
10-Mar	A	CLAPTON	1-1	IL		TRAPP CS	BOWER MB	FELLOWES AE	FRIZZELL FG
24-Mar	H	OXFORD CITY	1-1	IL		ELLENGOWAN S	LOMAX D	SMITH FV	WILLIAMS LC
31-Mar	A	OXFORD CITY	2-2	IL		ELLENGOWAN S	LOMAX D	SMITH FV	GLENISTER CE
14-Apr	H	TOOTING TOWN	1-3	SCSSF		ELLENGOWAN S	LOMAX D	SMITH FV	WILLIAMS LC
21-Apr	H w	NUNHEAD	6-1	IL		TRAPP CS	LOMAX D	MORRIS AE	BULMAN BM
23-Apr	A	LEYTONSTONE	2-1	IL		ELLENGOWAN S	MORRIS AE	PROBYN FC	VAN DER BORGH M
26-Apr	A	DULWICH HAMLET	0-4	IL		ELLENGOWAN S	MORRIS AE	PROBYN FC	VAN DER BORGH M
03-May	A	ILFORD	0-2	IL		ELLENGOWAN S	FRIZZELL FG	MORRIS AE	WILLIAMS LC
05-May	H @	WYCOMBE W	1-3	IL		ELLEHGOWAN S	FRIZZELL FG	MORRIS AE	WILLIAMS LC

Friendly Matches

DATE	VEN	OPPONENTS	RES	COMP	ATT	1	2	3	4
29-Oct	H	OXFORD UNIVERSITY	3-3	F		BENNETT CT	FRIZZELL FG	HESLOP RH	GLENISTER CE
12-Nov	H	SHEPPEY UNITED	6-0	F	400	MCBRIDE WM	FRIZZELL FG	IRWIN HC	HERMON JS
16-Nov	H	CAMBRIDGE UNIV	1-5	F		BENNETT CT	PROBYN FG	FRIZZEL FG	HERMON JS
26-Nov	A	SITTINGBOURNE	2-3	F		WAKEFORD RP	FRIZZELL FG	IRWIN HC	GLENISTER CE
15-Dec	H	LONDON UNIVERSITY	0-6	F		MCBRIDE WN	SNOW PS	LOMAX D	VAN DER BORGH M
04-Jan	H	PUBLIC SCHOOLS XI	2-1	F		ELLANGOWAN S	EMUS SH	ONIONS CT	VAN DER BORGH M
25-Jan	A	CAMBRIDGE UNIV	2-8	F		BENNETT CT	FLEMING J	SERGEANT PA	VAN DER BERGH M
01-Mar	A	OXFORD UNIVERSITY	3-2	F		BENNETT CT	ENTHOVEN HJ	FIELDMAN A	NICHOLLS H
17-Mar	H	NORTHAMPTON NOMADS	2-4	F		WILKINSON AM	LOMAX D	SMITH FV	FELLOWES AE

1928 - Tour to France

DATE	VEN	OPPONENTS	RES	COMP	ATT	1	2	3	4
06-Apr	A	STADE HARAIS	?-?	F					
08-Apr	A	ROUEN	?-?	F					
09-Apr	A	LE HAVRE ATHLETIC	?-?	F					

5	6	7	8	9	10	11
EWER FH	VAN DER BORGH M	PARKER CA	KNIGHT JG	JENKINS RG 2	GLENISTER CE 2	JANSEN A
EWER FH	VAN DER BORGH M	PARKER CA	KNIGHT JG 2	JENKINS RG	GLENISTER CE 1	JANSEN A
EWER FH	GLENISTER CE	PARKER CA	KNIGHT JG	JENKINS RG	WILLIAMS LC	JANSEN A
EWER FH	SANDERS FR	JENKINS RG 1	KNIGHT JG 1	ROBINS RWV	GLENISTER CE	JANSEN A
KNIGHT JG	GLENISTER CE	PARKER CA	JANSEN A	JENKINS RG	WILLIAMS LC	GENDERS CH
KNIGHT JG	GLENISTER CE	JENKINS RG	TERRY AE 2	ROBINS RWV 1	WILLIAMS LC 1	GENDERS CH
WHEWELL WT	BULMAN BM	JENKINS RG	KNIGHT JG	ROBINS RWV	WILLIAMS LC	JANSEN A
GLENISTER CE	BULMAN BM	TERRY AE	WILLIAMS LC	ROBINS RWV	FLETCHER GS	ZABELL NF 1
KNIGHT JG	BULMAN BM	ROBINS RWV	GLENISTER CE	JENKINS RG 2	FLETCHER GS	ZABELL NF
KNIGHT JG	BULMAN BM	PARKER CA	TERRY AE 1	PRITCHARD HK 1	WILLIAMS LC	COUCH DH
KNIGHT JG	BULMAN BM	PARKER CA	WATSON GS 1	PRITCHARD HK	WILLIAMS LC	JANSEN A
KNIGHT JG	BULMAN BM	VAN DER BORGH M	WATSON GS	GERMAN AC 2	CREE A 1	GALBALLY JW
KNIGHT JG	BULMAN BM	VAN DER BORGH M	WATSON GS 1	GERMAN AC 1	CREE A	COUCH DH
KNIGHT JG	BULMAN BM	VAN DER BORGH M	MASSEY JA	WATSON GS	WILLIAMS LC	GALBALLY JW
KNIGHT JG	BULMAN BM	VAN DER BORGH M	MASSEY JA 1	GERMAN AC 3	WATSON GS	GALBALLY JW
KNIGHT JG	BULMAN BM	VAN DER BORGH M	MASSEY JA 1	HERMON J 1	CREE A	GALBALLY JW
KNIGHT JG	BULMAN BM	JENKINS RG	WATSON GS 1	GERMAN AC 1	MASSEY JA	GALBALLY JW
SANDERS FR	BULMAN BM	VAN DER BORGH M	MASSEY JA	ROBINS RWV	KNIGHT JG 1	GALBALLY JW
KNIGHT JG	BULMAN BM	VAN DER BORGH M	JENKINS RG 2	MAYER ER	MASSEY JA	WATSON GS
KNIGHT JG 1	BULMAN BM	VAN DER BORGH M	JENKINS RG 1	GERMAN AC 5	WATSON GS 1	ACHESON-GRAY
KNIGHT JG	BULMAN BM	VAN DER BORGH M	MASSEY JA 2	GERMAN AC 1	WATSON GS 1	GALBALLY JW
KNIGHT JG	JOHNSON TC	VAN DER BORGH M	MASSEY JA	GERMAN AC 1	WATSON GS 1	GALBALLY JW
GLENISTER CE	FRIZZELL FG	VAN DER BORGH M	MASSEY JA 1	TERRY AE	WATSON GS	SERGEANT PA
KNIGHT JG	BULMAN BM	VAN DER BORGH M	MASSEY JA	GERMAN AC 2	WATSON GS	GALBALLY JW
JOHNSON TC	FRIZZELL FG	BARBER A	MASSEY JA	CREE A 1	WATSON GS	WILLIAMS LC
KNIGHT JG	SANDERS FR	BARBER A	MASSEY JA	GERMAN AC 1	WATSON GS	GALBALLY JW
GLENISTER CE	SANDERS FR	FRIZZELL FG	MASSEY JA	CREE A	WATSON GS 1	JANSEN A
KNIGHT JG	JOHNSON TC	JENKINS RG 1	MASSEY JA	GERMAN AC	WATSON GS 1	GALBALLY JW
JOHNSON TC	WATTS MA	VAN DER BORGH M	MASSEY JA	HERMON J	WATSON GS 1	GALBALLY JW
EWER FH	JOHNSON TC	JENKINS RG 1	MASSEY JA 1	PRICE WF 2	WATSON GS	ISAAC AH 2
EWER FH	PLAISTOWE FH	JENKINS RG	MASSEY JA	PRICE WF	WATSON GS 1	ISAAC AH 1
WOOSNAM M	STEVENSON JG	LINDSAY KM	JANSEN A	JEACOCKE A	WATSON GS	ISAAC AH
GLENISTER CE	WORCESTER GL	JENKINS RG	MASSEY JA	WOOSNAM M	VAN DER BORGH M	ISAAC AH
GLENISTER CE	WORCESTER GL	JENKINS RG	MASSEY JA 1	WOOSNAM M	VAN DER BORGH M	ISAAC AH

5	6	7	8	9	10	11
KNIGHT JG 1	BULMAN BM	VAN DER BORGH	TERRY AE	KEMP MF	MORRIS JR 1	GALBALLY JW 1
GERMAN AC 1	BULMAN BM	VAN DER BORGH 1	WATSON GS 2	CREE A	FLETCHER GS 2	GALBALLY JW
KNIGHT JG	PLAISTOWE FH	VAN DER BORGH	WATSON GS	CREE A 1	MORRIS JR	GALBALLY JW
KNIGHT JG	BULMAN BM	VAN DER BORGH	MASSEY JA 1	GERMAN AC 1	WATSON GS	GALBALLY JW
MANN J	MACE N	HEPBURN S.F	MASSEY JA	GERMAN AC	WATSON GS	GALBALLY WC
HERMAN J	WATTS MA	HEPBURN S.F	WATSON GS 2	ISAAC AH	JEACOCKE A	CRONIN AR
WHEWELL WT	MELLOR PE	HEPBURN S.F	WATSON GS	LOWE RGH 1	JEACOCKE A 1	JANYEN A
FRIZZELL FG	FELLOWS A	HEPBURN S.F 1	MASSEY JA 1	WATSON GS 1	TERRY A	CROUN AR
KNIGHT JG	SANDERS FR	FRIZZELL F.G	MASSEY JA 1	CREE A 1	WATSON GS	GALBALLY JW

5	6	7	8	9	10	11

1928/29

DATE	VEN	OPPONENTS	RES	COMP	ATT	1	2	3	4
06-Sep	A	NUNHEAD	2-0	IL	og	ELLENGOWAN S	LOMAX D	IRVIN HC	BULMAN BM
08-Sep	H	TUFNELL PARK	1-3	IL		ELLENGOWAN S	LOMAX D	IRVIN HC	WILLIAMS LC
12-Sep	H	KINGSTONIAN	2-10	CC		ELLENGOWAN S	MORRIS AE	IRVIN HC	GLENISTER CE
15-Sep	H	ST.ALBANS CITY	4-0	IL		TRAPP CS	LOMAX D	MORRIS AE	GLENISTER CE
19-Sep	H	LONDON CALEDONIANS	0-1	IL		ELLENGOWAN S	LOMAX D	ROBINSON HF	HERMON J
22-Sep	A	DULWICH HAMLET	0-1	IL		ELLENGOWAN S	LOMAX D	COLEBROOK D	GLENISTER CE
27-Sep	A	LONDON CALEDONIANS	1-4	IL		ELLENGOWAN S	LOMAX D	COLEBROOK D	VAN DER BORGH M
29-Sep	H	ILFORD	3-1	IL		ELLENGOWAN S	LOMAX D	COLEBROOK D	GLENISTER CE
06-Oct	A	NUNHEAD	0-4	LCC1		ELLENGOWAN S	LOMAX D	COLEBROOK D	FELLOWES AE
13-Oct	H	LEYTONSTONE	2-4	IL		ELLENGOWAN S	LOMAX D	HESLOP RH	WILLIAMS LC
20-Oct	A	WOKING	2-2	IL		ELLENGOWAN S	HESLOP RH	COLEBROOK D	COOKE T
03-Nov	A	CIVIL SERVICE	6-3	IL		ELLENGOWAN S	BOWER MB	COOKE T	GLENISTER CE 1
10-Nov	A	LEYTONSTONE	2-4	IL		ELLENGOWAN S	ENTHOVEN HJ	COLEBROOK D	COOKE T
24-Nov	A	CLAPTON	1-5	IL		ELLENGOWAN S	ENTHOVEN HJ	FELLOWES AE	FRIZZELL FG
01-Dec	A	OXFORD CITY	1-7	IL		WAKEFORD RP	FRIZZELL FG	BARKER JT	WILLIAMS LC
08-Dec	H	WYCOMBE W	1-1	IL		WAKEFORD RP	WATSON GS	FELLOWES AE	GLENISTER CE
15-Dec	A	SOUTHWICK	2-2	AC1		TRAPP CS	LOMAX D	COOKE T	BULMAN BM
22-Dec	A	SOUTHWICK	2-3	AC1r		TRAPP CS	LOMAX D	LOMAX D	EWER FH
29-Dec	A	ILFORD	7-6	IL		BONHAM-CARTER AD	COOKE T	LOMAX D	MASSEY JA
05-Jan	A	KINGSTONIAN	0-1	SCS1		BONHAM-CARTER AD	SNOW RJ	STEVENSON JG	WILLIAMS LC
19-Jan	H	WOKING	0-2	IL		GARLAND-WELLS HM	LOMAX D	STEVENSON JG	WILLIAMS LC
26-Jan	H	KEW ASSOCIATION	7-0	SSC1	og	GARLAND-WELLS HM	MORRIS AE	IRWIN HC	WILLIAMS LC
02-Feb	A	CLAPTON	4-2	IL		GARLAND-WELLS HM	BOWER MB	LOMAX D	WILLIAMS LC
09-Feb	H	WIMBLEDON	0-3	IL		GARLAND-WELLS HM	LOMAX D	MORRIS AE	WILLIAMS LC
16-Feb	H	EPSOM TOWN	1-3	SSC2		GARLAND-WELLS HM	MORRIS AE	IRWIN HC	WILLIAMS LC
23-Feb	A	WIMBLEDON	1-1	IL		GARLAND-WELLS HM	LOMAX D	MORRIS AE	WILLIAMS LC
02-Mar	H	NUNHEAD	1-2	IL		GARLAND-WELLS HM	BOWER MB	MORRIS AE	WILLIAMS LC
16-Mar	H	TUFNELL PARK	3-2	IL		GARLAND-WELLS HM	LOMAX D	MORRIS AE	WILLIAMS LC
23-Mar	A	WYCOMBE W	0-0	IL		GARLAND-WELLS HM	MORRIS AE	IRWIN HC	WILLIAMS LC
20-Apr	A	ST.ALBANS CITY	2-3	IL		GARLAND-WELLS HM	LOMAX D	MORRIS AE	GLENISTER CE
27-Apr	H	OXFORD CITY	4-0	IL		BONHAM-CARTER AD	MORRIS AE	PROBYN FC	WILLIAMS LC
01-May	H	CIVIL SERVICE	0-0	IL		BONHAM-CARTER AD	PROBYN FC	PLAISTOWE FH	WILLIAMS LC
04-May	H	DULWICH HAMLET	1-3	IL		BONHAM-CARTER AD	PROBYN FC	IRWIN HC	WILLIAMS LC

Friendly Matches

DATE	VEN	OPPONENTS	RES	COMP	ATT	1	2	3	4
27-Oct	A	OXFORD UNIVERSITY	5-1	F		ELENGORN B	FELLOWES AE	ENTHOVEN HJ	GLENISTER CE
15-Nov	H	LONDON UNIVERSITY	1-3	F		HILDER AL	WILKINSON WF	SNOW PS	BARBER A
17-Nov	W	CAMBRIDGE UNIV	2-5	F		TRAPP CS	ENTHOVEN HJ	FELLOWES AE	GLENISTER CE
02-Jan	H	PUBLIC SCHOOLS XI	5-1	F		BONHAM-CARTER AD	WATSON GS	WATTS MA	VAN DER BORGH M

5	6	7	8	9	10	11
EWER FH	KNIGHT JG	SANDERS FR	VAN DER BORGH M	FABIAN AH	JENKINS RG 1	ISAAC AH
SANDERS FR	BULMAN BM	VAN DER BORGH M	MASSEY JA	JENKINS RG 1	WATSON GS	ISAAC AH
EWER FH	BULMAN BM	VAN DER BORGH M	MASSEY JA	JENKINS RG	WATSON GS 1	ISAAC AH 1
KNIGHT JG	EWER FH	JENKINS RG	FABIAN AH 1	CREEK FNS 2	WATSON GS 1	ISAAC AH
EWER FH	BULMAN BM	JENKINS RG	FABIAN AH	WATSON GS	MASSEY JA	ISAAC AH
KNIGHT JG	HERMON J	LOWE DGA	FABIAN AH	HESLOP RH	WATSON GS	SMITH FV
HERMON J	BULMAN BM	FABIAN AH 1	JENKINS RG	LOWE RGH	WATSON GS	SMITH FV
KNIGHT JG	EWER FH	ROBINS RWV	JENKINS RG	GERMAN AC 3	WATSON GS	ISAAC AH
KNIGHT JG	EWER FH	VAN DER BORGH M	JENKINS RG	GERMAN AC	WATSON GS	ISAAC AH
JOHNSON TC	BULMAN BM	FRIZZELL FG	VAN DER BORGH M	WATSON GS	JEACOCKE A 1	SMITH FV 1
PLAISTOWE FH	BULMAN BM	FRIZZELL FG	PRICE WF 1	LOWE RGH 1	WATSON GS	SMITH FV
JOHNSON TC 1	BULMAN BM	WATSON GS 1	MASSEY JA 2	MORRIS JR 1	FLETCHER GS	ISAAC AH
BULMAN BM 1	WILLIAMS LC	WATSON GS	PRICE WF	LOWE RGH 1	FLETCHER GS	MASSEY JA
KNIGHT JG	BULMAN BM	WATSON GS	MASSEY JA	MORRIS JR	FLETCHER GS	WHEELER F 1
YOUD CS	BULMAN BM	WATSON GS	FABIAN AH	MASSEY JA	CRUMP RD	WHEELER F 1
KNIGHT JG 1	BULMAN BM	SLEIGHTHOLME CH	CREE A	LOWE RGH	FLETCHER GS	WHEELER F
KNIGHT JG	EWER FH	FABIAN AH	JENKINS RG	LOWE RGH	FLETCHER GS 2	WATSON GS
KNIGHT JG 1	BULMAN BM	JENKINS RG	CREEK FNS	GERMAN AC 1	LOWE RGH	VAN DER BORGH M
WHEWELL WT	BULMAN BM	FABIAN AH 1	KEMP-WELCH GD	LOWE RGH 2	FLETCHER GS 2	WATSON GS 2
BOWER MB	BULMAN BM	FABIAN AH	MASSEY JA	REEVES FK	JEACOCKE A	WATSON GS
ROSS T	BULMAN BM	FABIAN AH	PRICE WF	GERMAN AC	MASSEY JA	WATSON GS
SOPER MR	BULMAN BM	WATSON GS 1	MASSEY JA 2	LOCKTON JH 1	CREE A 1	WHEELER F 1
JOHNSON TC	BULMAN BM	FABIAN AH 1	MASSEY JA 1	KEMP-WELCH GD 2	FLETCHER GS	WHEELER F
KNIGHT JG	BULMAN BM	WATSON GS	MASSEY JA	LOWE RGH	CREE A	MASTERS A
SOPER MR	BULMAN BM	WATSON GS	MASSEY JA	LOWE RGH	FLETCHER GS 1	WHEELER F
EWER FH	BULMAN BM	ROBINS RWV	STEVENSON JG	HALLOWS EH 1	WATSON GS	WHEELER F
KNIGHT JG	JOHNSON TC	JANSEN A	STEVENSON JG 1	KEMP-WELCH GD	FLETCHER GS	COLLINS GAK
SOPER MR	STEVENSON JG	WATSON GS	MASSEY JA 1	LINGLEBACH WE	KEMP-WELCH GD 2	COLLINS GAK
GLENISTER CE	BULMAN BM	WATSON GS	KNIGHT JG	SLEIGHTHOLME CH	DOGGART AG	WHEELER F
KNIGHT JG	BULMAN BM	STEVENSON JG	WILLIAMS LC	SLEIGHTHOLME CH 1	MASSEY JA 1	WHEELER F
GLENISTER CE	BULMAN BM	STEVENSON JG	MASSEY JA 1	SLEIGHTHOLME CH 2	KNIGHT JG 1	WHEELER F
ROSS T	BROCKLESBY SV	STEVENSON JG	MASSEY JA	WOOSNAM M	KNIGHT JG	COLLINS GAK
GLENISTER CE	BULMAN BM	BARKER JT	MASSEY JA 1	ROSS T	KNIGHT JG	FRIZZELL FG

5	6	7	8	9	10	11
KNIGHT JG	BULMAN BM	WATSON GS	FORDER CP 2	LOWE RGH 2	MORRIS JR 1	ISAAC AH
HERMON J	FRANCIS WL	HEPBURN SF	FABIAN AH 1	JEACOCKE A	MASTERS ML	WATSON GS
KNIGHT JG	BULMAN BM	FABIAN AH	PRICE WF	LOWE RGH 1	FLETCHER GS	WATSON GS 1
SOPER WG	INGALL J	HEPBURN SF	FABIAN AH 1	LOCKTON JH 2	KEMP-WELCH GD 2	JEACOCKE A

1929/30

DATE	VEN	OPPONENTS	RES	COMP	ATT	1	2	3	4
05-Sep	A	NUNHEAD	0-1	IL		GARLAND-WELLS HM	MORRIS AE	EVANS FL	WILLIAMS LC
07-Sep	H	CLAPTON	5-0	IL	1,000	GARLAND-WELLS HM	TURNBULL JR	MORRIS AE	GLENISTER CE
11-Sep	H	KINGSTONIAN	1-2	CC		GARLAND-WELLS HM	TURNBULL JR	SOPER MR	WILLIAMS LC
14-Sep	A	WYCOMBE W	2-3	IL		GARLAND-WELLS HM	EVANS FL	MORRIS AE	GLENISTER CE
19-Sep	A	LONDON CALEDONIANS	0-1	IL		GARLAND-WELLS HM	TURNBULL JR	MORRIS AE	GLENISTER CE
21-Sep	H	LONDON CALEDONIANS	5-0	IL		GARLAND-WELLS HM	MORRIS AE	KNIGHT JG	GLENISTER CE
28-Sep	A	KINGSTONIAN	1-1	SCS1		GARLAND-WELLS HM	LOMAX D	MORRIS AE	WILLIAMS LC
05-Oct	A	DULWICH HAMLET	2-2	LCC1		GARLAND-WELLS HM	BOWER MB	MORRIS AE	GLENISTER CE
12-Oct	A	ST.ALBANS CITY	2-2	IL		GARLAND-WELLS HM	KNIGHT AE	FLEMING J	GLENISTER CE
19-Oct	H	KINGSTONIAN	1-2	IL		RUSSELL AM	KNIGHT AE	FLEMING J	GLENISTER CE
02-Nov	A	OXFORD CITY	1-3	IL		RUSSELL AM	MORRIS AE	FLEMING J	GLENISTER CE
06-Nov	H	DULWICH HAMLET	0-4	LCC1r		MACKENZIE NI	COOPER EH	MALYON RT	MANDER AW
09-Nov	H	TUFNELL PARK	1-1	IL		RUSSELL AM	MORRIS AE	FLEMING J	GLENISTER CE
23-Nov	A	DULWICH HAMLET	2-2	IL		RUSSELL AM	STEVENSON JG	MORRIS AE	GLENISTER CE
27-Nov	H	KINGSTONIAN	0-2	SCS1r		COBB BB	LIEPER W	BARKER JT	DIXON GH
30-Nov	A	LEYTONSTONE	5-2	IL		RUSSELL AM	KNIGHT AE	MORRIS AE	BULMAN BM
07-Dec	H	WYCOMBE W	2-2	IL		RUSSELL AM	KNIGHT AE	MORRIS AE	GLENISTER CE
14-Dec	H @	DULWICH HAMLET	0-4	AC1		RUSSELL AM	COOCH RH	MORRIS AE	CREE A
21-Dec	A	ILFORD	0-7	IL		RUSSELL AM	KNIGHT AE	SERGEANT	WILLIAMS LC
28-Dec	H	WIMBLEDON	2-3	IL		RUSSELL AM	KNIGHT AE	EVANS FL	BRYANT BE 2
04-Jan	A	KINGSTONIAN	1-1	IL		RUSSELL AM	KNIGHT AE	EVANS FL	STEVENSON JG
18-Jan	A	CLAPTON	1-2	IL		RUSSELL AM	KNIGHT AE	MORRIS AE	BARBER HN
25-Jan	H	MITCHAM WANDERERS	2-1	SSC1	og	RUSSELL AM	STEVENSON JG	MORRIS AE	WILLIAMS LC
01-Feb	H	ILFORD	5-3	IL		RUSSELL AM	KNIGHT AE	MORRIS AE	WILLIAMS LC
08-Feb	A	TUFNELL PARK	1-0	IL		RUSSELL AM	KNIGHT AE	MORRIS AE	LING KS
15-Feb	H	OXFORD CITY	2-1	IL		RUSSELL AM	MORRIS AE	STEVENSON JG	WILLIAMS LC
22-Feb	H	TOOTING TOWN	6-1	SSC2		RUSSELL AM	STEVENSON JG	MORRIS AE	SOPER M
01-Mar	H	ST.ALBANS CITY	1-0	IL		RUSSELL AM	STEVENSON JG	MORRIS AE	GLENISTER CE
08-Mar	A	WOKING	1-3	IL		RUSSELL AM	KNIGHT AE	MORRIS AE	GLENISTER CE
22-Mar	A	KINGSTONIAN	3-2	SSCsf		RUSSELL AM	KNIGHT AE	MORRIS AE	GLENISTER CE
29-Mar	H	WOKING	2-2	IL		RUSSELL AM	KNIGHT AE	MORRIS AE	WILLIAMS LC
12-Apr	H	LEYTONSTONE	5-3	IL	og	RUSSELL AM	EVANS FL	MORRIS AE	HORNE
16-Apr	H	NUNHEAD	1-1	IL		RUSSELL AM	EVANS FL	MORRIS AE	WILLIAMS LC
21-Apr	A	WARMINSTER	5-1	WCC					
26-Apr	H	DULWICH HAMLET	2-3	IL		RUSSELL AM	TURNBULL JR	MORRIS AE	LING KS
03-May	A	WIMBLEDON	0-3	IL		RUSSELL AM	MORRIS AE	EVANS FL	TIDSWELL GH
10-May	N g	NUNHEAD	2-1	SSCf	3,000	RUSSELL AM	STEVENSON JG	EVANS FL	LING KS

Friendly Matches

DATE	VEN	OPPONENTS	RES	COMP	ATT	1	2	3	4
26-Oct	H	OXFORD UNIVERSITY	1-3	F		RUSSELL AM	SNOW PS	MORRIS AE	WILLIAMS LC
14-Nov	H	LONDON UNIVERSITY	2-4	F		LEAVER KM	MERCER H	SMITH FB	LING KS
16-Nov	H	CAMBRIDGE UNIV	1-8	F	og	RUSSELL AM	MORRIS AE	KNIGHT AE	FLEMING J
01-Jan	H	PUBLIC SCHOOLS XI	3-0	F		LISTER BB	BARKER JT	SOPER MR	BRYANT BE
21-Jan	A	CAMBRIDGE UNIV	1-6	F		HILDER AL	BARKER JT	RUMSEY C	MELLOR PEM
27-Feb	A	OXFORD UNIVERSITY	3-1	F					
15-Mar	A	HITCHIN TOWN	0-4	F		BROWN W	STEVENSON J	MORRIS AE	GLENISTER CE

5	6	7	8	9	10	11
EWER FH	BULMAN BM	FABIAN AH	BARBER HN	JENKINS RG	FLETCHER GS	PUNNETT E
EWER FH	BULMAN BM	FABIAN AH 1	BARBER HN 2	EWER FH 1	FLETCHER GS 1	PUNNETT E
KNIGHT JG	BULMAN BM	FABIAN AH	BARBER HN 1	EWER FH	JENKINS RG	PUNNETT E
EWER FH	BULMAN BM	FABIAN AH	JENKINS RG	DYE-RASON	LEWIS RT 1	PUNNETT E 1
EWER FH	BULMAN BM	SOPER MR	ASHTON CT	JENKINS RG	LEWIS RT	PUNNETT E
EWER FH	BULMAN BM	FABIAN AH	MASSEY JA 2	ASHTON CT 3	DOGGART AG	PUNNETT E
BRYANT BE	BULMAN BM	FABIAN AH	VAN DER BORGH M	MASSEY JA	CREE A	COLLINS GAK 1
EWER FH	BULMAN BM	FABIAN AH	MASSEY JA	WHEWELL WT 1	KNIGHT JG	JENKINS RG 1
MANDER AW	BULMAN BM	FABIAN AH	HEAVEN CI	MASSEY JA 2	FLETCHER GS	PUNNETT E
SOPER MR	BULMAN BM	FABIAN AH 1	SHEARER EDR	MASSEY JA	FLETCHER GS	JENKINS RG
SOPER MR	BULMAN BM	FABIAN AH 1	MASSEY JA	JENKINS RG	FLETCHER GS	PARKER WS
EWER FH	BULMAN BM	HEAVEN CI	SHEARER EDR	DYE-RASON	VAN DER BORGH M	FABIAN AH
SOPER MR	BULMAN BM	FABIAN AH	STEVENSON JG	FLETCHER GS 1	PARKER WS	GRAVES J
TIDSWELL GH	BULMAN BM	JENKINS RG	CREE A	DYE-RASON	FLETCHER GS 1	GRAVES J 1
MELLOR PE	LANE AJ	FLINT W	BENNETT JA	DYE-RASON	SHEARER EDR	GRAVES J
EWER FH	GLENISTER CE	ROBINS RWV 2	KNIGHT JG 2	DOGGART AG 1	FLETCHER GS	JENKINS RG
TIDSWELL GH	BULMAN BM	STEVENSON JG	BARBER HN 1	CREE A	FLETCHER GS 1	GRAVES J
LING KS	BULMAN BM	VAN DER BORGH M	JENKINS RG	LOCKTON JH	FLETCHER GS	GRAVES J
LING KS	BULMAN BM	JENKINS RG	VAN DER BORGH M	HEAVEN CI	BRYANT BE	DYE-RASON
LING KS	BULMAN BM	FABIAN AH	BARBER HN	SHEARER EDR	FLETCHER GS	STEVENSON JG
SOPER MR	BULMAN BM	YEMM C	DIXON GH 1	VAN DER BORGH M	FLETCHER GS	FABIAN AH
LING KS	BULMAN BM	FABIAN AH	JENKINS RG	SOPER MR	FLETCHER GS 1	BARTY-KING GI
LING KS	BULMAN BM	WATSON GS 1	VAN DER BORGH M	SOPER MR	FLETCHER GS	GRAVES J
BEARE R	BULMAN BM	FABIAN AH	SHEARER EDR 2	SOPER MR 2	FLETCHER GS 1	GRAVES J
EWER FH	BULMAN BM	SOPER MR 1	CREE A	KNIGHT JG	DOGGART AG	STEVENSON JG
LING KS	BULMAN BM	SOPER MR	BROGDEN H	SHEARER EDR 1	FLETCHER GS 1	GRAVES J
KNIGHT JG	EWER FH	WATSON GS 1	BARBER HN 2	JENKINS RG 3	FLETCHER GS	GRAVES J
SOPER MR	GREEN GAR	WATSON GS	JENKINS RG 1	REEVES FK	FLETCHER GS	FABIAN AH
KNIGHT JG	EWER FH	JENKINS RG	BROGDEN H	SOPER MR 1	DOGGART AG	GRAVES J
STEVENSON JG 1	SOPER MR	WATSON GS	BARBER HN 1	JENKINS RG	FLETCHER GS 1	BARTY-KING GI
MANDER AW	TIDSWELL GH	JENKINS RG	BARBER HN 2	TOPPIN CG	FLETCHER GS	ABRAMS HCD
SOPER MR	TIDSWELL GH	FABIAN AH	JENKINS RG 1	REEVES FK 1	FLETCHER GS 2	WEBSTER WH
GREEN GAR	TIDSWELL GH	FABIAN AH	JENKINS RG	REEVES FK 1	FLETCHER GS	WEBSTER WH
GREEN GAR	TIDSWELL GH	FABIAN AH	STEVENSON JG	REEVES FK 1	SHEARER EDR 1	JENKINS RG
LING KS	STEVENSON JG	REEVES FK	SHEARER EDR	SOPER MR	PUNNETT E	BARTY-KING GI
EWER FH	WILLIAMS LC	REEVES FK 1	BARBER HN	SOPER MR 1	SHEARER EDR	PUNNETT E

5	6	7	8	9	10	11
SOPER MR	BULMAN BM	FABIAN AH	MASSEY JA	JENKINS RG 1	FLETCHER GS	PARKER WS
MELLOR PE	PERLZWEIG M	ROGERS M	DIXON GH	FAULKNER RG 2	WALER H	GUTHRIE R
GLENISTER CE	BULMAN BM	ROBINS RWV	JENKINS RG	MASSEY JA	PARKER WS	STEVENSON JG
MELLOR P	JONES WS	HEPBURN SF	REEVES FK 1	LOCKTON JH 1	WEBSTER WH 1	FABIAN AH
ROBINSON HF	BRYANT BE	REEVES FK	MAYES J	CREE A 1	GRAVES J	HAMMOND JT
				SHEARER EDR 2		GUTHRIE R 1
POSTILL R	TIDSWELL G	RICKETT L	BROGDEN H	FLETCHER G	GRAVES J	REEVES F

1930/31

DATE	VEN	OPPONENTS	RES	COMP	ATT	1	2	3	4
04-Sep	A	NUNHEAD	2-2	IL		RUSSELL AM	EVANS FL	STEVENSON JG	GRIFFITHS A
06-Sep	A	CLAPTON	5-3	IL		VAUGHAN M	EVANS FL	STEVENSON JG	MANDER AW
10-Sep	H	KINGSTONIAN	1-3	HC	og	RUSSELL AM	EVANS FL	MORRIS AE	MANDER AW
13-Sep	A	WYCOMBE W	3-3	IL		RUSSELL AM	EVANS FL	STEVENSON JG	GRIFFITHS A
18-Sep	A	LONDON CALEDONIANS	1-3	IL		RUSSELL AM	EVANS FL	STEVENSON JG	LING KS
20-Sep	H	REDHILL	3-1	FAC P		RUSSELL AM	EVANS FL	STEVENSON JG	GRIFFITHS A
24-Sep	H	LONDON CALEDONIANS	0-0	IL		RUSSELL AM	EVANS FL	STEVENSON JG	GERMAN AC
27-Sep	A	TUFNELL PARK	0-2	IL		RUSSELL AM	EVANS FL	STEVENSON JG	GRIFFITHS A
01-Oct	H	NUNHEAD	2-1	IL		RUSSELL AM	EVANS FL	MORRIS AE	GRIFFITHS A
04-Oct	A	WOKING	0-4	FAC1Q		RUSSELL AM	EVANS FL	STEVENSON JG	GRIFFITHS A
11-Oct	A	ST ALBANS CITY	5-4	IL	og	RUSSELL AM	EVANS FL	STEVENSON JG	GRIFFITHS A
18-Oct	A	ILFORD	3-5	IL		RUSSELL AM	EVANS FL	STEVENSON JG	GRIFFITHS A
25-Oct	A	KINGSTONIAN	1-3	IL		RUSSELL AM	EVANS FL	STEVENSON JG	GRIFFITHS A
01-Nov	H	DULWICH HAMLET	1-1	IL		WAKEFORD RP	EVANS FL	STEVENSON JG	ROSS T
08-Nov	H	OXFORD CITY	4-2	IL		WAKEFORD RP	EVANS FL	STEVENSON JG	ROSS T
15-Nov	A	WOKING	1-0	IL		WAKEFORD RP	EVANS FL	BOWER MB	GRIFFITHS A
22-Nov	H	WIMBLEDON	2-3	IL		WAKEFORD RP	EVANS FL	STEVENSON JG	ROSS T
29-Nov	H	WOKING	1-2	IL		RUSSELL AM	BARKER JT	BOWER MB	THOMPSON HW
06-Dec	A	DULWICH HAMLET	3-3	IL		RUSSELL AM	BOWER MB	STEVENSON JG	ROSS T
13-Dec	A	ROYAL MARINES	4-3	AC1		RUSSELL AM	BOWER MB	STEVENSON JG	GRIFFITHS A
27-Dec	H	KINGSTONIAN	6-1	IL		RUSSELL AM	EVANS FL	STEVENSON JG	GRIFFITHS A
03-Jan	H	TUFNELL PARK	5-3	IL		RUSSELL AM	RUSSELL GW	YOUNG AJ	GLENISTER CE
17-Jan	H	ILFORD	2-4	AC2	og	RUSSELL AM	EVANS FL	STEVENSON JG	GRIFFITHS A
24-Jan	A	MITCHAM WANDERERS	0-4	SSC1		RUSSELL AM	EVANS FL	STEVENSON JG	LING KS
31-Jan	H	LEYTONSTONE	5-1	IL		RUSSELL AM	EVANS FL	STEVENSON JG	GRIFFITHS A
07-Feb	A	OXFORD CITY	0-2	IL		RUSSELL AM	RUSSELL GW	CREE A	LING KS
21-Feb	A	LEYTONSTONE	3-1	IL		RUSSELL AM	ROSS T	RUSSELL GW	LING KS
28-Feb	H	ILFORD	3-2	IL		RUSSELL AM	ROSS T	STEVENSON JG	JOY B
07-Mar	A	WIMBLEDON	4-5	IL		RUSSELL AM	ROSS T	RUSSELL GW	BRYANT BE 1
28-Mar	H	ST ALBANS CITY	2-2	IL		RUSSELL AM	ROSS T	STEVENSON JG	GRIFFITHS A
22-Apr	H	WYCOMBE W	3-0	IL		RUSSELL AM	LAKE A	TURNBULL JR	LING KS
25-Apr	H	CLAPTON	6-2	IL		RUSSELL AM	LAKE A	TURNBULL JR	LING KS

Friendly Matches

DATE	VEN	OPPONENTS	RES	COMP	ATT	1	2	3	4
30-Aug	A	HASTINGS ST.L	2-2	F		KINGSTON 1	SOPER 1		
19-Nov	A	OXFORD UNIVERSITY	5-5	F	og	GARLAND-WELLS HM	TURNBULL JR	MANDER AW	HERMAN J
25-Nov	A	CAMBRIDGE UNIV	4-0	F		THORPE AG	WHITE G	STEVENSON JG	ROBINSON HF
17-Dec	H	LONDON UNIVERSITY	0-4	F		GARLAND-WELLS HM	BARKER JT	YOUNG AJN	GRIFFITH A
31-Jan	H	PUBLIC SCHOOLS XI	4-1	F		HILDER AL	BRADLEY JH	TIDSWELL EH	JACKSON PH
10-Jan	A	WYCOMBE W	2-6	F		LEAVER KW	TIDSWELL GH	GRIFFITHS A	LING KS
20-Jan	A	CAMBRIDGE UNIV	3-3	F					
26-Feb	H	OXFORD UNIVERSITY	3-1	F		GARLAND-WELLS	BARKER JT	BEADLE A	JOY B
14-Mar	H	LONDON UNIVERSITY	3-3	F		WAKEFORD RP	STEVENSON JG	RUSSELL GW	BRIGGS TM
11-Apr	H	WEALDSTONE	2-3	F		RUSSELL AM	BARKER JT	TIDSWELL GH	BRYANT E

5	6	7	8	9	10	11
LING KS	WILLIAMS LC	REEVES FK	BARBER HN	SOPER MR 2	SHEARER EDR	DAVIES G
LING KS	GRIFFITHS A	REEVES FK	BARBER HN 2	BENNETT G 1	SHEARER EDR 1	DAVIES G 1
LING KS	BEARE R	REEVES FK	BARBER HN	SOPER MR	SHEARER EDR	DAVIES G
LING KS	WILLIAMS LC	PUNNETT E	SOPER MR	REEVES FK 1	SHEARER EDR 2	GRAVES J
KNIGHT JG	WILLIAMS LC	PUNNETT E	BARBER HN	REEVES FK 1	SHEARER EDR	GRAVES J
LING KS	WILLIAMS LC	PUNNETT E	SOPER MR	REEVES FK 1	SHEARER EDR 1	KINGSTON LJ 1
LING KS	WILLIAMS LC	FABIAN AH	BARBER HN	REEVES FK	WILLIS RB	WEBSTER WH
LING KS	WILLIAMS LC	REEVES FK	WILLIS RB	JENKINS RG	SOPER MR	FABIAN AH
LING KS	WILLIAMS LC	FABIAN AH	REEVES FK	ROSSAGE P 2	SOPER MR	KINGSTON LJ
LING KS	WILLIAMS LC	JENKINS RG	SHEARER EDR	ROSSAGE P	SOPER MR	DAVIES G 1
LING KS	SOPER MR	FABIAN AH	SHEARER EDR 2	ROSSAGE P	JENKINS RG 1	DAVIES G 1
LING KS	SOPER MR	VAN DER BORGH M	SHEARER EDR 2	JENKINS RG	FLETCHER JH	KINGSTON LJ 1
LING KS	SOPER MR	WRIGHT JH	SHEARER EDR 1	JENKINS RG	FLETCHER JH	KINGSTON LJ
LING KS	GRIFFITHS A	JENKINS RG	SHEARER EDR 1	BOSWELL FT	CREE A	GRAVES J
LING KS	GRIFFITHS A	JENKINS RG	SHEARER EDR 3	SOPER MR	CREE A 1	GRAVES J
ROSS T	STEVENSON JG	JENKINS RG	SHEARER EDR	CREE A	BARRETT HW 1	GRAVES J
LING KS	GRIFFITHS A	WRIGHT JH	SHEARER EDR 1	CREE A	BENKA HF 1	BARRETT FH
ROSS T	GRIFFITHS A	JENKINS RG	CREE A	SHEARER EDR 1	BARRETT HW	GRAVES J
GRIFFITHS A	WRIGHT JH	JENKINS RG 1	CREE A	SHEARER EDR 2	EVANS FL	KINGSTON LJ
MANDER AW	MCMANUS A	FABIAN AH	BARBER HN 2	SHEARER EDR	JENKINS RG	KINGSTON LJ 2
MANDER AW	MCMANUS A	JENKINS RG 1	BARBER HN	SHEARER EDR 3	CREE A 1	DAVIES G
GRIFFITHS A	BRYANT BE	JENKINS RG 2	MORRIS JR 1	SHEARER EDR 1	BARRETT FH	KINGSTON LJ 1
MANDER AW	MCMANUS A	FABIAN AH	BARBER HN 1	SHEARER EDR	JENKINS RG	DAVIES G
ROSS T	GRIFFITHS A	KINGSTON LJ	CREE A	ROSSAGE P	SHEARER EDR	ROGERS VM
ROSS T	BRIGGS TM	REEVES FK 2	MORRIS JR 1	BARRETT HW 2	CREE A	DAVIES G
ROSS T	GRIFFITHS A	WRIGHT JH	MORRIS JR	SHEARER EDR	JENKINS RG	KINGSTON LJ
BRAMIDGE L	GRIFFITHS A	PUNNETT E 1	LEWIS RF	SHEARER EDR 1	CREE A	EVERETT S 1
MANDER AW	MCMANUS A	JENKINS RG	BARBER HN	SHEARER EDR 2	CREE A 1	SCHOFIELD DL
WOODBRIDGE DL	BRIGGS TM 1	FABIAN AH	MOXON GR 1	SHEARER EDR 1	JENKINS RG	DAVIES G
LING KS	BRIGGS TM	FABIAN AH	DOGRELL D	SHEARER EDR	CREE A 1	JENKINS RG 1
BRAMIDGE L	HOWE AW	JENKINS RG	KITTEL FW	CREE A 2	WHEELER F	GUTHRIE RB 1
ROSS T 1	COUCHMAN LT	BENNETT FA 2	BARBER HN	JENKINS RG 1	WHEELER F 2	DAVIES G

5	6	7	8	9	10	11
THOMPSON HW	BEER RR	MACKENZIE M 3	LEWIS RT	CREE A	BENKA HS 1	KINGSTON LJ
MANDER AW	MCMANUS A	BEATTIE PH	CREE A 1	MORRIS JR 2	BENKA HF 1	BARRETT FH
BRYANT BE	PLAISTOWE FH	REEVES FK	FABIAN AH	MORRIS JR	BARRETT HW	KINGSTON LJ
GILBERT JH	INGELL JB	SERGEANT PA	CREE A 1	SOPER MR 2	COLLINS GLK 1	KINGSTON LJ
ROSS T	GLENISTER CE	KINGSTON LJ 1	MORRIS JR	DYE-RAYSON F 1	WILLIAMS SE	REEVES K
				SHEARER EDR 1	BARRETT HW 2	
O'BRIEN PK 1	DROSSO M	GOWERS RW	SCOFIELD DL 1	WALTER HG 1	MASON G	GRAVES J
GRIFFITHS A	LING KS	KINGSTON LJ 1	CREE A 1	SHEARER EDR	DOGRELL D 1	JENKINS RG
LING KS	GRIFFITHS A	FABIAN AH 1	DOGRELL D	BROWN H	CREE A 1	DAVIES G

1931/32

DATE	VEN	OPPONENTS	RES	COMP	ATT	1	2	3	4
29-Aug	A	OXFORD CITY	3-4	IL		KINGSTON LJ	ROSS T	EVANS FL	JOY B
02-Sep	A	KINGSTONIAN	1-2	IL		RUSSELL AM	ROSS T	EVANS FL	JOY B
05-Sep	H	WOKING	4-0	IL		RUSSELL AM	TURNBULL JR	EVANS FL	JOY B
09-Sep	H	KINGSTONIAN	3-2	IL		RUSSELL AM	TURNBULL JR	EVANS FL	JOY B
12-Sep	H	TUFNELL PARK	5-4	IL		RICKETTS GR	TURNBULL JR	EVANS FL	JOY B
17-Sep	A	LONDON CALEDONIANS	5-0	IL		WAKEFORD RP	TURNBULL JR	EVANS FL	JOY B
19-Sep	A	MITCHAM WANDERERS	2-6	FACP		RUSSELL AM	TIDSWELL GH	RUSSELL GW	JOY B
23-Sep	H	LONDON CALEDONIANS	4-0	IL		RUSSELL AM	TURNBULL JR	EVANS FL	JOY B
26-Sep	H	LEYTONSTONE	2-1	IL		RUSSELL AM	RUSSELL GW	ROSS T	JOY B
03-Oct	A	NUNHEAD	2-2	IL	og	RUSSELL AM	RUSSELL GW	ROSS T	JOY B
10-Oct	H	WYCOMBE W	1-2	IL		RUSSELL AM	ROSS T	RUSSELL GW	JOY B
24-Oct	A	WOKING	1-4	IL		RUSSELL AM	ROSS T	COLEBROOKE D	GRIFFITHS A
07-Nov	H	NUNHEAD	3-2	IL		RUSSELL AM	ROSS T	BOWER MB	MANDER AW
14-Nov	A	CLAPTON	0-5	IL		RUSSELL AM	ROSS T	COLEBROOKE D	BRYANT BE
21-Nov	A	LLOYDS BANK	3-0	AFAC1		RUSSELL AM	ROSS T	COLEBROOKE D	CREE A
28-Nov	A	DULWICH HAMLET	0-4	IL		COUCHMAN LT	ROSS T	COLEBROOKE D	BRYANT BE
05-Dec	H	CLAPTON	3-2	IL		TEWKESBURY KC	ROSS T	COLEBROOKE D	LONG CG
12-Dec	A	WALTHAMSTOW AVE	2-4	AC1		CLOKE HP	ROSS T	BOWER MB	JOY B
19-Dec	A	WIMBLEDON	0-1	IL		TEWKESBURY KC	ROSS T	COLEBROOKE D	BRYANT BE
02-Jan	A	ILFORD	3-8	IL		CLOKE HP	TIDSWELL GH	COLEBROOKE D	BRYANT BE
16-Jan	A	MERTON	1-0	AFAC2		CLOKE HP	ROSS T	TIDSWELL GH	BRYANT BE
23-Jan	A	NUNHEAD	3-4	SSC1		CLOKE HP	ROSS T	EVANS FL	GRIFFITHS A
30-Jan	A	DERBYSHIRE AMATEURS	2-3	AFA3		CLOKE HP	ROSS T	WAY GA	COUCHMAN LT
13-Feb	A	ILFORD	0-4	IL		CLOKE HP	ROSS T	OWEN WV	BRYANT BE
20-Feb	H	OXFORD CITY	5-1	IL		CLOKE HP	ROSS T	CREE A	COUCHMAN LT
27-Feb	A	LEYTONSTONE	2-2	IL		WAKEFORD RP	ROSS T	CREE A	COUCHMAN LT
05-Mar	A	TUFNELL PARK	1-2	IL		WAKEFORD RP	ROSS T	BRIGGS TM	BRYANT BE
12-Mar	A	ST ALBANS CITY	3-3	IL		CLOKE HP	ROSS T	RUSSELL GW	COUCHMAN LT
19-Mar	H	ST ALBANS CITY	4-4	IL		WAKEFORD RP	ROSS T	RUSSELL GW	HOWE AW
02-Apr	H	DULWICH HAMLET	4-2	IL		WAKEFORD RP	EVANS FL	BRIGGS TM	SOPER MR
23-Apr	A	WIMBLEDON	0-2	IL		WAKEFORD RP	ROSS T	EVANS FL	SOPER MR
07-May	A	WYCOMBE W	0-2	IL		HUDDLE LT	ROSS T	LAKE A	SOPER MR

Friendly Matches

DATE	VEN	OPPONENTS	RES	COMP	ATT	1	2	3	4
17-Oct	A	ALDERSHOT COMMAND	2-4	F		RUSSELL AM	ROSS T	COLEBROOKE D	O'BRIEN TK
19-Oct	A	OXFORD UNIVERSITY	1-4	F		ROGERS TP	TURNBULL JR	LAKE AB	JOY B
30-Dec	H	AFA PUBLIC SCHOOLS XI	8-4	F		HILDER AL	COOK JA	HOLLEBONE TA	BARKER JT
09-Jan	A	CAMBRIDGE TOWN	3-9	F		KIMBER TL	ROSS T	EVANS FL	GLENISTER CE
19-Jan	A	CAMBRIDGE UNIV	2-1	F		HILDER AL	BARTER JT	MARYLON RT	TIDSWELL GH
03-Feb	H	OXFORD UNIVERSITY	1-0	F		TRAPP CS	DEAN HE	MARYLON RT	COUCHMAN LT
06-Feb	H	ROYAL MARINES	2-0	F		CLOKE HP	GRIFFITHS A	CREE A	BRYANT BE
17-Feb	A	CAMBRIDGE UNIV	1-2	F		HILDER AL	ELWELL AH	CREE A	NICHOLLS HJ
25-Feb	H m	GRASSHOPPERS	0-4	F		CLOKE HP	ROSS T	TURNBULL JR	JOY B
25-Mar	A	FROME TOWN	5-4	F	%				
27-Mar	A	CHIPPENHAM	6-0	F	%				

5	6	7	8	9	10	11
MANDER AW	COUCHMAN LT	JENKINS RG	BARBER HN	SHEARER EDR 2	WHEELER F	DAVIES G 1
MANDER AW	LING KS	FABIAN AH	BARBER HN	SHEARER EDR	JENKINS RG 1	KINGSTON LJ
LING KS	COUCHMAN LT	PUNNETT E	JENKINS RG	SHEARER EDR 4	RICHARDS GC	DAVIES G
LING KS	GRIFFITHS A	PUNNETT E	COUCHMAN LT 1	BENKA HF 1	RICHARDS GC 1	KINGSTON LJ
BRAMIDGE L	GRIFFITHS A	PUNNETT E	COUCHMAN LT	ASHTON CT 3	BENKA HF 2	KINGSTON LJ
LING KS	GRIFFITHS A	FABIAN AH 1	BARBER HN 1	BENKA HF 1	COUCHMAN LT 2	KINGSTON LJ
LING KS	GRIFFITHS A	JENKINS RG 1	COUCHMAN LT 1	BENKA HF	WHEELER F	DAVIES G
LING KS	GRIFFITHS A	FABIAN AH	BARBER HN 1	BENKA HF 1	WEBSTER WH 1	COUCHMAN LT
LING KS	TIDSWELL GH	FABIAN AH	CREE A	JENKINS RG	BENKA HF 2	KINGSTON LJ
LING KS	GRIFFITHS A	FABIAN AH	CREE A	BRYANT BE	JENKINS RG 1	DAVIES G
LING KS	GRIFFITHS A	TEPPER CH	CREE A	MORRIS JR 1	JENKINS RG	DAVIES G
LING KS	STEVENSON JG	KINGSTON LJ	JOY B 1	BENKA HF	CREE A	BRYANT BE
LING KS	BRYANT BE	TEPPER CH	BARBER HN	CREE A	JENKINS RG 3	DAVIES G
LING KS	LONG CG	TEPPER CH	MORRIS JR	MUIR RT	CREE A	DAVIES G
LING KS	BRYANT BE	TEPPER CH 1	JENKINS RG	ROSSAGE P 2	BARRITT HW	SERGEANT RA
LING KS	LONG CG	TEPPER CH	REEVES FK	ROSSAGE P	SERGEANT EF	DAVIES G
LING KS	BRIGGS TM 1	KINGSTON LJ 1	BRYANT BE	REEVES FK 1	JENKINS RG	DAVIES G
LING KS	BRIGGS TM	TEPPER CH	JENKINS RG 1	REEVES FK	BRYANT BE 1	DAVIES G
JOY B	BRIGGS TM	KINGSTON LJ	CREE A	LING KS	JENKINS RG	DAVIES G
JOY B	LONG CG	KINGSTON LJ	COUCHMAN LT	WEBB JOW 1	WEBSTER WH 2	DAVIES G
COUCHMAN LT	LONG CG	TEPPER CH	CREE A	MUIR RT	KINGSTON LJ	DAVIES G 1
COUCHMAN LT	LONG CG	REEVES FK 1	KINGSTON LJ	SOPER MR 2	WHEELER F	DAVIES G
JOY B	LONG CG	REEVES FK	KINGSTON LJ	WEBB JOW 1	WEBSTER WH 1	DAVIES G
COUCHMAN LT	LONG CG	REEVES FK	KINGSTON LJ	SOPER MR	JENKINS RG	DAVIES G
GRIFFITHS A	BRIGGS TM 1	JENKINS RG 1	SOPER MR 2	REEVES FK	KINGSTON LJ	DAVIES G 1
GRIFFITHS A	BRIGGS TM	KINGSTON LJ	SOPER MR 2	REEVES FK	WHEELER F	GRAVES J
GRIFFITHS A	COUCHMAN LT	JENKINS RG	SOPER MR	REEVES FK 1	KINGSTON LJ	DAVIES G
SOPER MR	LONG CG	TEPPER CH 1	KINGSTON LJ 2	REEVES FK	WEBB JOW	DAVIES G
COUCHMAN LT	JONES DM 1	KINGSTON LJ	SOPER MR	REEVES FK	JENKINS RG 3	DAVIES G
COUCHMAN LT	RUSSELL GW	KINGSTON LJ	FABIAN AH	COOPER KHL 1	WEBSTER WH	COLLINS GAK 2
GRIFFITHS A	COUCHMAN LT	REEVES FK	FABIAN AH	COOPER KHL	KINGSTON LJ	COLLINS GAK
GRIFFITHS A	COUCHMAN LT	KINGSTON LJ	REEVES FK	BENKA HF	JENKINS RG	DAVIES G

5	6	7	8	9	10	11
LING KS	GRIFFITHS A	TEPPER CH	GILLIES R	BRYANT BE 2	BUCHANNAN G	DAVIES G
O'BRIEN TK	GRIFFITHS A 1	BUCHANNAN G	KINGSTON LJ	BENKA HF	WEBB JOW	BELL CR
YOUNG PS	WREFORD-BROWN G	PICTON-WARLOW WR 2	KINGSTON LJ	HOOPER KHL 4	COLLINS GAK 2	BARKER TF
COUCHMAN LT	TIDSWELL GH	TEPPER CH	BRYANT BE	CREE A 3	DUTHIE RB	KINGSTON LJ
MANDER AW	LONG CG	FABIAN AH 1	COUCHMAN LT	WEBB JOW	COLLIN GA	KINGSTON LJ 1
GRIFFITHS A	CREE A	REEVES FK 1	SOPER MR	MORRIS JR	COLLIN GA	KINGSTON LJ
JOY B	COUCHMAN LT	REEVES FK	KINGSTON LJ	SOPER MR 2	JENKINS RG	DAVIES G
MANDER AW	LONG CG	REEVES FK	FABIAN AH	SOPER MR 1	COLLIN GA	KINGSTON LJ
GRIFFITHS A	BRIGGS TMR	KINGSTON LJ	CREE A	BENKA HF	COLLINS GAK	DAVIES G

1932/33

DATE	VEN	OPPONENTS	RES	COMP	ATT	1	2	3	4
27-Aug	A	ST ALBANS CITY	2-3	IL		CLOKE HP	ROSS T	EVANS FL	HOWE AW
31-Aug	H	LONDON CALEDONIANS	1-0	IL		HUDDLE LT	ROSS T	EVANS FL	LING KS
03-Sep	A	KINGSTONIAN	1-0	IL		HUDDLE LT	ROSS T	EVANS FL	JOY B
10-Sep	H	WYCOMBE W	2-1	IL		HUDDLE LT	ROSS T	EVANS FL	COUCHMAN LT
12-Sep	A	LONDON CALEDONIANS	1-0	IL		HUDDLE LT	ROSS T	EVANS FL	COUCHMAN LT
17-Sep	A	OXFORD CITY	3-0	IL		HUDDLE LT	ROSS T	EVANS FL	SOPER MR
24-Sep	A	KINGSTONIAN	0-3	IL		HUDDLE LT	ROSS T	EVANS FL	JOY B
01-Oct	A	WIMBLEDON	1-3	IL		HUDDLE LT	ROSS T	EVANS FL	JOY B
08-Oct	H	WIMBLEDON	4-2	IL		HUDDLE LT	ROSS T	EVANS FL	LAMPARD M
15-Oct	A	TUFNELL PARK	4-0	IL		HUDDLE LT	ROSS T	EVANS FL	LAMPARD M
22-Oct	H	UNITED GLASS BLOWERS	2-0	LSC3Q		HUDDLE LT	ROSS T	EVANS FL	LAMPARD M
29-Oct	A	LEYTONSTONE	1-0	IL		HUDDLE LT	ROSS T	EVANS FL	GRIFFITHS A
12-Nov	H	WEALDSTONE	4-2	LSC4Q		HUDDLE LT	ROSS T	EVANS FL	LAMPARD M
19-Nov	A	DULWICH HAMLET	1-3	IL		HUDDLE LT	ROSS T	EVANS FL	COUCHMAN LT
26-Nov	H	OXFORD CITY	4-0	AFASC1		HUDDLE LT	LAMPARD M	EVANS FL	COUCHMAN LT
03-Dec	A	EASTBOURNE	1-2	AFASC1		HUDDLE LT	ROSS T	LAMPARD M	GRIFFITHS A
10-Dec	A	MET POLICE	3-2	AC1		HUDDLE LT	ROSS T	EVANS FL	LAMPARD M
17-Dec	A	ILFORD	1-2	IL		HUDDLE LT	ROSS T	HISCOCK CH	O'BRIEN PK
31-Dec	A	WALTHAMSTOW AVE	0-7	LSC1		HUDDLE LT	ROSS T	YOUNG AJ	GRIFFITHS A
14-Jan	H	NUNHEAD	0-1	AC2		HUDDLE LT	ROSS T	EVANS FL	LAMPARD M
28-Jan	A	TUFNELL PARK	0-1	IL		TRAPP CS	ROSS T	GILBERT TH	GRIFFITHS A
04-Feb	H	ST ALBANS CITY	4-1	IL		HUDDLE LT	ROSS T	EVANS FL	O'BRIEN PK
11-Feb	A	WYCOMBE W	2-2	IL		HUDDLE LT	ROSS T	EVANS FL	O'BRIEN PK
25-Feb	A	NUNHEAD	0-1	IL		HUDDLE LT	ROSS T	EVANS FL	O'BRIEN PK
04-Mar	A	WOKING	0-1	IL		HUDDLE LT	ROSS T	EVANS FL	O'BRIEN PK
11-Mar	H	ILFORD	2-3	IL		HUDDLE LT	ROSS T	EVANS FL	O'BRIEN PK
18-Mar	H	LEYTONSTONE	1-2	IL		GRANT RS	STEVENSON JG	WEBB T	BEAVIS J
01-Apr	H	WOKING	5-3	IL		HUDDLE LT	ROSS T	EVANS FL	O'BRIEN PK
08-Apr	H	NUNHEAD	0-0	IL		HUDDLE LT	ROSS T	GRIFFITHS A	O'BRIEN PK
14-Apr	H	KINGSTONIAN	2-0	CC		HUDDLE LT	ROSS T	GRIFFITHS A	STANDALOFT A
22-Apr	H	DULWICH HAMLET	2-3	IL		HUDDLE LT	ROSS T	EVANS FL	O'BRIEN PK
29-Apr	A	CLAPTON	1-2	IL		HUDDLE LT	GRIFFITHS A	EVANS FL	LANGMAID VF
01-May	H	CLAPTON	5-0	IL		HUDDLE LT	ROSS T	EVANS FL	O'BRIEN PK

Friendly Matches

DATE	VEN	OPPONENTS	RES	COMP	ATT	1	2	3	4
20-Oct	A	OXFORD UNIVERSITY	1-4	F		HUDDLE LT	WHEELER SAT	LAKE AB	LAMPARD M
05-Nov	H	TUNBRIDGE WELLS R	3-3	F		TRAPP CS	ROSS T	TURNBULL JR	LAMPARD M
23-Nov	H	LONDON UNIVERSITY	2-1	F		TRAPP CS	ROSS T	LAKE AB	O'BRIEN PK
28-Dec	H	AFA PUBLIC SCHOOLS XI	5-3	F		HILDER AL	YOUNG AJN	WHEELER SAT	WREFORD-BROWN AJ
07-Jan	H	BANK OF ENGLAND	6-3	F		TRAPP CS	HISCOCK CH	EVANS FL	LAMPARD M 1
02-Feb	A	CAMBRIDGE UNIV	3-3	F		MILES R	LIDDLE E	TAYLOR R	O'BRIEN PK
08-Feb	H	OXFORD UNIVERSITY	1-2	F		CLOKE HP	LIDDLE E	TIDSWELL GH	GILBERT IH
15-Feb	H	CAMBRIDGE UNIV	2-1	F		TRAPP CS	O'BRIEN PK	TIDSWELL GH	LUETCHFORD RJ
18-Feb	A	BECKENHAM	3-1	F		HUDDLE LT	ROSS T	EVANS FL	O'BRIEN PK
15-Apr	A	ST ALBANS CITY	2-4	F		WHITE D	ROSS T	TURNBULL JR	GRIFFITHS A
17-Apr	A	WIMBLEDON	0-0	F		HUDDLE LT	DIXON LA	ROSS T	FRANKLIN WM

$ REPLACED BY GN LOWREY

1933 - Tour to France

DATE	VEN	OPPONENTS	RES	COMP	ATT	1	2	3	4
19-Mar	A	STADE RENNAIS	0-1	F		HUDDLE LT	ROSS T	EVANS FL	O'BRIEN PK

5	6	7	8	9	10	11
JOY B	BRIGGS TM 1	KINGSTON LJ	COUCHMAN LT 1	REEVES FK	WEBB JOW	DAVIES G
JOY B 1	BRIGGS TM	REEVES FK	KINGSTON LJ	SOPER MR	JENKINS RG	DAVIES G
LING KS	BRIGGS TM	KINGSTON LJ	SOPER MR	WEBB JOW 1	COUCHMAN LT	DAVIES G
LING KS	BRIGGS TM	KINGSTON LJ 1	JENKINS RG	WEBB JOW	SOPER MR 1	DAVIES G
LING KS	BRIGGS TM	KINGSTON LJ	FABIAN AH	COOPER KHL 1	SOPER MR	DAVIES G
LING KS	COUCHMAN LT	KINGSTON LJ 2	FABIAN AH 1	COOPER KHL	WEBB JOW	DAVIES G
LING KS	BRIGGS TM	KINGSTON LJ	FABIAN AH	COUCHMAN LT	WEBB JOW	DAVIES G
LING KS	BRIGGS TM 1	KINGSTON LJ	FABIAN AH	WEBB JOW	COUCHMAN LT	DAVIES G
LING KS	GRIFFITHS A	KINGSTON LJ	COUCHMAN LT 3	WEBB JOW 1	WHEELER F	DAVIES G
LING KS	O'BRIEN PK	KINGSTON LJ 1	COUCHMAN LT	WEBB JOW 3	WHEELER F	DAVIES G
LING KS	O'BRIEN PK	KINGSTON LJ 1	COUCHMAN LT	WEBB JOW 1	WHEELER F	DAVIES G
LING KS	O'BRIEN PK	KINGSTON LJ	COUCHMAN LT	LAMPARD M	WHEELER F	SERGEANT FA 1
LING KS	O'BRIEN PK	KINGSTON LJ 2	COUCHMAN LT	WEBB JOW 1	WHEELER F 1	DAVIES G
LING KS	O'BRIEN PK	KINGSTON LJ	LOCKEY WG 1	WEBB JOW	WHEELER F	DAVIES G
LING KS	O'BRIEN PK	KINGSTON LJ	FABIAN AH 3	WEBB JOW 1	WHEELER F	DAVIES G
LING KS	O'BRIEN PK	KINGSTON LJ	COUCHMAN LT 1	WEBB JOW	WHEELER F	DAVIES G
LING KS	GRIFFITHS A	KINGSTON LJ	FABIAN AH 2	WEBB JOW	COUCHMAN LT 1	DAVIES G
LING KS	COUCHMAN LT	ROGERS VM	FABIAN AH	KINGSTON LJ 1	WHEELER F	DAVIES G
LING KS	O'BRIEN PK	ROGERS VM	COUCHMAN LT	KINGSTON LJ	WEBB JOW	DAVIES G
LING KS	GRIFFITHS A	KINGSTON LJ	COUCHMAN LT	WEBB JOW	WHEELER F	DAVIES G
HISCOCK CH	O'BRIEN PK	KINGSTON LJ	ZABELL NF	SOPER MR	WHEELER F	DAVIES G
HISCOCK CH	GRIFFITHS A	ROGERS VM 2	LING KS 1	WEBB JOW 1	COUCHMAN LT	DAVIES G
HISCOCK CH	GRIFFITHS A	ROGERS VM	LING KS	WEBB JOW	COUCHMAN LT 1	DAVIES G 1
HISCOCK CH	GRIFFITHS A	KINGSTON LJ	LING KS	WEBB JOW	COUCHMAN LT	DAVIES G
HISCOCK CH	COUCHMAN LT	REEVES FK	LING KS	SOPER MR	WEBB JOW	DAVIES G
HISCOCK CH	GRIFFITHS A	KINGSTON LJ	COUCHMAN LT	REEVES FK	WEBB JOW 2	DAVIES G
READY A	COUCHMAN LT	LING KS	WALTER HGB	SOPER MR	WHEELER F 1	DAVIES G
HISCOCK CH	GRIFFITHS A	KINGSTON LJ 1	ROGERS VM 1	COUCHMAN LT 2	WHEELER F	DAVIES G 1
HISCOCK CH	COUCHMAN LT	KINGSTON LJ	ROGERS VM	WEBB JOW	WHEELER F	DAVIES G
HISCOCK CH	READY A	KINGSTON LJ	ROGERS VM 1	COUCHMAN LT 1	WEBB JOW	DAVIES G
HISCOCK CH	GRIFFITHS A	COOPER KHL 2	WIGGINS M	REEVES FK	COUCHMAN LT	KINGSTON LJ
HISCOCK CH	READY A	ROGERS VM	COOPER KHL 1	ROSS T	COUCHMAN LT	KINGSTON LJ
HISCOCK CH	GRIFFITHS A	ROGERS VM 1	FABIAN AH	COOPER KHL 1	COUCHMAN LT 3	KINGSTON LJ

5	6	7	8	9	10	11
GRIFFITHS A	O'BRIEN PK 1	KINGSTON LJ	COUCHMAN LT	COLLINS GAK	BRABBAN D	DAVIES G
LING KS	O'BRIEN PK	KINGSTON LJ	COUCHMAN LT 2	WEBB JOW 1	WHEELER F	DAVIES G
GEORGE RW	HIBBERT CL	KINGSTON LJ	GILBERT IH	WEBB JOW 2	LYMAN MJ	SERGEANT EA
WREFORD-BROWN GD	LONG CGD	WALLACH HL	CREE A 3	KINGSTON LJ	STOWE CG 2	MOSS WF
ROSS T	GRIFFITHS A	KINGSTON LJ	COUCHMAN LT 2	WEBB JOW 2	WHEELER F 1	DAVIES G
COUCHMAN LT	LONSDALE EHG	GILDERSON E 2	PASHLEY W	MORRIS JR 1	WEBB JOW	KELSEY J
HISCOCK CH	BRABBAN D	SMITH GLM	PASHLEY W 1	BROWN H	COUCHMAN LT	KINGSTON LJ
HISCOCK CH	WIGGINS M	COOPER KHL	SOPER MR 1	WEBB JOW 1	SCHOFIELD KS	SCHOFIELD DL
HISCOCK CH	GRIFFITHS A	ROGERS VM	LING KS	WEBB JOW 2	COUCHMAN LT	DAVIES G 1
HISCOCK CH	READY A	JEFFRIES A	KINGSTON LJ	BARBER HN 2	PENNANT-JONES M S	DAVIES G
HISCOCK CH	HIBBERT G	KINGSTON L	ROGERS V	ROGERS T	LAWRIE A	DAVIES G

5	6	7	8	9	10	11
HISCOCK CH	GRIFFITHS A	KINGSTON LJ	THORNTON J	FEUVRE EJ	WEBB JOW	GUTHRIE R

1933/34

DATE	VEN	OPPONENTS	RES	COMP	ATT	1	2	3	4
26-Aug	H	TUFNELL PARK	3-0	IL		HUDDLE LT	ROSS T	EVANS FL	JOY B
06-Sep	H	ILFORD	3-1	IL		HUDDLE LT	ROSS T	EVANS FL	JOY B
09-Sep	A	WYCOMBE W	1-3	IL		HUDDLE LT	ROSS T	EVANS FL	JOY B
14-Sep	A	ILFORD	2-1	IL		HUDDLE LT	ROSS T	EVANS FL	JOY B
16-Sep	A	KINGSTONIAN	0-0	IL		HUDDLE LT	ROSS T	EVANS FL	JOY B
23-Sep	H	ST ALBANS CITY	2-0	IL		HUDDLE LT	ROSS T	EVANS FL	JOY B
30-Sep	A	WOKING	1-2	IL		HUDDLE LT	ROSS T	EVANS FL	JOY B
07-Oct	A	LEYTONSTONE	0-1	IL		HUDDLE LT	DAVIES LA	EVANS FL	JOY B
14-Oct	A	LONDON CALEDONIANS	0-0	IL		HUDDLE LT	DAVIES LA	EVANS FL	WHEWELL WT
21-Oct	H	KINGSTONIAN	2-2	IL	4,000	HUDDLE LT	ROSS T	EVANS FL	JOY B
04-Nov	A	ST ALBANS CITY	4-0	IL		HUDDLE LT	ROSS T	EVANS FL	O'BRIEN PK
11-Nov	H	PO ENGINEERS	3-0	LSC3Q		HUDDLE LT	ROSS T	EVANS FL	LAMPARD M
18-Nov	H	HOXTON MANOR	2-2	LSC4Q		HUDDLE LT	ROSS T	EVANS FL	O'BRIEN PK
25-Nov	H	HOXTON MANOR	4-2	LSC4Q		HUDDLE LT	ROSS T	EVANS FL	KINGSLEY PGT
02-Dec	A	CLAPTON	0-0	LSC5Q		HUDDLE LT	ROSS T	DAVIES LA	LAMPARD M
09-Dec	A	ILFORD	1-1	AC1		HUDDLE LT	ROSS T	EVANS FL	KINGSLEY PGT
16-Dec	A	ILFORD	3-0	AC1r		HUDDLE LT	ROSS T	EVANS FL	GREEN GAR 2
23-Dec	H	CLAPTON	1-1	LSC5Q		HUDDLE LT	ROSS T	MCLAREN JEE	ADLARD GH
30-Dec	N1	CLAPTON	1-4	LSC5Q		HUDDLE LT	ROSS T	EVANS FL	O'BRIEN PK
06-Jan	H	OLD WESTMINSTERS	3-4	AFASC1		HUDDLE LT	ROSS T	EVANS FL	O'BRIEN PK
13-Jan	Ni	TUFNELL PARK	2-1	AC2		HUDDLE LT	ROSS T	EVANS FL	KINGSLEY PGT
20-Jan	H	OXFORD CITY	4-3	IL		HUDDLE LT	ROSS T	EVANS FL	KINGSLEY PGT
27-Jan	A	OXFORD CITY	2-2	IL		HUDDLE LT	MCLAREN JEE	EVANS FL	KINGSLEY PGT
03-Feb	A	BOURNEMOUTH GW	5-1	AC3	og	HUDDLE LT	ROSS T	EVANS FL	WHEWELL WT
10-Feb	H	WYCOMBE W	2-0	IL		CLOKE HP	ARGYLE JD	BOWER MB	WINLAW AWE
17-Feb	A	CLAPTON	1-2	IL		TRAPP CS	OWEN WW	MCLAREN JEE	WINLAW AWE
24-Feb	H	DULWICH HAMLET	1-2	AC4		HUDDLE LT	ROSS T	EVANS FL	WHEWELL WT
03-Mar	A	NUNHEAD	1-0	IL		HUDDLE LT	ROSS T	HISCOCK CH	GARROW AD
10-Mar	H	LEYTONSTONE	3-1	IL		HUDDLE LT	OWEN WW	EVANS FL	HISCOCK CH
17-Mar	H	WIMBLEDON	3-3	IL		HUDDLE LT	STRASSER GA	EVANS FL	O'BRIEN PK
24-Mar	A	TUFNELL PARK	0-2	IL		HUDDLE LT	ROSS T	EVANS FL	GREEN GAR
14-Apr	H	CLAPTON	6-1	IL		HUDDLE LT	ROSS T	EVANS FL	O'BRIEN PK
21-Apr	A	WIMBLEDON	2-1	IL	3,500	HUDDLE LT	ROSS T	EVANS FL	JOY B
23-Apr	H	WOKING	2-0	IL		STRINGER EJ	JOY E	EVANS FL	LISTER WHL
28-Apr	H	LONDON CALEDONIANS	1-2	IL		STRINGER EJ	ROSS T	EVANS FL	GRIFFITHS A
02-May	H	DULWICH HAMLET	1-3	IL		CLOKE HP	PARTRIDGE GM	EVANS FL	GRIFFITHS A
03-May	A	DULWICH HAMLET	0-2	IL		TRAPP CS	PARTRIDGE GM	EVANS FL	HISCOCK CH
05-May	H	NUNHEAD	1-0	IL		HUDDLE LT	STRASSER GA	EVANS FL	HISCOCK CH

Friendly Matches

DATE	VEN	OPPONENTS	RES	COMP	ATT	1	2	3	4
02-Sep	A	TUNBRIDGE WELLS R	2-3	F		TRAPP CS	ROSS T	EVANS FL	JOY B
28-Oct	H	OXFORD UNIVERSITY	3-3	F		STRINGER EJ	DIXON LA	EVANS FL	LAMPARD M
07-Apr	A	BASINGSTOKE	1-3	F		TRAPP CS	EVANS FL	JOY E	YARROW AD

5	6	7	8	9	10	11
HISCOCK CH	COUCHMAN LT	COOPER KHL	CRAYTHORNE JR	SCHOFIELD AC 2	WEBB JOW 1	KINGSTON LJ
HISCOCK CH	COUCHMAN LT	COOPER KHL 1	FABIAN AH 1	SCHOFIELD AC	ROGERS VM	KINGSTON LJ 1
HISCOCK CH	COUCHMAN LT	COOPER KHL	FABIAN AH	REEVES FK 1	WEBB JOW	BENEST HV
COUCHMAN LT	O'BRIEN PK	COOPER KHL	FABIAN AH	COLLINS GAK 1	GUTHRIE RB	KINGSTON LJ 1
COUCHMAN LT	O'BRIEN PK	COOPER KHL	FABIAN AH	WHEWELL WT	COLLINS GAK	KINGSTON LJ
COUCHMAN LT	O'BRIEN PK	COOPER KHL	FABIAN AH	MOXON GR 1	COLLINS GAK 1	KINGSTON LJ
COUCHMAN LT	O'BRIEN PK	COOPER KHL	FABIAN AH	MOXON GR	COLLINS GAK 1	KINGSTON LJ
COUCHMAN LT	BARBER AT	COOPER KHL	FABIAN AH	MOXON GR	WEBSTER WH	KINGSTON LJ
COUCHMAN LT	O'BRIEN PK	KINGSTON LJ	HASLEWOOD JSO	SHEARER EDR	KINGSLEY PGT	WEBSTER WH
COUCHMAN LT	O'BRIEN PK	KINGSTON LJ	MOXON GR	WEBB JOW 1	WEBSTER WH	COLLINS GAK 1
BRADSHAW WH	COUCHMAN LT	KINGSTON LJ 1	FABIAN AH	WEBB JOW 1	KINGSLEY PGT	COLLINS GAK 2
JOY B	COUCHMAN LT	COOPER KHL	FABIAN AH	WEBB JOW 2	WEBSTER WH	COLLINS GAK 1
JOY B	COUCHMAN LT	COOPER KHL	FABIAN AH 1	WEBB JOW	WEBSTER WH 1	COLLINS GAK
JOY B	COUCHMAN LT	MOXON GR 1	FABIAN AH 1	WEBB JOW	WEBSTER WH 1	COLLINS GAK 1
HISCOCK CH	COUCHMAN LT	KINGSLEY PGT	SHEARER EDR	WEBB JOW	MOXON GR	JOHNSTON H
JOY B	COUCHMAN LT	FABIAN AH	SHEARER EDR 1	WEBB JOW	WEBSTER WH	COLLINS GAK
JOY B	COUCHMAN LT	KINGSTON LJ	KINGSLEY PGT	WEBB JOW	CRAYTHORNE JR 1	COLLINS GAK
HISCOCK CH	KINGSLEY PGT	KINGSTON LJ	SHEARER EDR 1	WEBB JOW	CRAYTHORNE JR	GUTHRIE RB
HISCOCK CH 1	MCLAREN JEE	COOPER KHL	HASLEWOOD JSO	WEBB JOW	KINGSLEY PGT	COLLINS GAK
BRADSHAW WH	COUCHMAN LT	CRAYTHORNE JR	HASLEWOOD JSO	MOXON GR 2	WEBB JOW	JOHNSTON H 1
JOY B	COUCHMAN LT	FABIAN AH 1	LOCKEY WG 1	SHEARER EDR	WEBB JOW	COLLINS GAK
O'BRIEN PK	COUCHMAN LT	LOCKEY WG	FABIAN AH 1	FROST KAF 2	WEBB JOW 1	JOHNSTON H
O'BRIEN PK	COUCHMAN LT	KINGSTON LJ 1	LOCKEY WG	FROST KAF 1	WEBB JOW	BENEST HV
JOY B	COUCHMAN LT	FABIAN AH	LOCKEY WG	SHEARER EDR 1	WEBB JOW	COLLINS GAK 3
JOY B	COUCHMAN LT	WILLEY FT	LOCKEY WG	WINLAW RW 1	WHEELER F	KINGSTON LJ 1
HISCOCK CH	COUCHMAN LT	WILLEY FT	LOCKEY WG	FROST KAF	GUTHRIE RB	KINGSTON LJ 1
JOY B	KINGSLEY PGT	FABIAN AH	LOCKEY WG	SHEARER EDR 1	WEBB JOW	COLLINS GAK
BRADSHAW WH	COUCHMAN LT	KINGSTON LJ	LOCKEY WG	COOPER KHL	ROGERS VM	COLLINS GAK 1
JOY B	O'BRIEN PK	KINGSTON LJ	ROGERS VM 2	COUCHMAN LT 1	GUTHRIE RB	COLLINS GAK
JOY B	COUCHMAN LT 1	FABIAN AH	LOCKEY WG	COOPER KHL 2	WEBSTER WH	KINGSTON LJ
HISCOCK CH	MCLAREN JEE	ROGERS VM	LOCKEY WG	COUCHMAN LT	WEBB JOW	KINGSTON LJ
HISCOCK CH	COUCHMAN LT	LYWOOD F 1	ROGERS VM	FROST KAF 3	WEBB JOW 1	KINGSTON LJ 1
HISCOCK CH	COUCHMAN LT	COOPER KHL	FABIAN AH 1	FROST KAF 1	WEBB JOW	KINGSTON LJ
JOY B	COUCHMAN LT	COOPER KHL	FABIAN AH 1	FROST KAF	WEBB JOW	KINGSTON LJ 1
HISCOCK CH	COUCHMAN LT	KINGSTON LJ	ROGERS VM	FROST KAF 1	WEBB JOW	GUTHRIE RB
HISCOCK CH	COUCHMAN LT	ROGERS VM	ROGERS T	FROST KAF 1	WEBB JOW	KINGSTON LJ
JOY B	COUCHMAN LT	COOPER KHL	FABIAN AH	FROST KAF	WEBB JOW	KINGSTON LJ
ROSS T	GRIFFITHS A	COOPER KHL	LISTER WHL	WEBB JOW 1	GUTHRIE RB	COLLINS GAK

5	6	7	8	9	10	11
HISCOCK CH	COUCHMAN LT	KINGSTON LJ 1	CRAYTHORNE JR	SCHOFIELD AC 1	WEBB JOW	BENEST HB
COUCHMAN LT 1	WREFORD-BROWN AJ	COOPER KHL	HASLEWOOD JSO 1	MOXON GR	KINGSTON LJ 1	BENEST HV
ROSS T	COUCHMAN LT	KINGSTON LJ 1	RODGERS F	COOPER K	GUTHRIE RB	COLLINS GAK

1934/35

DATE	VEN	OPPONENTS	RES	COMP	ATT	1	2	3	4
25-Aug	A	WYCOMBE W	1-3	IL		HUDDLE LT	ROSS T	EVANS FL	COUCHMAN LT
29-Aug	H	DULWICH HAMLET	1-3	IL		HUDDLE LT	ROSS T	EVANS FL	COUCHMAN LT
01-Sep	H	TUFNELL PARK	1-0	IL		HUDDLE LT	ROSS T	EVANS FL	HISCOCK CH
06-Sep	A	DULWICH HAMLET	1-3	IL		HUDDLE LT	ROSS T	EVANS FL	COUCHMAN LT
08-Sep	A	ST.ALBANS CITY	1-2	IL		HUDDLE LT	ROSS T	EVANS FL	O'BRIEN PK
15-Sep	H	KINGSTONIAN	3-5	IL	3,000	HUDDLE LT	ROSS T	EVANS FL	O'BRIEN PK
22-Sep	A	NUNHEAD	0-3	IL		STRINGER EJ	ROSS T	EVANS FL	O'BRIEN PK
29-Sep	H	WOKING	2-2	IL		STRINGER EJ	ROSS T	EVANS FL	O'BRIEN PK
13-Oct	A	CLAPTON	1-2	IL		JOLLIFFE CA	DIXON LA	EVANS FL	O'BRIEN PK
20-Oct	A	KINGSTONIAN	0-1	IL		JOLLIFFE CA	ROSS T	EVANS FL	O'BRIEN PK
27-Oct	H	CLAPTON	1-0	IL		JOLLIFFE CA	DIXON LA	EVANS FL	O'BRIEN PK
03-Nov	A	OXFORD CITY	2-3	IL		JOLLIFFE CA	DIXON LA	EVANS FL	O'BRIEN PK
24-Nov	A	LEYTONSTONE	0-2	IL		JOLLIFFE CA	DIXON LA	EVANS FL	COUCHMAN LT
01-Dec	A	KINGSTONIAN	0-2	LSC1		JOLLIFFE CA	ROSS T	EVANS FL	HISCOCK CH
08-Dec	A	OLD CHOLMELIANS	4-1	AFASC1		JOLLIFFE CA	ROSS T	DIXON LA	GILBERT HG
15-Dec	H	OXFORD CITY	1-3	IL		JOLLIFFE CA	ROSS T	DIXON LA	HISCOCK CH
22-Dec	A	TUFNELL PARK	1-5	IL		JOLLIFFE CA	DIXON LA	EVANS FL	PARTRIDGE GM
29-Dec	H	WYCOMBE W	4-4	IL	og	JOLLIFFE CA	DIXON LA	EVANS FL 1	HISCOCK CH
05-Jan	A	HASTINGS ST.L	1-3	AFASC2		JOLLIFFE CA	ROSS T	DIXON LA	PARTRIDGE GM
12-Jan	A	OXFORD CITY	1-0	AC1	3,000	HUDDLE LT	ROSS T	EVANS FL	HISCOCK CH
19-Jan	A	LEYTONSTONE	2-0	IL		HUDDLE LT	HOLLEBONE GT	EVANS FL	GILBERT HG
02-Feb	A	FROME TOWN	4-2	AC2		HUDDLE LT	HOLLEBONE GT	EVANS FL	HISCOCK CH
09-Feb	H	WIMBLEDON	0-2	IL		HUDDLE LT	ROSS T	PARTRIDGE GM	HISCOCK CH
16-Feb	H	LONDON CALEDONIANS	1-2	IL		HUDDLE LT	ROSS T	EVANS FL	HOLLEBONE GT
23-Feb	A	HITCHIN TOWN	1-0	AC3		HUDDLE LT	HOLLEBONE GT	EVANS FL	SUTCLIFFE J
02-Mar	H	NUNHEAD	1-0	IL		HUDDLE LT	ROSS T	OWEN WV	HISCOCK CH
09-Mar	A	BISHOP AUCKLAND	0-1	AC4	7,640	HUDDLE LT	HOLLEBONE GT	EVANS FL	FELDING I
16-Mar	A	WOKING	2-0	IL		HUDDLE LT	ROSS T	EVANS FL	O'BRIEN PK
23-Mar	H	ILFORD	0-3	IL		HUDDLE LT	ROSS T	EVANS FL	O'BRIEN PK
13-Apr	A	ILFORD	2-2	IL		HUDDLE LT	HISCOCK CH	EVANS FL	MCLAREN JEE
22-Apr	H	KINGSTONIAN	0-4	SCSsf		HUDDLE LT	DIXON LA	EVANS FL	GILBERT HG
24-Apr	A	WIMBLEDON	1-1	IL		HUDDLE LT	ROSS T	EVANS FL	TURNER JRT
29-Apr	A	LONDON CALEDONIANS	3-3	IL		HUDDLE LT	STEVENSON JG	EVANS FL	MCLAREN JEE
01-May	H	ST.ALBANS CITY	5-3	IL		STRINGER EJ	PARTRIDGE GM	EVANS FL	ALLEN G

Friendly Matches

DATE	VEN	OPPONENTS	RES	COMP	ATT	1	2	3	4
06-Oct	A	ALEXANDRA PARK	4-2	F		STRINGER EJ	ROSS T	EVANS FL	O'BRIEN PK
10-Nov	H	OXFORD UNIVERSITY	2-3	F		TRAPP CS	DIXON LA	EVANS FL	O'BRIEN PK
17-Nov	H	CAMBRIDGE UNIV	1-1	F		TRAPP CS	ROSS T	EVANS FL	O'BRIEN PK
06-Apr	A	ROMFORD	1-3	F		HUDDLE LT	DIXON LA	EVANS FL	O'BRIEN PK
20-Apr	H	STOCKTON	4-0	F		HUDDLE LT	DIXON LA	EVANS FL	MURRAY CW
04-May	A	OXTED & DISTRICT	2-0	F		JOLLIFFFE CA	GIBSON LA	EVANS FL	SERGEANT TA

5	6	7	8	9	10	11
JOY B	MCLAREN JEE	COOPER KHL	CRAYTHORNE JR 1	WEBB JOW	GUTHRIE RB	KINGSTON LJ
JOY B 1	MCLAREN JEE	REEVES FK	CRAYTHORNE JR	WEBB JOW	COOPER KHL	KINGSTON LJ
JOY B	COUCHMAN LT	REEVES FK	GUTHRIE RB	WEBB JOW	COOPER KHL	KINGSTON LJ 1
JOY B	MCLAREN JEE	COOPER KHL	FABIAN AH 1	WEBB JOW	COLLINS GAK	KINGSTON LJ
HISCOCK CH	COUCHMAN LT	COOPER KHL 1	GUTHRIE RB	WEBB JOW	COLLINS GAK	KINGSTON LJ
JOY B	MCLAREN JEE	COOPER KHL	FABIAN AH	WEBB JOW 1	COUCHMAN LT 2	COLLINS GAK
JOY B	KINGSLEY PGT	COOPER KHL	KINGSTON LJ	COUCHMAN LT	LENTON PH	COLLINS GAK
JOY B	COUCHMAN LT 1	COLLINS GAK	KINGSTON LJ	MENDL D 1	SYMINGTON JW	BYRNE CJ
COUCHMAN LT	CLEGG AB	COOPER KHL	SYMINGTON JW	MENDL D	REEVES FK	TAYLOR RA 1
JOY B	COUCHMAN LT	KINGSTON LJ	ROGERS VM	MENDL D	O'BRIEN RB	TAYLOR RA
ROSS T	COUCHMAN LT	HIRST KG	KINGSLEY PGT	MENDL D	O'BRIEN RB 1	TAYLOR RA
ROSS T	COUCHMAN LT	KINGSTON LJ 1	RAYNES HM	MENDL D	O'BRIEN RB 1	TAYLOR RA
FELDING I	SUTCLIFFE J	TAYLOR RA	O'BRIEN RB	MENDL D	TERRY AE	KINGSTON LJ
JOY B	O'BRIEN PK	LYWOOD F	FABIAN AH	COUCHMAN LT	KINGSTON LJ	TAYLOR RA
JOY B	HISCOCK CH	LENTON PH	KINGSTON LJ	COUCHMAN LT 3	LYWOOD F 1	TAYLOR RA
JOY B 1	PARTRIDGE GM	LYWOOD F	KINGSTON LJ	COUCHMAN LT	TERRY AE	TAYLOR RA
ROSS T	COUCHMAN LT	LYWOOD F	WEBB JOW	MENDL D	KINGSLEY PGT	KINGSTON LJ 1
STEVENSON JG	COUCHMAN LT	JENKINS RG 1	SAYER C	MENDL D 1	KINGSLEY PGT	COLLINS GAK
HISCOCK CH	JOY B	LYWOOD F 1	SAYER C	COUCHMAN LT	WEBB JOW	KINGSTON LJ
JOY B	SUTCLIFFE J	JENKINS RG	FABIAN AH	COUCHMAN LT	KINGSLEY PGT	COLLINS GAK 1
HISCOCK CH	KINGSLEY PGT	JENKINS RG	FABIAN AH	COUCHMAN LT 2	WEBSTER WH	COLLINS GAK
JOY B	SUTCLIFFE J	KINGSTON LJ 1	GILBERT HG	COUCHMAN LT 1	WEBSTER WH 1	COLLINS GAK 1
JOY B	GUISE JL	KINGSTON LJ	GARNE J	COUCHMAN LT	ROSE H	COLLINS GAK
HISCOCK CH	COUCHMAN LT	JENKINS RG	FABIAN AH 1	WHEWELL WT	SAYER C	COLLINS GAK
JOY B	KINGSLEY PGT	JENKINS RG	FABIAN AH	COUCHMAN LT 1	WEBSTER WH	COLLINS GAK
FELDING I	PARTRIDGE GM	JENKINS RG	ROSE H	COUCHMAN LT	KINGSTON LJ	COLLINS GAK 1
JOY B	SUTCLIFFE J	KINGSTON LJ	ROSE H	COUCHMAN LT	WEBSTER WH	COLLINS GAK
HISCOCK CH	PARTRIDGE GM	KINGSTON LJ	FABIAN AH 1	FROST KAF	ROSE H	COLLINS GAK 1
HISCOCK CH	PARTRIDGE GM	KINGSTON LJ	FABIAN AH	COUCHMAN LT	ROSE H	COLLINS GAK
JOY B	SUTCLIFFE J	COOPER KHL	ALLEN G 1	ROSE H 1	WEBSTER WH	KINGSTON LJ
FAULKNER RG	TAYLOR HR	ROGERS VM	FABIAN AH	ALLEN G	LOCKEY WG	KINGSTON LJ
JOY B	HARLAND SW	WALTER HGB	RILEY F	LOCKEY WG 1	ALLEN G	KINGSTON LJ
SUTCLIFFE J	TAYLOR HR	COLLINS GAK	ALLEN G 2	RILEY F 1	LOCKEY WG	KINGSTON LJ
TURNER JRT	ROSE H	COOPER KHL	FABIAN AH 1	RILEY F 2	LOCKEY WG	KINGSTON LJ 2

5	6	7	8	9	10	11
TURNER JRT	KINGSLEY PGT	KINGSTON LJ	SYMINGTON J 2	MENDL D 2	LENTON PH	TAYLOR RA
ADLARD GH	COUCHMAN LT	MOSS JC	KINGSTON LJ 1	MENDL D 1	RAYNE HM	COLLINS GAK
HISCOCK CH	COUCHMAN LT	KINGSTON LJ	GAMINARA AW	MENDL D	O'BRIEN RB 1	TAYLOR RA
JOY B	SUTCLIFFE JA	LYWOOD F	ROSE H 1	FROST KAF	O'BRIEN RB	COLLINS GAK
SUTCLIFFE JS	MCLAREN JEE	KINGSTON LJ	RILEY F	ALLEN G 2	LOCKEY WG 2	GUTHRIE G
SUTCLIFFE JT	MCLAREN JEE	INGALL IB	ROSE H 1	COOPER KHL	LOCKEY WG 1	KINGSTON LJ

1935/36

DATE	VEN	OPPONENTS	RES	COMP	ATT	1	2	3	4
31-Aug	H	KINGSTONIAN	3-1	IL		HUDDLE LT	ROSS T	EVANS FL	COOPER F
04-Sep	A	WOKING	2-1	IL		HUDDLE LT	ROSS T	EVANS FL	COOPER F
07-Sep	A	ILFORD	1-0	IL		HUDDLE LT	ROSS T	EVANS FL	COOPER F
14-Sep	H	ST.ALBANS CITY	1-3	IL		HUDDLE LT	ROSS T	EVANS FL	COOPER F
19-Sep	H	WOKING	1-1	IL		HUDDLE LT	COOPER F	PARTRIDGE GM	COUCHMAN LT
21-Sep	A	WIMBLEDON	2-1	IL	7,600	HUDDLE LT	ROSS T	WHEWELL WT	COUCHMAN LT
28-Sep	H	TUFNELL PARK	1-1	IL		HUDDLE LT	ROSS T	EVANS FL	COUCHMAN LT
05-Oct	A	LEYTONSTONE	1-0	IL		HUDDLE LT	ROSS T	EVANS FL	O'BRIEN PK
19-Oct	H	LEYLAND MOTORS	0-1	SSC2Q		HUDDLE LT	PARTRIDGE GM	EVANS FL	PHILLIPS E
26-Oct	A	KINGSTONIAN	4-3	IL		HUDDLE LT	WHEWELL WT	EVANS FL	STANTON RG
09-Nov	A	DULWICH HAMLET	4-1	IL		HUDDLE LT	ROSS T	EVANS FL	PARTRIDGE GM
23-Nov	A	LONDON CALEDONIANS	1-3	IL		JOLLIFFE CA	ROSS T	EVANS FL	PARTRIDGE GM
30-Nov	H	KINGSTONIAN	0-1	LSC1		JOLLIFFE CA	ROSS T	EVANS FL	PARTRIDGE GM
14-Dec	H	OXFORD CITY	5-1	IL		HUDDLE LT	ROSS T	EVANS FL	ALLEN G
21-Dec	A	CLAPTON	1-1	IL		HUDDLE LT	ROSS T	EVANS FL	ALLEN G
28-Dec	H	ILFORD	6-2	IL		HUDDLE LT	PARTRIDGE GM	EVANS FL	ALLEN G
04-Jan	H	HORSHAM	4-1	AC1	2,900	HUDDLE LT	ROSS T	EVANS FL	ALLEN G
11-Jan	A	TUFNELL PARK	4-0	IL		HUDDLE LT	ROSS T	EVANS FL	ALLEN G
18-Jan	A	WYCOMBE W	5-2	IL		HUDDLE LT	ROSS T	EVANS FL	COOPER F
01-Feb	A	WYCOMBE W	2-0	AC2		HUDDLE LT	ROSS T	EVANS FL	ALLEN G
08-Feb	H	DULWICH HAMLET	2-2	IL		HUDDLE LT	ROSS T	EVANS FL	HISCOCK CH
22-Feb	H	BISHOP AUCKLAND	4-0	AC3	4,500	HUDDLE LT	ROSS T	EVANS FL	ALLEN G
29-Feb	A	ST.ALBANS CITY	1-5	IL		HUDDLE LT	HOLLIS J	EVANS FL	PARTRIDGE GM
07-Mar	H	ICI ALKALI	3-0	AC4	7,050	HUDDLE LT	ROSS T	EVANS FL	ALLEN G
14-Mar	H	WYCOMBE W	2-3	IL		HUDDLE LT	ROSS T	EVANS FL	HARLAND SW
21-Mar	A	OXFORD CITY	2-5	IL		HUDDLE LT	WHEWELL WT	EVANS FL	HARLAND SW
28-Mar	N dh	ROMFORD	3-2	Acsf		HUDDLE LT	WHEWELL WT	EVANS FL	ALLEN G
04-Apr	H	LEYTONSTONE	2-1	IL		HUDDLE LT	PARTRIDGE GM	EVANS FL	ALLEN G 1
11-Apr	H	LONDON CALEDONIANS	4-0	IL		STRINGER EJ	HOPKINS PG	EVANS FL	PARTRIDGE GM
13-Apr	A	KINGSTONIAN	0-2	SCSsf		STRINGER EJ	HOPKINS PG	EVANS FL	PARTRIDGE GM
18-Apr	N cp	ILFORD	1-1	AC f	27,146	HUDDLE LT	WHEWELL WT	EVANS FL	ALLEN G
20-Apr	H	NUNHEAD	1-3	IL		HUDDLE LT	WHEWELL WT	PARTRIDGE GM	SUTCLIFFE J
23-Apr	A	NUNHEAD	1-1	IL		BROWN WE	DIXON LA	EVANS FL	TURNER JRT
25-Apr	H	CLAPTON	2-1	IL		STRINGER EJ	STEVENSON JG	PARTRIDGE GM	GILBERT TH
27-Apr	A	WIMBLEDON	1-3	IL		HUDDLE LT	DIXON LA	EVANS FL	PALMER RE
02-May	N wh	ILFORD	2-0	AC f	28,000	HUDDLE LT	WHEWELL WT	EVANS FL	ALLEN G

Friendly Matches

DATE	VEN	OPPONENTS	RES	COMP	ATT	1	2	3	4
12-Oct	A	LLOYDS BANK	4-5	F		KING JH	ROSS T	EVANS FL	PHILLIPS E
02-Nov	H	OXFORD UNIVERSITY	2-1	F	og	HUDDLE LT	ROSS T	EVANS FL	COUCHMAN LT

5	6	7	8	9	10	11
TUNNINGTON E	COUCHMAN LT	LYWOOD F	FABIAN AH	RILEY F 1	ALLEN G	KINGSTON LJ 2
TUNNINGTON E	COUCHMAN LT	LYWOOD F 1	FABIAN AH	RILEY F	ALLEN G	KINGSTON LJ 1
COUCHMAN LT	ALLEN G	COOPER KHL	FABIAN AH	RILEY F 1	GUTHRIE RB	MCSWEENEY N
TUNNINGTON E	COUCHMAN LT	LYWOOD F 1	FABIAN AH	RILEY F	ALLEN G	COLLINS PT
WHEWELL WT	SUTCLIFFE J	LYWOOD F	ALLEN G	RILEY F	WEBB JOW 1	O'BRIEN J
JOY B	SUTCLIFFE J	KINGSTON LJ	ALLEN G	WARFIELD JM 1	WEBSTER WH	RILEY F 1
WHEWELL WT	PARTRIDGE GM	LYWOOD F	RILEY F	WARFIELD JM	WEBSTER WH 1	O'BRIEN RB
COOPER F	PARTRIDGE GM	LYWOOD F	HASLEWOOD JSO	CLEMENTS BA 1	RILEY F	KINGSTON LJ
HISCOCK CH	O'BRIEN PK	LYWOOD F	ALLEN G	CLEMENTS BA	O'BRIEN RB	KINGSTON LJ
JOY B 1	PARTRIDGE GM	RAYNER CD 1	FABIAN AH 1	CLEMENTS BA	WEBSTER WH 1	RILEY F
BRADLEY JH	O'BRIEN PK	SHEARER EDR 1	FABIAN AH 1	CLEMENTS BA 1	RILEY F	KINGSTON LJ 1
TARRANT A	O'BRIEN PK	RAYNER CD	HISCOCK CH	CLEMENTS BA	ROSE J	KINGSTON LJ 1
HISCOCK CH	O'BRIEN PK	JENKINS RG	FAIRBAINE RD	CLEMENTS BA	O'BRIEN RB	KINGSTON LJ
JOY B	HISCOCK CH	KINGSTON LJ	FABIAN AH 1	CLEMENTS BA 4	WEBSTER WH	RILEY F
JOY B	COUCHMAN LT	KINGSTON LJ	FABIAN AH	CLEMENTS BA	RILEY F	KINGSLEY PGT
BRADLEY JH	COUCHMAN LT	KINGSTON LJ 1	KINGSLEY PGT	CLEMENTS BA 4	LOCKEY WG 1	SERGEANT EA
JOY B	SUTCLIFFE J	KINGSTON LJ 1	FABIAN AH 2	CLEMENTS BA	WEBSTER WH	RILEY F 1
JOY B	COUCHMAN LT	KINGSTON LJ	FABIAN AH	CLEMENTS BA 3	WEBSTER WH	RILEY F 1
HISCOCK CH	COUCHMAN LT	RAYNER CD 1	SAYER C 1	CLEMENTS BA 2	RILEY F	KINGSTON LJ 1
JOY B	COUCHMAN LT	KINGSTON LJ	FABIAN AH 1	CLEMENTS BA	WEBSTER WH	RILEY F 1
JOY B	COUCHMAN LT	KINGSTON LJ	SAYER C 1	RILEY F	ALLEN G	O'BRIEN RB 1
WARFIELD JM	COUCHMAN LT	SHEARER EDR	FABIAN AH 1	CLEMENTS BA 3	WEBSTER WH	RILEY F
BRADLEY JH	COUCHMAN LT	KINGSTON LJ	FABIAN AH	MEAHCOTE LH	KINGSLEY PGT	O'BRIEN RB 1
JOY B	COUCHMAN LT	KINGSTON LJ	FABIAN AH	CLEMENTS BA 3	WEBSTER WH	RILEY F
HISCOCK CH	COUCHMAN LT	SCOTT HS	FAIRBAINE RD	CLEMENTS BA 2	ENTWISTLE J	KINGSTON LJ
COOPER F	COUCHMAN LT	SAYER C	HASLEWOOD JSO	WARFIELD JM 2	SHEPHERD A	COLLINS PT
JOY B	COUCHMAN LT	SHEARER EDR 2	FABIAN AH	CLEMENTS BA 1	WEBSTER WH	RILEY F
COOPER F	CALDWELL KPS	KINGSTON LJ	FAIRBAINE RD	COUCHMAN LT 1	WEBSTER WH	RILEY F
COOPER F	COUCHMAN LT	KINGSTON LJ	ALLEN G	CLEMENTS BA 2	GUTHRIE RB 2	O'BRIEN RB
COOPER F	COUCHMAN LT	ROGERS VM	ALLEN G	CLEMENTS BA	O'BRIEN RB	KINGSTON LJ
JOY B	COUCHMAN LT	SHEARER EDR	FABIAN AH	CLEMENTS BA	WEBSTER WH	RILEY F 1
TUNNINGTON E	COUCHMAN LT	KINGSTON LJ	FAIRBAINE RD	CLEMENTS BA 1	ALLEN G	RILEY F
TUNNINGTON E 1	COUCHMAN LT	COLLINS PT	FAIRBAINE RD	BENNETT M	GUTHRIE RB	KINGSTON LJ
TURNER JRT	PALMER RE	KINGSTON LJ	ALLEN G 2	LEE J	ENTWISTLE J	O'BRIEN RB
STEVENSON JG	PARTRIDGE GM	COLLINS PT	GUTHRIE RB	WEBB JOW	O'BRIEN RB	KINGSTON LJ 1
JOY B	COUCHMAN LT	SHEARER EDR 1	FABIAN AH	CLEMENTS BA	WEBSTER WH 1	RILEY F

5	6	7	8	9	10	11
PARTRIDGE GM	O'BRIEN PK	KINGSTON LJ	FAIRBAIRN RD	CLEMENTS BA 1	O'BRIEN RB 3	COLLINS PT
BRADLEY JH	PARTRIDGE GM	KINGSTON LJ	FAIRBAIRN RD	CLEMENTS BA 1	ASTON AC	O'BRIEN RB

1936/37

DATE	VEN	OPPONENTS	RES	COMP	ATT	1	2	3	4
29-Aug	A	KINGSTONIAN	0-2	IL		HUDDLE LT	WHEWELL WT	PARTRIDGE GM	COOPER F
03-Sep	H	DULWICH HAMLET	0-4	IL		STRINGER EJ	WHEWELL WT	PARTRIDGE GM	COOPER F
05-Sep	H	ST.ALBANS CITY	4-0	IL		HUDDLE LT	HOPKINS PG	WHEWELL WT	COUCHMAN LT
09-Sep	A	DULWICH HAMLET	2-1	IL	og	HUDDLE LT	HOPKINS PG	WHEWELL WT	CALDWELL KPS
12-Sep	H	WYCOMBE W	4-0	IL		WOOLCOCK AH	HOPKINS PG	WHEWELL WT 1	SUTCLIFFE J
16-Sep	N	KINGSTONIAN	2-2	CC	2,000	WOOLCOCK AH	HOPKINS PG	WHEWELL WT	CALDWELL KPS
19-Sep	A	ILFORD	2-0	IL		HUDDLE LT	SUTCLIFFE J	WHEWELL WT	PETTIT DEA
26-Sep	A	TUFNELL PARK	2-1	IL		HUDDLE LT	HOPKINS PG	WEBB FM	PARTRIDGE GM
03-Oct	A	LONDON CALEDONIANS	3-1	IL		HUDDLE LT	HOPKINS PG	WEBB FM	PARTRIDGE GM
10-Oct	A	WYCOMBE W	1-2	IL		JOLLIFFE CA	HOPKINS PG	WEBB FM	PARTRIDGE GM
17-Oct	H	OXFORD CITY	2-2	IL		JOLLIFFE CA	HOLLEBONE GT	WEBB FM	PARTRIDGE GM
31-Oct	H	WIMBLEDON	2-3	IL		JOLLIFFE CA	HOLLEBONE GT	PARTRIDGE GM	ALLEN G
07-Nov	A	NUNHEAD	0-4	IL		JOLLIFFE CA	BELLE BH	WEBB FM	PARTRIDGE GM
14-Nov	H	WOKING	3-3	IL		JOLLIFFE CA	HOLLEBONE GT	WEBB FM	PARTRIDGE GM
21-Nov	A	WIMBLEDON	0-3	IL		HILL HHC	HOPKINS PG	EVANS FL	PARTRIDGE GM
05-Dec	A	CLAPTON	1-2	IL		HUDDLE LT	WEBB FM	EVANS FL	PARTRIDGE GM
12-Dec	H	KINGSTONIAN	4-1	IL		HUDDLE LT	PARTRIDGE GM	EVANS FL	ALLEN G
19-Dec	A	CLAPTON	3-1	LSC1		HUDDLE LT	WHEWELL WT	EVANS FL	COOPER F
02-Jan	H	LONDON CALEDONIANS	2-1	IL		JOLLIFFE CA	PARTRIDGE GM	SUTCLIFFE J	COOPER F
09-Jan	H	OXFORD CITY	4-1	AC1		HUDDLE LT	STRASSER GA	WHEWELL WT	PETTIT DEA
16-Jan	A	WIMBLEDON	6-1	LSC2		JOLLIFFE CA	STRASSER GA	EVANS FL	PARTRIDGE GM
23-Jan	H	TOOTING & M	3-0	SSC1		JOLLIFFE CA	WEBB FM	EVANS FL	PALMER RE
30-Jan	H	CLAPTON	4-3	IL		JOLLIFFE CA	WHEWELL WT	EVANS FL	STRASSER GA
06-Feb	A	DULWICH HAMLET	0-1	AC2	16,200	JOLLIFFE CA	WHEWELL WT	SUTCLIFFE J	PETTIT DEA
13-Feb	H	BARNET	4-2	LSC3		SESSIONS WK	STRASSER GA	EVANS FL	PARTRIDGE GM
20-Feb	A	WOKING	3-4	IL		SESSIONS WK	STRASSER GA	BELLE BH	PARTRIDGE GM
27-Feb	N i	WALTHAMSTOW AVE	2-2	LSC sf	5,500	SESSIONS WK	SUTCLIFFE J	ALLEN G	COUCHMAN LT 1
06-Mar	A	ILFORD	1-4	IL		SESSIONS WK	WEBB FM	MORELAND CR	PARTRIDGE GM
13-Mar	H	SUTTON UNITED	3-1	SSC2		SESSIONS WK	WEBB FM	EVANS FL	PARTRIDGE GM
20-Mar	A	OXFORD CITY	2-3	IL	1,800	SESSIONS WK	PARTRIDGE GM	MORELAND CR	ALLEN G
03-Apr	A	LEYTONSTONE	0-6	IL		HUDDLE LT	STRASSER GA	MORELAND CR	PARTRIDGE GM
10-Apr	A	DULWICH HAMLET	0-2	SSC sf		SESSIONS WK	WEBB FM	EVANS FL	ALLEN G
17-Apr	N	WALTHAMSTOW AVE	3-12	LSC sf		SESSIONS WK	FAULKNER EA	WEBB FM	ALLEN G
22-Apr	A	ST.ALBANS CITY	0-2	IL		SESSIONS WK	FAULKNER EA	WEBB FM	PARTRIDGE GM
24-Apr		TUFNELL PARK	2-0	IL		SESSIONS WK	PARTRIDGE GM	MORELAND CR	CHEATLE CA
26-Apr	A	GUILDFORD CITY	0-1	SCC f	750	SESSIONS WK	CALDWELL EO	PARTRIDGE GM	CHEATLE CA
28-Apr	H	NUNHEAD	1-1	IL		SESSIONS WK	PARTRIDGE GM	MORELAND CR	CHEATLE CA
01-May	H	LEYTONSTONE	1-5	IL		SESSIONS WK	PARTRIDGE GM	WHEWELL WT	CHEATLE CA

No Surrey Combination Cup semi final has been traced, it is possible as it was a small competition that Casuals received a bye to the final

Friendly Matches

DATE	VEN	OPPONENTS	RES	COMP	ATT	1	2	3	4
01-Sep	H cp	CHINA	5-2	F		HUDDLE LT	SUTCLIFFE JA	WHEWELL WT	TUNNINGTON E
24-Oct	H	CAMBRIDGE UNIV	0-3	F		JOLIFFE CA	HOLLEBONE GT	WEBB FM	PARTRIDGE GM
28-Dec	H	AFA PUBLIC SCHOOLS XI	5-1	F		BROWN WE	BARKER JT	MORELAND CR	CHEATLE CA

5	6	7	8	9	10	11
JOY B	SUTCLIFFE J	KINGSTON LJ	FABIAN AH	CLEMENTS BA	COUCHMAN LT	GUTHRIE RB
TUNNINGTON E	COUCHMAN LT	KINGSTON LJ	COOPER KHL	WHALEY PF	GUTHRIE RB	RILEY F
COOPER F	SUTCLIFFE J 1	COLLINS PT	FABIAN AH 1	COOPER KHL 1	ALLEN G	RILEY F 1
TUNNINGTON E	COOPER F	PARTRIDGE GM	GUTHRIE RB	COUCHMAN LT 1	RILEY F	MCSWEENEY N
JOY B	CALDWELL KPS	COLLINS PT	COUCHMAN LT 1	COOPER KHL 1	RILEY F 1	MCSWEENEY N
TUNNINGTON E	COLLINS GAK	SCOTT HS	COUCHMAN LT 1	LEE J	GUTHRIE RB 1	MCSWEENEY N
JOY B	COUCHMAN LT	COLLINS PT	RILEY F 1	WARFIELD JM 1	WEBSTER WH	MCSWEENEY N
COOPER F	COUCHMAN LT	KINGSTON LJ	FABIAN AH	RILEY F 1	WEBSTER WH 1	SERGEANT EA
COOPER F	COUCHMAN LT	COLLINS PT 3	O'BRIEN RB	LEE J	CLEMENTS BA	KINGSTON LJ
COOPER F	COUCHMAN LT	COLLINS PT	WATERBURY CS	CLEMENTS BA	ROSE H	KINGSTON LJ 1
BRADLEY JH	COUCHMAN LT	COLLINS PT 1	ALLEN G	CLEMENTS BA 1	GUTHRIE RB	KINGSTON LJ
BRADLEY JH	COUCHMAN LT	COLLINS PT	GROVES RW	EDWARDS R 1	KINGSTON LJ	STOKES NB 1
HUNTER PDV	COUCHMAN LT	COLLINS PT	KINGSLEY PGT	EDWARDS R	CLEMENTS BA	KINGSTON LJ
GROVES RW 1	COUCHMAN LT	COLLINS PT 1	KINGSLEY PGT	EDWARDS R	CLEMENTS BA	KINGSTON LJ 1
BELLE BH	WEBB FM	COLLINS PT	SHEPHERD A	CLEMENTS BA	KINGSTON LJ	SERGEANT EA
HUNTER PDV	COUCHMAN LT	SCOTT HS	FABIAN AH	CLEMENTS BA	ALLEN G 1	KINGSTON LJ
SUTCLIFFE J	COUCHMAN LT	COLLINS PT 2	FABIAN AH	CLEMENTS BA	RILEY F 1	KINGSTON LJ 1
JOY B	SUTCLIFFE J	COLLINS PT 1	ALLEN G	CLEMENTS BA 1	GUTHRIE RB	KINGSTON LJ 1
JOY B	CHEATLE CA	COLLINS PT	HASLEWOOD JSO 2	CLEMENTS BA	ENTWISTLE J	KINGSTON LJ
JOY B	CALDWELL KPS	COLLINS PT	FABIAN AH 1	CLEMENTS BA 2	ALLEN G	RILEY F 1
WHEWELL WT	COOPER F	COLLINS PT	FABIAN AH	CLEMENTS BA 4	KINGSLEY PGT 1	KINGSTON LJ
HUNTER PDV	PARTRIDGE GM	COLLINS PT 1	FABIAN AH	CLEMENTS BA 2	KINGSTON LJ	SERGEANT EA
JOY B	KINGSLEY PGT	COLLINS PT 1	FABIAN AH	CLEMENTS BA 1	WEBSTER WH 1	KINGSTON LJ 1
JOY B	ALLEN G	COLLINS PT	FABIAN AH	CLEMENTS BA	WEBSTER WH	RILEY F
WHEWELL WT	CALDWELL KPS	COLLINS PT 1	LAWREY EM	CLEMENTS BA 2	KINGSLEY PGT	KINGSTON LJ 1
BRADLEY JH	CHEATLE CA	COLLINS PT	FABIAN AH	CLEMENTS BA 2	WEBSTER WH	KINGSTON LJ 1
WHEWELL WT	CALDWELL KPS	COLLINS PT	FABIAN AH	CLEMENTS BA 1	KINGSLEY PGT	JENKINS RG
CALDWELL KPS	DAVIES HA	DAVIS FK 1	COUCHMAN LT	SINGLETON A	O'BRIEN RB	COLLINS GAK
STEVENSON JG	GUTHRIE RB	COLLINS PT	SHEPHERD A	CLEMENTS BA 2	O'BRIEN RB 1	COLLINS GAK
COUCHMAN LT	CALDWELL KPS	COLLINS PT	ROSE H 1	EDWARDS R	RILEY F 1	COLLINS GAK
WHEWELL WT	COUCHMAN LT	KINGSTON LJ	ALLEN G	CLEMENTS BA	LOCKEY WG	RILEY F
SUTCLIFFE J	CALDWELL KPS	COLLINS PT	RILEY F	CLEMENTS BA	LOCKEY WG	KINGSTON LJ
COUCHMAN LT	PARTRIDGE GM	COLLINS PT 1	STEVENSON JG	CLEMENTS BA 2	WEBSTER WH	COLLINS GAK
LIDDLE TR	CALDWELL KPS	KINGSTON LJ	SHEPHERD A	EDWARDS R	LOCKEY WG	SERGEANT EA
WHEWELL WT	CALDWELL KPS	COLLINS PT	LOCKEY W 1	CLEMENTS BA	WEBSTER WH 1	ROSE H
WHEWELL WT	CALDWELL KPS	EDWARDS R	ALLEN G	CLEMENTS BA	LOCKEY WG	SMITH EA
SERGEANT EA 1	CALDWELL KPS	COLLINS PT	SHEPHERD A	CLEMENTS BA	LOCKEY WG	COLLINS GAK
LIDDLE TR	CALDWELL KPS	COLLINS PT 1	KINGSTON LJ	CLEMENTS BA	LOCKEY WG	COLLINS GAK

5	6	7	8	9	10	11
JOY B 1	COUCHMAN LT	COLLINS PT 2	FABIAN AH	LEE J	ALLEN G 1	RILEY F 1
HUNTER PDV	COUCHMAN LT	COLLINS PT	SHEPHERD A	CLEMENTS BA	O'BRIEN RB	MCGREGOR R
GRIFFITHS A	WREFORD-BROWN A	COLLINS PT 1	FABIAN AH	CREED AGM 2	WHALEY PF 2	GUTHRIE RB

1937/38

DATE	VEN	OPPONENTS	RES	COMP	ATT	1	2	3	4
02-Sep	A	LEYTONSTONE	0-6	IL		BROWN WE	PARTRIDGE GM	MORELAND CR	HARRISON FW
11-Sep	H	ILFORD	2-4	IL		WOOLCOCK AH	STRASSER GA	SUTCLIFFE J	HARRISON FW
18-Sep	H	WIMBLEDON	0-2	IL		WOOLCOCK AH	BELLE BH	SUTCLIFFE J	HARRISON FW
25-Sep	A	DULWICH HAMLET	2-5	LCC1		WOOLCOCK AH	WHEWELL WT	SUTCLIFFE J	COUCHMAN LT
02-Oct	H	WYCOMBE W	3-2	IL		WOOLCOCK AH	FAULKNER EA	STRASSER GA	DAVIES HA
07-Oct	A	MILLWALL	1-4	LChc1		WOOLCOCK AH	STRASSER GA	WHEWELL WT	DAVIES HA
09-Oct	A	WOKING	2-2	IL		WOOLCOCK AH	BELLE BH	STRASSER GA	PARTRIDGE GM
16-Oct	A	LONDON CALEDONIANS	1-2	IL		BROWN WE	FAULKNER EA	MORELAND CR	HARRISON FW
23-Oct	A	KINGSTONIAN	1-5	IL		WOOLCOCK AH	STRASSER GA	WHEWELL WT	CALDWELL KPS
30-Oct	H	NUNHEAD	2-4	IL		WOOLCOCK AH	BELLE BH	STRASSER GA	CALDWELL KPS
06-Nov	A	ILFORD	0-6	IL		BROWN WE	PARTRIDGE GM	MCLAREN JEE	HARRISON FW
13-Nov	A	TUFNELL PARK	0-2	IL		REED HF	FAULKNER EA	MORELAND CR	COUCHMAN LT
20-Nov	H	LEYTONSTONE	2-4	IL		WOOLCOCK AH	STRASSER GA	WHEWELL WT	CALDWELL KPS
27-Nov	A	KINGSTONIAN	2-2	IL		REED HF	PARTRIDGE GM	MORELAND CR	CHEATLE CA
04-Dec	H	CLAPTON	7-3	IL		REED HF	FAULKNER EA	PARTRIDGE GM	HARRISON FW
11-Dec	A	CLAPTON	2-1	IL		REED HF	PARTRIDGE GM	MORELAND CR	HARRISON FW
18-Dec	H	PINNER	5-1	LSC1		WOOLCOCK AH	PARTRIDGE GM	WHEWELL WT	CHEATLE CA
01-Jan	H	OXFORD CITY	6-0	IL	og	NAYLOR JW	PARTRIDGE GM	ALLEN J	COUCHMAN LT 1
08-Jan	A	BARNET	2-7	LSC2		WOOLCOCK AH	PARTRIDGE GM	MORELAND CR	CHEATLE CA
15-Jan	H @	FINCHLEY	1-4	AC1		NAYLOR JW	STRASSER GA	ALLEN J	PETTIT DEA
22-Jan	A	PO ENGINEERS	0-1	SSC1		REED HF	STRASSER GA	PARTRIDGE GM	CHEATLE CA
29-Jan	H	DULWICH HAMLET	1-2	IL		REED HF	ALLEN J	BOTTOM J	SIMSON MR
05-Feb	H	TUFNELL PARK	1-4	IL		REED HF	FAULKNER EA	MORELAND CR	CHEATLE CA
19-Feb	H	WOKING	4-2	IL		NAYLOR JW	STRASSER GA	ALLEN J	PETERS H
26-Feb	A	WYCOMBE W	4-0	IL		WOOLCOCK AH	ALLEN J	MORELAND CR	CALDWELL KPS
05-Mar	A	OXFORD CITY	2-3	IL		WOOLCOCK AH	PARTRIDGE GM	ALLEN J	CALDWELL KPS 1
12-Mar	H	LONDON CALEDONIANS	3-4	IL	og	WOOLCOCK AH	FAULKNER EA	WHEWELL WT	PARTRIDGE GM
19-Mar	A	WIMBLEDON	1-8	IL		REED HF	HOLROYD JH	ALLEN J	PETERS H
02-Apr	A	NUNHEAD	0-4	IL		NAYLOR JW			
23-Apr	A	ST ALBANS CITY	1-0	IL		WOOLCOCK AH	PARTRIDGE GM	WHEWELL WT	PETERS H
25-Apr	H	ST ALBANS CITY	2-0	IL		WOOLCOCK AH	COUCHMAN LT	STRASSER GA	PETERS H
30-Apr	A	DULWICH HAMLET	2-2	IL		WOOLCOCK AH	STRASSER GA	ALLEN J	PETERS H

Friendly Matches

DATE	VEN	OPPONENTS	RES	COMP	ATT	1	2	3	4
07-May	A	WALTHAMSTOW AVE	0-3	F		WOOLCOCK AH	PARTRIDGE GM	ALLEN J	PETTIT DEA

1937 - Joint Corinthians and Casuals Tour of Jamaica

DATE	VEN	OPPONENTS	RES	COM	ATT	1	2	3	4
04-Aug	A	ST GEORGE'S OLD BOYS	3-1	F	5,000	SESSIONS WK	FAULKNER EO	PARTRIDGE GM	BURROWES JT
07-Aug	A	JAMAICA 1ST COLONY	3-0	F		SESSIONS WK	FAULKNER EO	PARTRIDGE GM	BURROWES JT
09-Aug	A	KINGSTON CLUB	1-2	F		SESSIONS WK	MORELAND CR	PARTRIDGE GM	DAVIES HA
11-Aug	A	JAMAICA 2ND COLONY	1-0	F		SESSIONS WK	FAULKNER EO	MORELAND CR	DAVIES HA
14-Aug	A	SHERWOOD FORESTERS	2-2	F		SESSIONS WK	MORELAND CR	PARTRIDGE GM	DAVIES HA
16-Aug	A	SHERWOOD FORESTERS	2-0	F		SESSIONS WK	FAULKNER EO	MORELAND CR	DAVIES HA

5	6	7	8	9	10	11
LIDDLE TR	COOPER F	SCOTT HS	GUTHRIE RB	CLEMENTS BA	LEE J	KINGSTON LJ
WHEWELL WT 1	CALDWELL KPS	SCOTT HS	EDWARDS R	CLEMENTS BA 1	ALLEN G	COLLINS PT
WHEWELL WT	CALDWELL KPS	COLLINS PT	GROVES RW	CLEMENTS BA	WEBSTER WH	GUTHRIE RB
PETTIT DEA	DAVIES HA	GUTHRIE RB	WEBSTER WH	LEE J 1	HARRISON FW	COLLINS PT 1
WHEWELL WT	PARTRIDGE GM	COLLINS PT 1	SCHOFIELD D	LEE J 1	ROSE H 1	RILEY F
PETTIT DEA	SUTCLIFFE J	EDWARDS R	FABIAN AH	LEE J 1	ALLEN G	CLEMENTS BA
COUCHMAN LT	DAVIES HA	COLLINS PT	FABIAN AH	LEE J 2	SHEARER EDR	RILEY F
HUNTER PDV	PARTRIDGE GM	KINGSTON LJ	SHEPHERD A	SCHOFIELD D	COUCHMAN LT 1	LEIPER WA
WILLIAMS PH	SUTCLIFFE J	SHEARER EDR 1	SCHOFIELD D	LEE J	WEBSTER WH	RILEY F
SUTCLIFFE J	ROSE H	COLLINS PT	FABIAN AH	LEE J 2	WEBSTER WH	RILEY F
WILLIAMS PH	COUCHMAN LT	MULRENAN J	SCHOFIELD D	HAYWOOD JS	RILEY F	KINGSTON LJ
DARWELL-SMITH J	MCLAREN JEE	MULRENAN J	SCHOFIELD D	JOHNSTON K	SERGEANT EA	KINGSTON LJ
WILLIAMS PH 1	COUCHMAN LT	COLLINS PT	SCHOFIELD D	LEE J 1	RILEY F	MULRENAN BW
COUCHMAN LT	BURROWES JT	COLLINS PT	SCHOFIELD D	BARREL JM 2	ROSE H	MULRENAN BW
HUNTER PDV	CALDWELL KPS	SCHOFIELD D	COUCHMAN LT 4	RILEY F	WHALEY PF 1
PENNINGTON K	WHEWELL WT	MULRENAN BW 1	TRAPNELL P	COUCHMAN LT	RILEY F	WHALEY PF
COUCHMAN LT	BURROWES JT	MULRENAN BW	SCHOFIELD D 3	LEE J	RILEY F 1	WEBB JKG 1
WHEWELL WT	DAVIES HA	FABIAN AH 1	ALLEN G	SEAFORD HS 3	WASHINGTON ES	MULRENAN BW
WHEWELL WT	BURROWES JT	MULRENAN BW	FABIAN AH	COUCHMAN LT	SCHOFIELD D	WHALEY PF 2
WHEWELL WT	CALDWELL KPS	SHEARER EDR	FABIAN AH	LEE J 1	RILEY F	MULRENAN BW
WHEWELL WT	COUCHMAN LT	MULRENAN BW	LAWREY EM	SEAFORD HS	ALLEN G	WHALEY PF
PETERS H	BURROWES JT	MULRENAN BW	COUCHMAN LT	LEE J 1	HARRISON K	RILEY F
HOLLIS RM	WILLIAMS PH	WATKINS A	COLLINS PT	LEE J 1	COUCHMAN LT	WHALEY PF
WHEWELL WT	PARTRIDGE GM	COLLINS PT	HARRISON K	LEE J 3	RILEY F 1	MULRENAN BW
STRASSER GA	PARTRIDGE GM	COLLINS PT	FABIAN AH 3	LEE J	RILEY F 1	MULRENAN BW
STRASSER GA	DAVIES HA	COLLINS PT	FABIAN AH	WHEWELL WT 1	RILEY F	MULRENAN BW
WILLIAMS PH	DAVIES HA	MULRENAN BW	FABIAN AH 1	LEE J 1	RILEY F	SERGEANT EA
PENNINGTON K	WHEWELL WT	MULRENAN BW	HARRISON K	SEAFORD HS 1	GUTHRIE RB	REED A
			ALLEN G		WHEWELL WT	
WILLIAMS PH	PETTIT DEA	MULRENAN BW	ALLEN G	HEAD R	LOCKEY WG 1	RILEY F
WILLIAMS PH	PETTIT DEA	MULRENAN BW 1	ALLEN G	WHEWELL WT 1	LOCKEY WG	SERGEANT EA
WILLIAMS PH	PETTIT DEA	MULRENAN BW	ALLEN G	SERGEANT EA 2	ELLAM A	SMAILES S

5	6	7	8	9	10	11
COUCHMAN LT	SHACKLETON F	MULRENAN BW	WINGFIELD A	LEE J	WOODCOCK RG	SARGENT EA

5	6	7	8	9	10	11
WILLIAMS PH	CALDWELL KPS	COLLINS PT	FABIAN AH 1	EDWARDS 1	ALLEN G 1	DAVIES HA
WILLIAMS PH	CALDWELL KPS	COLLINS PT	FABIAN AH	EDWARDS 3	ALLEN G	DAVIES HA
WILLIAMS PH 1	BURROWES JT	COLLINS PT	GROVES RWE	EDWARDS	SEAFORD HS	ALLEN G
WILLIAMS PH	CALDWELL KPS	COLLINS PT	FABIAN AH	EDWARDS 1	ALLEN G	SEAFORD HS
WILLIAMS PH	CALDWELL KPS	COLLINS PT	FABIAN AH 1	SEAFORD HS	ALLEN G 1	GROVES RWE
WILLIAMS PH	CALDWELL KPS	COLLINS PT	EDWARDS 1	SEAFORD HS	ALLEN G	GROVES RWE 1

1938/39

DATE	VEN	OPPONENTS	RES	COMP	ATT	1	2	3	4
27-Aug	A	WYCOMBE W	2-2	IL	3,000	WOOLCOCK AH	STRASSER GA	SUTCLIFFE J	PETERS H
03-Sep	H	ILFORD	0-2	IL	1,000	WOOLCOCK AH	STRASSER GA	SUTCLIFFE J	PETERS H
08-Sep	A	ST ALBANS CITY	3-2	IL		WOOLCOCK AH	WHEWELL WT	SUTCLIFFE J	PETTIT DEA
10-Sep	A	CLAPTON	4-3	IL		WOOLCOCK AH	STRASSER GA	WHEWELL WT	COUCHMAN LT
14-Sep	H	ST ALBANS CITY	2-1	IL		WOOLCOCK AH	STRASSER GA	WHEWELL WT	CHEATLE CA
17-Sep	A	LEYTONSTONE	0-2	IL		WOOLCOCK AH	STRASSER GA	WHEWELL WT	COUCHMAN LT
24-Sep	A	OXFORD CITY	2-0	IL		WOOLCOCK AH	STRASSER GA	WHEWELL WT	PETTIT DEA
01-Oct	H	WOKING	0-3	IL		WOOLCOCK AH	STRASSER GA	WHEWELL WT	CHEATLE CA
08-Oct	A	LONDON CALEDONIANS	1-1	IL					
15-Oct	H	NUNHEAD	2-3	IL		WOOLCOCK AH	ALLEN J	MORELAND CR	PETTIT DEA
22-Oct	A	KINGSTONIAN	2-3	IL		BIRTLES S	BELLE BH	BOTTOM J	SHACKLETON H
05-Nov	H	LEYTONSTONE	1-4	IL		WOOLCOCK AH	STRASSER GA	WHEWELL WT 1	PETTIT DEA
19-Nov	H	KINGSTONIAN	1-2	IL		REED HF	ALLEN J	BOTTOM J	CHEATLE CA
26-Nov	A	WIMBLEDON	4-3	IL		REED HF	ALLEN J	BRADLEY JH	SHACKLETON H
03-Dec	H	CLAPTON	2-3	IL	og	WOOLCOCK AH	ALLEN J	BOTTOM J	SHACKLETON H
10-Dec	A	ILFORD	1-1	IL	2,500	WOOLCOCK AH	STRASSER GA	ALLEN J	CHEATLE CA
17-Dec	A	TUFNELL PARK	0-2	LSC1		WOOLCOCK AH			
31-Dec	H	TUFNELL PARK	3-1	IL		REED HF	BELLE BH	ALLEN J	PETERS H
07-Jan	H	WYCOMBE W	4-2	IL		WOOLCOCK AH	STRASSER GA	ALLEN J	PETTIT DEA
14-Jan	A	HARWICH & PARKESTON	9-1	AC1		WOOLCOCK AH	STRASSER GA	ALLEN J	DAVIES HA
21-Jan	A	SUTTON UNITED	4-4	SSC1	og	WOOLCOCK AH	WHALEY PF	ALLEN J	PETTIT DEA
28-Jan	A	SUTTON UNITED	0-1	SSC1		WOOLCOCK AH	STRASSER GA	ALLEN J	DAVIES HA
04-Feb	A	LEYTON	0-1	AC2		REED HF	STRASSER GA	ALLEN J	DAVIES HA
11-Feb	H	LONDON CALEDONIANS	4-0	IL		REED HF	STRASSER GA	ALLEN J	KILKENNY JC
18-Feb	A	NUNHEAD	1-1	IL		REED HF	STRASSER GA	ALLEN J	PETTIT DEA
04-Mar	A	WOKING	1-1	IL		REED HF	STRASSER GA	ALLEN J	CHEATLE CA
11-Mar	A	TUFNELL PARK	4-1	IL		REED HF			
18-Mar	H	OXFORD CITY	4-1	IL		WOOLCOCK AH	BELLE BH	ALLEN J	CHEATLE CA
01-Apr	A	DULWICH HAMLET	1-5	IL	7,000	WOOLCOCK AH	STRASSER GA	MORELAND CR	DAVIES HA
15-Apr	H	DULWICH HAMLET	1-1	IL		WOOLCOCK AH	STRASSER GA	ALLEN J	PETTIT DEA
26-Apr	A	GOLDERS GREEN	2-0	WMC	og	WOOLCOCK AH	STRASSER GA	ALLEN J	TEMPLAR F
06-May	H	WIMBLEDON	4-3	IL		WOOLCOCK AH	STRASSER GA	ALLEN J	GRIFFITHS AH

Friendly Matches

DATE	VEN	OPPONENTS	RES	COMP	ATT	1	2	3	4
19-Oct	H	READING UNIVERSITY	2-0	F	%				

5	6	7	8	9	10	11
HUNTER PDV	PETTIT DEA	COLLINS PT	ALLEN G	LEE J 1	COUCHMAN LT	WHALEY PF 1
HUNTER PDV	COUCHMAN LT	COLLINS PT	ALLEN G	WHEWELL WT	ENTWISTLE J	WHALEY PF
HUNTER PDV	ALLEN G	CHEATLE CA	EDELSTON M	LEE J 3	ENTWISTLE J	SERGEANT EA
PETERS H	SUTCLIFFE J	PHILLIPS NJ	ALLEN G	LEE J 4	ENTWISTLE J	SERGEANT EA
HUNTER PDV	COUCHMAN LT	PHILLIPS NJ 1	THWAITES PN 1	LEE J	WHALEY PF	SERGEANT EA
PETERS H	DAVIES HA	COLLINS PT	PETTIT DEA	LEE J	ENTWISTLE J	SERGEANT EA
PETERS H	DAVIES HA	COLLINS PT	THWAITES PN	LEE J 2	ENTWISTLE J	LOMAS JM
PETERS H	SUTCLIFFE J	COLLINS PT	THWAITES PN	LEE J	ENTWISTLE J	WEBSTER WH
					KELLY J 1	
HOLLIS RM	JAMES H	COLLINS PT	SHEPHERD A	LEE J	WEBSTER WH 1	O'BRIEN RB 1
WILLIAMS PH	PETERS H	COLLINS PT 1	SHEPHERD A	SETTLE A	ENTWISTLE J 1	SERGEANT EA
PETERS H	CALDWELL KPS	COLLINS PT	CARNEY LF	LEE J	KELLY J	ENTWISTLE J
WILLIAMS PH	PETERS H	COLLINS PT 1	GRIBBLE A	JAMES A	SHEPHERD A	MULRENAN BW
HOLLIS RM	CHEATLE CA	CALDWELL KPS	WATTS-SMITH DS	KELLY J 3	JOHNSON J 1	SERGEANT EA
HUNTER PDV	CHEATLE CA	SHEPHERD A 1	THWAITES PN	LEE J	KELLY J	COLLINS PT
COUCHMAN LT	PETTIT DEA	COLLINS PT 1	SHEPHERD A	LEE J	WASHINGTON ES	ENTWISTLE J
				LEE J	O'BRIEN RB	COLLINS PT
WHEWELL WT	COUCHMAN LT	FINLAY DO	JOHNSTON J	GOMM BA 1	WASHINGTON ES 1	COLLINS PT 1
WHEWELL WT	COUCHMAN LT 1	FINLAY DO 1	WATTS-SMITH DS	LEE J 2	SHEPHERD A	COLLINS PT
WHEWELL WT	COUCHMAN LT	COLLINS PT 1	SHEPHERD A	LEE J 4	WASHINGTON ES 2	RILEY F 2
COUCHMAN LT 1	ENTWISTLE J	COLLINS PT 1	FABIAN AH	LATHAM JW 1	SHEPHERD A	RILEY F
WHEWELL WT	PETTIT DEA	FINLAY DO	WATTS-SMITH DS	LEE J	SHEPHERD A	ENTWISTLE J
WHEWELL WT	COUCHMAN LT	COLLINS PT	ENTWISTLE J	LEE J	WASHINGTON ES	RILEY F
SUTCLIFFE J	COUCHMAN LT	ROGERS VM 1	HASLEWOOD JSO	LEE J 3	ENTWISTLE J	WHALEY PF
SUTCLIFFE J	COUCHMAN LT	FINLAY DO	SHEPHERD A 1	LEE J	BINCH JH	ENTWISTLE J
WHEWELL WT	WHALEY PF	COLLINS PT	SHEPHERD A	LEE J	BINCH JH 1	ENTWISTLE J
WHEWELL WT				LEE J 3	BINCH JH 1	
WILLIAMS PH	SCOTT JKC	CREED AJM	ENTWISTLE J 1	LEE J 2	BINCH JH 1	MULRENAN BW
SUTCLIFFE J	PETTIT DEA	PETTIT HE	SHEPHERD A	GOMM BA	LEES RW 1	RILEY F
WHEWELL WT	WILLIAMS PH	FINLAY DO	EDELSTON M	LEE J 1	LOCKEY WG	RILEY F
COUCHMAN LT	PETTIT DEA	BREMNER D	EDELSTON M	LEE J 1	LOCKEY WG	WEBSTER WH
BRADLEY JH	WILLIAMS PH	SHEPHERD A 1	EDELSTON M 1	LEE J	LOCKEY WG 1	RILEY F 1

5	6	7	8	9	10	11

CASUALS ALL TIME APPEARANCES

NAME	APPS	GOALS
ABRAMS HCD	1	0
ACHESON-GRAY	1	0
ACKLAND BM	2	1
ACKROYD E	1	0
ADAMS FA	1	0
ADAMS FE	65	9
ADAMS HF	1	0
ADAMS HN	3	1
ADAMS JR	1	0
ADAMS NP	21	0
ADAMS O	1	0
ADAMS WG	34	1
ADAMS WP	1	0
ADDISON JS	9	0
ADLARD GH	1	0
ADLER H	1	0
ADMIRAL JG	1	0
AGAIR CH	3	1
AINGER WH	34	30
AIREY TAA	4	0
ALCOCK WG	1	0
ALEXANDER CL	23	16
ALEXANDER CW	110	77
ALEXANDER EB (1)	1	0
ALEXANDER EB (2)	1	1
ALEXANDER ER	2	0
ALINGTON CL	2	0
ALLAN HC	1	0
ALLARD FM	1	0
ALLEN AR	1	0
ALLEN B	1	0
ALLEN G	55	7
ALLEN HC	10	0
ALLEN J	26	0
ALSTON GP	1	0
ALSTON HN	25	7
ALSTON NH	1	1
AMOS A	7	0
AMOS HGM	1	0
ANDERSON EP	7	0
ANDERSON ET	1	0
ANDERSON FJ	2	0
ANDERSON KB	2	0
ANDERSON W	2	2
ANDERSON WC	1	0
ANDREWS	1	0
ANDREWS A (1)	1	0
ANDREWS A (2)	1	0
ANDREWS E	1	0
ANDREWS F	5	0
ANDREWS FA	1	0
ANDREWS HG	1	0
ANDREWS HE	1	0
ANDREWS WH	17	9
ANTILL DS	12	0
APPLETON JA	1	0
APPLETON RM	1	0
ARGYLE JD	1	0
ARKWRIGHT CH	4	2
ARLINGTON GH	1	0
ARMSTRONG FC	1	0
ARMSTRONG FP	1	0
ARMSTRONG PM	1	1
ARTHUR SR	16	1

NAME	APPS	GOALS
ARUNDEL AD	9	6
ASHBURNER WT	1	0
ASHBY G	1	0
ASHCROFT JM	3	1
ASHLEY FA	1	0
ASHLEY FN	1	0
ASHTON CT	21	20
ASHTON G	2	2
ASHTON HO	2	0
ASHTON NC	3	0
ASTE GA	1	0
ASTLEY FW	1	1
ASTON FM	1	1
ATHERINGTON H	1	0
ATHERLEY H	2	0
ATKINSON AG	1	0
ATKINSON EH	4	0
ATWOOD WH	1	0
AUSTEN HCM	1	0
AUSTEN WAE	3	0
AUSTIN AE	1	0
AUSTIN HN	1	0
AUSTIN WSB	1	0
AUTOUEY R	1	0
BACHE HG	7	6
BADHAM JT	1	0
BAGNALL R ST V	1	0
BAGSHAW EC	11	0
BAGSHAW F	1	0
BAGSHAW NC	1	0
BAGSHAW WH	13	0
BAGSHAWE GC	1	0
BAILEY NC	2	2
BAIN FW	4	1
BAINES AGP	20	0
BAIRD F	1	1
BAKER B	1	0
BAKER J	1	0
BAKER JM	1	0
BAKER W	1	0
BALDWIN WW	1	0
BALFOUR AJ	1	0
BALFOUR AM	18	0
BALFOUR RN	27	0
BALFOUR-MELVILLE JE	2	1
BALLANTINE T	1	0
BAMBRIDGE EC	4	9
BANN	1	0
BARBER A	2	0
BARBER AT	1	0
BARBER HN	25	16
BARBOUR RE	1	0
BARDEN VM	1	0
BARDEN YMH	2	0
BARENS E	1	1
BARFORD RF	1	0
BARKER AR	24	8
BARKER JT	5	1
BARKER MM	1	0
BARKER RA	1	0
BARKER RR	243	15
BARKERS S	1	0
BARLOW MY	1	0

NAME	APPS	GOALS
BARMBY FJ	1	0
BARNABY	1	0
BARNARD	1	0
BARNARD FH	5	1
BARNARD RL	16	0
BARNBY AC	1	0
BARNBY LY	3	1
BARNETT RO	1	0
BARNETT WM	1	0
BARNETT-STUART E	1	0
BARNIE-ADSHEAD WR	7	0
BARNLEY	1	0
BARRACLOUGH HC	24	13
BARRATT L	1	0
BARREL JM	1	2
BARRETT FH	2	0
BARRETT FJ	1	0
BARRETT HR	149	10
BARRETT HW	4	3
BARRETT-HAMILTON GE	7	0
BARROW FR	1	0
BARROW J	1	0
BARRY	1	0
BARRY CF	1	0
BARTLETT (SUB)	1	0
BARTLETT V	1	0
BARTLEY A	1	0
BARTLEY EH	2	0
BARTLEY PR	1	0
BARTLEY TR	2	0
BARTON A	3	1
BARTON CT	1	0
BARTON EH	1	0
BARTON GB	2	2
BARTON GD	1	0
BARTY-KING GI	3	0
BARWELL	1	0
BARWELL CSW	1	0
BARWELL FR	12	5
BARWELL WT	6	1
BATCHELOR AE	4	0
BATEMAN W	1	0
BATHURST JA	8	2
BATTEN J	1	0
BATTERSEY HF	1	0
BAXTER	1	0
BAZELL H	5	2
BAZELL R	4	1
BEARDSLEY GL	3	0
BEARDSLEY HL	28	1
BEARE R	2	0
BEASLEY C	3	1
BEASLEY EH	2	0
BEASLEY HOC	7	1
BEASLEY J	2	2
BEAUMONT H	1	0
BEAVIS J	1	0
BECK PL	11	1
BECKET SW	1	0
BECKWITH EC	1	0
BECKWITH EG	1	0
BEDFORD AER	12	0
BEESON NW	3	0

292

NAME	APPS	GOALS
BELCHER AH	1	0
BELCHER BA	1	0
BELCHER C	1	0
BELCHER EA	2	0
BELCHER G	2	0
BELCHER RA	1	1
BELL BW	6	1
BELL OB	1	0
BELLE BH	9	0
BELLHOUSE	1	0
BELLHOUSE EW	9	0
BELLHOUSE GW	2	0
BELLHOUSE JW	3	0
BELLHOUSE TW	3	0
BENEST HV	2	0
BENKA HF	9	8
BENNET EO	1	0
BENNETT CT	1	0
BENNETT FA	1	2
BENNETT G	1	1
BENNETT JA	1	0
BENNETT JH	5	4
BENNETT M	1	0
BENSON EPS	1	0
BENTON T	1	0
BENWELL JO	2	0
BERRY EA	3	0
BERWICK REH	3	0
BETHEL V	1	0
BEVAN CO	1	0
BEWRING W	1	0
BICKLE AG	1	0
BICKLEY F	259	42
BIGGS WH	1	0
BILBY EV	3	0
BILSTOW ES	1	0
BINCH JH	4	3
BIRCH AE	33	0
BIRCH JF	1	0
BIRCH WG	3	0
BIRD FA	2	1
BIRD FN	2	2
BIRD HJ	1	0
BIRD WS	3	1
BIRKS AH	47	20
BIRRELL HA	26	1
BIRTLES S	1	0
BISS JCV	1	0
BISSEKER EG	22	15
BISSEKER H	1	0
BLACK R	1	0
BLACK W	1	2
BLACKBURN W	6	5
BLACKSTONE AF	1	0
BLAGDEN EJ	1	0
BLAGDEN JJ	1	0
BLAIN CF	2	0
BLAIN GF	1	0
BLAINE T	1	0
BLAKE GC	1	0
BLAKER AP	1	0
BLAKER H	1	2
BLAKER HR	83	9
BLAKER RNR	11	11
BLANE	1	0
BLASSON CA	3	0
BLASSON CH	2	0
BLASSON CO	4	1
BLASSON EA	1	0
BLENKIRON TW	109	8
BLEWITT R	1	0
BLISS EC	4	0
BLOUNT GB	11	0
BLOUNT R	4	0
BLUNT E	1	0
BLUNT F	1	0
BLUNT RA	38	5
BLUNT RG	1	0
BODDINGTON HC	3	0
BODDINGTON N	6	0
BOISSIER AP	1	0
BOLTON HE	1	0
BOMPAS HS	1	0
BOND CH	1	0
BOND F	1	0
BONE J	5	1
BONHAM-CARTER AD	6	0
BONSELL AD	1	0
BONSEY WH	1	0
BONSFORD AF	1	0
BOOKER AJN	1	0
BOOKER C	1	0
BOREHAM HR	1	0
BOROUGH J	7	0
BOROUGH RJ	1	0
BORROW SW	1	0
BORROW WS	1	0
BOSANQUET J	1	0
BOSTOCK AH	1	0
BOSTOCK AN	1	0
BOSTOCK FH	1	0
BOSWELL FJ	1	3
BOSWELL FT	2	0
BOSWORTH-SMITH BN	11	5
BOTTOM J	4	0
BOUCHER C	1	0
BOUCHER N	1	0
BOULTON	1	0
BOULTON A	1	0
BOURNE AC	3	0
BOUSTEAD RN	32	0
BOUSTEAD WH	1	0
BOUTTON L	1	0
BOWDLER EH	1	1
BOWDLER JCH	1	0
BOWER AG	42	1
BOWER MB	13	0
BOWRING FH	2	0
BOWRING W	1	0
BOX AR	1	0
BRADLEY JH	8	0
BRADSHAW WH	3	0
BRAITHWAITE PP	29	4
BRAMIDGE L	3	0
BRAMLEY FH	4	0
BRAMLEY HR	7	0
BRANDON C	2	0
BRANSTON GC	1	0
BRAY EH	26	3
BRAY JE	6	2
BREALEY H	3	1
BREMNER D	1	0
BREMNER K	1	0
BRENAN AR	3	0
BRERETON	1	0
BRIGGS C	1	0
BRIGGS H	1	0
BRIGGS TM	17	5
BRIGHT AS	1	0
BRIGHT CH	1	2
BRIGHTON R	1	0
BRISLEY CE	62	42
BRITTAN EM	4	0
BRITTEN	1	0
BRITTEN AF	1	0
BROAD JD	14	6
BROADBENT HJ	1	1
BROCKLESBY SV	1	0
BRODIE HW	20	12
BRODIE TR	1	0
BRODIE WS	3	0
BROGDEN H	2	0
BROOK AK	51	1
BROOKER AGN	1	0
BROOKS	1	0
BROOKS AH	1	0
BROOKS HT	1	0
BROUGHTON H	1	0
BROUGHTON L (sub)	1	0
BROWN A	1	0
BROWN CH	1	0
BROWN E	1	0
BROWN FH	1	0
BROWN GD	1	0
BROWN H	1	0
BROWN J (1)	1	0
BROWN J (2)	1	1
BROWN RP	4	0
BROWN TH	10	1
BROWN WE	4	0
BROWN WL	1	0
BROWNLOW JR HON	2	0
BRUCE	1	0
BRUCE FJ	1	0
BRUCE TJ	7	0
BRUCE WW	7	4
BRUCE-HALL M	1	0
BRUCE-HALL R	9	0
BRUNDETT JO	1	0
BRUNNER	1	0
BRUTTON HL	2	0
BRYANT	1	0
BRYANT BE	18	4
BRYANT FE	7	5
BRYANT FH	42	29
BRYANT HJ	10	5
BRYANT LH	1	2
BRYDON P	10	4
BRYDONE RM	13	12
BUCKINGHAM HC	3	0
BUCKLEY PF	10	1
BUCKMASTER WS	2	0
BUDD CT	1	0
BUDGE PP	13	11
BULL DR	1	0
BULL OB	2	0
BULLER AF	3	0
BULLOCK	1	2
BULLOCK GF	1	1
BULMAN BM	81	1
BULTEN	1	0
BUNTROY HE	3	0
BURDON NE	1	0
BURGE F	22	5
BURNETT-STUART G	2	0
BURNUP CJ	20	7
BURROWS	1	0
BURROWS FR	1	0
BURROWS JT	4	0
BURROWS LR	1	0
BURT CCF	1	0
BURT WJ	1	0
BURTENSHAW G	1	0
BURTON FE	1	2
BURY HV	7	0
BURY L	1	0
BUSH JT	2	0
BUTCHER AH	6	0
BUXTON SJ	5	0
BUZZARD AD	3	1
BUZZARD EF	20	4

NAME	APPS	GOALS
BYRNE CJ	1	0
CADMAN PSC	5	1
CALDWELL EO	1	0
CALDWELL KPS	26	1
CAMERON J	1	0
CAMPBELL FC	1	0
CAMPBELL IPF	20	0
CAMPBELL JA	1	0
CAMPBELL LN	2	0
CAMPBELL RR	1	0
CAMPBELL W	10	0
CANDLER AL	1	0
CANDY WF	1	0
CANE J	2	0
CANNING GH	1	0
CANNON TH	1	0
CANNY GB	16	1
CARDEW AE	12	4
CAREY HL	2	2
CAREY HR	3	0
CARLTON FH	9	2
CARLTON FR	1	0
CARLTON FW	30	6
CARLTON JE	1	0
CARLTON WF	1	0
CARLYON S	2	0
CARNEY LF	1	0
CARPENTER CE	8	0
CARPMAEL WP	18	0
CARR	1	0
CARR AJ	14	0
CARR AL	5	0
CARR AT	5	0
CARR JL	1	0
CARR LC	1	0
CARRINGTON HW	13	7
CARSON HJ	2	0
CARTER AJ	5	1
CARTER CC	1	0
CARTER EB	1	0
CARTER GC	1	0
CARTER KB	1	0
CARTER RD	1	1
CARTER WL	2	1
CARTMAN PC	1	0
CARTWRIGHT EH	1	0
CASSWELL AE	1	1
CASTLES A	1	0
CASTLEY EG	1	0
CATER GH	1	0
CATTLEY JF	4	2
CATTLEY TF	7	0
CATTLEY W	1	0
CAUDWELL E	1	1
CAUDWELL LS	2	1
CAUSTON	1	1
CAVILL WV	7	0
CAWSTON E	3	0
CHADDER AH	3	0
CHADWICK GE	1	0
CHAMPNEYS J	2	0
CHAPMAN EL	1	0
CHAPMAN WG	1	0
CHARLES CJ	1	0
CHARLES MJ	1	0
CHARLES W	1	0
CHARMAN FH	1	0
CHARRINGTON E	26	0
CHARRINGTON FA	1	0
CHARRINGTON FH	1	0
CHATTERTON AF	1	0
CHATTERTON FV	1	0
CHATTERTON HF	1	0
CHATTERTON RB	1	0
CHATTERTON W	1	1
CHAUNCE KN	1	0
CHEADE AR	4	0
CHEALES F	1	0
CHEATLE CA	20	0
CHEVELLY HC	1	0
CHOON HU	1	0
CHOWCHOW R	1	0
CHRISTIAN FW	1	0
CHURCH MB	5	0
CHURCH MR	4	0
CHURCHILL GS	6	0
CHUTE JC	1	0
CIOWAN WM	1	0
CLARK AM	1	0
CLARK HN	26	0
CLARK J	1	0
CLARK TP	1	0
CLARKE A	2	0
CLARKE B	1	0
CLARKE DH	6	2
CLARKE HR (SUB)	1	0
CLARKE MH	57	19
CLARKE TBA	11	9
CLARKESON ES	1	0
CLARKSON (SUB)	1	0
CLARKSON F	1	0
CLEAVE A	5	0
CLEAVE JR	4	0
CLEAVE R	100	3
CLEAVES CF	1	3
CLEGG AB	1	0
CLEMENTS BA	53	48
CLEMENTS CT	2	1
CLIFFORD EC	1	1
CLOKE HP	12	0
CLOUSTON OR	1	0
CLUXON A	1	0
COAST JP	5	0
'COATS' P	1	0
COBB BB	1	0
COBBETT PG (SUB)	1	0
COBBOLD WN	5	2
COCHRANE J	2	0
COCKBURN GE	5	1
COCKELL FH	1	1
COLDHAM JM	1	0
COLEBROOK D	10	0
COLEBROOKE D	7	0
COLEBY AT	3	2
COLEMAN S	1	2
COLERIDGE GD	4	0
COLERIDGE HON. JC	1	0
COLES WT	1	0
COLEY GH	1	0
COLLIER CBG	1	0
COLLIER GCB	1	0
COLLIER HJ	18	22
COLLIER JS	3	0
COLLIN ALLEN H	1	0
COLLINS CH	1	1
COLLINS EH	2	0
COLLINS GAK	48	19
COLLINS PT	62	21
COLLISON C	1	0
COLVILLE PC	1	0
COMPTON ED	26	14
CONNOLLY	1	0
CONOY FD	1	0
COOCH RH	1	0
COODE AP	2	0
COODE AT	5	0
COODE CP	5	0
COOK H	5	0
COOK JA	1	0
COOKE AT	2	0
COOKE CP	1	0
COOKE EM	1	0
COOKE HHA	13	0
COOKE RC	1	0
COOKE T	5	0
COOKE WH	1	0
COOKSON CF	1	0
COOKSON RT	1	0
COOPER	1	0
COOPER EC	2	2
COOPER EH	1	0
COOPER F	22	0
COOPER FH	3	0
COOPER FJ	5	0
COOPER HES	5	0
COOPER KHL	38	13
COOPER L	1	0
COOPER LJ	1	0
COOPER LP	2	0
COOPER NC	6	0
COOPER RG	1	0
COOPER SB	1	3
COPPELSTON JH	1	0
CORBETT A?	2	0
CORBETT AG	22	0
CORBETT AL	52	26
CORBETT BO	13	7
CORBETT LOWE	1	0
CORBETT R	6	7
CORFIELD A	1	0
CORFIELD EB	1	1
CORNELIUS NS	3	3
CORNELIUS-BROWN JG	1	0
CORNFORD JH	1	0
CORNISH HG	2	0
CORNISH HH	3	0
CORNWALLIS AW	2	0
CORNWALLIS FSW	1	0
CORRY HB	1	0
COTTERILL CH	1	0
COTTERILL GH	6	2
COTTERILL LL	7	3
COTTON R	1	0
COUCH DH	24	5
COUCHMAN LT	192	42
COUCHMAN RH	2	0
COULTHURST TT	5	0
COUPAR SE	1	1
COUPER SB	1	0
COURT PH	5	0
COVENTRY CJ	2	0
COVERDALE H	1	0
COVINGTON CK	1	0
COWAN DC	7	0
COWAN T	1	0
COWIE A	1	0
COWIE HN	1	0
COWIE RM	11	0
COWLEY J	1	0
COWLEY HC	1	0
COWPER SH	4	0
COX AG	12	0
COX JR	1	0
COX LL	34	9
COX NJ	1	1
COX S	31	9
CRABTREE H	1	1
CRAIG ?	1	0
CRAIG JD	64	3
CRAIG RD	62	1
CRAIK HD	2	0
CRAIK JD	1	0

NAME	APPS	GOALS
CRANSTOUN JC	1	0
CRAWFORD RC	1	1
CRAWFORD RO	14	10
CRAWLEY (SUB)	1	0
CRAWLEY E	1	0
CRAWLEY EC	3	0
CRAWLEY FHP	1	0
CRAWLEY HH	13	2
CRAWLEY PAS	9	0
CRAYTHORNE JR	6	2
CREE A	37	9
CREED AJM	1	0
CREEK FNS	4	3
CRESSWELL	1	0
CRESSWELL CE	29	6
CREWS AC	1	0
CREWS AE	12	0
CREWS CB	11	0
CRISP	1	0
CROFT T de C	1	0
CROLE-REES HB	3	1
CROLY HP	1	0
CROMMELIN-BROWN JL	8	0
CRONDY WM	1	0
CROPPER C	1	0
CROPPER CE	1	0
CROSDALE G	2	5
CROSS AB	1	0
CROSS FJK	40	10
CROSSLAND GL	2	0
CROWDY C	1	0
CROWTHER CNB	1	0
CRUIKSHANK G	8	6
CRUIKSHANK WJ	2	0
CRUIKSHANK WR	8	1
CRUMMACK RW	17	11
CRUMP CW	1	0
CRUMP RD	4	1
CRUMP W	1	0
CULLING G	1	0
CUMMING G	7	1
CURREY ES	3	0
CURREY GE	2	0
CURRIE CE	14	14
CURTIS GF	4	1
CURWEN WJH	6	0
CUTCHIE B (SUB)	1	0
CUTHBERTSON H	2	0
CUTTER H	1	3
CUTTER RC	103	52
DADLEY AB	1	0
DAFT HB	3	1
DAKINS HF	1	0
DALGLEISH EF	2	0
DALTON GT	1	1
DANIEL AM	2	0
DANIELL J	1	0
DANIELS GP (sub)	2	0
DANKES SH	1	0
DARBYSHIRE CS	3	0
D'ARCY-THOMPSON P	1	0
DARVELL S	18	0
DARVELL TJ	1	0
DARWELL-SMITH J	1	0
DASHWOOD L	2	2
DAVIDSON JL	8	3
DAVIDSON JLM	9	0
DAVIDSON W	1	0
DAVIES AO	3	0
DAVIES AT	2	1
DAVIES G	60	7
DAVIES GL	1	0
DAVIES H	1	0
DAVIES HA	14	0
DAVIES HH	1	0
DAVIES LA	3	0
DAVIES LI	13	11
DAVIES NH	1	0
DAVIES PH	1	1
DAVIES SJ	1	0
DAVIES V	2	0
DAVIS A (SUB)	1	0
DAVIS CJ	1	0
DAVIS FK	1	1
DAVIS V	1	0
DAW JW	4	0
DAWBARN GM	8	0
DAWE LS	15	3
DAWSON GW	2	0
DAWSON P	1	0
DAY AP	7	0
DAY AT	1	0
DAY GD	1	0
DAY SE	2	0
DAY SH	4	4
DE KOVEN R	4	0
DE LABAT C	8	5
DE PUTIE A	1	0
DEACON FL	1	0
DEACON PL	1	0
DEAN E	2	0
DEANE F	2	0
DEANS G	1	0
DEANS R	1	0
DECHI SF	1	0
DECON PL	1	0
DEED A	1	2
DEED SC	3	0
DEERING SB	1	0
DELL HC	1	0
DENISON-PENDER JC	21	7
DENNING	1	0
DENSHAM JB	18	1
DENT WH	1	0
DESSEN CO	1	0
DEUCHAR JD	1	0
DEWBARN GM	2	0
DEWDNEY EL	16	0
DEWHURST GP	4	0
DEXTER AJ	1	0
DICKINSON	1	0
DICKINSON CF	1	0
DICKINSON GN	1	1
DICKINSON HHR	1	0
DICKINSON SC	11	1
DICKSON JE	1	0
DICKSON JF	1	1
DICKSON SF	1	0
DIED CV	1	0
DISBROWE EJ	13	0
DIVER EJ	1	0
DIXON	1	0
DIXON A	1	0
DIXON AS	7	0
DIXON CA	1	0
DIXON CE	2	0
DIXON CW	1	0
DIXON EF	11	4
DIXON GF	188	49
DIXON GH	2	1
DIXON LA	12	0
DIXON S	1	0
DOBSON ED	1	0
DOBSON HL	1	0
DOCKER GAM	11	0
DODD EJ	29	13
DOGGART AG	34	21
DOGRELL D	1	0
DOLL MHC	43	2
DONALDSON CH	1	0
DONALDSON JG	9	3
DONALDSON LL	1	0
DONALDSON N	1	0
DONALDSON OC	1	0
DONALDSON TH	2	0
DONALDSON TN	1	0
DONALDSON WL	7	4
DONKIN HAL	3	0
DORRICK	1	0
DOW MK	1	0
DOWEN RC	1	0
DOWER EL	1	0
DOWER GL	2	0
DOWER JF	1	0
DOWER LF	7	0
DOWER RW	63	18
DOWSON ?	2	0
DOWSON A	1	0
DOWSON FN	36	6
DOWSON TN	1	0
DOYLE NHC	1	0
DRAKE AB	1	0
DRAKE CD	1	0
DRAKE CF	207	55
DRAKE EP	1	1
DRAKE HB	4	1
DRAKE RE	2	0
DRAN G	1	0
DREW N	1	0
DRIFFIELD LT	65	0
DRINKWATER AS	1	0
DRUMMOND EH	3	0
DRUMMOND GH	8	11
DUBUIS HF	134	32
DUDLEY-SMITH W	1	0
DUNKERLEY CL	1	0
DUNN ATB	5	1
DUNNETT HW	3	0
DURELL ED	1	0
DURRANT RB	116	82
DURRELL HLV	5	0
DUVELL PD	2	0
DYAS GE	5	0
DYER R	1	0
DYE-RASON	5	0
DYKES WR	2	0
DYNE JB	1	0
EAGEN R	1	0
EARLE FA	4	0
EASTERBROOK TE	31	1
EASTON EG	1	0
EASYWOOD AE	1	0
EBDEN FR	5	0
ECCLES A	8	0
EDDIS BEG	1	0
EDDIS KH	3	1
EDELSTON M	4	1
EDGAR SC	11	0
EDGE AS	5	0
EDGINTON AE	1	1
EDMUNDS A	1	0
EDMUNDS HW	4	0
EDWARDS	1	0
EDWARDS (SUB)	1	0
EDWARDS CS	1	0
EDWARDS FGB	1	0
EDWARDS HC	1	0
EDWARDS LS	1	0
EDWARDS O	1	0
EDWARDS R	9	1
EDWARDS V	55	55

NAME	APPS	GOALS
EDWARDS WG	14	1
EDWARDS WT	1	0
EKINS	1	0
ELIOT MG	2	0
ELLAM A	1	0
ELLENGOWAN S	21	0
ELLIOTT AE	4	0
ELLIOTT C	1	0
ELLIOTT-SMITH J	4	0
ELLIS H	1	0
ELLIS J	1	0
ELLISON HB	1	0
ENGLAND GF	12	0
ENGLAND RD	1	0
ENTHOVEN HJ	2	0
ENTWISTLE J	19	2
ESCOMBE RL	1	0
ESDAILE EGK	14	0
ESTRIDGE	1	1
EVANS (1)	1	0
EVANS (2)	4	5
EVANS AN	1	0
EVANS FL	169	1
EVANS LR	2	1
EVANS R (1)	1	1
EVANS R (2)	1	0
EVANS RS	2	0
EVANS WA	1	1
EVELYN EC	8	2
EVELYN WA	3	0
EVERETT S	1	1
EVORS CA	2	1
EWER FH	112	2
FABER	2	0
FABIAN AH	124	40
FAIRBAINE RD	5	0
FAIRBAIRN T	1	1
FANE FL	2	0
FARDELL ES	5	1
FARMER C	1	0
FARMER FR	10	1
FARMER H	3	0
FARMER JH	80	12
FARMER MS	3	0
FARNFIELD AS	1	0
FARNIE MS	1	0
FARRANT	1	0
FARRAR PF	1	1
FARRELL CL	1	1
FARRER CR	1	1
FARRER FE	1	0
FARRER HM	1	0
FARRINGTON JM	1	0
FAULKNER EA	8	0
FAULKNER RG	1	0
FAWKS RAH	1	0
FELDING I	3	0
FELLOWES AE	8	0
FENDER PGH	50	0
FEREDAY F	2	0
FERNIE (1)	1	0
FERNIE ?	2	1
FERNIE AE	22	6
FERNIE FE	18	6
FERNIE H	1	0
FERNIE JF	64	52
FERNIE PT	1	1
FERRERS GUY AW	1	0
FERRIS W	18	1
FEVEZ AL	19	0
FIE FM	1	1
FIELD WV	1	0
FIENNES HEW	3	0

NAME	APPS	GOALS
FILOCE AA	2	3
FINCHAM E	2	1
FINCHAM W	1	0
FINLAY DO	5	1
FINLAY JK	7	0
FINLAY RV	14	10
FINNEY CE	1	0
FINNEY WW	4	0
FISH AFB	3	0
FISHER LG	4	0
FITZGIBBON DF	8	1
FITZHUGH	1	0
FLEMING AL	2	1
FLEMING J	24	0
FLETCHER GS	37	18
FLETCHER JH	2	0
FLETCHER RH	6	0
FLINN OS	8	0
FLINT W	1	0
FLOWER H	1	0
FLOWER N	1	0
FLOWERS AD	1	0
FOESTON C	1	0
FOLEY AL	2	2
FOLEY B	7	1
FOLEY CP	1	0
FOLEY CW	2	0
FOLLETT RV	1	1
FONDER A de	1	0
FORBES	1	0
FORBES J	1	0
FORBES RAV	1	0
FORBES W	1	0
FORD FGJ	5	2
FORD FGL	1	0
FORD HA	25	7
FORDER FG	1	0
FORDYCE AD	5	0
FORDYCE AS	1	0
FORDYCE RD	2	1
FOREMAN H	1	2
FORMER JN	1	0
FORT CR	9	0
FORT HR	1	0
FOSTER A (1)	2	0
FOSTER A (2)	1	0
FOSTER AW	8	10
FOSTER BS	9	14
FOSTER FJN	1	0
FOSTER GN	10	11
FOSTER HK	3	0
FOSTER RE	2	1
FOSTER WL	4	1
FOULKES CH	16	0
FOWLER TH	4	0
FOX	1	0
FOX CJM	38	14
FOX EH	1	0
FOX GH	2	0
FOX RH	1	0
FOX RHB	1	0
FOX S	1	0
FOX WE	1	0
FOX WF	2	0
FOX WILMER B	18	3
FOX-WILMER B	1	0
FOY CA	7	0
FOY CW	1	0
FOY EH	2	0
FOY HC	13	0
FOY RB	1	0
FOY RH	48	0
FOYNE SM	1	0
FRANCIS CK	1	0

NAME	APPS	GOALS
FRANCIS HW	13	0
FRANCIS JA	2	1
FRANCIS PO	3	0
FRANK FH	1	0
FRANKS F	1	0
FRASER FR	1	1
FREEBORN G	1	0
FREELAND HE	1	0
FREEMAN	1	1
FREEMAN AC	3	1
FREEMAN H	2	0
FREEMAN W	2	0
FREER AE	3	0
FRERE A	2	0
FRERE E	1	0
FRERE EC	2	0
FRERE GL	1	0
FRERE JWC	1	0
FRERE WH	2	0
FRIEND RSI	2	1
FRIZZELL FG	60	1
FROAT L	1	0
FROST F	2	1
FROST KAF	10	9
FROST L	1	0
FROST R	2	0
FROST RH	1	0
FRY CB	59	5
FRYER FA	1	0
FRYER PA	8	6
FULFORD CR	1	0
FULTON R	1	0
FURBER ?	2	2
FURBER AL	3	0
FURBER S	76	49
GALBALLY JW	12	0
GALE D (SUB)	1	0
GANDAR-DOWAR E	2	1
GANDAR-DOWAR RD	9	5
GANDAR-DOWAR RW	4	2
GARDINER JW	2	0
GARLAND-WELLS HM	19	0
GARNE J	1	0
GARNETT AW	1	0
GARNETT EN	6	1
GARNEY AH	1	0
GARRETT-CLARKE H	1	0
GARROW AD	1	0
GASKIN AL	1	0
GATES HW	2	0
GAY LH	1	0
GEDDES EA	1	0
GENDERS CH	2	0
GERMAN AC	33	25
GETHING HB	17	13
GIBBS F	1	0
GIBSON GH	1	0
GIBSON LH	1	0
GIBSON RR	3	0
GIEVE RW	1	0
GIFFARD WJ	2	0
GILBERT A	1	0
GILBERT EW	2	1
GILBERT H	3	2
GILBERT HG	4	0
GILBERT TH	2	0
GILLESPIE FW	9	14
GILLETT EF	4	0
GILLIATT DE	1	0
GILLIATT W	38	1
GILLIATT WE	2	0
GIMINGHAM CH	3	0
GLASGOW SG	1	0
GLASSCOCK F	1	0

NAME	APPS	GOALS
GLENDALL AF	1	0
GLENISTER CE	84	8
GLENURE	1	0
GLOSSOP AGB	50	12
GODDARD LJ	20	0
GODSELL F	1	0
GODWIN H (SUB)	1	0
GODWIN WP	9	0
GOLDBERG HW	1	0
GOLDSMITH BE	1	0
GOMM BA	2	1
GOOD GB	1	0
GOOD RH	1	0
GOODMAN GW	1	0
GOODMAN J	32	2
GOODWIN A	1	0
GORDON (SUB)	1	0
GORDON CW	1	0
GORDON HH	2	1
GORDON WG	1	1
GOSLING WS	4	1
GOSTLING EV	24	0
GOTTING H	1	0
GRAHAM WM	1	0
GRANT AS	48	0
GRANT CW	1	0
GRANT DF	2	0
GRANT RS	1	0
GRANT-WILSON CW	26	0
GRAST JC	1	0
GRAVES J	17	1
GRAY	1	0
GRAY DHA	26	9
GRAY KR	1	0
GREARE H	1	0
GREATOREX	1	2
GREATOREX P	37	1
GREATOREX TA	5	0
GREEN BG	2	0
GREEN E	8	0
GREEN G	55	2
GREEN GAR	5	2
GREEN GE	1	0
GREEN MA	43	31
GREEN PA	18	13
GREENE HW	2	0
GREENE R de V	1	0
GREENSTOCK JW	1	0
GREENWELL E	3	1
GREENWOOD E	5	0
GREENWOOD WW	1	0
GREGORY SH	1	0
GREIG	1	0
GREIG A	1	0
GREIG CL	1	0
GREIG G	1	0
GREIG H	1	0
GREIG JL	6	0
GREIG RA	22	0
GRESSON CHR	6	1
GRESWELL EA	6	1
GRESWELL R	1	0
GREY CE	1	0
GREY JN	1	1
GRIBBLE A	1	0
GRICE OG	1	0
GRIEG RA	3	0
GRIEVESON JE	39	1
GRIFFIN LG	1	0
GRIFFITHS A	58	1
GRIFFITHS AH	1	0
GRIFFITHS C	1	0
GRIMSDELL E	1	0
GRIMSDELL RE	48	3
GRIMSDELL RG	1	0
GROOM AH	1	0
GROOM RG	3	0
GROSS RHW	1	1
GROSS RM	6	1
GROSVENOR RL	1	0
GROVES RW	3	1
GRUNDTVIG A	1	0
GRUNDTVIG HT	34	10
GUGGISBERG FG	30	0
GUISE JL	1	0
GUNN AH	1	0
GUNNERY WR	1	1
GUNTER RC	1	1
GUTHRIE RB	24	4
GUY AN	18	13
GUY C	1	0
GUY H	1	0
GUY HM	1	0
GUY JK	4	2
HACKING EM	13	1
HAIG-BROWN A	1	0
HAILEY H	1	0
HALE G	1	0
HALE JR	2	0
HALFORD FB	1	0
HALFORD GT	2	0
HALL AL	1	0
HALL CPA	1	0
HALL EF	4	0
HALL GC	2	0
HALL J	4	0
HALL KL	3	0
HALL RC	1	0
HALL RS	4	0
HALLAM	1	0
HALLEY HA	1	0
HALLOWS EH	2	1
HALSTEAD WF	2	0
HAMBLETON HA	7	3
HAMILTON GH	3	3
HAMILTON JB	1	0
HAMILTON KA	1	0
HAMILTON RE	1	0
HAMMELL N	1	0
HAMMILL N	1	0
HAMMILL V	1	0
HAMMOND A	6	0
HAMMOND CR	7	1
HAMMOND LG	5	0
HAMTIL N	1	0
HANCOCK	1	0
HANGHAM HE	1	0
HANNAFORD CH	39	8
HANNARD F	2	1
HANNAY WA	4	0
HANSARD H	1	0
HANSELL AL	2	0
HARDCASTLE ET	1	0
HARDMAN CES	1	3
HARDMAN CJS	2	0
HARDMAN ET	10	2
HARDY N	4	0
HARE A	1	0
HARE BF	1	0
HARKNESS CL	1	0
HARLAND SW	3	0
HARMSWORTH AH	1	0
HARMSWORTH G	1	0
HARMSWORTH J	1	0
HARMSWORTH SL	1	2
HARPER EA	1	0
HARPER HA	1	0
HARRIS G	1	0
HARRIS GH	1	0
HARRIS GS	41	31
HARRIS JB	6	1
HARRIS PS	1	0
HARRIS SS	4	3
HARRISON (1)	1	0
HARRISON (2)	1	0
HARRISON A?	1	0
HARRISON AE	77	0
HARRISON AH	23	0
HARRISON CI	1	0
HARRISON EH	1	0
HARRISON FW	8	0
HARRISON H	50	5
HARRISON HA	8	0
HARRISON J	1	0
HARRISON K	3	0
HARRISON RHA	1	0
HARRISON S	1	0
HARRISON WFN	1	0
HARTLAND EL	1	0
HARTLEY A	1	0
HARVEY RM	4	0
HARWOOD CS	1	1
HARWOOD J	3	0
HASELTON WE	3	0
HASKETT-SMITH A	1	1
HASKETT-SMITH B	2	1
HASKETT-SMITH F	5	2
HASKETT-SMITH GB	3	1
HASKETT-SMITH H	2	0
HASKETT-SMITH TB	1	0
HASKETT-SMITH WE	1	0
HASKETT-SMITH WF	1	1
HASKETT-SMITH WP	28	7
HASKETT-SMITH WR	1	0
HASLEWOOD JSO	7	2
HASLOP RM	1	0
HASTINGS F (sub)	1	0
HATHORNE AA	1	0
HATTON COS	135	15
HAUGHTON AJ	4	0
HAVART HH	1	0
HAWE DK	1	0
HAWES DM	5	2
HAWKER ML	1	0
HAWKSWORTH M	1	0
HAY	1	0
HAY A	2	1
HAY AS	4	2
HAY AT	1	0
HAYCOCK T (sub)	1	0
HAYDEN AJF	1	0
HAYES EA	1	0
HAYES F	19	0
HAYMAN WHP	1	0
HAYTER	1	0
HAYTER F	1	0
HAYWOOD JS	1	0
HAZELHURST FA	1	0
HEAD R	1	0
HEATH AJ	5	0
HEATH AS	2	0
HEATH CRW	8	2
HEATH FV	1	0
HEAVEN CI	3	0
HEBERT HR	1	1
HEIGHAM AF	1	0
HEMMERDE AF	1	2
HEMMERDE AJ	12	1
HEMMERDE CL	9	0
HEMMERDE H	1	0
HEMMERDE I	3	1
HENDERSON	2	0

NAME	APPS	GOALS
HENDERSON H	1	0
HENDERSON J	2	0
HENDERSON M	1	0
HENDERSON TB	25	14
HENLEY AK	2	2
HENLEY FAH	9	0
HENNAN GC	1	0
HEPBURN SF	26	1
HEPPELL	1	0
HEPPLE TW	2	0
HERBERT G	1	0
HERMAN AE	13	1
HERMAN GL	17	0
HERMON J	6	1
HERRING J	1	0
HERVEY RM	1	0
HERYCE V	1	0
HESELTINE C	1	0
HESLOP RH	9	0
HETHERINGTON RE	1	0
HEWETSON J	4	1
HEWETT H	1	0
HEWETT HT	1	0
HEWITT CD	22	7
HEWITT HW	14	2
HEYSMAN A	1	0
HEYWOOD N	1	0
HIBBERT A	1	0
HIBERT HR	1	3
HICKLEY CL	1	0
HICKLEY N	3	0
HICKS FM	1	0
HICKSON	1	0
HIGSON TA	16	0
HILDYARD ED	1	0
HILL	1	0
HILL HHC	1	0
HILL JE	14	1
HILL JG	1	0
HILL LG	1	0
HILL PG	1	0
HILL T	1	0
HILLEARY EL	36	0
HILLEARY R	13	3
HILLEARY RL	2	1
HILLEARY RM	113	14
HINMERS EC	1	0
HINMERS W	2	3
HIRST KG	1	0
HISCOCK CH	52	1
HOARE AR	1	1
HOARE G	2	0
HOBART H	1	0
HOBART RC	2	0
HOBBS WB	1	0
HOCKING	1	0
HOCKING EM	1	0
HODGES HF	2	1
HODGKINSON GS	1	0
HODSOLL B	1	0
HOFFMEISTER CE	10	7
HOGARTH A	1	0
HOGARTH AH	1	0
HOGARTH H	1	0
HOGARTH RG	13	9
HOLDEN-WHITE C	17	2
HOLDSWORTH C	1	0
HOLDSWORTH RL	18	12
HOLFORD F	1	0
HOLFORD GT	6	0
HOLLAND H	1	0
HOLLAND LT	1	0
HOLLEBONE GT	8	0
HOLLINGTON ET	1	0

NAME	APPS	GOALS
HOLLINGTON T	1	0
HOLLINS AF	1	1
HOLLINS AM	3	0
HOLLINS FH (1)	1	0
HOLLINS FH (2)	1	0
HOLLINS PL	8	3
HOLLIS J	1	0
HOLLIS RM	3	0
HOLLOCOMB JC	1	0
HOLMAN HM	16	4
HOLMES CB	2	0
HOLMES EB	1	0
HOLMES NT	3	0
HOLROYD JH	1	0
HOOPER E	1	0
HOOPER FH	4	0
HOOPER J	1	0
HOPE RB	32	21
HOPEWELL ER	4	0
HOPGOOD C	1	0
HOPKINS JC	1	1
HOPKINS PG	10	0
HOPKINS W	1	0
HOPKINS WH	1	1
HOPPER AW	1	0
HORLICK OP	3	1
HORNE	1	0
HORNER JF	2	0
HORTON L	1	0
HOSIE AL	7	2
HOSIE SL	3	2
HOSKINS CC	2	0
HOSKINS F	6	1
HOSSACK AH	10	1
HOTHAM FW	4	0
HOUGHTON AJ	1	0
HOWARD JE	4	0
HOWARD R	1	0
HOWARD TA	1	0
HOWE AW	3	0
HOWELL DL	3	2
HOWELL EL	1	0
HOWELL M	124	37
HOWELL RGD	1	0
HOWELL-JONES HG	48	11
HOWLETT	1	0
HOWSE CA	1	0
HUBBARD LW	1	0
HUDDLE LT	124	0
HUGHES FW	1	0
HUGHES HJ	1	0
HUGHES HS	1	0
HUGHES JL	2	0
HUGHES JR	3	1
HUGHES JS	5	0
HUGHES-DAVIES HE	1	0
HUGHES-ONSLOW H	4	1
HULL	1	0
HULL CPA	6	0
HUMPHREY EJ	6	2
HUMPHREYS CE	4	0
HUMPHREYS CM	6	0
HUMPHREYS H	1	1
HUMPHRYS CG	3	0
HUNNARD F	5	0
HUNT	1	0
HUNT KRG	7	1
HUNT R	1	1
HUNTER	1	0
HUNTER CB	1	0
HUNTER EI	1	0
HUNTER JW	5	0
HUNTER PDV	10	0
HURST AR	6	2

NAME	APPS	GOALS
HURST J	2	0
HYME WM	5	0
HYNE WM	5	0
IBBS RS	8	4
INGE-GARDINER CH	1	0
INGRAM ?	2	0
INGRAM CF	3	2
INGRAM FM	12	10
INGRAM RA	3	0
INGRAM W	1	1
IRWIN HC	10	0
ISAAC AH	17	4
ISAAC HF	1	0
ISWICK-PARKER CH	1	0
IZARD HC	2	0
JACKSON CH	17	2
JACKSON E	3	0
JACKSON F	1	0
JACKSON FH	2	0
JACKSON FM	1	0
JACKSON H	1	0
JACKSON HA	1	0
JACKSON NL	1	0
JACKSON W	1	2
JACQUES (SUB)	1	0
JAMES A	1	1
JAMES AC	2	0
JAMES HC	1	0
JAMES NF	1	0
JAMESON EM	3	0
JAMESON GD	1	1
JAMESON H	9	0
JAMIESON W	2	0
JANSEN A	25	3
JANSEN FW	1	0
JANSON FW	16	4
JANSON JH	6	0
JANSON JW	1	0
JARDINE DR	1	0
JEACOCKE A	3	1
JEACOCKE A	2	1
JENDWINE (SUB)	1	0
JENKINS RG	93	37
JENNER ACW	4	5
JESSOP GL	2	0
JOBSON WS	2	0
JOHNSON	2	0
JOHNSON AF	4	0
JOHNSON B	1	0
JOHNSON CB	15	2
JOHNSON EA	1	0
JOHNSON GL	1	0
JOHNSON H	2	0
JOHNSON HL	1	0
JOHNSON P	42	0
JOHNSON SM	1	1
JOHNSON TC	9	1
JOHNSON WL	1	0
JOHNSON WW	1	0
JOHNSTON H	3	1
JOHNSTON K	1	0
JOHNSTON R	1	0
JOLLIFFE CA	18	0
JONES A	1	0
JONES C	1	0
JONES D	1	0
JONES DM	1	1
JONES FET	2	0
JONES GV	1	0
JONES GW	1	0
JONES HA	1	0
JONES R	1	0
JOSEPH EH	2	0
JOSEPH GA	30	1

NAME	APPS	GOALS
JOSSHOUSE A	1	0
JOURDAIN RO	4	0
JOY B	84	5
JOY E	1	0
JOYCE R	1	0
JULIAN CR	31	13
KAY AW	4	2
KELLY J	4	4
KELLY JD	2	0
KEMP-WELCH GD	4	4
KENNEDY AGO	1	0
KENT-LEMON AC	1	0
KENYON MA	1	0
KER AWW	7	5
KER J	3	0
KERREY C	1	0
KERRY AHG	7	4
KER-SEYMER E	1	0
KESTON HN	1	0
KEYSELL FS	5	0
KIDD HB	27	0
KILBY TA	1	0
KILKENNY JC	1	0
KILLICH H	1	0
KING A	1	0
KING AH	20	0
KING AL	1	0
KING AN	1	1
KING AR	4	0
KING BW	1	0
KING CE	1	0
KING CH	3	0
KING EL	1	0
KING FJ	1	0
KING FL	11	0
KING FR	2	0
KING PV	1	0
KING RM	10	0
KING SL	518	3
KINGHORNE (sub)	1	0
KNIGHT C	1	0
KINGSLEY PGT	28	1
KINGSTON LJ	158	48
KIRBY A	1	0
KIRBY AC	18	0
KIRWAN BR	4	1
KIRWAN RO	1	0
KITCHENER HV	1	0
KITCHING AL	2	0
KITTEL FW	1	0
KITTERMASTER FJ	2	0
KNAPP T	1	0
KNIGHT A (SUB)	1	0
KNIGHT AE	13	0
KNIGHT C	14	1
KNIGHT JG	135	25
KNOX H	93	46
KNOX JJ	1	0
KORTRIGHT CJ	2	0
KYLE J	5	0
LABAT C de	7	1
LACY-SCOTT G	18	0
LAIDMAN WE	4	0
LAIRD RH	5	4
LAKE A	3	0
LAMBERT CN	9	0
LAMBERT WR	1	0
LAMDIN	1	0
LAMING J	1	0
LAMING P	1	0
LAMPARD M	11	0
LAMPTON WL	1	0
LANDALE N	33	0
LANDALE W	3	0
LANDON HE	19	8
LANE AJ	1	0
LANG LCV	3	0
LANG REV	1	0
LANGDEN JE	1	0
LANGLEY C	1	0
LANGLEY CK	13	0
LANGLEY LE	5	0
LANGMAID VF	1	0
LANGTON JM	1	0
LAPIN AB	1	0
LARDMAN WE	1	0
LAST CH	8	0
LATHAM JW	1	1
LATTEN RC	1	0
LAURENCE HC	1	0
LAURIE CC	1	0
LAW H	4	0
LAWRIE K	1	0
LAWN CF	1	0
LAWRENCE	1	0
LAWRENCE AGS	58	0
LAWRENCE GH	1	0
LAWRENCE HC	7	0
LAWREY EM	2	0
LAWSON MB	6	0
LE MESURIER G	3	0
LEA SE	26	2
LEACH R	3	4
LEACH-LEWIS AF	17	8
LEAK CS	1	0
LEAKE CL	16	7
LEANARD L	1	0
LEARMAN VS	1	0
LEBAT W de	1	0
LEBROCQ CN	1	0
LECKER WA	1	0
LECKY JG	16	0
LEDWARD GH	4	0
LEDWARD RH	7	0
LEE	1	0
LEE J	42	41
LEE RT	10	1
LEELE S	1	1
LEES RW	1	1
LEETE A	1	0
LEETE N	6	3
LEETE W	2	0
LEIPER WA	1	0
LEMAN AC	1	1
LEMAN DC	47	15
LEMAN GC	7	0
LEMAN RC	22	9
LENTON PH	2	0
LEPPELL H	1	0
LESLIE KD	5	3
LETTE N	1	0
LETTS HM	1	1
LETTS SE	2	2
LEWIS CE	2	0
LEWIS EL	4	2
LEWIS HG	3	0
LEWIS RF	1	0
LEWIS RP	1	0
LEWIS RT	2	1
LEXHAM AH	3	0
LIDDELL	1	0
LIDDELL FF	2	0
LIDDELL NO	3	0
LIDDLE TR	3	0
LEONARD RL	1	0
LIEPER W	1	0
LIGHT F	1	1
LIGHT P	1	0
LILL BA	1	0
LINDLEY T	2	1
LINDSAY KM	11	0
LING KS	73	1
LINGARD FC	6	0
LINGLEBACH WE	1	0
LINSELL MG	1	0
LION	1	0
LIPPELL DP	1	0
LISS FJ	1	0
LISTER LH	11	7
LISTER LR	1	1
LISTER RH	1	0
LISTER WHL	2	0
LITCHFIELD ACA	1	0
LITCHFIELD PC	1	2
LITTLE E	1	0
LITTLEJOHN E	1	1
LLEWELLYN-DAVIES J	1	0
LLOYD	2	0
LLOYD TGA	1	1
LOCKE EJ	1	0
LOCKER A	1	0
LOCKER WA	42	3
LOCKEY WG	28	7
LOCKHART-MUIR-IVES J	1	0
LOCKTON JH	66	39
LODGE LV	22	0
LOMAS JM	1	0
LOMAX D	32	0
LOMAX E	1	0
LONG CG	9	0
LOOKER WH	7	0
LORAINE WS	21	1
LORD ENCOMBE	1	0
LORD NORJOO	1	0
LOVEGROVE CD	4	0
LOW HH	22	0
LOW RA	3	0
LOWE C	1	0
LOWE DGA	9	1
LOWE HA	14	1
LOWE HP	1	0
LOWE RGH	11	4
LOWE WW	4	7
LOWES E	55	29
LOWES G	1	0
LOWNDES MJ	7	2
LOWNDES RG	2	1
LOWTHER HA	3	0
LOWTHER HC	8	0
LOWTHER L	1	0
LUBBOCK HT	2	0
LUCAS AL	1	0
LUDOLPH FJ	1	0
LUKER SG	22	0
LUSHINGTON G	11	1
LUSHINGTON T	1	0
LYMBERY	1	0
LYNCH F	1	0
LYONS JH	1	4
LYWOOD F	13	5
MACDONALD CJ	1	1
MACDONALD CL	1	1
MACDONALD CN	5	0
MACDONALD DR	2	0
MACDONALD IM	2	0
MACDONALD WIF	1	0
MACDONALD CH	2	0
MACDONNELL J	1	0
MACE N	7	1
MACINTOSH C	5	2
MACKAY GR	1	0
MACKAY RJ	2	0

NAME	APPS	GOALS
MACKEAN S	1	1
MACKENZIE J	1	0
MACKENZIE NI	1	0
MACKIE S	1	0
MACKINTOSH C	14	2
MACKLIN W	1	0
MACKRILL OW	3	0
MACLEAN A	2	0
MAGNAY CBW	7	0
MAINWARING CM	4	1
MAIR WDK	4	5
MALDEN AC	1	0
MALDEN AW	18	0
MALLETT KL	1	0
MALLETT ML	1	0
MALLINSON	1	0
MALLORY TC	2	0
MALTBY FE	2	0
MALYON RT	1	0
MANDER AW	12	0
MANDER RJ	4	0
MANLY JH	11	2
MANN R	7	2
MANNERS J	1	0
MAORIE H	1	0
MAPLES RC	1	1
MAQUAY CB	3	0
MARCH JW	2	0
MARCH RC	1	0
MARDEN	1	0
MARRABLE SA	1	0
MARRETT HF	1	0
MARRIOTT HM	1	0
MARSH EC	2	0
MARSH JW	2	0
MARSHALL	1	0
MARSHALL AH	3	0
MARSHALL C	1	0
MARSHALL EJ (SUB)	1	0
MARSHALL EM	6	1
MARSHALL EW	37	9
MARSHALL FJ	2	1
MARSHALL FJ	1	0
MARSHALL HM	1	1
MARSHALL HW	1	0
MARSHALL PE	1	0
MARSHALL RW	1	0
MARSHALL W	2	0
MARSON L	1	0
MARTEN AB	10	0
MARTIN AR	1	0
MARTIN E	41	25
MARTIN EB	1	0
MARTIN WM	1	0
MARTYN AJK	2	0
MARTYN O	1	0
MARTYN RV	1	0
MARWOOD G	1	1
MASCALL WH	1	0
MASON E	1	0
MASON FW	1	0
MASON G	1	0
MASON L	1	0
MASON S	1	1
MASSEY JA	44	20
MASTER R	1	0
MASTERMAN HA	1	0
MASTERMAN HW	3	0
MASTERS A	1	0
MATHER JW	1	0
MATTHEWS CC	10	5
MAXWELL TA	3	0
MAY PR	59	1
MAY RC	2	0

NAME	APPS	GOALS
MAYER ER	12	7
MAYNARD J	1	0
MAYNARD-TAYLOR ?	1	0
MAYNARD-TAYLOR C	1	0
MAYNARD-TAYLOR DC	2	0
MAYNARD-TAYLOR EG	1	0
MAYNE J	1	0
MCALPIN J	1	0
MCBRIDE WN	15	0
MCCALL MM	4	0
MCCALL RF	25	2
MCCANCE HJ	1	0
MCCOWAN W	9	0
MCDONALD CR	1	0
MCGAW JT	6	0
MCINTOSH A	1	0
MCINTOSH TW	1	1
MCINTOSH W	1	1
MCIVER CD	98	46
MCKAY RG	1	0
MCKEAN H	11	1
MCKERROW	1	0
MCLAREN J	1	0
MCLAREN JEE	13	0
MCMANUS A	4	0
MCNAIR JR	1	0
MCNEIL H	1	0
MCSWEENEY N	5	0
MEAHCOTE LH	1	0
MECKLIN CB	1	2
MEEK RG	2	0
MEERS DH	1	0
MEERS RH	31	0
MELLIN GL	2	1
MELLOR AA	1	0
MELLOR PE	6	0
MELVILLE AS	6	0
MENDL D	8	2
MENZIES T	1	0
MENZIES WK	1	0
MERK C	1	0
MERK FH	5	1
MERK T	1	0
MERRALL W	1	0
MERTONS R	1	0
MESELTINE C	1	0
MIDDLEBOE N	14	0
MIDDLEDITCH B	2	0
MILBURN LE	1	0
MILLAR B	1	0
MILLAR-INGLISS KA	6	0
MILLEN GMF	1	0
MILLER A	1	0
MILLER GT	3	0
MILLER H	9	3
MILLER JS	11	16
MILLER RW	4	9
MILLER WW	1	0
MILLS	1	0
MILLS HM	5	0
MILLS RO	1	0
MILLS WG	11	0
MILLS-ROBERTS RH	13	0
MILMAN LCP	1	0
MILTON HA	43	4
MINNS SC	1	0
MITCHELL A (SUB)	1	0
MITCHELL B	1	0
MITCHELL EJD	33	0
MITCHELL HA	1	0
MITCHELL JF	2	0
MITCHELL JP	1	0
MITCHELL RJD	3	0
MITCHELL WG	3	0

NAME	APPS	GOALS
MITCHELSON TR	1	0
MOIR DE	1	0
MOIR JP	1	0
MONTGOMERY H	1	0
MONTGOMERY PJ	98	38
MONTGOMERY RM	48	0
MONTGOMERY W	1	0
MOODY RH	3	0
MOODY WH	1	1
MOODY WR	1	1
MOON CT	1	0
MOON EG	22	4
MOON LJ	22	17
MOON RG	1	0
MOON WR	30	6
MOORE AG	1	0
MOORE AJ	41	0
MOORE CA	30	1
MOORE HL	1	0
MOORE JD	5	0
MOORE JG	1	0
MOORE TD	1	0
MOORHOUSE AC	1	0
MOORHOUSE CP	1	0
MOORHOUSE HC	8	7
MOORS RH	2	0
MORELAND CR	15	0
MORGAN GC	2	0
MORGAN J (1)	1	0
MORGAN J (2)	1	0
MORGAN JL	1	0
MORGAN JS	17	4
MORGAN T	1	0
MORGAN WM	3	1
MORGAN-OWEN H	1	0
MORGAN-OWEN JG	3	2
MORGAN-OWEN M	79	12
MORICE CS	1	0
MORICE HF	1	1
MORLEY HA	16	0
MORRIS	1	0
MORRIS AE	47	0
MORRIS CW	1	0
MORRIS E	1	0
MORRIS H	3	0
MORRIS HJ	1	0
MORRIS HM	21	14
MORRIS JF	4	5
MORRIS JR	6	4
MORRISON ?	1	0
MORRISON CL	1	0
MORRISON JSF	1	0
MORRISON WG	8	2
MORTEN AB	1	0
MORTIMER H	2	0
MORTIMER RG	5	0
MORTON L	1	0
MORTON PH	1	0
MOSELEY A	1	0
MOSER G	10	2
MOSS HK	2	0
MOSS W	1	0
MOSSER G	5	0
MOULD WAH	1	0
MOUNSEY OR	9	1
MOUNT SC	10	0
MOXON GR	8	5
MUGLISTON FH	16	0
MUGLISTON HG	2	0
MUIR RT	2	0
MULRENAN BW	20	4
MULRENAN J	2	0
MUNDAHL HS	29	0
MUNN JS	1	0

NAME	APPS	GOALS
MUNRO CE	2	0
MUNRO H	1	0
MUNRO HH	2	0
MURDOCH C	1	0
MURPHY G	1	0
MURPHY JK	2	0
MURRAY G	1	0
MUSPRATT C	1	0
MUSPRATT FC	5	0
MUSPRATT PC	1	0
MUSPRATT WE	7	1
MYTTON A	2	0
MYTTON GH	1	0
MYTTON H	2	0
MYTTON HF	1	0
NASH CHC	1	0
NASH RW	1	0
NASON FW	1	0
NAYLOR JW	4	0
NAYLOR WA	8	0
NEIL MACDONALD C	1	0
NEILL B	1	0
NELSON AF	1	0
NELSON GL	1	0
NELSON JC	1	0
NELSON JL	23	2
NELSON MG	38	6
NELSON TL	82	6
NESBITT P	4	0
NESON F	1	0
NEWBERRY HC	9	7
NEWBERRY RE	3	0
NEWBOLD JC	4	1
NEWBOLD JH	2	0
NEWBURY	1	0
NEWCOME SL	1	1
NEWHAM OE	1	0
NEWITT JRH	4	3
NEWMAN D	9	0
NEWMAN GG	10	0
NEWNHAM A	1	0
NEWPORT GB	5	7
NICHOL GN	1	0
NICHOLAS FW	3	0
NICHOLAS FWH	1	0
NICHOLLS EP	33	5
NICHOLLS H	3	1
NICHOLLS PS	4	0
NICHOLS	1	0
NICHOLSON F	5	0
NICHOLSON JCD	2	0
NICHOLSON RS	1	0
NICIN BA	1	0
NICKISSON F	1	0
NICKISSON JL	21	0
NIX JS	10	0
NIXON AC	113	43
NOLAN-WHELAN GN	1	0
NOLAN-WHELAN JV	1	0
NORMAN L	1	0
NORMAN NC	1	0
NORRIS GH	7	0
NORTH	1	1
NOTCUTT SA	1	0
NOTES WJ	2	0
NOTT BOWER RE	12	0
NUGENT CN	1	0
OAKLEY WJ	55	0
OATES M	1	0
O'BRIEN C	3	2
O'BRIEN CW	24	13
O'BRIEN J	1	0
O'BRIEN PK	54	2
O'BRIEN RB	14	4
O'BRIEN T	1	0
O'CONNOR D	1	0
O'CONNOR J	1	0
O'KELLY D	1	0
O'KELLY JW	1	0
OLIVER	1	1
OLIVER CM	1	0
OLIVER FG	28	1
OLIVER K	1	0
OLIVER TJ	1	0
OLIVEY GS	1	0
ONSLOW HH	1	0
OPENSHAW J	1	0
ORAMS E	1	0
ORMSBY MH	3	0
ORR E	1	0
ORTEN L	1	0
ORTON L	6	0
OSBORN JENKIN CO	2	0
OSBOURNE SE	1	0
OSMOND JE	1	0
OWEN F	1	0
OWEN JD	1	0
OWEN JH	1	0
OWEN JW	1	0
OWEN ML	1	0
OWEN RCD	10	0
OWEN RH	2	0
OWEN TD	1	0
OWEN WV	2	0
OWEN WW	2	0
OWENS T	1	0
PACKFORD CW (SUB)	1	1
PAGDON EH	1	0
PAGE C	25	2
PAGE H	3	0
PAGET-TOMLINSON EE	13	2
PAINE HN	1	0
PAINTON ER	1	0
PALAIRET LCH	1	1
PALLDITCH PH	1	0
PALMER AB	3	0
PALMER B	3	0
PALMER H (SUB)	1	0
PALMER RE	3	0
PARAVICINI PJ	1	0
PARES B	60	7
PARES CB	1	0
PARES ET	1	0
PARES GL	9	7
PARKER CA	33	5
PARKER O	4	2
PARKER WS	2	0
PARKES O	1	0
PARKS JH	1	0
PARNELL HS	3	0
PARRY AF	1	0
PARRY CF	5	0
PARRY CW	7	0
PARRY JH	3	1
PARSONS E	4	1
PARSONS FW	1	0
PART CK	4	3
PARTON EG	2	0
PARTON FJ	1	0
PARTRIDGE GB	11	4
PARTRIDGE GM	72	0
PASCOE M	1	0
PATER A	1	0
PATERSON D	1	0
PATERSON JN	1	0
PATRICK D	18	8
PATTERSON N	1	0
PAUL ?	2	0
PAUL JE	33	17
PAUL JP	34	0
PAULL JD	4	0
PAULL JH	1	0
PAULL JR	5	0
PAWSON AC	1	0
PAWSON AG	1	0
PAWSON FW	33	29
PAXTON GN	1	0
PAYNE HG	129	0
PEAKE HE	1	0
PEARCE	1	0
PEARCE BG	28	14
PEARCE H	1	0
PEARCE HC	1	0
PEARLESS SH	1	0
PEARS AF	2	0
PEARS HT	3	0
PEARSON CW	3	0
PECK C	1	0
PECK HC	23	8
PECK HR	1	0
PECK JH	27	9
PEERS HC	1	0
PEILE AB	2	0
PELLY FR	116	1
PEMMER A	1	0
PENDER JCD	1	0
PENNEY J	1	0
PENNING VH	1	0
PENNINGTON K	2	0
PERKE FH	1	0
PERKINS HW	2	2
PERKINS N	7	4
PERKINS TN	42	38
PERKISS FCL	1	0
PERKS H	1	0
PERKS JE	19	3
PESHALL F	1	0
PETER J	1	1
PETERS H	16	0
PETTIT DEA	23	0
PETTIT HE	1	0
PETTITT	1	0
PEYERS P	1	0
PHELPS GI	1	0
PHELPS J	1	0
PHELPS N	1	0
PHILLMORE JE	2	0
PHILLIPS D	1	0
PHILLIPS E	6	2
PHILLIPS FW	1	0
PHILLIPS J	1	0
PHILLIPS NJ	2	1
PHILLIPS S (SUB)	1	0
PICKERING HJ	79	2
PICKERING S	1	0
PIDCOCK RG	1	0
PIERCE A	1	0
PIGGOTT MT	5	4
PIKE	1	0
PIKE SA	2	1
PILDITCH PH	6	0
PINFIELD RG	110	19
PINGINS AR	1	0
PINGUIS RG	1	0
PINK HS	17	6
PIPER HF	33	2
PIPER SA (SUB)	1	0
PIRKIS FCL	25	6
PLAISTOWE FH	53	0
PLATT GM	1	0
PLATT W	1	0

NAME	APPS	GOALS
PLATTS A	26	0
PLAYER G	6	0
PLOWMAN A	1	0
PLOWMAN J	1	0
PLUMMER EN	7	0
PLUMPTREE E	2	0
PLUMPTREE HP	8	4
POLEHAMPTON EH	39	1
POLEHAMPTON FW	10	0
POLLOCK J	1	0
POLLOCK-HODSOLL GB	189	11
POLLOCK-HODSOLL HE	15	1
POLLOCK-NOTT HE	1	0
POPE WH	3	0
POPHAM BG	15	2
POPHAM CH	5	0
POPHAM RF	9	0
POTTER	1	0
POTTER A	1	0
POTTER GP	3	0
POTTER R	3	0
POTTS	1	1
POTTS AE	1	0
POTTS R	2	0
POWELL C	1	0
POWELL EO	4	0
POWELL GL	1	0
POWELL HA	3	1
POWELL HN	1	0
POWELL JGT	1	0
POWELL JP	1	0
POWELL NA	2	0
POWELL WA	4	0
POWELL WG	11	0
POYSER AV	11	6
PREST HEW	3	0
PRESTON AL	1	0
PRESTON WD	1	0
PRETTO DH	6	0
PRICE HC	13	3
PRICE WF	5	3
PRICE WG	2	1
PRICKETT H	1	0
PRIDEAUX	1	2
PRIDHAM HR	1	0
PRINCEP	1	0
PRITCHARD HK	3	1
PROBYN FC	5	0
PROBYN PC	25	5
PROBYN S	1	0
PROCTER H	1	2
PROTHERO AG	11	0
PRYCE-JONES AW	8	0
PRYCE-JONES WE	10	1
PRYCE-WHITE	1	0
PUNNETT E	16	2
PUTY AD	1	0
PYKE AC	1	0
QUICK CF	1	0
RABONE M	1	0
RADFORD T	3	0
RAIKES GB	15	0
RAIKES KC	60	1
RAILTON NG	6	0
RAILTON WJ	1	0
RANT JCG	1	0
RAPAND C	4	0
RATHBONE B	1	0
RATHBONE EP	8	4
RATHBONE P	1	0
RATHBONE R	1	0
RAUTHMELL AW	6	0
RAUTHMELL HA	43	1
RAUTHMELL LC	1	0

NAME	APPS	GOALS
RAUTHMELL RA	2	0
RAWLEY HC	1	0
RAWLINSON JFP	1	0
RAYMOND L	1	0
RAYNER CD	3	2
RAYNER J	3	1
RAYNES HM	1	0
RAYNOR K	35	3
READY A	3	0
REAVE J	1	0
REBOW MG	7	1
RECANO CM	2	0
REDDY B	1	0
REDDY F	1	0
REDFORD	1	0
REED A	1	0
REED HF	16	0
REES RM	1	0
REEVE WG	16	6
REEVES EA	1	0
REEVES FK	39	13
REISS RQ	3	0
REMNANT JF	1	0
RENDELL BA	1	0
RENSHAW JAK	2	0
REUNERT F	1	0
REYNOLDS LW	4	0
RHODES C	1	0
RHODES HA	41	11
RHODES TB	14	7
RICE-OXLEY AE	1	0
RICHARDS CJR	1	0
RICHARDS GC	2	1
RICHARDS HW	1	0
RICHARDSON AG	2	0
RICHARDSON FJ	8	0
RICHARDSON JN	2	0
RICKETT G	1	0
RICKETTS GR	1	0
RILEY F	62	23
RIMMINGTON H	43	0
RITCHIE (SUB)	1	0
RIVER-SMITH S	1	0
ROBERSON AJE	2	0
ROBERTS AW	15	2
ROBERTS FR	3	3
ROBERTS FW	21	9
ROBERTS GD	7	6
ROBERTSON (SUB)	1	0
ROBERTSON ARG	13	0
ROBERTSON F	1	0
ROBERTSON FG	1	0
ROBERTSON GE	1	0
ROBINS RM	6	8
ROBINS RWV	9	3
ROBINSON CA	25	7
ROBINSON F	4	0
ROBINSON GM	10	4
ROBINSON HF	2	0
ROBINSON WE	1	0
ROBSON ST (sub)	1	0
ROCK AC	1	0
ROE WN	18	0
ROFFEY GW	1	0
ROGER RS	1	0
ROGERS R	19	2
ROGERS T	1	0
ROGERS VM	21	8
ROGERSON W	1	0
ROLAND H	1	0
ROLLER CT	6	3
ROOKE A	2	4
ROOKE BE	25	5
ROPER C	1	0

NAME	APPS	GOALS
ROPER RE	3	3
ROPER RG	36	23
ROPER WF	1	0
ROSE H	13	3
ROSE J	1	0
ROSS	1	0
ROSS T	139	1
ROSSAGE P	6	4
ROUGEMONT CH	6	0
ROUSE AH	1	0
ROUSE WH	1	0
ROUSE WS	3	2
ROUTLEDGE C	3	0
ROUTLEDGE MH	23	0
ROWE GH	1	0
ROWLANDSON TS	20	0
ROWLEY R	2	1
RUDD CI	1	0
RUDD CT	1	0
RUDD GB	3	6
RUISER AB	3	0
RUSSELL AM	72	0
RUSSELL D	1	0
RUSSELL EC	4	0
RUSSELL GW	11	0
RUSSELL H	1	0
RUSSELL SH	1	0
RUSSELL WH	1	0
RUTHERFORD PW	1	0
RUTTER ?	1	0
RUTTER EC	16	0
RUTTER NC	1	0
RUTTER RC	4	0
RYAN JH	5	4
RYDE FC	23	1
RYDER CF	1	0
RYDER GW	1	0
RYDER JS	3	0
RYDER TA	17	0
RYDON AL	1	0
RYDON HL	21	0
SADDISON J	2	0
SAINSBURY PC	11	0
SALE EW	6	0
SALE FA	1	0
SALE HB	8	0
SALE RB	6	0
SALE RW	9	0
SALMON SL	1	0
SALMON SW	1	0
SALMON T	7	0
SALT RJ	1	0
SALT RN	1	0
SALWEY A	8	0
SAMSON EM	15	0
SAMSON WL	4	1
SANDER MR	1	0
SANDERS FE	1	0
SANDERS FR	21	0
SANDERSON WB	1	0
SANDILANDS RR	22	13
SANDROVD A	1	0
SANGER GFD	2	0
SAREL WG	1	0
SAUL FJ	1	0
SAUNDERS FE	4	0
SAVILL L	5	0
SAVILLE AC	11	0
SAWYER GS	1	0
SAWYER T	1	0
SAYER C	6	2
SAYER GR	20	5
SCHOFIELD AC	2	2
SCHOFIELD D	10	4

NAME	APPS	GOALS
SCHOFIELD DL	1	0
SCHOFIELD EH	2	0
SCOLLEAT	1	0
SCOONES FJ	1	0
SCOONES O	7	0
SCOTT A	1	0
SCOTT AL	8	0
SCOTT BJ	3	0
SCOTT HS	5	0
SCOTT HW	14	4
SCOTT JKC	1	0
SCRIVEN J	1	0
SEAFORD HS	3	4
SEDGWICK AV	1	0
SEEDORFF FJ	38	0
SERGEANT	1	0
SERGEANT EA	16	3
SERGEANT EF	1	0
SERGEANT FA	1	1
SERGEANT PA	195	5
SERGEANT RA	1	0
SESSIONS WK	13	0
SETH SMITH DF	1	0
SETON WJ	93	2
SETTLE A	1	0
SEVERN AH	1	0
SEVIER-DAVIES G	1	0
SEWELL ?	1	0
SEWELL COH	7	3
SEWELL EB	8	1
SEWELL FW	1	0
SEWELL RB	1	0
SEYMOUR	1	0
SEYMOUR HJ	1	0
SHACKLETON H	3	0
SHARP GF	1	0
SHARP TS	2	0
SHARPE CA (SUB)	2	0
SHARPE CC	1	0
SHARPE HA	1	0
SHARPLES J	11	0
SHARPLEY H	1	0
SHATTOCK GO	5	0
SHAW CL	1	0
SHAW GL	1	0
SHAW NF	10	0
SHEARER EDR	53	44
SHEARMAN V	1	0
SHEEN F (SUB)	1	0
SHEPHARD AS	1	0
SHEPHARD JHD	1	0
SHEPHERD A	19	3
SHEPHERD GS	1	0
SHEPHERD J	1	0
SHEPHERD NJ	7	0
SHEPHERD NP	3	2
SHEPHERD W	3	0
SHEPHERD WE	1	0
SHEPPARD ?	1	0
SHEPPARD G	1	0
SHEPPARD H	1	0
SHEPPARD JH	9	0
SHEPPARD JHD	1	0
SHEPPARD NF	1	0
SHEPPARD SN	2	0
SHEPPARD WF	10	0
SHEPSTONE RA	1	0
SHILCOCK GW	13	1
SHILLITOE FR	2	0
SHILLITOE H	1	0
SHINE EB	1	0
SHIPTON CH	12	0
SHORT HS	3	1
SIEWART JG	5	0

NAME	APPS	GOALS
SILVERTOP FS	1	0
SIMKINS WA	24	17
SIMMONDS A	1	0
SIMMONDS SR	4	5
SIMMONS G	1	1
SIMONDS	1	1
SIMONDS ER	1	1
SIMONDS F	1	0
SIMONDS J	83	17
SIMONDS JF	1	1
SIMONDS LR	1	2
SIMONDS SR	21	14
SIMPKINS H	1	0
SIMPSON FA	5	0
SIMPSON FC	1	0
SIMPSON GH	12	0
SIMPSON H	1	0
SIMPSON L	10	0
SIMPSON WH	1	0
SIMPSON-HAYWOOD GH	1	0
SIMSON MR	1	0
SINGER	2	0
SINGER AM	1	1
SINGER CW	2	0
SINGER S	1	0
SINGLETON A	1	0
SIRETT W	1	0
SKEWES V	1	0
SKEY HO	6	0
SKILBECK W	1	0
SLAUGHTER	1	0
SLEIGH GB	7	0
SLEIGHTHOLME CH	59	23
SLINGER CW	1	0
SLOCOCK R	1	1
SLOLEY R	11	6
SMAILES S	1	0
SMIT HN	2	0
SMIT NA	1	0
SMIT NH	2	0
SMITH	1	1
SMITH ?	1	1
SMITH A	1	0
'SMITH' A	1	0
SMITH A (SUB)	1	0
SMITH AE	24	5
SMITH AF	1	1
SMITH AG	1	0
SMITH AR	1	1
SMITH AS	2	1
SMITH BF	1	0
SMITH C	8	1
SMITH CA	14	10
SMITH CM	1	1
SMITH DH	1	0
SMITH Dr J	16	12
SMITH E	1	0
SMITH EA	1	0
SMITH ER	1	0
SMITH FV	62	2
SMITH G	1	0
SMITH GO	29	42
SMITH GS	1	0
SMITH HF	1	0
SMITH HR	7	1
SMITH J	1	0
SMITH JG	1	0
SMITH NH	1	0
SMITH RM	1	1
SMITH RT	2	0
SMITH RW	2	0
SMITH V	1	0
SMITH W	1	0
SMITH WD	2	1

NAME	APPS	GOALS
SMITH WP	3	0
SNELL HS	43	24
SNELL IE	18	5
SNOW PS	5	0
SNOW RJ	1	0
SOMERS-COCKS HL	2	0
SOMES FH	7	1
SOOLE AS	1	0
SOPER MR	50	14
SOPER NT	1	0
SOPPITT C	1	0
SORENSON IM	1	0
SOWLER T	5	0
SPACKMAN L	1	0
SPILSBURY BW	1	0
SPOOKE	1	0
SPOONER FD	2	0
SPOONER WT	1	0
SPRATT H	4	0
SPRING-RICE G	4	0
SQUIRE CE	4	8
SQUIRE RT	7	0
SQUIRES AE	1	0
SQUIRES RT	5	0
STANBROUGH LK	6	1
STANBROUGH MH	22	8
STANBROUGH WF	7	2
STANCOMB FW	1	0
STANDALOFT A	1	0
STANTON RG	1	0
STAPLES EP	1	0
STATTER RC	1	0
STEDIAN F	1	0
STEELE HS	4	0
STEELE M	1	0
STEER G	1	0
STEPHEN GP	1	0
STEPHENS A	10	0
STEPHENS GF	1	0
STEPHENS L	1	0
STEPHENSON FL	1	0
STERN A	1	0
STEVENS EH	1	0
STEVENS FH	1	0
STEVENS GF	2	1
STEVENS GP	13	5
STEVENS H	1	1
STEVENSON	1	0
STEVENSON JG	80	8
STEWART HC	4	4
STIRLING W	1	0
STOATS H	1	0
STOCKEN HR	1	0
STOCKS CL	7	0
STOCKS FC	5	0
STOCKS FL	1	0
STOCKS FW	1	0
STOKEN HS	1	1
STOKES A	1	0
STOKES B	1	0
STOKES EF	27	13
STOKES NB	1	1
STOKES RF	3	6
STONE ACS	9	0
STONE AE	1	0
STONE AG	1	0
STONE RN	1	0
STONE S	1	0
STOUT PW	6	1
STRACHAN A	1	0
STRASSER GA	42	0
STRATTON JC	1	0
STREET FC	3	0
STREET F	5	1

NAME	APPS	GOALS
STREET G	1	0
STREET MG	1	0
STRINGER EJ	9	0
STUART	1	0
STUART JG	1	0
STUART VD	1	0
STUART-LOVE C	1	0
STUBBINGS	1	0
STURGESS-JONES TO	1	0
STURROCK WD	1	0
SUGG FH	1	0
SULLIVAN SH	1	0
SULMAN H	2	0
SULMAN SW	21	14
SULS W	1	0
SUMMERS TH	6	0
SUTCLIFFE J	35	1
SUTTON AN	1	0
SUTTON EW	1	0
SUTTON NP	2	0
SWAINSON CG	1	0
SWISS J	1	0
SYMES-THOMPSON AH	13	4
SYMINGTON JW	2	0
SYMINGTON TP	10	4
SYMMS JM	4	2
SYMNS R	1	0
SYMONDS J	2	1
SYMONDS JW	1	0
SYMONDS RH	1	0
SYMONS CBO	7	4
SYMONS CT	8	0
SYMONS H?	1	0
SYMONS HF	1	0
SYMONS HJ	33	9
SYMONS JA	10	0
SYMONS LI	1	0
SYMONS SJ	2	2
SYMONS SR	1	0
TABERNACLE G	1	3
TARRANT A	1	0
TAUNTON ?	1	0
TAUNTON EH	2	0
TAUNTON HG	14	4
TAUNTON HJ	1	0
TAYLOR CM	7	0
TAYLOR GMC	13	0
TAYLOR HR	2	0
TAYLOR HS	1	0
TAYLOR J	1	0
TAYLOR RA	8	1
TAYLOR SG	1	0
TAYLOR SS	68	49
TEALE MA	8	1
TEMPLAR F	1	0
TEMPLETON J	1	0
TEPPER CH	8	2
TERRY AE	6	3
TETLEY JCD	6	0
TEWKESBURY KC	2	0
TEWSEY HJ	1	0
TEWSON S	8	0
THEW VG	11	0
THINN F	1	0
THINN GA	1	0
THOMAS CM	1	1
THOMAS FG	1	0
THOMAS LS	1	0
THOMAS R	1	2
THOMAS RM	1	0
THOMAS TS	5	1
THOMAS W	1	0
THOMPSON (1)	1	0
THOMPSON (2)	1	0

NAME	APPS	GOALS
THOMPSON AF	1	1
THOMPSON AHS	1	0
THOMPSON C	1	0
THOMPSON CB	10	0
THOMPSON DLN	1	0
THOMPSON FL	1	0
THOMPSON G	1	0
THOMPSON H	1	0
THOMPSON HW	1	0
THOMPSON J	8	0
THOMPSON JS	2	0
THOMPSON RG	1	0
THOMPSON RS	1	0
THOMPSON SJ	1	0
THOMPSON SL	1	0
THOMPSON W	1	1
THORBURN J	1	0
THORNE FG	29	7
THORNE WC	5	0
THORNE WRP	2	0
THORNTON CF	2	0
THORNTON RG	7	0
THORNTON RJ	1	0
THURWELL ES	1	0
THWAITES H	26	0
THWAITES PN	4	1
THWAITES TW	1	0
TIDSWELL GH	10	0
TILLETT SJ	1	0
TILLEY A	1	0
TIMBS PA	11	0
TIMMIS RB	1	0
TIMMIS WU	7	0
TIMONEY F	1	0
TOMBLESON JB	2	0
TOMLINSON FW	10	0
TOMPSON AH	1	0
TOMSON DV	15	0
TONKIN RS	1	0
TOONE G	1	0
TOONE P	1	0
TOONE WP	78	44
TOPHAM ?	1	4
TOPHAM AG	58	3
TOPHAM HG	1	0
TOPHAM R	46	30
TOPLIS NJ	1	0
TOPPIN CG	1	0
TOVEY	3	0
TOVEY AG	1	0
TOVEY CH	33	0
TOWLE AF	1	0
TOWNE WD	4	0
TOWNSEND FW	7	0
TOWNSEND M	35	0
TOWNTON HC	1	0
TOYNE SM	15	3
TRAPNELL P	1	0
TRAPP CS	54	0
TRECKMAN CL	1	0
TRECKMAN O	1	0
TREISMAN WB	1	0
TRELEAVEN CW	3	0
TRENT	1	0
TRESTALL EA	9	0
TREVOR W	1	1
TRINGHAM E	1	0
TRINGHAM J	1	0
TROWEL JW (SUB)	1	0
TRYWICK JA	1	0
TUBBS NH	21	1
TUDOR-OWEN E	1	0
TUDOR-OWEN FHG	26	3
TUFF B	43	28

NAME	APPS	GOALS
TUFF CT	6	5
TUFF FN	2	1
TUFNELL NC	3	1
TULL JE	1	0
TUNKS GW	1	0
TUNNINGTON E	8	1
TUPPER GH	1	0
TUPPER GL	4	1
TUPPER GW	20	1
TURNBULL ER	2	0
TURNBULL H	4	0
TURNBULL HM	1	0
TURNBULL JR	11	0
TURNBULL RM	1	0
TURNER (SUB)	1	0
TURNER AE	1	0
TURNER H	1	0
TURNER JRT	4	0
TURNER PF	1	0
TURNER R	41	42
TURNER RJ	1	0
TURNER TR	1	0
TURNOUR	1	0
TWISS AQ	1	0
TWISS HW	3	0
TWIST A	1	0
TYLER CH	1	0
UDAL NR	4	0
UNWIN G	1	0
UNWIN HR	19	8
UNWIN LL	1	1
UNWIN SR	5	3
UPTON A	1	0
UPWARD HA	1	0
USILL HV	1	0
VACHELL FT	26	0
VAN DER BORGH M	71	0
VAN DER BORGH M	1	0
VAN LANGENBERG F	3	0
VAN THIEL HF	14	0
VAN WART RB	7	0
VANN BW	12	8
VARDY AT	23	0
VASSALL GC	10	4
VASSALL SH	1	0
VAUGHAN M	1	0
VEITCH HM	2	0
VEITCH JG	33	29
VENABLES FL	1	0
VERNON DF	1	0
VERNON HD	3	3
VERREY BT	4	2
VIAN AR	2	0
VIAN BA	8	0
VICKERS H	9	1
VIDAL	1	0
VIDAL HSG	2	0
VIDAL LA	2	2
VIDLER JS	3	3
VINTCENT CH	3	2
VINTCENT G	1	0
VINTCENT J	1	0
VINTCENT LA	3	4
VOGEL FL	6	0
VOGEL JF	1	0
VOGEL JL	2	0
WACE A	1	0
WACE C	3	0
WACE FH	2	0
WACE HC	12	0
WACE LH	3	0
WACE R	9	1
WACE V	1	0
WADDINGTON CW	1	0

NAME	APPS	GOALS
WADE CH	19	0
WADE PV	2	0
WAKEFORD RP	17	0
WALCH E	1	0
WALDRON LM	2	1
WALFORD PF	3	1
WALKER A	6	0
WALKER AR	2	0
WALKER EH	1	0
WALKER HJD	1	0
WALKER HK	8	1
WALKER HW	1	1
WALKER J	1	0
WALKER PF (SUB)	1	1
WALKER RH	2	0
WALKER T	1	0
WALL A	1	0
WALL C	1	0
WALLACE A	1	0
WALLACE AW	6	0
WALLER HK	3	1
WALLICH AD	2	0
WALLIS RWD	1	0
WALLIS SR	1	0
WALSH AH	1	0
WALSH FA	1	0
WALTER A	1	1
WALTER FA	1	1
WALTER FH	45	2
WALTER HGB	2	0
WALTER JH	1	0
WALTERS AM	38	14
WALTERS CR	1	0
WALTERS HM	26	36
WALTERS JH	4	2
WALTERS PM	27	0
WALTON GF	3	0
WALTON-EVANS J	1	0
WARD	1	0
WARD CB	2	0
WARD ED	1	0
WARD ER	1	0
WARD ES	84	26
WARD F	1	0
WARD FJ	1	0
WARD HO	1	0
WARD HP	1	0
WARD JM	1	0
WARD OW	1	2
WARD VE	1	0
WARD VF	44	14
WARD VG	31	19
WARD-CLARKE HM	1	0
WARDE HP	1	0
WARE LH	1	0
WARE RC	1	0
WARFIELD JM	5	4
WARNER AC	3	4
WASHINGTON ES	5	3
WASSELL H	1	0
WATERBURY CS	1	0
WATERFIELD N	1	0
WATERHOUSE R	5	4
WATERS PB	2	0
WATHAN AR	2	0
WATKINS A	1	0
WATKINS PMC	1	1
WATKINS WF	1	0
WATKINSON WS	21	0
WATSON GS	63	21
WATSON HJ	1	0
WATSON TW	1	0
WATSON WA	1	0
WATT J	10	0

NAME	APPS	GOALS
WATTS MA	1	0
WATTS-SMITH DS	3	0
WAUGH AJ	10	8
WAY GA	1	0
WEATHERHEAD HTC	1	0
WEATHERHEAD TC	3	0
WEAVER LT	15	2
WEBB FM	14	0
WEBB JKG	1	1
WEBB JOW	62	23
WEBB T	1	0
WEBDALE CF	1	0
WEBSTER WH	47	14
WEIGHTMAN H	1	0
WELCH FCB	4	1
WELCHLAND P	1	0
WELLS E	1	0
WELLS WC	6	0
WELSH	1	0
WELSH F	1	0
WELSH FCB	1	0
WENTWORTH F	2	1
WEST H	1	0
WEST J (SUB)	1	1
WESTBY A	1	0
WESTBY HP	18	1
WESTON W	1	0
WESTON WA	1	0
WESTRAIL AE	1	0
WETHERED P	1	0
WETHERED WP	1	0
WETHERED WT	1	0
WETTON H	21	2
WEY A	1	0
WHALEY PF	12	4
WHARTON AW	1	0
WHARTON LE	6	0
WHEATEAR	1	0
WHEELER A	1	0
WHEELER F	31	7
WHEWELL WT	74	6
WHINNEY E	1	1
WHINNEY H	1	0
WHISH C	2	0
WHITE FS	1	0
WHITE J	12	0
WHITE K	3	0
WHITE RSM	5	2
WHITE WN	4	0
WHITEINGTON B	1	0
WHITTAKER LE	9	4
WHITTING AG	16	2
WHITTOW A	1	0
WHURR GT	1	0
WIGGINS M	1	0
WIGRAM EF	3	0
WIGRAM R	1	3
WIGRAM T	1	0
WIILSON CH	1	0
WILBERFORCE FR	2	0
WILBERFORCE S	1	0
WILD CH	16	0
WILKINS FC	1	0
WILKINSON	1	0
WILKINSON AM (1)	12	3
WILKINSON AM (2)	54	0
WILKINSON CL	19	2
WILKINSON GE	12	0
WILKINSON LR	2	0
WILLES	1	0
WILLETT BH	19	0
WILLETT JA	1	0
WILLETT P	3	1
WILLEY FT	2	0

NAME	APPS	GOALS
WILLIAM F (SUB)	1	0
WILLIAMS (SUB)	1	1
WILLIAMS ACR	4	0
WILLIAMS AW	4	0
WILLIAMS C	2	0
WILLIAMS CA	5	0
WILLIAMS CH	2	0
WILLIAMS GA	1	0
WILLIAMS HR	9	0
WILLIAMS JG	6	0
WILLIAMS LC	54	3
WILLIAMS LG	1	0
WILLIAMS LS	4	1
WILLIAMS MB	1	0
WILLIAMS MR	1	0
WILLIAMS PH	13	1
WILLIAMS RH	4	0
WILLIAMS RW	16	4
WILLIAMS SS	2	0
WILLIAMS WJ	1	0
WILLIAMS WL	1	0
WILLIS RB	2	0
WILMER-FOX B	1	0
WILSON	2	0
WILSON AB	3	0
WILSON AP	2	0
WILSON CE	107	0
WILSON CH	11	0
WILSON CP	52	5
WILSON CT	1	0
WILSON EG	2	0
WILSON GL	10	22
WILSON GO	1	3
WILSON GP	41	17
WILSON HJ	2	0
WILSON W	1	0
WILTSHIRE HP	10	2
WIMBLE HD	2	1
WINCH AB	2	0
WINCH GB	4	0
WINCH HS	5	5
WINCKWORTH DN	1	0
WINCKWORTH DP	5	0
WINCKWORTH WB	3	0
WINCKWORTH WN	13	1
WINGER E	1	1
WINGFIELD M	1	0
WINLAW AWE	2	0
WINLAW RW	1	1
WINSLOE (SUB)	1	0
WINSLOW G	6	1
WINSLOW HP	7	1
WINSTON RC	1	0
WIPPELL DP	7	1
WISE W (SUB)	1	0
WITH PA	11	0
WITHERINGTON C	1	0
WITHERINGTON GW	1	0
WITHERINGTON IG	6	0
WITHERINGTON JG	6	0
WITHERS A	1	1
WOLFENDEN E	2	3
WOLFENDOE VJ	1	0
WOOD	1	0
WOOD GR	3	1
WOOD H	1	1
WOOD JL	2	1
WOOD L	2	0
WOODARD EH	5	0
WOODARD EN	4	0
WOODBRIDGE AR	25	6
WOODBRIDGE CM	1	0
WOODBRIDGE DL	1	0
WOODBRIDGE GH	4	0

NAME	APPS	GOALS
WOODBRIDGE MJ	1	0
WOODGATE GE	1	0
WOODHOUSE	2	1
WOODHOUSE OW	1	0
WOODHOUSE WM	13	4
WOODMAN A	1	0
WOODRUFF GG	33	0
WOODRUFFE W	1	0
WOODS A	1	0
WOOLCOCK AH	41	0
WOOLFENDER AR	3	3
WOOLLACOMBE W	1	0
WOOLLAN EB	1	0
WOOSNAM M (1)	10	5
WOOSNAM M (2)	4	0
WORCESTER BL	8	1
WORCESTER GL	3	0
WORCESTER LO	4	0
WREFORD-BROWN C	16	0
WREFORD-BROWN G	2	0
WREFORD-BROWN OE	5	0
WRIGHT B	1	0
WRIGHT CW	1	1
WRIGHT EG	1	0
WRIGHT EGD	1	0
WRIGHT HE	1	0
WRIGHT HW	1	0
WRIGHT JH	4	0
WRIGHT OW	2	0
WRIGHT RG	128	84
WRIGHT RW	1	0
WRIGHT W	3	0
WRIGHT WR	53	9
WRY ?	1	0
WYATT CP	5	0
WYLD	1	3
WYLD HJ	1	0
WYLD WH	2	0
WYLDE HS	3	0
YATES HG	16	6
YEMM C	1	0
YOUD CS	1	0
YOULE JS	3	1
YOUNG ?	2	1
YOUNG AJ	2	0
YOUNG CS (SUB)	1	0
YOUNG D	1	0
YOUNG E	2	0
YOUNG F	3	0
YOUNG R	4	1
YOUNG RA	13	2
YOUNG SG	1	0
YOUNG W	45	6
ZABELL NF	5	1

Appendix
Final League Tables

1905/06	P	W	D	L	F	A	PT
London Caledonians	10	7	1	2	25	8	15
Clapton	10	6	1	3	11	13	13
Casuals	**10**	**3**	**4**	**3**	**14**	**14**	**10**
Civil Service	10	4	1	5	16	20	9
Ealing Association	10	3	2	5	15	19	8
Ilford	10	1	3	6	5	12	5

1906/07	P	W	D	L	F	A	PT
Ilford	10	8	2	0	26	9	18
London Caledonians	10	6	0	4	19	14	12
Clapton	10	4	3	3	18	11	11
Civil Service	10	3	1	6	11	19	7
Ealing Association	10	3	1	6	12	22	7
Casuals	**10**	**2**	**1**	**7**	**15**	**26**	**5**

1907/08	P	W	D	L	F	A	PT
New Crusaders	16	13	2	1	80	15	28
Richmond Association	16	11	0	5	39	25	22
Ealing Association	16	7	5	4	47	34	19
Civil Service	16	7	4	5	28	20	18
Casuals	**16**	**6**	**5**	**5**	**36**	**29**	**17**
Eastbourne	16	6	4	6	35	46	16
Ipswich Town	16	5	4	7	36	40	14
Townley Park	16	2	3	11	25	46	7
Croydon	16	1	1	14	12	83	3

1908/09	P	W	D	L	F	A	PT
New Crusaders	16	13	1	2	66	21	27
Civil Service	16	11	4	1	38	22	26
Eastbourne	16	6	6	4	44	43	18
Ealing Association	16	8	2	6	38	39	18
Casuals	**16**	**5**	**3**	**8**	**34**	**31**	**13**
Ipswich Town	16	5	3	8	25	43	13
Reigate Priory	16	4	3	9	33	46	11
Richmond Association	16	4	2	10	20	43	10
Crouch End Vampires	16	2	4	10	23	33	8

1909/10	P	W	D	L	F	A	PT
New Crusaders	16	11	2	3	35	11	24
Civil Service	16	9	3	4	38	21	21
Ealing Association	16	6	5	5	35	28	17
Eastbourne	16	7	3	6	37	43	17
Casuals	**16**	**5**	**5**	**6**	**33**	**29**	**15**
Townley Park	16	5	4	7	29	35	14
Ipswich Town	16	6	1	9	26	37	13
Reigate Priory	16	4	4	8	19	36	12
Norsemen	16	4	3	9	21	33	11

1910/11	P	W	D	L	F	A	PT
New Crusaders	16	11	4	1	40	12	26
Civil Service	16	9	6	1	34	18	24
Townley Park	16	8	3	5	23	20	19
Hampstead	16	8	2	6	25	28	18
Casuals	**16**	**7**	**2**	**7**	**27**	**28**	**16**
Ipswich Town	16	7	0	9	30	37	14
Ealing Association	16	5	0	11	22	52	10
Eastbourne	16	4	1	11	25	31	9
Tunbridge Wells	16	4	0	12	33	33	8

1911/12	P	W	D	L	F	A	Pts
Civil Service	16	11	1	4	44	23	23
New Crusaders	16	8	4	4	30	21	20
Hampstead	16	8	3	5	19	18	19
Ealing Association	16	8	2	6	24	23	18
Ipswich Town	16	6	5	5	34	31	17
Oxford	16	5	6	5	23	23	16
Casuals	**16**	**4**	**5**	**7**	**25**	**25**	**13**
Townley Park	16	3	6	7	25	28	12
Alleyn Old Boys	16	1	4	11	14	46	6

1912/13	P	W	D	L	F	A	Pts
New Crusaders	14	13	0	1	40	8	26
Civil Service	17	12	0	5	42	16	24
Hampstead	18	10	2	6	32	20	22
Ealing Association	18	7	4	7	26	36	18
Ipswich Town	18	9	0	9	38	42	18
Casuals	**16**	**7**	**2**	**7**	**29**	**20**	**16**
L.C.W. & Parr's Bank	17	3	9	5	19	26	15
Townley Park	17	5	2	10	19	40	12
Oxford	15	3	5	7	12	25	11
Eastbourne	18	3	0	15	28	52	6

1913/14	P	W	D	L	F	A	Pts
Civil Service	16	12	3	1	49	13	27
Casuals	**16**	**7**	**7**	**2**	**36**	**16**	**21**
Ealing Association	16	6	6	4	29	22	18
Ipswich Town	16	8	2	6	36	35	18
Crouch End Vampires	16	8	2	6	23	25	18
L.C.W. & Parr's Bank	16	7	1	8	33	35	15
Hampstead	16	5	1	10	23	40	11
Reigate Priory	16	3	3	10	22	34	9
Townley Park	16	2	3	11	19	50	7

1919/20	P	W	D	L	F	A	PT
Dulwich Hamlet	22	15	3	4	58	16	33
Nunhead	22	14	5	3	48	26	33
Tufnell Park	22	12	4	6	45	32	28
Ilford	22	13	1	8	63	42	27
Oxford City	22	12	3	7	63	51	27
London Caledonians	22	10	3	9	32	30	23
Leytonstone	22	8	3	11	50	43	19
Clapton	22	8	3	11	38	44	19
Civil Service	22	7	4	11	35	40	18
Woking	22	6	3	13	36	42	15
West Norwood	22	5	4	13	19	53	14
Casuals	**22**	**3**	**2**	**17**	**20**	**88**	**8**

1920/21	P	W	D	L	F	A	PT
Ilford	22	16	4	2	70	24	36
London Caledonians	22	13	5	4	45	17	31
Tufnell Park	22	14	3	5	43	24	31
Nunhead	22	12	5	5	53	33	29
Dulwich Hamlet	22	11	6	5	60	30	28
Oxford City	22	12	3	7	56	38	27
Leytonstone	22	8	6	8	36	29	22
Clapton	22	7	7	8	33	52	21
Civil Service	22	3	7	12	28	45	13
Woking	22	3	5	14	16	43	11
Casuals	**22**	**3**	**3**	**16**	**31**	**87**	**9**
West Norwood	22	2	2	18	18	67	6

1921/22	P	W	D	L	F	A	PT
Ilford	26	17	4	5	66	34	38
Dulwich Hamlet	26	14	8	4	65	24	36
London Caledonians	26	16	4	6	41	21	36
Nunhead	26	12	5	9	65	41	29
Clapton	26	13	3	10	51	46	29
Tufnell Park	26	10	7	9	44	39	27
Oxford City	26	12	2	12	48	47	26
Wycombe Wanderers	26	12	2	12	61	64	26
Civil Service	26	9	8	9	40	48	26
Woking	26	10	6	10	39	49	26
Leytonstone	26	9	6	11	41	48	24
West Norwood	26	8	5	13	43	57	21
Wimbledon	26	7	4	15	52	56	18
Casuals	**26**	**0**	**2**	**24**	**25**	**107**	**2**

1922/23	P	W	D	L	F	A	PT
Clapton	26	15	7	4	51	33	37
Nunhead	26	15	5	6	52	32	35
London Caledonians	26	13	7	6	43	26	33
Ilford	26	11	7	8	57	38	29
Casuals	**26**	**12**	**5**	**9**	**68**	**51**	**29**
Civil Service	26	9	10	7	39	36	28
Wycombe Wanderers	26	11	4	11	61	61	26
Dulwich Hamlet	26	9	7	10	60	44	25
Leytonstone	26	9	7	10	45	56	25
Tufnell Park	26	9	5	12	41	45	23
Wimbledon	26	10	2	14	49	50	22
Woking	26	7	6	13	42	67	20
Oxford City	26	6	5	15	45	68	17
West Norwood	26	5	5	16	25	71	15

1923/24	P	W	D	L	F	A	PT
St Albans City	26	17	5	4	72	38	39
Dulwich Hamlet	26	15	6	5	49	28	36
Clapton	26	14	5	7	73	50	33
Wycombe Wanderers	26	14	5	7	88	65	33
London Caledonians	26	14	3	9	53	49	31
Civil Service	26	12	5	9	52	47	29
Casuals	**26**	**13**	**1**	**12**	**65**	**54**	**27**
Ilford	26	9	6	11	56	59	24
Nunhead	26	8	8	10	41	46	24
Wimbledon	26	8	4	14	43	62	20
Tufnell Park	26	8	2	16	38	53	18
Woking	26	5	8	13	31	62	18
Oxford City	26	7	2	17	53	74	16
Leytonstone	26	6	4	16	41	68	16

1924/25	P	W	D	L	F	A	PT
London Caledonians	26	18	5	3	76	36	41
Clapton	26	19	1	6	64	34	39
St Albans City	26	16	2	8	69	39	34
Tufnell Park	26	11	4	11	47	41	26
Ilford	26	11	4	11	46	42	26
Leytonstone	26	12	2	12	55	63	26
Casuals	**26**	**12**	**1**	**13**	**55**	**58**	**25**
Wycombe Wanderers	26	11	2	13	58	61	24
Civil Service	26	10	4	12	52	64	24
Nunhead	26	9	5	12	45	43	23
Wimbledon	26	10	2	14	50	54	22
Dulwich Hamlet	26	8	5	13	42	57	21
Oxford City	26	9	2	15	38	71	20
Woking	26	5	3	18	33	67	13

1925/26	P	W	D	L	F	A	PT
Dulwich Hamlet	26	20	1	5	80	49	41
London Caledonians	26	18	1	7	81	44	37
Clapton	26	14	4	8	64	50	32
Wycombe Wanderers	26	14	3	9	97	83	31
St Albans City	26	12	6	8	76	54	30
Nunhead	26	13	4	9	49	43	30
Ilford	26	13	2	11	81	70	28
Leytonstone	26	12	1	13	75	63	25
Woking	26	8	6	12	56	73	22
Tufnell Park	26	8	5	13	36	53	21
Casuals	**26**	**8**	**4**	**14**	**48**	**61**	**20**
Wimbledon	26	9	1	16	61	77	19
Oxford City	26	8	1	17	48	76	17
Civil Service	26	5	1	20	43	99	11

1926/27	P	W	D	L	F	A	PT
St Albans City	26	20	1	5	96	34	41
Ilford	26	17	0	9	76	57	34
Wimbledon	26	15	3	8	72	45	33
Nunhead	26	11	8	7	51	33	30
Woking	26	12	6	8	68	60	30
London Caledonians	26	11	7	8	58	47	29
Clapton	26	11	4	11	58	60	26
Leytonstone	26	11	1	14	54	78	23
Dulwich Hamlet	26	9	4	13	60	58	22
Wycombe Wanderers	26	10	2	14	59	86	22
Tufnell Park	26	8	4	14	45	55	20
Oxford City	26	7	5	14	46	72	19
Casuals	**26**	**8**	**3**	**15**	**37**	**78**	**19**
Civil Service	26	6	4	16	48	65	16

1927/28	P	W	D	L	F	A	PT
St Albans City	26	15	5	6	86	50	35
London Caledonians	26	12	9	5	63	38	33
Ilford	26	14	4	8	72	54	32
Woking	26	13	5	8	72	56	31
Nunhead	26	13	2	11	57	54	28
Wimbledon	26	12	3	11	57	48	27
Leytonstone	26	13	1	12	53	56	27
Clapton	26	8	10	8	52	47	26
Dulwich Hamlet	26	8	9	9	56	49	25
Casuals	**26**	**8**	**8**	**10**	**54**	**58**	**24**
Wycombe Wanderers	26	9	5	12	60	69	23
Oxford City	26	7	7	12	36	57	21
Civil Service	26	8	4	14	38	76	20
Tufnell Park	26	4	4	18	38	82	12

1928/29	P	W	D	L	F	A	PT
Nunhead	26	15	6	5	47	35	36
London Caledonians	26	15	4	7	65	33	34
Dulwich Hamlet	26	14	6	6	65	34	34
Wimbledon	26	9	10	7	66	54	28
Ilford	26	12	3	11	67	52	27
Clapton	26	11	5	10	60	55	27
Tufnell Park	26	11	5	10	58	55	27
St Albans City	26	12	3	11	63	69	27
Leytonstone	26	11	3	12	56	79	25
Wycombe Wanderers	26	10	3	13	58	60	23
Oxford City	26	10	3	13	61	71	23
Casuals	**26**	**8**	**5**	**13**	**49**	**60**	**21**
Woking	26	8	3	15	39	65	19
Civil Service	26	4	5	17	39	71	13

1929/30	P	W	D	L	F	A	PT
Nunhead	26	19	3	4	69	36	41
Dulwich Hamlet	26	15	6	5	74	39	36
Kingstonian	26	15	4	7	57	37	34
Ilford	26	16	1	9	84	60	33
Woking	26	11	5	10	66	65	27
Wimbledon	26	11	2	13	64	66	24
Wycombe Wanderers	26	10	4	12	49	52	24
Casuals	**26**	**8**	**7**	**11**	**50**	**51**	**23**
Oxford City	26	10	3	13	45	60	23
St Albans City	26	9	4	13	54	77	22
Clapton	26	8	4	14	47	57	20
London Caledonians	26	8	3	15	49	69	19
Leytonstone	26	8	3	15	48	68	19
Tufnell Park	26	6	7	13	35	54	19

1930/31	P	W	D	L	F	A	PT
Wimbledon	26	18	6	2	69	37	42
Dulwich Hamlet	26	12	9	5	51	39	33
Wycombe Wanderers	26	12	6	8	67	45	30
Casuals	**26**	**12**	**6**	**8**	**71**	**56**	**30**
St Albans City	26	11	7	8	67	66	29
Ilford	26	10	6	10	70	62	26
Oxford City	26	10	5	11	43	48	25
London Caledonians	26	8	8	10	43	53	24
Kingstonian	26	10	4	12	49	64	24
Tufnell Park	26	9	5	12	45	61	23
Nunhead	26	9	4	13	49	54	22
Woking	26	9	4	13	56	63	22
Clapton	26	7	4	15	62	75	18
Leytonstone	26	6	4	16	46	65	16

1931/32	P	W	D	L	F	A	PT
Wimbledon	26	17	2	7	60	35	36
Ilford	26	13	9	4	71	45	35
Dulwich Hamlet	26	15	3	8	69	43	33
Wycombe Wanderers	26	14	5	7	72	50	33
Oxford City	26	15	2	9	63	49	32
Kingstonian	26	13	3	10	71	50	29
Tufnell Park	26	9	7	10	50	48	25
Nunhead	26	9	7	10	54	61	25
Casuals	**26**	**10**	**4**	**12**	**59**	**65**	**24**
Clapton	26	9	5	12	50	57	23
Leytonstone	26	9	3	14	36	61	21
St Albans City	26	8	4	14	57	78	20
Woking	26	6	5	15	44	64	17
London Caledonians	26	2	7	17	24	74	11

1932/33	P	W	D	L	F	A	PT
Dulwich Hamlet	26	15	6	5	71	45	36
Leytonstone	26	16	4	6	66	43	36
Kingstonian	26	15	2	9	77	49	32
Ilford	26	14	0	12	60	58	28
Casuals	**26**	**12**	**2**	**12**	**48**	**36**	**26**
Tufnell Park	26	11	3	12	51	51	25
St Albans City	26	12	1	13	57	63	25
Clapton	26	10	5	11	51	65	25
Oxford City	26	9	6	11	49	54	24
Woking	26	10	4	12	53	61	24
Wycombe Wanderers	26	10	4	12	47	56	24
Nunhead	26	8	6	12	42	50	22
Wimbledon	26	8	5	13	55	67	21
London Caledonians	26	5	6	15	35	64	16

1933/34	P	W	D	L	F	A	PT
Kingstonian	26	15	7	4	80	42	37
Dulwich Hamlet	26	15	5	6	68	36	35
Wimbledon	26	13	7	6	63	35	33
Tufnell Park	26	14	5	7	55	50	33
Ilford	26	15	2	9	60	56	32
Casuals	**26**	**13**	**5**	**8**	**47**	**32**	**31**
Leytonstone	26	13	3	10	55	48	29
Nunhead	26	10	5	11	48	44	25
London Caledonians	26	7	8	11	29	51	22
Wycombe Wanderers	26	9	2	15	57	60	20
St Albans City	26	8	4	14	44	75	20
Oxford City	26	7	4	15	45	57	18
Clapton	26	5	6	15	35	62	16
Woking	26	6	1	19	43	81	13

1934/35	P	W	D	L	F	A	PT
Wimbledon	26	14	7	5	63	30	35
Oxford City	26	14	4	8	69	50	32
Leytonstone	26	15	2	9	49	36	32
Dulwich Hamlet	26	11	7	8	66	45	29
Tufnell Park	26	11	7	8	53	44	29
Kingstonian	26	11	6	9	44	40	28
Nunhead	26	10	7	9	35	34	27
London Caledonians	26	9	7	10	40	41	25
St Albans City	26	9	6	11	61	80	24
Ilford	26	9	6	11	40	56	24
Clapton	26	7	7	12	46	48	21
Woking	26	9	3	14	44	68	21
Wycombe Wanderers	26	7	6	13	51	69	20
Casuals	**26**	**6**	**5**	**15**	**37**	**57**	**17**

1935/36	P	W	D	L	F	A	PT
Wimbledon	26	19	2	5	82	29	40
Casuals	**26**	**14**	**5**	**7**	**60**	**45**	**33**
Ilford	26	13	3	10	67	47	29
Dulwich Hamlet	26	10	8	8	64	47	28
Nunhead	26	11	6	9	51	40	28
Wycombe Wanderers	26	13	2	11	60	68	28
Clapton	26	11	5	10	42	46	27
Oxford City	26	11	4	11	60	58	26
St Albans City	26	11	2	13	59	64	24
Woking	26	9	4	13	43	62	22
Tufnell Park	26	9	3	14	42	61	21
London Caledonians	26	9	3	14	35	52	21
Kingstonian	26	9	2	15	43	56	20
Leytonstone	26	7	3	16	34	67	17

1936/37	P	W	D	L	F	A	PT
Kingstonian	26	18	3	5	63	43	39
Nunhead	26	17	3	6	77	32	37
Leytonstone	26	16	4	6	71	42	36
Ilford	26	14	5	7	86	39	33
Dulwich Hamlet	26	12	6	8	64	48	30
Wycombe Wanderers	26	10	5	11	55	52	25
Wimbledon	26	9	7	10	52	53	25
Clapton	26	10	5	11	42	51	25
Casuals	**26**	**10**	**3**	**13**	**46**	**58**	**23**
Woking	26	9	4	13	53	69	22
Oxford City	26	8	5	13	56	89	21
St Albans City	26	7	5	14	44	62	19
Tufnell Park	26	4	7	15	43	74	15
London Caledonians	26	5	4	17	26	66	14

1937/38	P	W	D	L	F	A	PT
Leytonstone	26	17	6	3	72	34	40
Ilford	26	17	3	6	70	39	37
Tufnell Park	26	15	2	9	63	47	32
Nunhead	26	14	3	9	52	44	31
Wycombe Wanderers	26	12	5	9	69	55	29
Dulwich Hamlet	26	13	3	10	57	46	29
Kingstonian	26	12	4	10	51	48	28
Clapton	26	9	6	11	49	53	24
Wimbledon	26	10	3	13	62	49	23
London Caledonians	26	9	4	13	44	55	22
Oxford City	26	7	7	12	35	71	21
Casuals	**26**	**8**	**3**	**15**	**51**	**74**	**19**
Woking	26	7	2	17	41	72	16
St Albans City	26	4	5	17	31	60	13

1938/39	P	W	D	L	F	A	PT
Leytonstone	26	18	4	4	68	32	40
Ilford	26	17	4	5	68	32	38
Kingstonian	26	17	3	6	62	39	37
Dulwich Hamlet	26	15	5	6	60	32	35
Wimbledon	26	14	3	9	88	56	31
Nunhead	26	11	6	9	54	44	28
Casuals	**26**	**11**	**6**	**9**	**54**	**51**	**28**
Clapton	26	12	2	12	69	61	26
Wycombe Wanderers	26	10	6	10	62	62	26
St Albans City	26	8	5	13	44	50	21
Woking	26	9	2	15	35	56	20
Oxford City	26	4	4	18	44	84	12
Tufnell Park	26	4	4	18	33	87	12
London Caledonians	26	3	4	19	26	81	10

Appendix
Casuals Reserve Team Record 1922-1939

Season	P	W	D	L	F	A	Pts	Pos	League
1922/23	26	10	4	12	42	52	24	8	IL
1923/24	26	10	6	10	44	38	26	6	IL
1924/25	26	10	2	14	55	60	22	10	IL
1925/26	26	14	6	6	58	46	34	4	IL
1926/27	26	9	5	12	67	76	23	8	IL
1927/28	26	10	1	15	50	77	21	10	IL
1928/29	26	7	2	17	45	88	16	14	IL
1929/30	26	17	2	7	75	48	36	2	IL
1930/31	26	16	3	7	74	46	35	2	IL
1931/32	26	16	2	8	84	67	34	2	IL
1932/33	26	7	5	14	44	83	19	12	IL
1933/34	26	9	4	13	63	77	22	11	IL
1934/35	26	10	4	12	51	60	24	9	IL
1935/36	26	13	3	10	57	55	29	5	IL
1936/37	26	8	5	13	53	65	21	10	IL
1937/38	26	6	6	14	37	60	18	12	IL
1938/39	26	7	6	13	46	64	20	11	IL
Total	442	179	66	197	945	1062	425		

Bibliography & Thanks

Books & Brochures

Alcock, C.W.	Football Annual 1882	The Cricket Press	1882
Bevan, Hibberd & Gilbert	To the Palace for the Cup	Replay Publishing	1999
Fabian, A.H. & Green, G.	Association Football	Caxton Publishing Co.	1960
Hallows, T.	Casuals Jubilee Brochure	Casuals F.C.	1933
Hollans, J.	Spurs – A History of Tottenham Hotspur F.C.	Sportsmans Book Club	1957

Newspapers

Acton Gazette, Bath Herald, Berkshire Chronicle, Birmingham Daily Post, Bolton Chronicle, Boro" of West Ham, East Ham, and Stratford Express, Bucks Examiner, Bucks Free Press, Burnley & East Lancashire Mid-Weekly Gazette, Croydon Advertiser, Daily Gazette (Islington), Derby Daily Telegraph, Derby Express, Dorking & Leatherhead Advertiser, Dumfries & Galloway Courier & Herald, Ealing Gazette, Ealing Gazette and West Middlesex Observer, Eastbourne Gazette, East Anglian Daily Times, Edinburgh Evening News, Erith Times, Belvedere & Abbey Wood Chronicle, Evening Argus (Brighton), Evening Times (Glasgow), Evening North Wiltshire Herald, Falkirk Mail, Fife Advertiser, Fife Free Press, Football News (Nottingham), Glasgow Herald, Grimsby Express, Grimsby News, The Guardian, Hampstead & Highgate Express, Hants and Berks Gazette and Middlesex and Surrey Journal, Harrow Gazette, Hertfordshire Express and Hitchin, Letchworth & Stevenage Gazette, Ilford Recorder, Islington Gazette, Kentish Express, Kettering Guardian and North Northants Advertiser, Kidderminster Sun, The Launceston Weekly News, and Cornwall & Devon Advertiser, Lincolnshire Chronicle, Lincolnshire Echo, Liverpool Daily Post, Liverpool Mercury, Long Eaton Advertiser and Ilkeston and Erewash Weekly News, Luton News, Maidenhead Advertiser, Mansfield and North Notts Advertiser, The Mansfield Reporter and Sutton-in-Ashfield Times, Middlesex Advertiser and County Gazette, Middlesbrough and Stockton Evening Telegraph, Middlesex & Buckinghamshire Advertiser, Middlesex Gazette, Newbury Express, Berks, Hants, Wilts, and Oxon Courier, Newcastle Daily Chronicle, News Chronicle, Northern Daily Mail (Hartlepool), Northern Daily Mail and South Durham Herald, The North Star, Nottingham Daily Express, Nottingham Evening News, The Observer, Oxford Times, Paisley & Renfrewshire Gazette, Preston Herald, Reading Standard, Retford, Worksop, Isle of Axholme & Gainsborough News, Scarborough Evening News, The Scarborough Post, Scottish Sport, Sheffield Daily Telegraph, South London Press, Southern Echo and Bournemouth Telegraph, Southport Standard, The Sportsman, Staffordshire Post, Staffordshire Sentinel, Stirling Observer, Stratford Express, Streatham News Sunderland Echo, Surrey Advertiser, Surrey Comet, Surrey Mirror, The Times, Tottenham & Wood Green Star, Uxbridge Gazette, Uxbrudge Review & District Record, Walthamstow & Leyton Guardian, West London Advertiser and West London News, West London Observer, West Somerset Free Press, Westminster Gazette, The Weymouth Telegram, Woodford Times, Woking Herald, Woking Observer, Yorkshire Post

Websites

www.rsssf.com
www.guardian.co.uk
www.salarchives.co.uk

Thanks

Colindale Newspaper Library, Emma Rummins, Tim Bell, Brian & Roger Phillips, Viv Bourne, Barry Glynn (East Molesey CC), Christopher Sweeney (Islington Local History Centre), Sarah Bowden (Wandsworth Local History Archive), Anne Wheeldon (Hammersmith Local History Archives), Tom Blackbourn, David Bromich, Gillian Johnson (Burton Library), Len Reilly (Lambeth Archive), Jan Marsh (Bournemouth Libraries), Mark Stubbs (Luton Central Library), Bob Thompson (Harrow Central Library), Val Bryant (Redbridge Archives), Hammersmith & Fulham Archives, Newcastle City Archives, Mishi D. Morath, Rachel Simon (Bucks Archives), Richard Yates, John Laurence, Mrs Heater (Brighton College), Ann Wheeler (Charterhouse School), Oliver Pollard (Forest School), Thelma Cavallini, Norman Epps, Rachael Guy (Berkhamsted School), Marian F Delfgou (Chigwell School), Terry Heard (City of London School), S.J. Mann (Cranleigh School), Penny Hatfield (Eton College), Christopher Dawkins (Felsted School), Rita Boswell (Harrow School), Anne Drewery (Lancing College), Norman Rosser (Malvern College), Paul Stevens (Repton School), Jackie Wilkie (Old Aldenhamian Society), Michael Morrogh (Shrewsbury School), Sally Todd (St. John's School, Leatherhead), Edward Minchinton (Wellingborough School), Suzanne Foster (Winchester College), John Blackmore, Roisin O'Connor, Mike Wilson, Colin Walton

REFERENCES

Chapter One
1 *Casuals Jubilee Book* 1933 p3
2 *Football Annual* 1882 p147
3 *Derby Express* 27.12.1884 p3
4 *Association Football* volume 1 p256
5 Wall, F.J. Fifty years of Football p3
6 *The Sportsman* 2.10.1883 p4
7 *The Sportsman* 10.11.1883 p7
8 *Berkshire Chronicle* 15.11.1884 p2
9 *The Times* 13.2.1885 p12
10 *The Sportsman* 27.10.1885 P4
11 *A History of Tottenham Hotspur* p28
12 *The Sportsman* 28.10.1885 p8
13 *The Sportsman* 31.3.1887 p4
14 *The Sportsman* 7.4.1887 p4
15 *The Sportsman* 28.3.1887
16 *The Sportsman* 14.10.1887 p4
17 *The Sportsman* 20.2.1888 p4
18 *The Sportsman* 2.4.1888 p4
19 *The Sportsman* 4.3.1889 p4
20 *The Sportsman* 12.1.1889 p7
21 *The Sportsman* 26.9.1889 p4
22 *The Sportsman* 17.4.1890 p4

Chapter Two
1 *The Sportsman* 14.11.1890 p4
2 *The Sportsman* 28.11.1890 p4
3 *Paisley & Renfrewshire Gazette* 10.1.1891 p3
4 *The Times* 22.7.1890 p11
5 *Birmingham Daily Mail* 17.1.1891 p3
6 *The Sportsman* 20.4.1891 p4
7 *The Sportsman* 27.4.1891 p4
8 *The Sportsman* 17.2.1892 p7
9 *The Sportsman* 19.2.1892 p5
10 *The Sportsman* 20.2.1892 p7
11 *The Sportsman* 17.11.1892 p4
12 *The Sportsman* 23.1.1893 p4
13 *The Sportsman* 27.3.1893 p4
14 *Brighton College Magazine* April 1893
15 *Morning Post* 14.12.1932
16 *The Sportsman* 5.2.1894 p4
17 *The Sportsman* 19.2.1894 p4
18 *The Sportsman* 19.3.1894 p7
19 *The Times* 9.4.1894 p10
20 *The Times* 23.4.1894 p6
21 *The Sportsman* 9.11.1894 p4
22 *The Sportsman* 8.11.1894 p4
23 *The Times* 17.10.1894 p11
24 *Woodford Times* 8.3.1895 p2
25 *Woodford Times* 15.3.1895 p8
26 *The Sportsman* 1.5.1895 p7

Chapter Three
1 *The Sportsman* 17.4.1896 p4
2 *The Sportsman* 25.9.1896 p4
3 *The Sportsman* 16.11.1896 p3
4 *The Sportsman* 18.1.1897 p7
5 *The Sportsman* 11.4.1898 p4
6 *The Sportsman* 14.3.1898 P3
7 *The Sportsman* 24.3.1898 p4
8 *The Times* 31.1.1898 p11

Chapter Four
1 *The Sportsman* 25.3.1901 p3
2 *The Sportsman* 26.1.1903 p3
3 *The Sportsman* 25.1.1904 p4
4 *The Times* 22.2.1904 p12
5 *The Sportsman* 27.2.1905 p7
6 *The Sportsman* 15.4.1905 p3

7 *The Sportsman* 19.9.1905 p4
8 *The Sportsman* 5.3.1906 p3
9 *The Sportsman* 8.10.1906 p3
10 *The Times* 29.4.1907 p12
11 *The Sportsman* 10.4.1907 p8

Chapter Five
1 *The Sportsman* 30.9.1907 p8
2 *The Times* 12.4.1908 p11
3 *The Times* 5.4.1909 p6
4 *The Times* 10.4.1911 p13
5 *The Times* 14.4.1913 p12

Chapter Six
1 *The Times* 4.1.1918 p5
2 *The Times* 19.4.1919 p5
3 *Morning Post* 14.12.1932 p20
4 *The Times* 8.3.1920 p6
5 *The Times* 23.8.1920 p4
6 *Morning Post* 14.12.1932 p20
7 *Morning Post* 14.12.1932 p20
8 *The Sportsman* 9.11.1920 p2
9 Bevan, Hibberd & Gilbert *To the Palace for the Cup* p133
10 *The Times* 1.5.1922 p7
11 *Surrey Advertiser* 29.4.1922 p7
12 *The Times* 13.4.1922 p5

Chapter Seven
1 *The Times* 23.10.1922 p6
2 Bevan, Hibberd & Gilbert *To the Palace for the Cup* p134
3 *The Times* 29.8.1922 p10
4 *The Sportsman* 17.1.1923 p2
5 Bevan, Hibberd & Gilbert *To the Palace for the Cup* p136
6 *The Times* 4.9.1924 p5
7 *The Times* 29.12.24 p4
8 *Westminster Gazette* 7.5.1925 p10
9 Bevan, Hibberd & Gilbert *To the Palace for the Cup* p137

Chapter Eight
1 *The Times* 29.8.1925 p4
2 *Surrey Comet* 2.9.1925 p 4
3 *Surrey Comet* 2.12.1925 p4
4 *Morning Post* 14.12.1932 p20
5 *Surrey Comet* 17.11.1926 p4
6 *Herts Advertiser* 20.11.1926 p15
7 *Surrey Comet* 30.3.1927 p4
8 *Surrey Comet* 27.4.1927 p5
9 *Surrey Comet* 4.1.1928 p3
10 *Surrey Comet* 25.1.1928 p3
11 *Surrey Comet* 9.5.1928 p2
12 *The Guardian* 13.3.1928 p4
13 *The Times* 19.11.1928 p6
14 *Surrey Comet* 20.2.1929 p2
15 *Surrey Comet* 8.5.1929 p4
16 *The Times* 23.11.1938 p5

Chapter Nine
1 *The Times* 22.10.1929 p7
2 *Morning Post* 14.12.1932 p20
3 *Surrey Comet* 1.1.1930 p3
4 *Surrey Comet* 14.5.1930 p2
5 *Surrey Comet* 13.9.1930 p4
6 *The Times* 12.8.1931 p6
7 *The Times* 21.9.1931 p6
8 *Surrey Comet* 30.9.1931 p3
9 *The Times* 26.2.1932 p6
10 *Morning Post* 14.12.1932 p20
11 *The Times* 24.9.1932 p5
12 *Surrey Comet* 12.4.1933 p2

Chapter Ten
1 *The Times* 25.8.1933 p4
2 *News Chronicle* 24.8.1933 p9
3 *Surrey Comet* 18.10.1933 p4
4 *The Times* 26.3.1934 p6
5 *Surrey Comet* 7.3.1934 p4
6 *Surrey Comet* 19.12.1934 p2
7 *Association Football* volume 1 p255
8 *Surrey Comet* 13.3.1935 p2
9 *The Observer* 15.9.1935 p28
10 *Surrey Comet* 8.1.1936 p2
11 *The Times* 3.2.1936 p6
12 *The Times* 24.2.1936 p6
13 *The Times* 9.3.1936 p6
14 *The Times* 30.3.1936 p6
15 *Surrey Comet* 15.4.1936 p2
16 *The Times* 20.4.1936 p5
17 *The Times* 4.5.1936 p7
18 *Surrey Comet* 6.5.1936 p2
19 *The Times* 11.5.1936 p6

Chapter Eleven
1 *News Chronicle* 2.9.1936 p13
2 *Surrey Comet* 28.4.1937 p2
3 *Surrey Comet* 6.3.1937 p4
4 *The Times* 10.3.1937 p6
5 *The Times* 23.6.1937 p6
6 *The Gleaner* 13.8.1937 p12
7 *South London Press* 12.10.37 p2
8 *South London Press* 5.4.38 p2
9 *The Guardian* 5.1.1939 p3

SUBSCRIBERS

Thank you to the following people who made the production of this book possible. Your support is much appreciated.

Richard Kreider
Derek Sale
Robert Woolridge
Claire Short
Gerard McGreevy
John Mills
Fay and Derek Pedder
Derek Earley
Tony Slade
David Harrison
Rod Fraser
Steve Menary
Keith Dennis
Neville Evans
Peter William Brown
Barbara Pratt
Rod Harrington
Barry Green
Peter Drake
Dil Porter
Jon
Glynn Hyatt
John Blackmore
John Ringrose
Ivan Page
Stan Nathan
Richard Lambert
Andy Jennings
Richard Shore
Peter Miles
David Hetherington
Raymond Flood
Bob Lilliman
Peter Kolodziej
John Cracknell
David Bowell
David Downs
London Football Association
Brian Ellis
Keith Reynolds
Gloria Coyne
Mark Tyler
Richard Wells
Norman Epps
Phil Pepperrell
Keith Betts
Vince Huggett
Roger Robinson
Keith Holloway
Brian Vandevilt
Colm Kerrigan

Andy Sakseide
Futuremore Barizly
Philip H Whitehead
James Goodwin
David Brealey
Mark Pope
Malcolm Hamer
Alfred Sills
Roger Hillman
Charterhouse Archive
Colin Timbrell
Gareth Owen
Malcolm Wederell
Geoff Hewitson
Tony Mason
Anita Cavallini
Mike Wilson
E & E Blackbourn
Peter Cavallini
Justin Carcavella
Rodney O'Donnell
John Grimme
Charles Banks
Renato Cot
Daniel Cot*
Nick Overend
Craig Tyreman
Rafael Fernandes Goncalves
Enrico Vito Ranieri
Rob Pearce
Robert Ewing
Steve Martin
Colin Walton
Chris Parrott
Alex Mitchell
John Metcalfe
Sherrill Burrows
David Ian Chapman
Michael Cavallini
Vincenzo Regoli
Morgyn Chipres
Morgyn Chipres
Mishi Morath
Ronnie McNamara
Gerry Young
Niall Watt
John Levy
John Levy
Geoff Harvey
Rachel Cripps